C000066426

Blackstone's

Counter-Terrorism
Handbook

Blackstone's
Counter-Terrorism
Handbook

Authors:
Police National Legal Database
Andrew Staniforth

Consultant Editors:
Clive Walker and John Parkinson

OXFORD
UNIVERSITY PRESS

OXFORD
UNIVERSITY PRESS

Great Clarendon Street, Oxford OX2 6DP

Oxford University Press is a department of the University of Oxford.
It furthers the University's objective of excellence in research, scholarship,
and education by publishing worldwide in

Oxford New York

Auckland Cape Town Dar es Salaam Hong Kong Karachi
Kuala Lumpur Madrid Melbourne Mexico City Nairobi
New Delhi Shanghai Taipei Toronto

With offices in

Argentina Austria Brazil Chile Czech Republic France Greece
Guatemala Hungary Italy Japan Poland Portugal Singapore
South Korea Switzerland Thailand Turkey Ukraine Vietnam

Oxford is a registered trade mark of Oxford University Press
in the UK and in certain other countries

Published in the United States
by Oxford University Press Inc., New York

British Library Cataloguing in Publication Data
Data available

Library of Congress Cataloging-in-Publication Data

Staniforth, Andrew.
    Blackstone's counter-terrorism handbook / author, Andrew Staniforth;
consultant editors, Cive Walker and John Parkinson.
    p. cm.
    Includes bibliographical references and index.
    ISBN 978-0-19-955980-0 (flexicover : alk. paper) 1. Terrorism—Great
Britain—Prevention. 2. Terrorists—Legal status, laws, etc.—Great Britain.
3. Terrorism—Prevention. I. Walker, Clive. II. Parkinson, John. III. Title.
IV. Title: Counter-terrorism handbook. V. Title: Counter terrorism handbook.
    KD8039.S73 2009
    344.4105'325—dc22

                                                                    2009004029

Typeset by Laserwords Private Limited, Chennai, India
Printed in Italy on acid-free paper by
Legoprint S.p.A.

ISBN 978–0–19–955980–0

1 3 5 7 9 10 8 6 4 2

Foreword

A paramount concern of mine since I became Independent Reviewer of Terrorism Legislation in 2001 has been that police officers at all levels should understand the extent and limitations of counter-terrorism laws. My mantra is that terrorism law should be used only for terrorism purposes. Every step outside those purposes provides terrorists with an argument. All in authority are required never to forget that such laws are a step outside the norms of criminal justice legislation: the right to stop and search in the street in a way different from, and more extensive than a non-terrorism intervention is a power to be exercised with caution. The obtaining of an authority to cordon an area is a potentially serious interference with the private and economic lives of law-abiding citizens. Accessing details of a bank account is an infringement of customary privacy.

The authors of this excellent book have drawn together the body of counter-terrorism legislation in a form accessible to all stakeholders. Although designed for police officers, I have no doubt that it will be an essential part of a wider range of libraries. That it is up to date including the Counter-Terrorism Act 2008 is an achievement in itself.

The authors have included in the book a detailed description of what terrorism is (and therefore what is not included). The first chapter really is required reading, from which all will emerge with an understanding enhanced by the exceptional clarity of the writing. I commend it to Ministers, civil servants, and lawyers, as well as to those for whom the book is designed.

The use of case studies provides outstanding illustrations which can be translated into almost any situation an officer is likely to encounter. In training sessions for non-specialist officers, the case studies will prove invaluable.

Non-specialist officers will face terrorism issues from time to time. When major events with a potential for terrorist interest are taking place, sometimes officers are drafted in from outside forces, with little local knowledge and only basic acquaintance with counter-terrorism law. Sometimes they will have to be briefed very quickly indeed. This volume will facilitate such briefings. All officers should read about sections 43 and 44. The limitations of the power to stop and search without suspicion have been overstepped too often. Other stop and search powers exist, and are generally preferable.

The references to international events provide an alarming but accurate historical context, illustrated by the events in Mumbai during November 2008. The reality that violent Jihadists all over the world are working together against the established order, and that with rare exceptions there are links of some kind to weave all the terrorist cells into an international destructive tapestry, is well argued in the book.

Profiling of potential terrorists is another subject the authors have faced squarely. There is always the risk of potential discrimination in the selection of suspects or persons to be searched. This is avoided if sound intelligence analysis has taken place. Training in the rapid behavioural analysis of travellers has been developed, not least by the British Transport Police. Nevertheless the majority of travellers stopped under Schedule 7 will be entirely innocent people. The incidence of stops of the innocent should not be exacerbated by a misguided attempt to balance the statistics by interventions against those who plainly are not terrorists. Complaints against officers are time-consuming as well as unwelcome. A better understanding of the law, including such details as when Schedule 7 comes into play at a port of entry, will serve likewise the efficiency of the legislation and the effectiveness of individual officers. In this context too the book is clear and illustrative.

The Counter-Terrorism Act 2008 proved very controversial in Parliament, principally because of the proposed increase in the maximum period of detention before charge from 28 to 42 days. That proposal was withdrawn by the government after defeat in the House of Lords. The absolute maximum remains at 28 days. The means and stages by which interviewing and investigating officers approach that maximum from the time of arrest is analysed carefully in the book. It is unlikely that non-specialist officers will be involved at that stage, but it may arise. Some may only have served in Special Branch or other specialized units for a short time—especially promoted senior officers—when a critical incident arises. Custody officers may find themselves thrust into the complex detention issues surrounding terrorism suspects with a variety of religious, dietary, and language rights. Advance reading of this volume will repay itself fully for any officer or lawyer finding themselves in the tense police custody atmosphere after terrorism arrests, often under the glare of the media.

In all, I commend this important contribution to understanding counter-terrorism law.

Lord Carlile of Berriew QC
Independent Reviewer of Terrorism Legislation

Notes from the Editors

The UK faces a continuing threat from extremists who believe they can advance their aims through acts of terrorism. This threat is both serious and enduring, being international in scope and involving a variety of groups, networks, and individuals who are driven by violent and extremist beliefs.

In response to the challenges posed by this threat, a new police counter-terrorism landscape has been established to protect the UK. This enhanced police structure compliments the work of partner intelligence agencies to protect national security, but even they cannot tackle terrorism without the commitment of the wider police service or support from members of the public.

Major counter-terrorism operations are complex having reach, scale, and complexity beyond other criminal investigations. That said, national security depends upon the security of communities and the police service has focused its attention on a multi-agency approach to neighbourhood policing. It is recognized that the police service represents one of many bodies who together can improve the safety and security for individuals and communities. It is this local contact that is required not just to prevent gun crime, knife crime, and anti-social behaviour but also to identify those who encourage extremist views and engage in terrorist related activity.

We must however, put the threat from terrorism and violent extremism in perspective. When compared against other types of criminal activity, terrorism remains a relatively rare occurrence but the impact of terrorist attacks demands a focused and determined response from the whole police service and its partners.

To tackle the present threat effectively, police colleagues are required to develop their knowledge and understanding of terrorism, extremism, and associated legislation. The *Blackstone's Counter-Terrorism Handbook* provides practical and operational guidance that will assist all police colleagues and partners to meet the challenges of the terrorist threat, so members of the communities we serve can go about their business freely, safely and with confidence.

John Parkinson
Detective Chief Superintendent
Counter-Terrorism Unit

The policing of political violence, characterized as intelligence-led and politically sensitive, has tended to generate structures which have been remote from locality, secretive, and specialist. This tendency was evident in the establishment of the Metropolitan Police's Special Irish Branch, formed in 1883 as one of the earliest detective police units. The same disposition remained still true nearly a century later with the work of what became the Anti-Terrorist Branch. Many such elements of security policing persist today.

Yet, the contemporary phase of terrorism has evolved important new trends and demands a new policing stance. Contemporary terrorism may involve embedded citizens—neighbours from your locality—as much as foreign extremists. That phenomenon may not be new to Ireland or to other parts of the world, but it certainly represents a change in Britain. A modified policing stance is also warranted by the need to anticipate the risk of terrorism, the delivery of which can now involve mass human casualties and swathes of property damage. Good intelligence to monitor and to prevent terrorism has therefore risen to the fore and has been added to the more traditional tactic of the pursuit through criminal law processes. The imperative to refocus and to take account of new trends has been made manifest in the CONTEST strategy document, eventually published by the Home Office in 2006, which reflects not only concerns for 'Prevent' and 'Pursuit' but also 'Prepare' and 'Protect'.

Bringing these responses together, there are palpable movements towards expansion and localism in the policing of political violence. Both features are evidenced above all by the setting up of police Counter-Terrorism Units, but that development is backed by others. In the policing sphere, there is the network of Counter-Terrorist Security Advisors, and, beyond policing alone, there is involvement in the Local Resilience Forums and other planning groups, set up under the Civil Contingencies Act 2004, as well as work on the 'Preventing Extremism Together' initiative which began in 2005 and demands constant involvement with local community agencies and groups. Our understandings of how the processes of radicalization emanate in extremism remain far from perfect, but if 'Prevent' is to have impact in at least interdicting the most savage excesses of extremism, then it is vital that policing of political violence can draw upon the information and goodwill of communities from which aberrant extremists are drawn. To be tough on terrorism and on the causes of terrorism is a very ambitious undertaking and has inevitably encouraged the mainstreaming of counter-terrorism policy and action. Concepts such as community involvement, multi-agency working, and public assurance, now widely accepted and practised in local policing, must find a translation into the policing of political violence. All police officers, and not just those assigned to CTUs, must share in those tasks. Terrorism policing thus becomes for all the police and for all the public.

In the light of that conclusion, this Handbook offers an excellent guide to policing practitioners who are involved in operational and community aspects of countering terrorism and to other agencies who recognize their concerns and involvement in this arena. It is reflective of the remarkable changes now taking place in the policing of terrorism that some of its practitioners have been willing to talk candidly about terrorism and about the legislative frameworks—the Terrorism Acts—under which they operate. There is much to gain from reading their very accessible descriptions of the countering of terrorism which form the body of this important new handbook.

Clive Walker
Professor of Criminal Justice Studies
University of Leeds

Preface

The way in which the police service counters terrorism is developing in direct response to the present threats from international terrorism. This response has, over recent years, resulted in the creation of national strategies, new police departments, and the introduction of new anti-terrorism legislation. Countering terrorism and preventing violent extremism is no longer the sole responsibility of specialist policing departments; the whole police service and members of its extended family all have an important role in protecting communities from terrorist and extremist related activity.

There are a number of unique challenges that confront police officers when attempting to increase their awareness of terrorism and extremism issues. The perceived complexity of the subject, the sensitivity of operational information, and the nature of specialist policing roles are contributing factors. The *Blackstone's Counter-Terrorism Handbook* has been specifically designed to meet the needs of all police officers and other professional practitioners who are required to broaden their knowledge and understanding of this subject.

The handbook is formulated and written by operational practitioners and anti-terrorism legal advisors. It clearly explains the concept of terrorism, extremism, and associated legislation providing the wording of offences, points to prove, meanings, explanatory notes, relevant cases, and practical considerations. While not disclosing secret or sensitive policing techniques this book, for the very first time, provides the operational police officer with details of counter-terrorism investigations, profiles of outlawed terrorist groups, and practical guidance and advice to assist in the interpretation and application of anti-terrorism legislation.

The Handbook is fully up to date as of January 2009 and includes all recent legislative developments and changes in the law. Whilst every care has been taken to ensure that the contents of this Handbook are accurate, neither the publisher nor the authors can accept any responsibility for any action taken, or not taken, on the basis of the information contained within this Handbook.

Andrew Staniforth
Counter-Terrorism Unit

Acknowledgements

The *Blackstone's Counter-Terrorism Handbook* would not have been created without the foresight and determination of Andrew Staniforth (Counter-Terrorism Unit) and Nigel Hughes (Head of PNLD), the hard work of Marnie Ratcliffe and Christiane Rabenstein (PNLD Legal Advisors), and the guidance of John Parkinson and Clive Walker (Consultant Editors).

Thanks are also extended to the team at Oxford University Press for sharing their expertise and the support provided by Lord Carlile of Berriew QC, the Independent Reviewer of Terrorism Legislation.

Acknowledgements

Contents

Part 1   An Introduction to Terrorism

Contents

Tables of Legislation

Tables of Legislation

Tables of Legislation

European Union

United States of America

International

Tables of Secondary Legislation, Codes of Practice, and Home Office Circulars

Secondary legislation

Secondary legislation - European Union

Codes of Practice

Home Office Circulars

List of Figures and Tables

Figures

Tables

List of Abbreviations

ACPO (TAM) Association of Chief Police Officers (Terrorism & Allied Matters)
ACPOS Association of Chief Police Officers, Scotland
AI Ansar Al Islam
AIAI Al Ittihad Al Islamia
ANO Abu Nidal Organisation
ANPR Automatic Number Plate Recognition
AR Animal Rights
ARE Animal Rights Extremism
AS Ansar Al Sunna
ASG Abu Sayyaf Group
ASU Active Service Unit
ATCSA Anti-terrorism Crime and Security Act 2001
BIA Border Immigration Agency
BK Babbar Khalsa
BLA Baluchistan Liberation Army
BMP Border Management Programme
BTP British Transport Police
C18 Combat 18
CAA Civil Aviation Authority
CAC Continuity Army Council (Irish Republican Army)
CBRN Chemical, Biological, Radiological, and Nuclear
CCTV Close Circuit Television
CEFO Community Engagement Field Officer
CIA Central Intelligence Agency
CIRA Continuity Irish Republican Army
CJS Criminal Justice System
CO Cabinet Office
COBRA Cabinet Office Briefing Room 'A'
CONTEST Government's International Counter-Terrorism Strategy: 'Prevent, Pursue, Protect & Prepare'
CoP Codes of Practice
CP Counter Proliferation
CPI Commission, Preparation, Instigation
CPNI Centre for the Protection of National Infrastructure
CNI Critical National Infrastructure
CT Counter-Terrorism
CTA Common Travel Area (Ports Policing)

List of Abbreviations

CTC Counter-Terrorism Command (SO15 Metropolitan Police)
CTIU Counter-Terrorism Intelligence Unit
CTSA Counter-Terrorism Security Advisor
CTU Counter-Terrorism Unit
DE Domestic Extremism
DfT Department for Transport (Ports Policing)
DHKP-C Revolutionary Peoples' Liberation Party – Front (Devrimici Halk Kurtulus Patisi - Cephesi
DIS Defence Intelligence Staff
EIJ Egyptian Islamic Jihad
EKP Economic Key Point
ETA Basque Homeland & Liberty (Euskadi ta Askatasuna)
EO Examining Officer, Schedule 7 Terrorism Act 2000
FIS Foreign Intelligence Services
GAC General Army Council (Irish Republican Army)
GCHQ Government Communications Headquarters
GDF Good Friday Agreement
GI Al-Gama'at al-Islamiya
GIA Armed Islamic Group (Groupe Islamique Armée)
GICM Groupe Islamique Combatant Marocain
GPMS Government Protective Marking Scheme
GSPC Salafist Group for Call & Combat (Groupe Salafiste pour la Prédication et le Combat)
HIG Hezb-E Islami Gulbuddin
HM Harakat Mujahideen
HMRC Her Majesty's Revenue & Customs
HME Home Made Explosive
HMIC Her Majesty's Inspectorate of Constabulary
HMG Her Majesty's Government
HMP Her Majesty's Prison
HO Home Office
HUJI Harakat Ul Jihad Islami
HUJI-B Harakat Ul Jihad Islami (Bangladesh)
HuM/A Harakat Ul Mujahideen/Alami & Jundallah
IAA Islamic Army of Aden
ICT International Counter-Terrorism
IED Improvised Explosive Device
IICD Independent International Commission on Decommissioning
IJU Islamic Jihad Union
IMU Islamic Movement of Uzbekistan
INLA Irish National Liberation Army
IPCC Independent Police Complaints Commission

IPLO Irish People's Liberation Organisation
IRA Irish Republican Army
IRSM Irish Republican Socialist Movement
IRSP Irish Republican Socialist Party
IRT Irish Republican/Related Terrorism
ISC Intelligence Services Committee
ISYF International Sikh Youth Federation
JBOC Joint Border Operations Centre (e-Borders)
JeM Jaish e Mohammed
JI Jeemah Islamiyah
JMB Jammat-ul Mujahideen Bangladesh
JTAC Joint Terrorism Analysis Centre
JuF Jamaat Ul-Furquan
LeJ Lashkar-E Jhangvi
LIFG Libyan Islamic Fighting Group
LT Lashkar e Tayyaba
LTTE Tamil Tigers
LVF Loyalist Volunteer Force
MI5 Military Intelligence 5 known as the Security Service
MI6 Military Intelligence 6 former name of the Secret Intelligence Service
MIP Millat-E Islami Pakistan
MNF-I Multi-National Forces-Iraq
MNLF Moro National Liberation Front
MoD Ministry of Defence
N17 17 November Revolutionary Organisation
NaCTSO National Counter-Terrorism and Security Office
NCTT National Community Tension Team
NDET National Domestic Extremism Team
NETCU National Extremism Tactical Co-ordination Unit
NI Northern Ireland
NIPP Northern Ireland Peace Process
NIM National Intelligence Model
NPAC National Ports Analytical Centre
NSAC National Security Advice Centre
NPIA National Police Improvement Agency
NPOIU National Public Order Intelligence Unit
NTFIU National Terrorist Financial Investigation Unit
NWFP North West Frontier Province (Pakistan)
OSCT Office of Security & Counter-Terrorism
PACE Police & Criminal Evidence Act 1984
PBIED Person Borne Improvised Explosive Device (suicide bomb)
PIJ Palestinian Islamic Jihad - Shaqaqi

List of Abbreviations

PIRA Provisional Irish Republican Army
PKK Kongra Gele Kurdistan
PLO Palestine Liberation Organization
PNLD Police National Legal Database
POAC Proscribed Organisations Appeal Committee
POT Prevention of Terrorism Act 2005
PSA Public Service Agreement
PSNI Police Service of Northern Ireland
PVE Preventing Violent Extremism
RIRA Real Irish Republican Army
RIPA Regulations of Investigatory Powers Act 2000
RoI Republic of Ireland
SB Special Branch
SIS Secret Intelligence Service (formerly known as MI6)
SO15 Specialist Operations 15 Counter-Terrorism Command
SOCA Serious & Organised Crime Agency
SPO Senior Ports Officer
SSP Sipah-E Sahba Pakistan
TACT Terrorism Act (2000 & 2006)
TAK Teyre Azadiye Kurdistan
TNSM Tehrik Nefaz-e Shari-at Muhammadi
UDA Ulster Defence Association
UDP Ulster Democratic Party
UFF Ulster Freedom Fighters
US United States
UVF Ulster Volunteer Force
VBIED Vehicle Borne Improvised Explosive Device
VSS Vulnerable Sites and Sectors

Counter-Terrorism Act 2008—Summary

The Counter-Terrorism Act 2008 received Royal Assent on 26 November 2008 when this book was nearly completed. This is a summary of the parts of the Act that are most relevant to the topics covered in the book. At the time of writing, most of the Act was not in force.

Part I of the Act introduces new powers to gather and share information. Sections 1–9 provide new additional powers to remove documents for examination, etc. in the context of a police search under existing terrorism legislation search powers. These include provision for articles subject to legal privilege, the creation of records of removal, the retention of documents seized, access to seized documents, copying of documents, and the return of seized documents. A new power to take fingerprints and samples from persons subject to control orders is also added. Provision is made for the retention and use of fingerprints and samples, including in the Counter-Terrorism DNA Database. The Act also deals with the disclosure of information between the police and the intelligence services.

Part II of the Act (sections 22–27) makes provision for post-charge questioning of a person if the offence is a terrorism offence or the offence has a terrorist connection. Any post-charge questioning must be authorized by a judge of the Crown Court and must not exceed a period of 48 hours. Adverse inferences can be drawn in the same circumstances as in interviews pre-charge.

Part III (sections 28–39) deals with the prosecution and punishment of terrorist offences. This includes provisions regarding jurisdiction, consent to prosecution, and sentencing for terrorist offences (the terrorist element must be treated as an aggravating factor). Sections 34–39 make further provisions with regards to forfeiture. Section 34 of the Act amends the whole of section 23 of the Terrorism Act 2000 (TACT) and in doing so widens its parameters. Section 35 inserts section 23A into TACT which allows forfeiture in terrorism offences other than sections 15–18, such as weapons training and inciting terrorism outside the UK. Section 36 inserts section 23B into TACT which mainly replaces section 23(7) (court hearing from person other than convicted person claiming to be owner of property) which does not appear in the revised section 23. Section 37 of the Act amends Schedule 4 to the Terrorism Act 2000 to allow victims to be compensated by the courts in certain circumstances.

Part IV of, and Schedules 4 and 5, to the Act (sections 40–61) make provision for notification requirements and foreign travel restriction orders for persons sentenced or made subject of a hospital order in connection with a terrorism legislation or terrorism-related offence. If the offence was committed in the UK, the application is automatic; if the offence was committed abroad, the police must apply to a magistrates' court. The requirements include initial notification of certain information to the police within three days of being sentenced, notification of any change of name or address, requirements for re-notification, method of notification and creates offences relating to notification requirements. Foreign travel restriction orders can only be imposed on a person subject to notification requirements, cannot last for more than six months and it is an offence to breach one.

Parts V and VI concern terrorist finance and money laundering as well as financial restrictions decisions: these sections affect mainly the Treasury when seeking to freeze assets and are not directly relevant to the police.

Further miscellaneous provisions are included in Part VII: Section 75 amends the definition of 'terrorism' to include action for the purpose of advancing a *racial* cause. Sections 76 inserts a new section 58A into the Terrorism Act 2000 which makes it an offence to elicit, publish, or communicate information about members of the armed forces, etc. Sections 78–81 of the Act make amendments to the provisions relating to control orders. Section 78 inserts sections 7A–7C into the Prevention of Terrorism Act 2005 which creates powers of entry and search for those subject to control orders. These are a power of entry and search for—

- section 7A—absconding
- section 7B—failure to grant access to premises
- section 7C—monitoring compliance with order (warrant required).

Sections 79–81 make further amendments to the provisions relating to control orders which include a change to the definition of terrorism-related activity and changes to the Schedule relating to the anonymity of controlled persons.

Notes have been added into the relevant parts of the book identifying the changes brought by this Act and references have been made to the PNLD, which enable the reader to check what is in force. It should be noted that, in its final version, the Act did not change the period of pre-charge detention which remains at a maximum of 28 days.

Marnie Ratcliffe and Christiane Rabenstein

Icons List

AG✓ **Attorney General's consent required**
Proceedings may only be started by or with the consent of the Attorney General.

DPP✓ **Director of Public Prosecutions' consent required**
Proceedings may only be started with the consent of the Director of Public Prosecutions. In some cases the permission of the Attorney General is also required.

Mode of Trial: Summary
To be tried in the magistrates' court.

Mode of Trial: Indictable
To be tried in the Crown Court.

Time Limit for Prosecution
The time limit allowed for submission of the file (laying of information).

Part 1
An Introduction to Terrorism

Chapter 1

Terrorism

1.1 Concept of Terrorism

Protecting the public remains the highest priority of the police service, but the perceived growing risk of terrorism over recent years has resulted in the public's protection being severely threatened. No community is immune from the global reach of international terrorism and the UK is a prime target for extremists who believe they can advance their aims through acts of violence. This threat is considered to be both serious and enduring, being international in scope and involving a variety of individuals, groups, and networks who are driven by extremist beliefs.

The way in which the UK counters terrorism is developing in response to the present threat. This area of policing is no longer the sole responsibility of specialist departments. To counter the threat effectively, all police officers are therefore required to broaden their knowledge and understanding of terrorism. To investigate terrorist related matters, set policy, devise strategy and make informed decisions, a clear understanding of terrorism as a concept is required. Developing an understanding of terrorism will ensure that police officers are better prepared to identify and respond to terrorist related incidents.

1.1.1 Defining terrorism

Terrorism is nothing new. Its origins can be traced back in time for centuries but it remains a much contested concept to this day. There is no universally accepted definition of terrorism. Academic opinion and international bodies remain divided upon its most accurate description. Much philosophical debate surrounds the definition of terrorism and its different perspectives. This includes concepts of what is 'good' and what is 'evil' being captured in the common phrase that 'one man's terrorist is another man's freedom fighter'. There are hundreds of different definitions of terrorism in use today but many of them lack legal credibility to be used in domestic or international law. Lord Carlile of Berriew QC, the independent reviewer of terrorism legislation in the UK, presented a report to Parliament in March 2007 which focused upon the legal definition of terrorism. The report identified that a definition of terrorism is of real practical and operational significance as it triggers many powers as well as contributing to the description of offences.

POINT TO NOTE—DEFINING TERRORISM

Defining terrorism is important. Saying that the threat from terrorism is severe or that terrorist-related incidents are increasing annually, has little meaning unless we are clear what terrorism actually is. Defining terrorism provides focus for those with the responsibility of making key strategic decisions. It ensures that law enforcement partners and government agencies understand from the outset what it is they are protecting the public from. A clear definition is also important for international co-operation as terrorism may have different meanings in other countries around the world. For terrorism to be prevented nationally and internationally a shared understanding of terrorism is required. A clear definition of terrorism is also vital so that the police can distinguish adequately between legitimate and illegitimate activities related to political policies. The special laws devised to deal with terrorism, which will often be Draconian in impact compared to 'normal' laws, should not affect legitimate political activity, even if it is highly aggressive or unpopular.

As a starting point for his report, Lord Carlile highlighted the definition of terrorism which was included in the Prevention of Terrorism (Temporary Provisions) Act 1989. It described terrorism as: 'the use of violence for political ends, and includes any use of violence for the purpose of putting the public or any section of the public in fear'.

This definition had major drawbacks as new forms of terrorist activity began to emerge and develop through the 1990s. Most importantly the definition did not require a serious level of violence or serious damage or risk to health and safety or electronic disruption. In a review of terrorism legislation during 1996, Lord Lloyd of Berwick recommended that a different definition should be adopted. He suggested the operational definition used at the time by the Federal Bureau of Investigation (FBI) of the United States would be better suited for UK legislation which defined terrorism as: 'The use of serious violence against persons or property, or threat to use such violence, to intimidate or coerce a government, the public or a section of the public, in order to promote political, social or ideological objectives'.

The definition used by the FBI extends the description of terrorism to promote political, social, and ideological causes. Following much debate legislators concluded that it did not cover issues associated with vital electronic systems such as damage to air traffic control systems or other critical infrastructure systems. The pursuit of a more accurate description continued as independent reviewers of terrorism legislation agreed that there were great difficulties in finding a satisfactory definition. Following substantial research, analysis, and debate, the legal definition of terrorism which has been subsequently amended by the Terrorism Act 2006 and the Counter-Terrorism Act 2008 can now be found in Section 1 of the Terrorism Act 2000 which states:

Definition box—Legal definition of terrorism

'Terrorism' means the use or threat of action where;

a) it involves serious violence against a person, involves serious damage to property, endangers a persons life (other than that of the person committing the action), creates a serious risk to the health or safety of the public, or a section of the public, or is designed seriously to interfere with or seriously to disrupt an electronic system;

b) it is designed to influence the government, or an international government organisation, or to intimidate the public or a section of the public; and;

c) is made for the purpose of advancing a political, religious, radical or ideological cause.

See also **4.1**.

The legal definition provided by Section 1 is broad and is designed to capture the diverse range of activities associated with terrorism, which others have used as a precedent. On the other hand, international law definitions, such as in the UN Terrorism Finance Convention of 1999 and the European Council Framework Decision on Combating Terrorism of 2002, have adopted a markedly different and arguably clearer approach which focuses upon listed criminal offences. During 2006 the Minister of State at the Home Office, Tony McNulty MP, expressed the view that the definition is 'comprehensive and effective' having been 'approved following extensive debate in Parliament'. You can clearly see the influence provided by previous definitions from UK and US legislation with the inclusion of phrases such as 'serious violence' and 'section of the public in fear'. These key phrases can also be found in many other legal definitions of terrorism which have often used the UK Act as a precedent. On the other hand, international law definitions, such as those in Section 1 provide a detailed description of what acts are involved in terrorism, what the acts are designed to do and for what purpose, but does the definition really help us to clearly understand what terrorism actually is?

POINTS TO NOTE—WHAT IS TERRORISM?

First and foremost terrorism is a crime, a crime which has serious consequences and one which requires to be distinguished from other types of crime, but a crime nonetheless. Individuals who commit terrorist-related offences are subject to the processes of the criminal justice system and those who are otherwise believed to be involved in terrorism are subject to restrictive executive actions. However, the key features of terrorism that distinguish it from other forms of criminality are its core motivations. Terrorism may be driven, as the legal definition provided Section 1 of the Terrorism Act 2000 states, by:

- Politics
- Religion
- Ideology

These objectives are unlike other criminal motivations such as for personal gain or in the pursuit of revenge. Terrorists may be driven by any one or any combination of the three core motivations but the primary motivator is political as the diagram below shows. Individuals who are driven by religious or ideological beliefs have to gain some political ground to compel others to conform to their point of view, especially if they are operating within a democratic society.

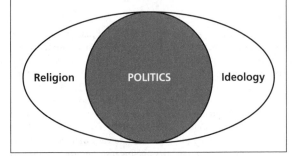

Acts of terrorism whether motivated by politics, religion, or ideology convey a message. This message attempts to persuade its audience or force them to accept their views and beliefs. The victims of terrorism are often distinct from this audience, victims may be passers-by on a train or those travelling on a plane but a political audience would be a government or the electorate. Terrorism therefore has a three-way relationship between the terrorist, the victim, and the audience, which is not usually the case in other types of crime. This relationship also means that a greater degree of control and oversight is required to counter terrorism so innocent and non-combatant victims are protected. Terrorism is a very powerful way in which to promote beliefs and has potentially serious consequences for society. If allowed to grow and flourish terrorism can undermine national security, it can cause instability to a country, and in the most extreme of circumstances can lead to war. These are a very different set of outcomes when compared against other types of crime. This is the reason why policing terrorism is different to policing other types of crime and why it requires a different approach to prevent it.

1.1.2 Politics

Understanding the political motivations of terrorist groups is key to countering their activities. Politics is central in society, it is the way in which governance and authority within society is managed. The Oxford English Dictionary defines politics as follows:

Definition box—Politics

1. (a) the art and science of government
   (b) public life and affairs as involving authority and government
2. (a) particular set of ideas, principles or commitments in politics
   (b) activities concerned with the acquisition or exercise of authority or government
   (c) an organisational process or principle affecting authority, status etc.

The police service is itself the focus of much political debate. Fighting crime, tackling terrorism and protecting the public are fundamental issues within a democratic society. Members of the public will have many different political views on how the police service should best serve society. In a liberal, pluralist, and democratic society, which the police have a duty to defend, a wide range of political views are acceptable and desirable, even views which may offend others, are aggressively pursued, or are highly unpopular.

An understanding of the spectrum of politics is important for police officers and especially for those engaged in countering terrorism and extremism. Political views that are at the extreme ends of the political spectrum can cause serious issues within society as people who hold such views cannot often tolerate others.

POINT TO NOTE—DISTINGUISH BETWEEN EXTREMISM AND TERRORISM

Police officers should continue to distinguish between extremism and terrorism; one does not necessarily lead to another, and simply to hold extremist views is not an offence and is not terrorism. To be terrorism, there must be elements of violence or intimidation or the planning of it.

1.1.2.1 *Extreme right-wing*

Right-wing political extremism can take various forms. Some individuals and groups seek strong centralized government and the preservation of their national domestic culture. Others, such as militia in the US, believe in the preservation of personal rights, including strong forms or personal property and privacy and the right to bear arms, with central government becoming weak. Extreme right-wing views are often associated with fascism and racism. They are individuals and groups who advocate severe, stringent and immoderate measures using violence and intimidation to promote their beliefs and their priority over other cultures and communities.

1.1.2.2 *Extreme left-wing*

Left-wing political extremism also takes various forms. A common theme is to bring about what they perceive as a more equal distribution of power and wealth, whether in a particular locality, in the country as a whole, or on an international scale. Existing instruments of power and wealth, such as governmental structures and international organizations, therefore become targets.

1.1.3 Religion

Religion can be a key component of terrorist motivations. Defining religion and understanding its complexities and potential links to terrorist activity in modern society presents a real challenge for those engaged in preventing terrorism. An awareness of world faiths and cultures is required to counter terrorism and extremism effectively. Religion is a face of society having its own historical development which is often set in a specific social and economic climate. Individuals find religion can guide them through life and is often described as a treasure for those within a faith who find hope, comfort, and blessing. The powerful belief of followers of different faiths requires to be recognized especially by extremists who twist the truth of religious teachings and scriptures to legitimise the pursuit of their aims. A clear definition of religion can be found in the Oxford English Dictionary:

Definition box—Religion

1. the belief in a superhuman power, in a personal God of gods entitled to obedience and worship
2. the expression of this in worship
3. a particular system of faith and worship
4. life under monastic vows
5. a thing that one is devoted to.

There are many different religions in the world today. Some have millions of followers and are steeped in centuries of tradition and ritual. There are however many new and emerging religions of small numbers of individuals who collectively discover and develop their religious purpose. There are also many examples of dissent within major religions and the formation of self-appointed and self-directing groups who assert religious justification for their actions even if their views are not shared by the majority in their religion.

The following table provides a brief summary of the most prominent religions which shows the diversity of belief systems in world faiths.

Table 1.1: Religions

Buddhism	Buddhism is a religion that began in the sixth century in India that is without a God, a spiritual or ethical path. It is often referred to as a 'philosophy of life' from its followers rather than a religion. Buddhists believe that there is a circle of rebirth and the soul only escapes this by detachment from all that causes suffering. The key symbol of Buddhism is the 'wheel of rebirth' which represents Buddhism teachings and the way to enlightenment which was first taught by the first Buddha, Siddhartha Gautama.

Christianity   Christianity is a faith based upon 'the Christ' believed to be Jesus of Nazareth. Jesus was a Jew who lived in the first century. Christians believe that Jesus was God and man at the same time, a sublime unity of heaven and earth. They believe in God as a Trinity, that is, three persons in one, Father, Son and Holy Spirit. Christians use the Hebrew Scriptures, the Old Testament and the New Testament which contains 27 books including 21 letters. Christians believe that Jesus died for humankind.

Hinduism   Hinduism is a very ancient religion of which there is no one single identified founder though it has developed over the centuries. Hindus believe that God is within and behind all things. Some Hindus see God as personal, some impersonal. Hindus believe that the way to God is through good deeds, meditation and detachment or devotion. Hindus have vegetarianism as an ideal and will avoid eating beef as the cow is sacred. The key symbol of Hinduism represents the energy created by the universe.

Islam   Muslims believe that Islam has always been taught by God's true prophets throughout history. Islam as we know it today appeared in Arabia during the 17th century. Muslims believe that there is one God who is known as Allah in Arabic and that the first prophet of Allah was Adam, the first man. The final prophet, Muhammad, received the Qur'an in a series of revelations. Muslims believe that you have to earn your own salvation and forgiveness from Allah by following his guidance and commandments.

Judaism   Orthodox Jews trace their faith to the dawn of time with the first man, Adam. The prophets are teachers who follow the Tenakh, the Hebrew Bible, which is a collection of 39 books split into the three sections of the Torah, the Prophets and the Writings. There is no one single founder of the faith although Moses (1400–1200) takes on a role closest to that as he received the Torah on Mount Sinai. Jews believe that God has called them to follow his commandments.

Shinto   Shinto is an ancient faith of Japan. There are no founders, only legends in an age-old system of folk belief. Shinto is 'the way of the Kami' often translated as 'the way of the gods'. Kami are more than gods in the traditional sense and are believed to be spiritual beings or enlightened humans who have become immortal. Shinto aims to seek approval from the Kami where the blessing of rice planting and harvest is regarded as an important aspect for its followers.

Sikhism	Sikhism began in India during the fifteenth century being founded by Guru Nanak (1469–1539) who sought to unite Muslims and Hindus in a synthesis of their main beliefs. Nine other Gurus succeeded him who developed the faith further. Sikhs believe that there is one God who is to be worshipped. Gurus are teachers of Sikhism, chosen by the grace of God who follow the Guru Granth Sahib which is a collection of hymns from the different Gurus.
Taoism	Taoism began in the sixth century and its roots can be traced to ancient Chinese culture and folklore. Taoism is a complex amalgam of traditions from which there are many Gods. The Tao is a mystical force within life and Taoism appeals for harmony within the Tao where its followers seek to live in peace with nature and society. Ambition and lust for power are wrong within Taoism as they disrupt harmony and flow. Taoism was founded by the 'Old Master' Li Erh Tan who is said to have written 'The Classic Text of the Way of Virtue', the scriptures of Taoism.

POINT TO NOTE—RELIGIOUS MOTIVATIONS FOR TERRORISM

Most terrorist action based upon religion could be counted also as political but it is possible that violence wholly within a small religious sect might not be characterized in that way, and so the definition of terrorism has been expanded to include religious motivations.

1.1.4 Ideology

An ideology is an organized collection of ideas. Understanding the context of a particular ideology will assist in tackling the justifications offered by terrorists who seek to legitimize their actions. The Oxford English Dictionary defines ideology as:

Definition box—Ideology

1. the system of ideas at the basis of an economic or political theory
2. the manner of thinking characteristic of class or individual
3. visionary speculation
4. the science of ideas.

The key purpose of an ideology is to offer a change in society which is different from the common or normal perspective. Individuals or organizations that promote their ideology do so believing it will provide a better life in society. There are many types of ideology but the most prominent is the collection of political ideologies which may contain certain ideas on the best form of government, legal, and economic systems. It is therefore difficult to conceive that there can be ideological terrorism which is not political terrorism. Most terrorist groups want to trigger action of some form and not just to change mindsets.

1.2 Terrorism Classification

There are different types of terrorism and extremism and it is important to identify which type of terrorism an individual or group belongs to in order to counter it effectively. Terrorism and extremism can be classified into six broad categories which include:

- Political
- Religious
- Ideological
- Nationalist
- State-sponsored
- Single-issue.

POINT TO NOTE—IDENTIFYING TYPES OF TERRORISM AND/OR EXTREMISM

Identifying the type of terrorism or extremism an individual or group belongs to is an important step in beginning to understand what it is they actually want to achieve. This understanding forms the basis of how we can most effectively employ counter measures. It provides an insight into what the key characteristics of the individual or group may be and what tactics may be used to convey their message and promote their beliefs.

1.2.1 Political and religious terrorism

Political and religious terrorism perceives itself as acting upon orders of a higher or divine authority. They are often the most violent and robust of terrorism organizations as they believe their actions are sanctioned by this higher authority. They believe that their actions are morally justified and that they will be vindicated of any wrongdoing when carrying out orders in pursuit of their objectives.

1.2.2 Ideological terrorism

Ideological terrorism and extremism seeks to change the social, economic and political systems of a country. Ideological terrorists and extremists are violent individuals and groups who can come from either the extreme left-wing or extreme right-wing of the political spectrum. Ideological terrorism objectives are set very high and attempt to achieve a great deal. In order to achieve these objectives it often requires a full social revolution to take place and the term 'social-revolutionary' is often used to describe this grouping.

1.2.3 Nationalist terrorism

Nationalist terrorism groups claim to be the authentic voice of a national culture. Through acts of violence they attempt to restore their lands back to one single larger country or seek complete independence from it by creating a new separate state. Well known nationalist terrorist organizations include the Irish Republican Army (IRA) and Euskadi Ta Askatasuna (ETA) of Spain.

1.2.4 State-sponsored terrorism

State-sponsored terrorism requires a state to support terrorism activities in pursuit of achieving its political objectives. These terrorist activities are sometimes carried out in the state's own territory or conducted in a third or neighbouring country. This tactic is often used to fulfil political agendas as any allegations of state involvement in terrorism can be easily denied or disassociated from political parties when such acts are conducted in other countries.

1.2.5 Single-issue terrorism and extremism

Single-issue terrorism and extremism focuses on a specific policy, practice or procedure. The key objective is to change, block or at the very least disrupt or deter one issue from continuing in its present form. Unlike purely ideological terrorism and extremism, single-issue groups do not seek a full-scale political revolution but they do want real action and changes to be made.

1.3 Terrorism Characteristics

Terrorism may be the only tactic used by an individual or group to further their particular cause but it may also be used as part of a much wider strategy which includes non-violent or legitimate components. So, terrorists have been associated with legitimate political movements, such as the relationship between the IRA and Sinn Fein. There are three common characteristics of terrorism wherever it is used throughout the world which are:

- Pre-meditated
- Indiscriminate
- Breach human rights.

1.3.1 Pre-meditated

The very nature of terrorist acts can reveal that maximizing casualties and raising fear amongst a wider audience is meticulously calculated throughout attack planning activities. To evidence the level of forethought within terrorist organizations we need only observe the activities of the Al-Qaeda inspired terrorist cell responsible for the Madrid train bombings in 2004.

Case study—Madrid, Spain, 2004

On the morning of Thursday, 11 March 2004 terrorist cell members placed ten rucksack improvised explosive devices (IEDs) packed with nails on four separate commuter trains in Madrid. Within a space of three minutes all of the devices were detonated on busy carriages during the rush hour at El Pozo Station, Calle Tellez, Atocha Station and Santa Eugenia Station.

The co-ordinated explosions claimed 191 lives leaving more than 1,800 injured. The victims came from 17 countries including Spain, France, Bulgaria and Poland, but they also came from as far as Brazil, Peru, Chile and Cuba making this attack truly global in scale, an attack that so far remains Europe's worst terrorist incident this century.

This attack was planned to coincide with the Spanish general elections, occurring three days before voting commenced. The timing of this attack also had greater significance, being committed exactly 911 days after the 9/11 terrorist attacks in the United States. Was this just a coincidence of attack planning of the Al-Qaeda inspired cell? Or part of the powerful delivery of their message?

1.3.2 Indiscriminate

The second common characteristic found in acts of terrorism throughout the world is the indiscriminate nature of attacks. A target-rich environment is offered to those terrorist groups who seek civilian casualties. They can carefully select a target and decide when and how to attack for maximum impact. There are many tactical options available to terrorist groups. Some of the most commonly used tactical options are indiscriminate by their very nature, including vehicle devices and suicide bombings. Even if a terrorist organization selects what it perceives to be a 'legitimate target' such as a military installation or government building, innocent civilians are often killed or injured. The sheer number of potential targets and tactical options therefore provides the terrorists with a high probability of success, and where desired, with the very minimum of risk.

Case study—Warrington Bombings, 1993

At 4 am on Friday, 26 February 1993 terrified residents in Warrington were evacuated from their homes following explosions which ripped through the local gas works on Winwick Road. Several hours before the explosions, Police Constable Mark Toker was shot and injured following a routine vehicle check of a van. The occupants of the van sped away from the scene later hi-jacking a Ford Escort forcing the driver into the boot. Following the incident, members of the Provisional Irish Republican Army (PIRA), Pairic MacFloinn, John Kinsella and Denis Kinsella were arrested and later jailed for their part in the attack.

Possibly in retaliation for the arrests, members of PIRA returned to Warrington on Saturday, 20 March 1993, just 20 days after the attack on the gas works. Explosive devices were placed in two waste bins on

Bridge Street, one outside Boots and the other outside Argos. A warning was given, but too late for action to be taken. The bombs exploded at 12.12 pm on what was a busy day for shoppers prior to Mothers' Day. Two children died in the attack, they were the only fatalities. The first victim, three-year-old Jonathan Ball died at the scene as he was caught up in the blast whilst shopping for a Mothers' Day card with his babysitter. The second victim, Timothy Parry, was shopping for a pair of football shorts when the devices exploded and he died in Liverpool's Walton Hospital five days later as a result of his injuries. A further 56 people were injured, many of them seriously. Despite a huge police operation the perpetrators of the attack have never been caught and brought to justice.

POINT TO NOTE—WHAT THE CASE STUDIES SHOW US

The case study of the two Warrington bombings shows how terrorist organizations are indiscriminate in their choice of targets and methods of operating. On both occasions no concern was shown for the potential loss of innocent life. The attacks also remind us that in our recent history it is not only military personnel and police officers who have been murdered by acts of terrorism on the UK mainland but also, and in far greater numbers, members of the public. To tackle new and emerging terrorist threats we need first to reflect upon previous terrorist attacks. Learning the lessons from history will assist in providing solutions to develop counter-terrorism measures for the future.

1.3.3 Human rights

The third common characteristic to be found in acts of terrorism throughout the world is their disregard for fundamental human rights. Terrorist attacks themselves cross the boundaries set by society. They deliberately breach human rights to maximize fear amongst communities so that we may be forced to make concessions in order to prevent further attacks. The Human Rights Act 1998 now guarantees fundamental rights and freedoms that are contained within the European Convention of Human Rights agreed by the Council of Europe at Rome, on 4 November 1950. It is these very rights that terrorist activity can often breach. The conventions contained within separate Articles include:

Table 1.2: Human Rights Articles

Article 2	Right to life
Article 3	Prohibition of torture
Article 4	Prohibition of Slavery & Forced Labour
Article 5	Right to Liberty & Security
Article 6	Right To A Fair Trail
Article 7	No Punishment Without Law
Article 8	Right To Respect Private/Family Life
Article 9	Freedom of Thought, Conscience & Religion
Article 10	Freedom of Expression
Article 11	Freedom of Assembly & Association
Article 12	Right To Marry
Article 14	Prohibition of Discrimination

For terrorist organizations to successfully pursue their extremist causes and influence governments to change policy, they operate outside of the framework of domestic and international law. Breaching human rights is therefore a direct consequence of taking such action, including what might be viewed as the prime right to life. This record of breach of rights does not, however, justify breaches of rights by the security authorities, including the police. Activities such as torture, illegal detentions and threats against political activists are counter-productive to the aim of upholding the values of a liberal, pluralist democracy, and they damage confidence in the police, especially amongst the communities from which the terrorists are drawn and which might otherwise help the police. There are many terrorist organizations that have engaged in sustained and bloody campaigns but none more so than the Liberation Tigers of Tamil Eelam.

Case study—Liberation Tigers of Tamil Eelam

The Liberation Tigers of Tamil Eelam (LTTE) are commonly known as the 'Tamil Tigers' and are one of the most violent terrorist organizations operating in the world today. LTTE is a militant Tamil nationalist organization that has waged a sustained campaign of violence since the 1970s against the government of Sri Lanka in order to create a separate Tamil state.

LTTE is an outlawed terrorist organization in 32 countries including the UK as it does not display the respect for human rights or adhere to the conduct expected of resistance movements. LTTE has been associated with the murder of innocent civilians, the kidnap of children for use as soldiers and the assassination of political figures. LTTE has also focused its attacks on non-military targets including commuter trains and buses, farming villages and mosques, resulting in the death and serious injury of a large number of civilians.

To conduct many of these attacks successfully the LTTE has developed the use of suicide bombers. The most feared section of the LTTE is the 'Black Tigers', a suicide commando unit which is responsible for large scale attacks and close-quarter assassination of political leaders. They are regarded as having pioneered the use of concealed suicide bomb vests which are now utilized by other terrorist groups around the world.

The LTTE has strongly denied the kidnap, recruitment and indoctrination of children in their terrorist activities, however, the use of children as front-line troops was proved in 2003 when 25 LTTE members aged 13 to 17 surrendered to the Sri Lankan forces. This incident sparked international controversy and amidst international pressure the LTTE were forced to announce that it would stop conscripting child soldiers. Further human rights contraventions linked to this brutal terrorist organization include strategies of ethnic cleansing, forcibly removing the Sinhalese and Muslim inhabitants from areas under the Tamil Tigers control, and the execution of prisoners of war despite making a declaration in 1998 that it would abide by the Geneva Conventions.

POINT TO NOTE—IDENTIFYING TERRORIST CHARACTERISTICS

Identifying the characteristics of an individual or group provides an insight of the terrorists' determination to achieve their objectives. It is then possible to make informed decisions on the most effective ways to protect the public and counter potential threats.

1.4 Terrorist Motivations

Taking steps to understand why terrorists do what they do is an important aspect of countering terrorism. Understanding elements of terrorist beliefs may facilitate an ability to tackle those drawn to commit acts of terrorism. Identifying what drives people towards terrorism and identifying the climate which provides such extreme beliefs to grow and flourish, may present an opportunity to tackle terrorism at its source.

1.4.1 Intervention

The psychology of terrorism is the subject of much academic debate. It is widely accepted that no one is born with extremist beliefs but is rather something which develops over time. It is this period of development which provides an opportunity to identify where extremist beliefs are emerging. There are many factors which may influence an individual including parenting, social inclusion, education, employment, health, and poverty. It is also important to acknowledge that their treatment at the hands of government agencies, including discriminatory and abusive treatment by the police, can also give rise to extremist behaviour, such as occurred in Northern Ireland. Many of these factors are social issues for the wider government and society to address but all may contribute in their own way to pushing individuals towards an extremist perspective. Identifying those who are most vulnerable to accepting and adopting extremist beliefs could lead to the implementation of intervention strategies designed to channel individuals away from extremist activity.

Case study—Osama bin Laden

Osama bin Laden will not have been born with the extremist views he holds today. So how did he become the most notorious terrorist in the world?

Osama, which means 'Young Lion' in Arabic, was born on 10 March 1957 in Saudi Arabia. He was the seventeenth son of Mohammed, a self-made construction multi-millionaire who had more than 50 sons and daughters to several wives. Mohammed founded his construction company in 1931 and the company has helped to re-build mosques and renovate holy places in Jerusalem, Mecca and Medina. Mohammed died in a plane crash in 1967 when bin Laden was 10 years old. At the age of 17, bin Laden married a Syrian relative who was to be the first of his four wives and began his studies at the prestigious King Abdul-Aziz University in Jeddah. During 1981 bin Laden completed his degrees in Economics and Public Administration.

Whilst at university, bin Laden became acquainted with extremist groups and was introduced to Abdullah Azzam and Muhammed Quth. It is reported that the teachings of Azzam and Quth significantly

---

influenced bin Laden's beliefs and that whilst at university he became absorbed in the writings of extremist individuals to the extent that he too developed radical views. At that time, bin Laden would have been aware of major changes taking place in the Middle East, none more so than the invasion of Afghanistan by the Soviet Union in December 1979. Muslims from around the world were drawn to fight the Soviets in Afghanistan in the 1980s which reportedly cost more than a million Afghan lives and resulted in a further five million Afghans being displaced. At the age of 22, bin Laden was drawn to fight in Afghanistan. He headed to Pakistan and there met with Afghan leaders who were calling for support.

Over several years bin Laden assisted in the recruitment of individuals to join the Afghan cause. He also supplied hundreds of tons of construction equipment from his family business used by the mujahedeen to build roads, dig tunnels and build hospitals. Following years of violent conflict the Soviet Union eventually withdrew from Afghanistan.

The war profoundly affected bin Laden and he developed the view that the conflict did not end with the removal of the Soviets but widened his agenda to cover the 'liberation' of Palestine and the removal of Western and modernist influences from Arab countries. In this way, his conflict took on religious and cultural aspects as well as political goals. In an interview with CNN in May 1997 bin Laden stated that, 'I have benefited so greatly from the jihad in Afghanistan that it would be impossible for me to gain such a benefit from any other chance. What we benefited from most was that the glory and myth of the superpower was destroyed.'

POINT TO NOTE—RADICALIZATION

Individuals can be recruited to support a cause by being systematically exposed to extremist beliefs. The way in which people move towards extremist beliefs is often referred to as 'radicalization'. It is simply a process by which people adopt an interpretation of religious, political or ideological belief that ultimately leads to them legitimising the use of violence through acts of terrorism. However, it is not an offence or terrorism to be 'extreme' or 'radical'.

1.4.2 Justification

An important aspect of a terrorist's motivation lies in their 'belief system'. As terrorists develop extremist beliefs of their particular cause they do so seeking justification for their actions. Individuals who teach, preach, and promote extremist beliefs often provide a single narrative of events. They are able to skilfully convince individuals that their manipulated version of events are true and alternative opinions are false.

POINT TO NOTE—JUSTIFICATION OF BELIEFS AND ACTIONS

Whatever the motivation, terrorists claim justification for their beliefs and actions. Individuals and groups who claim that a terrorist act is justified means that they pursue a purpose which they believe is 'just' and one that they believe can be given a reasonable explanation.

Many terrorist organizations see their enemy as the stronger body, the more dominant power. Usually, this assessment is true; their ability to access and use force and the apparatus of force is far less than the means possessed by state forces. This position then allows terrorists to justify the use of terrorist tactics against this dominant power. Terrorists justify and legitimize their acts in this way even though the use of force is illegitimate and there are, at least in the UK, democratic and peaceful ways to pursue political agendas. Al-Qaeda has a strong belief in their actions which is promoted to new recruits. It is this belief that over time becomes a duty, a duty that must be fulfilled. This was highlighted in January 2007 when Ayman al-Zawahiri, Al-Qaeda second in command and spiritual leader, stated in a recording that: 'It is your duty today to bear arms and to support those who are bearing arms, Jihad is the obligation of our time'.

It is important not to underestimate the powerful delivery of some of these messages. They seek to influence individuals who may feel disappointed with their standing in life, individuals who believe that they are not part of a community, who may feel that they have no identity or voice in their society, with no hopes or future life aspirations. It may be difficult to understand why people would be influenced in this way but it is very real, as evidenced by the attacks in London on 7 July 2005.

Case study—Mohammed Siddique Khan (MSK)

Mohammed Siddique Khan from Leeds, the oldest of the four suicide bombers, provides some justification for his actions whilst recording a 'martyrdom' message prior to the attacks. He stated that, 'Our drive and

---

motivation does not come from tangible commodities this world has to offer—your democratically elected governments continuously perpetuate atrocities against my people all over the world and your support of them makes you directly responsible—we will not stop this fight, we are at war and I am a soldier, now you too will taste the reality of this situation'.

1.4.3 Profile

A profile of a terrorist, or a person vulnerable to the process of radicalization would directly assist the police, partner agencies and communities to identify potential individuals, after all, there are many areas of policing where a profile of a suspect or group of criminals would be developed to assist in the identification of offenders. There is however no one single profile that would assist front line police officers or members of the community to identify a terrorist. This view is supported by the government's official account of the bombings in London on 7 July 2005 which states that: 'there is not a consistent profile to help identify who may be vulnerable to radicalisation'.

The Prevent Strategy launched by the government during 2008 aims to stop people becoming or supporting terrorists and violent extremists. It identifies that experience in the UK and elsewhere in the world has provided a lot of information as to why people are drawn into the world of violent extremism, either as actors or supporters. The assessment from the government is that violent extremism is caused by a combination of interlocking factors which include:

- An **ideology** which justifies terrorism by manipulating theology as well as history and politics;
- **Radicals and their networks** which promote violent extremism through a variety of places, institutions and media;
- **Individuals who are vulnerable** to the messages of violent extremists;
- **Communities**, which are sometimes poorly equipped to challenge and resist violent extremism; and;
- **Grievances**, some genuine and some perceived, and some of course directed very specifically against government.

POINTS TO NOTE—DANGERS OF A SINGLE PROFILE

Every single person who engages with terrorist activity does so for a variety of reasons. It is often a personal and individual journey as individuals move towards developing extremist beliefs. Terrorists come from a variety of cultural and religious backgrounds, social standing, education and with a variety of life experience. The real danger in establishing one single generic profile of a terrorist is that whilst seeking positive indicators on a profile it may overlook an individual or group failing to identify them as a potential threat.

Terrorists want to blend into our communities; they operate beneath the radar not wishing to draw attention to themselves or their activities. To bring them out into the open, a thorough understanding of what patterns of behaviour are routine and common needs to be developed so that changes can be identified.

1.5 **Terrorist Organizations**

Schedule 2 of the Terrorism Act 2000 provides a list of terrorist organizations that are outlawed in the UK. The Home Secretary has the power to proscribe organizations that are concerned with terrorism. The terrorist organizations that are proscribed under the 2000 Act include groups that are banned under powers introduced by the Terrorism Act 2006 as glorifying terrorism. An additional 14 organizations in Northern Ireland are proscribed under previous temporary and emergency provisions. The outlawed organizations range from global networks such as Al-Qaeda, to nationalist groups such as the Provisional Irish Republican Army (PIRA).

The command and control systems within these terrorists' organizations vary. Many nationalist terrorist groups are well structured and conduct their activities with tight operational security. Terrorist organizations often demand that their operatives are well-trained, that they have military discipline, that they are able to follow complex plans and can successfully overcome tactical and technical challenges during operations. However, Al-Qaeda and ideological groups often operate on a much looser, network basis. The core group provides ideology and assistance, but cells may be self-forming, using the name of the core group as if it were a franchise.

See also **4.2.1**.

POINT TO NOTE—TERRORIST ORGANIZATIONS

Understanding how terrorist organizations operate, focusing on their structure, lines of communication and command and control systems will provide an opportunity to assess the level of threat they pose. A greater understanding will also identify effective ways to counter their operations and reduce the threat. Knowledge and understanding of terrorist organizations are both key elements in being able to police terrorism.

Terrorist organizations operating throughout the world today can be broadly categorized as having either one of the following structures:

- Centralized

or

- Decentralized

1.5.1 Centralized organizations

Centralized organizations have a hierarchical structure often with a military command and control regime. This structure offers a high degree of control to its leaders ensuring the activities of its members do not undermine the tactical and strategic objectives of the group. They are however prone to infiltration as their regimented and inflexible structure can make them vulnerable to attack. Their command and control functions can be predictable allowing law enforcement and intelligence agencies with an opportunity to counter future threats.

Case study—Irish Republican Army

The Irish Republican Army (IRA) has a centralized structure having defined procedures and specific roles for its operatives. It is led by the General Army Council who passes its instructions through the command chain to the Army Executive, the Army Council and the General Headquarters Staff who tactically deliver the agreed strategies. This structure provides control to senior IRA members where operations have to be sanctioned. The IRA terrorists are generally regarded as being disciplined and their attack planning thoroughly researched providing them with a high level of certainty that their activities will be successful.

Terrorist attacks by the IRA are designed to increase political pressure on the government and to gain additional support for their cause. An effective example of this includes the vehicle bomb that was detonated on Whitehall in London during 1991. The location of the device delivered a powerful message to the government that they were able to strike at the heart of the UK when they pleased. The vehicle was parked close to the Ministry of Defence premises, not far from 10 Downing Street, Horse Guards Parade and the Houses of Parliament in Westminster. This attack gained considerable support for the IRA as its aim appeared not to be the killing of innocent members of the public. It was seen as a 'legitimate target' and the type of operation that would have been controlled and commanded by the tight centralized structure in support of the overall political motivations of the IRA. To evidence why such control is required by nationalist groups we need only to examine the events that took place in Omagh during 1998, Northern Ireland's worst terrorist atrocity.

Case study—Omagh Bombing 1998

On 15 August 1998 members of the Real IRA (RIRA) parked a stolen Vauxhall Cavalier containing 500 lbs of explosives outside a clothes shop on Omagh's Market Street. The device detonated at 3 pm in a crowded shopping area. A series of warnings were provided but the location of the bomb was not clear. To add to the confusion it appeared that the vehicle had been parked some distance away from its intended target. The police led members of the public away from what they perceived to be the location of the device but people were actually led towards the direction of the Vauxhall Cavalier.

It is still not clear as to whether the primary intention of RIRA was to maximize casualties from the outset, or whether a series of mistakes about the exact location of the vehicle had been made. In either case 29 people were killed in the attack which included men and women from both Protestant and Catholic faiths. Nine children were also killed, as well as a woman who was expecting twins. There was a huge public reaction and condemnation of RIRA for this attack. The then Prime Minister, Tony Blair described the attack as an 'appalling act of savagery and evil'. RIRA lost support and local opinion was swayed in support of the peace process, the very process which RIRA was intending to destabilize.

The events of Omagh go some way to proving why control is required for terrorists groups that are in some way answerable to the public. Attacks which are not in support of the wider group's motivations can be turned against them to such an extent that they may never recover the political ground they have lost. An important lesson here is that there is a difference between indiscriminate attacks and mass attacks. Only in the case of Al-Qaeda has there sometimes been a clear desire for mass casualties, since they neither value the lives of those being victimized nor seek popular support.

There are a number of centralized structures which terrorist organizations have adopted, though it should be realized that structures often cohere around personalities and friendships, so the rationalization which follows represents ideal types rather than the reality of many groups. Some of these structures will have formed naturally as terrorist groups grow and gain support but others will have been purposefully created. There are three key centralized structures which include:

- Duo-cell
- Tri-cell
- Corporate cell.

1.5.1.1 *Duo-cell*

The Duo-cell is a very simple centralized structure. Terrorist A is the leader of the cell commanding and controlling the activities of Terrorist B. There is a strict line of communication which ensures operational security is tight but a Duo-cell requires Terrorist B to gain considerable insight into the attack plans of Terrorist A. This makes Terrorist B and the cell structure vulnerable to infiltration. A Duo-cell is difficult to detect and penetrate as the activities of only two members can be easily concealed. The primary advantage for the leader of a Duo-cell is that if their activities have been well planned, Terrorist A can withdraw from Terrorist B at any time without detection.

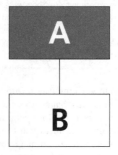

Figure 1.1: Duo-cell structure

1.5.1.2 *Tri-cell*

A Tri-cell is another simple centralized structure but it provides the leader of the cell with more resilience as simultaneous activities can be conducted. The lines of communication are important for a Tri-cell which adopts the 'need to know' principle. Terrorist A can provide orders to Terrorist B and C independently so that they are not aware of each other's activities. In certain circumstances Terrorist B and C may never meet and never know each other's identity. This ensures that operational security is tight and that following any suspicion of the cell being infiltrated by agents the leader of the cell can quickly identify any informants. The advantage for the leader of a Tri-cell is that if their activities have been well planned Terrorist A can withdraw from Terrorist B or C at any time without detection. If two independent attacks are being planned the compromise of only one attack will not prevent the second attack from progressing.

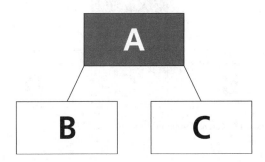

Figure 1.2: Tri-cell structure

1.5.1.3 *Corporate cell*

The corporate cell is the most sophisticated centralized terrorist structure in operation today. The diagram below shows a very simple structure but it encompasses the advantages of both the Duo-cell and the Tri-cell. A corporate cell provides its leader or leaders with greater operational scope. The corporate cell of major centralized terrorists' organizations can be as complex as any organizational structure of commercial companies. A corporate cell relies upon clear lines of communication with each member having a specific role and responsibility. Activities of a particular strand of a corporate cell under the directorship of terrorist B can be conducted in complete isolation from terrorist B and C. Despite the corporate cell providing numerous opportunities for agents to infiltrate the sheer scale of structures ensures the protection and anonymity of its leader can be achieved. The key disadvantage of such a large centralized terrorist organization is the management of its members ensuring that no activity is conducted without the appropriate approval. Rogue elements that do not follow instructions within such groups are not tolerated as their actions may have a detrimental impact upon the strategic progression of the wider terrorist group. To keep its members in line large terrorist groups which operate a corporate cell structure have robust internal methods of security and policing.

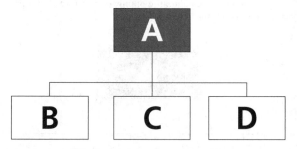

Figure 1.3: Corporate-cell structure

1.5.2 Decentralized organizations

Decentralized organizations are described as networks with no vertical chain of command. They require a minimum degree of control by their leaders and are extremely difficult to locate and penetrate. A network structure offers flexibility to terrorist groups with an opportunity to plan and conduct multiple attacks which stretches law enforcement resources. Al-Qaeda are the most prominent terrorist group who currently operate a decentralized structure being best described as a 'network of networks'.

Case study—Al-Qaeda

Al-Qaeda has been forced to change the way in which they are structured in order to survive. During the Afghan conflict and throughout the 1980s Al-Qaeda operated within a centralized structure. There were two key elements which led them to change their method of operating. First, following the end of the Afghan conflict Al-Qaeda re-focused its objectives when Osama bin Laden declared war on the West. A centralized structure would not be able to achieve this goal as communication channels around the world would not be easily achieved and a loss of control of operatives and their activities was inevitable. A decentralized structure offered an alternative solution.

Creating a loose coalition of networked groups operating under the banner of Al-Qaeda would make multiple attacks in numerous countries all around the world a possibility. Al-Qaeda had been structured like other hierarchical terrorist groups having a number of strands. The military section focused upon recruitment, training, procurement and operations. The finance section of Al-Qaeda sought revenue whilst religious and legal sections drafted justification for their extreme ideologies.

It became clear during the 1990s that the decentralized global network operation of Al-Qaeda had spread into Europe and the UK as Khala-al-Fawwaz was arrested in London for the US embassy bombings in Kenya and Tanzania in 1998 which claimed 300 lives. Prior to his arrest Khala-al-Fawwaz was managing the Al-Qaeda European press and public relations office operating from London.

The second element which led to Al-Qaeda to change its structure was as a direct result of coalition forces action and the struggle against terrorism that continues to this day. In order to operate effectively Al-Qaeda was forced to split. It now operates as a series of networks which makes it very difficult to track. As Al-Qaeda lost much of its base in Afghanistan it has gained ground elsewhere. Al-Qaeda is reported to be operating in over 60 countries. To achieve this global reach Al-Qaeda has relinquished its central management system so cells dotted all over the world can now operate independently claiming to have conducted attacks in the name and ideological brand of Al-Qaeda terrorism.

POINT TO NOTE—DECENTRALIZED STRUCTURES

One of the most potent threats from international terrorism is that cells inspired by Al-Qaeda can form anywhere. These cells do not have to seek approval from the core leadership of Al-Qaeda. They can conduct their operations from within their own local communities, a threat which is very real in the UK with home-grown terrorists. Such autonomous cells can operate independently having no direct links to the core of Al-Qaeda.

The decentralized structure of Al-Qaeda is an effective way of operating. Not only does it limit the opportunities for intelligence agencies to intercept and disrupt attack planning activity but it also protects the core leadership of Al-Qaeda whilst attacks continue in their name.

There are a number of decentralized structures which terrorist organizations have adopted. Some of these structures will have formed organically as terrorist groups grow and gain support but others will have been purposefully created. There are four key decentralized structures which include:

- Link Cell;
- Star Cell;
- Fused Cell; and
- Lone Wolf.

1.5.2.1 *Link cell*

The Link Cell is a simple linear structured network with no hierarchy. The lines of communication flow in one direction ensuring the anonymity of Terrorist A as instructions, guidance, or information passes through the links to Terrorist H. Despite there being many lines of communication which may be prone to interception, terrorists forming part of a Link Cell are well protected. If its

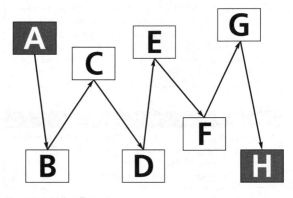

Figure 1.4: Link-cell structure

members follow strict security guidance then they will not know each other's identities nor will they be in a position to identify the instigator of terrorist activities within their network. The Link Cell is common amongst serious and organized criminal gangs, especially in the movement of drugs and firearms. The Link Cell relies upon its members to trust the network asking no questions about from whom or where instructions have originated.

1.5.2.2 *Star cell*

The Star Cell is a decentralized structure which has a prominent leader at its centre. Information from terrorist A is communicated to other members. This information flows around the structure of the star which at any time can be fed back to the centre. The prominent leader is the key driver of this structure often providing propaganda, spiritual guidance and encouragement for its network to develop and deliver terrorist attacks. There are no formal lines of communication between each member making the

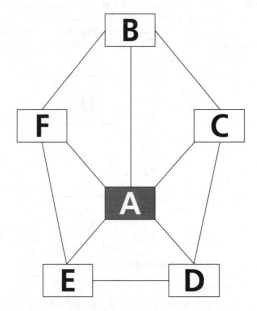

Figure 1.5: Star-cell structure

identification of the network difficult. The primary advantage of a Star Cell lies in its ability to regenerate following the disruption or compromise of any if its members. As one member is removed, attacks continue by other members and if the prominent leader is removed any one of the members can assume primacy and move into the centre. To disrupt or remove a Star Cell structure all of its component parts have to be tackled together.

1.5.2.3 *Fused cell*

A Fused Cell is the most complex of decentralized structures which has no real prominent force leading its activities. It is best described as a fully linked network of networks where each member is linked to one another by numerous lines of communication. They do not take direction from any specific individual but decide for themselves what activities they are going to be concerned in to further their cause. The key advantage of a Fused Cell is that it can be driven by external influences and can grow quickly across countries and continents as the rhetoric of its members is promoted on a global scale. It is not that individual Fused Cells are difficult to track once identified it is the way in which they can suddenly appear that creates the greatest challenges for law enforcement agencies who seek to get ahead of its growth aiming to prevent new cells from forming.

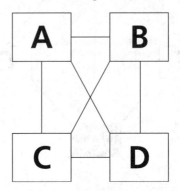

Figure 1.6: Fused-cell network structure

1.5.2.4 *Lone wolf*

The most potent threat of any centralized or decentralized terrorist structure is that of the individual who has no direct lines of communication with any terrorist group. Described as a Lone Wolf hunting away from any pack a single individual can plan and prepare an attack in complete isolation if tight operational security measures are followed. The Lone Wolf provides the greatest terrorist threat as they can suddenly appear without warning. Individual terrorists who operate alone often first come to the attention of intelligence agencies and law enforcement once their attacks have been conducted.

Figure 1.7: Lone wolf

The Lone Wolf may engage in terrorist activity for a variety of reasons having a number of personal motivations. They may also have been encouraged to develop violent and extremist beliefs having been exposed to terrorist propaganda and extremist material. The Lone Wolf is vulnerable to those who pedal hate and recruit new operatives for their cause. Preventing an environment where extremist beliefs are allowed to take route is the long term method of tackling this threat.

POINTS TO NOTE—FRAMEWORKS

The centralized and decentralized structures outlined provide a simple analysis of some of the frameworks that have been adopted by terrorist organizations. It is by no means a complete list of all potential structures that new and emerging terrorist groups may adopt. It is also important to note that a single terrorist organization may be made up of one or any combination of the structures. Al-Qaeda, for example, may operate as a Star Cell in certain countries but it may also have connecting nodes to a series of Fused Cell structures in other locations. The ideology of Al-Qaeda has also captured the hearts and minds of the Lone Wolf. There is much debate amongst counter terrorism professionals and academics across the world about the actual structure of Al-Qaeda and whether its ideology poses a greater threat than the attack planning activities of its core leadership. Whatever the result of the debate it is clear that Al-Qaeda inspired terrorism continues to gather momentum.

Terrorist organizations can also change and adapt their structure and method of operating, particularly if they sense their operational security is under threat. This was observed during 1977 as the IRA, believing that its organization had been infiltrated by agents working for the government, changed its structure from organized companies and brigades to small cells that although commanded from the centre had more autonomy. This new structure was implemented quickly, another key advantage of a centralized structure as decisions are swiftly followed and translated throughout the organization.

1.6 Terrorist Tactics

Terrorists and their organizations choose which tactic they wish to deploy. There are many factors which influence this decision which includes the nature of the intended target, the abilities of its operatives and the hostile environment in which they operate. Whatever target is chosen the terrorists are spoilt by an abundance of methods at their disposal to bring about a successful conclusion.

Over time and often by accident (trial and error) rather than design, terrorist organizations develop a preferred method of operating often referred to as their 'signature' or 'hallmark'—this would be a tactic that they trusted and had refined through operational experience. The threat from international terrorism however embraces a variety of tactics where no single technique can be solely attributed to a specific grouping. It would also be dangerous for us to believe that a particular terrorist group operates in a certain way which could lead to other plans being dismissed. Terrorist activities throughout the world include the following:

- Arson
- Assassinations
- Bombings
- Hi-jacking
- Hoaxes and threats
- Hostage-taking
- Hostile reconnaissance
- Infiltration
- Kidnap

- Propaganda
- Recruitment
- Training
- Sabotage
- Suicide missions.

Terrorist organizations may use these activities alone or as part of a much broader strategy. Tactics such as propaganda, threats, or hoaxes are designed to raise fear and tensions within communities. Criminal activities are also used to support terrorist organizations particularly for raising funds. Terrorists have also used toxic agents to conduct attacks, though this is extremely rare and the risk of the terrorist use of chemical, biological, radiological, or nuclear weapons is low because of the difficulties of obtaining and deploying such materials and Al-Qaeda aside, most terrorist groups do not seek innocent mass casualties. Many of the terrorist tactics described above have been used in the UK.

POINT TO NOTE—THE SAME PLACE CAN BE ATTACKED TWICE

History tells us that once a place has been attacked it is more likely to be attacked again. The reason relates to the political symbolism of these targets, the understanding of which increases after each attack. The World Trade Centre is a prime example of this, being first attacked in 1993 by a vehicle borne device located in an underground car park. It was attacked again eight years later in 2001 by suicide terrorists hi-jacking commercial flights and using them as weapons. Not only did the events of 7 July 2005 in London represent the first use of suicide bombers in the UK, but two weeks later on 21 July 2005, a failed suicide attack also targeted the London Underground as part of a similar plot.

It is important for police colleagues to increase their awareness of terrorist tactics so that they can respond effectively to them. We should not fall into the trap of thinking that just because a place has been attacked by a specific tactic that it will not be attacked again in the same way or by an alternative method. Neither should we assume that a tactic which has not been used before is not under development and will not be used in the near future. Transport systems, international aircraft, iconic sites, and state buildings will always be prime targets alongside other premises forming part of a country's critical infrastructure such as power stations and key utilities.

1.6.1 **Recruitment**

Terrorist organizations seek to spread their political, religious or ideological motivations to new individuals who are recruited to their cause. One of the most alarming threats that has developed over recent years is the number of UK citizens travelling to Iraq and Afghanistan to join insurgent groups to fight coalition forces. Individuals from our communities are being recruited for this cause.

Case study—Iraq British Brigade

In June 2006 the Sunday Times reported that 'up to 150 radicals from Britain have travelled to Iraq to join up with the 'British Brigade' that has been established by Al-Qaeda leaders to fight coalition forces'. It went on to say that, 'the flow of young men from Western Europe to Iraq has increased dramatically over the last two years'.

The International Institute for Strategic Studies published a report in 2006 entitled, 'The Military Balance'. In this report, it was estimated that one in ten of the 20,000 insurgents in Iraq were foreign-born. The Sunday Times also reported that this was not only an issue for the UK but that other European countries were also encountering a similar problem, stating that, 'In May 2006 Pierre de Bousquet de Florian, the head of the French domestic security service, said that about 15 young French people remained in and around Iraq and at that at least nine had died'.

POINTS TO NOTE—RETURNING RECRUITS

Police officers must be aware of the wider implications of these issues. Not all of the recruits who join the insurgents will die during combat in Iraq and Afghanistan; some will survive and may return home to their communities having received military training and combat experience. What will they do when they return back to the UK? This is a specific threat which you may not have previously considered but it provides some evidence of the broad types of activity that may potentially impact upon the threat to the UK from international terrorism.

See also **4.3**.

1.6.2 **Training**

Terrorist organizations throughout the world conduct training to develop and improve their capabilities. Training camps are often a place where further recruitment and indoctrination is conducted. Terrorist training camps have long been established in parts of the Middle East but there has been a growing number of training activities taking place in the UK in support of international terrorism.

Case study— Operation OVERAMP

Operation Overamp was a two-year joint Security Service (MI5) and police investigation focusing upon Attila Ahmet and Mohammed Hamid. Ahmet and Hamid incited others to commit murder during meetings at Hamid's house and at terrorist training camps in the British countryside. At Woolwich Crown Court on 26 February 2008 seven men linked to these terrorist activities were convicted of terrorism related offences. The landmark case brought the first conviction under Section 8 of the Terrorism Act 2006 which created an offence to provide terrorist training or attend a place for terrorist training.

Deborah Walsh, Deputy Head of the Crown Prosecution Service Counter Terrorism Division stated that, 'No one should be in any doubt as to how serious Hamid and Ahmet were in encouraging their recruits to inflict casualties on innocent people. Hamid is a man for whom the indiscriminate killing of 52 people on 7 July 2005 was, in his own words: "not even breakfast for me"'. The defendants were filmed by each other undertaking serious military style training, including manoeuvres that replicated Taliban and Al-Qaeda training methods.

1.6.3 Hostile reconnaissance

Hostile reconnaissance involves the gathering of information for use in a terrorist attack. It forms an integral part of the attack planning process as terrorists seek to obtain a profile of a target. Hostile reconnaissance is a feasibility study to identify what method of attack would be most appropriate and when would be the preferred time of attack to ensure an operation is successfully completed. Identifying hostile reconnaissance is important as it very often provides the first indication that a terrorist cell is planning an attack. A number of terrorist plots in the UK that have been disrupted by the police have revealed evidence of hostile reconnaissance being conducted. An example of how important hostile reconnaissance is to terrorist attack planning is evident in the attack which took place during the Munich Olympic Games in 1972.

Case study—Munich Massacre, Olympic Games 1972

Munich won the bid to host the 1972 Olympics during the 64th International Olympics Committee Session in Rome on 26 April 1966. At the time of the announcement, the world was still recovering from the impact of the Nazi regime and the new and emerging West German democratic government were keen to promote a very different Germany. On 26 August 1972 the West German President, Gustav Heinemann, officially opened the Games at the Olympic Stadium in Munich. More than 7,000 competitors took part from 121 countries in the Games that carried the motto 'the Happy Games'. Unbeknown to German authorities, members of the terrorist group Black September had already infiltrated the Olympic Village securing employment weeks prior to the opening ceremony. They were well placed to conduct hostile reconnaissance and began plotting their attack against the Israeli Olympic team.

Black September was a Palestinian militant terrorist organization. They took their name from the events of September 1970 where thousands of Palestinians were killed during fighting in Jordan. The Jordanians wished to expel the Palestinians from their country having provided them with refuge several years before. Their presence in Jordan had begun to threaten the authority of King Hussein and force was sanctioned to ensure their removal. The fighting was brutal and many Palestinians fled to Israel seeking asylum or imprisonment rather than face the Jordanians. This period of history proved to be a challenging time in the Middle East. As an uneasy peace settled in Jordan, Black September was established which began to engage in acts of assassination and bombings of Jordanian targets before turning its attention to Israel.

Members of Black September were individuals devoted to their cause and they were willing to sacrifice themselves for what they believed in. The Munich Games provided Black September with an opportunity to seek their revenge. German authorities did not expect such determined individuals to infiltrate their Olympic Village despite concerns being raised from the Israeli security officials about the location of their teams accommodation and general lack of visible security measures. Members of Black September working within the Olympic Village identified the location of the Isreali teams accommodation and assessed weaknesses in security. It is reported that security within the Olympic Village was intentionally relaxed, believed to be part of the German authorities' plan to present a new demilitarized country. As a direct result athletes by-passed security controls, jumping over perimeter fencing and not presenting or carrying appropriate identification.

Members of Black September operated within tight self-contained cells which were difficult to penetrate. Leadership was provided from outside of the cell which protected the anonymity of those providing strategic direction. Operating a need-to-know security regime and armed with detailed plans, the Black September Munich cell were in place, unde-tected, and were ready to use the element of surprise on their targets.

During the early hours of 5 September, almost two weeks into the Games, eight terrorists scaled the perimeter fence to the Olympic Village wearing tracksuits and carrying duffel bags containing AK47 assault rifles, pistols and grenades. They made their way to two of the Israeli Olympic team apartments at 31 Connollystrasse. At approximately 4.30 am, using stolen keys from their previous employment, the terrorists entered and ambushed the athletes. During initial exchanges members of the Israeli team were overpowered and wrestling coach Mosche Weinberg and weightlifter Yossef Romano were shot and killed. The terrorists were left with nine living hostages. As the German authorities responded to reports of the incident the terrorists delivered their demands which included the release of 234 Palestinians jailed in Israel. To show their determination the body of murdered Mosche Weinberg was thrown out of the front door of the apartment. The Israeli government quickly confirmed their position; there would be no negotiation with terrorists. Life within the Olympic Village away from the immediate vicinity of 31 Connollystrasse continued as normal. The sporting events also continued throughout that day until mounting pressure on the IOC led to the suspension of the Games which triggered mass media attention towards the Olympic Village. German bor-der police officers armed with sub-machine guns were plotted around the apartments as members of Black September, just 12 hours into the siege, increased their demands by requesting safe passage to Cairo in Egypt.

The German authorities believed that movement by the terrorists would provide them with an opportunity to attempt a rescue operation. The plan was to collect the terrorists and their hostages in a bus which would take them to two helicopters. They would then be transported to a nearby NATO airbase at Furstenfeldbruck. At this airbase German police snipers would be ready to intercept the terrorists as they boarded the plane which would also contain a small contingent of firearms offi-cers dressed as flight crew. The plan would prove to be an unmitigated disaster from start to finish. The rescue operation was developed on the basis that there were no more than five terrorists, it was clear that an accurate intelligence picture had not been appropriately established. As the hostages and members of Black September boarded a bus to take them to the helicopters the German authorities realized there were actually eight terrorists who were heavily armed. There was little time to inform the operation at the airbase and no flexibility in their planning to increase the capacity of firearms resources. For a reason that remains unresolved and subject to much debate to this day the firearms unit within the waiting aircraft decided to leave their posts and retreat from their advanced positions within the aircraft without informing their cen-tral command. This decision was to prove fatal.

At approximately 10.30 pm, the helicopters landed at the airbase. Unfortunately they did not land as instructed and instead of providing a clear line of sight for the snipers they actually obstructed views which gave the terrorists an advantage. The snipers did not have radio communications and as a result could not co-ordinate their fire. Two terrorists left the helicopters and made their way to the waiting Boeing 727 aircraft. As they entered the plane they saw no cabin crew and it was at this point that they must have realized the agreement struck with the German authorities was a trap. The two terrorists raced back to the helicopters to inform the rest of the terrorist cell as the snipers seized upon their opportunity and opened fire. The snipers were, however, poorly equipped, poorly trained and in bad light with no telescopic sights or infra-red capability they missed their targets and the terrorists were quick to respond with their superior AK47s. A German sniper was shot and killed instantly, followed by the shooting of two terrorists who had held the helicopter pilots hostage at gunpoint. As a chaotic gunfight ensued the helicopter pilots escaped but the hostages who were bound together remained inside the helicopters unable to get out.

The German authorities had not made any contingency plans which included the use of armoured vehicles. As the gunfight raged members of Black September found cover beneath the helicopters making it increasingly difficult for the snipers to select their targets. A decision was made to call for armoured vehicles but due to heavy traffic on the route to the airbase there was a significant delay. The arrival of the armoured vehicles appeared to provide the remaining terrorists with the realization that their attack was nearing defeat. Shortly after midnight on the morning of 6 September the terrorists opened fire at close range on the hostages in the helicopters and threw hand grenades into the cockpit. The resulting explosion incinerated the nine remaining Israeli team members which included Ze'ev Friedman, David Berger and Yakov Springer from the weightlifting team, Mark Slavin, Eliezer Halfin and Yossef Gutfreud from the wrestling team and Andre Spitzer the fencing coach and Amitzur Shapira the track coach. Three terrorists, Yusuf Nazzal, Jamal Al Gashey and Mohammed Safady survived the crossfire and were arrested. News was slow to reach the world about the massacre, initial reports were positive stating that all hostages had been rescued but it was US ABC channel broadcaster Jim McKay that broke the news to the world stating that, 'Our worst fears have been realised tonight. They've now said that there were eleven hostages. Two were killed in their rooms yesterday morning, nine were killed at the airport tonight. They're all gone'.

The impact of the terrorist attack on the 1972 Olympics was devastating. All remaining Israeli athletes withdrew from the Games following the memorial service held on 6 September in the

Olympic Stadium. Calls were made to cancel the remainder of the events but the final decision was to continue although the atmosphere was very different. Security was tightened with all Jewish sportsmen and women having personal protection. In response to the murder of 11 of its athletes Israeli planes bombed Palestinian targets in Syria and Lebanon three days later on 9 September. The Israeli government sought its revenge via other avenues and identified a series of undercover agents who were reported to be tasked with assassinating individuals believed to be connected in the planning of the Munich attack. This operation lasted for many years and has been recently captured on film in Steven Spielberg's movie, 'Munich'. The German authorities were also engaged in further counter-terrorism operations directly linked to the violent events of the Olympic Games. On 29 October, just seven weeks after the arrest of the three surviving Black September members, terrorists hi-jacked a German Lufthansa passenger jet demanding their immediate release. To guard against any further embarrassment the German authorities met their demands in full and all three surviving members were provided safe passage to Libya without ever standing trial for their part in the Munich massacre.

The massacre in Munich was made possible because terrorists conducted hostile reconnaissance of the Olympic Village and planned their attack in detail. No one reported any suspicious activity and the attack planning progressed undetected.

The types and methods of obtaining or gathering intelligence during hostile reconnaissance are wide and varied and may include any of the activities documented in the following table:

Table 1.3: Gathering intelligence in hostile reconnaissance

Suspicious Sightings	Presence at a place which appears unusual or unnatural.
Surveillance	Recording or monitoring of activities which includes the use of cameras, mobile phone cameras and other vision-enhancing devices.
Security Tests	Attempts to measure security systems, protocols, or responses.
Elicitation	Attempts to gain information in person or by electronic means.
Dry Run	Rehearsal to test attack plans.

POINTS TO NOTE—REPORTING SUSPICIOUS ACTIVITY

Police officers must be aware of the importance of recording and reporting suspicious activity. At all times members of the public should be encouraged to report any information which they believe to be unusual. If something strikes you as being out of place, trust your instincts and report it. In an emergency which may present an immediate threat then the **999** emergency service telephone number should be used but the confidential anti-terrorism hotline number, **0800 789321**, which is staffed around the clock by specialist counter-terrorism police officers and staff, provides an additional service and is waiting to receive information. The terrorist threat remains real and there is no room for complacency, the public and the police need to remain alert and be aware of their surroundings.

1.6.4 Bombings

Bombings are closely associated with acts of terrorism around the world. There are a wide variety of bombing techniques that continue to be used from letter bombs designed to target an individual, concealed pipe bombs to attack small groups in specific locations and vehicle and person borne devices which can penetrate at the heart of a terrorist group's enemy. Knowledge, expertise, and access to the relevant materials are required before a bombing attack of any nature can be conducted. This provides an opportunity for authorities to identify and intercept terrorist attack planning as commercial and military grade explosives are tightly controlled and regulated in the UK. Terrorists are increasingly creative in their design and delivery of bomb attacks and now utilize quantities of chemicals found in non-commercial and non-military products to make their own home-made explosives (HMEs). The most devastating terrorist attack in the UK was achieved through the use of a bomb located on Pan Am Flight 103 during December 1988.

Case study—Lockerbie, Pan Am Flight 103, 21 December 1988

At 6.25 pm on Wednesday, 21 December 1988, Pan American Flight 103, a Boeing 747 aircraft named 'Clipper Maid of the Seas', took off from London Heathrow Airport destined for JFK airport in New York. Moments after 7.02 pm, as the flight was over Scotland, the airliner's transponders stopped replying. At that time the 747 was calculated as flying at 31,000 feet and

---

at a speed of 580km per hr. The subsequent investigation revealed that an explosion had ripped through the front fuselage section of the aircraft ultimately causing it to rip into several pieces. Investigators believe that within three seconds of the explosion, the cockpit, fuselage and the third engine were falling separately. The fuselage continued moving forward and down until it reached 19,000 feet at which point its dive became almost vertical. As the aircraft fell it broke into smaller pieces resulting in debris being scattered over an area of 2 km.

The initial explosion and the impact of the aircraft upon parts of Lockerbie, Scotland, resulted in the death of 270 people. All 243 passengers were killed, together with 16 air crew. Eleven people in Lockerbie were killed as large sections of the fuselage fell in and around the town. Victims on the aircraft came from 21 countries, including 180 from the US and 41 from the UK. The attack remains the deadliest terrorist incident in the UK and until the events of 9/11 was also the largest loss of American life due to acts of terrorism.

The explosion was believed to have been caused by a bomb concealed in a suitcase that was placed on the flight by the interline baggage system. The suitcase was unaccompanied at the time of detonation. On 3 May 2000 two Libyan men were tried for murder, Abdelbaset Ali Mohmed Al Megrahi and Lamin Khalifah Fhimah. Fhimah was found not guilty but Megrahi was convicted of murder on 31 January 2001 and sentenced to life imprisonment. Although his first appeal was rejected on 14 March 2002 Megrahi continues to appeal against his conviction through the Scottish Criminal Cases Review Commission (SCCRC).

1.6.5 Suicide missions

Suicide terrorism is an extremely impactive terrorist tactic. Like precision-guided missiles suicide terrorists whether on foot, vehicles, boats, or aircraft can strike at the heart of their target causing maximum casualties. Academic research in this field indicates that suicide attacks kill four times more individuals than other conventional tactics. Suicide terrorism is effective; it is inexpensive and is symbolic, drawing considerable attention to the cause of the perpetrators. There is no exit strategy to plan and prepare for suicide missions saving considerable time and effort. If suicide missions are successful there is little evidence left for authorities to gain information on key terrorist cell members. It is also important to highlight that suicide terrorism is not a tactic that is only used as a last resort or by the weaker group: it has, on a small number of occasions, been used by terrorist organizations who may only briefly hold a strong position within a struggle but who wish to exploit weaknesses in their enemy.

POINTS TO NOTE—SUICIDE TERRORISM

We must begin to understand what drives people to kill themselves in this way. Understanding suicide terrorism is a challenge in itself. Whilst suicide terrorists in the UK, Israel, and Iraq may share many characteristics, they are also unique. Suicide terrorists are often described as 'products of their own environment' and findings from research into what drives a particular individual towards suicide terrorism as to other forms of terrorist activity cannot be readily used to draw conclusions for all suicide terrorists operating across the world.

Case study—Mike's Place, Tel Aviv, Israel, 2003

The first significant attack by a British home-grown suicide bomber occurred thousands of miles away in Israel two years before 7/7. At 1 am on 30 April 2003 a suicide bomber attacked Mike's Place, a bar on the Tel Aviv seafront. Three people were killed and a further 60 were injured. Waiting outside the bar was another suicide bomber whose device failed to detonate. As the emergency services arrived the second bomber fled. In a nearby rubbish bin police later found two passports which identified the bombers as being British. Asif Mohammed Hanif, aged 21, martyred himself at Mike's Place whilst his accomplice, Omar Khan Sharif, aged 27, ran away from the scene. Two weeks later the body of Sharif was found floating in the sea off Tel Aviv. Both Sharif and Hanif had travelled to Israel from the UK.

1.6.6 Infiltration

Terrorist organizations seek information about their enemies. As part of hostile reconnaissance they will attempt to elicit information about an identified target or test security measures to analyse reaction and responses. Terrorists are aware that an effective method of gathering this information is to infiltrate the ranks of its target.

Case study—Castlereagh, Belfast, 2002

On St Patrick's Day, just after 10 pm on Sunday, 17 March 2002, intruders entered Castlereagh Police Station in Belfast. They made their way to 'Room 2-20', reportedly an area designated for the storage of sensitive Special Branch files. A police officer was overpowered and documents were stolen. Initial investigations revealed no sign of a forced entry.

As media speculation grew it emerged that 'Room 2-20' had recently been moved to that location from another part of the building due to refurbishment. All indications suggested that the intruders had received instructions from an insider. The documents were believed to contain highly sensitive information concerning the covert human intelligence source activities of the police.

Following the attack, Sammy Wilson, a member of the Policing Board of Northern Ireland stated that he had serious concerns about security at Castlereagh which up until 1999 was believed to have been used to conduct interviews of terrorist suspects. He said that 'People who have given information to Special Branch and understood it was given in the strictest confidence would have grave concerns', concluding that 'if a police station can be robbed in this way, what chance do the ordinary punters have who are manning petrol stations late at night and people manning post office counters'.

Suspicions were directed to the potential involvement of the Provisional Irish Republican Army (PIRA) and the then Secretary for Northern Ireland, Dr John Reid, was swift to appoint a former civil servant, Sir John Chilcot to head a government inquiry which was to run in parallel with the criminal investigation. Dr John Reid stated that 'It is essential that we establish the facts surrounding this incident as quickly as possible and ensure, in the national interest, that all necessary steps have been taken'.

The attack put pressure on the already fragile peace process particularly as the IRA was planning a second act of weapons decommissioning. If the incident was to be placed at the door of PIRA and they were responsible for the theft of its 'enemy's' secrets, then this could be viewed as a clear breach of the complete cessation of military operations which was outlined as an integral part of the peace process. Ulster Unionist MP David Burnside declared that 'If the Provisional IRA who are inside this process and in government of Northern Ireland, unionists and my party colleagues are going to have to re-examine their whole approach'. The BBC outlined that Sinn Fein had said republicans played 'no part in the raid on Castlereagh'.

1.6.7 Chemical, biological, radiological, and nuclear

Whilst suicide terrorism can claim mass casualties the most dangerous terrorist tactic is the potential use of chemical, biological, radiological, or nuclear agents.

Case study—Sarin Gas Attack, Tokyo Underground, 1985

On 20 March 1995 the Japanese cult Aum Shinrikyo (Supreme Truth) placed containers of the toxic Sarin gas on five trains of the Tokyo underground network. The trains were destined to stop at the Kasumigaseki station which serviced many government offices. Twelve people were killed in the attack leaving over 5,500 wounded. The attack was carefully planned but was rushed to be put in place earlier than anticipated as members of the cult believed that the authorities were aware of their activities. The Sarin was not pure and it was distributed in polythene bags which had been punctured. Officials believed that minor adjustments to attack plans would have resulted in many more deaths.

The UK has also witnessed some interest in toxic attacks with the intended use of Ricin (but no actual attack or remotely viable attack) and the US has also investigated (without success) the use of anthrax in late 2001.

POINTS TO NOTE— IDENTIFYING TERRORIST ACTIVITY

It is important for police officers to note that the spectacular images that may be seen of vehicles exploding and devices being detonated account for less than 1% of the terrorist attack plan process. These images are the final result of a much wider effort but often, they are the images we remember. For a terrorist to use the tactics we have discussed requires a number of ways of operating, ways which provide us with an early indication that attack planning is being developed.

Police officers must seize upon these opportunities and identify terrorist activity taking place.

Members of the public, police officers, and partners are required to report information about terrorism. Thousands of people take photos everyday, but what if you see something that appears out of place? Terrorists use surveillance to plan attacks; they take photos and make notes about security measures such as the location of CCTV cameras. Terrorists require effective communications to develop attacks, they often collect and use many anonymous pay-as-you-go phones, as well as swapping SIM cards and handsets. Terrorists live within our communities; they require accommodation for planning attacks, storing equipment and

---

chemicals. They require protective equipment for handling such chemicals such as gloves, masks, and goggles. Terrorists also use multiple identities to conceal their activities and use false documentation to achieve this. They also require meeting rooms, training facilities paid for by funds raised as part of cheque and credit card fraud. Terrorists also require vehicles to assist in the transportation of such equipment or to assist them to blend into the community whilst conducting hostile reconnaissance. If you suspect any of this activity is taking place, think about terrorist tactics and report it.

See also **5.5**.

1.7 **Terrorist Communications**

We live in a technological age that provides the ability to access information anywhere in the world. The media has changed the way in which we now view the world and the development of the internet and the constant feeds from 24-hour news channels now form part of our everyday lives. While these advances have brought improvements to social, educational, and commercial communications they are also used by terrorist and extremist groups. Police colleagues are required to develop an awareness and understanding of how communication technology and the media are used by such groups. The extent of their usage is vast creating a new threat referred to as 'cyber-terrorism' and its impact should not be underestimated.

Case study—Cyber-Terrorist 007

When police officers raided a flat in West London during October 2005, they arrested a young man, Younes Tsouli. The significance of this arrest was not immediately clear but investigations soon revealed that the Moroccan born Tsouli was the world's most wanted cyber-terrorist. Tsouli adopted the user name 'Irhabi 007', Irhabi meaning Terrorist in Arabic and his activities grew from posting advice on the internet on how to hack into mainframe computer systems to assisting those in planning terrorist attacks.

Tsouli trawled the internet searching for home movies made by US soldiers that would reveal the inside of US military bases. Over time these small pieces of information were collated and passed to those planning attacks. This virtual hostile reconnaissance provided insider data; no longer do terrorists need to conduct physical reconnaissance if information can be pieced together from the internet.

Police investigations revealed that Tsouli had 2.5million Euros worth of fraudulent transactions passing through his accounts used to support and finance terrorist activity. Pleading guilty to charges of incitement to commit acts of terrorism Tsouli received a 16-year custodial sentence to be served at Belmarsh High Security Prison in London, where, unsurprisingly he has been denied access to the internet.

The then National Co-ordinator for Terrorist Investigations Peter Clarke stated that Tsouli 'provided a link to core Al-Qaeda, to the heart of Al-Qaeda and the wider network that he was linking into through the internet' going on to say that 'What it did show us was the extent to which they could conduct operational planning on the internet. It was the first virtual conspiracy to murder that we had seen'.

POINTS TO NOTE— MEDIA COVERAGE

Terrorism is aimed at impacting upon more people than the immediate victims of violence. Mass media coverage forms a critical source of information about terrorism and irresponsible media coverage can magnify the efforts of terrorists in creating a climate of fear. Terrorists understand the value of using the media which serves as a channel through which their propaganda can be circulated. Media coverage allows terrorists groups not only to justify their actions but also to generate international sympathy for their cause.

As constant pressure is placed upon news channels to fill gaps within their 24-hour live coverage, unbalanced and inaccurate reporting may polarize public opinion and undermine governments. News channels are strictly controlled in their coverage of terrorism and there is little evidence of unbalanced and inaccurate reporting in the UK but terrorist organizations understand the value of international media coverage. During the troubles in Ireland the then Prime Minister Margaret Thatcher realized the full potential of terrorist organizations' exploitation of the media, stating: 'terrorists should be denied the oxygen of publicity that they need to breathe'.

To prevent terrorists from freely promoting their ideologies through the media, standards of responsible media coverage of terrorist events are in place. The volume of news coverage of a terrorist attack is required to be balanced providing context, background, and different perspectives. The use of inflammatory terminology may seriously damage community relations and no platform should be afforded to terrorists to make any demands.

Terrorist incidents involving hostages provide additional challenges for the media, as the protection of the lives of the hostages is paramount and the respect and privacy of hostages and their families should be maintained. To manage these communications effectively requires authorities to engage with and respond to the media. Terrorism is no longer a taboo subject, and whilst sensitive operational information should not be disclosed there is now a greater willingness to share more information with the media. Wherever possible, factual information should be provided to the media to prevent any vacuum being filled with speculation. Expert press liaison and news management is being made an intrinsic part of the police response to counter terrorism which makes use of an effective public information policy with an appropriate utilization of the mass media's power.

POINTS TO NOTE— INTERNET AND COMPUTERS

Terrorists will seek to effectively use the internet and the media. It is important that we do not lose focus on this issue. It is not the internet or the media that is the root cause of this problem. Terrorists existed before the internet and mass media were created, they would also continue their activities if mass media and the internet ceased to operate. The use of the media and the internet provides evidence of how quickly terrorists develop their tactics providing new challenges for those responsible for countering such threats. The internet and computers have equally become prime sources of evidence and intelligence about what terrorists are thinking and planning. They are major aids to police and intelligence agency investigations, as well as being tools for terrorists.

Chapter 2
Countering Terrorism

2.1 Counter-Terrorism Strategy

To combat terrorism in all of its forms, governments are required to devise effective strategies which have to be comprehensive and wide-ranging. The prevention of terrorist attacks remains the primary objective of such strategies, but they must also prepare emergency services to respond to the consequences of terrorism. In addition counter-terrorism strategies need to be able to protect the public, having robust criminal justice systems in place to arrest and prosecute terrorists. Devising such a strategy is complex as a free and democratic society offers terrorists the same freedoms in which to operate. A counter-terrorism strategy must therefore preserve the very freedoms that the terrorists wish to exploit. This is a very difficult balance to achieve as human rights and civil liberties have to be maintained. Governments across the world devise counter-terrorism strategies considering two broad responses which include the use of the military or the use of a criminal justice system.

2.1.1 Military system

A military system is used by governments to tackle terrorists who pose a significant threat to national security. Terrorist groups who possess and utilize conventional weapons and aspire to possess chemical, biological, radiological, or nuclear capabilities require a robust response which the military can offer. A military system for countering terrorism may also be required when domestic law enforcement agencies can no longer contain a specific terrorist threat. Armed forces have an increased capability of managing severe threats. Governments allow their military to plan and implement counter-terrorism strategies in such circumstances.

POINTS TO NOTE—MILITARY SYSTEM

The use of the military to counter terrorism very often meets the demand of the public and media for swift and tough action to be taken against terrorists and their sponsors. The military can deliver a clear message to those who seek to further their cause through acts of violence but using the military effectively requires strong support from domestic intelligence and law enforcement agencies. Military units that engage in street by street urban conflicts to combat terrorist activity are required to adapt to this type of environment. Governments are aware of the challenges when deploying military measures to counter terrorism which may have severe and long-term consequences if not carefully considered and implemented. A military response may increase the likelihood of further innocent casualties, which could lead to sympathy and support for the terrorist group and the potential of an escalation of violence. The actions of the military may therefore undermine democracy and raise concerns about human rights—the very values being protected. Military action taken in response to terrorist activity may actually lose support for their measures, leaving society to question the validity of the action taken.

Deciding to use the military to combat a terrorist threat is a significant step for any government to take. This may however be absolutely necessary to protect innocent civilians and preserve national security. The current 'War on Terror' following the events of 9/11 has made governments review their military response. It is now understood that military interventions to counter terrorism may produce false expectations of an early success and that the use of the military alone may not be completely effective in tracking terrorist groups.

2.1.2 Criminal justice system

A criminal justice system can be employed to counter terrorism. It provides the scope for trial and conviction of suspected terrorists. The foundation of a democratic criminal justice system is the premise that an individual is innocent until proven guilty and the process is conducted in a recognized court of law, following a fair trial with legal representation. Using criminal justice to counter terrorism protects the democratic values of the prosecuting states while ensuring the rights of all concerned are maintained.

POINTS TO NOTE—CRIMINAL JUSTICE SYSTEM

The use of a criminal justice system to counter terrorism ensures that the process of dealing with terrorist suspects is legitimate. A criminal justice approach has a number of key advantages; none more so than the element of trust in a system which ensures that an individual's human

---

rights are maintained when comparative to the use of military measures to combat terrorism.

A criminal justice system depends upon effective domestic law enforcement agencies and their ability to conduct complex terrorist investigations. Countering a global terrorist threat via a criminal justice system also depends upon efficient bi-lateral and multi-national co-operation.

The most significant challenge in establishing and maintaining an effective criminal justice system to counter terrorism is ensuring that robust legislation is in place that has the scope to keep pace with new and emerging terrorist threats but yet remains a necessary, appropriate and proportionate response.

To effectively tackle the threats from international terrorism governments are required to use a variety of effective measures from both the military and criminal justice systems. Counter-terrorism strategies have been developed by governments around the world because of the events that unfolded in the US on the morning of 11 September 2001. The events of 9/11 are widely regarded as the beginning of the 'new age of terror'. Developing an understanding of the attacks and the subsequent lessons learned is vital for those now engaged in policing terrorism and extremism.

2.2 **11 September 2001**

Nearly 3,000 people died in the terrorist attacks on 11 September 2001. In lower Manhattan, on a field in Pennsylvania, and along the Banks of the Potomac, the US suffered the single largest loss of life from an enemy attack on its soil. Within two hours, four commercial jets would be simultaneously hi-jacked as part of a co-ordinated attack on the US. The nature of the tactics used and the devastation caused marked the dawning of a new era in international terrorism. As news channels beamed images around the world of aircraft crashing into the World Trade Centre's 'twin towers', viewers could hardly comprehend the events they were witnessing. The shock waves of such a simple yet savage attack vibrated around the world. Governments realized that if terrorists embracing the ideology of Al-Qaeda could strike at the heart of the US they could strike anywhere.

Alongside the thousands of people that perished many more were seriously injured, both physically and psychologically.

Members of the public, emergency services, and other professional organizations working that day had to call upon all of their natural instincts, training, and resourcefulness to save the lives of others. The series of co-ordinated attacks set a new precedent and people caught up in the horror had to rise to the challenges they faced. Many lives were saved as people displayed bravery and courage, none more so than the cabin crews and passengers on board the hi-jacked flights.

Case study—American Airlines Flight 11

American Airlines flight 11 provided a non-stop service from Boston to Los Angeles. Nine flight crew and 81 passengers were on board which took off as scheduled at 7.59 am on 11 September 2001. The weather conditions were fine, nothing unusual or suspicious had been reported to the crew, this was a routine flight, business as usual. Nobody knew that five terrorists were amongst the passengers who intended killing themselves and everybody onboard.

Just 15 minutes into the flight, at approximately 8.14 am, the terrorists, who were sat in business class, had commenced their attack by stabbing cabin crew and taking control of the aircraft. The terrorists sprayed a chemical irritant in the first class cabin to force passengers and flight attendants to the rear of the plane. At that time American Airlines cabin crew Betty Ong and Madeline Sweeney were able to contact their reservations office in North Carolina via an air phone. This was the first of several occasions on 9/11 that flight attendants reported events on board that however distressing to hear, provided US investigators with detailed information on how the hi-jacks were conducted.

Approximately 20 minutes into the flight Ong reported that 'The cockpit is not answering, somebody's stabbed in business class and I think there's mace—that we can't breathe—I don't know, I think we're getting hi-jacked'. For the next 25 minutes Ong and Sweeney provided descriptions of the suspected hi-jackers including their seat numbers. Ong reported that the aircraft was 'flying erratically'. Sweeney also reported that 'something is wrong. We are in rapid descent, we are all over the place'. Sweeney was directed to look out of the window to potentially identify where they were. Sweeney stated that 'We are flying very, very low. We are flying way too low'. Seconds later she said 'Oh my God we are way too low.'

At 8.46 am, American Airlines flight 11 crashed into the North Tower of the World Trade Centre in New York City. All on board, along with an unknown number of people in the tower, were killed instantly. Al-Qaeda had commenced its first wave of attacks on America, in America, and worse was to follow later that morning.

The role of the first emergency responders is critical for the preservation of life. Understanding the challenges that confronted them during 9/11 reveals the true horror of terrorist attacks. Their experiences must be analyzed to enable any operational learning to occur for the development of emergency and protective services responses in the future.

Case study—9/11 First line responders

235 New York Fire Department fire-fighters arrived at the North Tower of the World Trade Centre disaster area in just 15 minutes. They were soon to realize the true extent of the events unfolding before them. One of the first fire units to arrive was Ladder 6, based in the China Town district of New York led by Captain Jay Jonas, a veteran with 20 years service as a fireman. During a documentary screened on Channel 4 in 2006 Captain Jonas recalled his thoughts as he arrived at the World Trade Centre, stating that 'It put a knot in your stomach going across and seeing that, something that you thought you would never see, the North Tower of the World Trade Centre, the top 20 floors in flames'.

When Lieutenant Jim McGlynn and his fire crew of Engine 39 arrived at the North Tower the tragedy was all too real. One of the first hazards they faced was the bodies of 'jumpers' crashing to the ground. Lieutenant McGlynn also recalled what he observed at that time stating that, 'I saw people jumping, you heard them hit the pavement and you realized the utter desperation that these people must be going through to jump to their death'.

Fire Chiefs at the North Tower encountered badly burned civilians who had been caught in the path of a fireball which had ripped through a lift shaft from the 93rd to the 95th floor to the ground level. The initial assessment on the extent of the fire-fighter operation was provided by the Division Chief for Lower Manhattan, Peter Hayden. He stated that they were aware of people trapped in lifts and on upper floors estimating that between 25,000 and 50,000 civilians could be in the building. The North Tower of the World Trade Centre was 110 stories high, each floor measuring a massive acre square. The assessment was clear that this operation was not to be a fire-fighting operation but a rescue mission. Fire Department Chiefs had a very strong sense that they would lose fire-fighters that day.

2.3 **9/11 Commission Report**

During November 2002 the United States Congress and President George Bush established the National Commission on Terrorist Attacks Upon the United States. Known as the 9/11 Commission, this independent, bipartisan panel was directed to examine the facts and circumstances surrounding the 11 September attacks. Its aim was to identify lessons learned and provide recommendations to safeguard against future acts of terrorism. In pursuing their mandate the 9/11 Commission reviewed more than 2.5 million pages of documents, interviewed more than 1,200 individuals in ten countries and conducted hearings over 19 days taking public testimony from 160 witnesses. The 9/11 Commission report concluded that:

> the domestic agencies were not mobilised in response to the threat. They did not have direction, and they did not have a plan to institute. The borders were not hardened. Transportation systems were not fortified. Electronic surveillance was not targeted against a domestic threat. State and local law enforcement were not marshalled to augment the Federal Bureau of Investigations efforts. The public was not warned.

The 9/11 Commission report was critical of the US government in a number of key areas. It questioned how 19 suicide terrorists could be imported into America without examination; how they were able to live undetected within local communities for several months whilst seeking English language classes and flight instruction; and why they were not identified by US agencies working overseas in the first instance. Most importantly however, the 9/11 Commission focused upon how the US, having learned from its experiences, could develop their response to tackle this new threat and protect its citizens in the future. The report focused upon four key areas which included imagination, policy, capabilities, and management:

Table 2.1: Primary focus of the 9/11 Commission Report

Imagination	What could the US authorities have foreseen? What could they have been reasonably expected to anticipate?
Policy	What policies, plans, protocols, and procedures were in place? Were they correctly followed? Were they robust? Had they been tested? Were they fit for purpose?
Capabilities	What skills, knowledge, expertise, and resources were available?
Management	Who had responsibility and ownership? Who, what, when, where, and why were key decisions made?

From this analysis the report highlighted flight training, finance, and foresight, amongst others, as key areas to be addressed.

2.3.1 Flight training

A key component in the success of the terrorists' attack plan lay in their ability to overpower and take control of the aircraft. This provided an opportunity for the suicide pilots to fly towards identified targets. Some of the flying skills had been acquired in flight training establishments within the US general aviation sector. The US has the largest flight training industry in the world. Students are attracted by the country's climate, its location but fundamentally, by the competitive rates charged by their flight instructors. As a result large numbers of prospective flying students arrive in the US from all corners of the world. Seeking flight training was therefore not unusual and the 9/11 suicide pilots blended into the large diverse and transient flight training population. They were well placed to conduct their activities beneath the radar of US authorities.

See also **4.3.7**, **4.3.8** and **5.4.12**.

POINT TO NOTE—AUTHORITIES AND SUICIDE HIJACKING OF AIRCRAFT PRIOR TO 9/11

US authorities had already debated suicide hijacking of aircraft prior to 9/11 but these were dismissed on the grounds that there would have been no opportunity for dialogue with the hijackers. This dismissal was based on the notion that any suicide hijackers would wish to communicate to authorities to make demands, or outline their intentions or motivations.

US authorities also discussed the possibility of a hi-jacked airliner coming from overseas and crashing into the Pentagon. It was however decided that there would be sufficient time to identify the target and scramble interceptors to shoot it down before it reached the US coastline. No one imagined that four aircraft could be forcibly commandeered in flight within US air space and used to such devastating effect.

The 9/11 terrorist cell thoroughly researched its use of aircraft. The Commission highlighted that a large extent of the damage at the World Trade Centre was initially caused by considerable amounts of burning aviation fuel. It is believed that all the hi-jackers targeted internal flights that were to cover long distances in the US thereby maximizing the amount of fuel on board at the time of impact. In addition, several of the hi-jackers conducted hostile reconnaissance on internal US flights where considerable information was gained to support their attack planning. On these reconnaissance flights the hi-jackers carried rudimentary weapons such as box cutters to identify what they could easily get past airport security. They also selected specific aircraft and assessed the exact time at which it would be best to take control of the flight. The 9/11 plot was carefully planned and executed. Thousands of dollars in cash was paid to training providers of flight simulators. Two terrorist cell members sought flying lessons but were not interested in commencing with small aircraft but instead wished to learn how to fly Boeing commercial jets. A number of different flight instructors stated that the suicide pilots wished to focus upon controlling the aircraft in flight but took little interest in take-off or landing procedures.

POINT TO NOTE—THREAT LEVEL POST 9/11

As a result of 9/11 and the use of commercial aircraft as weapons, the aviation industry has undergone an unprecedented period of reviewing security measures. It is clear that Al-Qaeda continue to seek large-scale spectacular attacks using aircraft. The threat level within the global aviation sector remains high. It serves to underline the need for increased vigilance from authorities not just within the commercial scheduled and charter sectors but also within the general aviation business including flying schools and associated training.

2.3.2 Finance

The US government had committed enormous resources to protect national security to specifically counter terrorism. In the fiscal year 2001 it spent $157 billion on defence, homeland security, and international affairs. To put this into perspective Home Office figures reveal that UK spending on security for the same period was just £1 billion. Prime Minister Gordon Brown announced in November 2007 that the security budget, currently set at £2.5 billion, would increase to £3.5 billion by 2011. Countering terrorism is not cheap and requires a substantial financial commitment from governments.

POINT TO NOTE—STRATEGY

The size of the US security budget does highlight the fact that no matter how many resources are dedicated to countering terrorism it is the way in which it is spent that has to be effective. A counter-terrorism strategy has to be based upon a thorough knowledge and understanding of terrorist organizations, their tactics and the current threat they pose.

The US government counter-terrorism focus was overseas and not within its borders, therefore the domestic US agencies engaged in law enforcement, security and intelligence did not co-ordinate their internal response. They were not driven to counter terrorism on a local level. With no plan to implement, no contingencies in place, and having no training to rehearse such responses, US agencies were not prepared to manage or respond to the attacks as effectively as they could have been.

2.3.3 Foresight

Everything is clear when we can see with hindsight, but before the events of 9/11 what could the US authorities reasonably be expected to have known? The US is no stranger to suicide aeroplane attacks following the events at Pearl Harbour, but this attack was carried out by a major power during the process of a conventional and recognizable war. In contrast, 9/11 was carried out by a small group of individuals with relatively few resources being sanctioned from a remote location in Afghanistan.

At the time of the terrorist attacks the US seemed a safe place to be. The Cold War was over, defence spending had been cut and the US remained the world's 'super power'. During the 2000 Presidential campaign terrorism was hardly mentioned, nor was it reported heavily in the media. A 1995 intelligence report did however make reference to new and emerging threats predicting future attacks against the US at home and abroad. The report described the greatest danger as coming from a transient grouping of individuals that lacked strong organization. It also stated that this group, operating outside of traditional circles, had access to a worldwide network. This network was Al-Qaeda and by the mid-1990s the US intelligence community was aware of an 'Osama bin Laden' led terrorist group which was involved in attacks on US interests abroad. At this time however little was made of this terrorist group and despite many subsequent briefings on the Al-Qaeda network no predictions were made as to the real threat they posed to the US at this time. The 9/11 Commission reveals that analysts clearly saw the threat but had difficulty convincing other parts of the government. This was despite terrorist attacks on US targets which had been directly linked to Al-Qaeda and Osama bin Laden.

Case study—1998 US Embassy bombings in Africa

On the morning of 7 August 1998 two suicide truck bombs exploded outside US embassies in Africa. The first device detonated at 10.30 am adjacent to the embassy in Nairobi, Kenya. The bomb ripped through the building killing 213 people and injuring 5,000 leaving extensive damage and destruction to the embassy and surrounding buildings. Twelve Americans died in the attack, the majority of victims being Kenyan, local people who were going about their daily business. The second car bomb exploded at 10.39 am outside the US embassy in Dar es Salaam, the capital city of Tanzania. This device also caused massive devastation killing 11 Tanzanians and wounding 85.

The attacks are widely regarded as the first co-ordinated terrorist atrocities on Western targets by Al Qaeda following the public fatwa declared by Osama bin Laden in February that same year. The fatwa encouraged the murder of any American, anywhere on earth, believing it to be 'the individual duty of every Muslim who can do it in any country in which it is possible to do it'.

POINT TO NOTE—ANTICIPATING ATTACKS

Bureaucracies do not easily do 'imagination' but wider thinking may have allowed consideration regarding the possible use of suicide planes by terrorists. Therefore, little seems to have been considered to avoid such attacks. Credible threats were followed up but no one seemed to examine the wider possibilities of such a 9/11 type of attack. What warning systems the US had in place of such attacks were not tested fully to see if they were adequate to meet these new threats.

The US strategy for dealing with terrorists was robust trial and punishment for individuals and war or sanctions against rogue states. The current threat though came from individuals who were difficult to categorize. Briefings in early 2001 concluded that the only way to stop Al-Qaeda operating was to remove their sanctuary in Afghanistan. Prior to 9/11 a military invasion into Afghanistan was seen as inconceivable. The threat from Al-Qaeda was not a high priority for the US at that time.

Covert action against Osama bin Laden was conducted prior to 9/11 but it never progressed beyond the intelligence-gathering stages. The 9/11 Commission Report was struck by the 'narrow and unimaginative menu of options for action offered to the President'. The government was trying to solve the Al-Qaeda problem with post-Cold War tactics and institutions. The nature of the threat from Al-Qaeda was completely different and they had done little to reform their working practices to meet the needs of these 21st century problems. This was particularly surprising as the World Trade Centre had previously been attacked by a vehicle bomb which was placed in an underground car park in 1993 by terrorists sharing a similar ideology with Al-Qaeda.

The 9/11 Commission highlighted deficiencies in the ability of its intelligence and law enforcement agencies to share information. It was identified that they were working in isolation. A key issue concerning the lack of joint working and information sharing puzzled many US commentators. These very same agencies had mobilized their responses together two years prior to 9/11 to prevent threats to US national security from the perceived 'Millennium Bug'.

Case study—'The Millennium Bug'

Governments from across the world were concerned about potential computer viruses, loss of data and the vulnerability of networks to hacking from cyber-terrorists as internal computer clocks switched from 1999 to 2000. To minimize risk and prepare for the potential consequences information sharing amongst the US intelligence community was widespread. Agencies who traditionally never shared intelligence were doing so on a local, regional, and national level.

Following intense media coverage highlighting the potential threats, the public were alive to 'Millennium Bug' issues. They effectively became the 'eyes and ears' for the intelligence community passing concerns to US authorities. As the millennium passed without major disruption, terrorism and intelligence became secret again, it was out of the public domain and back to being protected by individual agencies. The partnership working evidenced by US agencies proved that in a time of need they were capable of mobilizing themselves against a potential terrorist threat, and most importantly, they were able to share their intelligence.

In summer 2001 certain quarters within the US administration did try to sound the alarm over Al-Qaeda activity but the 'Millennium Bug' experience was not repeated. There was little reporting in the media and the public were not alerted to the emerging threats. The intelligence remained the preserve of those secretive agencies once more. Recommendations were made by the 9/11 Commission concluding a 'unity of purpose and unity of effort are the way forward'.

POINT TO NOTE—DEVELOPING A NATIONAL PICTURE

It is difficult to comprehend the failure of the US authorities to recognize the signs that a major terrorist plot was taking place within their communities. The sheer size and scale of the US security machine did not correctly analyze, assess and prioritize intelligence on a national level. A large number of agencies that held critical data did not share its information. These organizations were working in isolation each with their own 'need to know' principles and limited 'need to share' protocols. A full national picture of the emerging threat was not put together. Like a giant jigsaw puzzle many of the smaller pieces were missing that would have provided US authorities with a greater opportunity to identify and disrupt the plot. Despite collating intelligence to develop a picture of unfolding events the US authorities were behind the activities of the terrorist cell and as the Al-Qaeda 'Planes Operation' drew into its final phases in September 2001, time simply ran out.

2.3.4 Lessons learned

In the wake of 9/11, the US government was quick to enact the Aviation and Transportation Security Act. The American Attorney General announced the 'Flight Training Candidate Check Programme' where any non-federal provider of flight instruction in the US, seeking to train an alien in the operation of an aircraft over 12,500 pounds, must first have the candidate vetted by the Attorney General. The programme also extends to disclosures about training given to those who already know how to fly and includes a requirement to provide fingerprints and submit to a criminal records based check. The legislation also requires that all flight schools conduct a Security Awareness Programme for flight school employees. This programme has been established to increase awareness of suspicious circumstances focusing on the activities of individuals enrolling in or attending flight schools. The US Transportation Security Administration website has certificated on-line flight school and flight simulator security awareness learning programmes. Taken together with the necessity for student pilots to undergo vetting, the US now has a tighter control of flight training, therefore denying terrorists this opportunity in the future.

POINT TO NOTE—9/11 COMMISSION REPORT

Amongst a series of recommendations the 9/11 Commission Report highlighted one of the key lessons to learn for authorities and members of the public was that:

> In the new age of terror, we are the primary targets. The losses America suffered that day demonstrated both the gravity of the terrorist's threat and the commensurate need to prepare ourselves to meet it. The first responders today live in a world transformed by the attacks of 9/11. Because no one believes that every conceivable form of attack can be prevented, civilians and first responders will again find themselves on the frontlines. We must plan for that eventuality. A rededication to preparedness is perhaps the best way to honour the memories of those we lost that day.

The 9/11 Commission Report presents a realistic view of preventing further terrorist attacks. It identifies the significant unfair advantage that terrorist groups have when preparing their attacks. An effective strategy to counter terrorism must therefore not only proactively pursue terrorists disrupting their activities but accept and make provision for the reality that some attacks will succeed. Although an uncomfortable truth, it simply makes sense to plan and prepare for 'worst case scenario' so that in the event of another attack we are better placed to respond.

2.3.5 The global response to 9/11

As news broke across the world that the US was under attack, many countries implemented their emergency contingency plans to protect their borders. US authorities were also quick to react by removing the President from his official engagements to board Air Force One. The action taken by US authorities on that morning to minimize and prevent further attacks had an immediate impact upon other countries.

Case study—Canada responds to 9/11

The Canadian government responded quickly to support its neighbour during 9/11. As the US closed its airspace to incoming flights Canadian traffic control accepted 224 diverted flights within 45 minutes of the attacks at the World Trade Centre. The diverted flights, which contained 33,000 passengers, were provided with landing slots at airports across Canada. Remarkably, small communities like Gander, Newfoundland and Labrador accommodated 12,000 of these passengers despite their

---

population of only 10,000. The response of Canada to come to the aid of its neighbour has to be recognized as an important part of preparing for the wider consequences of international terrorism. It has to be remembered that the Canadian government accepted these diverted flights with no absolute guarantee that they did not contain further suicide terrorists.

The then Canadian Prime Minister, Jean Chrétien, urgently established an ad-hoc cabinet committee on Public Safety and Anti-Terrorism which began to review policies, legislation, regulations, and programmes across the Canadian government. Their aim was to strengthen all aspects of their approach to fight terrorism and ensure public safety. From this committee they developed a new counter-terrorism strategy known as the Anti-Terrorism Plan which continues to be used to this day.

2.3.6 **The UK response to 9/11**

In the weeks that followed 9/11 the UK government focused its attention on developing the UK's response to international terrorism. The Office of Security and Counter-Terrorism, together with other intelligence and law enforcement agencies began to formulate a strategy. It became clear that the new terrorist threat would not be resolved in the short term so a variety of measures had to be considered. Intelligence agencies drew upon their experience of managing the threat from Irish-related terrorism for over 30 years. Finances were quickly made available to the emergency services to initially develop the capability and capacity to respond to terrorist attacks. They included:

- £85.5 million to the National Health Service to counter bio-terrorism;
- £56 million to the Fire Service for decontamination programmes;
- £132 million to the Fire Service for search and rescue equipment;
- £49 million to the Metropolitan Police; and
- £12 million to national police forces.

Once the initial short-term measures had been put in place the government focused on creating a long-term strategy to protect the UK from the new and emerging threat from international terrorism.

2.4 **The Contest Strategy**

The 'Contest' strategy (an acronym of COuNter-TErrorism STrategy) was established in 2003 and subject to a review in 2006 following the attacks in London on 7 July 2005. The key aim of the strategy is 'to reduce the risk from international terrorism so that people can go about their business freely and with confidence'.

Developing and delivering Contest involves numerous departments from across the government which includes the emergency services, voluntary organizations, the commercial sector and partners from around the world. The strategy is divided into four key pillars which provide the scope to counter terrorism effectively. The four pillars are commonly known as the four Ps which are Prevent, Pursue, Protect and Prepare.

2.4.1 **Prevent**

The 'Prevent' strand of Contest is concerned with tackling the radicalization of individuals. It aims to do this by addressing structural problems in the UK and overseas that may contribute to radicalization, such as inequalities and discrimination. To prevent terrorism and its underlying causes requires a long-term approach. The strategy intends to deter those who facilitate terrorism and deter those who encourage others to become terrorists. This requires a change in the environment where extremists and those radicalizing others operate. The Prevent strand also aims to engage in the battle of ideas, to win hearts and minds by challenging the ideologies that extremists believe can justify the use of violence.

Preventing violent extremism, often referred to as the 'PVE' agenda, is a key area of Contest. Preventing terrorism and extremism is the proactive element of the strategy which has received significant investment from the government. In November 2007 it was announced that an additional £240 million would be made available to the police service to prevent violent extremism. This includes funding for the training of 3,500 Neighbourhood Policing Teams to address radicalization in their local communities. During April 2008 the government launched a new Prevent strategy which outlined how local partners, such as the police service and local authorities could work together to stop people becoming or supporting terrorists and violent extremists.

2.4.1.1 *The Prevent strategy*

The government believes that the UK, like many other countries, faces a challenge from terrorism and violent extremism where a very small minority seek to harm innocent people in the name of an ideology which causes division, hatred, and violence. The role of the government is to take tough security measures needed to keep people safe but a security response alone is not enough, a response led and driven by local communities is vital. The very essence of the Prevent strategy seeks to engage partners to work together to challenge and expose the ideology that sanctions and encourages indiscriminate violence. There is a pressing need to stop people, especially young people, getting drawn into illegal activities associated with violent extremism. The Prevent strategy states that:

> We need to expose and isolate the apologists for violence and pro-
> tect the places where they operate. Local authorities, the police,
> and their partners in schools, other educational institutions and
> elsewhere, have a critical role in preventing violent extremism. They
> understand the local context. They are in a unique position to talk to
> local communities, hear their concerns and enable people to stand
> shoulder to shoulder, confident in their rejection and condemnation
> of violence.

The Prevent strategy highlights that everyone has a right to live in a safe and welcoming neighbourhood where they feel they belong. At the same time it identifies that no neighbourhood can truly succeed unless local people define their future by working together to tackle the challenges they face. The government firm-ly believes that when people have a say in the design and delivery of public services, those services better meet their needs. Places where local people have the opportunities, skills and confidence to come together and address the problems they face are more likely to resolve them.

The Prevent strategy has five key strands aimed at achieving the overall aim of stopping people becoming or supporting terrorists and violent extremists. They are:

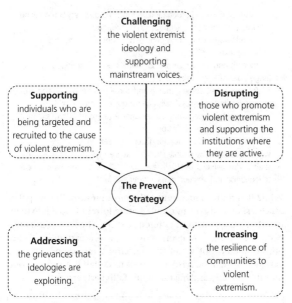

Figure 2.1: Primary strands of Prevent

The Prevent strategy identifies the most significant terrorist threat to the UK as being from Al-Qaeda and its affiliated groups. Al-Qaeda uses a distorted interpretation of Islam, history and contemporary politics to justify attacks against civilians in the UK and overseas, an issue addressed by the Home Secretary Jacqui Smith during the first national conference on radicalization and political violence in January 2007 where she stated that:

> We need to challenge the ideology of violent extremism, that misreading of Islam and view of history and contemporary politics justifies terrorism.
>
> Studies of experiences in this country and elsewhere has told us a lot about why people are drawn into the world of violent extremism, either as actors or supporters.
>
> Our best estimate is that in this country, as in others, violent extremism is caused by a combination of interlocking reasons:
>
> By an ideology, by which I mean both a misinterpretation of religion and a view of contemporary politics and history;

By ideologues and propagandists for this cause, very often taking advantage of the open institutions in this country;

By vulnerability in young people, of a kind that I recognise from other contexts;

By communities which are sometimes poorly equipped to challenge violent extremism; and

By grievances, some genuine and some perceived, and some of course directed very specifically against government.

Our strategy to deal with radicalisation and violent extremism must therefore focus on these factors.

I do not wish to discourage dissent or seek political conformity. I will not dictate how people should practise their religion or express their lawful opinions. But I will never accept any argument which seeks to legitimise and sanction mass murder.

While it is right to focus upon the most pressing threats police officers should also be mindful of other forms of violent extremism that are also damaging to our society. The PVE agenda recognizes that there are many forms of violent extremism. Police officers should not forget the powerful messages preached by extreme far-right activists who seek to destabilize trusted community networks and fracture multi-faith partnerships.

Case study—Right-wing extremist

During November 2007 police officers searched premises for child pornography but as they raided Martin Gilleard's East Yorkshire flat, they uncovered ammunition, weapons, home-made bombs, and a large amount of white extremist literature. Police officers seized a diary belonging to Gilleard where he wrote his intentions stating that: 'I'm so sick and tired of hearing Nationalists talk of killing Muslims, of blowing up Mosques, of fighting back, only to see these acts of resistance fail to appear. The time has come to stop the talk and start to act.'

It appeared that Gilleard was preparing for an ethnic war, his aim to protect the purity of the white race. Frustrated by a perceived lack of action Gilleard started to collect dozens of weapons. He had made four nail bombs and hid them underneath his bed, bizarrely he would make his young son sleep on this bed whenever he came to visit. At the time his premises were searched Gilleard was not at home prompting a large 'man hunt' operation as Gilleard went on the run. Police officers successfully located Gilleard three days later in Dundee, Scotland, where he was arrested for terrorism offences.

This case revealed that Counter-Terrorist Units, together with their local force Special Branch counterparts are increasingly having to investigate far right groups. Gilleard was one of the first right-wing extremists to be prosecuted under counter-terrorism legislation. The Head of the

---

Counter-Terrorism Unit—Leeds, Detective Chief Superintendent John Parkinson stated that:

Martin Gilleard is a very dangerous individual and not only did he express his intentions to carry out acts of terrorism, he had the capacity to do so. Terrorism in its rawest form is someone who possesses those extreme views who then moves onto violence or threats of violence for an ideological or political cause and that is equally applicable to right-wing extremism or to an Islamist cause.

A judge at Leeds Crown Court stated that he believed that Martin Gilleard intended to cause havoc with the devices found by police under his bed. Gilleard was found guilty of terrorist offences and possessing child pornography and was sentenced to 16 years' imprisonment.

POINT TO NOTE—THE PREVENT STRATEGY

If allowed a platform to promote their views extreme right-wing activists will attempt to frustrate community cohesion. Police officers who are engaging with the community are required to identify where issues of extremism are developing, this requires a thorough understanding of the people and places they serve. A key element of the Prevent strategy is the engagement of the police with partner agencies and the community. New police officer roles are being established known as 'Community Engagement Field Officers' (CEFOs) who will work to channel those individuals vulnerable to exposure from violent and extremist views away from such harm.

The Prevent strategy has a long-term approach which now recognizes the difference between governments and Al-Qaeda's perception of successfully achieving desired outcomes within certain timeframes. Government strategies to counter terrorism generally work within a maximum five-year plan yet Al-Qaeda shares a long-term generational view for achieving its objectives. Bridging this gap is important as one aspect which is very clear from intelligence agencies and governments around the world is that the present threat posed by Al-Qaeda has the potential to last a considerable period of time. Conflicts between governments and terrorist groups who are driven by political, religious, or ideological motivations may last for decades. The Prevent strategy acknowledges this uncomfortable truth. It identifies preventing violent extremism as the key challenge to tackling terrorism so that the next generation of our communities can go about their business freely and with confidence.

2.4.2 Pursue

The 'Pursue' strand of CONTEST is concerned with reducing the terrorist threat to the UK and to UK interests overseas by disrupting terrorists and their operations. To achieve this the 'Pursue' strand focuses upon gathering intelligence and improving the ability to identify and understand the terrorist threat. It also aims to take action to frustrate terrorist attacks and to bring terrorists to justice through developing a legal framework. Home Office statistics reveal that 1,165 individuals were arrested under the provisions of the Terrorism Act 2000 from 11 September 2001 to 31 March 2007. This represents an average of 17 arrests every month under the 2000 Act for that period, a figure that significantly increased during 2007 as 42 people were convicted of terrorist offences which were related to 16 separate operations. New legislation, such as the Terrorism Act 2006, greatly assists in the pursuit of terrorists but bringing them to justice also involves international co-operation and the joint-working with partners and allies overseas. This is an important element of the 'Pursue' strand which also aims to reduce the global threat by strengthening the intelligence effort to achieve disruption of terrorists and their operations outside of the UK.

See also Chapters 4 and 5.

POINT TO NOTE—TERRORISM ACT 2006

The government is working hard to provide the police service with the necessary powers to be able to tackle terrorism effectively. The introduction of the Terrorism Act 2006 extended police powers to counter the threat from international terrorism with the creation of nine new offences. It has significantly lowered the threshold for persons to be arrested for terrorism offences. On 30 March 2006, the then Home Secretary Charles Clarke stated that:

The Government is determined to do everything possible to protect our citizens from those who seek to destroy our society, way of life and our freedoms.

These updated laws will create a more hostile environment in which terrorists find it more difficult to operate and assist us in tackling every part of the terrorist network.

It is key for the prevention of terrorism that all police officers have an understanding of terrorism offences, powers and procedures. The new offences created under the 2006 Act which includes encouraging terrorism and possession of terrorist publications will be evidenced in the main by uniform colleagues who observe incidents or seize such items.

Many of the new powers introduced by the government are now being tested. It is very often that large scale anti-terrorism cases receive most of the media's attention. The successful prosecutions of other offences appear to fade into the background but they provide strong evidence that the current anti-terrorism legal framework is effective at countering the diverse threats from international terrorism. An example of this in practice was the case against Abu Bakar Mansha who, on 22 December 2005, was convicted for possessing documents which contained information likely to be useful to a person committing or preparing an act of terrorism under provisions provided by the Terrorism Act 2000. The prosecution focused upon Mansha's intention to kill or wound a corporal of the 1st Battalion, Princess of Wales Royal Regiment who was awarded the Military Cross after leading an attack in Iraq in which five insurgents died.

See also **4.3.6** and **4.3.11**.

POINT TO NOTE—USING POLICE POWERS

Police colleagues must use the full extent of the powers they have been provided with if terrorism and the prevention of violent extremism is to be addressed effectively. Complex terrorism cases can regularly take 18 months to two years to get to trial, trials which may last six months or more. As the number of arrests, charges and convictions rise in the UK for terrorism-related offences, a huge source of data is available and lessons about terrorist tactics, planning, recruitment, and training can be gained. Many suspected terrorists are awaiting trial in the UK providing evidence of the severe level of threat the UK continues to endure.

2.4.3 Protect

The 'Protect' strand of Contest is concerned with reducing the vulnerability of the UK and UK interests overseas. It aims to strengthen border security, protect key utilities, transport infrastructures and crowded places. Protecting the UK is a vital component of the strategy as target-hardening key and vulnerable sites will deter terrorist attacks from taking place. It will also help to reduce the risks to the public in the event of an attack. Considerable developments have already been made by the government to protect the UK which includes the introduction of a new threat level system, a Border Management Programme (BMP) to co-ordinate joint working at ports and borders, and emphasis on reducing the threat to the UK's Critical National Infrastructure (CNI).

2.4.3.1 *Informing the public*

The Intelligence and Security Committee Report to the London Terrorists Attacks on 7 July 2005 recommended that 'a greater transparency of the threat level and alert systems as a whole, and in particular that more thought is given to what is put in the public domain about the level of threat and required level of alert. After the July attacks there is an even greater need for members of the public to be better informed.' As a result of the recommendation, a review of the Threat Level System was undertaken including an analysis of how the government and security professionals respond. The review has simplified the Threat Level System for security practitioners and clarifies the process for the general public without causing alarm. The government now has a clear vision for the future that they should say more publicly about its general analysis of the terrorist threat and broad approach to protective security.

POINT TO NOTE—KEEP UPDATED

The UK threat level may change. To keep updated on the current level of threat to the UK from international terrorism access the Home Office website at:
<http://www.homeoffice.gov.uk/security/current-threat-level>

2.4.3.2 *Border Management Programme*

A key work stream to protect the UK from international terrorism is to strengthen border security. A Border Management Programme (BMP) has been established which is a cross-government initiative aimed at developing and implementing closer and more effective joint-working in order to strengthen border security while minimizing the impact of legitimate traffic. The strategic objectives of the programme are to:

- Improve intelligence-sharing in support of border agencies
- Jointly identify and manage risks
- Provide a more effective border control
- Minimize the impact on legitimate traffic and business partners.

2.4.3.3 *Critical National Infrastructure*

Other key areas of the 'Protect' strand aim to reduce the vulnerability to attack of the UK's Critical National Infrastructure (CNI) including its transport systems and of crowded places. Risks are assessed and identified through a national process which considers the possibility of an attack and the impact on the UK. Identifying the priorities in order to protect the UK through proportionate security measures and technological advances will reduce the likelihood of a terrorist attack.

**POINT TO NOTE—PRIVATE AND PUBLIC SECTORS
WORKING TOGETHER**

The 'Protect' strand acknowledges the contribution of the private sector
which is crucial in protecting the UK and UK interests overseas against
terrorism. This involves the public sector working closely with key utilities
such as energy and water, and with key services, such as transport and
finance, within a framework of advice and regulation that aims to help
businesses operate safely.

2.4.4 Prepare

The 'Prepare' strand of Contest is concerned with ensuring that
the UK is ready as it can be to manage the consequences of a
terrorist attack. It aims to identify the potential risks that the UK
faces from terrorism and assesses its impact. It also aims to build
the necessary capabilities to respond to any attacks and will con-
tinually evaluate and test preparedness.

Achieving the aims of the 'Prepare' strand involves developing
the resilience of the UK to withstand such attacks. This requires
improving the ability of the UK to respond effectively to the direct
harm caused by a terrorist attack, and in particular those individuals affected by it. It must also develop the UK's ability to quickly
recover those essential services which are disrupted by an attack
and to be able to absorb and minimize wider indirect disruption.
The key elements of the strand are:

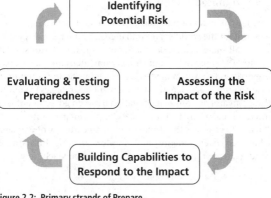

Figure 2.2: Primary strands of Prepare

Preparing for emergency incidents and planning for 'worst-case scenario' will reduce the impact of a terrorist attack. The government has responded quickly to recognize the potential threat from terrorist groups seeking chemical, biological, radiological, or nuclear (CBRN) capabilities by establishing a cross-government initiative called the CBRN Resilience Programme.

Case study—CBRN Resilience Programme

The CBRN Resilience Programme aims to ensure that fewer lives will be risked or lost in the event of a terrorist or accidental CBRN incident. To achieve this the programme ensures that the response to a CBRN incident will be quick and effective having emergency services that are appropriately trained and equipped to manage such incidents. Under the programme, the government have provided the following:

- 360 mobile decontamination units for use around the country by Ambulance and Accident & Emergency Departments
- 7,250 personal protection suits for key health workers, with an extra 2,500 additional personal protective suits stockpiled
- Stockpiles of emergency medical equipment, strategically stored around the country and available at 24 hours' notice
- 7,000 police officers with special training to deal with CBRN incidents
- 4,400 new high performance gas-light suits for fire-fighters.

See also **5.5**.

2.4.5 A united response

It is no coincidence that many of the counter-terrorism strategies around the world share similar goals and terminology, after all, we all share a common interest in combating terrorism. The events of 9/11 proved that the threat from international terrorism is global and that its tentacles can reach out to any community in any country. As such, the development of strategies to counter these threats has been a collaboration between governments and international organizations. A vital component in countering terrorism effectively is the deployment of an early-warning system which can covertly identify and monitor emerging threats, a role conducted to protect the UK by its 'Intelligence Machinery'.

2.5 **The Intelligence Machinery**

The National Intelligence Machinery is often referred to as the 'intelligence community'. It is the name provided to the group of agencies who gather and assess secret intelligence to protect national security on behalf of the government. The 'intelligence community' includes the Cabinet Office (CO), Secret Intelligence Service (SIS), Government Communications Headquarters (GCHQ), Security Service (MI5), Defence Intelligence Staff (DIS), and the Joint Terrorism Analysis Centre (JTAC).

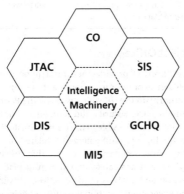

Figure 2.3: Intelligence Machinery

Each agency has a specific function to support national counter-terrorism efforts. They all act within the law and their operations are conducted within a framework of legislation that defines their roles and activities.

POINT TO NOTE—COMMUNITY FOCUS

Countering international terrorism on a global scale requires a united and co-ordinated response but it also requires a local community focus. Many police officers and members of the public may not fully appreciate their role in countering terrorism. Information passed by members of the public and the police across the UK assists specialist police departments and partner agencies to counter terrorism. Police officers may not also realize the value and importance of the information they provide. It is often for reasons of operational security that receipt of information may not be readily acknowledged. This does not mean that information is not acted upon, or that it is not significant, on the contrary, the data supplied may be of considerable value now or at some point in the future. This information may be used to provide background details, it may provide new lines of enquiry and it could corroborate existing intelligence which independently corroborates other sources. It might also be the final piece of a much larger jigsaw that many colleagues have been searching for. Information provided by members of the public and police officers is a vital component in countering terrorism, information which feeds the 'UK Intelligence Machinery'.

2.5.1 Cabinet Office

The Cabinet Office (CO) provides the central support and direction for the 'intelligence community'. It represents the highest counter-terrorism authority in the UK which is led by the Permanent Secretary for Intelligence, Security and Resilience. The Permanent Secretary is directly responsible to the Prime Minister for advising on security, intelligence, and emergency-related matters. A key responsibility of the Secretary is to ensure that the 'intelligence community' has a clear strategy and system in place for prioritizing collection and analysis of information. This information supports the government's national security policies which aims to protect the UK from a range of threats including terrorism. The Secretary also has the responsibility to Chair the Joint Intelligence Committee (JIC) which as part of the Cabinet Office is responsible for providing Ministers and senior officials with intelligence assessments. The JIC provides guidance on the collection, analysis and assessment of secret intelligence, which each year establishes requirements and priorities for the agencies of the 'intelligence community'. The assessments provided by the JIC are strategic, assessments which direct the efforts of other agencies within the 'Intelligence Machinery'.

2.5.2 Secret Intelligence Service

The Secret Intelligence Service (SIS) is commonly known as MI6 (Military Intelligence section 6). It is Britain's secret service and provides the government with a global covert capability to promote and defend the national security and economic well-being of the UK. SIS operates throughout the world to collect secret foreign intelligence in accordance with the requirements and priorities established by the Joint Intelligence Committee. It collects its intelligence through human and technical sources and liaises with a wide range of intelligence and security service agencies overseas.

SIS was established in 1909 in response to German espionage activity and the threat of Germany's military and naval expansion. The first tasks of SIS were to counter foreign espionage in the UK and to collect secret intelligence abroad. To meet these demands SIS was divided into two sections, the Home Section, which later became the Security Service (MI5) and the Foreign Section, which later became SIS as we know it today. The role of SIS is now governed by the Intelligence Service Act 1994 which placed SIS on a statutory basis for the first time. The Act formalizes the Foreign Secretary's responsibility for the work of SIS as it protects national security with particular reference to government defence and foreign policies.

The role of SIS is fact and not fiction. It provides crucial high-grade intelligence from countries worldwide. International terrorism is global, SIS are in place to provide early warnings and are our first line of defence in identifying plots overseas which may target the UK or UK interests. The development of air travel and communications technology such as the internet has made the world a much smaller place.

POINT TO NOTE—SIS

Police colleagues need to be aware that what takes place thousands of miles away can have a direct impact upon events within communities we serve. The role of SIS in providing secret foreign intelligence given the current level of threat from international terrorism has never been more crucial.

2.5.3 Security Service (MI5)

The Security Service (MI5) is responsible for protecting the UK against the threats to national security. The focus of this work is within the UK, they are the lead domestic intelligence agency. The Security Service has a broad responsibility. It aims to frustrate terrorism, prevent damage to the UK from foreign espionage and to frustrate the proliferation of materials, technologies, and expertise relating to the development of weapons of mass destruction. In addition the Security Service watch out for new and re-emerging types of threat, they offer security advice to a range of organizations and protect government assets.

The role of the Security Service is defined by the Security Service Act 1989 which put the Service onto a statutory footing for the first time. In collecting and assessing intelligence the Service is guided by the requirements and priorities established by the Joint Intelligence Committee. Since the creation of the Serious Organised Crime Agency the Service has suspended work on serious crime in order to concentrate more resources to counter terrorism.

The work of the Security Service requires considerable secrecy. It is only in recent years, following the growth of international terrorism and subsequent threats to the UK, that has resulted in the Service embarking upon a new era of openness. The Service has responded to a shift in priorities from Irish-related terrorism to international terrorism within a very short time frame. This has required a substantial increase in resources which was recognized by Prime Minister Gordon Brown when speaking in the House of Commons on 14 November 2007, who stated: 'Because of the terrorist threat, the size of the Security Service, which was under 2,000 in 2001 and is now 3,300, will rise beyond 4,000, twice the size of 2001.'

This growth provides the level of resources required by the Service to meet the challenges posed by terrorist activity in the UK.

2.5.4 Government Communications Headquarters

The Government Communications Headquarters, commonly known as GCHQ, is an intelligence and security organization. It has two key missions, Signals Intelligence and Information Assurance. Signals Intelligence relates to the interception of communications and GCHQ is often described as the UK's listening post. Signals Intelligence protects the vital interests of the UK providing information to support government decision-making processes in the fields of national security, military operations, and law enforcement. Information Assurance assists the government communications and information systems and keeps them safe from hackers and other terrorist-related threats.

As a civil service department GCHQ reports to the Foreign Secretary, and like SIS it was also placed on a statutory basis by the Intelligence Services Act 1994. This Act defines the boundaries of GCHQ activities. Within these boundaries the choice of what to intercept and report to the government and military commands is based on the intelligence requirements established by the Joint Intelligence Committee.

GCHQ provide a vital service to support national efforts to counter terrorism which embraces new technologies. However, the work of GCHQ does not come cheap. Having recently moved into new purpose-built premises at a cost of £1.2 billion it represents the largest Private Finance Initiative project undertaken to date. The value of GCHQ's products is however well established. Formerly the Government Code and Cipher School in 1919 it adopted the name of GCHQ in 1946 when its headquarters were at Bletchley Park during the Second World War. Its code-breaking activities during this period, especially in relation to the German 'Enigma' coding device are well known. Modern terrorist organizations use new and developing global communications. Their level of expertise in this area should not be underestimated. The role of GCHQ is to keep the UK one step ahead of its adversaries.

2.5.5 Defence Intelligence Staff

The Defence Intelligence Staff (DIS) is very different to the other agencies forming part of the 'intelligence community'. The DIS is a constituent part of the Ministry of Defence which brings together expertise from the Army, Air Force, and Navy. It conducts intelligence analysis from both overt and covert sources providing intelligence assessments which are used by the military and the government. The DIS collects intelligence in direct support of military operations as well as supporting operations by members of the 'intelligence community'. The DIS is an integral part of the 'intelligence community' providing access to intelligence collected on the ground during military operations.

2.5.6 Joint Terrorism Analysis Centre

The Joint Terrorism Analysis Centre (JTAC) was established in 2003 to analyze and assess all intelligence relating to international terrorism, at home and overseas. The creation of JTAC brought together expertise from the police and key government departments and agencies. As a truly joint organization it ensures that the sharing of information across separate organizations is achieved. Poor information sharing between agencies was highlighted as a deficiency of the US government during the build-up to the terrorist attacks in 2001 by the 9/11 Commission, a deficiency that the UK government was quick to identify and rectify in the UK with the creation of JTAC.

JTAC also sets the threat levels for the UK from international terrorism. It issues warnings of threats and other terrorist-related subjects for customers from a wide range of government departments and agencies. JTAC also produces more in-depth reports on trends, terrorist networks and capabilities. They are an integral part of the 'Intelligence Machinery' and this is where information gathered by the police service is fed into the national picture for analysis.

2.6 **Home Office**

The role of the Home Office changed in May 2007 as it took on the responsibility for leading the government's Contest strategy to counter terrorism in the UK. It accepted this additional role alongside existing responsibilities for policing, crime reduction, borders and immigration, identity and passports. At the same time, responsibility for prisons, probation, criminal law and sentencing moved to the new Ministry of Justice. More than ever before, the changes focus the Home Office on its core role of protecting the public, with the aim of safeguarding the fundamental rights and freedoms of UK citizens.

The Ministerial duties of the Home Secretary were outlined in a speech provided by Home Secretary, Jacqui Smith in January 2008 stating that:

> My duty as Home Secretary is to protect the security of our citizens and the freedoms they enjoy. The purpose of terrorism is to use indiscriminate killing to dictate the way we think and act, both as individuals and as governments. But it is a weakness of terrorism as a tactic that the way we respond determines the impact that it will have. Whether terrorists ultimately succeed or not is up to us, not up to them.

We should not forget that we operate from a position of strength, for these values are shared by the overwhelming majority of people living in Britain. In Britain our response to preventing terrorism should therefore preserve both our security and the values on which our society depends. And in this country we will uphold our common values by pursuing terrorists as criminals through our criminal justice system. They will get the justice that they deny others.

2.6.1 Home Office Strategy 2008–11

The new purpose of the Home Office is outlined in the Home Office Strategy 2008–11 'Working Together To Protect The Public'. The Home Office recognizes that to protect the public they need to work better with all of its partners including the police, intelligence agencies, local authorities, voluntary bodies, other departments, and other governments. The Home Office now works towards seven key objectives to:

- Help people feel secure in their homes and local communities;
- Cut crime, especially violent, drug and alcohol-related crime;
- Lead visible, responsive and accountable policing;
- Support the efficient and effective delivery of justice;
- Protect the public from terrorism;
- Secure our borders and control migration for the benefit of our country;
- Safeguard people's identity and the privileges of citizenship.

POINT TO NOTE—HOME OFFICE AND TERRORISM

The Home Office identifies that terrorism is one of the gravest threats the UK currently faces. It recognizes that it is a threat that manifests itself both overseas and in the UK requiring a local, national, and international response to tackle it. The re-focus of the Home Office now taking responsibility to protect the UK from terrorism provides an indication of the level of threat the UK continues to endure and the commitment of the government to reduce it.

The Home Office three-year strategy for 2008–11 commits to achieving eight high-level objectives which will be measured by the counter-terrorism Public Service Agreements (PSAs) whose aim is to 'reduce the risk to the UK and its interests overseas from international terrorism'. The high-level objectives include the following, outlined in the table below:

Table 2.2: Home Office Objectives

1	**Refresh Contest**	Building on our knowledge and experience of the developing threat, and tackling any particular vulnerabilities.
2	**Prevent Radicalization**	Putting a new focus on preventing radicalization. This will involve challenging the ideology of violent extremism; addressing radicalization in prisons; working with educational institutions to counter extremism, and tackling the use of the internet to radicalize and groom young people. It will build on the work of the Department for Communities and Local Government to build more resilient communities and support local people and organizations who are willing to challenge anti-Islamic activity.
3	**Work With ACPO**	Work with the Association of Chief Police Officers to develop a Prevent policing plan, building on the successful work already done by the police to develop local policing and support community cohesion. The completion of the national coverage of neighbourhood policing teams provides new opportunities to develop this work.
4	**Develop OSCT**	Complete the establishment of the Office of Security & Counter-Terrorism, bringing into the Home Office a wider range of skills and experience.
5	**Improve Protection**	Improve the protection of crowded public places, our transport infrastructure, in line with Lord West's recommendations and in conjunction with the Centre for the Protection of National Infrastructure (CPNI) and Counter-Terrorism Security Advisors.
6	**Improve UK Borders**	Improve the security of our borders with the formation of the UK Border Agency and the introduction of e-borders, enabling us to check people in and out of the UK.

| 7 | **Improve Legal Framework** | Improve the legal framework for investigating and prosecuting terrorists through a new Counter-Terrorism Bill, whilst developing a broad public consensus behind its key principles. |
| 8 | **Develop CT Policing** | Develop police counter-terrorist capabilities and resources. |

2.6.2 Office of Security and Counter-Terrorism

For over 30 years, the Office of Security and Counter-Terrorism (OSCT) have led the work on counter-terrorism in the UK engaging with the police and security services. The OSCT report directly to the Home Secretary and the Minister of State for the Home Office. The OSCT currently have responsibility for:

- Developing and co-ordinating the Contest Strategy
- Exercising the UK's response to a terrorist incident
- Developing security measures and protection packages for public figures
- Ensuring that the UK's critical national infrastructure is protected from attack (including electronic attack)
- Ensuring the UK is prepared to deal with a chemical, biological, or nuclear release
- Liaising with government and emergency services during terrorist incidents or counter-terrorism operations
- Overseeing the Regulation of Investigatory Powers Act 2000 (RIPA)
- Overseeing the Security Service Acts 1989 and 1996
- Overseeing Home Office related elements of the Intelligence Services Act 1994.

One of the primary functions of the OSCT is to exercise the UK's response to a terrorist incident. Under the Prepare strand of Contest the OSCT have developed a dynamic national counter-terrorism exercise programme which enables the government to test the UK's ability to respond to terrorist incidents and to identify ways in which the ability to respond can be improved. Counter-terrorism exercises are a vital part of the UK's resilience and contingency planning. It allows systems to be tested thoroughly, providing training opportunities for front line responders highlighting any vulnerabilities. The OSCT exercise programme includes:

- Three annual large-scale live exercises, involving police forces, other government departments and agencies

- Strategic-level decision-making by senior government officials
- Paper exercises where decisions are explored, rather than played out.

2.6.3 UK Border Agency

During November 2007 Prime Minister Gordon Brown announced a wide range of measures to counter terrorism which included a new approach to strengthening UK borders. These measures included the creation of the UK Border Agency in April 2008 which brings together the work of three key agencies which include:

- Border and Immigration Agency (BIA)
- UK Visas
- HM Revenue and Customs (HMRC).

The new agency has 25,000 staff present in 135 countries. It has been established to address recommendations of the 2007 Cabinet Office Review 'Security in a Global Hub'. The Review called for the implementation of a unified passport and customs checkpoint and identified a number of issues around policing at borders. The government had previously set out a new philosophy of border control for the UK in March 2007 stating that:

> Border control can no longer just be a fixed line on a map. Using new technology, particularly biometrics, and new approaches to managing risk and intelligence, we must create a new offshore line of defence, checking individuals as far from the UK as possible and through each stage of their journey. Our aim is to make legitimate travel easier, yet prevent those who might cause us harm from travelling here.

The UK Border Agency aims to protect the UK with a simple system of triple checks which include:

1. New offshore controls including pre-arrival screening;
2. A stronger UK border; and
3. Tougher checks at UK borders.

The Minister of State for Borders and Immigration, Liam Byrne MP set out the government's plans in the 2008 UK Border Agency report 'A Strong New Force At The Border' stating that:

> The purpose of the UK Border Agency is clear—to secure our border and control migration for the benefit of our country. That means we will protect our borders and our national interests.

The public will notice border controls that are stronger. They will see our customs and immigration staff in a single uniform. They will see a primary checkpoint at passport control where they will be asked about the travel documents they have and the goods they are carrying. They will see our new force with the purpose, the power and the punch to protect our border in the 21st Century.

The UK Border Agency and the police co-operate closely at ports. The UK Border Agency is the first line of border defence. Checks overseas, including watch lists, ensure that individuals and goods which could cause harm to the UK are prevented from travelling here. Individual police forces will often act on an electronic alert, based upon those watch lists against passengers or suspect goods on arrival. The UK Border Agency staff are also trained to watch out for unusual behaviour or possessions which may indicate criminal or immigration abuse where they will alert police colleagues if required. The UK Border Agency will meet its aim to protect the UK by:

Offshore Border Control

Significant activity will take place away from the UK Border, prior to the individual travelling. Activities include checks carried out to gain biometrically-enabled Visa and checks against passenger manifests which will inform their intervention.

Screening Pre-Arrival

As the individual or cargo is en route, checks are taking place. Individuals and freight can be identified and resources are deployed at the border to intercept those of interest based on risk.

In The UK

Using powers from the UK Borders Act 2007 which includes identity cards for foreign nationals, national identity cards, E-Passports and through Automatic Number Plate Recognition (ANPR)

At The UK Border

New systems and enhanced screening are able to more accurately identify individuals and freight of interest when they arrive at the UK border. Biometric documentation will be used to increase security and to facilitate the passage of legitimate passengers and trade.

Figure 2.4: Key aims of the UK Border Agency

UK Border Agency officers are now better equipped to protect the country from illegal immigration and other crime with tough powers which enable them to:

- Board and search vehicles, planes, or trains to search for people or goods
- Stop and question
- Detain an individual and
- Arrest individuals where necessary.

See also **5.4**.

POINTS TO NOTE—UK BORDER AGENCY'S POWERS

The Home Office highlights that where needed, the UK Border Agency's front-line staff will be able to support police officers in exercising their powers under counter-terrorism legislation. In addition, the Home Office are working towards increased UK Border Agency and police co-operation at UK ports especially in the areas of:

- Joint threat assessments and operations, including deploying UK Border Agency staff to the police-run National Ports Analytical Centre (NPAC)
- Developing joint structures at international, national, regional, and local levels
- Strengthening intelligence co-operation
- Cross-agency training
- Joint support for delivery of the UK Contest Strategy to counter international terrorism.

According to Home Office statistics released in 2008, the UK Border Agency is already proving to be a considerable success. Working in collaboration with police colleagues, the UK Border Agency during early 2008 had:

- Prevented almost 6,000 illegal migrants from entering Britain at juxtaposed controls;
- Seized over £80 million worth of illegal drugs, including almost 200 separate seizures of cocaine and heroin;
- Seized more than 200 million cigarettes worth more than £6.5 million;
- Taken off the streets almost 800 dangerous weapons including firearms, stun guns and hundreds of knives.

2.7 **Protecting National Security**

Terrorists and extremists may attack vital information or commu-nications systems to cause disruption and economic damage. The government places a high value on ensuring that the UK is well protected against such attacks. Our national infrastructure is the underlying framework of facilities, systems, sites, and networks necessary for the functioning of the country and the delivery of essential services. They are often the very services which we take for granted and include water, energy, and food which if attacked could lead to severe economic loss, social damage or in the most extreme cases large scale loss of life. Key sites within the UK also include airports which have been the target of numerous terrorist attacks across the world, including the attack on Glasgow Airport in Scotland during June 2007.

Case study— Glasgow Airport, 30 June 2007

At approximately 3.11 pm on Saturday, 30 June 2007 a dark green-coloured Jeep Cherokee loaded with propane cylinders was driven into the glass doors of the Glasgow International Airport terminal. Initial reports indicated that protective security steel bollards had prevented the vehicle from entering the terminal. The vehicle contained two men, Kafeel Ahmed and Bilal Talal Samad Abdulla who were both arrested at the scene. Ahmed suffered 90% burns to his body and died at Glasgow Royal Infirmary as a result of his injuries several days later. Although people assisting police officers at the scene of the attack suffered injuries themselves, miraculously, no other casualties arose from this attempted suicide attack.

The attack came a day after the Metropolitan Police were also engaged in a counter-terrorism investigation following a controlled explosion carried out on a car also packed with gas cylinders in the Haymarket area of London on 29 June 2007. An ambulance crew had reportedly seen smoke coming from the green Mercedes at 1.30 am that morning which had been parked near to a nightclub. Two major incidents within the space of 48 hours raised concerns that the UK was the target of a potential series of co-ordinated terrorist attacks. Alex Salmond, the First Minister of Scotland, stated that, 'The incident at Glasgow Airport today as well as recent events in London show that we face threats both north and south of the border, and both the Scottish and UK Governments are united in our determination to stand up to that threat and protect our communities.'

> The attack was the first to specifically target Scotland providing evidence that no community is immune from the global reach of international terrorism.
>
> Images of the unfolding events at Glasgow Airport were beamed around the world by 24-hour news channels within minutes of the attack. Airports in the UK were also quick to respond taking measures to increase their security while other countries also implemented their counter-terrorism contingency plans. United States Secretary of Homeland Security, Michael Chertoff, stated that 'We have been in close contact with our counterparts in the UK regarding today's incident at the Glasgow airport and yesterday's car bomb discoveries in London. Our law enforcement and intelligence officials are closely monitoring the ongoing investigations'.

The terrorist attacks in London and Glasgow during June 2007 triggered an immediate response from the government. As part of a series of measures Prime Minister Gordon Brown asked Lord West to conduct a review of security.

2.7.1 Lord West review 2007

During 2007, as a direct result of the failed terrorist attacks in London and Glasgow in June that same year, Lord West, the Minister for Homeland Security and Counter-Terrorism, conducted a review of security within the UK. The review specifically focused upon the protection of our strategic infrastructure, stations, ports and airports, and other crowded places. There were three key findings from the review which included:

- A need for a new 'risk-based' strategic framework to reduce vulnerability of crowded places;
- Focused effort on reducing the vulnerability of the highest risk crowded places by working with private and public sector partners at a local level;
- New efforts to 'design in' counter-terrorism security measures are needed, building on good practice from crime prevention.

During a keynote speech at the Government Conference on Homeland and Border Security during July 2008 Lord West stated that:

The protection and security of the UK is always on my mind—I have been hugely impressed by the hard work and dedication of the men and women in our police and security services and of the many others—in government, private and voluntary sectors—who contribute to the safety of the UK and the wider international community. Countering terrorism is not just about the work of the police, security service and intelligence agencies—it relies upon everyone to play their part.

We need to build more resilient enterprises and a resilient society where our values and freedoms can survive and thrive in the face of this complex and serious terrorist threat.

To do this, and to make sure that our response is proportionate and necessary, is an enormous challenge, but I am confident that we shall continue to succeed. By working together we shall ensure that violent extremists and terrorists find neither support nor sanctuary anywhere in the UK.

2.7.2 National security strategy

During March 2008 Prime Minister Gordon Brown announced the publication of the first National Security Strategy for the UK. The strategy highlights the nature of the new security challenges, how they have changed and how the UK is responding. It identifies that providing security for the nation and for its citizens remains the most important responsibility of the government. The strategy acknowledges that since the end of the Cold War, the international landscape has been transformed highlighting that the opposition between two power blocs has been replaced by a more complex and unpredictable set of relationships.

The strategy outlines that whilst the international landscape as a whole is increasingly complex and unpredictable no state directly threatens the UK. The introduction of the strategy is the first time that a single overarching framework has been brought together to include key objectives and plans of all government departments, agencies and forces concerned in protecting the national security of the UK. The primary objective of the strategy is 'to protect the UK and its interests, enabling its people to go about their daily lives freely and with confidence, in a more secure, stable, just and prosperous world'.

The primary objective of the strategy is supported by eight guiding principles which include the following, outlined in the Checklist below:

Checklist—National security strategy

- Our approach to national security is clearly grounded in a set of core values.
- We will be hard-headed about the risks, our aims, and our capabilities.
- Wherever possible, we will tackle security challenges early.
- Overseas, we will favour a multilateral approach.
- At home, we will favour a partnership approach.
- Inside government, we will develop a more integrated approach.
- We will retain strong, balanced and flexible capabilities.
- We will continue to invest, learn and improve to strengthen our security.

2.7.3 Centre for the Protection of National Infrastructure

The Centre for the Protection of National Infrastructure (CPNI) is a government authority which provides protective security advice to businesses and organizations across the UK's national infrastructure. They assist members of the national infrastructure to manage the risks to their services who require an accurate assessment of the current threats from terrorism. A definition of what constitutes the UK's Critical National Infrastructure was provided to Parliament by Baroness Scotland in 2004 who stated that:

> the critical national infrastructure includes those assets , services or systems that support the economic , political and social life of the UK, whose importance is such that any loss or compromise would have life-threatening, serious economic or other grave social consequences for the community, or would otherwise be of immediate concern to Government.

The CPNI was formed on 1 February 2007 through a merger of the National Infrastructure Security Co-ordination Centre, the National Security Advice Centre and departments of the Security Service MI5. Although only formed in 2007 it has always been part of the UK government's strategy to disrupt threats to national security and protect its key sites. The CPNI now provides integrated security advice and is accountable to the Director General of the Security Service MI5 operating under the Security Service Act 1989. The CPNI have established a 'top ten' list of security guidelines which includes the following, outlined in the Checklist below:

Checklist—CPNI Security Guidelines

- Assess the risks to your business.
- Consider security first when planning building works.
- Establish a security culture in your business.
- Keep premises clean and tidy.
- Control access points and use staff and visitor passes.
- Install physical measures eg locks, alarms, CCTV, lighting, etc.
- Establish good mail handling procedures.
- Recruit carefully, checking identities and following up references.
- Take proper IT security precautions.
- Test your business continuity plans regularly.

2.7.4 National Counter-Terrorism Security Office

The National Counter-Terrorism Security Office (NaCTSO), on behalf of the Association of Chief Police Officers (Terrorism and Allied Matters) (ACPO TAM) works in partnership with the Security Service MI5 to reduce the impact of terrorism in the UK by:

- Protecting the UK's most vulnerable and valuable sites and assets.
- Enhancing the UK's resilience to terrorist attack.

NaCTSO aims to:

- Raise awareness of the terrorist threat and the measures that can be taken to reduce risks and mitigate the effects of an attack.
- Co-ordinate national service delivery of protective security advice through the Counter-Terrorism Security Adviser (CTSA) network and monitor its effectiveness.
- Build and extend partnerships with communities, police and government stakeholders.
- Contribute to the development of national and international counter-terrorism policy and advice.

Since 2002, NaCTSO has established, co-ordinated and tasked a network of CTSAs throughout the UK. CTSAs provide advice in person to the public and the private sector including businesses, communities and other stakeholders at a force level. During 2007 the Prime Minister Gordon Brown outlined proposals to strengthen the work of the CTSAs by creating new posts and investing a further £1.5 million by April 2008 which has now been achieved. The role of the CTSAs include:

- Identifying and assessing local critical sites within their force area that might be vulnerable to terrorist or extremist attack
- Devising and developing appropriate protective security plans to minimize impact on key sites and the surrounding community
- Promoting awareness of the terrorist threat and develop positive ongoing relationships by appropriate discussion of changes in the prevailing terrorist threat and commensurate resources
- Engaging with police departments to encourage a co-ordinated approach to ensure counter-terrorism protective security advice is incorporated in general crime prevention regimes.

CTSAs are able to achieve the core functions of their roles as a result of having regular access to counter-terrorism threat assessments and related intelligence. In addition they receive comprehensive specialist training in areas such as explosives and pre-curser chemicals, pathogens and toxins, radiological sources, site and vulnerable point surveying, business continuity and disaster recovery, information and personal security, integrated security systems, designing out vehicle borne terrorism and the threat from CBRN attack.

See also 5.5.

POINT TO NOTE—NACTSO AND CTSA

The role of NaCTSO and the network of CTSAs is vital for the protection of the UK as it not only raises awareness of the terrorist threat but builds and extends partnerships with communities, the police and government stakeholders who all contribute to target hardening the UK.

2.8 **Threat Levels**

On 1 August 2006 the government made information available to the public on the terrorism threat level system in the UK. The then Home Secretary, Dr John Reid, stated that: 'Previously, the Government has not made public the way in which this system works or the national threat level that emerges from it. Following a review, we have decided to inform the general public about the process and the national threat level, which applies to the UK as a whole'.

This decision now recognizes the important role the public plays in countering terrorism when confronted with such a sustained and heightened threat. The government has a duty of care to protect the UK which is a key component in its national strategy to counter international terrorism. The government continues to maintain a state of readiness in response to the threats. It remains the government's policy to issue warnings or advice if ever it became necessary to protect the public in the event of a specific and credible terrorist threat. However, there is a delicate balance to maintain between keeping the public informed of current threats, whilst ensuring the secrecy and security of covert operations. Information which is made available to the public is also available to terrorists and the challenge is to keep the public updated whilst not providing an unnecessary advantage to terrorist cells. Disclosing too much information to the public may alert terrorists to police or intelligence agency activities. There is a need to share information with the public so that we can all adjust our security measures according to specific threats, but this has to be communicated sensitively and has to be put into a broader context.

POINT TO NOTE—THE PUBLIC

It is important that the public are informed about terrorist activity but in doing so it should not increase their perceived fear of terrorism which may become disproportionate to the actual threat, thereby potentially provoking an over-reaction which may be neither necessary nor justified. The government encourages the public at all times to be alert to, but not alarmed by, terrorist threats.

2.8.1 National threat level system

The terrorist threats to the UK are diverse which requires a dedicated response to assessing such threats effectively. The Joint Terrorism Analysis Centre (JTAC), provides analysis and assessment of information relating to the threats from international terrorism. A new system has been created to keep the public informed and is designed to give a broad indication of the likelihood of a terrorist attack. The threat levels are:

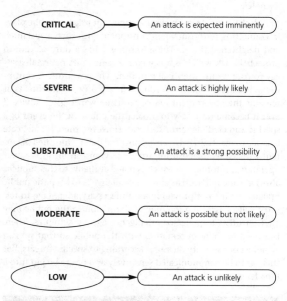

CRITICAL	An attack is expected imminently
SEVERE	An attack is highly likely
SUBSTANTIAL	An attack is a strong possibility
MODERATE	An attack is possible but not likely
LOW	An attack is unlikely

Figure 2.5: National threat level system

POINT TO NOTE—THREAT LEVEL

The UK threat level may change. To keep updated on the current threat to the UK from international terrorism access the Home Office website at <http://www.homeoffice.gov.uk/security/current-threat-level>.

The threat to the UK has consistently been assessed as being 'severe' since its introduction but it has also been increased to 'critical'. The alleged plot to attack trans-Atlantic commercial jets in the summer of 2006 was an occasion when the UK was put on high alert as a terrorist attack was expected.

Case study—Trans-Atlantic airline plot, 10 August 2006

On the morning of 10 August 2006 the aviation industry and passengers arriving at UK airports suffered major disruption following the overnight arrest of a terrorist cell suspected of planning a co-ordinated suicide attack on several trans-Atlantic flights. Unprecedented security measures were put in place to protect the public which prevented passengers from carrying liquids on flights. The alleged plot focused upon the potential use of 18 suicide bombers who are thought to have constructed viable improvised explosive devices using everyday items such as drinks bottles concealing their actual intended use. The then Home Secretary Dr John Reid stated that, 'overnight the police, with the full knowledge of Ministers, have carried out a major counter-terrorism operation to disrupt what we believe to be major threats to the UK and international partners'. He went on to say that 'at 2 am this morning the Joint Terrorism Analysis Centre raised the UK threat state to critical'.

Speaking to the world's press from outside New Scotland Yard Metropolitan Police Deputy Commissioner Paul Stephenson stated that 'if successful the plot would have caused mass murder on an unimaginable scale'.

2.8.2 Assessing the threat

It is rare that a single source of information relating to an event that can be relied upon is available. More often, judgements about the threat will be based on a wide range of information which is often fragmented. Small pieces of information are required to be put together which includes analysis of previous attacks and similar events in other countries. Intelligence is not an exact science and it will never reveal the whole picture which is why information supplied by police partners and members of the public is important no matter how insignificant it may appear to be at the time. It just might provide corroboration and strengthen analytical judgements. The former Director General of the Security Service MI5, Baroness Eliza Manningham-Buller stated in an Intelligence and Security Committee Report into the London Terrorist Attacks on 7 July 2005 that:

> Intelligence rarely tells you all you want to know. Often difficult decisions need to be made on the basis of intelligence which is fragmentary and difficult to interpret. In sum, some is gold, some dross and all of it requires validation, analysis and assessment. When it is gold it shines and illuminates, saves lives, protects nations and informs policy. When identified as dross it needs to be rejected: that may take some

confidence. At the end of the day it requires people of integrity not only to collect it but also to prioritise, sift, judge and use it.

Assessing the threat includes the gathering and analysis of information around four core areas: the terrorist's intention, their capabilities, timescales and the vulnerability of the chosen target. The table below offers more detail.

Table 2.3: Assessing the threat from terrorism

Intent	What are the intentions of the terrorist group? What is their plan? Is the plan achievable? What is the target? What do they aim to achieve? What methods are they going to use?
Capability	Do they have the expertise to carry out their intended plan? Do they have sufficient resources? Do they require support? Have they received specific training?
Timescale	When are they going to carry out their plan? When will they be ready to carry out their plan? Do they have any alternative dates in mind? What are the time constraints of their attack plan?
Vulnerability	Does the intended attack plan strike at an area that is potentially vulnerable? Can effective measures be put in place to decrease its vulnerability? Are there existing mechanisms in place to disrupt or deter the attack?

Identifying answers to some of the questions above will inform an assessment of the 'actual' as opposed to the 'perceived' threat of a specific terrorist group. Intelligence gathered concerning their intentions and an assessment of whether their aims are achievable or realistic given their capabilities are key to this process. Timescales are also a crucial element of assessing threat levels as knowing when a terrorist group is to strike may provide a higher degree of urgency to respond to unfolding events. Once this data is captured an analysis of the potential vulnerability to such an attack can be conducted. Compiling a picture to make an accurate assessment of the actual threat is a real challenge and one that requires a thorough understanding of terrorism-related activity. The following formula, which is used in other areas of business to identify **'threat'** and **'risk'** is used to assess specific terrorist related threats:

(Intent + Capability + Timescale) = THREAT

(Threat + Vulnerability) = RISK

Figure 2.6: Threat and risk formula

2.9 **Chapter Summary**

The government can never guarantee that attacks will not happen in the future, but its security effort is dedicated to reducing the risk as much as possible. It is important that the police and the public do not become complacent about the seriousness of the level of the threat that 'severe' represents. Just because a terrorist threat which is described as being 'highly likely' has not manifested itself in a successful major attack does not mean to say that the threat is any less potent.

The threat from international terrorism remains very real in the Uk and overseas. The terrorist attacks in Mumbai, India, during November 2008, in which 200 people were killed provides further evidence of the potent threat of terrorism and its power in drawing global attention to a particular cause. The co-ordinated attacks in Mumbai were well planned and executed, a threat from organized terrorists groups that Jonathan Evans, the Director General of the Security Service MI5 was keen to highlight whilst speaking in Manchester during November 2007 stating that:

> It is important that we recognize an uncomfortable truth; terrorist attacks we have seen against the UK are not simply random plots by disparate and fragmented groups. The majority of the attacks, successful or otherwise, have taken place because Al-Qaeda has a clear determination to mount terrorist attacks against the UK. This remains the case today and there is no sign of it reducing.

Chapter 3

Policing Terrorism

3.1 **A Brief History**

Policing terrorism is nothing new. It was once the sole responsibility of small specialist departments but this is no longer the case. The nature of the threat from international terrorism demands a greater level of commitment from the whole of the police service. In 1883, the then Home Secretary, Sir William Vernon Harcourt, was confronted with meeting the challenges presented by Irish republicans who had conducted a series of bombings in London. He stated that 'This is not a temporary emergency requiring a momentary remedy, this will last far beyond the term of my life and must be met by a permanent organisation to detect and control it'.

Sir William called for the creation of a specialist policing unit to manage the threats posed by Irish republicans to protect the public from further harm. The police service in the UK has countered terrorism and extremism throughout its history. This area of policing has previously been shrouded in secrecy but the level of sustained threat from international terrorism must now be tackled by all assets of the police service and its partners.

POINT TO NOTE—LEARNING FROM HISTORY

The way in which the police service now tackles terrorism is developing. It is developing in response to the severe threat we currently face. The statement from Sir William Harcourt is just as relevant today as the threat from international terrorism is not a temporary emergency and a momentary remedy will not prevent it.

HM Government is investing significant resources into the police service specifically to counter terrorism and extremism but what is really new about how the police service counters terrorism and extremism today? To answer this, we need to reflect upon over 125 years of policing terrorism in the UK.

3.1.1 Creation of Special Branch

The 1860s saw resurgence in Irish nationalism and a growing support for the 'Fenian' movement who sought to create a Republican Ireland which was independent of the UK. 'Fenianism' was a generic title assumed at the time by many Irish Republican militants ('Fianna' is Gaelic for 'warrior'), in succession to various such groupings which had existed for around a century. Within the Fenian movement, in the 1850s and 1860s, there was formed an Irish Republican Brotherhood in Ireland (which was the basis for the Irish Republican Army when it was established in 1919) and the Fenian Brotherhood (later Clan na Gael) in the United States. As part of a broad political campaign, violence and intimidation was used to gain support for their cause, but the wider movement included lawful political movements such as Home Rule Leagues and Land Leagues. To counter these new and emerging threats the UK government mounted a number of secret operations against the Fenians, and as a result of the counter-action but also owing to poor organization, a Republican rebellion in 1867 was successfully thwarted. The Fenian activities including attacks in England in which 13 people died, included a police sergeant in Manchester. The Republican bombings resurged in the early 1880s, and a dedicated response was required to counter the threats.

The Home Office created a fully-fledged Secret Service Department under the command of a young Anglo-Irish lawyer called Robert Anderson. Anderson recruited a Briton who had close contacts with the Republicans in America. Anderson's contact was recruited as an agent and was able to infiltrate the ranks of the IRA. Anderson's agent was rapidly promoted, first to Military Organizer of the IRA and later to Inspector General, feeding Anderson with every detail of the IRA's operations. The tactics used by Anderson, to identify and recruit an informant proved successful, a tactic that would continue to be used against the IRA.

In March 1883 the Metropolitan Police established a Special Irish Branch with a network of agents run by Major Nicholas Gosselin. The new department conducted a number of successful operations which frustrated the IRA who responded by detonating a bomb in the public lavatory below the Special Irish Branch office in Scotland Yard. The explosion ripped through the building. Police officers and staff were injured in the attack but the Branch survived and in 1887 it became known as the Special Branch with responsibility for all politically motivated crime.

Despite a wealth of policing expertise in this field and countering an organization that had been infiltrated by government agents at the highest levels, successful attacks were conducted on the UK mainland. Attacks occurred with alarming regularity and increasing impact. Public figures, military personnel and police officers were some of the targets, but the main victims were ordinary citizens such as people in railway stations and public houses. Locations were chosen where improvised explosive devices were sited to deliver a powerful political message. Such devices were used to attack Harrods, the BBC Television Centre, government Ministries, the Houses of Parliament, the Old Bailey and 10 Downing Street. Road and rail networks were targeted. Funding was mainly derived from sympathizers within both parts of Ireland, but organized crime and overseas funding was also secured to finance the paramilitary activities. Between 1969 and 1999, there were 3,667 deaths related to political violence in Northern Ireland; 303 were police officers, 709 were soldiers, 536 terrorists (although this figure is disputed) and the remainder and vast majority were civilians. There were 300 terrorist-related deaths in Britain during the same period. Damage to property and the cost of additional security was a further substantial cost to the public.

3.1.2 From threat to threat

The threat from Irish-related terrorism was only interrupted last century during the First and Second World Wars. Officers from Special Branch found that their covert policing skills made them valuable assets in countering German espionage activity. They also assisted the French Resistance to frustrate the Nazi occupation of France during the Second World War. As the UK recovered from the wider impact of the war, further threats from the IRA began to emerge. During the late 1960s, Special Branch, together with the Security Service (MI5), embarked upon a period of 40 years dedicated to countering threats from the IRA.

We must not forget that police officers, military personnel, members of the Royal family, and innocent members of the public, including children were killed and injured during this period.

Case study—Harrods, London, 17 December 1983

At approximately 12.44 pm on 17 December 1983 the central London branch of the Samaritans organization received an Irish Republican Army (IRA) code word from a caller stating that there were vehicle bombs placed outside Harrods. As police officers arrived at the scene the bomb, placed in a blue Austin GT car containing 14kg of explosives, was detonated by a timing device at approximately 1.21 pm. The force of the blast ripped the vehicle roof clean off blowing it on to the top of a nearby five-storey building. Nick Lawrence was a witness to the bombing being inside the Harrods store at the time the device detonated. He recalled what happened during that busy afternoon of Christmas shopping:

> I had crossed the whole of London to get to Harrods after failing to get the book I wanted for my Dad for Christmas. I figured Harrods must have it. I had just walked past a first-floor window when the bomb went off in the street outside. It was literally a 'bang' sound, but furiously loud. The window blew in but the glass was caught by the special net curtains, weighted at the bottom. If it hadn't I would have been cut to pieces.

Six people were killed in the blast which included three members of the public and three police officers. The members of the public who perished included Philip Geddes (aged 24), Kenneth Salvesen (aged 28) and Jasmine Cochrane-Patrick (aged 25). Police Constable Jane Arbuthnot (aged 22) and Police Sergeant Noel Lane (aged 28) also died and Police Inspector Stephen Dodd (aged 34) was fatally injured and died on 24 December. Approximately 90 people were injured in the blast including Police Constable Jon Gordon who lost both his legs and part of his hand as a result of the attack. A memorial that marks the spot where the police officers gave their lives to protecting the public is located at Harrods on Hans Crescent.

The IRA admitted to planting the bomb stating that a clear warning about the explosion had been given. Hundreds of extra police officers were drafted into London to protect the public from the possibility of further attacks. Harrods re-opened three days later stating that it would not be defeated by acts of terrorism.

Case study—Brighton Bomb, 12 October 1984

At 2.54 am on 12 October 1984 a bomb planted at the Grand Hotel in Brighton by members of the Provisional Irish Republican Army (PIRA) exploded. The primary target of the attack was Prime Minister Margaret Thatcher who was staying at the hotel together with senior members of the Cabinet and members of the Conservative Party for their annual Conservative Party Conference. At the time of the attack the Prime Minister was reported to be working on her conference speech. Although the 30 pound bomb ripped through the hotel it only damaged the bathroom suite where the Prime Minister was staying failing to penetrate her sitting room and bedroom. Although the bomb did not kill the Prime Minister or any of her Ministers, five people perished in the attack including Sir Donald McLean and Sir Anthony Berry. PIRA admitted responsibility for the attack stating that: 'Mrs Thatcher will now realise that Britain cannot occupy our country and torture our prisoners and shoot our people in their own streets and get away with it. Today we were unlucky but remember we only have to get lucky once. You will have to be lucky always. Give Ireland peace and there will be no more war'.

Margaret Thatcher, undeterred from the morning's events began the next session of the Conservative Party Conference as planned, claiming that the bombing was:

> an attempt to cripple Her Majesty's democratically elected Government. That is the scale of the outrage in which we have all shared, and the fact that we are gathered here now—shocked, but composed and determined—is a sign not only that this attack has failed, but that all attempts to destroy democracy by terrorism will fail.

During September 1986, Patrick Magee, was found guilty of planting the bomb. Under the false name of Roy Walsh, Magee had checked into the Grand Hotel 24 days earlier placing the bomb underneath a bath equipped with a long-delay timer. Magee received eight life sentences but under the terms of the Good Friday Agreement, having served only 14 years, he was released from prison in 1999.

The important issues to draw from the police response in tackling Irish-related terrorism is that many covert and overt investigations were successfully conducted and terrorists were brought to justice. Despite many attacks taking place the work of Special Branch throughout the UK together with the Metropolitan Police Anti-Terrorist Branch was highly regarded. In 2002 HM Inspectorate of Constabulary conducted a thematic inspection of Special Branch and Ports, concluding that 'Special Branch extends the reach of National agencies by utilising the close link between local police and the communities they serve. This link is a major strength of the UK national security structure and the envy of other countries.'

3.1.3 Responding to international terrorism

During 2007, the former Deputy Assistant Commissioner of the Metropolitan Police, and National Co-ordinator for Terrorist Investigations, Peter Clarke, outlined his observations on the changing terrorist threat as part of a lecture in memory of the late Chief Constable of West Yorkshire Police, Colin Cramphorn. The lecture focused upon countering terrorism in the UK since 9/11 in which he said:

> So what has happened since 9/11? I think it is no exaggeration to say that there has been a complete change in our understanding of the terrorist threat. For 30 years or more we had been facing a deadly campaign of terrorism conducted by utterly ruthless people intent on wreaking death and destruction. But it was different to that which we now face.
>
> Colleagues from around the world often say to me that the long experience that we have in the UK of combating a terrorist threat must have stood us in good stead; that experience gained during some 30 years of an Irish republican terrorist campaign would have equipped us for the new challenges presented by Al-Qaeda and its associated groups. To an extent that is true—but only to an extent. The fact remains that the Irish campaign operated within a set pf parameters that helped to shape our response to it.
>
> It was essentially a domestic campaign using conventional weaponry, carried out by terrorists in tightly-knit networks who were desperate to avoid capture and certainly had no wish to die. The use of warnings restricted the scale of the carnage, dreadful though it was. The warnings were cynical and often misleading, but by restricting casualties were a factor in ultimately enabling the political process to move forward, however haltingly.
>
> I believe that if you take the reverse of many of these characteristics, you are not far away from describing the threat we face today. It is global in origin, reach and ambition. The networks are large, fluid, mobile and incredibly resilient. We have seen how Al-Qaeda has been able to survive prolonged multinational assault on its structures, personnel and logistics. It has certainly retained its ability to deliver centrally directed attacks here in the UK.

The threat from the IRA had clear political objectives and the organization itself had a military structure which used recognizable military tactics and methods of operating. The IRA avoided the loss of their own operatives and although they did not succeed on every occasion, they attempted to strictly avoid civilian casualties. This was evidenced by the use of coded warnings provided to the police identifying where explosive devices had been deployed. This threat is very different to the one posed by Al-Qaeda and its affiliates. Al-Qaeda today has little structure, and is best described as a network of networks operating globally. They have a wide range of targets and no defined method of operating. They have no particular signature that can be attributed to their activities. Most importantly, they seek mass casualties in order to maximize the impact of their attacks. They also enthusiastically embrace the use of suicide operations. The key differences between the threats posed by the IRA and Al-Qaeda are outlined in the table below.

Table 3.1: Differences in threats posed by the IRA and Al-Qaeda

Irish-Related Terrorism	International Terrorism
Clear political objectives within a religious cultural divide.	Global clash of political, religious, cultural and economic identity.
Highly structured hierarchical military organization.	Global network of networks with little structure.
Conflict within familiar Western historical and cultural framework and context.	Conflict within unfamiliar context and framework.
Specific targets to further clear political aims and objectives.	Wide range of targets to inflict maximum damage with unclear aims.
Recognizable military modus operandi and signature.	Undefined military modus operandi or signature.
Civilian casualties were not a primary target.	Seek mass civilian casualties in order to maximize effect of attack.
Avoided loss of operatives.	Enthusiastically embrace suicide martyrdom operations.

The government was improving the UK's response to counter-terrorism after 9/11 by developing a strategy to counter international terrorism and commencing a regional structure to gather and assess counter-terrorism intelligence to support and co-ordinate the work of Special Branches.

The UK had also established the Joint Terrorism Analysis Centre to assess threats to the UK. Additional resources had been made available to protect the UK, new legislation had been put in place and both the police and partner agencies had recruited additional personnel to meet the demands of the growing threat.

Despite many lessons being learned and an unprecedented period of growth and investment in counter-terrorism resources, the police service and its partners were unable to prevent four 'home-grown' terrorists committing the worst attack London had witnessed since the events of the Second World War on the morning of 7 July 2005.

3.1.4 July 2005

July 2005 was already proving to be a busy period for those engaged in policing and protecting national security. The G8 Summit based at the Gleneagles Hotel in Scotland was well underway. One of the largest police operations the UK had ever undertaken was proving successful as a result of many months planning and preparing to meet the challenges of potential terrorist and extremist threats.

The world's most powerful and influential Heads of State had gathered to discuss a variety of world issues. They included discussions concerning the poverty and rising debts in Africa, which were highlighted by many pressure groups as crippling the country's opportunity to regenerate and prosper. This issue became centre stage for the summit resulting in a massive demonstration of 250,000 people on the streets of Edinburgh in support of the 'Make Poverty History' campaign which was calling for trade justice, better aid and debt relief for those countries in severe poverty. On 6 July, the International Olympic Committee announced that the 2012 Olympics Games would be staged in London. Members of the public and supporters of the London Olympic bid who had gathered at Trafalgar Square in London erupted in cheers as the news was broadcast live on large screens. Celebrations continued well into the night as Prime Minister Tony Blair expressed his gratitude for the work and dedication of the team engaged in bringing the Olympics to London.

3.1.5 7 July 2005

The UK woke on the morning of Thursday, 7 July with a strong positive feel. The early morning rush hour had started as normal, there were some delays but nothing unusual to report. However, later that morning news would reach the media of an unfolding national critical incident, an incident that would shape the way in which the government protects its citizens from terrorist attacks.

Case study—7 July 2005, London bombings

The initial report of the Official Account of the Bombings in London presented to the House of Commons on 11 May 2006 provides a detailed picture of the bombers movements on the morning of 7 July 2005:

3.58 am: A light blue Nissan Micra vehicle is caught on CCTV cameras in Hyde Park Road, Leeds, West Yorkshire, prior to joining the M1 motorway outside Leeds. This car was hired by Shehzad Tanweer (ST) and is believed to have been carrying ST, Mohammed Siddique Khan (MSK) and Hasib Hussain (HH). Hyde Park Road is close to 18 Alexandre Grove, the flat which appears to have been the bomb factory.

4.54 am: The Nissan Micra stops at Woodall Services on the M1 motorway to fill up with petrol. ST goes into pay. He is wearing a white T-shirt, dark jacket, white tracksuit bottoms and a baseball cap. He buys snacks, quibbles with the cashier over his change, looks directly at the CCTV camera and leaves.

5.07 am: A red Fiat Brava arrives at Luton train station car park, Jermaine Lindsay (JL) is alone in this car. During the 90 minutes or so before MSK, HH and ST arrive, JL gets out of the car and walks around, enters the station, looks up at the departure board, comes out and moves the car a couple of times. There are a handful of other cars in the car park. A few more arrive during this period.

6.49 am: The Nissan Micra arrives at Luton and parks next to the Fiat Brava. The four men get out of their respective cars, look in the boots of both, and appear to move items between them. They each put on rucksacks which CCTV shows are large and full. The four men are described as if they were going on a camping holiday.

One car contained explosive devices of a different and smaller kind from those in the rucksacks. It is not clear what they were for, but they may have been for self-defence or diversion in case of interception during the journey given their size; that they were in the car rather than the

---

boot; and that they were left behind. Also left in the Nissan Micra were other items consistent with the use of explosives. A 9mm handgun was also found in the Fiat Brava. The Nissan Micra had a day parking ticket in the window, perhaps to avoid attention, the Fiat Brava did not.

7.15 am: JL, HH, ST and MSK entered the Luton train station and went through the ticket barriers together. It is not known where they bought their tickets or what sort of tickets they possessed, but they must have had some to get on to the platform.

7.21 am: JL, HH, MSK and ST are all caught on CCTV cameras together heading to the platform for the King's Cross Thameslink train. They are casually dressed, apparently relaxed. ST's posture and the way he pulls the rucksack on to his shoulder as he walks, suggests he finds it heavy. It is estimated that in each rucksack was 2–5 kg of high explosive. ST is now wearing dark tracksuit bottoms. There is no explanation for this change of clothing at present.

7.40 am: The London King's Cross train leaves Luton station. There are conflicting accounts of their behaviour on the train. Some witnesses report noisy conversations, another believes he saw two of them standing silently by a set of train doors. JL, MSK, HH and ST stood out a bit from usual commuters due to their luggage and casual clothes, but not enough to cause suspicion. This was the beginning of the summer tourist period and Luton station serves Luton Airport.

8.23 am: The train arrives at King's Cross, slightly late due to a delay further up the line. JL, MSK, HH and ST are captured on CCTV cameras at 8:36 am on the concourse close to the Thameslink platform and heading in the direction of the London Underground system. At around 8.30 am four men matching the description of JL, MSK, HH and ST are seen hugging. They appear happy, even euphoric. They then split up. MSK must have gone to board a westbound Circle Line train, ST an eastbound Circle Line train and JL a southbound Piccadilly Line train. HH also appeared to walk towards the Piccadilly Line entrance.

8.50 am: CCTV cameras show the platform at Liverpool Street with the eastbound Circle Line train alongside seconds before it is blown up. ST is not visible, but he must have been in the second carriage from the front. The images show commuters rushing to get on the train and a busy platform. Some get on, some just miss it. The train pulls out of the station. Seconds later smoke billows from the tunnel. There is shock and confusion on the platform as people make for the exits.

Forensic evidence suggests that ST was sitting towards the back of the second carriage with the rucksack next to him on the floor. The blast killed eight people, including ST, with 171 injured.

At Edgware Road, MSK was also in the second carriage from the front, mostly likely near the standing area by the first set of double doors. He was probably also seated with the bomb next to him on the floor.

Shortly before the explosion, MSK was seen fiddling with the top of the rucksack. The explosion killed seven people, including MSK, and injured 163.

On the Piccadilly Line, JL was in the first carriage as it travelled between King's Cross and Russell Square. It is unlikely that he was seated. The train was crowded, with 127 people in the first carriage alone, which makes it difficult to position those involved. Forensic evidence suggests the explosion occurred on or close to the floor of the standing area between the second and third set of seats. The explosion killed 27 people, including JL, and injured over 340.

8.55 am: HH walks out of King's Cross Underground onto Euston Road. Telephone call records show that he tried unsuccessfully to contact MSK, JL and ST on his mobile telephone over the next few minutes. His demeanour over this period appears relaxed and unhurried.

9.00 am: HH goes back into King's Cross station through Boots and then goes into W H Smith on the station concourse to purchase a 9 volt battery. It is possible that a new battery was needed to detonate the device, but this is only speculation at this stage.

9.06 am: HH goes into McDonald's on Euston road, leaving ten minutes later.

9.19 am: HH is seen on Grays Inn Road. Around this time, a man fitting HH's description was seen on the no 91 bus travelling from King's Cross to Euston Station, looking nervous and pushing past people.

It was almost certainly at Euston that HH switched to the no 30 bus travelling eastwards from Marble Arch. This bus was crowded following the closures on the underground. HH sat on the upper deck, towards the back. Forensic evidence suggests the bomb was next to him in the aisle or between his feet on the floor. A man fitting HH's description was seen on the lower deck earlier, fiddling repeatedly with his rucksack.

09.47 am: The bomb goes off, killing 14 people, including HH, and injuring over 110. It remains unclear why the bomb did not go off at 8.05 am alongside the others. It may be that HH was intending to go north from Kings Cross but was frustrated by delays on the Northern Line. Another possibility, as he seems to have bought a new battery, is that he was unable to detonate his device with the original battery.

The co-ordinated terrorist attacks of 7 July reveal patterns of behaviour from the suicide terrorists which remain the subject of much research today. To know and understand one's enemy is a well established principle within the field of countering terrorism. It is now widely acknowledged that simply knowing who the enemy is cannot prevent terrorist activity in the long term—understanding the enemy has become just as, or even more, important.

The actions of Shezhad Tanweer at 4.54 am on 7 July at Woodall Services whilst travelling to Luton provides evidence of behaviour many may find unusual. Having appeared to accept his fate, knowing the devastation he would personally cause several hours later, he still took time to quibble with the cashier about the change he had been given for the purchase of goods. Why would he do this knowing that he was to die? Was it just a natural reaction? There are many speculative responses to account for the reaction of Shezhad Tanweer at that time but all appeared to be normal just hours before the attack. None of the cell members that morning displayed any patterns of behaviour that would appear to be uncharacteristic, unusual or that would raise any concern or suspicion. Knowing and understanding terrorist behaviour, specifically suicide terrorist behaviour are the keys to being able to identify potential triggers that may alert authorities to impending danger.

The actions of Hasib Hussain, the youngest of the four bombers at the age of 18 shows how he was able to rectify the fault with his rucksack device by the purchase of a new 9 volt battery from WH Smiths at King's Cross Station. This behaviour has to be put into context. Having failed to detonate his device did Hasib Hussain flee from the scene? No. Did he attempt to conceal any evidence and destroy the faulty device? No. Did he attempt to conceal his identity from CCTV? No. Did he appear to panic? No. Instead Hasib Hussain walked back to King's Cross Station passing members of the public, emergency services and London Underground employees. Not only was he able to rectify the problem with the device, displaying a technical capability and presence of mind, but he also showed a determination to complete his mission identifying an opportunity to detonate his device whilst seeking mass casualties on an alternative method of public transport.

POINT TO NOTE—MOTIVATIONS

It is important to identify that the individual behaviours and group dynamics of the 7/7 terrorist cell are not wholly typical of other terrorist attacks. Not all terrorists successfully completed their missions—some terrorists have withdrawn from attacks, some have failed to detonate their explosive devices for technical or other reasons. In addition, individual terrorists may be wholly committed to the group's cause, while others may not be as firmly committed but are motivated by their bond to other cell members.

> The primary lesson to learn from the patterns of behaviour from the 7/7 terrorist cell bombers is that in order to deploy effective counter measures, understanding their motivations, ideologies and intentions is essential. This is the real long term challenge of countering terrorism to prevent further attacks and protect the UK.

World leaders, politicians, religious and community leaders reacted strongly to the terrorist attacks. Prime Minister Tony Blair broke away from his G8 engagements to provide the following statement:

> It is important that those engaged in terrorism realise that our determination to defend our values and our way of life is greater than their determination to cause death and destruction to innocent people in a desire to impose extremism on the world. Whatever they do it is our determination that they will never succeed in destroying what we hold dear in this country and in other civilised nations throughout the world.

The then Lord Mayor of London, Ken Livingstone, also provided a statement which captured the early reactions of many people that day. He stated that:

> This was not a terrorist attack against the mighty and the powerful. It was not aimed at Presidents or Prime Ministers. It was aimed at ordinary working-class Londoners, black and white, Muslim and Christian, Hindu and Jew, young and old. Indiscriminate slaughter irrespective of any consideration for age, class, religion, whatever. That isn't an ideology. It isn't even a perverted faith. It is just an indiscriminate attempt at mass murder.

3.1.6 21 July 2005

As Londoners returned to their normal rush hour routines, life in the capital appeared to return to some sense of normality. Unbeknown to commuters a further suicide terrorist cell planned to seek mass casualties again attempting to disrupt the public transport infrastructure of London. The following series of explosions, outlined in the timeline below, were conducted.

Time	Event
12.26	An explosion occurred on a train at Shepherd's Bush London Underground tube station on the Hammersmith and City Line in West London.
12.30	An explosion occurred on a train at the Oval London Underground tube station on the Northern Line.
12.45	An explosion occurred on a Victoria Line train at Warren Street tube station of the London Underground.
13.30	An explosion occurred in East London on the number 26 bus travelling from Waterloo to Hackney Wick, on Hackney Road at the junction with Columbia Road in Shoreditch, London.

Figure 3.1: 21 July 2005 Timeline

All of the devices failed to explode as only the detonator caps had fired, which did not ignite the bombs. Miraculously there were no casualties as London was once again the subject of a co-ordinated suicide terrorist attack. A massive police counter-terrorism investigation was launched, resulting in the release of CCTV images of four men on 22 July. The four men had been seen running away from the scenes of the explosions by witnesses. The four men were later identified as Osman Hussain, Yasin Hassan Omar, Ramzi Mohammed and Muktar Said Ibrahim. Following one of the largest 'manhunts' the UK police service has ever undertaken all four men, together with an identified fifth bomber, Manfo Kwaka Asiedu, were all charged with conspiracy to murder amongst other offences.

POINTS TO NOTE—21 JULY FAILED SUICIDE ATTACK

The 21 July failed suicide attack reveals two key issues concerning the prevention of terrorism and the protection of sites. First, the history of terrorism reveals that once a location has been attacked it is just as likely, if not even more likely to be the target of a further attack. The World Trade Centre in 1993 and 2001 and the London Underground on 7/7 and 21/7 are just two of the higher profile attacks. It is not appropriate to consider that just because a place has been attacked it is somehow immune from further targeting—efforts to protect the site and the public use of it need to be developed.

Secondly, a major development in the arrest of one of the 21/7 cell members was the discovery of empty peroxide bottles by a caretaker

---

of a flat which they frequented. Peroxide was a constituent part of the bombs that the cell members prepared. Providing more information to local authorities and partners about chemicals which may be used to make Home Made Explosives (HME) will increase the likelihood of identifying and intercepting terrorist activity. Police officers also need to be aware of such items, so they too can correctly report quantities of such substances that appear suspicious.

3.1.7 **22 July 2005**

At 10.06 am on Friday, 22 July 2005 during the course of a major Metropolitan Police Service anti-terrorist operation called Operation THESEUS, a number of undercover surveillance officers from S012 Special Branch and a number of officers from CO19 specialist firearms unit followed Jean Charles de Menezes onto the north bound Northern Line platform at the Stockwell tube station of the London Underground. Mr de Menezes had been under surveillance since 9.33 am that morning when he left a block of flats at 21 Scotia Road, London. Mr de Menezes stepped into the third coach of a stationary train and within moments two CO19 officers, aiming at his head, shot and killed him. An Independent Police Complaints Commission (IPCC) investigation into the death of Mr de Menezes revealed that the armed officers held the professed belief that he was a suicide bomber.

Mr de Menezes had been followed from 21 Scotia Road in the erroneous belief that he was one Hussain Osman, one of the convicted terrorists responsible for the failed suicide attack the previous day who was on the run. Mr de Menezes had nothing to do with terrorism and was, at the time of his death, travelling to work from his home address. He was unarmed; he was not carrying an explosive device.

The IPCC carried out two investigations following Mr de Menezes' death. The first investigation, known as Stockwell One, concerned the circumstances of the fatal shooting itself. The second investigation, known as Stockwell Two, concerned the complaints about the Metropolitan Police Service's handling of public statements following the fatal shooting. During November 2007 the IPCC Stockwell One report was published, then Commissioner of the Metropolitan Police, Sir Ian Blair in response to its release stated that:

> The Metropolitan Police has never sought to avoid accountability for the death of Jean Charles de Menezes. We killed an innocent man. Hardly a day goes by when I have not thought about how things could have been done differently and thus Mr de Menezes would still have been alive. I know that many of the officers involved reconsider the events of the day, again and again. Some mistakes or communications by different individuals led to a disastrous result.
>
> It is important to remember that no officer set out that day to shoot an innocent man—the death was a result of a culmination of actions that must be viewed against the unprecedented threat in this capital city. Fifty-two innocent people had just been killed and hundreds had been injured. Now, four failed suicide bombers were on the run and there was a very real fear they would strike again and more innocent lives would be lost.
>
> Tragically, Jean Charles de Menezes died at the hands of the Metropolitan Police. We do not shy from that but we do ask that people understand the nature of the policing operation and the actions of the men and women who did their best to protect the public in such testing circumstances. We have apologised to the family and friends of Jean Charles de Menezes many times in the past and I take this opportunity again to express our deep regret for his death.

3.1.8 Stockwell One Report

On 27 July 2005, five days after the death of Mr de Menezes, the IPCC commenced their investigation into the shooting of John Charles de Menezes. On 19 January 2006, the IPCC concluded its investigation submitting its findings to the Crown Prosecution Service contained within the Stockwell One report. The terms of reference of this report included:

- Examination of the information that led to the surveillance of the block of flats in which Jean Charles de Menezes lived.
- Examination of the Regulation of Investigatory Powers Act 2000 compliance and associated risk assessment.
- The command structure of the operation to include details of the numbers and types of specialist officers deployed, and the tactics available to them.
- The qualification and training of those involved, including the command team, and their suitability to carry out their role.

- Details of the briefing given to the officers involved and any description or photograph of any suspect made available.
- Whether or not the operation was designated as a 'KRATOS' operation and the policy, operational tactics and authority levels of 'KRATOS', a firearms response for tackling deadly and determined attacks.
- The details of the mobile surveillance operation.
- The details of police action once Jean Charles de Menezes had reached the Stockwell London Underground tube station.
- Establishing the manner in which the family of Jean Charles de Menezes were treated by Metropolitan Police officers following his death.
- An examination of whether or not the policy and operational authorities of 'KRATOS' were followed and were effective, and whether 'KRATOS' is compliant with Article 2 of the European Convention of Human Rights (ECHR).

The investigation produced 16 recommendations divided into police use of firearms, operational considerations, surveillance operations, post-incident management, and community reassurance which included:

Police use of Firearms

1.	**Concern:** Despite Commander Dick making it clear she was in command of all aspects of the firearms operation, there remains the potential for confusion between the respective roles of gold, silver and designated senior officer.
	Recommendation: To review existing policy and guidance in relation to the command and control of firearms operations to ensure there is absolute clarity of role and responsibility within the chain of command, particularly when a designated senior officer is deployed. This should include deployments conducted under the auspices of Operation Kratos and Operation C.
2.	**Concern:** Despite being appointed as the designated senior officer, the strategic briefing chaired by Commander McDowall commenced before Commander Dick's arrival due to inaccurate information being provided to her regarding the location of where the briefing was to be held.

	Recommendation: To review existing guidance and practice to ensure gold, silver and bronze commanders have a clear and common understanding of the circumstances surrounding future firearms operations, the overall strategy and the key tactical options under consideration.
3.	**Concern:** No formal recording was made of any of the briefings prior to the deployment of firearms and surveillance officers. Thereafter, there was no audio recording of what was communicated within the operations room. Such recordings would have provided an audit trail regarding the information that was received by the room and the decisions that were then transmitted. Some staff working in the operations room expressed concerns regarding the noise generated within it and how that may have affected its effectiveness.
	Recommendation: To review existing practice to ensure that, at a corporate level, robust and appropriate facilities and mechanisms exist to maintain the effective command and control of future operations of a similar nature. Particular attention should be paid to ensuring that key briefings, strategic and tactical decisions are fully recorded or documented and in any event capable of audit.
4.	**Concern:** The strategy set by the gold commander was not implemented. The strategy made it clear that all persons leaving Scotia Road would be stopped either as suspects or as potential intelligence sources. Six persons left the flats before Mr de Menezes. Due to insufficient resources being in place, none were stopped.
	Recommendation: To review the existing mechanisms and policy for ensuring that sufficient and robust channels of communication exist that provide commanders with 'real-time' updates on intelligence, operational and resourcing issues that could adversely impact the successful implementation of the overall strategic parameters and the identified tactical options and that robust procedures are in place to ensure that the necessary fast-time action is taken in the early stages of an incident to achieve this.

| 5. | **Concern:** There was no threat assessment and the risk assessments undertaken for this operation did not consider the risk of misidentification or uncertainty regarding the identification of a suspect. The assessment did not consider a suspect leaving the premises before firearms resources were in place. |
| | **Recommendation:** To review existing procedures and training for carrying out assessments for operations of this nature incorporating lessons learned from this incident. |

Operational Considerations

6.	**Concern:** There was a substantial delay between the time the firearms team were requested and when they were deployed. By the time Mr de Menezes left Scotia Road at 9.33 am, CO19 officers were still not in place despite being initially requested at 5.05 am.
	Recommendation: To review existing policy and practice to ensure that, when in pursuance of an armed operation, it is necessary to stop or otherwise detain potential subjects of a surveillance operation, and that appropriate firearms support is in place to expedite a prompt and safe resolution of the encounter.
7.	**Concern:** There was a lack of clarity about the command to 'stop' the suspect given the likely mindset of the firearms officers. They were deployed on an anti-terrorist operation the day after unsuccessful attempts were made to cause explosions within the underground system. They had been issued with special ammunition. They knew a designated senior officer was in command.
	Recommendation: To review existing policy and guidance to ensure absolute clarity exists in the use of operationally specific terminology. Particular attention is to be paid to ensuring the terminology used for deployments under the auspices of Operations Kratos and Operation C are entirely consistent with the common language of command for regular firearms deployments in response to serious crime operations.

Surveillance Operations

8.	**Concern:** The SO12 surveillance team, the CO19 specialist firearms officers and those in command were not used to working together and were not sufficiently familiar with each other's working practices.
	Recommendation: To review existing policy and operational capability in relation to the deployment of surveillance teams on firearms operations to ensure that deployment fully complements and supports rapid armed intervention should such subsequently become necessary.
9.	**Concern:** It was only the views of the surveillance team leader that were communicated in relation to the identification of the suspect. The fact that two surveillance officers believed that the person being followed was not the suspect should have been communicated to the designated senior officer, as it may have assisted her decision making.
	Recommendation: To review existing policy and practice to ensure joint firearms and surveillance operations are fully integrated and that channels exist to ensure salient developments, such as doubts over a target's identity, can be swiftly communicated to relevant strategic and operational commanders.
10.	**Concern:** The completion of the supplementary surveillance log has been proved to involve alterations which changed the meaning of the entry.
	Recommendation: To review existing policy and practice to ensure that at a corporate level robust facilities and processes exist to demonstrate the integrity of evidence gathered during the course of surveillance operations. Particular attention should be paid to the continued utility of surveillance logs.

Post-incident Management

11.	**Concern:** The incident was not referred until 3.21 pm on Monday, 25 July and until that time the IPCC was prevented from starting an investigation on the instruction of the Commissioner of the Metropolitan Police. The rationale given by the Commissioner for this decision relating to the IPCC's powers and duties was not correct.
	At the present time the Police (Complaints and Misconduct) Regulations 2004 require the police to refer complaints and allegations of misconduct that are subject to mandatory referral (such as death and serious injuries) to the IPCC no later than the end of the working day following the day on which the complaint was made or the conduct came to the attention of the appropriate authority.
	Recommendation: That all mandatory referrals to the IPCC should occur, particularly in the case of death or serious injury, as soon as possible but in any event not later than the end of the day following the incident, complaint or misconduct and that the Police (Complaints and Misconduct) Regulations 2004 should be amended accordingly.
12.	**Concern:** The difference in the treatment of police and civilian witnesses to this incident are not acceptable or justifiable. Members of the public were expected to be interviewed and make statements soon after witnessing a most traumatic incident without being able to confer with other witnesses and provide a joint account. The police officers involved were allowed to return to their own base, refresh themselves and confer. This was and is accepted practice. However, the IPCC has raised its concerns regarding the post-incident procedures put in place after other incidents where police firearms are discharged.
	Recommendation: To review existing guidance and practice to ensure that appropriate and robust mechanisms exist to secure an accurate and auditable record of 'hot' and team/group debriefs.

13.	**Concern:** Officers involved in the incident wrote up their notes together. This is current practice but makes those accounts less credible. Such practices were agreed in the protocol between the police service and the IPCC in July 2004.
	Recommendation: To review efficacy of existing post-incident management policy, guidance and practice to ensure an appropriate balance exists between being right-ly held to account for one's actions whilst discharging the office of constable and the rights of the principal officers. Particular attention should be paid to the need to ensure that individual accounts are obtained in a proximate and transparent manner that is consistent with the rules of evidence, the duty of care to staff and the need to secure public confidence. Post-incident procedures should be revised to ensure that officers do not write up their notes together.

Communications Infrastructure

14.	**Concern:** Command and control of this incident was inevitably lost when CO19 officers entered the underground. Had there been any update regarding the uncertainty surrounding the identification at this point it would have been impossible to communicate.
	Recommendation: That, in collaboration with partners in Transport for London and British Transport Police, the Metropolitan Police Service undertake to ensure that communications are harmonised and facilitate the command and control of operations conducted within the London Underground network.

Training and Exercises

15.	**Concern:** Events during July 2005 confronted the Metropolitan Police Service with a series of challenges that had not been experienced before. Whilst terrorist attacks on the transport system had been predicted, the MPS relied on the ACPO firearms manual and the Kratos policy to combat such an attack. It is apparent that more was required. The IPCC wants to ensure that the police service and individual police officers have learnt as much as possible from the events of 22 July and have the best possible preparation for dealing with similar situations in future.
	Recommendation: The MPS, HMIC, ACPO, the National Policing Improvement Agency (NPIA), the Home Office and other relevant agencies should revise planning, exercises and training provided for those involved in anti-terrorist policing to ensure such processes fully incorporate all the learning from the events of 22 July. As soon as legal procedures permit, the experience of those officers directly involved, including staff from the IPCC, should be fed into those reviews.

Community Reassurance

16.	**Concern:** The IPCC has noted the positive response given by members of the Community Reference Group and other community representatives to the steps taken by the then Lambeth Borough Commander and other statutory bodies to provide community reassurance in the aftermath of all the events in July 2005. The IPCC witnessed some of this at first hand. We commend Chief Superintendent Martin Bridger and his officers for an excellent job facing the communities directly, listening to their concerns and seeking to restore their confidence. It was reported to us that this had been achieved as a result of the community police liaison arrangements.
	Recommendation: The good practice in place in Lambeth, which ensured effective community reassurance should be noted by the MPS and HMIC. Steps should be taken to ensure that, where appropriate, this good practice is replicated in other BCUs (Basic Command Units).

POINTS TO NOTE—STOCKWELL ONE REPORT

The Stockwell One Report highlights many of the issues that law enforcement agencies encounter while keeping pace with a changing terrorist threat. The introduction of simultaneous, co-ordinated and multiple suicide attacks in the UK provided the police service with new tactical, strategic command and control challenges.

The scope of the Stockwell One recommendations reveal that it is not only specialist counter-terrorism departments or their associated operations that require development. The recommendations focused upon the very heart of policing critical incidents from start to finish which is day-to-day core business of the police service. The events of 22 July 2005 have proven to be a catalyst for change.

It is important for police officers to learn from the events of July 2005 and specifically the fatal shooting of John Charles de Menezes. The impact of these events upon how the police delivers its service in the future to protect the public from harm is profound. July 2005 is widely acknowledged as the beginning of a new reality for policing the UK as the actual threat from international terrorism was realized.

3.1.9 A new reality

The events of July 2005 tested the capability and capacity of the UK police resources to respond to all of the challenges it encountered. The police service asked whether its current structure and wide-ranging responsibilities were 'fit for purpose' considering whether there was an alternative way to police this new world. The former Metropolitan Police Commissioner Sir Ian Blair expressed his views at a televised Dimbleby Lecture on 15 September 2005, stating that:

> Terror has changed its methods, or more accurately, brought some of its existing methods to Britain for the first time, and whilst the 6th of July represents an aspiration, 7th July represents a fact. Britain remains a target of the highest possible priority to Al-Qaeda and its affiliates. We are in a new reality, the sky is dark, the terrorists seek mass casualties and are entirely indiscriminate. Every community is at risk.
>
> The police will need authority, tactics and equipment to deal with attacks similar to those of 7th July and far, far worse. Most important of all however, is we will need to draw that authority from a public that understands us and the dilemmas we face. In effect the police faces

a widening mission. If I can emphasise this with a single statement is that the Met deploys officers everyday in Barking and in Kensington tasked specifically to prevent truancy and graffiti. It also usually has officers on the ground in Baghdad and Kabul. Properly to respond to all that mission, to move to neighbourhood policing while responding to terror without losing current mainstream services, the police will have to alter the way we work, change the make-up of our workforce and seek out new partnerships with the public, together with new methods of democratic accountability.

So the questions are; What kind of police service do you want? Who should decide that? And how? We need a wide-spread and fundamental debate. I will begin with some propositions. First we want a single police service not a multiplicity of them, by that I don't necessarily mean a single, national police force, but one holistic service to cover the whole of the mission. What we should seek to avoid at all costs is a separation of local neighbourhood policing from either serious criminal investigations or counter-terrorism investigations. Every lesson of every police enquiry is that, not only the issues that give rise to anti-social behaviour but also those which give rise to criminal activity and to terrorism begin at the most local level.

One example followed the failed bombings of 21st July. A local authority worker identified the flat where the three men, shown on CCTV images, had frequented. This was the bomb factory. However, he also mentioned that he had found dozens of empty peroxide bottles in the waste bins. Had we had one of our neighbourhood policing teams in place then he would probably have told us about what he found. Peroxide is the basis of the bombs. Thus national security depends on neighbourhood security. It will not be a Special Branch officer at Scotland Yard who first confronts a terrorist, but a local cop or a local community support officer. It is not the police and the intelligence agencies who will defeat crime and terror and anti-social behaviour, it is communities.

As the government responded to the July 2005 terrorist attacks, specialist police counter-terrorism units across the UK were engaged in a series of investigations. This was a sustained period of terrorist activity that had not been seen before. The UK remained on high alert as terrorists cells associated to the ideology of Al-Qaeda were identified, disrupted, and arrested. A picture of terrorist attack planning was being pieced together.

Case study—Kidnap and beheading plot 2007

On 31 January 2007 police officers raided a series of premises to disrupt a terrorist plot to kidnap and behead a Muslim British Army soldier. The focus of the police operation was in Birmingham where cell leader Pervaiz Khan was arrested. The Home Office stated that:

'We can confirm that a major counter-terrorist operation took place earlier today led by West Midlands Police. Eight arrests under the Terrorism Act have been made to date during this nationwide operation. The Home Secretary was fully briefed on the operation and is receiving regular updates as developments occur.'

During February 2008 Pervaiz Khan, together with four other individuals, were found guilty of committing terrorism offences. Khan admitted his guilt to charges of conspiracy to murder and kidnap being sentenced to life imprisonment. The plot represented a change in the tactics being used by UK based terrorists which was reported in an article appearing in The Times on 1 February 2007 which stated:

How Al-Qaeda 'tried to bring Baghdad to Birmingham'

Not long back from his six-month tour in Iraq, the young Muslim soldier was puzzled when police called at his family home in Birmingham. What they had to say left him speechless with disbelief. Officers described how a gang from his home town was allegedly plotting to abduct the soldier and then force him on film to 'apologise' for what he had done in Iraq.

After this propaganda coup, the gang intended to video themselves executing their hostage. His murder would be seen worldwide on the internet as a warning to other British Muslims regarded by the kidnappers as 'traitors'.

The terrorist plot provides evidence of how terrorist tactics used in other countries are being brought to the UK. It is an insight to the challenges encountered by the intelligence and law enforcement agencies who are required to quickly adapt to new and emerging tactics. The threat from international terrorism continues to evolve, a threat that the police service and its partners are working hard to reduce.

3.2 **Counter-Terrorism Policing Structure**

Following the events of 9/11, the government realized the way the police service was structured needed to be developed in order to counter terrorism. A gradual increase of counter-terrorism policing resources began with the implementation of Regional Intelligence Cells located at strategic sites across the UK. They were designed to gather and assess intelligence from local forces, analysing issues on a regional basis to inform the national intelligence picture. Further funding was also made available so that local forces could build their own capacities by strengthening their Special Branch departments. This included national funding for additional Ports Officers to protect UK borders and Counter-Terrorism Security Advisors to offer security and prevention advice to business to further 'target harden' the UK from terrorist attack.

Despite substantial investment and the commencement of a re-focus on community-based policing, the developing policing structure could not prevent the events of 7 July 2005. The government and the police service realized that the increase of counter-terrorism policing assets over a number of years should be accelerated in order to protect the UK. The developments which have taken place to police terrorism since 2005 have been unprecedented. There has never been such a rapid period of change or growth in the way in which the police service now responds to terrorism, since the creation of specialist police units in the 1880s. One of the most significant developments which is widely acknowledged as a catalyst for the changes we are seeing today, was the merger of the Metropolitan Police Special Branch and the Anti-Terrorist Branch to establish a Counter-Terrorism Command (CTC) in October 2006. For the first time it brought both counter-terrorism 'covert' and 'overt' policing assets together under one single command structure.

Traditionally countering terrorism had been conducted in two halves: covertly and overtly. The intensity of the new threat from international terrorism required the fusion of expertise from both covert and overt counter-terrorism investigators, who would pursue terrorists together. The benefits of this new close joint-working were soon realized, however: it was increasingly clear that terrorist cells were operating throughout the UK. London was no longer the only intended target of terrorist attacks, neither was it the only place where terrorist cells were conducting their attack planning activities. Further investment and re-structuring had to be made to meet the challenges from international terrorism, developments lead by the Association of Chief Police Officers (ACPO) for Terrorism and Allied Matters (TAM).

3.2.1 ACPO (TAM)

The Association of Chief Police Officers (ACPO) is an independent, professionally-led strategic body. In the public interest and in equal and active partnership with the government and the Association of Police Authorities (APA), ACPO leads and co-ordinates the direction and development of the Police Service in England, Wales, and Northern Ireland. In times of national need ACPO co-ordinates the strategic policing response on behalf of all Chief Officers.

ACPO's day-to-day work on policing policy issues are carried out through a number of Business Areas headed by a senior ACPO officer. These Business Areas include Terrorism and Allied Matters (TAM). The ACPO (TAM) Committee provides a bridge between the government direction on counter-terrorism and the operational implementation. It has responsibility for co-ordinating national activity and provides guidance to forces on counter-terrorism and allied matters, whilst funding, devising and driving forward development plans and projects. Committee members include ACPO officers, senior representatives from government departments and other agencies including the Security Service. The Committee reports to ACPO and the government.

The work of ACPO (TAM) is directly aligned to the priorities and themes of Contest, the government's strategy to counter international terrorism and supports the mission areas set out in the Contest strategy of Prevent, Pursue, Protect, and Prepare.

3.2.2 Building capacity

In response to the challenges posed by the developing terrorist threat and to increase and maintain policing resilience to terrorism, ACPO (TAM) is funding and developing a new UK counter-terrorism landscape, designed to strengthen the UK's response to the threat of terrorism and significantly increase capacity and capability. This structure consists of a Counter-Terrorism Command (CTC) Counter-Terrorism Units (CTUs) and Counter-Terrorism Intelligence Units (CTIUs) based at strategic sites across the UK. Prime Minister Gordon Brown reported to the House of Commons in November 2007 that, 'We have now constituted dedicated regional counter-terrorism units with in total more than 2,000 police and support staff, responsible for overseeing investigations into those who recruit terrorists and promote hate'.

Specialists available within the CTC, CTUs and CTIUs are advised on tasking through a national structure. The tasking is delivered in partnership with the Security Service to deliver and support counter-terrorism work locally, regionally, and nationally. It also advises on the direction of resources for its wider business activity, incorporating allied matters such as domestic extremism and other protective security issues. To support the tasking structure, ACPO (TAM) provides funding at a local level, for operational priorities identified through the tasking process.

3.2.3 Counter-Terrorism Units

There are currently four Counter-Terrorism Units based at different sites across the UK. These Units are nationally aligned assets, regionally based to meet the current threat and have been implemented and resourced by 'Lead' police forces. The Units complement and enhance the work and capability of Special Branch, who already provide the link between locally-based policing. The role of the Units is to provide co-ordination and specialist support to police across the country, and in particular, to forces in their own region. The Unit gathers intelligence and evidence to help prevent and disrupt terrorist activities and contributes on a regional level into the national intelligence and evidence picture. The CTUs have a wide range of expertise including; skilled detectives, financial investigators, community contact teams, intelligence analysts, forensic specialists, and high-tech investigators. This expertise enhances the regional capability and capacity to deal with the current threat. There are currently four Units regionally based in the following areas:

- **Birmingham** (Lead force West Midlands Police)
- **Leeds** (Lead force West Yorkshire Police)
- **Manchester** (South West) Lead force Greater Manchester Police
- **South East** (Lead force Thames Valley Police).

3.2.4 Counter-Terrorism Command

In addition to the Counter-Terrorism Units, the Metropolitan Police Service has a Counter-Terrorism Command (CTC). This is responsible for proactive intelligence-led operations to prevent and disrupt acts of terrorism and reactive investigations of acts or attempted acts of terrorism in London and the South-East of England. The

CTC works in partnership with intelligence and security agencies to gather, assess, analyse and develop intelligence to drive operational activity to protect London and the UK from the threat of terrorism, extremism, and subversion. The CTC also has a national and international role and is the police service single point of contact for international partners in counter-terrorism matters.

3.2.5 Counter-Terrorism Intelligence Units

The Counter-Terrorism Intelligence Units (CTIUs) carry out similar functions to the CTUs and CTC. Their primary objective is to co-ordinate and support forces within their region and to gather and develop intelligence and evidence, supported by their own surveillance capability. They do not have an investigative role. There are currently four CTIUs which are also national assets based in strategic locations across the UK:

- East Midlands (Lead force—Derbyshire Constabulary);
- Eastern (Lead force—Essex Police);
- Wales (Lead force—South Wales Police); and
- South West (Lead force—Avon and Somerset Constabulary).

POINTS TO NOTE—LOCAL POLICING PLANS

The new counter-terrorism structure will support the 'intelligence community'. However, neither counter-terrorism policing units or the intelligence agencies can detect, disrupt or deter terrorist activity without the commitment of the wider police service.

A key development in the response to tackling terrorism has been the introduction of terrorism and extremism on local policing plans sharing ownership of the challenges the police service encounters. Sir Norman Bettison, the Chief Constable of West Yorkshire Police stated at an ACPO (TAM) conference during February 2008 that 'Borough Commanders should make themselves "champions" in the counter-terrorism effort'.

This statement recognizes the integral role that local policing plays in countering the current threat. Local Special Branch departments provide the bridge between local policing to the regional CTUs and CTIUs. Countering terrorism on a local level relies upon the practical policing skills of all police officers, who are therefore required to identify and report any unusual or suspicious activity. This is not easy as terrorists attempt to blend into their surroundings wherever possible. A knowledge and understanding of how terrorists and their organizations operate is required, together with a detailed understanding of the communities local policing serves—a vital role of Neighbourhood Policing Teams.

3.2.6 **Neighbourhood policing**

Neighbourhood policing is at the heart of policing the UK. Over recent years the government has re-focused its attention towards local community based multi-agency approached policing. It is now recognized that the police service represents one of many bodies who can improve the quality of lives for individuals and their communities. It is this local contact that is also required to prevent acts of terrorism, a vital element in the government's Contest strategy to counter international terrorism. Chief Constable Matt Baggott form the national Neighbourhood Policing Programme in 2007 explained the important role of Neighbourhood Policing stating that:

> Neighbourhood Policing is much more than increasing visibility in communities. It provides a real and unique opportunity to put the public 'centre stage', influencing regeneration, cohesion and significant improvements in quality of life. Neighbourhood Policing works. Confidence in local policing is improving and levels of anti-social behaviour are diminishing. The importance and value of Neighbourhood Policing should not be underestimated, and we must ensure promises are kept and opportunities grasped.

Neighbourhood policing is often described as a business approach that aims to ensure improved performance on a range of policing outcomes. If properly implemented, Neighbourhood policing will make people feel safe by delivering improvements in:

- Crime reduction
- Public confidence
- Feelings of safety and
- Perceptions of anti-social behaviour.

These outcomes will result from neighbourhood policing activity which includes:

Visibility
Increased visibility and familiarity of officers/Police Community Support Officers in the local area which allows

Engagement
Engagement with the community to identify their priorities for action which allows

Targeting
Targeted problem-solving with partners and communities to tackle the issues which matter the most in communities.

Figure 3.2: Neighbourhood policing activity

POINTS TO NOTE—TEAM EFFORT

Communities will defeat terrorism. Neighbourhood policing teams and their partners are at the forefront of countering terrorism and extremism in the UK. They are the first point at which a new terrorist cell or an individual who is moving towards extremist views can be identified. Countering terrorism is a team effort, the intelligence agencies and specialist counter-terrorism police departments cannot protect the UK alone, the wider police family and partners all have a part to play in reducing the present threat so that future communities can go about their business freely and with confidence.

3.3 **Tackling Domestic Extremism**

In recent years the UK has seen an increasing protest activity directed at a broad range of 'causes'. It is important for the police service to manage these potential threats: whilst they may not reach the threshold of terrorist activity or seriously threaten issues of national security, they can cause harm to communities and the economic well-being of the UK. It is important to keep the threat from 'domestic extremists' in perspective. The majority of protests in the UK are perfectly peaceful, lawful and undertaken in pursuance of the right of assembly and freedom of speech that we all enjoy as part of living in a democratic society. There is however a more complex side to extremists who wish to further their cause by committing criminal acts, being involved in incidents of public disorder and using violence and intimidation. It is these individuals who are of concern to the police service. It must be recognized that some extremists will, under certain circumstances, adopt a 'soft' style of protest, behaving in a perfectly law abiding manner being part of a legitimate and peaceful protest. Their attendance at such events may however have different motives as they progress a more extreme agenda.

3.3.1 **Categorization**

There are a broad range of individual causes that individuals can be engaged in. These include anti-globalization, animal experimentation, medical research, the pharmaceutical industry, the food industry, hunting, sports involving animals, the financial industry, environmental issues, and many more which have been the subject of attention and protest. Protests have also been directed at commercial premises, city centres as well as employees away from their place of work in addition to suppliers of those targeted companies, shareholders, and financial institutions providing funding. The key 'domestic extremist' groups are categorized in the table below.

Table 3.2: Key 'domestic extremist' groups

Anarchism	Anarchism is the political belief that society should have no government, laws, police, or other authority, but should be a free association of all its members. Anarchism rests on the doctrine that no man has a right to control by force the action of any other man.

Animal Rights

Animal rights, which is also referred to as animal liberation, is an ideology based upon the very basic interests of animals. There are a wide variety of individual belief structures within this movement but principally persons who support this cause believe that animals should be afforded the same consideration as humans in that they should not suffer harm, that they should not be considered as property, used as food, clothing or the subject of experimental research or for entertainment. A widely accepted view amongst animal rights activists is that all animals should be regarded as legal persons and members of the moral community.

Anti-Capitalism

Capitalism is a term used to describe the economic system which promotes private ownership for profit operating within a free market. Those that oppose this system of economics are described as anti-capitalists who seek a fair central economic system based on the principles of safeguarding individual employees' rights.

Anti-Globalization

Globalization is the term used to describe the process or transformation of local or regional issues that rise into a global phenomena. Anti-globalization is the term used to describe those individuals with a political stance that oppose what is often an economic issue concerning the power, influence and impact of large multi-national corporations and the spread of migration, technology, and investment.

Anti-War

Anti-war protestors should be distinguished from 'peace' movements. Anti-war activists are engaged in more protest activities aiming to put an end to a nation's decision to begin or continue an armed conflict. There are a variety of belief strands within this category of domestic extremism as some anti-war protestors may believe that both sides of the conflict should discontinue their activities while others may only support the withdrawal of one side of the conflict which is often the more powerful body widely seen as the aggressor or invader.

Environmentalism	The protection of our planet has become a social movement centred upon the primary concern for the conservation and improvement of the natural environment. An extreme environmentalist is a person who would advocate unlawful activity to sustain the management of resources and steward-ship of the natural environment through changes in policy or individuals or group direct action.
Fascism	Fascism is a political ideology that seeks to regenerate the social, economic, and cultural life of a country by basing it on heightened sense of national belonging or ethnic identity. Fascists reject liberal ideas such as freedom and individual human rights and democracy. Fascism is often associated with right-wing fanaticism, racism, and violence. Nazism, the short name for national socialism is considered to be a form of fascism focusing upon the belief in the superiority of an Aryan race. The term Neo-Nazism refers to post World War II activities and those who now seek to resurrect those social movements and ideologies in place during that time.

3.3.2 Tactics

Extremist groups use a wide variety of tactics. They are creative in their approach to disrupting the activities of businesses and targeting employees. Police officers need to be aware of these tactics when deciding and developing responses. The targeting of protest activity is directed towards 'Primary' and 'Secondary' sites consisting of:

- **Day-to-day activities**—protests by local group members at the primary and sometimes secondary sites; and
- **Regional and national days of action**—where substantially larger numbers of protesters gather together or in organized groups. They will target both primary and secondary sites. Often the majority of the protesters are not local people and there is more likelihood of more extremist involvement.

'Primary and 'secondary' sites are defined as per the table below:

Table 3.3: Primary and secondary sites

Primary	Primary sites consist of the main target premises or organization where the activity of that business is the primary issue against which the protest is directed. It has to be recognized that protesters will sometimes deliberately target another site, which is less prepared for such an eventuality. If a place is identifiable as being connected or associated to a particular organization protesters may regard it as a target.
Secondary	Secondary sites consist of all other sites, which are linked in any way whatsoever to the primary target site. For example, home addresses of directors, shareholders, employees of primary and secondary targets, suppliers or customers of primary and secondary targets, local authorities, solicitors, banks, shops and public places. The list of potential secondary targets is extensive. It is generally any target that will have a direct impact or assist in the continuing and increasing pressure to bring about the closure of the primary target organization.

Domestic extremism groups have used a wide variety of tactics to progress their cause. The following table provides examples of some of the tactics that have been used by extremist groups in the UK.

Table 3.4: Tactics used by extremist groups in the UK

Mass Demonstrations	Organized and pre-planned mass demonstrations covering a large area, for example city centre May Day protests.
Spontaneous Demonstrations	Spontaneous or pre-planned demonstrations at specific locations, for example, outside company addresses.
Home Address Demonstrations	Pre-planned or spontaneous demonstrations at an individual's home address, or immediate neighbourhood.
Bomb Telephone Threats	Bomb or other malicious telephone threats to a third party, company premises, or an individual's home address.

Improvised Explosive Devices	Improvised Explosive Devices (IEDs), for example in shops or upon vehicles at distribution centres.
Hoax Devices	Real or hoax devices left at company premises or an individual's home address.
Intrusions	Intrusions into company premises for 'sit ins', obtaining information, for example, details of staff or supplying companies, or releasing or stealing animals.
Malicious Mail	Real, hoax, or malicious mail sent to company premises or an individual's home address.
Harassment	Harassment of staff at or away from company premises.
Intimidation	Intimidation of staff at or away from company premises.
Unsolicited Goods	The sending of unsolicited goods to company and individual employee addresses.
Assault	Physical assault on individuals.
Switchboard Jamming	Telephone switchboard-jamming campaigns.
Fax Machine Blockades	Fax machine blockade—a continuous piece of black paper is faxed to the machine.
E-mail Saturation	E-mail saturation campaigns.
Infiltration	Social engineering and infiltration, for example, organizations unwittingly employing extremists or sympathizers.

3.3.3 Police response

Domestic extremism has become a concern to many organizations because it targets people and their homes, as well as business premises. Domestic extremists move beyond the bounds of legitimate protest to intimidate individuals engaged in lawful activity and to impose economic costs on legal businesses. As such, it presents a criminal threat that is national in its scope to the UK and its citizens. The UK police service is working hard to tackle domestic extremism and to respond effectively and appropriately to their criminal activities. The tactic of targeting suppliers, contractors, financial service providers means that single, criminal domestic extremist incidents in local force areas are often part of a series of linked crimes. Local police forces deal with domestic extremist crime and incidents locally. National police units ensure that the police service has a comprehensive picture of domestic-related extremist crime to provide a co-ordinated, effective, and consistent approach to policing. No one single police department can tackle the challenges of domestic extremism alone. A national framework of specialized units who support the work of local police forces is in place to tackle these challenges. They include the following:

- **National Extremism Tactical and Co-ordination Unit (NETCU)** acts as a central support service for business and the academic sector targeted by domestic extremists. NETCU assesses risk and provides one-to-one tactical guidance, security advice, and support on dealing with domestic extremist campaigns.
- **National Domestic Extremism Team (NDET)** integrates with other units and organizations to help develop, prioritize, and co-ordinate investigations concerning individuals and extremist groups.
- **National Public Order Intelligence Unit (NPOIU)** liaises with Special Branch teams and Counter-Terrorism Units within the police service to maintain a strategic overview of domestic extremism-related public order issues.

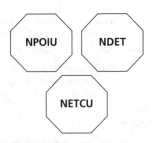

Figure 3.3: Specialist units tackling domestic extremism

The national framework to counter the threats from domestic extremism provide a valuable service to business to protect the economic well-being of the UK. Their work is often supported by the National Counter-Terrorism Security Office (NaCTSO) and the network of Counter-Terrorism Security Advisors (CTSAs). The work of all three police units combines to:

- Uphold the law and protect those engaged in lawful business and employment, while upholding the right to peaceful protest

- Bring to justice domestic extremists who commit crime as part of a campaign
- Ensure victims and potential victims of crime and criminal activity by domestic extremists get the protection and support they need.

3.4 **Terrorism Legal Framework**

See also **5.8.1**

A robust criminal justice system is an essential part of countering terrorism. Within any criminal justice system which seeks to counter terrorism, a delicate balance has to be maintained. As terrorists wish to exploit the very freedoms a democratic society enjoys, legislators can inadvertently impinge upon the civil liberties and human rights of the very people they aim to protect. They can introduce powers and procedures which may not be justified, proportionate and which may not be able to reduce the current threat. The UK has extensive experience of implementing anti-terrorism legislation. As with most pieces of legislation that appears on the statute books it provides an insight of what was happening in society at the time. Following the Dynamite War of 1883 where ten bombs exploded in London alone, legislators found it necessary to provide a robust response to ongoing threats from the Fenian movement. The Explosive Substances Act 1833 was developed to provide a mechanism to deal with these challenges, a piece of legislation that has stood the test of time which is still being used to this day.

3.4.1 **Miscarriages of justice**

A criminal justice system within a democratic society is judged by both its successes and failures. Over many years the police and the Crown Prosecution Service have worked together to bring terrorists to justice. Despite these many successes against international and Irish-related terrorists the criminal justice system in the UK has also witnessed serious miscarriages of justice.

Case study—The Guildford Four

On 19 October 1989 the 'Guildford Four' had their convictions quashed by the Court of Appeal. An extensive inquiry into the original police investigation of the bombings of public houses in Guildford, Surrey, in 1974, which left five people dead and over 100 injured unveiled serious improprieties. As each of the men received mandatory life sentences for murder Mr Justice Donaldson expressed regret that they had not been charged with treason which at the time carried a mandatory death penalty. Upon their release then Home Secretary Douglas Hurd stated that: 'We must all, I believe, feel anxiety, regret and deep concern at what has occurred'.

Further terrorist-related cases from the 1970s were also deemed 'unsafe'. The 'Maguire Seven' were arrested in 1974 for possessing nitroglycerine which had allegedly been passed to the IRA to make bombs. They were convicted in 1975 receiving custodial sentences ranging from five to 14 years. Amongst the 'Maguire Seven' was Patrick Conlon, the father of Gerald Conlon, one of the 'Guildford Four'.

Patrick Conlon had travelled from Belfast to help his son during the trial of the Guildford bombings. In 1991 the verdicts against the Maguire Seven were repealed well after their release from prison, however, during January 1980 Patrick Conlon died in prison, the circumstances of which were made into an Oscar and BAFTA nominated movie in 1993, 'In The Name Of The Father'. On 9 February 2005, 25 years after their original convictions, Tony Blair became the only Prime Minister to apologize to the Guildford Four and the Maguire Seven stating that, 'I am very sorry that they were subject to such an ordeal and such an injustice, they deserve to be completely exonerated'.

The case of the Guildford Four was not the only serious miscarriage of justice during the height of the troubles. The case study below outlines another such miscarriage.

Case study—The Birmingham Six

On 21 November 1974, two bombs exploded in Birmingham which were later attributed to the Provisional Irish Republican Army (PIRA). The first device detonated at 8.25 pm and killed ten people at the Mulberry Bush public house. The second device detonated at the Tavern-In-Town public house at 8.27 pm killing 11 people. 182 people were injured in the co-ordinated attacks. A third device which was located outside a bank failed to detonate. The attacks were the bloodiest conducted on the UK mainland at that time and a large counter-terrorism investigation was launched. On that same evening, Special Branch officers working at Heysham ports routinely examined five men, John Walker, Paddy Joe

Hill, Richard McIlkenny, Gerry Hunter and Billy Power. All five had left Birmingham earlier that evening being seen off at the local station by a sixth man, Hugh Callaghan. The men were travelling to Belfast to attend the funeral of James McDade, an IRA member who had accidentally killed himself while planting a bomb in Coventry. As Special Branch officers were conducting their examination news came through about the bombs in Birmingham and the men were subsequently arrested. The attack led to the Prevention of Terrorism (Temporary Provisions) Act of 1974. This Act provided the first statutory regime regulating the detention of terrorists suspects providing the maximum detention period before charge of up to seven days. These new powers completed their passage through Parliament within two days of the Birmingham attacks.

On 12 May 1975 following forensic examination and a series of interviews all six men were charged with murder and conspiracy to cause explosions. Despite claiming that they had been beaten, threatened and forced to sign statements the police evidence was admitted and the trial began on 9 June 1975 in Lancaster Castle. The jury found all defendants guilty of murder and the judge, Justice Bridge sentenced each of them to life imprisonment expressing regret that capital punishment was no longer an option.

Dubbed the 'Birmingham Six' the men continued to protest their innocence and following three appeals and allegations of mistreatment by prison staff the Crown withdrew most of its case against them. New evidence of fabrication, suppression of evidence, discrediting of the confessions and forensic evidence were key elements which revealed this miscarriage of justice. On 14 March 1991 all six men were released and they celebrated their freedom outside of the Old Bailey in London. In front of the world's media and a large crowd that had gathered to greet them Paddy Hill stepped up to the microphone and stated that, 'For 16 and a half years we have been used as political scapegoats. The police told us from the start they knew we hadn't done it, they didn't care who had done it'.

Having been convicted of a crime they did not commit the Birmingham Six waited a further ten years before they were granted any compensation.

The collapse of the cases against the Guildford Four and the Birmingham Six caused the Home Secretary to establish a Royal Commission on Criminal Justice in 1991 which led to the Criminal Appeal Act of 1995 and the Criminal Cases Review Commission in 1997. It is important for police colleagues who are working with terrorism legislation to understand this vital period of history which sent shockwaves through the criminal justice system. The profound impact of these cases can still be seen today as terrorist legislation is robustly contested through its passage onto the statute books.

During 1995 Lord Lloyd of Berwick conducted a review of terrorism legislation. His report was part of the process which led to the creation of the Terrorism Act 2000. He concluded that though the threat of terrorism centred on Northern Ireland could be expected to diminish, the global terrorist threat was likely to intensify. The Terrorism Act 2000 drew together many new areas of anti-terrorism legislation and it remains the cornerstone of the new terrorism legal framework currently being built in the UK. Not only did the 2000 Act define what 'terrorism and 'terrorist' were it also outlawed terrorist organizations, provided new offences and procedures for port and border controls.

As the threat from international terrorism emerged in the UK following the events of 9/11, new powers were introduced by the Anti-terrorism Crime and Security Act of 2001 to cut off terrorist funding and protect the aviation and nuclear industry. However, it was the events of 7 July 2005 that required an urgent response from the government to protect the UK from a real dynamic threat which resulted in control orders being established through the introduction of the Prevention of Terrorism Act 2005. The introduction of the Terrorism Act 2006 extended police powers to counter the new threat from international terrorism. With the creation of nine new offences it significantly lowered the threshold for persons to be arrested for terrorism offences.

The government is keeping to its commitment under the strategy to counter international terrorism in providing new legislation to pursue terrorists so that they can be brought to justice. The Counter-Terrorism Act 2008 was introduced to the House of Commons as a Bill on 24 January 2008. It amends anti-terrorism law and includes new proposals to strengthen the terrorism legal framework.

3.4.2 Proscribed organizations

The UK has long been an attractive prospect for terrorist groups in a variety of ways. The financial benefits such as fundraising and fraud were historically viewed as the main attraction for such groups. This, together with a relaxed and democratic climate, the encouragement for freedom of speech and respect for human rights, provides terrorist organizations with a public platform on which to perform. The government has attempted to restrict these actions by publishing a list of terrorist organizations making their existence illegal in the UK. In effect, it outlaws organizations that are openly engaged in activities ensuring the UK does not become a base for international terrorists and their supporters.

POINTS TO NOTE—AWARENESS OF TERRORIST GROUPS

Police colleagues need to be aware of the terrorist groups that are outlawed, what mechanisms are in place to achieve this and what they can practically do to assist in enforcing the anti-terrorism legislation.

3.4.2.1 *Proscription*

The proscription of terrorist organizations contributes towards making the UK a hostile environment for terrorists and sends a strong message that the UK totally rejects such organizations and any claims to legitimacy. Proscription is a tough power as it has the effect of outlawing previously lawful activity. Once an organization is proscribed it is a criminal offence to belong to, support, or display support for a proscribed organization. The Terrorism Act 2000 also allows the police to seize all property of a proscribed organization.

Schedule 2 of the Terrorism Act 2000 provides the Secretary of State with the power to outlaw any organization which he believes 'is concerned in terrorism'. An organisation is 'concerned in terrorism' if it commits or participates in acts of terrorism, prepares for terrorism, promotes or encourages terrorism, or is otherwise concerned in terrorism either in the UK or abroad. 'Organisation' is defined as including 'any association or combination of persons'. Once the statutory criteria are satisfied, the Secretary of State then has discretion whether or not to proscribe a particular organization. In reaching a decision, the Home Secretary also takes into account a number of factors, including those in the checklist below.

Checklist—Deciding factors in proscribing organizations

- The nature and scale of an organization's activities
- The specific threat that it poses to the UK
- The specific threat that it poses to British nationals overseas
- The extent of the organization's presence in the UK
- The need to support other members of the international community in the global fight against terrorism.

See also **4.3.1**.

The Terrorism Act 2006 amended the Terrorism Act 2000 to allow the proscription of organizations which glorify terrorism. It would also deal with proscribed organizations which change their names in an attempt to evade the law, by continuing the ban to the renamed organization. On 10 October 2005 the then Home Secretary Charles Clarke, following the proposed inclusion of additional groups stated:

> Proscription is an important power, and not one to be used lightly. The list of proscribed organisations is kept under constant review and, after careful consideration of all the relevant factors, I am satisfied that these groups should now be added to it [he went on to say that] I am also determined to act against those who, while not involved in committing acts of terrorism, provide succour or support for terrorist groups and their acts. That is why I intend to bring forward further legislation to amend the current threshold of proscription to make it possible to proscribe any organisation which glorifies terrorism.

See also **4.2.1**.

3.4.2.2 *Membership*

Offences which a person can commit are wide-ranging: from membership of an organization, supporting or assisting in the activities of an organization or the wearing in a public place of clothing or articles suggesting the membership of an organization. Punishment, if convicted on indictment, may result in a term of imprisonment not exceeding ten years and on summary conviction could result in six months imprisonment, a fine or both.

Proscribed organizations can at any time make an application to the Secretary of State for de-proscription. Should an application be unsuccessful, the organization or any person affected by their proscription can then appeal to the Proscribed Organizations Appeal Commission (POAC), set up under Section 5 and Schedule 3 of the Terrorism Act 2000.

POINTS TO NOTE—PROSCRIBED ORGANIZATIONS

It is clear that the government is seizing all opportunities to tackle the threat from international terrorism. The continued review of proscribed organizations must remain a major tool ensuring terrorist activities are disrupted and that the UK remains a hostile environment for terrorists to operate.

So how do you know whether an individual is a member of an outlawed terrorist group? After all, they will not be carrying a placard that declares their membership. There may be other indicators, some of which may not be entirely discreet. Much is made of the covert nature of individuals who are concerned in the commission, preparation or instigation of acts of terrorism. Whilst it is generally true that terrorists and extremists wish to operate beneath the radar to avoid identification, their strong beliefs and motivations can at times lead to an unwitting disclosure of their allegiances. This is something all police colleagues should be aware of as terrorist offences may be being openly committed. Paying close attention to what individuals say, do, and what they wear are all potential indicators of the support or membership of a terrorist group.

Case study—Section 11 of the Terrorism Act 2000

In January 2000 James Rankin was returning from a trip to Belfast travelling by ferry to Troon Ferry Port in Ayrshire. At the time he was wearing items of jewellery which brought him to the attention of police officers working at the port. On his wedding finger Rankin was wearing a ring which displayed the initials of the Ulster Volunteer Force, 'UVF'. The UVF, a Loyalist group within Northern Ireland are a proscribed organization under anti-terrorism legislation who were originally formed in 1914. Their profile was raised on 21 May 1966 as they openly declared war on the Irish Republican Army (IRA) and are alleged to be responsible for more than 400 deaths during the Troubles.

Rankin was charged and found guilty of rousing suspicion that he was a member or supporter of a terrorist group under Section 11 of the Terrorism Act 2000. Rankin denied the allegations describing the ring as a wedding present from his wife denying association with the Loyalist group. The court heard that Rankin carried the Union flag in a flute band and attended Belfast's 12 July parades. Following his conviction at Ayr Sheriff Court Rankin lodged an appeal where his counsel, Chris Shead, said that the Terrorism Act 2000 should not be interpreted in a way that would criminalize behaviour like the wearing of apparel, which could be regarded as 'bravado'. Mr Shead went on to inform the court that there had to be more than an indication of an interest in the proscribed organization. Lord Hamilton, who heard the appeal with Lord Abernethy and Lord Philip disagreed stating that the UVF ring could be easily seen and was widely known to represent the Ulster Volunteer Force paramilitaries. He said: 'While the manner and circumstances of the offending in this case may, as reflected by the sheriff's proposal, be at the least serious end of the spectrum of conduct against which the section strikes, it is not, in our view, out of the range of legislative intent'.

The case against Rankin highlights the scope of Section 11 providing an example of how this legislation has been used. What is clear is that the knowledge and expertise of the officers concerned identified and proved their links to a proscribed organization. What symbols, marks or abbreviations are you aware of that may indicate a person's support or membership of a terrorist group? A person is guilty of Section 11 of the Terrorism Act 2000 if they belong to or profess to belong to a proscribed organization. Do you know which terrorist groups are banned in the UK? Section 11 relies upon the knowledge and understanding of police colleagues to identify, translate, and contextualize symbols, marks, and abbreviations evidenced by the successful conviction of Rankin. Section 11 reinforces Schedule 2 of the Terrorism Act 2000 which provides a list of outlawed terrorist groups. The key statutory defence is to prove that the organization was not outlawed when they became a member.

See also **4.2.2–4.2.4**.

3.4.2.3 *Profiles of proscribed organizations*

There is a broad range of terrorist organizations that are outlawed in the UK. The following provides a profile for each of these groups that have been banned under the Terrorism Act 2000, Terrorism Act 2006 and under provisions of former terrorism legislation.

POINT TO NOTE—KEEP UPDATED ON PROSCRIBED ORGANIZATIONS

The list of proscribed organizations may change. To keep updated on the current list of outlawed terrorist groups in the UK access the Home Office website following the links at:

<http://www.homeoffice.gov.uk/security/terrorism-and-the-law/terrorism-act/proscribed-groups>

---

17 November Revolutionary Organization

Aims:

November 17 aims to highlight and protest at what it deems to be imperialist and corrupt actions of the Greek Military Junta. The group holds an anti-US view blaming the US for supporting the Junta.

Background:

November 17 was formed in 1974 and is a radical leftist group following a Marxist ideology. Members believe that capitalism is based on the exploitation of workers and so are committed to a 'workers' revolution'. November 17, which is often referred to as 'N17', opposes the Greek government and Western interests. The group's name refers to the final day of the 1973 Athens Polytechnic uprising in which a series of protests against the Greek Military Junta ended when security forces stormed the Polytechnic campus.

The first attack to be attributed to N17 was the assassination of Richard Welch, a US Central Intelligence Agency (CIA) attaché based in Athens. During December 1975 four N17 gunmen shot Welch in front of his wife and driver. Assassinations were a tactic that NI7 members used throughout its sustained campaign.

At approximately 7.48 am on 8 June 2000, Brigadier Stephen Saunders, a British Army Officer and the UK military attaché was driving through Athens traffic on his way to work at the British Embassy. At that time he was shot and killed by an N17 motorcycle gunman. The investigation into the assassination of Brigadier Saunders led to an unprecedented level of co-operation between Greek and UK police services who after a lengthy investigation arrested several members of N17 and brought them to trial.

Abu Nidal Organization (ANO)

Aims:

The principal aim of the Abu Nidal Organization terrorist group is the destruction of the state of Israel. It is also hostile to 'reactionary' Arab regimes and states supporting Israel.

Background:

Abu Nidal was a Palestinian political leader and during the height of his reign during the 1970s and 1980s he was widely regarded as the world's most dangerous terrorist. Following the rejection of a peace settlement with Israel, the Abu Nidal Organization, which is often referred to as 'ANO', was established following a split with the Palestine Liberation Organization (PLO) in 1974.

ANO has operated against Israeli and Western targets. Abu Nidal is widely recognized as being a mercenary and responsible for ordering terrorist attacks and assassinations conducted in over 20 countries resulting in the death or injury of over 900 people.

ANO, which is mainly based in Lebanon and Libya, is believed to have operated under other names such as the Fatah Revolutionary Council and Black September. Black September took its name from the events of September 1970 where thousands of Palestinians were killed during fighting in Jordan. Members of Black September were responsible for the kidnap and murder of 11 Israeli athletes from the Olympic village during the 1972 Olympic Games in Munich.

See also **1.6.3**.

Abu Sayyaf Group (ASG)

Aims:

The aim of the Abu Sayyaf Group is to fight for an independent Islamic state in the Southern Philippine island of Mindanao.

Background:

The Abu Sayyaf Group is also referred to as 'ASG'. It is one of a number of militant separatist groups based in and around the southern islands of the Philippines where groups have been engaged in an insurgency to create a state independent of the predominantly Catholic Philippines.

A Congressional Research Report submitted for discussion in 2002 to US authorities from the Foreign Affairs, Defence and Trade Division stated that ASG was the target of Philippine and US anti-terrorism co-operation. The report indicates that ASG emerged as a splinter group during 1990 composed of former Moro National Liberation Front (MNLF) fighters and Filipinos who had fought in Afghanistan. The research indicated that ASG had resorted to terrorist tactics, including kidnappings, executions of civilians, and bombings. The findings of the Congressional Research Report also indicated that during 2000 and 2001 ASG had raided resorts in Malaysia and the Philippine island of Palawan, kidnapping foreign nationals. This resulted in ASG receiving large ransom payments for releasing these hostages. ASG is said to have had links with Osama bin Laden and Al-Qaeda in the early 1990s but Philippine officials have provided conflicting assessments of current links. The report states that US officials have asserted that there is evidence of existing links between ASG and Al-Qaeda.

To prevent further attacks the Philippine government policy was to use military pressure upon ASG. The research concludes that such operations have been constrained by several factors including difficult terrain, inadequate Philippine military equipment, and consideration of the safety of hostages.

Al-Gama 'at al-Islamiya (GI)

Aims:

The main aim of the proscribed terrorist group, Al-Gama 'at al-Islamiya, is to overthrow the Egyptian government and replace it with an Islamic state. Some members of Al-Gama 'at al-Islamiya also wish to achieve the removal of Western influence from the Arab world.

Background:

Al-Gama 'at al-Islamiya, also referred to as 'GI' formally organized in 1973 in the Upper Nile regions of Al-Minya, Asyu't, Qina and Sohaj in Egypt. It is Egypt's largest militant group having several thousand members at the height of its notoriety. Sheikh Omar Abdel a-Rahman, commonly known as the 'Blind Sheikh', became the spiritual leader of GI providing the moral grounds for the group's criminal and terrorist activity.

Sheikh Omar Abdel al-Rahman was jailed in the US for the 1993 World Trade Centre bombings and was associated with Al-Qaeda following an alliance formed in 1998 by Al-Qaeda and other militant Islamic terrorist groups. GI is widely recognized as being an offshoot of the Muslim Brotherhood who sought to overthrow Egypt's secular regime to create an Islamic state. GI members however believe that they will only achieve their objectives through violent jihad, having no place for diplomacy or negotiation.

On 17 November 1997, Deir el-Bahri, an archaeological site and famous tourist destination in Egypt, witnessed a massacre of tourists at the hands of GI. Six terrorists armed with automatic firearms and knives disguised themselves as security forces and trapped tourists within a temple area. The systematic murder of 63 tourists lasted 45 minutes. Among the fatalities were six Britons, of which one was a five-year old boy and four Japanese couples on their honeymoons. The terrorists fled following the massacre later to be found together in a cave where they were believed to have committed suicide. The massacre, orchestrated by individuals such as Ayman al-Zawahiri, who is now the spiritual leader of Al-Qaeda, believed that a terrorist attack on tourists would devastate the Egyptian economy reducing support for the government.

Al Ghurabaa

Aims:

Al Ghurabaa is a splinter group of Al-Muajiroon and disseminates materials that glorify acts of terrorism.

Background:

On 17 July 2006, Al Ghurabaa, also referred to as 'AG', was outlawed in the UK under new provisions of the Terrorism Act 2006 for glorifying terrorism. Then Home Secretary, Dr John Reid, announced the banning of AG stating that the new provisions meant that Government could make it even more difficult for terrorists to operate. He said that:

> I am determined to act against those who, while not directly involved in committing acts of terrorism, provide support for and make statements that glorify, celebrate and exalt the atrocities of terrorist groups. I am also committed to ensuring that those organizations that change their name do not avoid the consequences of proscription.

AG is a UK-based organization believed to be a splinter group from Al-Muajiroon, a former organization led by the cleric Omar Bakri Mohammed. AG was proscribed as a terrorist group following its organization of a protest on 3 February 2006 in response to the Danish cartoons depicting the Prophet Mohammed. The march was conducted from the London Central Mosque to the Danish Embassy in London. Protestors carried placards which stated 'Kill those who insult Islam' and 'Europe you will pay, 9/11 is on its way'.

A spokesman for AG is Abu Izzaden, who on 20 September 2006, heckled the then Home Secretary Dr John Reid at a public meeting in East London calling him an 'enemy' of Islam and stating, 'How dare you come here to a Muslim area.' Abu Izzaden was ejected from the meeting by police and was subsequently arrested in February 2007 and again in April 2007 in connection with counter-terrorism investigations concerning allegations of inciting others to commit acts of terrorism and terrorist fundraising. On 17 April 2008 Abu Izzadeen was convicted alongside other men at Kingston Crown Court for supporting terrorism and is currently serving a four and a half-year custodial sentence.

Al Itihaad Al Islamia

Aims:

The main aims of Al Itihaad Al Islamia are to establish a radical Sunni Islamic state in Somalia and to regain the Ogaden region of Ethiopia as Somali territory via an insurgent campaign.

Background:

Al Itihaad Al Islamia, which is often referred to as 'AIAI', is Somalia's largest militant Islamic organization, rising to power in the early 1990s following the collapse of the Siad Barre regime. It is reported that Osama bin Laden assisted in funding AIAI with the goal of creating an Islamist state in the Horn of Africa. It is this association between militant elements within AIAI and Osama bin Laden that AIAI aligned itself with the 'global jihad' ideology of Al-Qaeda. AIAI is also suspected of having operated in support of Al-Qaeda in the East Africa region.

AIAI is believed to be responsible for a series of bomb attacks in public places in Addis Ababa during 1996 and 1997 in addition to the kidnapping of several relief workers in 1998. At the height of its operations AIAI militia was believed to have exceeded 1,000. A small percentage of the group is considered to be militant. AIAI is recognized as sponsoring Islamic social programs, such as orphanages and schools, and provides pockets of security in Somalia.

According to US intelligence officials, AIAI co-operated with Al-Qaeda linked terrorists who conducted the US Embassy bombings in Africa. On the morning of 7 August 1998 two suicide truck bombs exploded outside US embassies. The first device detonated at 10.30 am adjacent to the embassy in Nairobi, Kenya. The bomb ripped through the building killing 213 people, injuring 5,000, leaving extensive damage and destruction to the embassy and surrounding buildings. Twelve Americans died in the attack but the majority of victims being Kenyan, they were local people going about their daily business. The second car bomb exploded at 10.39 am outside of the US embassy in Dar es Salaam, the capital city of Tanzania. This device also caused massive devastation killing 11 Tanzanians and wounding 85.

Al-Qaeda

Aims:

The core aim of Al-Qaeda is to establish an Islamic Caliphate throughout the world by working with allied Islamic extremist groups to overthrow apostate regimes expelling Westerners and non-Muslims from Muslim countries.

Background:

Al-Qaeda is an international terrorist network led by Osama bin Laden. Established around 1988 by bin Laden, Al-Qaeda helped finance, recruit, transport, and train thousands of fighters from dozens of countries to be part of an Afghan resistance to defeat the Soviet Union. In February 1998, Al-Qaeda issued a statement under the banner of 'The World Islamic Front for Jihad Against the Jews and Crusaders'. Al-Qaeda claimed it was the duty of all Muslims to kill US citizens, civilian or military, and their allies everywhere. During June 2001 Al-Qaeda merged with Egyptian Islamic Jihad (Al-Jihad) led by Ayman al-Zawahiri, now the spiritual leader of Al-Qaeda. The group has targeted US and other Western interests during a sustained period of global violence, some of the attacks include;

1993	New York World Trade Centre bombing.
1998	Bombings of U.S. embassies in Kenya and Tanzania
2000	U.S.S. Cole bombing in Aden, Yemen
2001	9/11 attacks on the World Trade Centre and the Pentagon
2002	Nightclub bombing in Bali, Indonesia
2003	Car bomb attacks on residential compounds in Saudi Arabia
2004	Bomb attacks on the transport network in Madrid
2005	7/7 Suicide attacks on transport networks in London
2005	21/7 failed suicide attacks on transport networks in London
2006	Failed suicide plot to destroy UK trans-Atlantic flights.
2006	Failed suicide plot at Glasgow Airport, Scotland
2007	Failed plot to kidnap a Muslim British Army officer

Al-Qaeda is also referred to as 'AQ' or the Arabic translation as 'the Base'. While it is widely accepted that 'core' Al-Qaeda operating in Afghanistan has limited capability as a direct result of the 'war on terror', it is now a fractured global network of networks whose ideology is recruiting new, young and vulnerable individuals to further its cause.

See also **1.3.1**, **1.4.1**, **1.5.2**, **1.7**, **2.2**, **2.3.3**.

Ansar al Islam

Aims:

Ansar al Islam is a radical Sunni Salafi group from the northeast of Iraq around Halabja. The group is anti-Western and opposes the influence of the US in Iraqi Kurdistan and the relationship between the Kurdistan Democratic Party (KDP), the Patriotic Union of Kurdistan (PUK), and the US government.

Background:

Ansar al Islam, which is also referred to as AI, translated in Arabic as 'Supporters' or 'Partisans' of Islam, is one of a number of Sunni Islamist groups based in the Kurdish-controlled northern provinces of Iraq. AI promotes a radical interpretation of Islam, close to the official Saudi ideology of Wahhabism applying strict Sharia law.

AI is based in and around the villages of Biyara and Tawela, which lie northeast of the town of Halabja in the Hawraman region of Sulaimaniya province bordering Iran. AI came together as a group in September 2001, initially under the name of Jund al-Islam (Soldiers of Islam), but its constituent factions have existed for several years.

AI is believed to comprise a mixture of Iraqis and non-Iraqi elements, mainly Arabs and Kurds. The group is believed to operate a facilitation network in Iran. Since its establishment, the group's armed fighters have engaged in intermittent clashes with the forces of the Patriotic Union of Kurdistan (PUK), in whose strongholds are located in Biyara and Tawela. AI has also been closely associated with operations against Multi-National Forces-Iraq (MNF-I), Iraqi Security Forces (ISF) and the Kurdish security apparatus. The group is highly mobile and resilient, fighting in small units and undertaking assassinations of key figures.

The group has links to Al-Qaeda but remains an independent terrorist organization. The Patriotic Union of Kurdistan claims that Al-Qaeda has provided funds to assist the group progress its activities. AI remains closely associated with the insurgency and terrorism occurring in Iraq. AI was responsible for the detonation of a suicide car bomb on 22 March 2003 which killed Australian journalist Paul Moran. The group is also thought to have been responsible for an attempted bombing on 9 September 2003 of a US Department of Defence office in Arbil which killed three people.

Ansar Al Sunna

Aims:

Ansar al-Sunna is a fundamentalist Sunni Islamist extremist group based in Iraq whose aim is to expel all foreign influences from Iraq and to create a fundamentalist Islamic state.

Background:

Ansar al-Sunna, which is also referred to as 'AS', was founded on 20 September 2003 after declaring its existence on the internet. AS is believed to contain Kurdish Ansar al-Islam operatives, foreign Al-Qaeda terrorists and Iraqi Sunnis. AS adheres to a rigid Salafi ideology which calls upon Muslims to support its activities in Iraq describing it as their duty to do so. AS has claimed responsibility for numerous suicide bombings in Iraq for which it is notorious. AS killed 109 people on 1 February 2004 during one of the bloodiest attacks of the conflict on Kurdistan Democratic Party (KDP) and Patriotic Union of Kurdistan (PUK) offices in Irbil. AS has also claimed responsibility for the following attacks at the height of its activities during 2003 and 2004:

- **29 November 2003**
  ambush of two vehicles carrying Spanish intelligence officers (killing seven).
- **31 January 2004**
  Bombing of the al-Taqafah Police Centre on Mosul (killing nine).
- **23 February 2004**
  Bombing of the Rahimawa Police Station in Kirkuk (killing 13).

Groupe Islamique Armée (Armed Islamic Group) (GIA)

Aims:

The aim of the Armed Islamic Group is to overthrow the regime in Algeria replacing it with a Salafist Islamic state under Sharia law.

Background:

The Armed Islamic Group, which is also referred to as 'GIA', began its violent activities in early 1992 after the government prevented the electoral victory of the Islamic Salvation Front (FIS). GIA has called for the killing of anyone collaborating with or supporting the authorities including teachers, government employees, and civil servants. The GIA is a particularly violent terrorist organization using intimidation as its primary weapon being notorious for its campaign to prevent people from voting in elections using slogans such as 'one vote, one bullet'.

On 14 December 1999, Ahmed Ressam, a GIA member, was arrested at the US and Canadian border. Officers discovered bomb making materials in the boot of his rented car together with sufficient explosives to make at least four high-powered bombs. US authorities stated that the bombs were to attack the Los Angeles airport during the Millennium celebrations. Ressam, dubbed the 'Millennium Bomber' by the US media, was convicted of a conspiracy to commit a terrorist act and smuggling explosives. Ressam received a prison term of 22 years but he was not initially sentenced due to his co-operation with US authorities. Ressam has reportedly identified more than 100 people with alleged links to Al-Qaeda and providing information concerning training camps in Afghanistan.

Asbat Al-Ansar

Aims:

The aim of Asbat al-Ansar is to overthrow the government in Lebanon and enforce its extremist interpretation of Islamic law within Lebanon.

Background:

Asbat al-Ansar, translated in Arabic as 'League of Partisans' or 'Band of Helpers' sometimes uses the aliases of 'The Abu Muhjin' or 'Jama'at Nour'. Asbat al-Ansar is based in Lebanon, described as a Sunni extremist group composed primarily of Palestinians. The group follows an extremist interpretation of Islam that justifies violence against civilian targets to achieve political ends. Some of those goals include overthrowing the Lebanese government and thwarting perceived anti-Islamic and pro-Western influences in the country.

Asbat al-Ansar has conducted numerous terrorist attacks in Lebanon since it first emerged in the early 1990s. The group has been held responsible for the assassination of Lebanese religious leaders. It has also conducted a series of low-level attacks against domestic targets such as churches, bars, casinos, and theatres. The group is accused of bombing a customs building and killing four judges in 1999. It has also been linked to a string of murders perpetrated against rival Palestinian and Islamist groups operating in southern Lebanon together with assassinations of Lebanese religious leaders.

During 2000 Asbat al-Ansar was believed to have received funding from the Al-Qaeda leader, Osama bin Laden. As a result of this support Asbat al-Ansar began to increase the profile of its attacks. On 3 January 2000, Abu Kharab, an Asbat al-Ansar member, fired rocket-propelled grenades at the Russian embassy in Beirut in an alleged act of solidarity with Chechen rebels. The attack resulted in the death of a Lebanese policeman and the injury of seven others before the gunman was shot and killed. A further attack on 20 January 2000, reportedly saw Asbat al-Ansar leaders organizing and funding a failed coup near Tripoli, Lebanon, that was staged by their allies, a Sunni fanatic group called Takfir wal-Hijra. The coup lasted several days involving 150–200 rebels against 3,000 Lebanese troops. This incident resulted in the deaths of 45 people, including 11 soldiers and five civilians. More recently in 2003, Asbat al-Ansar members have been accused of conducting a series of bomb attacks on fast-food restaurants including a car bomb attack on a McDonald's outlet in a suburb of Beirut.

Babbar Khalsa (BK)

Aims:

Babbar Khalsa is a Sikh movement that aims to establish an independent Sikh state called 'Khalistan' within the Punjab region of India.

Background:

Babbar Khalsa, which is also referred to as 'BK', fights for the liberation of Khalistan, the Sikh homeland in Punjab Province, which declared its independence in 1987. BK conducts attacks in India which are mounted against Indian officials and facilities as well as civilians.

BK was most active during the 1970s and 1980s. Prior to the 9/11 attacks in the US, BK was attributed as conducting the world's worst terrorist attack bombing Air India Flight 182 on 23 June 1985. The Boeing 747 aircraft was operating on a Montreal to New Dehli flight stopping over at London Heathrow Airport when it exploded at an altitude of 31,000 feet killing all 329 passengers and crew. A bomb, hidden inside a suitcase, had been placed in the forward cargo hold. The suitcase had been previously booked in by terrorists who did not depart with the aircraft. The main suspects for the bombings were members of BK and following a 20-year investigation only one person, Inderit Singh Reyat, has been found guilty of manslaughter for constructing the bomb. Reyat was living on Vancouver Island, Canada, prior to the attack working as an auto mechanic and electrician.

During the early 1990s the Indian government conducted a crackdown on Sikh militant organizations and although BK has conducted recent low-level attacks in India its capability and capacity has been greatly weakened.

Basque Homeland and Liberty, (Euskadi ta Askatasuna) (ETA)

Aims:

The aim of Euskadi ta Askatasuna is to create an independent socialist Basque Country. Their core objectives were outlined in the 'Democratic Alternative' paper published in 1995 which states that they seek to force the governments of Spain and France to recognize the rights of the Basque Country ensuring that Basque citizens are also uniquely recognized whilst providing an amnesty for all of its members, prisoners and those currently exiled. They also seek respect for a democratic process offering a total ceasefire when all conditions have been met.

Background:

Euskadi ta Askatasuna, commonly known as 'ETA', was founded in 1959 to fight for an independent homeland, principally in Spain's Basque region. Terrorist attacks of ETA are designed to increase political pressure on the Spanish and French governments and to gain additional support for their cause. It is estimated that ETA has killed over 800 people through a series of bombings and assassinations.

Holiday makers in Spain during June 2007 reading the 'Costa Blanca News' would have been anxious seeing the 'Security Hike' headline as the Spanish government called for calm as ETA broke its ceasefire threatening to kill again. The report stated that the Home Office in the Alicante Province had increased its security measures following the announcement by ETA. It revealed how security experts in Spain claimed that ETA had rearmed themselves during the ceasefire and that it now had sufficient resources to carry out a sustained campaign anywhere in Spain with tourist hotspots being likely targets. The announcement broke a 'permanent ceasefire' which was declared by ETA on 22 March 2006 when they sent a DVD message to the media. ETA had however been responsible for the bombing of the Madrid Barajas International Airport on 30 December 2006. The activities of ETA continue to this day as they pursue their cause.

Baluchistan Liberation Army

Aims:

The Baluchistan Liberation Army comprises of tribal groups based in the Baluchistan area of Eastern Pakistan, and aims to establish an independent nation encompassing the Baluch dominated areas of Pakistan, Afghanistan and Iran.

Background:

The Baluchistan Liberation Army, which is often referred to as 'BLA', was listed as a proscribed organization together with other international terrorist groups by the government on 17 July 2006. The then Home Secretary, Dr John Reid stated that,

> Proscribing these groups, which are either engaged in terrorism or which glorify terrorist acts, sends a strong signal that the United Kingdom is not prepared to tolerate those who support terrorism here or anywhere in the world.

Targets of BLA include civilians, specifically those of Punjabi origin. During June 2000 a series of bomb attacks were conducted by BLA terrorists in the region of Quetta in Pakistan which is an area frequented by Pakistani military personnel. The attacks resulted in the deaths of 31 people, 26 of whom were soldiers.

The former Pakistani President Pervez Musharaff attempted to resolve grievances of the BLA with the publication of 32 recommendations to ease tensions. The three main recommendations focused upon a greater share of gas profits to the inhabitants of the region including more jobs in the exploitation of gas resources. It also outlined proposals of a payment of $100 million providing the region with a bigger part in the construction of a new deep water port on the province's coastline. Many of the recommendations have yet to be achieved. Violence linked to BLA continues as they seek to establish an independent nation.

Egyptian Islamic Jihad

Aims:

The main aim of Egyptian Islamic Jihad is to overthrow the Egyptian government and replace it with an Islamic state. It now also shares the ideology promoted by Al-Qaeda aiming to establish an Islamic Caliphate throughout the world by working with allied Islamic extremist groups to overthrow apostate regimes expelling Westerners and non-Muslims from Muslim countries.

Background:

Egyptian Islamic Jihad, also referred to as 'EIJ', is a militant Islamist group that was established in 1973 originally conducting armed attacks against the Egyptian government. During June 2001, EIJ merged with Al-Qaeda and that served to broaden its aims. EIJ has now largely been absorbed by Al-Qaeda.

The leader of EIJ, Ayman al-Zawahiri, is now the spiritual leader of Al-Qaeda. Zawahiri remains one of the most wanted terrorists to date having a US bounty of $25 million for his capture. He is strongly believed to have been involved in the operational planning of the 9/11 terrorist attacks in the US during 2001. In recent years, Zawahiri has emerged as one of Al-Qaeda's most prominent spokesmen encouraging Muslims to follow the ideology of Al-Qaeda.

The original EIJ was responsible for the assassination of Egyptian President Anwar Sadat in 1981. They also claimed responsibility for the attempted assassination of the Egyptian Prime Minister Atef Sidqi and Egyptian Interior Minister Hassan al-Alfi in 1993.

Groupe Islamique Combattant Marocain

Aims:

The Groupe Islamique Combattant Marocain's primary objective is the installation of a governing system of the Caliphate to replace the governing Moroccan monarchy. The group also has an Al Qaeda-inspired global extremist agenda.

Background:

Groupe Islamique Combattant Marocain, also referred to as 'GICM', was listed as a proscribed organization on 10 October 2005 together with 13 other international terrorist groups. GICM is one of a small number of North African terrorist groups growing out of Afghanistan during the tenure of the Taliban in the mid 1990s. It is believed that the capability and capacity of GICM in Morocco has been weakened following a series of arrests of its members in connection with the Casablanca suicide bombings on 16 May 2003 in which 45 people, including the bombers, were killed. The group is reported to have a presence in a number of European countries.

It is not clear to what extent the GICM was involved in the Casablanca bombings in May 2003, or the March 2004 Madrid train bombings killing 191 people, both of which have been attributed to the group in certain sections of the media. GICM was named by Spanish Interior Minister, Angel Acebes, as the priority for the investigation into the bombings which remains Europe's worst terrorist attack this century.

On the morning of Thursday, 11 March 2004, terrorist cell members placed ten rucksack-improvised explosive devices packed with nails on four separate commuter trains in Madrid. Within a space of three minutes all of the devices were detonated on busy carriages during the rush hour at El Pozo Station, Calle Tellez, Atocha Station and Santa Eugenia Station. The co-ordinated explosions claimed 191 lives leaving more than 1,800 injured. The victims came from 17 countries including Spain, France, Bulgaria, and Poland, but they also came from as far as Brazil, Peru, Chile, and Cuba making this attack truly global in scale, an attack that so far remains Europe's worst terrorist incident this century. This attack was planned to coincide with the Spanish general elections occurring three days before voting commenced. A little known fact however is that it was also committed exactly 911 days after the 9/11 terrorist attacks in the United States.

Hamas -Izz al-Din al-Qassem Brigades

Aims:

The aim of Hamas -Izz al-Din al-Qassem Brigades is to end Israeli occupation in Palestine to establish an Islamic state.

Background:

Hamas -Izz al-Din al-Qassem Brigades, often referred to as 'Hamas IDQ', is a military wing of the Palestinian Group Hamas. This specific brigade was established in 1992 to provide a co-ordinated military response for Hamas. A number of Palestinian groups emerged in the late 1980s to pursue the goal of establishing an Islamic Palestinian state in place of Israel.

Hamas IDQ have been responsible for many attacks against Israeli civilian and military targets including the kidnapping of Israeli soldier, Gilad Shalit, during 2006. Israel estimates that Hamas IDQ has 20,000 fighters in its brigade claiming they undertake training in the use of conventional but highly sophisticated weaponry such as rockets and missiles.

The Hamas IDQ brigade members are believed to operate in small independent cells which provide them with the level of operational security required to operate successfully in their environment. Militants of the brigade wear a characteristic black hood with a green headband. Hamas IDQ is believed to operate with an increased independence from the Hamas political wing within the Gaza Strip.

Harakat-Ul-Jihad-Ul-Islami

Aims:

The aim of Harakat-Ul-Jihad-Ul-Islami is to achieve accession of all Kashmir to Pakistan.

Background:

Harakat-Ul-Jihad-Ul-Islami, which is also referred to as 'HUJI' and translated in Arabic as 'The Islamic Holy War', was established in 1984 by Fazalur Rehman Khalil and Qari Saifullah Akhtar. HUJI is widely recognized to be the first Pakistan-based militant Islamic terrorist group formed during the Afghan-Soviet conflict. Following the withdrawal of Soviet forces from Afghanistan in 1989 HUJI merged with Harkat-ul-Mujahideen (HuM), another Pakistani militant group. HUJI and HuM are both proscribed organizations under the provisions of the Terrorism Act 2000.

HUJI aims to establish Islamic rule by waging war. Its beliefs derive from the Deobandi ideology, its recruits being indoctrinated in an extreme and radical interpretation of Islam. HUJI militants draw their inspiration from Osama bin Laden and as a result, like many other extremist groups in Pakistan and Afghanistan, broadly follow the ideologies of Al-Qaeda.

HUJI is regarded as one of the most violent and active terrorist groups operating in the Middle East and is suspected of a series of attacks over the last ten years. It has conducted its operations in Bangladesh, India, and Pakistan using a variety of tactics to fulfill its objectives which include bombings and assassinations.

During 1999 and 2000 members of HUJI were suspected of being involved in a series of failed assassination attempts on the then Prime Minister of Bangladesh, Sheikh Hasina. The attacks attributed to HUJI continued which saw bombing attacks near to the American Centre in Kolkata, India during January 2002 and the bombing of the Delhi-Poanta Shramjeevi Express at Jaunpur in India during June 2005.

More recently HUJI is suspected of being involved in a series of attacks in India which included co-ordinated attacks on court premises on 23 November 2007. HUJI militia were believed to have killed 15 people and injured 80 others in the attacks which occurred in the cities of Varanasi, Faizabad and Lucknow in Uttar Pradesh, India.

Harakat-Ul-Jihad-Ul-Islami Bangladesh

Aims:

The primary aim of Harakat-Ul-Jihad-Ul-Islami Bangladesh is to establish Islamic rule in Bangladesh.

Background:

Harakat-Ul-Jihad-Ul-Islami, which is also referred to as 'HUJI-B', draws its inspiration from Osama bin Laden and so broadly follows the ideology promoted by Al-Qaeda. HUJI-B has a strong Wahabi and Taliban influence. Members of HUJI-B oppose both Indian and Western influence in Bangladesh believing that Hindu and Christian cultural influences are damaging the Islamic culture.

HUJI-B was established in 1992 and like Harakat-Ul-Jihad-Ul-Islami (HUJI) is reported to have received assistance and guidance from Osama bin Laden. The activities of HUJI-B are focused in the coastal area of Bangladesh stretching from the port of Chittagong to the Myanmarese border which is notorious for piracy, smuggling and arms running.

To progress its cause HUJI-B targets both civilians and the military who challenge their militant ideology. Its targets have included academics, journalists, and politicians. HUJI-B is an active terrorist group with a series of attacks attributed to its activities from 1996. These have included an assassination attempt on Bangladesh's leading poet, Shansur Rahman in January 1999 and the stabbing of a journalist in June 2000 for the making of a documentary on the plight of Hindus in Bangladesh.

On 20 July 2000, during routine security checks, security forces recovered explosive devices weighing 76kg near to the locations where the then Prime Minister of Banladesh, Sheikh Hasina was to visit. The devices were discovered close to an area where the Prime Minister was to conduct a public speech in the Gopalganj district. The key suspect in the plot was Mufti Abdul Hanan who allegedly played an integral part in the manufacture of the explosives at a soap factory near Gopalganj.

Harakat ul Mujahideen/ Alami and Jundallah

Aims:

The aim of both Harakat ul Mujahideen/Alami and Jundallah is the rejection of democracy and to establish a caliphate based on Sharia law. Harakat ul Mujahideen/Alami and Jundallah also aims to achieve accession of all Kashmir to Pakistan.

Background:

Harakat ul Mujahideen/Alami, who is also referred to as 'HuM/A' is a Pakistani militant group being established in 1985 to oppose the Soviet invasion of Afghanistan. Translated in Arabic as the 'Order for Holy Warriors', the initial objectives of HuM/A were the provision of food and shelter for the Afghan refugees in the North West Frontier Province in Pakistan. Following the withdrawal of Soviet forces in 1989 HuM/A has continued to wage violent Jihad against secular Muslim governments and the West.

During 1993, HuM/A merged with Harakat-Ul-Jihad-Ul-Islami, another terrorist organization which is also outlawed in the UK under the provisions of the Terrorism Act 2000. This merger is reported to have failed to form an effective group to progress its cause. These two groups subsequently split but it shows how these groups have operated together in the past.

HuM/A is based in Muzaffarabad, Rawalpindi and numerous other towns in Pakistan and Afghanistan where it is believed to have several thousand armed supporters.

Harakat Mujahideen

(formerly known as Harakat ul-Ansar)

Aims:

The primary aim of Harakat Mujahideen is to seek independence for Indian-administered Kashmir.

Background:

Harakat Mujahideen, which is also referred to as 'HM', was previously known as Harakat ul-Ansar (HuA) formed as the result of a merger between Harkat-ul-Mujahideen (HuM) and Harkat ul-Jihad-al-Islami (HuJI). HuA was established in Karachi during 1980 primarily to send volunteers to Afghanistan to assist Afghan rebels to fight against Soviet forces. The headquarters of HuA were located in Punjab where they followed the Deobandi ideology of Islam.

HuA was reported to have several thousand armed supporters who are believed to be located in Azad Kashmir, Pakistan, and in the southern area of Kashmir and Doda regions of India. HuA operate from a base in Muzaffarabad, Pakistan, but its militia conduct attacks primarily in Kashmir.

The change from Harakat ul-Ansar to Harakat Mujahideen is believed to have been conducted to avoid identification of its activities and operatives following the proscription of Harkat ul-Ansar in 1997 by US authorities. HuA leadership was a signatory to the fatwa led by the leader of Al-Qaeda, Osama bin Laden during 1998. The fatwa called for worldwide attacks against US and Western interests. HM is considered to be the continuation of HuA and as such is an outlawed terrorist organization under the provisions of the Terrorism Act 2000.

Harakat Mujahideen has been engaged in violent acts to further its cause. A significant attack saw the kidnapping of Major Bhupinder Singh of the Border Roads Organisation from South Kashmir on 19 January 1994. The dead body of the major was recovered from a nearby roadside the day after the attack.

Hizzballah Military Wing

Aims:

Hizzballah is committed to the armed resistance for the state of Israel and aims to seize all Palestinian territories and Jerusalem from Israel.

Background:

Hizzballah, translated as the 'Party of God', is one of the most infamous terrorist organizations operating in the world today. Proscribed as a terrorist organization under provisions of the Terrorism Act 2000 its membership and activities are outlawed in the UK. Hizzballah was established in 1982 in Lebanon and was originally the militant wing of a religious group, the Ṣhi'a, designed to provide a pro-active arm in the protest against social and political deprivation. Hizzballah has expressed its objectives wishing to remove foreign influences from Lebanon to create an independent and Islamic Lebanon.

Members and supporters of Hizzballah strongly oppose the United States and Israel. They are driven essentially by Islamic religious ideologies but in pursuit of their objectives have used coercion, intimidation, and violence. Hizzballah has conducted bomb attacks not only to draw attention to its cause but to instill fear in others. These attacks have included the bombing of American and French army barracks of the Multinational Force in Beirut during 1983. Hizzballah has also engaged in hostage-taking, a tactic it continues to be closely associated with today. More than 20 individuals of Western origin were held in Lebanon between 1984 and 1990. Hizzballah also developed suicide missions which included the bombing of the Israeli Headquarters in Tyren which was destroyed by a vehicle device packed with explosives in 1983.

Hezb-E Islami Gulbuddin

Aims:

The primary aim of Hezb-E Islami Gulbuddin is to seek the creation of a fundamentalist Islamic State in Afghanistan.

Background:

Hezb-E Islami Gulbuddin, which is also referred to as 'HIG', was originally founded in 1977 by Gulbuddin Hekmatyar who remains the leader of this outlawed terrorist organization. During the invasion of Afghanistan by Soviet forces HIG operated near the Pakistani border where they had a strong presence in areas such as Kumar, Laghman, Jalabad, and Pakita. Gulbuddin Hekmatyar opposed the 2001 attack by the US on the Taliban in Afghanistan and as a result continues to launch attacks not only on US forces but also the US supported Karzai government.

HIG is widely assessed as being a major mujahideen group in the war against the Soviet forces. It is also believed that during this conflict HIG had contact with the leader of Al-Qaeda, Osama bin Laden. HIG is believed to have been involved in establishing a number of terrorist training camps and sending fighters to Islamic conflicts.

Following the withdrawal of Soviet forces in 1989 many Islamic extremist groups clashed violently as they each sought to gain control of Kabul. HIG was blamed for much of the death and destruction during this conflict which ultimately led many ordinary Afghans to welcome the emergence of the Taliban rule in Afghanistan. As the Taliban gained support they exerted their power and influence and HIG were forced to flee Kabul in 1996 where it sought refuge in Tehran, Iran.

HIG has staged a series of small attacks in its attempts to force the US to withdraw from Afghanistan. Many individuals detained at the US high security prison in Guantanamo are suspected of being members of, or are associated with, HIG.

International Sikh Youth Federation

Aims:

The International Sikh Youth Federation is an organization committed to the creation of an independent state of Khalistan for Sikhs within India.

Background:

The International Sikh Youth Federation, which is also referred to as 'ISYF', was founded in 1984 following the events of Operation Blue Star. On 3 June 1984, the then Prime Minister of India, Indira Ghandi, ordered the military to conduct Operation Blue Star, which provided a military response to remove the Sikh militants from the Golden Temple in Amristar, India. It was believed that Sikh militia had gained a stronghold within the Golden Temple complex resulting in a deterioration of law and order in the Punjab. Operation Blue Star is considered to be a political disaster as official Indian military figures reveal that 83 soldiers were killed with a further 248 being injured. These figures also indicate that 492 militants were killed together with innocent civilians including women and children.

The timing of the attacks did not appear to be planned as Sikhs regarded the date of the attack as a religious day where the Golden Temple was busy receiving Sikh visitors from all over the world. The battle lasted four days concluding on 6 June 1984. The consequences of the operation were soon realized as Sikhs who held government positions resigned from their posts. On 31 October that same year, the Sikh bodyguards of Indian Prime Minister, Indira Ghandi, assassinated her in the garden of the Prime Minister's Residence at No 1, Safdarjung Road in New Delhi. Indira Ghandi was the first female Prime Minister of India and had been the head of state for four consecutive terms from 1966 until her death in 1984. She was reportedly shot over 30 times at close range, a revenge killing for the deaths caused as a direct result of Operation Blue Star.

ISYF is led by Lakhbir Singh Rode, the nephew of Jarnail Singh Bhinderanwale who was a key figure in the fight for the creation of an independent state of Khalistan for Sikhs within India until he was killed by Indian military during Operation Blue Star. It is also believed that members of ISYF were involved in the plot that led to the mid-air explosion on board Air India Flight 182 from Montreal, Canada to London, which killed all 329 passengers and crew on 23 June 1985.

Islamic Army of Aden

Aims:

The primary aim of the Islamic Army of Aden is to overthrow the current Yemeni government and the establishment of an Islamic State following Sharia Law.

Background:

The Islamic Army of Aden, which is often referred to as 'IAA', emerged during 1998 following the release of a series of communications stating that it supported the ideology of Al-Qaeda and Osama bin Laden. It also expressed its intention to overthrow the Yemeni government calling for operations to be conducted against US and other Western interests in Yemen.

IAA has been engaged in a series of bomb attacks and kidnappings to progress its cause but its most notorious terrorist attack is the bombing of the USS Cole. At approximately 11.18 am on 12 October 2000 a small dinghy approached the port side of USS Cole where it exploded with its occupants on board. The suicide boat killed 17 US sailors and the two suicide bombers causing a 40ft by 40ft hole in the ship's port side. The USS Cole, a US Navy destroyer, was fuelling at the port of Aden when the attack occurred. The attack was believed to have been organized, supported and conducted by Osama bin Laden and affiliated groups in Yemen. President Clinton stated that:

> If, as it now appears, this was an act of terrorism, it was a despicable and cowardly act. We will find out who is responsible and hold them accountable.

During the aftermath of the attack on the USS Cole Yemeni authorities conducted a sustained crackdown on IAA which appears to have been successful although numerous attacks during 2003 were attributed to this outlawed terrorist group.

Islamic Jihad Union

Aims:

The primary aim of the Islamic Jihad Union is the elimination of the current Uzbek regime creating an Islamic-democratic state in Uzbekistan.

Background:

The Islamic Jihad Union, which is also referred to as 'IJU', is a proscribed terrorist organization in the UK under the provisions of the Terrorism Act 2000. On 13 October 2005, Hazel Blears MP testified before the House of Commons that IJU should be banned because it posed a threat to British interests overseas. Evidence to support the proscription of IJU was provided during the arrest of two men suspected of being members of IJU in Frankfurt, Germany on 18 September 2008. German prosecutors revealed that two men had been arrested on suspicion of links with the Pakistan based IJU which they described as a modern successor to Al-Qaeda.

German authorities reported that the two men were travelling to an IJU camp in the Afghanistan and Pakistan border area during 2007. They were reportedly taking supplies including binoculars, torches, and MP3 players to the remote camp. In addition, further information released by German prosecutors revealed that both men were believed to be associates of another male arrested by German authorities in 2007 in connection with a conspiracy to conduct car bomb attacks in Germany. The targets of the plot were reported to be the Frankfurt International Airport and the US military installations in Germany.

In an interview released on 23 May 2008 by the Nine Eleven Finding Answers Foundation with Mujahid Abdul Gaffar al-Almani, a German Islamic convert, questions were raised concerning the activities of IJU. Al-Almani was asked why Germany might expect attacks by Islamist organizations. He replied that IJU recognized that Germans were directly involved in the war which is taking place in Afghanistan and that a coalition forces base is being constructed in Uzbekistan to support supplies for the occupying forces. He was also asked about the current status of IJU to which he replied that the training of new recruits who were constantly arriving was going well, having assembled a group of recruits who were ready to commit acts of martyrdom.

Islamic Movement of Uzbekistan

Aims:

The primary aim of the Islamic Movement of Uzbekistan is to establish an Islamic state in Uzbekistan. It is also reported to have expressed an intention to establish a broader state over the entire Turkestan area.

Background:

The Islamic Movement of Uzbekistan, which is also referred to as 'IMU' or the Islamic Party of Turkestan, originally focused upon overthrowing the government of Uzbek President, Islam Karimov, planning to replace it with an Islamic state of Uzbekistan. The group is now believed to have expanded its aims by establishing an Islamic state in Uzbekistan to the creation of an Islamic state in all of Central Asia, which would include all of Kazakhstan, Tajikistan, Turkmenistan, Uzbekistan and China's Xinxiang province.

The IMU is believed to be made up of militant Islamist extremists who come from Uzbekistan but this organization includes other Central Asia nationalities and ethnic groups. During 2000 it was estimated that IMU had the support of over 2000 militia where they provided fighters to support the Taliban and fought alongside Al-Qaeda and Osama bin Laden.

During the 2001 coalition forces intervention in Afghanistan it is believed that the majority of IMU was largely destroyed while fighting alongside the Taliban. Despite being operationally inactive since this time it remains an outlawed terrorist organization in the UK under the provisions of the Terrorism Act 2000.

Jaish e Mohammed

Aims:

The primary aim of Jaish e Mohammed is to liberate Kashmir from Indian control. It has also expressed an intention to destroy America and India wishing to unify the various Kashmiri militant groups to achieve these objectives.

Background:

Jaish e Mohammed, which is also referred to as 'JeM' is an Islamist group based in Pakistan which focuses its terrorist activities within Kashmir. Jaish e Mohammed is translated into Arabic as the 'Army of Mohammed' whose leader is Maulana Masood Azhar. Azhar was a member of Harkat-ul-Mujahideen (HuM), another proscribed terrorist organization under the provisions of the Terrorism Act 2000, which received support and guidance from the leader of Al-Qaeda, Osama bin Laden. On 11 February 1994 Azhar was arrested by Indian authorities for being a member of HuM. As a result of his arrest supporters of Azhar founded Jaish e Mohammed which is now widely recognized to be the deadliest and principal terrorist organization operating in Jammu and Kashmir. Azhar was released by the Indian government in December 1999 in exchange for the safe return of passengers taken hostage on the hijacked Indian Airlines Flight 814 in Kandahar, Afghanistan. One of the hijackers was believed to be the brother of Azhar, Ibrahim Azhar.

Members of Jaish e Mohammed were believed to be responsible for the terrorist raid on the Indian Parliament on 13 December 2001. Five armed terrorists drove into Parliament House in a vehicle displaying identification marks of the Home Ministry and Indian Parliament. Once inside the complex they rammed the Vice President's vehicle and opened fire on guards. Two police officers were killed and all the terrorists were shot dead. No member of Parliament was harmed in the attack.

Jeemah Islamiyah

Aims:

The primary aim of Jeemah Islamiyah is the creation of a unified Islamic state in Singapore, Malaysia, Indonesia and the Southern Philippines.

Background:

Jeemah Islamiyah, which is also referred to as 'JI', is a proscribed terrorist organization being outlawed in the UK under the provisions of the Terrorism Act 2000. JI is a militant Islamic separatist movement suspected of killing hundreds of civilians, dedicated to the establishment of a fundamentalist Islamic state. JI is believed to have been established as a network of several Islamic groups by Abu Bakar Bashir and Abdullah Sungkar who propagated the belief of Darukl Islam, a conservative strain of Islam. JI formed as a network of terrorist cells that provided financial support to Al-Qaeda led by Osama bin Laden. JI has been involved in a number of terrorist attacks including bombings and assassinations, the most notorious being the Bali bomb.

At 11.05 pm on 12 October 2002 a suicide bomber detonated his backpack device inside the 'Paddy's Pub' nightclub in Kuta, Bali. This bomb was the first of three co-ordinated explosions which killed 202 and injured 209 innocent civilians. As people ran from the nightclub a vehicle device concealed in a parked Mitsubishi van was detonated by a further suicide bomber outside the Sari Club. This bomb was larger than the first, reportedly wired for remote detonation as a safeguard against technical malfunction or a change of heart from the suicide bomber. A further bomb was detonated outside the US consulate in Denpasar, but due to its size it did not kill anyone leaving only one individual with minor injuries and very little damage.

A Dutch student, Chris van der Draai described the panic that ensued following the explosions;

> We had a bit of panic, everybody panicked, but I think, with the first bomb, many people just stood up and everybody ran down to the beach and the second bomb went off, so I think some people were very lucky that both bombs weren't exploded together.

Several members of JI were arrested and found guilty of planning and assisting in the Bali bomb plot which killed innocent people visiting or working in Bali from 22 individual countries around the world.

Khuddam Ul-Islam & Jamaat Ul-Furquan

Aims:

The aim of both Khuddam Ul-Islam and Jamaat Ul-Furquan is to unite Indian administered Kashmir with Pakistan. It also aims to establish a radical Islamic state in Pakistan seeking to destroy India and the US. Khuddam Ul-Islam and Jamaat Ul-Furquan have stated that they will achieve their objectives by the recruitment of new jihadis and through securing the release of imprisoned Kashmiri militants.

Background:

Khuddam Ul-Islam, also referred to as (KuI) and Jamaat Ul-Furquan, also referred to as (JuF) are both proscribed terrorist organizations in the UK under the provisions of the Terrorism Act 2000. On 10 October 2005 the then Home Secretary, Charles Clarke announced that a further 15 terrorist organizations would be outlawed in the UK. These groups included Khuddam Ul-Islam and splinter group Jamaat Ul-Furquan. Charles Clarke stated that:

> Recent events in London and elsewhere in the world have shown all too clearly that the threat posed by global terrorism has not gone away. I am determined to act against those who, while not involved in committing acts of terrorism, provide support for terrorist groups and their acts.

KuI and JuF are believed to be engaged in supporting terrorist activity within Kashmir providing recruitment and training. They are both splinter groups of Jaish e Mohammed (JeM) which is also an Islamist group based in Pakistan which focuses its terrorist activities within Kashmir. Jaish e Mohammed is translated into Arabic as the 'Army of Mohammed' whose leader is Maulana Masood Azhar. Azhar was a member of Harkat-ul-Mujahideen (HuM), another proscribed terrorist organization under the provisions of the Terrorism Act 2000, which received support and guidance from the leader of Al-Qaeda, Osama bin Laden.

Kurdistan Workers' Party

Aims:

The aim of the Kurdistan Workers' Party is to seek an independent Kurdish state in southeast Turkey.

Background:

The Kurdistan Workers' Party is translated from Arabic as 'Partiya Karkerern Kurdistan' commonly referred to as 'PKK'. In Kurdish the PKK is also known as Kadek Kongra-Gel or 'KGK'. PKK has Marxist-Leninist roots and was formed in the late 1970s launching an armed conflict against the Turkish government in 1984 where it called for an independent Kurdish state within Turkey.

It is estimated that more than 37,000 people have died as a direct result of the PKK's struggle which reached a peak in the mid 1990s when thousands of villages were destroyed in the east and southeast of Turkey. The actions of the PKK forced hundreds of thousands of Kurds to flee to other cities in Turkey.

The PKK has been engaged in acts of terrorism and has used tactics such as assassinations, bombing attacks, chemical warfare, kidnapping, sabotage and suicide bombings. The PKK has been active in numerous locations but predominantly focuses its attention on planning attacks in Turkey. However, it has also been engaged in activities in Iraq, Iran, and Syria. Estimates concerning the size and strength of the PKK are unclear with numerous official bodies quoting between 3,000 and 6,000 members who are predominantly based in northern Iraq. During July 2007 the Turkish General Staff published a list of weapons and ammunition seized from PPK since 1984. It included a total of 4,500 AK47 Kalashnikovs, 5,713 rifles, 1,610 rocket launchers and 11,568 mines.

Lashkar e Tayyaba

Aims:

The primary aim of Lashkar e Tayyaba is to seek independence for Kashmir creating an Islamic state.

Background:

Lashkar e Tayyaba, which is also referred to as 'LeT', is believed to be the largest and most active militant group located in the Lahore region of Pakistan. Lashkar e Tayyaba is translated in Arabic as the 'Army of the Righteous' or the 'Army of the Pure'. LeT was formed in 1991 to support the military activities of other terrorist groups in Pakistan and Afghanistan. LeT is an active terrorist group having conducted a series of attacks on Indian armed forces in Jammu and Kashmir. LeT can be distinguished from other terrorist groups operating to liberate Kashmir for two reasons, first, its operations conducted against security forces are well-planned and executed, secondly, is its ruthless and bloody involvement in numerous massacres of innocent and unarmed non-Muslim villagers.

On 24 January 1998 in the village of Wandhama, close to the town of Ganderbal in Kashmir, a number of LeT terrorists dressed as Indian army soldiers were drinking tea with the villagers. Upon receipt of a radio message that declared all of the families had been covered, the villagers were brought together and executed, being shot with what was believed to be Kalashnikov rifles. In total 23 people were murdered in the massacre that included defenceless men, women, and children.

LeT is a proscribed terrorist organization in the UK under the provisions of the Terrorism Act 2000 and is also outlawed in the US, India, Pakistan, Australia, and Russia.

Liberation Tigers of Tamil Eelam

Aims:

The aim of the Liberation Tigers of Tamil Eelam is to seek a separate Tamil state in the North and East of Sri Lanka.

Background:

The Liberation Tigers of Tamil Eelam, which is also referred to as 'LTTE', or more commonly known as the 'Tamil Tigers', was founded in 1972 and has become the most powerful group in Sri Lanka fighting for a distinct Tamil state. LTTE is a militant Tamil nationalist organization that has waged a sustained campaign of violence since the 1970s against the government of Sri Lanka in order to create a separate Tamil state. LTTE has pursued an armed conflict in Sri Lanka involving the occupation of territories in the north of Sri Lanka. It is one of the most violent terrorist organizations operating in the world today.

LTTE is an outlawed terrorist organization in 32 countries including the UK being proscribed under the provisions of the Terrorism Act 2000. It is feared for its complete disregard of fundamental human rights. LTTE has been associated with the murder of innocent civilians, the kidnap of children for use as soldiers and the assassination of political figures. LTTE has also focused its attacks on non-military targets including commuter trains and buses, farming villages, and mosques. This activity has resulted in the death and serious injury of a large number of civilians.

To conduct many of these attacks successfully the LTTE has developed the use of suicide bombers. The most feared section of the LTTE is the 'Black Tigers', a suicide commando unit which is responsible for large-scale attacks and close-quarter assassination of political leaders. They are regarded as having pioneered the use of concealed suicide bomb vests which are now utilized by other terrorist groups around the world.

Palestinian Islamic Jihad – Shaqaqi

Aims:

The primary aim of Palestinian Islamic Jihad – Shaqaqi is to end the Israeli occupation of Palestine and to create an Islamic state.

Background:

The Palestinian Islamic Jihad – Shaqaqi, which is also referred to as 'PIJ', is a proscribed terrorist organization in the UK under the provisions of the Terrorism Act 2000. It is also outlawed in the US, Israel, the European Union, Japan, Australia, and Canada.

PIJ aims to end the Israeli occupation of Palestine and to create an Islamic state. It opposes the existence of the state of Israel, the Middle East Peace Process, and the Palestinian Authority and has carried out suicide bombings against Israeli targets. It was formed during the 1970s where a number of Shia groups based in the Gaza Strip were united in their commitment to create an Islamic Palestinian state leading to the destruction of Israel.

On 20 February 2003, US authorities arrested Dr Sami Al-Arian, a computer engineering professor from the University of South Florida on allegations of terrorist fundraising. Following a lengthy legal process Al-Arian pleaded guilty to one of the 17 charges against him. On 14 April 2006 Al-Arian admitted to conspiring to provide services to PIJ and was sentenced to 57 months imprisonment. US District Judge James Moody criticized Al-Arian stating that:

> 'You lifted not one finger. To the contrary, you laughed when you heard of the bombings. You were a leader of the PIJ.'

Revolutionary Peoples' Liberation Party – Front (Devrimci Halk Kurtulus Partisi-Cephesi)

Aims:

The aim of the Revolutionary Peoples' Liberation Party – Front is to establish a Marxist-Leninist regime in Turkey.

Background:

The Revolutionary Peoples' Liberation Party – Front, is also known as Devrimci Halk Kurtulus Partisi-Cephesi, more commonly referred to as 'DHKP-C'. DHKP-C is an outlawed terrorist organization in Turkey, the European Union, US, and the UK under the provisions of the Terrorism Act 2000. DHKP-C is a Turkish group whose origins can be traced back to the 1970s. Its operations have been mainly confined to Turkish targets in Turkey which have included attacks on Turkish security officials but during the 1990s it broadened its attack planning focusing upon foreign interests which included attacks on the US military, diplomatic personnel and facilities. These attacks have included:

13 August 1991:	assassination of Andrew Blake, the head of the British Commercial Union in Istanbul.
9 January 1996:	assassination of Ozdemir Sabanci, a prominent Turkish businessman.
24 July 2004:	suicide bombing of a bus in Istanbul killing four people including the bomber and injuring 15 others.

Teyre Azadiye Kurdistan

Aims:

The primary aim of Teyre Azadiye Kurdistan is to secure Kurdish secession from Turkey.

Background:

Teyre Azadiye Kurdistan, which is also referred to as 'TAK' and is translated as the Kurdistan Freedom Falcons, is a militant paramilitary organization which operates in southern Turkey and northern Iraq. TAK is a proscribed terrorist organization in the UK under the provisions of the Terrorism Act 2000. TAK is also outlawed by the US and the European Union. It is widely acknowledged that TAK is a splinter faction of Partiya Karkerern Kurdistan, commonly referred to as 'PKK'. PKK has Marxist-Leninist roots and was formed in the late 1970s launching an armed conflict against the Turkish government in 1984 where it called for an independent Kurdish state within Turkey.

On 28 August 2006 members of TAK were believed to be responsible for attacking the popular tourist port resort of Marmaris in Turkey. Three explosions were conducted from bombs hidden in litter bins. Two days later on 30 August 2006 a further explosion occurred from another bomb planted in a rubbish container in the town of Mersin, Turkey. The attacks prompted speculation of a co-ordinated terrorist campaign that appeared to target tourists, the tourism industry being a major source of revenue for the Turkish government. Although the Turkish government has made some concessions, the series of attacks in the summer of 2006 revealed that it may not have done enough to end Kurdish disaffection. Although there is little sign of TAK having similar strength to that which it had in the 1990s, it is clear that Kurdish separatists have seen lengthy ceasefires that have achieved little to further their cause. The attacks attributed to TAK during 2006 left three people dead and 47 injured, ten of whom were British.

Salafist Group for Call and Combat (Groupe Salafiste pour la Prédication et le Combat)

Aims:

The aim of the Salafist Group for Call and Combat is to create an Islamic state in Algeria.

Background:

The Salafist Group for Call and Combat, translated in French as Groupe Salafiste pour la Prédication et le Combat, is commonly referred to as 'GSPC'. The group, which is also known as the 'Hassan Hattab Faction', was founded by Hassan Hattab who was born in Rouiba, Algeria. Having trained as a paratrooper during his national service, Hattab joined the radical Islamist guerrilla movement, the Armed Islamic Group (GIA). He became a regional commander for GIA but broke away from GIA following disagreements over the killing of innocent civilians resulting in the creation of GSPC. Major attacks attributed to GSPC include:

11 December 2007: Co-ordinated car bomb attacks at the Algerian Supreme High Court and the United Nations High Commission for Refugees in Hydra killing 42 people, injuring a further 158.

2 January 2008: A suicide bomber drove a car bomb into a police station in Naciria, Algeria, killing four police officers.

29 January 2008: A suicide bomber detonated a car bomb while driving towards a police station killing three police officers in Thenia, Boumerdes, Algeria.

Saved Sect or Saviour Sect

Aims:

The primary aim of the Saved Sect is to encourage violent extremism through the dissemination of materials that glorify acts of terrorism.

Background:

The Saved Sect, which is also known as the Saviour Sect is a splinter group of Al-Muajiroon which disseminates materials that glorify acts of terrorism. The Saved Sect was established in November 2005 and believes that Muslims living in the western world do not follow traditional Islamic values and seeks to remind Muslims of true Islamic values.

The name of the group is taken from a tradition or 'hadith' ascribed to the Prophet Muhammed which states that:

My nation will be divided into 73 sects; all of them will be in the Fire except for one (the saved sect).

On 17 July 2006, the then Home Secretary Dr John Reid, announced that under the provisions provided by the Terrorism Act 2006, the Saviour Sect was an outlawed terrorist organization in the UK. This new legislation passed by the government was designed to protect the UK from groups who may not themselves be directly concerned in the commission, preparation or instigation of acts of terrorism, but may instead actively encourage others to take part in such acts, or glorify terrorist acts leading to others to commit criminal offences.

The introduction of the Terrorism Act 2006 and its provisions to proscribe terrorist organizations supports the government's 'Contest' strategy which sets out to pursue terrorists by strengthening the anti-terrorism legal framework in the UK.

Sipah-E Sahaba Pakistan (SSP) (aka Millat-E Islami Pakistan (MIP)—SSP was renamed MIP in April 2003 but is still referred to as SSP) and splinter group Lashkar-E Jhangvi (LeJ)

Aims:

The aim of both Sipah-E Sahaba Pakistan and Lashkar-E Jhangvi are to transform Pakistan to a Sunni state under Sharia law.

Background:

Sipah-E Sahaba Pakistan, which is also referred to as 'SSP', is also known as Millat-E Islami Pakistan (MIP). SSP was renamed MIP in April 2003 but may also be referred to as SSP. A splinter group of SSP is Lashkar-E Jhangvi (LeJ). All of these groups are proscribed organizations under the provisions of the Terrorism Act 2000.

SSP is also believed to seek all Shia Muslims be declared as Kafirs or non-believers expressing an intention to participate in the destruction of other religions including Judaism, Christianity, and Hinduism. SSP strongly opposes the US and Pakistani relationship following the 9/11 terrorist attacks and subsequent 'war on terror'. On 12 January 2002, the then President of Pakistan, Pervez Musharraf, declared SSP a terrorist organization banning its activities.

The SSP has been linked to the World Trade Centre bombing in New York on 23 February 1993. A vehicle bomb was driven into an underground car park and detonated below the North Tower. US authorities believed that the plan was to destabilize the North Tower so that it would collapse onto the South Tower bringing both towers crashing to the ground. The explosion caused extensive damage killing six people and injuring 1,042 others.

The World Trade Centre attack was conducted by a group of Islamic militants believed to have contacts with the SSP. The prime terrorist cell member was Ramzi Yousef who was arrested in 1995 at an alleged Al-Qaeda safe-house in Pakistan. The uncle of Yousef is Khaled Sheikh Mohammed who was suspected of financing the operation. Khaled Sheikh Mohammed, also referred to as 'KSM' was the principal architect of the 9/11 terrorist attacks in 2001 having links to the core leadership of Al-Qaeda and Osama bin Laden. Khaled Sheikh Mohammed was arrested by US authorities and remains in US custody.

Libyan Islamic Fighting Group

Aims:

The Libyan Islamic Fighting Group seeks to replace the current Libyan regime with a hard-line Islamic state. It is also believed to be part of the wider global Islamist extremist movement as inspired by Al-Qaeda.

Background:

The Libyan Islamic Fighting Group, which is also referred to as 'LIFG', was formed in the early 1990s in Afghanistan. The group relocated to Libya where it sought to overthrow Colonel Mu'ammar Kaddaffi. LIFG mounted several operations inside Libya in pursuit of its cause which included a failed attempt to assassinate Colonel Mu'ammar Kaddafi during 1996. The activities of LIFG did not manage to topple the Libyan regime.

On 10 October 2005 LIFG became an outlawed terrorist group in the UK being proscribed under the provision of the Terrorism Act 2000 together with 14 other international terrorist groups.

On 9 April 2008 Libyan authorities released 90 prisoners said to be reformed members of LIFG. A charity chaired by the eldest son of Colonel Kaddafi, organized the release of the prisoners who are believed to have renounced violence. The prisoners had been arrested and detained for their alleged membership of LIFG who had been serving prison terms from ten years to life imprisonment. The majority of the prisoners had served between six and eight years of their custodial sentences. The Libyan funded charity stated that the release of the 90 prisoners represented a third of the total number of inmates detained in Libya who are suspected of being members of LIFG.

On 7 February 2006 the United Nations embargoed five individual LIFG members and four separate corporations who had continued to operate in the UK until October 2005. The sanctions were brought against them following US State Department allegations that they were concerned in supporting terrorist activity. The majority of these accusations focused upon the transfer of funds and the creation of bogus charities as a front to disguise financial transactions that are believed to support terrorist activity.

Jammat Mujahideen Bangladesh

Aims:

The primary aim of Jammat Mujahideen Bangladesh aims to establish the rule of Islam in Bangladesh opposing the creation of democracy.

Background:

Jammat Mujahideen Bangladesh, which is also referred to as 'JMB', and translated from Arabic as the 'Party of the Mujahideen', is an Islamist terrorist organization operating within Bangladesh.

JMB first came to prominence on 20 May 2002 when eight of its members were arrested in the Parbatiput and Dinajpur districts of Bangladesh being found in possession of 25 petrol bombs. The group has claimed responsibility for numerous fatal bomb attacks across Bangladesh including a series of co-ordinated bomb attacks on 17 August 2005 at 300 separate locations in 30 cities. These attacks killed two people injuring 50 others but other attacks attributed to JMB have proved more deadly targeting police officers, judges and lawyers. Documents and leaflets discovered at various bomb sites on 17 August 2005 stated that:

> We are the soldiers of Allah. We have taken up arms for the implementation of Allah's law the way the Prophet, Sahabis and heroic Mujahideen have implemented for centuries.

An analysis of weaponry seized from JMB cadres and their hideouts provided by a South Asia Intelligence Review indicated that the outfit uses or has access to time bombs, detonators, petrol bombs and explosives. Militants of the JMB are known to receive extensive training in explosive making. The JMB's involvement in the 17 August 2005 country-wide bombings also provides an indication of its bomb making expertise.

The South Asia Intelligence Review also indicates that JMB is believed to be procuring its arms and explosives from militant groups based in Pakistan, Myanmar, Thailand, India, and China. As a result of its activities JMB remains an outlawed terrorist organization in the UK being proscribed under provisions of the Terrorism Act 2000.

Tehrik Nefaz-e Shari'at Muhammed

Aims:

The primary aim of Tehrik Nefaz-e Shari'at Muhammed is to seek the enforcement of Islamic Law in Pakistan.

Background:

Tehrik Nefaz-e Shari'at Muhammed, which is also referred to as 'TNSM', is translated from Arabic as the 'Movement for the Enforcement of Islamic Laws'. TNSM are dedicated to enforce the rule of Islamic Law in Pakistan and is widely regarded as one of the most dangerous terrorist groups operating within the North-West Frontier Province (NWFP).

TNSM has conducted regular attacks against coalition and Afghan government forces in Afghanistan who are believed to provide direct support to Al-Qaeda and the Taliban. In addition to foot operatives, TNSM is also believed to have supplied weaponry to support the Taliban activities arming their militia with rocket launchers, missiles, anti-aircraft guns, and hand-grenades. One faction of TNSM claimed responsibility for a suicide attack on an army training compound on 8 November 2007 in Dargai, Pakistan, in which 42 soldiers were killed.

The TNSM operates primarily in the tribal areas of Pakistan, such as Swat and the adjoining districts of the NWFP. Although well established in the NWFP, the TNSM has had only limited success in expanding its activities beyond the tribal areas of the province. It has substantial support in Malakand and Bajaur and includes activists that have fought in Afghanistan at some time during the past 25 years.

As a result of its activities TNSM is an outlawed terrorist organization in the UK being proscribed under the provisions of the Terrorism Act 2000. Then Prime Minister of Pakistan, Pervez Musharaf, banned TNSM in Pakistan on 12 January 2002.

Irish Republican Army (IRA)

Aims:

The Irish Republican Army has two key aims, first, it is devoted to removing British forces from Northern Ireland, and second, to unifying Ireland.

Background:

The Irish Republican Army, also referred to as the 'IRA' and translated from Irish as 'Oglaigh na hEireann', is the leading Republican paramilitary group in Ireland which has existed in one form or another since 1919. The IRA is a military organization descended from the Irish Volunteers.

The IRA is a proscribed terrorist organization, one of 14 such Irish groups outlawed under present anti-terrorism legislation in the UK. The original IRA, more commonly referred to as the 'Old IRA' was operational from 1922 until a split in 1970. The split brought about two main groups, the Provisional IRA and the Official IRA. The title 'IRA' which appears on the list of proscribed organizations is considered sufficient to cover the numerous splinter groups and breakaway factions of the IRA which include;

- **Provisional Irish Republican Army**: also referred to as 'PIRA', being formed in 1970 when the original Old IRA split.
- **Official Irish Republican Army**: also refereed to as 'OIRA', and described as the residual group being formed in 1970 when the original Old IRA split. OIRA has conducted few attacks since the ceasefire of 1972.
- **Real Irish Republican Army**: also referred to as 'RIRA', which emerged as a dissident faction opposed to the Peace Process of 1997.
- **Continuity Irish Republican Army**: also referred to as 'CIRA', which emerged as a dissident faction opposed to the Peace Process of 1997.

Section 3(1)(b) of the Terrorism Act 2000 confirms that an organization is proscribed if it operates under the same name as an organization listed in that Schedule which includes PIRA, OIRA, RIRA and CIRA.

The IRA conducted a sustained campaign of terrorist activity both in Ireland and on the UK mainland. Traditional IRA activities have included bombings, assassinations, kidnappings, punishment beatings, extortion, smuggling, and other organized criminality.

See also **1.3.2, 1.5.1, 1.6.6, 3.1.1, 3.4, 3.4.1, 3.4.2.2**.

Cumann na mBan (Union of Women)

Aims:

The primary aim of Cumann na mBan is to advance the cause of Irish liberty devoted to unifying Ireland.

Background:

Cumann na mBan is translated from Irish meaning 'Union of Women' or the 'League of Women' who were established in 1914 as an auxiliary of the Irish Volunteers. Throughout the struggles in Ireland, especially during the Easter Rising in 1916, the women of Cumann na mBan directly assisted the Irish Volunteers playing a vital role. They worked as First Aid posts tending to the wounded, prepared and delivered meals, gathered intelligence on scouting expeditions, carried messages, and transferred arms. The role of Cumann na mBan during the Easter Rising is reflected in the groups constitution which states that it will

> teach its members first aid, drill, signalling and rifle practice in order to aid the men of Ireland.

Members of Cumann na mBan were also engaged in supporting the terrorist activities of other Republican groups. The women of Cumann na mBan came from a variety of backgrounds, although the majority were described as working class, many also came from more privileged backgrounds being described as 'white-collar' workers and 'professional women'. Although an independent organization in its own right, the executive of Cumann na mBan were subordinate to the Irish Volunteers.

Members of Cumann na mBan have been engaged in frontline street-by-street combat with British soldiers during 'The Troubles'. They remain an outlawed terrorist group in the UK being proscribed under the provisions of the Terrorism Act 2000.

Fianna nah Eireann
(Warriors of Ireland)

Aims:

The primary aim of Fianna nah Eireann is to promote the objects, principles and exercises of scouting among the boys and girls of Ireland to cultivate, train and develop all faculties physical, intellectual and spiritual; to implant them with respect for themselves and a desire to give service to others, that may in the fullness of manhood grow into useful, honest, upright citizens, worthy of the land that bore them devoted to the unification of Ireland.

Background:

The Fianna nah Eireann which is translated as the 'Soldiery of Ireland' or the 'Warriors of Ireland', was founded in 1909 as a scouting organization that emphasized Irish nationalism as opposed to British nationalism. The members of Fianna nah Eireann pledge their allegiance to the Sovereign Independent Irish Republic proclaimed in 1916 following the Easter Rising. The militant character of the Fianna nah Eireann can be found in an early constitution from 1914 which included three clauses for membership as:

1) **Objects:** to re-establish the Independence of Ireland.
2) **Means:** the training of the youth of Ireland, mentally and physically. To achieve this object by teaching scouting and military exercises, Irish history, and the Irish language.
3) **Declaration:** I promise to work for the Independence of Ireland, never to join England's armed forces, and to obey my superior officer.

The international Scout movement has never recognized Fianna nah Eireann which, as a uniformed youth movement, contradicts the evolution of scouting worldwide which has moved towards emphasizing peace as opposed to division and further conflict.

The Red Hand Commandos

Aims:

The aim of the Red Hand Commandos is to fight to ensure that Ulster remains British and to defend the loyalist community from republican violence.

Background:

The Red Hand Commandos, which is also referred to as 'RHC' is a Northern Irish loyalist paramilitary group having close links with the Ulster Volunteer Force (UVF).

RHC was founded in 1970 in response to a series of violent attacks on a loyalist parade as they marched on Newtownards Road in Ulster. The parade was attacked by a series of stone throwers who caused disruption to the march. As the parade moved along Crumlin Road the stone throwers dispersed, believed to be making way for gunmen from the Irish Republican Army who opened fire on the parade resulting in the murder of three loyalists. As a result of the murders, a number of young loyalists from the Shankhill and Old Park areas of Ulster came together at a meeting where they formed the RHC to fight for a British Ulster and to defend loyalist communities from further republican violence.

RHC supported the conditions and signing of the Good Friday Agreement of 1998. Although renouncing violence and ceasing to operate as a paramilitary organization on 3 May 2007, it declared its intention to retain its weapons, stating that they would be placed out of reach and be inaccessible to its members. This did not satisfy the Independent International Commission on Decommissioning and the RHC remains a proscribed terrorist organization in the UK under the provisions of the Terrorism Act 2000.

Saor Eire (Free Ireland)

Aims:

The primary aim of Saor Eire is to achieve an independent revolutionary leadership for the working class and working farmers seeking to overthrow British imperialism and its ally, Irish capitalism.

Background:

Saor Eire, translated in Irish as 'Free Ireland' is a left-wing political organization established in September 1931 by members of the Irish Republican Army. Saor Eire is an organization of workers and working farmers which has been referred to as the 'Revolutionary Workers' Party'. The name 'Saor Eire' has been used occasionally since its foundation by various Republican factions. The key objectives of Saor Eire can be found in its constitution taken from their first conference at Iona Hall in Dublin on 26 September 1931 where they were stated as being:

1. To achieve an independent revolutionary leadership for the working class and working farmers towards the overthrow of British imperialism and its ally, Irish capitalism.
2. To organise and consolidate the Republic of Ireland on the basis of the possession and administration by the workers and working farmers, of the land, instruments of production, distribution, and exchange.
3. To restore and foster the Irish language, culture and games.

Saor Eire was seen as a dangerous communist group by both the right-wing press and the Catholic Church. Saor Eire seeks to change social authorities promoting an equal distribution of power and wealth. In more general terms it fights for equal opportunities for Republicans favouring radical socialism. This was met with strong opposition that has prevented it from becoming an effective political organization.

The Ulster Freedom Fighters

Aims:

The primary aim of the Ulster Freedom Fighters is to support the activities of the Ulster Defence Association which aims to defend the loyalist community from republican violence.

Background:

The Ulster Freedom Fighters, who are also referred to as 'UFF', is a loyalist paramilitary organization in Northern Ireland which emerged from the Ulster Defence Association (UDA) in the early 1970s being used to conduct their military tasks.

The activities of UFF have included attacks against civilians as well as members of the Irish Republican Army. As the military wing of the UDA, the UFF was originally intended to react and respond to acts of republican violence against Protestants in Northern Ireland.

During June 1973 Patrick Gerard Wilson, also known as Paddy Wilson, was murdered by John White, a member of UFF. Paddy Wilson was elected as a Republican Labour Party member of the Senate of Northern Ireland in 1969. During 1970 he became a founder member of the Social Democratic and Labour Party. In one of the most violent and brutal murders of 'The Troubles', John White hacked and stabbed Paddy Wilson to death. At the time of this attack he also stabbed and killed the assistant of Paddy Wilson, Irene Andrews, whose breasts were cut off in the attack. John White was arrested and later confessed to the murders in 1978 he then was sentenced to life imprisonment. White was released from prison in 1992 when he joined the Ulster Democratic Party. The UDA officially ended its campaign of violence in 2007 when it ordered the UFF to stand down.

The Ulster Volunteer Force

Aims:

The aim of the Ulster Volunteer Force is to fight to ensure that Ulster remains British and to defend the loyalist community from republican violence.

Background:

The Ulster Volunteer Force, which is also referred to as the 'UVF', is a loyalist paramilitary organization based in Northern Ireland which was formed in May 1966. The UVF has focused its activities around East Antrim, County Armagh and the Shankhill district of Belfast. The UVF is recognized as being one of the most active and violent loyalist groups that operated during 'The Troubles'. Statistics compiled by the University of Ulster reveal that the UVF is believed to be responsible for 426 killings between 1969 and 2001 of which 350 were civilians and 12 were republican paramilitaries.

On 3 May 2007 UVF declared that it had renounced violence and would cease to exist as a terrorist organization. This included a commitment from UVF that it would end all recruitment, training and targeting stating that Active Service Units (ASUs) had been deactivated. UVF leadership also stated that its weaponry would be put out of reach of its members although this did not satisfy the Independent International Commission on Decommissioning. Although the move was welcomed by all parties in Ireland the Police Service of Northern Ireland took a precautionary view stating that:

> Whilst we welcome today's announcement, individuals and organisations will be judged by their actions – actions always speak louder than words.

The Irish National Liberation Army

Aims:

The primary aim of the Irish National Liberation Army during 'The Troubles' was to protect members of the Irish Republican Socialist Movement from attacks by the Official Irish Republican Army who sought a 32-county socialist republic, free and independent from British control and run by the Irish working classes.

Background:

The Irish National Liberation Army, which is also referred to as the 'INLA' and is translated into Irish as 'Arm Saorise Naisiunta na hEirehame'. The INLA emerged in 1974, being founded as the army of the Irish Republican Socialist Party which was primarily established to defend attacks from Official Irish Republican Army activists.

The INLA was involved in the commission of many murders which were often conducted in retaliation for republican activities. It was these very murders that produced a series of linked attacks in what were often described as 'tit for tat' killings. The killings were at times so ruthless that members of the INLA earned themselves the nickname of 'mad dogs'.

A series of killings that appeared to spiral out of control occurred in December 1997 when three members of INLA imprisoned in Long Kesh assassinated Loyalist Volunteer Force (LVF) member, Billy Wright. This murder led loyalists to conduct a number of attacks on Catholics which in turn resulted in the INLA shooting dead the leader of the Ulster Defence Association, Jim Guiney. This period of 'The Troubles' temporarily damaged the Northern Ireland Peace Process.

On 6 December 1982 members of the INLA bombed the Droppin' Well disco and nightclub in Ballykelly in County Londonderry which was frequented by British Army soldiers. The blast of the bomb extensively damaged the structure of the building causing tonnes of rubble to fall upon people inside. Seventeen people were killed including 11 British soldiers and six civilians. A further 150 people were injured in the blast, some of whom were pulled from the rubble by the emergency services.

On 22 August 1998 the INLA declared a ceasefire acknowledging that its activities during 'The Troubles' may have been wrong and that as part of its support for the Good Friday Agreement, did not see a return to an armed struggle as a viable option at that time.

Irish People's Liberation Organization

Aims:

The primary objective of the Irish People's Liberation Organization is to destroy the Irish Republican Socialist Movement.

Background:

The Irish People's Liberation Organization is a small Irish republican paramilitary organization which is also referred to as 'IPLO'. IPLO emerged from a violent split with the Irish National Liberation Army (INLA) whose aim during 'The Troubles' was to protect members of the Irish Republican Socialist Movement from attacks by the Official Irish Republican Army. Factions of INLA based in Belfast and Dublin were in dispute following the Hunger Strike in 1981 where members of INLA sacrificed their lives for their cause to unify Ireland.

The INLA factions could not reconcile their differences. When INLA member Harry Kirkpatrick was arrested by police he turned 'super grass' and his evidence was used to implicate his former comrades, many of whom were convicted for terrorist and criminal activities. As a direct result of the aftermath of the 'super grass' revelations the INLA was near to collapse. Disaffected and expelled members of INLA were drawn together and in 1986 they formed the IPLO. Its first priority was to destroy the Irish Republican Socialist Movement from which it had ultimately split.

As violence and intimidation within rival republican groups emerged it proved to be a destructive part of 'The Troubles' for the wider republican movement. The Provisional Irish Republican Army (PIRA) was forced to take action to restore order within its own body of support. As the largest armed republican group in Ireland PIRA mounted an operation to resolve the problems. On

31 October 1992 an estimated 100 PIRA members closed the IPLO by killing the Belfast Brigade leader Sammy Ward and kneecapping others whose lives were spared in return for their surrender and disarmament. The IPLO was disbanded within days of the PIRA's operation.

The IPLO remain an outlawed terrorist organization in the UK being proscribed under the provisions of the Terrorism Act 2000. Throughout its operations, according to statistics compiled by the University of Ulster, it was responsible for 22 killings, 12 of which were of innocent civilians.

The Ulster Defence Association

Aims:

The aim of the Ulster Defence Association is to defend the loyalist community from republican violence rejecting the unification of Ireland while seeking independence for Ulster.

Background:

The Ulster Defence Association, which is also referred to as the 'UDA' is a loyalist paramilitary organization in Northern Ireland. The UDA was created in 1971 and operated as an umbrella organization for a number of militant loyalist groups. Until 10 August 1992 the UDA was a legal organization until it was outlawed following links to paramilitary attacks.

The military branch of the UDA was the Ulster Freedom Fighters (UFF). The primary aim of the UFF is to support the activities of the UDA. The activities of the UFF have included attacks against civilians as well as members of the Irish Republican Army. The UFF was originally intended to react and respond to acts of republican violence against Protestants in Northern Ireland.

The UDA supports unionism within Ireland favouring independence for Northern Ireland. The stance of the UDA was clear during 'The Troubles' as it stated that if the Provisional Irish Republican Army would stop its campaign of violence then the UDA would also withdraw from its activities.

On 11 November 2007 the UDA formally renounced violence but its leaders refused to surrender its weapons. The UDA is also suspected of developing strong links with fascist groups in the UK including Combat 18 (C18). The UDA remains an outlawed terrorist organization in the UK being proscribed under the provisions of the Terrorism Act 2000.

Loyalist Volunteer Force

Aims:

The Loyalist Volunteer Force seeks to prevent a political settlement with Irish nationalists in Northern Ireland by attacking Catholic politicians, civilians, and Protestant politicians who endorse the Northern Ireland Peace Process.

Background:

The Loyalist Volunteer Force, which is also referred to as the 'LVF' is a loyalist paramilitary group in Northern Ireland. LVF broke away from the Ulster Volunteer Force being led by Billy Wright, a former lay preacher, who was arrested and charged with menacing behaviour receiving an eight-year prison term. Whilst serving his sentence in the LVF wing of HMP Maze prison, members of INLA shot him dead on 27 December 1997.

The LVF conducted a series of attacks during 'The Troubles' engaging in bombings, kidnappings, and close-quarter shootings. On 3 May 2007 the LVF renounced violence declaring that it had ceased its military activities. The then Northern Ireland Secretary Peter Hain stated that:

> I have always said that the peace process must leave nobody behind and that those who are willing to change will have our support. In that context, today's commitments by the LVF signalling a fundamental change are very welcome.
>
> We must earnestly hope that there are no more victims and that future generations will live in enduring peace.

Continuity Army Council

Aims:

The aim of the Continuity Army Council is to lend support to those persons or organizations who seek to unify Ireland.

Background:

The Continuity Army Council was formed following an Irish Republican Army (IRA) General Army Convention (GAC) meeting which was conducted in September 1986. The GAC is the IRA's highest decision-making body and this was the first time in 16 years they had met. The meeting was called to discuss the constitution of the IRA. As a result of the discussions a number of IRA members, who were opposed to some of the changes to be made to the IRA constitution, established a new IRA Executive calling themselves the Continuity Army Council (CAC). The CAC was deemed the lawful Executive of the IRA. From this new Executive the Continuity IRA (CIRA) was created, which claims to be the legitimate continuation of the old IRA of 1969. CIRA have been engaged in paramilitary activities, its more recent actions include the following:

- **14 June 2008** A landmine attack on a Police Service of Northern Ireland patrol car in Rosslea, County Fermanagh which injured two officers.
- **26 May 2008** CIRA is believed to be responsible for carrying out a punishment shooting on a drug dealer in Armagh City.
- **16 August 2008** A rocket-propelled grenade attack on a Police Service of Northern Ireland (PSNI) police patrol in Lisnaskea, County Fermanagh leaving three police officers requiring treatment for minor injuries and shock.

- **26 August 2008** CIRA claimed responsibility for a sniper attack on a PSNI patrol in Craigavon during disturbances. Five shots were fired at the PSNI patrol. Blast bombs and petrol bombs were also thrown, damaging a number of police vehicles. At least five other vehicles were destroyed in the clashes.
- **13 September 2008** CIRA is suspected of leaving a 100 lb bomb outside Jonesborough in south Armagh. It is believed they were trying to lure police into an ambush.

The Orange Volunteers

Aims:

The primary aim of the Orange Volunteers is to ensure that Ulster remains British, defending the loyalist community from republican violence.

Background:

The Orange Volunteers, who are also referred to as 'OV', is an Ulster loyalist paramilitary group in Northern Ireland. The OV motto 'addaces fortuna juvat' translates from Irish as 'Fortune Favours the Bold'. OV was established in 1998 following the Drumcree conflict which is an ongoing dispute over parades in the town of Portadown in Northern Ireland. The route of the parade taken by the Protestant Orange Order is between the Portadown town centre and the Dumcree parish church to the north which is predominantly Catholic.

During the Orange Order parade of 1998 the Royal Ulster Constabulary and the British Army prevented the march and its supporters from returning to the town centre via Garaghy Road. This road was a familiar route for the parade but one which had previously raised tensions amongst the wider community often spilling over into violence. According to Royal Ulster Constabulary statistics, the following incidents occurred between 4 July 1988 and 14 July 1998:

- 2,561 recorded public order incidents
- 615 attacks on police officers
- 632 petrol bombs were thrown
- 24 shooting incidents occurred
- 45 bomb blasts were conducted
- 837 plastic bullet rounds were fired by police.

At the height of their activity OV was believed to have 20 members, some of whom were experienced in bomb making and munitions. During 2000 OV declared a ceasefire and it has not been active since that time.

Red Hand Defenders

Aims:

The Red Hand Defenders seek to prevent a political settlement with Irish nationalists opposing the peace process and maintaining the status of Northern Ireland as part of the United Kingdom.

Background:

The Red Hand Defenders are also referred to as 'RHD'. They are a loyalist paramilitary group which emerged following the series of violent clashes that occurred between loyalists and republicans as a result of the Dumcree crisis in July 1998. The violence began when the Protestant Orange Order was not allowed to march along its annual route in Portadown, Northern Ireland.

The RHD opposes the Irish Republican Army (IRA) and its supporters. It has conducted a number of violent attacks which have included arson, bombings, and murders. It has focused its activity upon civilian targets such as homes, churches, and private businesses. Its activities have been closely associated with other loyalist paramilitary groups operating in Northern Ireland specifically having close links with the Ulster Defence Association (UDA) and the Loyalist Volunteer Force (LVF), all of which are outlawed terrorist organizations being proscribed under the provisions of the Terrorism Act 2000.

During July 2002 a spate of shootings in Belfast resulted in the murder of Gerard Lawlor, a 19-year-old father who was walking home from Antrim Road towards the Whitewell Road when he was attacked at midnight. Witnesses close by to the incident heard four or five gun shots. Gerard Lawlor died at the scene. According to BBC reports on 22 July, members of RHD had admitted murdering a man in North Belfast during a night of sectarian violence. Irish Foreign Minister, Brien Cowen stated that:

> Last night's sickening murder of Gerald Lawlor, a young innocent man shot dead in a cowardly drive-by attack, is a stark reminder of where savage sectarian hatred can lead.

3.4.3 **Powers of arrest**

A broad power of arrest is provided under Section 41 of the Terrorism Act 2000. There is no requirement to fulfil any necessity test; only that officers reasonably suspect that the person is a terrorist. A 'terrorist' is defined as a person who is or has been involved in the commission, preparation or instigation of acts of terrorism or has committed an offence under the Act which includes amongst others, those linked to outlawed terrorists groups, terrorist property, weapons training and inciting terrorism.

POINT TO NOTE—SECTION 41

An arrest made under Section 41 should not be used indiscriminately. There must be real and reasonable suspicion. It is always advisable that wherever possible officers considering the use of these powers should contact local specialist units for advice, guidance, and support. Clearly, this will not always be operationally possible to achieve which is why knowledge of anti-terrorism legislation and confidence in its practical application is required by all police colleagues. In any event, an arrest of a person under Section 41 should be communicated to local specialist units as soon as practicable, time is very much of the essence and the sooner counter-terrorism officers can be informed the better.

See also 5.3.1.

3.4.4 **Detention of terrorist suspects**

An arrest under Section 41 of the Terrorism Act 2000 triggers other powers and procedures which are vital not only for the investigation but the treatment and detention of the suspect. The Terrorism Act 2000 under Schedule 8 provides specific procedures for the detention, treatment, review and extension of terrorist suspects which is the key difference between a criminal and a terrorist investigation. The Codes of Practice, Code C to the Police and Criminal Evidence 1984 deals with the detention, treatment and questioning of persons by police officers which also contained guidance on how to manage a suspect detained for terrorism.

From midnight on 24 July 2006 this changed and the detention, treatment and questioning of terrorist suspects is now governed by a new code, Code H. This new code only applies whereby an individual has been arrested under Section 41. The provisions of the code do not apply to any arrests made under other terrorist legislation.

See also **Appendix 1** and **5.3**.

3.4.5 **Stop and search**

Specific stop and search powers are provided under Sections 42, 43 and 44 of the Terrorism Act 2000. The Home Office have provided detailed guidance for police officers in relation to the appropriate use of terrorism stop and search powers. It specifically highlights that stop and search activity has raised concerns over the disproportionality of its use among black and ethnic minority groups. This is liable to be accentuated by its use in relation to terrorism, especially when countering the threat from international groups. It is not appropriate to stereotype people of a certain faith or ethnicity as terrorists but these factors may be significant when taken as part of a combination of other factors. It is known that some terrorists will adopt behaviours and appearances typical of local cultures to avoid identification and it is not therefore appropriate to use these factors as a preconceived basis for searches. It is important to remember that where profiles of suspects are available, they are subject to change and can become quickly outdated.

All officers conducting stop and search powers under terrorism legislation should be aware of the cultural sensitivities surrounding the removal of clothing and especially headgear. A thorough understanding of religious and cultural differences is an essential element of policing communities sensitively but effectively.

POINTS TO NOTE—PLAN

Prior to exercising stop and search powers under terrorism legislation police officers should seek to '**PLAN**' their action and be able to answer the following questions;

Proportionality

Is the use of the power a proportionate response?

Legality

Does the available information and intelligence establish appropriate legal grounds?

Accountability

Are decision-making and other processes documented and auditable?

Necessity

Is the use of the power necessary in the circumstances?

POINT TO NOTE—LORD CARLILE'S ANNUAL REPORT

Lord Carlile of Beriew is the government's independent reviewer of terrorism legislation. In his annual report on the operation of the Terrorism Act 2000 during 2007, in particular on stop and search powers under Sections 44 to 47, he warns that future authorizations are to be examined more critically by the Home Office and that those charged with a responsibility for deploying these powers on the ground must be accurately briefed, adequately trained and know what they are doing and why they are doing it, if the police service is to avoid future criticisms over its misuse of the power.

Lord Carlile indicates that he expects this power to be used less and consideration should be given to the use of other more appropriate stop and search powers where applicable, making the point that while arrests for other crimes have followed searches under the section, none of the many thousands of searches has ever related to a terrorism offence. He questions the need for certain authorizations in some force areas, whilst acknowledging that this power remains necessary and proportionate to the continuing and serious risk of terrorism.

3.4.6 Control orders

When the police service investigates terrorism its primary objective is to obtain evidence to put the suspected offenders through the criminal justice system. But what happens when a situation arises where there is intelligence but insufficient evidence to pursue a conviction through the criminal justice system process?

There are occasions where intelligence comes to the attention of the authorities but for various reasons it cannot be used. This may be due to legislative constraints or for matters of security. Where there is a strong intelligence case of such a nature that the authorities have formed reasonable grounds for suspecting that an individual presents a real threat to the public then a mechanism must be available to protect the public from harm. It is for such circumstances that control orders were introduced under the provisions of the Prevention of Terrorism Act 2005. There are two types of control order; derogating and non-derogating. They are defined as follows in the table below:

Table 3.5: Control Orders

Derogating Control Order	Derogating is one whereby the Secretary of State has to infringe the operation of the Human Rights Act 1998 (right to liberty) in order to impose it. This would effectively be such as 'house arrest'. It is worth noting that there has not been a derogating control order imposed under this legislation to date.
Non-Derogating Control Order	Non-derogating orders are where a set of 'conditions' are imposed on the individual restricting their life and movement. Under a non-derogating control order the individual is released with obligations in order for the authorities to try and keep some control over their movements and actions to prevent them continuing to be involved in alleged terrorism offences.

Control orders are a controversial piece of legislation as they directly challenge civil liberties and human rights. The key issue is that an individual subject to a control order is not involved in any criminal proceedings but is effectively living under an order from the court which restricts their lives. Despite much heated debate in the Houses of Parliament about the use of control orders, they actually provide a far greater solution to the immediate threat from international terrorism than other alternatives such as internment that has previously been used following heightened threats from terrorism. In times of severe threat every government has to do what it believes to be necessary to protect its people. This is not to say that control orders have been completely successful; on the contrary, intense media spotlight on this issue has highlighted deficiencies. During May 2007 the Daily Mail reported that three terror suspects who were subject of control orders had gone on the run. Shadow Home Secretary David Davis said; 'People are placed on control orders on the basis that they are terror suspects who pose a serious risk. It is shocking that another three have absconded'.

See also **5.6**.

3.4.6.1 *Control order process*

The Secretary of State will apply to the court to impose a control order based on available intelligence. In an emergency the Secretary of State also has the power to make a provisional order although this will have to be reviewed by the court within seven days. The control orders can prohibit or restrict an individual's movement or impose an obligation on them to remain in a particular place. A control order may also require an individual to co-operate with any specific monitoring arrangements such as submitting to any required procedures, wearing or using any apparatus and complying with any directions. In addition a control order may also require an individual to provide advance information about their proposed movements or other activities. The Act provides a list of potential obligations which may also be imposed which include restrictions on their possessions or specified articles such as the use of the internet. Restrictions may also cover aspects of their work, associations, or communications. A control order may also restrict an individual's place of residence and curfew and restrict what persons can visit their premises. It may also stipulate specific access to the premises such as visits from the police and allow those persons to search their premises or remove any articles. The obligations which can be imposed are very stringent which is why every control order has to be judged on its owns merits focusing upon the threat and risk posed by the individual in question. The obligations of a control order are therefore specifically tailored to the individual case.

The conduct of the police in ensuring compliance with the order needs to be carried out reasonably so that these powers retain their integrity and the public has confidence that they are the best method of reducing risks. Lord Carlile, the Independent Reviewer of Terrorism Legislation submits an annual report to the government concerning the use and application of control orders. In response to Lord Carlile's review of control orders in February

2008 Home Secretary Jacqui Smith stated that 'control orders remain the best available means for managing the risk'.

3.4.7 Encouraging terrorism

The images of individuals openly supporting and encouraging terrorist activity in a public forum have been broadcast on British media over recent years. Following 9/11 and the London 7/7 bombings public speeches made by the likes of Abu Hamza Al Masri and Omar Bakri Muhammad selling their strong and opinionated messages has made national headlines.

The introduction of the Terrorism Act 2006 extended police powers to counter the threat from international terrorism. Section 1 of the Act focuses on deterring those who facilitate terrorism and those who encourage others to become terrorists. The Act makes it a criminal offence directly or indirectly to encourage the commission, preparation, or instigation of acts of terrorism or to disseminate terrorist publications. This offence includes statements or publications that glorify terrorism and carries a maximum penalty of seven years imprisonment. The introduction of this Act attracted much attention for the broad nature of its wording.

See also **4.3.1**.

POINT TO NOTE—SECTION 1 AND FREE SPEECH

Care must be taken when considering the use of Section 1 of the Terrorism Act 2006 and the issue of the right to free speech. The Crown Prosecution Service provides clear guidance on this issue stating that free speech includes the right to offend, furthermore the courts have ruled that behaviour that is merely annoying, rude or offensive may not constitute a criminal offence.

The wording of the Act states that a person may commit an offence whether intentional or reckless, members of the public are directly or indirectly encouraged or induced by the statement to commit, prepare or instigate acts of terrorism. In other words, it is not necessary to prove that their words or actions would definitely result in an act of terrorism.

During August 2005, the then Home Secretary Charles Clarke took a further step towards pursuing terrorists and extremists by publishing a list of certain types of 'Unacceptable Behaviours'. These behaviours form the basis for excluding and deporting individuals from the UK. It is aimed at those who would attempt to promote terrorism or provoke others to commit terrorist acts.

The list covers any non-UK citizen whether in the UK or abroad who uses any means or medium which includes writing, producing, publishing or distributing material, public speaking including preaching, the running of a website and using a position of responsibility such as teacher, community or youth leader to express views which:

- foment, justify or glorify terrorist violence in furtherance of particular beliefs
- seek to provoke others to terrorist acts
- foment other serious criminal activity or seek to provoke others to serious criminal acts
- foster hatred which might lead to inter-community violence in the UK.

3.4.8 Terrorism training

Over recent years there has been considerable focus upon terrorist training camps. It is important to understand what may constitute such a place. On one level they can relate to camps in the mountain regions of Pakistan or Afghanistan where individuals attend from all over the world. These camps are located in secure locations, they are lightweight, very mobile and often move around to avoid identification and capture. Given the terrain in which they are located they are also difficult to track by military units. It is estimated that at the time of the 9/11 attacks in 2001 there were over 120 training camps in Afghanistan alone. Individuals attending these camps would typically be trained for between one and six months. At the other end of the scale terrorist training camps may relate to an outward bound centre or paint-balling facilities located anywhere in the UK.

See also **4.3.7**.

POINT TO NOTE—TERRORIST TRAINING CAMPS

So what makes a paint-balling centre into a 'terrorist training camp'?

Anti-terrorism legislation relating to terrorist training revolves around the purpose why individuals are at that place at that time. Therefore, terrorist training camps do not need to be clandestine in nature and may be carried out in what is effectively the complete open. Persons attending these type of 'camps' do so in full view of everyone. Outward bound and activity centres are clearly legitimate ventures, however, it is the reason why these people attend which may bring them into conflict with the law.

See also **4.3.8**.

3.4.8.1 *Methodology*

So why would persons who are intent on radicalizing individuals, take them paint-balling or to a white water rafting centre, for example? Counter-terrorism investigations in the UK have revealed that a key purpose is to identify potential individuals, who are often vulnerable young men, who might be susceptible to radicalization by the 'mentor' of the group. There would be no point sending a young western male out to a mountain-based training camp in Afghanistan if he could not cope with the hardship of an outward bound centre in the UK. Many of the young people training in the UK have been brought up in relative comfort and trekking over hills and sleeping in tents may well be a novelty, but in reality is it something they could regularly adapt to? Many of these young people may wish to return home to their creature comforts of computers, video games, and DVDs. If the UK climate presents a tough challenge for some of them it provides an early indication of whether they could operate in harsher conditions to be found in Afghanistan training camps.

POINT TO NOTE—TYPES OF TRAINING

Police officers working in both urban and rural areas must be aware that terrorist training at the lowest level in the UK is most likely to involve outdoor activities as a means of testing potential recruits. It may not just relate to physical training; it can involve training via the use of books, manuals or via the use of the internet. It can also be conducted via 'virtual training camps' through a 'chat room' with individuals who do not know each other, have never met each other and who are potentially thousands of miles apart.

3.4.9 Ports and border policing

Policing the ports and borders of the UK is an integral part of protecting national security. There has been a Special Branch presence at UK ports since the Metropolitan Police Service first stationed its officers at 13 West and South Coast Ports to counter the subversive activities of anarchists intent on disrupting Queen Victoria's Jubilee celebrations in 1887. The Metropolitan Police

Service maintained its presence at UK sea and airports until the expansion of the National Ports Scheme during the 1970s and 1980s when provincial police forces, having formed their own Special Branches, then assumed responsibility for the policing of ports from a national security context.

Today, in the UK, there are over 150 licensed civil aerodromes handling in excess of 200 million passengers, 60 unlicensed airports, over 70 commercially significant sea ports handling over 50 million ferry passengers and around 600 million tonnes of freight per annum, not to mention, international rail termini, a further 3000 airfields or airstrips, a comparable number of small harbours, ports and jetties and our only international land border between Northern Ireland and the Republic of Ireland.

Policing these sites is the responsibility of Ports Officers who are warranted officers enjoying the same powers and privileges as their uniformed colleagues. The work of Ports Units is co-ordinated by ACPO (TAM). Each Ports Unit is lead by a Senior Ports Officer (SPO) who is usually the rank of Sergeant or Inspector, the rank depending upon the size and structure of the Ports Unit assessed by the size of its port policing requirements which include the number and type of actual ports, passengers, freight volumes, destinations and the potential threat to the UK posed by those or connecting destinations. Ports Officers acquire examination powers under Schedule 7 of the Terrorism Act 2000 and a code of practice for Examining Officers.

POINT TO NOTE—PORTS WORK

The Ports Officer, together with the assistance of colleagues from the UK Border Agency are effectively the first and the last line of defence in the fight against terrorism at ports and borders. The emphasis in ports work is now very much focused upon joint, smarter, intelligence led and technology driven working but there will always be a place for practical policing for those engaged at our ports and borders.

See also **5.4**

3.4.10 **Schedule 7 to the Terrorism Act 2000**

Schedule 7 to the Terrorism Act 2000 is reserved exclusively for deployment at UK ports and borders and is designed to identify those persons who are or have been concerned in the Commission, Preparation or Instigation of Acts of Terrorism (CPI). This is the power to 'examine' and an accompanying Code of Practice (CoP) for 'Examining Officers' (EO) under the Terrorism Act 2000, puts flesh on the bones of the legislation giving guidance on the conduct of an 'examination'. The legislation not only applies to UK sea and air ports, but also to the international rail termini in the UK associated with the Channel Tunnel and the land border between Northern Ireland (NI) and the Republic of Ireland (RoI). A draft revised CoP was issued for public consultation by the Home Office in 2007.

See also **Appendix 4**

The conventional meaning of what constitutes a 'port' presents no problems, however, the Schedule refers to a 'port' as a 'place' where an EO believes a person has gone for the purpose of embarking on or has arrived on disembarking from, a ship or aircraft. A 'place' in NI is in the 'border area' if it is within a mile of the border with the RoI, and in relation to cross-border train journeys, it is the first place in NI at which a train stops to set down passengers. Consequently definitions of a 'port' can be many and varied; eg a private helipad in the' back garden' of a private house, a small coastal jetty, even a suitable beach, or a farmer's field.

An EO requires no grounds to justify examining a person, but any questioning must be directed towards determining if that person appears to be someone who is or has been concerned in the commission, preparation, or instigation of acts of terrorism and if exclusively so used, the EO need not caution the examinee, unless he or she is being arrested. However, an EO must believe that a person's presence at a port or the border area is connected with his or her entering or leaving or travelling by air within, Great Britain (GB) or NI. There is no requirement to tape record an examination unless the examinee has been 'detained' under the schedule and is at a police station.

An examination commences as soon as a person or vehicle has been stopped and screening questions have been asked. The term 'examination' is a unique concept and is not restricted to an interview. In determining whether a person is or has been concerned in CPI terrorism there are powers to stop a person or vehicle, detain that person and authorise their removal from a vehicle, ship or aircraft. Additionally, an EO may search a person and his or her belongings whether they are with him or her, about to be on, are on, or have been on, a ship or aircraft and, for that purpose, may also search the ship or aircraft. The powers extend to boarding and searching ships, aircraft and vehicles in order to examine goods and containers, empowers other persons to carry out searches and examinations of goods on behalf of the EO, and in securing compliance, a constable may use reasonable force in exercising a power conferred under the Schedule.

The terms 'examination' and 'detention' do not mean the same, the schedule proposes two concepts—the first, an examination where the subject is fully co-operative and willing. The CoP requires that the length of this examination should be kept to the minimum practicable, and that after one hour the examinee be served with a Notice of Examination detailing the duties and the rights of the examinee. The second is an examination under detention, where the subject is unco-operative and unwilling to remain. The EO may 'detain' the subject, serve notices of 'examination' and 'detention', and continue the examination. The length of the examination should be kept to the minimum practicable however detention (and the examination) expires nine hours from the time the examination originally commenced.

Whilst in detention, a person may be photographed, measured, or 'identified'. If detained at a police station, he may also be fingerprinted and intimate and non-intimate samples taken. Detention in this case is not the same as detention under the provisions of the Police and Criminal Evidence Act 1984. Neither examination or detention (nor any combination of examination or detention) should exceed nine hours.

Examinations need not be conducted at the podium in the full glare of the public. The CoP advises police officers to make every reasonable effort to exercise powers in a way that minimizes embarrassment or offence to a person who may subsequently have no terrorist connections; this may include questioning and searches, etc in a private room. Examinees have the right to legal advice, to have someone informed, and to consult the CoP. The draft revised CoP proposes that an examination will not be suspended pending the arrival of a solicitor. During examination the subject is required to; give any information requested by the EO, produce a valid passport with a photograph or some other identity document, state whether he or she possesses those documents and produce them when requested.

The sanction for wilfully failing to comply with a duty, contravening a prohibition, obstructing or frustrating a search or examination under this Schedule is three months' imprisonment, and/or a level 4 fine.

POINT TO NOTE—POLICE, PORTS DUTY, AND SCHEDULE 7

Police officers are from time to time asked to perform duties at ports in addition to those officers permanently based there. These duties may be as a result of a specific local, regional or national operation or at time of a heightened national threat. It is important that all police officers are aware of their broad powers under Schedule 7 of the Terrorism Act 2000 which represents the first opportunity of disrupting terrorist activity upon entry to the UK.

See also **Appendix 4.**

3.5 Practical Counter-Terrorism Policing

Countering terrorism and extremism is a team effort. Terrorist activity is taking place within our communities and police officers should not believe that the area in which they work is immune from terrorist activity. Rural parts of the UK as well as densely populated towns and cities all make attractive locations for terrorists to operate. Simply hoping that the threat from terrorism will not result in activity in your communities or assuming that you will not be attacked because you have recently sustained an attack are the very complacencies that terrorists will exploit. Policing terrorism in the UK is developing, it is developing in response to the severe level of threat we continue to endure. Countering terrorism is being woven into the very fabric of policing. All police officers can contribute to countering terrorism and violent extremism but an understanding and awareness of counter-terrorism investigations, forensics, security and the 'need to know' principles are required.

3.5.1 Counter-terrorism investigations

Terrorism is a crime, but counter-terrorism investigations are very different to other types of criminal investigation. There are three key differences to consider. First of all, counter-terrorism investigations have a global reach. Every major counter-terrorism investigation has the potential for enquiries to be conducted in multiple locations. One enquiry for one single terrorist may lead investigators to several forces in separate regions of the UK to numerous countries in Europe, the Middle East and around the world as they track movements and associates. It may become evident in the very early stages of enquiries that the investigation has a global reach simply through electronic telecommunications. Secondly, the scale of an investigation can rapidly grow as multiple suspects are identified with intended targets not just in the UK but destinations anywhere in the world. To resource this level of investigation where there is a critical requirement for intelligence and evidence capture can quickly go beyond the capacity of major incident teams established for the most serious criminal offences. Finally, the complexity of such an investigation is not only evident in the cross-border of transnational protocols but that intelligence and evidence is being collected at the same time. Evidence is required to support successful prosecutions and intelligence may be required urgently to support ongoing covert operations for intelligence agencies around the world.

Counter-terrorism investigations are broadly split into two categories, covert and overt. A covert intelligence gathering operation is where the suspect is assumed to be unaware of activity which infringes upon their private life. This activity in the main involves some type of surveillance activity. Threats to national security, which include terrorism, espionage, and counter-proliferation is the primary responsibility of the Security Service MI5 as they are the lead intelligence gathering agency in the UK for these matters. The Security Service cannot achieve all of this on its own and so is supported by specialist police counter-terrorism units. The Security Service MI5 and the police service are two separate bodies each with their own responsibilities and structures. During covert terrorist investigations these two organizations combine their efforts and capabilities in order to achieve the common goal of preventing terrorist attacks. Throughout the course of a covert investigation positive action may have to be taken to arrest suspects for terrorist-related activity. The police service has the responsibility to conduct overt investigations and build prosecution cases as the Security Service does not have executive powers. The majority of arrests for terrorism offences are pre-planned operations carried out by specialist units but this will not always be the case as front line officers encounter terrorist activity.

POINT TO NOTE—INVESTIGATIVE WORK

Despite counter-terrorism investigations having reach, scale and complexity beyond that experienced in other large scale enquiries, it relies upon thorough investigative police work. Investigators in specialist counter-terrorism units do receive specific training to perform their roles but it is their attention to detail combined with a professional and practical application to their role that is key to investigating terrorism, skills that are commonly shared throughout the police service.

3.5.2 Forensic awareness

A major issue during terrorist investigations is forensic contamination, where the presence of some material which links the suspect to a scene or item is called into question. This is a very important area for police officers to consider as it is often the action taken by officers arresting a suspect or seizing items that allows doubt to be shed on the validity of where the material originated and the possibility of its being picked up somewhere else. In terrorism cases very small traces of explosives can result in a successful conviction if there are no contamination issues. A wealth of forensic experience exists within counter terrorism units and they should always be contacted as they have tried and tested methods of forensic recovery which have been developed over years of operational practice to manage the risk of contamination and transfer issues. In January 2007, the 'New Scientist' reported that:

> No one knows how easily such transfer of material could take place. But we can be certain that if anyone ends up in court with extremely small traces of explosives as part of evidence against them. Lawyers are going to have fun. [They went on to say that] ruling out accidental contamination might require knowledge of where the accused had been and some kind of statistical analysis of the chance of picking up an incriminating chemical.

Having an awareness of forensic issues is therefore an important part of terrorist investigations. During pre-planned operations careful consideration is exercised in the development of a forensic strategy where risks are managed.

The primary function should always be the protection of life and the evacuation of casualties before the preservation of any evidence. It will not always be possible to obtain the specialist advice and guidance of counter-terrorism forensic teams when confronted with a situation that is unfolding in front of police officers responding to or dealing with an incident. It is important that police officers exercise caution and risk assess their action, especially where unknown substances or chemicals are suspected. The action police officers take can be a crucial element in terrorist investigations. Michael Mansfield QC states that, 'forensic scientists rarely disagree on the facts, only on the interpretation of the facts. In other words not that the traces were there, but how they got there'.

3.5.3 Security

The security measures the police service puts in place to protect its assets is vital to the success of not only countering terrorism and extremism but of all other types of criminal activity. The police, like many other organizations invests millions of pounds on protective security including swipe card entry systems, CCTV, biometric identification, and information technology firewalls. All of these layers of protection are necessary to prevent hostile attacks from individuals with ulterior motives who seek information to further their cause. Despite this level of investment breaches of security occur because all protective measures are prone to some aspect of human behaviour. For example, why have an expensive alarm if someone neglects to set it? Why have biometric entry systems if people do not challenge someone they do not recognize tail-gaiting them inside? Developing a security culture and maintaining its effectiveness within the workplace is something police officers may all from time to time take for granted but it is an important element of police work. If police officers cannot protect the information they hold countering terrorism, extremism and protecting national security becomes increasingly difficult.

Police colleagues all have an important part to play in adopting and enforcing security measures. People are the most important asset that any organization has yet they are also the most vulnerable and they pose the greatest risk to security protocols. Every employee of every organization has gigabytes of information stored within their heads; information which, if accessed, could lead to serious compromise. Police officers need to understand that they have privileged access to sensitive information which terrorist and extremist groups would only be too willing to exploit.

One of the very first security measures organizations employ is the vetting of staff prior to confirmation of their new role as part of the recruitment process. It is wise to check references and other credentials to ensure as far as possible that the new member of any team is who they purport to be. Vetting is becoming increasingly robust but it only offers an 'acceptable' level of assurance that the applicant is 100% genuine, it can never provide an absolute guarantee of an individual's integrity or appropriateness for their new role. Very often companies recruit people because of another's personal recommendation or assurances are sought from friends or colleagues of the applicant. The new internet social networking sites provide a wealth of information about people. Websites that offer to re-unite you with old friends and colleagues rely upon its customers to disclose information about themselves, their family and their work. Police officers must exercise caution when choosing to establish such sites as information may be used by individuals for a variety of reasons. Police officers need to assess what information they may disclose on such sites and should ask themselves:

- What information have I put on these sites?
- What have I disclosed about my work?
- What have my friends or family put on these sites about me?

The police service has a duty of care to its employees, but in turn, police colleagues have a responsibility to adopt the very basic levels of confidentiality to minimize the risk to themselves, their colleagues, and the wider assets of the police. It is true that 'loose lips sink ships' and most importantly police colleagues may never realize the full impact of their disclosure.

Case Study—Wilful Misconduct In Public Office

During August 2007 The Times reported that an ex-police officer had been jailed for leaking terror attack secrets. The retired officer who had returned to the police as a member of support staff admitted wilful misconduct in public office by disclosing secret documents to a journalist. Information from this document was published in the Sunday Times in April 2007, information which was traced to a leaked report from the Joint Terrorism Analysis Centre (JTAC), part of the Intelligence Machinery in the UK. Upon sentencing Mr Justice Gross said: 'Disclosure of this nature should and ought to attract immediate custody.'

The Crown Prosecution Service, represented by Jonathan Sharpe stated that:

this is a report of intelligence that pools intelligence from every friendly power. It is unvarnished intelligence and that leads to its disclosure being so potentially damaging.

POINT TO NOTE—SECURITY ISSUES AND DISCLOSURE

The security issues concerning this disclosure are far broader than the immediate threats to the sources of information contained within the JTAC report.

There is an increasing willingness within the counter-terrorism environment to share sensitive information. This information is painstakingly assessed and where appropriate sanitized to protect its origins. This move towards sharing information was identified by the 9/11 Commission who highlighted deficiencies in the US government's response to the 2001 terrorist attacks. Despite declaring a willingness to share more information breaches in security and leaking of national secrets frustrates this process.

3.5.4 Need to know

There are two main reasons why sensitive areas of policing operate a 'need to know' principle. First, that an individual who knows everything about a specific operation is vulnerable. Secondly, the risks to the operation and individuals involved require to be tightly managed as compromise would lead to damaging consequences. All police colleagues should be aware of the potential consequences that could result following compromise of protectively marked assets. Information the police service and other law enforcement partners possess is assessed under the Government Protective Marking Scheme. This scheme provides a system which enables agencies to transfer information to each other whilst maintaining its protection. It also provides guidance highlighting the potential consequences if protectively marked information is compromised. The scheme states that the very lowest levels of protectively marked information if compromised could cause substantial stress to individuals, facilitate the commission of a crime, or prejudice an investigation. The very highest levels of protectively marked information if compromised may potentially raise international tension, directly threaten life and cause grave damage to the security of the UK. It is these factors which evidence the importance of the 'need to know' principles.

POINT TO NOTE—NEED TO KNOW PRINCIPLE

If there is not an operational need for all police officers to know about a specific operation or piece of information it is for a good reason.

Police officers may wish to know what is happening, they may be intrigued as to what is taking place but police officers must accept that the 'need to know' principle is there to protect everyone. Minimizing the risk of compromise is paramount and all police officers have a responsibility to keep all secrets secret.

3.5.5 Anti-terrorism hotline

One of the most important roles police officers and members of the public can conduct in support of countering terrorism is to report suspicious activity. This is vital not just for prevention of anti-social behaviour, public order or the detection of serious and organized crime but also for terrorism and violent extremism. The police service believes that communities will defeat terrorism and are now asking the public to trust their instincts and pass on information which could help stop terrorists in their tracks. Members of the public may unknowingly have information which could be a crucial piece of the investigative jigsaw. To achieve this however, police officers must be in a position to provide practical guidance and support to members of the public displaying a knowledge and understanding of terrorist-related activity. Police officers need to be aware of what the public should be alert to and what type of activity or incident should be reported. This will require officers to have an in depth knowledge of what their local force's intelligence requirements are for countering terrorism and extremism which is outlined in local policing plans and force level control strategies. Police officers also need to develop a sense of what information is a priority which requires an initial assessment of its potential importance and what force protocols are in place to report such information.

Police officers need to encourage the public to be aware of what is happening around them and to think about anything or anybody that has struck them as unusual in their day-to-day lives. Police officers also need to ask members of the public to think carefully about anyone they know whose behavior has changed suddenly.

What has changed? Could it be significant? What about the people they associate with? Have they noticed activity where they live which is not the norm? National anti-terrorism awareness campaigns identify key issues for the public and the police which will assist in tackling terrorism which are included in the Checklist below.

Checklist—If you suspect it, report it

- Terrorists need transport—If you work in commercial vehicle hire or sales, has any rental made you suspicious?
- Terrorists use multiple identities—Do you know someone with documents using different names for no obvious reason?
- Terrorists need communication—Anonymous, pay-as-you-go and sim card mobile phones are typical. Have you seen someone with large quantities of mobile phones that has made you suspicious?
- Terrorists need information—Observation and surveillance help terrorists attacks. Have you seen anyone taking pictures of security arrangements?
- Terrorists use chemicals—Do you know of someone buying large or unusual quantities of chemicals for no obvious reason?
- Terrorists use protective equipment—Handling chemicals is dangerous. Maybe you have seen goggles or masks dumped somewhere?
- Terrorists need funding—Cheque and credit card fraud are ways terrorists generate cash. Have you seen any suspicious transactions?
- Terrorists use computers—Do you know someone who visits terrorist-related websites?
- Terrorists need to travel—Meetings, training, and planning can take place anywhere. Do you know someone who travels but is vague about where they are going?
- Terrorists need storage—Lock-ups, garages, and sheds can all be used to store equipment. Are you suspicious of anyone renting a commercial property?

POINT TO NOTE—TRUST YOUR INSTINCTS

If you suspect that any of the suspicious activity described in the Checklist is taking place, or have received reports from members of the public about such activity, think about terrorist tactics, trust your instincts, and report it. In an emergency, which is believed as presenting an immediate threat, such as a person observed acting suspiciously, or a vehicle, unattended package or bag which might pose an imminent danger, then the **999** emergency services telephone number should be used by members of the public at all times. There should be no delay in responding to such a perceived threat. The confidential anti-terrorism hotline number, **0800 789 321**, which is staffed around the clock by specialist counter-terrorism police officers and staff, provides an additional service and is waiting to receive information. As an alternative to speaking directly to police officers or staff an online form is also available to complete which can be located at <http://www.met.police.uk/so/athotline>.

Police officers must be aware that the anti-terrorism hotline service is available for members of the public to confidentially report terrorism-related information. Members of the public may be concerned and have reservations about contacting the police, either because their friends or family may find out, or their suspicions may prove to have innocent explanations but police officers must reassure the public that all calls and information received by the anti-terrorism hotline number are treated in the strictest of confidence. All information received is thoroughly researched and investigated before any police action is taken.

Part 2

Legislative and Procedural Content

Chapter 4

Terrorist Activities

4.1 Introduction—Definition of Terrorism/Terrorist

Section 1 of the Terrorism Act 2000 is central to the current anti-terrorism legislation. It defines the term 'terrorism'. This definition is used not only in the Terrorism Act 2000, but also the Anti-terrorism, Crime and Security Act 2001, the Prevention of Terrorism Act 2005, the Terrorism Act 2006 and the Counter-Terrorism Act 2008. It has also been included in a number of different recent Acts, for example in the Civil Contingencies Act 2004.

Note that there is no general 'offence of terrorism' as such. The commission of an act of terrorism is not an offence, but the commission, preparation or instigation of acts of terrorism is an element of a number of specific offences, for example training for terrorism (see **4.3.7**), possession of an article for a purpose connected with terrorism (see **4.3.10**) and collection of information (see **4.3.11**). 'Act of terrorism' is also referred to in legislation which provides police powers, such as the power of arrest in section 41 of the Terrorism Act 2000 (see **5.3.1**).

4.1.1 Terrorism

Terrorism means the use or threat of actions where

1. the action
   - involves serious violence against a person *or*
   - involves serious damage to property *or*
   - endangers a person's life, other than that of the person committing the action *or*
   - creates a serious risk to the health or safety of the public or a section of the public *or*

- is designed seriously to interfere with or seriously disrupt an electronic system **and**
2. the use or threat is designed to influence the government or an international governmental organisation or to intimidate the public or a section of the public **or** involves the use of firearms or explosives **and**
3. the use or threat is made for the purpose of advancing a political, religious, racial [see note (g) below] or ideological cause.

Terrorism Act 2000, s 1(1) and (2)

Meanings

References to action, persons, property, the public and the government are not restricted to the United Kingdom but include actions outside the United Kingdom and property or persons wherever situated as well as the public or the government of foreign countries (Terrorism Act 2000, s 1(4)).

Actions taken for the purpose of terrorism include actions taken for the benefit of a proscribed organization, s 1(5) (see **4.2.1**).

Action

Includes omission (Terrorism Act 2000, s 121).

Firearm

Includes an air gun or air pistol (Terrorism Act 2000, s 121).

Explosive

Means—

(a) an article or substance manufactured for the purpose of producing a practical effect by explosion,
(b) materials for making an article or substance within paragraph (a),
(c) anything used or intended to be used for causing or assisting in causing an explosion, and
(d) a part of anything within paragraph (a) or (c) (Terrorism Act 2000, s 121).

Property

Includes property wherever situated and whether real or personal, heritable (ie inheritable) or moveable, and things in action (eg copyright, trademark, rights of repayment of loaned money) and other intangible (eg goodwill of business) or incorporeal property (eg mortgages, leases, etc) (Terrorism Act 2000, s 121).

Notes

(a) The definition of terrorism is very wide. It basically includes any use or threat of violence for political, but also for religious, racial or ideological reasons. It also covers acts that are not in themselves violent, but which may nevertheless have a devastating impact, such as disrupting key computer systems or interfering with the supply of water or power where life, health or safety may be put at risk. Some acts will also constitute criminal offences; other acts, such as those involving 'endangering another person's life' or 'creating a serious risk to the health or safety of the public or a section of the public' may involve conduct that would not itself be a criminal offence.

(b) The use or threat of action amounts to terrorism if it meets three elements. First, the action involves serious violence, damage, risk to the public, etc. Secondly, the use or threat of action has a certain purpose: to influence the government or intimidate the public (this does not have to be met if the action involves the use of firearms or explosives). And thirdly, the purpose of the threat is to advance a political, religious or ideological cause.

(c) The definition of terrorism is not restricted to 'domestic' terrorism; it extends to terrorist activities in the UK and abroad. This reflects the international nature of terrorism, and perhaps also the fact, that the UK wants to avoid becoming or appearing to be a safe haven for foreign terrorists wherever they want to or have committed their acts. Action against terrorism within a country's borders is also required by international law under UN Security Council Resolution 1373 of 2001. Many terrorism offences cover acts done abroad. See also **5.7.1**.

(d) The Terrorism Act 2006 amended the definition of terrorism to include the use or threat of action to influence international governmental organizations, such as the United Nations. This amendment eliminated the disparity between definitions of terrorism in UK law and the equivalent definitions in various international conventions.

(e) Campaigns using firearms or explosives are deemed to be terrorism whether or not the action is designed to influence the government or intimidate the public.

(f) See also Concept of Terrorism **1.1**, Terrorism Classification **1.2**, Terrorism Characteristics **1.3** and Terrorist Motivations **1.4**.

(g) *Counter-Terrorism Act 2008*—Section 75 amended the definition of terrorism to include the use or threat of action for the purpose of advancing a racial cause. Although a racial cause will in most cases be subsumed within a political or ideological cause, this amendment is designed to put the matter beyond doubt that such a clause is included.

Related cases

R v F [2007] EWCA Crim 243 The phrase 'government of a country other than the United Kingdom' in s 1(4) of the Terrorism Act 2000 is not restricted to representative or democratic governments. The meaning of the phrase is plain enough. It applies to all countries, even those which are governed by tyrants and dictators, such as Libya. There is no exemption from criminal liability for terrorist activities which are motivated or said to be morally justified by the alleged nobility of the terrorist cause. The terrorism legislation has an international dimension and citizens of certain countries governed by dictators are not excluded from the legal protection from terrorist activities. In recognition of this wide reach, the prosecution of some offences based on foreign actions must have the consent of the Attorney General (Terrorism Act 2006, s 19). See **5.7.4**.

PNLD reference numbers

D8701, C1441

4.1.2 **Acts of terrorism**

Acts of terrorism include anything constituting an **action** taken for the purposes of terrorism, within the meaning of the Terrorism Act 2000 (Terrorism Act 2006, s 20(2)).

That means it also includes actions taken for the purpose of a proscribed organization, Terrorism Act 2000, s 5(1), see **4.2.1**

Act/action

Includes omission (Terrorism Act 2000, s 121).

4.1.3 **Terrorist**

'Terrorist' means a person who is or has been concerned in the commission, preparation, or instigation of acts of terrorism **or** has committed an offence under any of the following sections of the Terrorism Act 2000;

Section 11 membership of a proscribed organization (see **4.2.2**)

Section 12 support of a proscribed organization (see **4.2.3**)

Section 15 invite, receive, provide funds (see **4.4.2**)

Section 16 use, possess money/property (see **4.4.3**)

Section 17 being concerned in the raising of funds (see **4.4.4**)

Section 18 money laundering (see **4.4.5**)

Section 54 weapons training (see **4.3.9**)

Section 56 directing terrorist organization (see **4.2.5**)

Section 57 possession for terrorism purposes (see **4.3.10**)

Section 58 collection of information (see **4.3.11**)

Section 59 inciting terrorism overseas (England and Wales) (see **4.3.5**)

Section 60 inciting terrorism overseas (Northern Ireland)

Section 61 inciting terrorism overseas (Scotland)

Section 62 terrorist bombing (see **5.7.1**)

Section 63 terrorist finance offences (see **5.7.1**)

Meanings

Commission

The act of committing.

Preparation

The act of preparing.

Instigation

The act of instigating, inciting.

Terrorism (see **4.1.1**).

Note

This applies retrospectively and so applies to anyone who has been involved in the commission, instigation, or preparation of terrorism acts before this act came into force (Terrorism Act 2000, s 40(2)).

4.2 **Proscribed Organizations**

This section sets outs the law relating to proscribed organizations, which can be found in sections 3 and 11–13 of the Terrorism Act 2000. Detailed information on proscribed organizations can be found at **3.4.2**.

4.2.1 **Proscription procedure**

Section 3 of the Terrorism Act 2000 sets out the proscription of organizations. It states that any organization listed in Schedule 2 to the Terrorism Act 2000, or any organization that operates under the same name as one listed in Schedule 2, is proscribed and that the Secretary of State can add to, delete from or amend the list at any time. A full list of proscribed organizations can be found at **3.4.2.3**.

An **organisation** may only be **proscribed** if the Secretary of State believes that the organisation is concerned in terrorism.

Terrorism Act 2000, s 3(4)

  (5) An organisation is concerned in terrorism if it—
      (a) commits or participates in acts of **terrorism,**
      (b) prepares for terrorism,
      (c) promotes or encourages terrorism, or
      (d) is otherwise concerned in terrorism.
  (5A) The cases in which an organisation promotes or encourages terrorism for the purposes of subsection (5)(c) include any case in which activities of the organisation-
      (a) include the unlawful **glorification** of the commission or preparation (whether in the past, in the future or generally) of acts of terrorism; or
      (b) are carried out in a manner that ensures that the organisation is associated with **statements** containing any such glorification.
  (5B) The glorification of any conduct is unlawful for the purposes of subsection (5A) if there are persons who may become aware of it who could reasonably be expected to infer that what is being glorified, is being glorified as-
      (a) conduct that should be emulated in existing circumstances, or
      (b) conduct that is illustrative of a type of conduct that should be so emulated.

Terrorism Act 2000, s 3(5),(5A),(5B)

Meanings

Organization

Includes any association or combination of persons (Terrorism Act 2000, s 121). This is a very wide definition which could be used to describe anything from a large well-organized collection of people to a small gathering of two people.

Proscribed

Outlawed, prohibited.

Terrorism (see **4.1**).

Glorification

Includes any form of praise or celebration.

Statement

Includes a communication without words consisting of sounds or images or both (ie includes videos, DVDs and CDs).

PNLD reference number

D8702

4.2.2 **Membership of proscribed organizations**

Section 11 of the Terrorism Act 2000 creates the offence of being a member of a proscribed organization.

Offence

A person commits an offence if he belongs to or professes to belong to a proscribed organisation.

Terrorism Act 2000, s 11(1)

Points to prove

✓ date and location
✓ belongs/professes to belong to a
✓ proscribed organization

Meanings

Proscribed organization (see **4.2.1**).

Defence

It is a defence for a person charged with an offence under subsection (1)
to prove—
(a) that the organisation was not proscribed on the last (or only) occasion
   on which he became a member or professed to be a member, and
(b) that he has not taken part in the activities of the organisation at any
   time while it was proscribed.

Terrorism Act 2000, s 11(2)

The prosecution must prove in the first instance that the person was
a member of the proscribed group. The defendant must then prove
the defence on the balance of probabilities.

Police powers

Power of arrest—section 41 of the Terrorism Act 2000 (see **5.3.1**)

Power to stop and search—section 43 of the Terrorism Act 2000 (see
5.2.1)

Related cases

**Sheldrake v Director of Public Prosecutions; Attorney General's
Reference (No 4 of 2002) 2004] UKHL 43** The burden in s 11(2) is
an evidential one and not a legal one. In order to make it compliant
with article 6.2 of the Convention on Human Rights, the burden
had to be an evidential type which meant the defence only had to
raise it in evidence as an issue as to the matter in question fit for
consideration by the court.

R v Hundal and Dhaliwal [2004] EWCA Crim 389 If a person joins an
organization in a country where the organization is not proscribed, he
still commits an offence if he is a member of that organization when he
travels to the UK.

Notes

(a) Section 11(4) lists a number of Acts for which the term 'proscribed' means any of those Acts. Most of those Acts have been
   or will be repealed, but this Act allows them to be the basis for a
   prosecution if evidence of membership of a proscribed organization relates to a pre-Act period.

(b) This offence applies to acts done outside the UK regardless of the nationality of the offender, Terrorism Act 2006, s17 (see **5.7.1**).

(c) See also support of proscribed organization (**4.2.3**) and wearing of uniform (**4.2.4**).

(d) There is a potential appeal under s 7 of the Terrorism Act 2000 which relates to the deproscription procedure so it is important to make a note of exact dates and times when the person was allegedly a member of a proscribed organization.

(e) See **3.4.2.2** for practical information.

(f) *Counter-Terrorism Act 2008*—Sections 22 to 27 of the Act make provision for post-charge questioning of a person if the offence is a terrorism offence or the offence has a terrorist connection. This offence is a terrorism offence for the purposes of the Act. See PNLD ref S1136 to check whether these sections are in force, see also p xxvii for a summary of the Act.

(g) *Counter-Terrorism Act 2008*—Section 28 makes provisions for this offence to be tried in any place in the UK if it was committed in the UK. See PNLD ref S1136 to check whether this section is in force, see also p xxvii for a summary of the Act.

(h) *Counter-Terrorism Act 2008*—Part IV of and Schedules 4 and 5 to the Act (ss 40–61) make provisions for notification requirements and foreign travel restriction orders for persons sentenced or made subject of a hospital order for this offence. See PNLD ref S1136 to check whether these sections are in force, see also p xxvii for a summary of the Act.

PNLD reference numbers

H3551, D8703

DPP✓ **DPP/AG consent required:** Terrorism Act 2000, s 117 (see **5.7.4**).

🕐 **Time limit for prosecution:** None.

♿ **Summary:** Maximum six months' imprisonment and/or a fine not exceeding the statutory maximum.

🏛 **Indictment:** Maximum ten years' imprisonment and/or a fine.

4.2.3 **Support of proscribed organizations**

Section 12 of the Terrorism Act 2000 provides for the offences of supporting a proscribed organization. There are three offences created by this section; invite support for a proscribed organization; arrange, manage or assist in arranging or managing a meeting to support a proscribed organization, or address a meeting in support of a proscribed organization.

Offences

(1) A person commits an offence if—
   (a) he invites support for a **proscribed organisation**, and
   (b) the support is not, or is not restricted to, the provision of money or other property (within the meaning of section 15).
(2) A person commits an offence if he arranges, manages or assists in arranging or managing a **meeting** which he knows is—
   (a) to support a proscribed organisation,
   (b) to further the activities of a proscribed organisation, or
   (c) to be addressed by a person who belongs or professes to belong to a proscribed organisation.
(3) A person commits an offence if he addresses a meeting and the purpose of his address is to encourage support for a proscribed organisation or to further its activities.

Terrorism Act 2000, s 12(1)–(3)

Points to prove

Section 12(1)

- ✓ date and location
- ✓ invited support for
- ✓ proscribed organization
- ✓ other than support with money/other property

Section 12(2)

- ✓ date and location
- ✓ arranged/managed/assisted in arranging/managing a meeting
- ✓ which you knew
- ✓ was to support/further the activities of/be addressed by a person who belonged/professed to belong to
- ✓ a proscribed organization

Section 12(3)

- ✓ date and location
- ✓ addressed a meeting
- ✓ to encourage support for/further activities of
- ✓ a proscribed organization

Meanings

Proscribed organization (see **4.2.1**).

Meeting

Means a meeting of three or more persons, whether or not the public are admitted, Terrorism Act 2000, s 12(5).

Defence

Where a person is charged with an offence under subsection (2)(c) in respect of a private meeting it is a defence for him to prove that he had no reasonable cause to believe that the address mentioned in (2)(c) would support a proscribed organisation or its activities.

Terrorism Act 2000, s 12(4)

This defence would, for example cover meetings between a government representative and a member of a proscribed organization.

A meeting is private if the public are not admitted, Terrorism Act 2000, s 12(5).

Police powers

Power of arrest—section 41 of the Terrorism Act 2000 (see **5.3.1**)

Power to stop and search—section 43 of the Terrorism Act 2000 (see **5.2.1**)

Notes

(a) The offence in s 12(1) is concerned with support 'other than money or other property' as that kind of support is dealt with in s 15 (see **4.4.2**).

(b) The intention behind this offence is to prevent public address and debate which would support and/or further the activities of a proscribed organization.

(c) See also membership of proscribed organization (**4.2.2**) and wearing of a uniform (**4.2.4**).

(d) *Counter-Terrorism Act 2008*—Sections 22 to 27 of the Act make provision for post-charge questioning of a person if the offence is a terrorism offence or the offence has a terrorist connection. This offence is a terrorism offence for the purposes of the Act. See PNLD ref S1136 to check whether these sections are in force, see also p xxvii for a summary of the Act.

(e) *Counter-Terrorism Act 2008*—Section 28 makes provisions for this offence to be tried in any place in the UK if it was committed in the UK. See PNLD ref S1136 to check whether this section is in force, see also p xxvii for a summary of the Act.

(f) *Counter-Terrorism Act 2008*—Part IV of and Schedules 4 and 5 to the Act (ss 40–61) make provisions for notification requirements and foreign travel restriction orders for persons sentenced or made subject of a hospital order for this offence. See PNLD ref S1136 to check whether these sections are in force, see also p xxvii for a summary of the Act.

PNLD ref numbers

H3552, H3553, H3555, D8704

DPP✓ **DPP/AG consent required:** Terrorism Act 2000, s 117 (see **5.7.4**).

🕐 **Time limit for prosecution:** None.

♿ **Summary:** Maximum six months' imprisonment and / or a fine not exceeding the statutory maximum.

▦ **Indictment:** Maximum ten years' imprisonment and / or a fine.

4.2.4 **Uniforms**

Section 13 of the Terrorism Act 2000 provides for the offence of wearing a uniform or insignia of a proscribed organization.

Offence

A person in a **public place** commits an offence if he—

(a) wears an item of clothing, or

(b) wears, carries or displays an article, in such a way or in such circumstances as to arouse reasonable suspicion that he is a member or supporter of a **proscribed organisation**.

Terrorism Act 2000, s 13

Points to prove

✓ date and location

✓ in a public place

✓ wore an item of clothing/wore/carried/displayed an article

> ✓ in such way/circumstances as to arouse
> ✓ reasonable suspicion
> ✓ that you were a member/supporter
> ✓ of a proscribed organization

Meanings

Public place

Means a place to which members of the public have or are permitted to have access, whether or not for payment.

Proscribed organization (see **4.2.1**).

Police powers

Power of arrest—section 41 of the Terrorism Act 2000 (see **5.3.1**)

Power to stop and search—section 43 of the Terrorism Act 2000 (see **5.2.1**)

Notes

(a) This offence can only be committed in a public place.

(b) This offence is wider that the one contained in section 1 of the Public Order Act 1936 which covers only the wearing of a uniform. Items such as badges or caps can also be prohibited under section 13.

(c) See also membership of proscribed organization (**4.2.2**) and support of proscribed organization (**4.2.3**).

(d) *Counter-Terrorism Act 2008*—Sections 22 to 27 of the Act make provision for post-charge questioning of a person if the offence is a terrorism offence or the offence has a terrorist connection. This offence is a terrorism offence for the purposes of the Act. See PNLD ref S1136 to check whether these sections are in force, see also p xxvii for a summary of the Act.

(e) *Counter-Terrorism Act 2008*—Section 28 makes provisions for this offence to be tried in any place in the UK if it was committed in the UK. See PNLD ref S1136 to check whether this section is in force, see also p xxvii for a summary of the Act.

Related cases

Rankin v Murray (Procurator Fiscal, Ayr) 2004 SLT 1164, 2004 SCCR 422 (HC of Justiciary) (Sc) The wearing of jewellery which prominently bore the initials UVF (Ulster Volunteer Force, a proscribed organization) whilst in a ferry terminal travelling from Belfast to Troon was enough to commit an offence under section 13 of the Terrorism Act 2000 even though there was no evidence to suggest that the person was a member of the organization (see **3.4.2.2**).

PNLD ref numbers

H3556, H3557, D8705

DPP/AG consent required: Terrorism Act 2000, s 117 (see **5.7.4**).

Time limit for prosecution: 6 months.

 Summary only: Maximum six months' imprisonment and/ or a fine not exceeding level five on the standard scale.

4.2.5 **Directing a terrorist organization**

Section 56 of the Terrorism Act 2000 creates the offence of directing a terrorist organization.

> ### Offence
> A person commits an offence if he **directs, at any level**, the activities of an **organisation** which is concerned in the commission of acts of **terrorism**.
>
> Terrorism Act 2000, s 56

> ### Points to prove
> ✓ date and location
> ✓ directed the activities of
> ✓ an organization
> ✓ which was concerned in the commission
> ✓ of acts of terrorism

Meanings

Directs

Not defined in the Act but should be given its ordinary meaning. To give commands, directions, to take charge or control of, to manage conduct the affairs of. It seems to embody the attributes of being able to order other people and of commanding some obedience from them.

At any level

Not defined in the Act but is aimed to encompassing all those who direct be it at a local, regional, or national level.

Organization

Includes any association or combination of persons (Terrorism Act 2000, s 121). This is a very wide definition which could be used to describe anything from a large well-organized collection of people to a small gathering of two people. The offence is not confined to the direction of proscribed organizations.

Terrorism (see **4.1**).

Police powers

Power of arrest—section 41 of the Terrorism Act 2000 (see **5.3.1**)

Power to stop and search—section 43 of the Terrorism Act 2000 (see **5.2.1**)

Notes

(a) The organization does not have to be proscribed to commit this offence.

(b) This offence is aimed at those who do not directly get involved in the commission of acts of terrorism but direct others to do so and who under previous legislation have escaped prosecution.

(c) The offence only relates to the commission (committing) of acts of terrorism and not the instigation, preparation, or encouragement (see **4.1**).

(d) It is the organization that must be involved in the commission of acts of terrorism and not the direction given. Therefore this is a very wide-ranging offence that would cover orders that are unlawful (purchase of firearms for example) but also those that are lawful, such as directing someone one to buy provisions for the terrorist organization.

(e) *Counter-Terrorism Act 2008*—Sections 22 to 27 of the Act make provision for post-charge questioning of a person if the offence is a terrorism offence or the offence has a terrorist connection. This offence is a terrorism offence for the purposes of the Act. See PNLD ref S1136 to check whether these sections are in force, see also p xxvii for a summary of the Act.

(f) *Counter-Terrorism Act 2008*—Section 28 makes provisions for this offence to be tried in any place in the UK if it was committed in the UK. See PNLD ref S1136 to check whether this section is in force, see also p xxvii for a summary of the Act.

(g) *Counter-Terrorism Act 2008*—Part IV of and Schedules 4 and 5 to the Act (ss 40–61) make provisions for notification requirements and foreign travel restriction orders for persons sentenced or made subject of a hospital order for this offence. See PNLD ref S1136 to check whether these sections are in force, see also p xxvii for a summary of the Act.

PNLD ref numbers

H3788, D8742

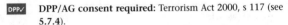 **DPP/AG consent required:** Terrorism Act 2000, s 117 (see 5.7.4).

 **Time limit for Prosecution:** None.

Indictment: Life imprisonment.

4.3 **Encouragement, Preparation, and Terrorist Training**

The Terrorism Act 2006 created various offences that cover actions that may take place before the actual terrorist act is committed, such as encouragement, preparing terrorist acts, possessing certain items, or terrorist training. Further related offences, such as weapons training and incitement, and offences relating to articles and records are included in the Terrorism Act 2000.

4.3.1 **Encouragement of terrorism**

Section 1 of the Terrorism Act 2006 creates the offence of encouragement of terrorism which covers direct encouragement and indirect encouragement, including glorification of terrorism.

Offence

(1) This section applies to a **statement** that is likely to be understood by some or all of the members of **the public** to whom it is **published** as a direct or indirect encouragement or other inducement to them to the commission, preparation or instigation of **acts of terrorism** or **Convention offences**.

(2) A person commits an offence if—

    (a) he publishes a statement to which this section applies or causes another to publish such a statement; and

    (b) at the time he publishes it or causes it to be published, he—

        (i) intends members of the public to be directly or indirectly encouraged or otherwise induced by the statement to commit, prepare or instigate acts of terrorism or Convention offences; or

        (ii) is reckless as to whether members of the public will be directly or indirectly encouraged or otherwise induced by the statement to commit, prepare or instigate such acts or offences.

Terrorism Act 2006, s 1(1) and (2)

> ## Points to prove
> ✓ date and location
> ✓ publish/cause another to publish
> ✓ statement that is likely to be understood
> ✓ by some/all members of the public to whom it was published
> ✓ as direct/indirect encouragement/other inducement
> ✓ to commit/prepare/instigate acts of terrorism/Convention offences
> ✓ intending/being reckless as to
> ✓ direct/indirect encouragement/other inducement by the statement
> ✓ to commit/prepare/instigate acts of terrorism/Convention offences

Meanings

Statement

References to a statement are references to a communication of any description, including a communication without words consisting of sounds or images or both (Terrorism Act 2006, s 20(6)). This means it also includes images such as videos.

The public

References to the public—

(a) are references to the public of any part of the UK or of a country or territory outside the UK, or any section of the public; and
(b) also include references to a meeting or other group of persons which is open to the public (whether unconditionally or on the making of a payment or the satisfaction of other conditions) (Terrorism Act 2006, s 20(3)).

Publishing a statement

References to a person's publishing a statement are references to—

(a) his publishing it in any manner to the public;
(b) his providing electronically any service by means of which the public have access to the statement; or
(c) his using a service provided to him electronically by another so as to enable or to facilitate access by the public to the statement (Terrorism Act 2006, 20(4)).

The definition in section 20(4)(b) includes internet service providers, the definition in section 20(4)(c) includes those who run websites that contain message boards and those that post messages on such message boards.

Terrorism/act of terrorism (see **4.1**).

Convention offence

Means an offence listed in Schedule 1 to the Terrorism Act 2006 or an equivalent offence under the law of a country or territory outside the UK and includes offences such as causing explosions, hostage-taking, or terrorist fund-raising (for a list see **5.7.3**).

Defence

In proceedings for an offence under this section against a person in whose case it is not proved that he intended the statement directly or indirectly to encourage or otherwise induce the commission, preparation or instigation of acts of terrorism or Convention offences, it is a defence for him to show—

(a) that the statement neither expressed his views nor had his endorsement (whether by virtue of section 3 or otherwise); and

(b) that it was clear, in all the circumstances of the statement's publication, that it did not express his views and (apart from the possibility of his having been given and failed to comply with a notice under subsection (3) of that section) did not have his endorsement.

Terrorism Act 2006, s 1(6)

The defence applies only if the defendant is alleged to have acted recklessly. The defence is intended, for example, to cover television companies, news broadcasters, and publishers. It imposes an evidential burden on the defendant. The defendant only has to adduce sufficient evidence to raise this defence. It then remains for the prosecution to prove or disprove it. However, the defence does not apply if a person has received a notice under section 3 (eg internet service provider has been required to modify terrorism-related article) and has failed to comply with it, because this is regarded as endorsement of the statement (for details about notices under section 3 see **4.3.3**).

Police powers

Power of arrest—section 41 of the Terrorism Act 2000 (see **5.3.1**)

Power to stop and search—section 43 of the Terrorism Act 2000 (see **5.2.1**)

Notes

(a) This offence has three elements:
   - the defendant must publish a statement or cause another to publish a statement, s 1(2)(a),
   - the statement must be likely to be understood by some or all members of the public to whom it is published as a direct or indirect encouragement to them to commit or prepare or instigate acts of terrorism or Convention offences, s 1(1), and
   - the defendant must have the necessary state of mind when publishing the statement/causing it to be published, he must act intentionally or recklessly, s 1(2)(b).

(b) The requirement of 'members of the public' means that statements made in private are not covered by this offence. However, if the statement is in writing, consider the offence of dissemination of terrorist publication (see **4.3.2**).

(c) Indirect encouragement/glorification.

Statements that are likely to be understood by members of the public as indirectly encouraging the commission or preparation of acts of terrorism or Convention offences include every statement which—

   (a) **glorifies** the commission or preparation (whether in the past, in the future or generally) of such acts or offences; and
   (b) is a statement from which those members of the public could reasonably be expected to infer that what is being glorified is being glorified as **conduct** that should be emulated by them in existing circumstances (Terrorism Act 2006, s 1(3)).

Glorification, glorify etc. include any form of praise or celebration (Terrorism Act 2006, s 20(2)).

Conduct includes conduct that is illustrative of a type of conduct that should be so emulated (Terrorism Act 2006, s 20(7)).

Section 1(3) gives an example for statements that indirectly encourage terrorism, those that glorify acts of terrorism, but it does not restrict indirect encouragement to glorification. What else might be covered is nowhere explained, and there will therefore be a danger that too wide an interpretation will breach rights to free expression under article 10 as not being 'in accordance with the law'. The offence can be committed by indirectly encouraging terrorism, either by glorifying terrorism, or by indirectly encouraging terrorism in any other way, even if the statement does not fall within section 1(3). In addition, section 1(3)(b) limits indirect encouragement to those statements from which the audience would conclude that they should do something that is similar to what has been glorified, and secondly that it must be possible for them to do such conduct in this day and age ('in existing circumstances'). That means that not every statement that glorifies terrorism is automatically regarded as indirect encouragement. Glorification of distant historical events is therefore unlikely to be caught, though it can be committed by reference to past acts so long as they resonate with the present.

Example: Where it is reasonable to expect members of the public to infer from a statement glorifying the bomb attacks on the London Underground on 7 July 2005 that what should be emulated is action causing severe disruption to London's transport network, this will be caught. This example also shows that the conduct glorified and the conduct to be emulated does not have to be exactly the same, only of the same type.

The inclusion of the expression 'to glorify' was much criticized when the Act was made; it has been regarded as too wide and too vague, the offence as not being sufficiently clearly defined. Some argue the offence might infringe the freedom of expression and therefore be incompatible with the Human Rights Act 1998.

(d) When determining how a statement is likely to be understood and what members of the public could reasonably be expected to infer from it, both the contents of the statement as a whole and the circumstances and manner of its publication have to be considered (Terrorism Act 2006, s 1(4)). This is meant to ensure that the context of a statement is taken into account. It would therefore make a difference whether a specific issue is dealt with in an academic thesis or in an inflammatory pamphlet.

(e) It is irrelevant whether the encouragement relates to specific acts of terrorism or Convention offences or to such acts or offences generally and whether anybody is in fact encouraged or induced by the statement (Terrorism Act 2006, s 1(5)). This means that the statement, or how it is likely to be understood, need not relate to specific acts of terrorism or Convention offences and the offence is committed even if no such act or offence has actually taken place.

(f) The offence can be committed *intentionally* or *recklessly*, s 1(2)(b). *Intention* requires that the defendant intends members of the public to be encouraged to commit, prepare, or instigate acts of terrorism or Convention offences. *Recklessness* requires that the defendant is reckless as to the possibility that the statement will have the effect of members of the public being encouraged. 'Reckless' should be interpreted in accordance with current case law on the meaning of recklessness. That means in order to be reckless the defendant has to be shown to be aware of the risk that an effect of the statement would be to encourage terrorism or Convention offences, and in the circumstances known to him, it was unreasonable for him to take that risk. **R v G and R** [2003] UKHL 50.

(g) For the application of this section to internet activity, etc see **4.3.3**.

(h) *Extra-territorial jurisdiction*—This offence applies to acts done outside the UK regardless of the nationality of the offender, in so far as it is committed in relation to the commission, preparation, or instigation of one or more Convention offences, not in respect of acts of terrorism, Terrorism Act 2006, s 17, see **5.7.1**.

Where an internet service provider established in the UK does anything in an EEA state (the EU states, Norway, Switzerland, and Liechtenstein) other than the UK, refer to the Electronic Commerce Directive (Terrorism Act 2006) Regulations 2007 (SI 2007/1550), see **4.3.3**.

(i) This offence supplements the offences of encouraging or assisting an offender (see **5.8.6**). Also consider offences such as soliciting to commit murder (see **5.8.4.1**). The use of the terms 'terrorism' or 'Convention offences' and the use of the terms 'encouragement', 'inducement', and 'glorifies' all cover activity much wider than the incitement of a specific offence. There is an overlap with the offence of dissemination of terrorist publications in section 2 of the Terrorism Act 2006, see **4.3.2 note (j)**.

(j) *Corporate liability*—For the liability of company directors etc. see section 18 of the Terrorism Act 2006 (see **5.7.2.1**).

(k) See also Recruitment **1.6.1**, and Encouraging Terrorism **3.4.7**.

(l) *Counter-Terrorism Act 2008*—Section 28 of the Act makes provision for this offence to be tried at any place in the UK if it was committed in the UK. See PNLD reference number S1136 to check whether this section is in force.

(m) *Counter-Terrorism Act 2008—notification requirements*—Sections 40 to 61 of the Act make provision for notification requirements for persons sentenced, or made subject to a hospital order. For a summary of the Act see p xxvii. See PNLD reference number S1136 to check whether these sections are in force.

PNLD reference numbers

H8450, D18570, C1203

 DPP/AG consent required: Terrorism Act 2006, s 19 (see **5.7.4**).

 Time limit for prosecution: None.

Summary: Maximum six months' imprisonment and/or fine not exceeding the statutory maximum.

 Indictment: Maximum seven years' imprisonment and/or fine.

4.3.2 **Dissemination of terrorist publication**

Section 2 of the Terrorism Act 2006 creates the offence of dissemination of terrorist publications.

Offences

(1) A person commits an offence if he engages in conduct falling within subsection (2) and, at the time he does so—

   (a) he intends an effect of his conduct to be a direct or indirect encouragement or other inducement to the commission, preparation or instigation of **acts of terrorism**;

   (b) he intends an effect of his conduct to be the provision of assistance in the commission or preparation of such acts; or

   (c) he is reckless as to whether his conduct has an effect mentioned in paragraph (a) or (b).

(2) For the purposes of this section a person engages in conduct falling within this subsection if he—

   (a) distributes or circulates a **terrorist publication**;

   (b) gives, sells or **lends** such a publication;

   (c) offers such a publication for sale or **loan**;

   (d) provides a service to others that enables them to obtain, read, listen to or look at such a publication, or to acquire it by means of a gift, sale or loan;

   (e) transmits the contents of such a publication electronically; or

   (f) has such a publication in his possession with a view to its becoming the subject of conduct falling within any of paragraphs (a) to (e).

Terrorism Act 2006, s 2(1) and (2)

Points to prove

✓ date and location
✓ distributed/circulated
✓ **or** gave/sold/lent/offered for sale/loan

> ✓ **or** provided a service to others that enabled them to obtain/read/listen to/look at or to acquire by means of gift/sale/loan
> ✓ **or** transmitted electronically the contents of
> ✓ **or** possessed with a view to it being distributed/circulated/given/sold/lent/offered for sale/loan/being part of a service/being transmitted electronically a terrorist publication
> ✓ at the time of doing so intended/reckless as to
> ✓ effect of conduct being direct/indirect encouragement/other inducement to the commission/preparation/instigation of acts of terrorism **or**
> ✓ effect of conduct being the provision of assistance in the commission/preparation of acts of terrorism

Meanings

Acts of terrorism (see **4.1.2**).

Publication

Means an **article** or **record** of any description that contains any of the following, or any combination of them—

(a) matter to be read;

(b) matter to be listened to;

(c) matter to be looked at or watched (Terrorism Act 2006, s 2(13)). This means that as well as books this section also covers, amongst other things, films and videos (with or without sound), cassette tapes, electronic books, material contained on CD-ROMs and photographs. This definition of publication is different from that provided for in section 20 of the Act which applies to section 1 (encouragement of terrorism, see **4.3.1**).

Article

Includes anything for storing data (Terrorism Act 2006, s 20(2)).

Record

Means a record so far as not comprised in an article, including a temporary record created electronically and existing solely in the course of, and for the purposes of, the transmission of the whole or a part of its contents (Terrorism Act 2006, s 20(2).

Terrorist publication

A publication is a terrorist publication, in relation to conduct falling within subsection (2), if matter contained in it is likely—

(a) to be understood, by some or all of the persons to whom it is or may become available as a consequence of that conduct, as a direct or indirect encouragement or other inducement to them to the commission, preparation, or instigation of acts of terrorism; or

(b) to be useful in the commission or preparation of such acts and to be understood, by some or all of those persons, as contained in the publication, or made available to them, wholly or mainly for the purpose of being so useful to them (Terrorism Act 2006, s 2(3)).

Matter that is likely to be understood by a person as indirectly encouraging the commission or preparation of acts of terrorism includes any matter which—

(a) **glorifies** the commission or preparation (whether in the past, in the future or generally) of such acts; and

(b) is matter from which that person could reasonably be expected to infer that what is being glorified is being glorified as conduct that should be emulated by him in existing circumstances (s 2(4)).

Glorification, glorify etc

Includes any form of praise or celebration (Terrorism Act 2006, s 20(1)).

On indirect encouragement and glorification see also **4.3.1**.

Lend/loan

Lend includes let on hire, and loan is to be construed accordingly (Terrorism Act 2006, s 2(13)).

Defence

In proceedings for an offence under this section against a person in respect of **conduct to which subsection (10) applies**, it is a defence for him to show—

(a) that the matter by reference to which the publication in question was a terrorist publication neither expressed his views nor had his endorsement (whether by virtue of section 3 or otherwise); and

(b) that it was clear, in all the circumstances of the conduct, that that matter did not express his views and (apart from the possibility of his having been given and failed to comply with a notice under subsection (3) of that section) did not have his endorsement.

Terrorism Act 2006, s 2(9)

Conduct to which subsection (10) applies

(10) This subsection applies to the conduct of a person to the extent that—

   (a) the publication to which his conduct related contained matter by reference to which it was a terrorist publication by virtue of subsection (3)(a) (i. e. matter contained in it was likely to be understood, by some or all of the persons to whom it is or may become available as a consequence of that conduct, as a direct or indirect encouragement or other inducement to them to the commission, preparation or instigation of acts of terrorism); and

   (b) that person is not proved to have engaged in that conduct with the intention specified in subsection (1)(a) (i. e. he intends an effect of his conduct to be a direct or indirect encouragement or other inducement to the commission, preparation, or instigation of acts of terrorism).

In relation to the defence in section 2(9), the defendant need only show that the part of the publication which satisfies the test of terrorist publication in section 2(3) did not express his views or have endorsement in order to establish part (a) of the defence.

If a person has received a notice under section 3 (eg an internet service provider has been required to modify a terrorism-related article) and has failed to comply with it, then this is regarded as endorsement of the publication, and the defence does not apply (for details about notices under section 3 see **4.3.3**).

Also note that the defence does not apply to an offence committed intentionally under section 2(3)(a) (publication is likely to be understood as encouragement or inducement to prepare, instigate, or commit acts of terrorism) or to any offence under section 2(3)(b) (publication is likely to be useful for the commission or preparation of such acts).

Police powers

Power of arrest—section 41 of the Terrorism Act 2000 (see 5.3.1)

Power to stop and search—section 43 of the Terrorism Act 2000 (see 5.2.1)

Power of search, seizure, and forfeiture of terrorist publications— section 28 of the Terrorism Act 2006 (see 4.3.4)

Notes

(a) The offence has three elements:
   • there must be a terrorist publication (s 2(3));

- the person must engage in a specific conduct (s 2(2)); and
- the person must have the necessary state of mind; the offence can be committed recklessly or intentionally (s 2(1)).

(b) For the purposes of this section the question whether a publication is a terrorist publication in relation to particular conduct must be determined as at the time of that conduct; and having regard both to the contents of the publication as a whole and to the circumstances in which that conduct occurs (s 2(5)). This means that account can be taken of the nature of the bookseller or other disseminator of the publication.

(c) In section 2(1) references to the effect of a person's conduct in relation to a terrorist publication include references to an effect of the publication on one or more persons to whom it is or may become available as a consequence of that conduct (s 2(6)). This means that the effect of a person holding a publication intending to disseminate it later, for example, by way of sale, will include the effect on the audience to whom it is intended it will be made available by a later act of dissemination, ie the sale itself. This is intended to cover the fact that if a person, for example, only holds a publication with the intention of disseminating it, the effect of that conduct is not to encourage terrorism or to be useful to terrorists, because only once the publication is disseminated can it have one of those effects.

(d) The offence covers not only bookshops but also those who sell books and publications over the internet whether the publication is in hard copy or electronic. It also applies to libraries and the distribution of leaflets and flyers. It is sufficient to possess for distribution (s 2(2)(f)), so there is no need in that case to prove actual publication. The offence covers commercial and non-commercial transactions.

(e) The purpose mentioned in section 2(1) (encouragement or inducement to commit, prepare, or instigate acts of terrorism or provision of assistance to commit or prepare such acts) may be one of several. A person may, for example, say his main purpose is to make money or to help his friend, but at the same time be reckless as to whether his conduct also encourages the commission of acts of terrorism. In that case he still commits the offence. (Compare: **R v Dooley** [2005] EWCA Crim 3093 para14: in this case on the possession of indecent photographs of a child *with a view to their being distributed* it was held to be sufficient that one of the purposes of the defendant's actions was the distribution of the photographs.)

(f) The offence is not committed where a person simply possesses a terrorist publication, but under certain circumstances he might commit an offence of 'possession of articles for terrorist purposes' (see **4.3.10**). The expression 'with a view' in section 2(2)(f) means less than a conditional intent, it might even cover a state of mind in which use is merely a contemplated possibility.

(g) It is irrelevant whether anything mentioned in subsections (1) to (4) is in relation to the commission, preparation, or instigation of one or more particular acts of terrorism, of acts of terrorism of a particular description or of acts of terrorism generally (s 2(7)). Only a part of the publication needs to satisfy the test in section 2(3) for the publication to be a terrorist publication. The whole publication will then be considered a terrorist publication.

(h) It is also irrelevant, in relation to matter contained in any article whether any person is in fact encouraged or induced by that matter to commit, prepare, or instigate acts of terrorism; or in fact makes use of it in the commission or preparation of such acts (s 2(8)).

(i) This offence can be committed *intentionally* or *recklessly*, s 1(2)(b). 'Reckless' should be interpreted in accordance with current case law on the meaning of recklessness (**R v G and R** [2003] UKHL 50). That means in order to be reckless the defendant has to be shown to be aware of the risk that an effect of his conduct would be direct or indirect encouragement or inducement to commit, prepare, or instigate acts of terrorism or provision of assistance to commit or prepare such acts, and in the circumstances known to him, it was unreasonable for him to take that risk. Whether the offence is committed intentionally or recklessly is a matter of importance to sentence (see related cases below).

(j) Many cases of dissemination of terrorist publications will also fall under section 1 'encouragement of terrorism' ('publishing a statement' in section 1 includes 'publishing it in any manner to the public', see **4.3.1**). But the definition of 'publication' in section 2 is wider than that of 'statement' in section 1.

(k) For the application of this section to internet activity, etc see **4.3.3**.

(l) The offence applies only to conduct in the UK. Where an internet service provider established in the UK does anything in an EEA state (the EU states, Norway, Switzerland, and Liechtenstein) other than the UK, refer to the Electronic Commerce Directive (Terrorism Act 2006) Regulations 2007 (SI 2007/1550), see **4.3.3**.

(m) *Corporate liability*—For the liability of company directors, etc see section 18 of the Terrorism Act 2006 (see **5.7.2.1**).

(n) *Counter-Terrorism Act 2008*—Section 28 of the Act makes provision for this offence to be tried at any place in the UK if it was committed in the UK. See PNLD reference number S1136 to check whether this section is in force.

(o) *Counter-Terrorism Act 2008—notification requirements*—Sections 40 to 61 of the Act make provision for notification requirements for persons sentenced, or made subject to a hospital order. For a summary of the Act see p xxvii. See PNLD reference number S1136 to check whether these sections are in force.

Related cases

R v Rahman; R v Mohammed [2008] EWCA Crim 1465 The Court of Appeal recognized that the circumstances in which section 2 can be committed vary widely and that factors relevant to sentence include not only the quality and quantity of publications but also all other circumstances including mens rea.

PNLD reference numbers

D18571, D18572, H8451, H8452, H8453, H8454, H8455

`DPP✓` **DPP/AG consent required:** Terrorism Act 2006, s 19 (see **5.7.4**).

🕐 **Time limit for prosecution:** None.

♿ **Summary:** Maximum six months' imprisonment and/or fine not exceeding the statutory maximum.

⊞ **Indictment:** Maximum seven years' imprisonment and/or fine.

4.3.3 Use of internet for encouragement of terrorism

Section 3 of the Terrorism Act 2006 contains additional provisions concerning the offences of encouragement of terrorism (see **4.3.1**) and dissemination of terrorist publications (see **4.3.2**) applying to the internet and other electronic services. It allows for the service of a notice by a constable, where he believes illegal terrorism-related material is available on a website. The person or persons responsible for that material may be required to secure that the material is not available to the public or is modified. The effect of the notice is that if the person does not comply with the notice, he cannot use the statutory defence and claim that the publication did not have his endorsement (see **4.3.1** and **4.3.2**). But non-compliance is not as such an offence.

Police powers

(1) This section applies for the purposes of sections 1 and 2 in relation to cases where—

    (a) a **statement** is published or caused to be **published** in the course of, or in connection with, the provision or use of a service provided electronically (section 1); or

    (b) conduct falling within section 2(2) was in the course of, or in connection with, the provision or use of such a service (section 2).

(2) The cases in which the statement, or the **article** or **record** to which the conduct relates, is to be regarded as having the endorsement of a person ('the relevant person') at any time include a case in which:

    (a) a constable has given him a notice under subsection (3);

    (b) that time falls more than two **working days** after the day on which the notice was given; and

    (c) the relevant person has failed, without reasonable excuse, to comply with the notice.

(3) A notice under this subsection is a notice which—

    (a) declares that, in the opinion of the constable giving it, the statement or the article or record is **unlawfully terrorism-related**;

    (b) requires the relevant person to secure that the statement or the article or record, so far as it is so related, is not available to **the public** or is modified so as no longer to be so related;

    (c) warns the relevant person that a failure to comply with the notice within two working days will result in the statement, or the article or record, being regarded as having his endorsement; and

    (d) explains how, under subsection (4), he may become liable by virtue of the notice if the statement, or the article or record, becomes available to the public after he has complied with the notice.

Terrorism Act 2006, s 3(1)–(3)

Meanings

Statement (see **4.3.1**).

Publishing a statement (see **4.3.1**).

Article

Includes anything for storing data (Terrorism Act 2006, s 20(2)).

Record (see **4.3.2**).

Working day

Means any day other than a Saturday or a Sunday; Christmas Day or Good Friday; or a day which is a bank holiday under the Banking and Financial Dealings Act 1971 in any part of the UK (s 3(9)).

Unlawfully terrorism-related

A statement or an article or record is unlawfully terrorism-related if it constitutes, or if matter contained in the article or record constitutes:

(a) something that is likely to be understood, by any one or more of the persons to whom it has or may become available, as a direct or indirect encouragement or other inducement to the commission, preparation, or instigation of acts of terrorism or Convention offences; or

(b) information which—
   (i) is likely to be useful to any one or more of those persons in the commission or preparation of such acts; and
   (ii) is in a form or context in which it is likely to be understood by any one or more of those persons as being wholly or mainly for the purpose of being so useful (s 3(7)).

Something that is likely to be understood as an indirect encouragement to the commission or preparation of acts of terrorism or Convention offences includes anything which is likely to be understood as—

(a) the glorification of the commission or preparation (whether in the past, in the future, or generally) of such acts or such offences; and

(b) a suggestion that what is being glorified is being glorified as conduct that should be emulated in existing circumstances (s 3(8)).

Glorification, glorify etc

Includes any form of praise or celebration (Terrorism Act 2006, s 20(2)). For indirect encouragement and glorification see also **4.3.1**.

The public (see **4.3.1**).

Notes

(a) The purpose of serving a notice is to achieve the quick removal or modification of unlawful terrorism-related content from the internet. The consequence of non-compliance with the notice is that the person cannot use the statutory defence because the statement or publication is regarded as having his endorsement (see **4.3.1** and **4.3.2**). Non-compliance as such is not an offence in itself.

(b) The power to serve a notice is only available to police officers. It can be initiated by any constable, but in practice (pursuant to the 'Guidance On Notices Issued Under Section 3 Of The Terrorism Act 2006', see note (e) below) it will normally be an officer of the Metropolitan Police Service Counter-Terrorist Command (SO15). The notice should be authorized by an officer of Superintendent rank or above after consultation with the ACPO TAM police lead, the National Co-ordinator of Special Branch, special branch of any force that might have a direct interest, and also the intelligence services.

(c) The notice must declare that the statement, article, or record in question is unlawfully terrorism-related (s 3(7)) in the view of the constable. This notice requires the relevant person, for example a webmaster, to ensure that the statement, article, or record is removed from public view or amended to ensure that it is no longer unlawfully terrorism-related. The notice must warn the person that he has two working days to comply with the notice, and that failure to do so will lead to that person being regarded as having endorsed the statement, article, or record. Such a notice will also explain how the relevant person may be liable if the statement, article, or record becomes available to the public again, following compliance with the notice. This final element relates to repeat statements (see note (f) below).

(d) Notices can be served on any person who is involved in the provision or use of electronic services, such as content provider, hosting internet service provider, webmaster, forum moderator, etc. They should mainly be used where material is not removed voluntarily. Where material might be removed voluntarily and there is no suspicion that the potential subject of the section 3 notice is involved in encouraging publication of the material, one should in the first place try to achieve voluntary removal, in particular where the material breaches the terms and conditions under which a service is provided (for example chat room rules, Acceptable Use Policy).

(e) The procedure for giving notices to persons, bodies corporate, firms, and unincorporated bodies or associations is set out in section 4 of the Terrorism Act 2006. Notices have to be given either in person or by recorded delivery. There is further 'Guidance On Notices Issued Under Section 3 Of The Terrorism Act 2006' agreed between ACPO and the Internet Service Providers

Association which is available on the Home Office Security website, including the question of when a notice should be issued, and the procedure for doing so. This guidance should be consulted before any notice is issued. (See <http://security. homeoffice.gov.uk/news-publications/publication-search/ terrorism-act-2006/2007-05-24-s3-guidance.pdf?view=Binary>)

(f) *Repeat statements*: Where a notice has been served and the person has complied with it, but subsequently publishes or causes to be published a so-called 'repeat statement' which is (practically) the same or to the same effect as the statement to which the notice related, or to matter contained in the article or record to which it related, the repeat statement is deemed to have the person's endorsement (s 3(4)). It is not necessary to serve another notice on that person in respect of a repeat statement. However, a person is not deemed to have endorsed the statement under two conditions: first, the person has to show that, before the publication of the repeat statement, he has taken every step he reasonably could to prevent a repeat statement from becoming available to the public and to ascertain whether it does. And secondly, if he was not aware of the publication of the repeat statement; or having become aware of its publication, has taken every step that he reasonably could to secure that it either ceased to be available to the public or was modified so as to be no longer unlawfully terrorism-related (Terrorism Act 2006, s 3(5)–(6)).

(g) Where a service provider established in the UK does anything in an EEA state (the EU states, Norway, Switzerland, and Liechtenstein) other than the UK please refer to the Electronic Commerce Directive (Terrorism Act 2006) Regulations 2007 (SI 2007/1550) and to the Home Office Guidance (see above note (e)). These Regulations ensure that UK law is compliant with EU law. They limit liability of intermediary internet service providers for offences under sections 1 and 2 (see **4.3.1** and **4.3.2**); they also implement the principle, that, within the EEA, internet services should be regulated by the country where the provider of the services is established.

PNLD reference numbers

D18573, D18574, D18575

4.3.4 **Search and seizure of terrorist publications**

Section 28 of the Terrorism Act 2006 provides powers for the search, seizure, and forfeiture of terrorist publications. These measures are directed against materials rather than persons, and so the objective insight is forfeiture rather than evidence-gathering.

Police power

(1) If a justice of the peace is satisfied that there are reasonable grounds for suspecting that **articles** to which this section applies are likely to be found on any premises, he may issue a warrant authorising a constable—

   (a) to enter and search the **premises**; and

   (b) to seize anything found there which the constable has reason to believe is such an article.

(2) This section applies to an article if-

   (a) it is likely to be the subject of conduct falling within sub-section (2)(a) to (e) of section 2 *(offence of dissemination of a terrorist publication, see **4.3.2**)*; and

   (b) it would fall for the purposes of that section to be treated, in the context of the conduct to which it is likely to be subject, as a terrorist publication.

(4) An article seized under the authority of a warrant issued under this section-

   (a) may be removed by a constable to such place as he thinks fit; and

   (b) must be retained there in the custody of a constable until returned or otherwise disposed of in accordance with this Act.

Terrorism Act 2006, s 28(1), (2) and (4)

Meanings

Article

Includes anything for storing data (Terrorism Act 2006, s 20(2)).

Premises

Includes any place and in particular, includes—

(a) any vehicle, vessel, aircraft or hovercraft;

(b) any offshore installation;

(ba) any renewable energy installation; and

(c) a tent or movable structure (Police and Criminal Evidence Act 1984, s 23).

Notes

(a) For the meaning of 'terrorist publication' and details on the offence of dissemination of terrorist publications, see **4.3.2**.

(b) Where an article is seized under this power under the authority of a warrant issued on an information laid by or on behalf of the Director of Public Prosecutions it is liable to forfeiture; and, if forfeited, may be destroyed or otherwise disposed of by a constable in whatever manner he thinks fit (Terrorism Act 2006, s 28(5)).

(c) For details regarding the procedure of seizure and forfeiture of articles refer to Schedule 2 of the Terrorism Act 2006 (not reproduced here).

(d) A person exercising the power conferred by a warrant may use such force as is reasonable in the circumstances for exercising the power (Terrorism Act 2006, s 28(3)).

(e) The power to seize articles attracts additional powers under the Criminal Justice and Police Act 2001, ss 51 and 55. This enables a bulk of material to be taken away to be read, rather than being examined on the premises, to see if it should be seized. This is needed for cases where large numbers of publications are held at a set of premises. For details see **5.1.2 (note (g))**.

(f) *Counter-Terrorism Act 2008*—Sections 1 to 9 of the Act provide further powers to remove documents for examination etc. See PNLD reference number S1136 to check whether these sections are in force.

PNLD reference number

D18588

4.3.5 **Incite terrorism overseas**

Section 59 of the Terrorism Act 2000 creates the offence of inciting terrorism overseas.

Offences

A person commits an offence if—

(a) he **incites** another person to commit an act of **terrorism** wholly or partly outside the United Kingdom, and

(b) the act would, if committed in England and Wales, constitute one of the **offences** listed in **subsection (2)**.

Terrorism Act 2000, s 59(1).

Points to prove

✓ date and location
✓ wholly/partly outside the UK
✓ incited
✓ another
✓ to commit an act of terrorism
✓ which if committed in the UK would constitute
✓ an offence of murder *or*
  an offence under section 18 of the Offences Against the Person Act 1861 *or*
  an offence under section 23 or 24 of the Offences Against the Person Act 1861 *or*
  an offence under section 28 or 29 of the Offences Against the Person Act 1861 *or*
  an offence under section 1(2) of the Criminal Damage Act 1971

Meanings

Incites

The Oxford English Dictionary defines it as 'encourage or stir up (violent or unlawful behaviour), urge or persuade to act in a violent or unlawful way'.

Terrorism (see **4.1.1**).

Offences listed in subsection (2)

Those offences are

(a) murder (see **5.8.4**),
(b) an offence under section 18 of the Offences Against the Person Act 1861 (wounding with intent, see **5.8.3.3**),
(c) an offence under section 23 or 24 of that Act (poison),
(d) an offence under section 28 or 29 of that Act (explosions), and
(e) an offence under section 1(2) of the Criminal Damage Act 1971 (endangering life by damaging property) (see **5.8.5**).

Police powers

Power of arrest—section 41 of the Terrorism Act 2000 (see **5.3.1**)

Power to stop and search—section 43 of the Terrorism Act 2000 (see **5.2.1**)

Notes

(a) It is irrelevant whether or not the person incited is in the UK or not when the incitement takes place (Terrorism Act 2000, s 59(4)).

(b) There is no criminal liability under this section for anyone acting on behalf of the Crown (Terrorism Act 2000, s 59(5)).

(c) Section 59 does not really create a new offence but extends jurisdiction for existing offences if they are committed for the purposes of terrorism.

(d) See also Recruitment, **1.6.1**.

PNLD reference numbers

H3789, D8745

 DPP/AG consent required: Terrorism Act 2000, s 117 (see **5.7.4**).

 Time limit for prosecution: None.

 Indictment: A person found guilty of an offence under this section will face the same penalty as for the offence listed in subsection (2) which he incites.

4.3.6 **Preparation of terrorist acts**

Section 5(1) of the Terrorism Act 2006 creates the offence of preparation of terrorist acts. This is intended to cover the steps taken in preparation for the carrying out of a terrorist act, including planning or other forms of preparation, prior to an attempt being made.

Offence

A person commits an offence if, with the intention of—

(a) committing **acts of terrorism**, or

(b) assisting another to commit such acts, he engages in any conduct in preparation for giving effect to his intention.

Terrorism Act 2006, s 5(1)

Points to prove

✓ date and location
✓ with the intention of committing/assisting another to commit acts of terrorism
✓ engaged in conduct in preparation for giving effect to your intention

---

Meanings

Acts of terrorism (see **4.1**).

Police powers

Power of arrest—section 41 of the Terrorism Act 2000 (see **5.3.1**)

Power to stop and search—section 43 of the Terrorism Act 2000 (see **5.2.1**)

Notes

(a) It is irrelevant whether the intention and preparations relate to one or more particular acts of terrorism, acts of terrorism of a particular description, or acts of terrorism generally (Terrorism Act 2006, s 5(2)). This makes the offence a very broad one.

(b) The offence consists of two elements: a person must have the necessary state of mind, which means he must have the intention to commit acts of terrorism or to assist another to do so, *and* he engages in any conduct in preparation for giving effect to his intentions.

(c) This is essentially an offence of facilitation and adds to existing common law offences of conspiracy to carry out terrorist acts (see **5.8.6.2**), and attempting to carry out such acts (see **5.8.6.5**). With the introduction of this offence more forms of preparatory acts are covered by the criminal law. This offence criminalizes acts at an earlier stage than the offence of attempt within the meaning of the Criminal Attempts Act 1981 which requires that the acts done are more than merely preparatory (see **5.8.6.5**). Conduct constitutes an offence at a stage before an attempted offence would be committed; this is similar to the offence of going equipped to steal, Theft Act 1968, s 25. The offence of conspiracy also requires more, namely that an agreement to commit an offence must have occurred (see **5.8.6.2**). In addition, both offences require that a specific offence is attempted or planned rather than just a general intention to carry out acts that amount to terrorism. The actus reus of

---

this offence is not specific and should be very easy to prove, even if there is not sufficient evidence to prove other criminal offences. The offence emphasizes the intention and criminal thoughts of the offender rather than actions.

(d) Examples: This offence covers acts of preparation with the relevant intention, for example if a person possesses items that could be used for terrorism, even if not immediately, and that person has the necessary intention. It is intended to catch those who, knowing the connection with terrorism and an intention to commit terrorist acts provide the facilities to do so. Another example for this offence would be if a person buys chemicals to make a poison in order to introduce it into the water supply with the intention to commit murder. He has at that stage not committed attempted murder because his actions would not be regarded as more than merely preparatory to the commission of the offence of murder. However, he intends to do an act that 'creates a serious risk to the health and safety of (a section of) the public'. If this is designed to intimidate the public and if the offender acts for the purpose of advancing a political, religious, or ideological reason, he has committed the offence of preparation of terrorist acts by merely buying the chemicals. Another example might be the provision of accommodation for terrorists knowing they were such.

(e) This offence does not apply to acts done outside the UK; it is not included in section 17 of the Terrorism Act 2006. See also **5.7.1**.

(f) Consider also other offences that cover preparatory acts, such as the common law offence of conspiracy to carry out terrorist acts which requires an agreement to commit an offence (see **5.8.6.2**); offences in relation to proscribed organisations (see **4.2.2** and **4.2.3**), in relation to articles (see **4.3.10**) and in relation to collection of information (see **4.3.11**). With regards to forms of assistance wider than these offences it will often be more difficult to prove intention under section 5(1) since, by definition there will be no tangible material and/or no tangible link to a proscribed group.

(g) *Corporate liability*—For the liability of company directors, etc see section 18 of the Terrorism Act 2006 (see **5.7.2.1**).

(h) *Counter-Terrorism Act 2008*—Section 28 of the Act makes provision for this offence to be tried at any place in the UK if it was committed in the UK. See PNLD reference number S1136 to check whether this section is in force.

(i) *Counter-Terrorism Act 2008—notification requirements*—Sections 40 to 61 of the Act make provision for notification requirements for persons sentenced, or made subject to a hospital order. For a summary of the Act see p xxvii. See PNLD reference number S1136 to check whether these sections are in force.

PNLD reference numbers

H 8456, D18576

`DPP✓` **DPP/AG consent required:** Terrorism Act 2006, s 19 (see **5.7.4**).

🕐 **Time limit for prosecution:** None.

▥ **Indictment:** Maximum life imprisonment.

4.3.7 **Training for terrorist acts**

Section 6 of the Terrorism Act 2006 creates two offences of terrorist training. Providing instruction or training for terrorist acts and receiving such instruction or training are covered by this section. These offences complement the offences of weapons training contained in section 54 of the Terrorism Act 2000 (see **4.3.9**) but allow for criminal prosecution of forms of training unrelated to weapons, such as surveillance or targeting techniques, or the handling of substances which might then be used in attacks.

Offences

(1) A person commits an offence if—
   (a) he provides instruction or training in any of the **skills mentioned in subsection (3)**; and
   (b) at the time he provides the instruction or training, he knows that a person receiving it intends to use the skills in which he is being instructed or trained—
      (i) for or in connection with the commission or preparation of **acts of terrorism** or **Convention offences**; or
      (ii) for assisting the commission or preparation by others of such acts or offences.
(2) A person commits an offence if—
   (a) he receives instruction or training in any of the skills mentioned in subsection (3); and
   (b) at the time of the instruction or training, he intends to use the skills in which he is being instructed or trained—
      (i) for or in connection with the commission or preparation of acts of terrorism or Convention offences; or
      (ii) for assisting the commission or preparation by others of such acts or offences.

Terrorism Act 2006, s 6(1) and (2)

Points to prove: offence in s 6(1)

✓ date and location
✓ provided training/instruction in a skill mentioned in section 6(3) of the Terrorism Act 2006
✓ knowing that a person receiving it intended to use the skills in which the person was instructed/trained
✓ for/in connection with the commission/preparation of acts of terrorism/Convention offence **or**
for assisting the commission/preparation by others of such acts/offences

---

Points to prove: offence in s 6(2)

✓ date and location
✓ received training/instruction in a skill mentioned in section 6(3) of the Terrorism Act 2006
✓ intending to use the skills in which you were instructed/trained
✓ for/in connection with the commission/preparation of acts of terrorism/Convention offence **or**
for assisting the commission/preparation by others of such acts/offences

Meanings

Skills mentioned in subsection (3) are

(a) the making, handling or use of a **noxious substance**, or of substances of a description of such substances;
(b) the use of any method or technique for doing anything else that is capable of being done for the purposes of terrorism, in connection with the commission or preparation of an act of terrorism or Convention offence or in connection with assisting the commission or preparation by another of such an act or offence; and
(c) the design or adaptation for the purposes of terrorism, or in connection with the commission or preparation of an act of terrorism or Convention offence, of any method or technique for doing anything (Terrorism Act 2006, s 6(3)).

Noxious substance

Means—

(a) a **dangerous substance**, this is anything which consists or includes a substance listed in Schedule 5 to the Anti-terrorism, Crime and Security Act 2001 and anything which is infected with or otherwise carries any such substance (substances listed in the Schedule include numerous viruses, bacteria, fungi, toxins, and animal pathogens); or

(b) any other substance which is hazardous or noxious or which may be or become hazardous or noxious only in certain circumstances (Terrorism Act 2006, s 6(7), and Anti-terrorism, Crime and Security Act 2001, s 58(4)).

Substance

Includes any natural or artificial substance (whatever its origin or method of production and whether in solid or liquid form or in the form of a gas or vapour) and any mixture of substances (Terrorism Act 2006, s 6(7)).

Acts of terrorism (see **4.1**).

Convention offence

Means an offence listed in Schedule 1 of the Terrorism Act 2006 or an equivalent offence under the law of a country or territory outside the UK and includes offences such as causing explosions, hostage-taking, or terrorist fund-raising (for a list see **5.7.3**).

Police powers

Power of arrest—section 41 of the Terrorism Act 2000 (see 5.3.1)

Power to stop and search—section 43 of the Terrorism Act 2000 (see 5.2.1)

Notes

(a) It is irrelevant whether any instruction or training that is provided is provided to one or more particular persons or generally; whether the acts or offences in relation to which a person intends to use skills in which he is instructed or trained consist of one or more particular acts of terrorism or Convention offences, acts of terrorism or Convention offences of a particular description or acts of terrorism or Convention offences generally; and whether assistance that a person intends to provide to others is intended to be provided to one or more particular persons or to one or more persons whose identities are not yet known (Terrorism Act 2006, s 6(4)).

(b) Despite section 6(4), it will remain difficult to prove an offence committed by the internet since section 6(1) requires knowledge that the recipient intends to use the learned skills in terrorism. If one does not even know who is receiving the material (as in section 6(4) 'persons whose identities are not yet known'), it will be difficult to establish how they will be using the information for purposes of terrorism. In that case, it might be better to use the offences of encouragement of terrorism, Terrorism Act 2006, s 1 (see **4.3.1**), or dissemination of a terrorism publication, Terrorism Act 2006, s 2 (see **4.3.2**), in connection with section 3 which makes additional provisions relating to those two offences where they are committed by means of the internet (see **4.3.3**).

(c) The range of skills in subsection (3) is very wide, comprising legitimate skills such as flying a plane, and unlawful skills, such as making a bomb to disperse a virus. The latter is an example for the skills relating to the making, handling, or use of a noxious substance, or of substances of a description of such substances (but note that this could also be charged under the offence of weapons training, see **4.3.9**).

(d) An example of a skill relating to the use of any method or technique for doing anything else that is capable of being done for the purposes of terrorism would be a technique for causing a stampede in a crowd; or for the design or adaptation of a method or technique: giving instructions about places where a bomb would cause maximum disruption.

(e) This offence applies to acts done outside the UK regardless of the nationality of the offender in so far as it is committed in relation to the commission, preparation, or instigation of one or more Convention offences, Terrorism Act 2006, s 17, see **5.7.1.1**. This is important because the places at which terrorist training is taking place are likely to be located abroad rather than in the UK.

(f) *Powers of forfeiture*—Where a person is convicted of this offence the court before which the person was convicted may order the forfeiture of anything that has been in the convicted person's possession for purposes connected with this offence. This could, for example, include various noxious substances and equipment designed for the handling, and production, of such substances. Such an order can only come into force when there is no possibility for an appeal against the order which would vary it or set it aside. The court may also make other provisions which are necessary to give effect to the forfeiture, such as about the retention, handling, or destruction of what is forfeited (Terrorism Act 2006, s 7). For forfeiture of terrorist cash in general see **4.4.12** and **4.4.17**.

(g) Also consider the offences of attendance at a place used for terrorist training (see **4.3.8**) and offences regarding weapons training (see **4.3.9**). Certain training may also be encouragement of terrorism (see **4.3.1**), and the provision of instruction could be dissemination of terrorism publications (see **4.3.2**).

(h) See also Training **1.6.2**, Flight training **2.3.1**, and Terrorism training **3.4.8**.

(i) *Corporate liability*—For the liability of company directors, etc see section 18 of the Terrorism Act 2006 (see **5.7.2.1**).

(j) *Counter-Terrorism Act 2008*—Section 28 of the Act makes provision for this offence to be tried at any place in the UK if it was committed in the UK. See PNLD reference number S1136 to check whether this section is in force.

(k) *Counter-Terrorism Act 2008—notification requirements*—Sections 40 to 61 of the Act make provision for notification requirements for persons sentenced, or made subject to a hospital order. For a summary of the Act see p xxvii. See PNLD reference number S1136 to check whether these sections are in force.

PNLD reference numbers

H8457, H8458, D18577, D18578, D10396

DPP✓ **DPP/AG consent required:** Terrorism Act 2006, s 19 (see **5.7.4**).

🕐 **Time limit for prosecution:** None.

⚖ **Summary:** Maximum six months' imprisonment and/or fine not exceeding the statutory maximum.

🏛 **Indictment:** Maximum ten years' imprisonment and/or fine.

4.3.8 **Attendance at a place used for terrorist training**

Section 8 of the Terrorism Act 2006 makes it an offence to attend at a place used for terrorist training. This complements the offences of training for terrorist acts and weapons training.

Offence

(1) A person commits an offence if—

    (a) he **attends** at any place, whether in the United Kingdom or elsewhere;

    (b) while he is at that place, **instruction or training of the type mentioned in section 6(1) of this Act** *(training for terrorist acts)* or **section 54(1) of the Terrorism Act 2000** *(weapons training)* is provided there;

    (c) that instruction or training is provided there wholly or partly for purposes connected with the commission or preparation of **acts of terrorism** or **Convention offences**; and

    (d) the requirements of subsection (2) are satisfied in relation to that person.

(2) The requirements of this subsection are satisfied in relation to a person if—

    (a) he knows or believes that instruction or training is being provided there wholly or partly for purposes connected with the commission or preparation of acts of terrorism or Convention offences; **or**

    (b) a person attending at that place throughout the period of that person's attendance could not reasonably have failed to understand that instruction or training was being provided there wholly or partly for such purposes.

Terrorism Act 2006, s 8(1) and (2)

Points to prove

- ✓ date and location
- ✓ attended at a place
- ✓ while instruction/training of the type mentioned in section 6(1) of the Terrorism Act 2006/section 54(1) of the Terrorism Act 2000 is provided there
- ✓ wholly or partly for purposes connected with the commission/preparation of
- ✓ acts or terrorism/Convention offences
- ✓ knowing/believing yourself *or* a person attending at that place throughout the period of your attendance could not reasonably have failed to understand
- ✓ that instruction/training was being provided there
- ✓ wholly/partly for purposes connected with the commission/preparation of acts of terrorism/Convention offences

Meanings

Attendance

Implies voluntary participation, a purpose or intention of being there. The offence does not extend to a person who has been kidnapped or held against his own will.

Instruction or training of the type mentioned in section 6(1) of the Terrorism Act 2006 (see **4.3.7**).

Instruction or training of the type mentioned in section 54 of the Terrorism Act 2000 (see **4.3.9**).

Acts of terrorism (see **4.1.2**).

Convention offence

Means an offence listed in Schedule 1 of the Terrorism Act 2006 or an equivalent offence under the law of a country or territory outside the UK and includes offences such as causing explosions, hostage-taking, or terrorist fund-raising (for a list see **5.7.3**).

Defences

In order to avoid loopholes in the law, no specific defence to this offence has been included, such as informing the police or attendance for legitimate research purpose. A journalist attending at a camp or a member of a non-governmental organization in a humanitarian capacity would therefore commit the offence. However, police informants and undercover police officers themselves, who would also be caught in the absence of any defence of lawful excuse, will be excused by operation of the refusal of the DPP to consent to a prosecution (see **5.7.4**).

Police powers

Power of arrest—section 41 of the Terrorism Act 2000 (see **5.3.1**)

Power to stop and search—section 43 of the Terrorism Act 2000 (see **5.2.1**)

Notes

(a) It is immaterial whether the person concerned receives the instruction or training himself; and whether the instruction or training is provided for purposes connected with one or more particular acts of terrorism or Convention offences, acts of terrorism or Convention offences of a particular description or acts of terrorism or Convention offences generally (Terrorism Act 2006, s 8(3)).

(b) Instruction or training being provided includes also instruction or training being made available (Terrorism Act 2006, s 8(6)).

(c) Terrorist training for the purposes of this offence is defined by reference to training that may be given under other offences, namely training for terrorism (see **4.3.7**) and weapons training (see **4.3.9**). For an offence to have been committed, all or part of the training in such a place would need to have been provided for purposes connected with terrorism or Convention offences.

(d) The place used for terrorist training can be outside the UK, Terrorism Act 2006, s 8(1)(a). Also, this offence applies to acts done outside the UK regardless of the nationality of the offender, Terrorism Act 2006, s 17 (see **5.7.1.1**). This is important because the places at which terrorist training is taking place are likely to be located abroad rather than in the UK.

(e) Also consider the offences of training for terrorism (see **4.3.7**) and weapons training (see **4.3.9**).

(f) *Corporate liability*—For the liability of company directors etc see section 18 of the Terrorism Act 2006 (see **5.7.2.1**).

(g) *Counter-Terrorism Act 2008*—Section 28 of the Act makes provision for this offence to be tried at any place in the UK if it was committed in the UK. See PNLD reference number S1136 to check whether this section is in force.

(h) *Counter-Terrorism Act 2008—notification requirements*—Sections 40 to 61 of the Act make provision for notification requirements for persons sentenced, or made subject to a hospital order. For a summary of the Act see p xxvii. See PNLD reference number S1136 to check whether these sections are in force.

PNLD reference numbers

H8459, D18579

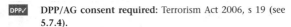 **DPP/AG consent required:** Terrorism Act 2006, s 19 (see **5.7.4**).

 **Time limit for prosecution:** None.

Summary: Maximum six months' imprisonment and/or fine not exceeding the statutory maximum.

Indictment: Maximum ten years' imprisonment and/or fine.

4.3.9 **Weapons training**

Section 54 of the Terrorism Act 2000 deals with weapons training. It makes it an offence to instruct or train another in the making or using of firearms, explosives or chemical, biological, or nuclear weapons and to receive such instruction or training. In addition to this, inviting another to receive such instruction or training is also an offence under this section.

Offences

(1) A person commits an offence if he **provides instruction** or training in the making or use of—
  (a) **firearms**,
  (aa) **radioactive material** or weapons designed or adapted for the discharge of any radioactive material,
  (b) **explosives**, or
  (c) **chemical, biological** or nuclear **weapons**.

(2) A person commits an offence if he receives instruction or training in the making or use of-
  (a) firearms,
  (aa) radioactive material or weapons designed or adapted for the discharge of any radioactive material,
  (b) explosives,
  (c) chemical, biological or nuclear weapons.

(3) A person commits an offence if he **invites** another to **receive instruction or training** and the receipt—
  (a) would constitute an offence under subsection (2), or
  (b) would constitute an offence under subsection (2) but for the fact that it is to take place outside the United Kingdom.

Terrorism Act 2000, s 54 (1)–(3)

Points to prove

✓ date and location
✓ provided/received instruction/training/invite another to receive training
✓ in use/making of
✓ firearms/radioactive material or weapons designed or adapted for the discharge of any radioactive material/explosives/chemical/biological/nuclear weapons

---

Meanings

Provision of instruction

Also includes making it available either generally or to one or more specific persons.

Invitation to receive instruction or training

May be either general or addressed to one or more specific persons (Terrorism Act 2000, s 54(4)).

Firearm

Includes an air gun or air pistol (Terrorism Act 2000, s 121).

Radioactive material

Means radioactive material capable of endangering life or causing harm to human health (Terrorism Act 2000, s 55).

Explosive

Means—

(a) an article or substance manufactured for the purpose of producing a practical effect by explosion,
(b) materials for making an article or substance within paragraph (a),
(c) anything used or intended to be used for causing or assisting in causing an explosion, and
(d) a part of anything within paragraph (a) or (c) (Terrorism Act 2000, s 121).

Chemical weapons

Chemical weapons are—

(a) **toxic chemicals** and their precursors;
(b) munitions and other devices designed to cause death or harm through the toxic properties of toxic chemicals released by them;
(c) equipment designed for use in connection with munitions and devices falling within paragraph (b).

An object is not a chemical weapon if the use or intended use is only for permitted purposes; and permitted purposes are—

(a) peaceful purposes;
(b) purposes related to protection against toxic chemicals;
(c) **legitimate military purposes**;
(d) purposes of enforcing the law.

Legitimate military purposes

Are all military purposes except those which depend on the use of the toxic properties of chemicals as a method of warfare in circumstances where the main object is to cause death, permanent harm or temporary incapacity to humans or animals.

A toxic chemical

Is a chemical which through its chemical action on life processes can cause death, permanent harm, or temporary incapacity to humans or animals; and the origin, method of production and place of production are immaterial.

A precursor

Is a chemical reactant which takes part at any stage in the production (by whatever method) of a toxic chemical.

References to an object include references to a substance.

(Chemical Weapons Act 1996, s 1)

Biological weapon

Means a biological agent or toxin (within the meaning of the Biological Weapons Act 1974) in a form capable of use for hostile purposes or anything to which section 1(1)(b) of that Act applies (Terrorism Act 2000, s 55). Section 1 of the Biological Weapons Act 1974 provides that this means—

(a) any **biological agent** or **toxin** of a type and in a quantity that has no justification for prophylactic, protective or other peaceful purposes; or

(b) any weapon, equipment or means of delivery designed to use biological agents or toxins for hostile purposes or in armed conflict. (Biological Weapons Act 1974, s 1(1)).

Biological agent

Means any microbial or other biological agent.

Toxin

Means any toxin, whatever its origin or method of production.

Defences

It is a defence for a person charged with an offence under this section in relation to instruction or training to prove that his action or involvement was wholly for a purpose other than assisting, preparing for or participating in **terrorism**.

Terrorism Act 2000, s 54(5)

Terrorism/act of terrorism (see **4.1**)

This defence covers activities, such as those of HM armed forces. The defence is fairly wide; the defendant does not have to prove a lawful purpose, it only needs to be a purpose other than terrorism.

Section 118 of the Terrorism Act 2000 shifts the burden of proof to the prosecution where the defendant adduces evidence that is sufficient to raise this defence (for details see **4.3.10**).

Police powers

Power of arrest—section 41 of the Terrorism Act 2000 (see **5.3.1**)

Power to stop and search—section 43 of the Terrorism Act 2000 (see **5.2.1**)

Notes

(a) The offence in subsection 54(1) does not require a recipient of the training or instruction. It could therefore cover someone who makes such information generally available, for example via the internet (see also the offences of encouragement of terrorism, **4.3.1**, and dissemination of terrorist publications, **4.3.2**).

(b) *Extraterritorial jurisdiction*—This offence applies to acts done outside the UK regardless of the nationality of the offender, Terrorism Act 2006, s 17, see **5.7.1.1**. This is important because such training is likely to take place abroad rather than in the UK.

(c) *Powers of forfeiture*—Where a person is convicted of this offence the court before which the person was convicted may order the forfeiture of anything that has been in the convicted person's possession for purposes connected with this offence. This could, for example, include various chemicals and equipment designed for the handling, and production, of such substances. Such an order can only come into force when there is no possibility for an appeal against the order which would vary it or set it aside (Terrorism Act 2000, s 54(7)–(9)). For forfeiture of terrorist cash in general see **4.4.12** and **4.4.17**.

(d) Also consider the offences of 'training for terrorism' (see **4.3.7**) and 'attendance at a place of terrorist training' (see **4.3.8**).

(e) *Counter-Terrorism Act 2008*—Section 28 of the Act makes provision for this offence to be tried at any place in the UK if it was committed in the UK. See PNLD reference number S1136 to check whether this section is in force.

(f) *Counter-Terrorism Act 2008—forfeiture orders*—Section 120A of the Terrorism Act 2000 as amended by section 38 of the Counter-Terrorism Act 2008 makes similar provision to those in section 54(7)–(9), which are repealed by the 2008 Act, regarding forfeiture of anything that the court considers to have been in the possession of the person for purposes connected with the offence. See PNLD reference numbers D20357 and D8741 to check whether the amendments are in force.

(g) *Counter-Terrorism Act 2008—notification requirements*—Sections 40 to 61 of the Act make provision for notification requirements for persons sentenced, or made subject to a hospital order. For a summary of the Act see p xxvii. See PNLD reference number S1136 to check whether these sections are in force.

PNLD reference numbers

H 3785, H 3786, H 3787, D8741, D22143

DPP/AG consent required: Terrorism Act 2000, s 117 (see **5.7.4**).

Time limit for prosecution: None.

Summary: Maximum six months' imprisonment and/or fine not exceeding the statutory maximum.

Indictment: Maximum ten years' imprisonment and/or fine.

4.3.10 Possession of articles for terrorist purposes

Section 57 of the Terrorism Act 2000 makes it an offence to possess articles connected with an act of terrorism.

Offence

A person commits an offence if he possesses an **article** in circumstances which give rise to a reasonable suspicion that his possession is **for a purpose connected with** the commission, preparation or instigation of an **act of terrorism.**

Terrorism Act 2000, s 57(1)

Points to prove
- ✓ date and location
- ✓ possess article
- ✓ in suspicious circumstances
- ✓ purpose of the commission/preparation/instigation of act of terrorism

Meanings

Article

Includes substance and any other thing (Terrorism Act 2000, s 121).

For a purpose connected with terrorism

Requires a direct connection between the article and the act of terrorism. See **R v Zafar, Butt, Iqbal, Raja and Malik** (see *related cases* below).

Act of terrorism (see 4.1.2).

Defence

It is a defence for a person charged with an offence under this section to prove that his possession of the article was not for a purpose connected with the commission, preparation or instigation of an act of terrorism.

Terrorism Act 2000, s 57(2)

Section 118 of the Terrorism Act 2000 shifts the burden of proof to the prosecution where the defendant adduces evidence that is sufficient to raise this defence. It imposes an evidential burden on the accused.

If the person adduces evidence which is sufficient to raise an issue with respect to the matter the court or jury shall assume that the defence is satisfied unless the prosecution proves beyond reasonable doubt that it is not (Terrorism Act 2000, s 118(2)).

The effect of this section is that, if a defendant adduces evidence to raise this defence, the burden of proof shifts to the prosecution of proving beyond reasonable doubt that the possession of the article was held for such purpose. That means that once the issue is raised by the accused, it remains for the prosecution to prove or disprove it.

Police powers

Power of arrest—section 41 of the Terrorism Act 2000 (see 5.3.1)

Power to stop and search—section 43 of the Terrorism Act 2000 (see 5.2.1)

Notes

(a) Burden of proof: There is a special provision regarding the burden of proof for some elements of this offence:

In proceedings for an offence under this section, if it is proved that an article—

> (a) was on any premises at the same time as the accused, or
> (b) was on premises of which the accused was the occupier or which he habitually used otherwise than as a member of the public, the court may assume that the accused possessed the article, unless he proves that he did not know of its presence on the premises or that he had no control over it (Terrorism Act 2000, s 57(3)).

> Where the prosecution adduces evidence regarding the article being on premises the court may make the assumption that the accused possessed the article unless the accused proves that he did not know of its presence or had no control over it. However, the accused then only has to adduce evidence which is sufficient to raise the issue whether he knew of the presence of the article or had control over it; it is then for the prosecution to disprove this beyond reasonable doubt (Terrorism Act 2000, s 118(4)). The issue remains for the prosecution to prove or disprove. This eases the evidential burden placed on the accused. He is simply required to raise the issue; this negates the presumption in the statute unless the prosecution can prove otherwise.

(b) *Extraterritorial jurisdiction*—This offence applies to acts done outside the United Kingdom if it is committed by a United Kingdom national or a United Kingdom resident (Terrorism Act 2000, s 63A(1)), see also 5.7.1.4.

(c) The possession of documentation may also fall within section 58 of the Terrorism Act 2000, to 'make/possess records or information useful to an act of terrorism' (see **R v Rowe** below and 4.3.11). Actions that might have been prosecuted under this offence might now be prosecuted under the Terrorism Act 2000, for example 'publishing statements to encourage terrorism' (see 4.3.1), 'preparation of terrorism acts' (see 4.3.6), or 'training for terrorism' (see 4.3.7). The courts accept that there

is overlap between sections 57 and 58, though there are important differences in wording between them.

(d) *Counter-Terrorism Act 2008*—Section 28 of the Act makes provision for this offence to be tried at any place in the UK if it was
committed in the UK. See PNLD reference number S1136 to
check whether this section is in force.

(e) *Counter-Terrorism Act 2008—forfeiture orders*—Section 120A of
the Terrorism Act 2000 as amended by section 38 of the Counter-Terrorism Act 2008 provides that the court may order the
forfeiture of any article that is the subject matter of the offence.
See PNLD reference number D20357 to check whether the
amendment is in force.

(f) *Counter-Terrorism Act 2008—notification requirements*—Sections
40 to 61 of the Act make provision for notification requirements for persons sentenced, or made subject to a hospital
order. For a summary of the Act see p xxvii. See PNLD reference
number S1136 to check whether these sections are in force.

Related cases

R v Zafar, Butt, Iqbal, Raja and Malik [2008] EWCA Crim 184 The
connection between the article and the intended acts of terrorism is
very important. The phrase 'for a purpose in connection with' is so
imprecise that it could lead to uncertainty of the law. Therefore it has
to be interpreted in a way that requires a direct connection between
the article and the act of terrorism. Section 57(1) should be read: 'A
person commits an offence if he possesses an article in circumstances
which give rise to a reasonable suspicion that *he intends it to be used
for the purpose of* the commission, preparation, or instigation of an act
of terrorism.' An example where there is a direct and obvious connection is an article that is intended to be incorporated in a bomb or
used as an ingredient of explosives designed for an act of terrorism.

Possessing a document for the purpose of inciting other persons
to commit an act of terrorism is sufficient; an indirect connection
between possession of the item and potential terrorist acts is not.
Examples: possessing an airline ticket to fly to a foreign country to
take part in terrorist training would not be an offence. It has to be
proved that the purpose of possessing the article is to incite another
person to commit acts of terrorism.

R v Rowe [2007] EWCA Crim 635 Documents and records, such
as books and computer discs, can be 'articles' for the purpose of this
offence. The court held that there is an overlap between this offence in
section 57 and the offence in section 58 of the Terrorism Act 2000 but
they deal with different characteristics of terrorist-related activities.

Section 57 deals with the possession of articles *for the purpose of terrorist acts* and section 58 with the collection or keeping of information *of a kind likely to be useful* to those involved in acts of terrorism. Only section 57 requires specific intent.

PNLD reference numbers

H3779, D8743, D8751, D8752, C1797, C1446

DPP✓   **DPP/AG consent required:** Terrorism Act 2000, s 117 (see 5.7.4).

🕐   **Time limit for prosecution:** None.

♿   **Summary:** Maximum six months' imprisonment and/or a fine not exceeding the statutory maximum.

🏛   **Indictment:** Maximum 15 years' imprisonment and/or fine.

For offences committed before 13 April 2006: Maximum 10 years' imprisonment and/or fine.

4.3.11 **Collection of information**

Section 58 of the Terrorism Act 2000 provides offences relating to the collection of information which may be useful to someone who commits or prepares acts of terrorism.

Offence

A person commits an offence if—
(a) he collects or makes a **record** of information of a kind likely to be useful to a person committing or preparing an **act of terrorism**, or
(b) he possesses a document or record containing information of that kind.

Terrorism Act 2000, s 58(1)

Points to prove
✓ date and location
✓ collect/make record of **or** possess document/record containing
✓ information likely to be useful to a person committing/preparing an act of terrorism

---

Meanings

Record

Includes a photographic or electronic record, Terrorism Act 2000, s 58(2).

Act of terrorism (see **4.1.2**).

Defence

It is a defence for a person charged with an offence under this section to prove that he had a reasonable excuse for his action or possession.

Terrorism Act 2000, s 58(3)

Section 118 of the Terrorism Act 2000 shifts the burden of proof to the prosecution where the defendant adduces evidence that is sufficient to raise this defence (for details see **4.3.10**).

See also **R v F** below.

Police powers

Power of arrest—section 41 of the Terrorism Act 2000 (see **5.3.1**)

Power to stop and search—section 43 of the Terrorism Act 2000 (see **5.2.1**)

Notes

(a) *Extraterritorial jurisdiction*—This offence applies to acts done outside the UK if it is committed by a UK national or a UK resident (Terrorism Act 2000, s 63A(1)), see also **5.7.1**.

(b) *Forfeiture*—Where a person is convicted of this offence the court may order the forfeiture of any document or record containing information of a kind likely to be useful to a person committing or preparing an act of terrorism, Terrorism Act 2000, s 58(5). See also **note (e)** below.

Before the court makes the order it must give an opportunity to be heard to any person, other than the convicted person, who claims to be the owner of or otherwise interested in anything which can be forfeited, Terrorism Act 2000, 58(6).

The forfeiture order must not come into force until there is no further possibility that it will be varied, or set aside, on appeal (disregarding any power of a court to grant leave to appeal out of time) Terrorism Act 2000, 58(7).

(c) Consider also the offence of possessing articles in connection with an act of terrorism in section 57 of the Terrorism Act 2000 (see **4.3.10 note (c)** and **R v Rowe**). Where documents encourage the commission of acts of terrorism consider the offence of encouragement of terrorism (see **4.3.1**), and the offence of dissemination of terrorist publications (see **4.3.2**).

(d) *Counter-Terrorism Act 2008*—Section 28 of the Act makes provision for this offence to be tried at any place in the UK if it was committed in the UK. See PNLD reference number S1136 to check whether this section is in force.

(e) *Counter-Terrorism Act 2008—forfeiture orders*—Section 120A of the Terrorism Act 2000 as amended by section 38 of the Counter-Terrorism Act 2008 makes similar provision regarding forfeiture to those mentioned in note (b) above. It provides that the court may order the forfeiture of any document or record containing information of the kind mentioned in subsection (1)(a). The 2008 Act repeals section 58(5) to (7). See PNLD reference numbers D20357 and D8741 to check whether the amendment is in force.

(f) *Counter-Terrorism Act 2008—notification requirements*—Sections 40 to 61 of the Act make provision for notification requirements for persons sentenced, or made subject to a hospital order. For a summary of the Act see p xxvii. See PNLD reference numbers D20357 and D8741 to check whether these sections are in force.

(g) *Counter-Terrorism Act 2008*—Section 77 of the Act inserts a new offence into the Terrorism Act 2000; new section 58A makes it an offence to elicit, publish, or communicate information about members of the armed forces or of the intelligence services or constables. See PNLD reference number D20367 for details.

Related cases

R v K [2008] EWCA Crim 185 This case interpreted the meaning of 'information of a kind likely to be useful to persons committing or preparing acts of terrorism'. The literature must be wholly or mainly useful to terrorism. Section 58 could not catch, for example, the A–Z of London even if it might be used by suicide bombers. The literature must be intrinsically relevant.

R v F [2007] EWCA Crim 243 It is not a reasonable excuse for the possession of documents for the purposes of section 58(3) that the documents originated as part of an effort to change an illegal or undemocratic regime. For more on this case and foreign government see also above **4.1**.

R v Rowe [2007] EWCA Crim 635 Guidance on prosecutions under sections 57 and 58 of the Terrorism Act 2000, see above **4.3.10**.

PNLD reference numbers

H3780, H3781, H3793, D8744, C1818, C1441, C1446

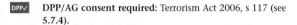 **DPP/AG consent required:** Terrorism Act 2006, s 117 (see **5.7.4**).

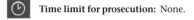 **Time limit for prosecution:** None.

Summary: Maximum six months' imprisonment and/or fine not exceeding the statutory maximum.

Indictment: Maximum ten years' imprisonment and/or fine.

4.4 Terrorist Property and Finance

Part III of the Terrorism Act 2000 and Parts I and II and Schedules 1 and 3 to the Anti-terrorism, Crime and Security Act 2001 provide for terrorist property and finance. These provisions are in addition to the normal powers of seizure under the Proceeds of Crime Act 2002 and powers to freeze property pursuant to UN law.

4.4.1 Definition and interpretation of terrorist property

Section 14 of the Terrorism Act 2000 provides the definition of terrorist property.

(1) In this Act 'terrorist property' means—
  (a) money or other property which is likely to be used for the purposes of **terrorism** (including any resources of a **proscribed organisation**),
  (b) proceeds of the commission of acts of terrorism, and
  (c) proceeds of acts carried out for the purposes of terrorism.
(2) In subsection (1)—
  (a) a reference to proceeds of an act includes a reference to any property which wholly or partly, and directly or indirectly, represents the proceeds of the act (including payments or other rewards in connection with its commission), and
  (b) the reference to an organisation's resources includes a reference to any money or other property which is applied or made available, or is to be applied or made available, for use by the organisation.

Terrorism Act 2000, s 14

Meanings

Terrorism (see **4.1.2**).

Proscribed
Outlawed, prohibited.

Organization
Includes any association or combination of persons (Terrorism Act 2000, s 121). This is a very wide definition which could be used to

describe anything from a large well-organized collection of people to a small gathering of two people.

Proscribed organization (see **4.2.1**).

Notes

(a) The definition in subsection 14(1) comes into play in section 18 (money laundering, see **4.4.5**) and the subsection makes it clear that terrorist property can include both property to be used for terrorism and proceeds of acts of terrorism.

(b) This section clarifies that the proceeds of an act of terrorism covers not only the money stolen in, for example a terrorist robbery, but also any money paid in connection with the commission of terrorist acts.

(c) This section also states that not only any use of resources for bomb making or arms purchase etc but also money set aside for other purposes such as paying rent, supporting the families of prisoners is included.

(d) *Counter-Terrorism Act 2008*—Sections 22 to 27 of the Act make provision for post-charge questioning of a person if the offence is a terrorism offence or the offence has a terrorist connection. This offence is a terrorism offence for the purposes of the Act. See PNLD ref S1136 to check whether these sections are in force, see also p xxvii for a summary of the Act.

(e) *Counter-Terrorism Act 2008*—Section 28 makes provisions for this offence to be tried in any place in the UK if it was committed in the UK. See PNLD ref S1136 to check whether this section is in force, see also p xxvii for a summary of the Act.

(f) *Counter-Terrorism Act 2008*—Part IV of and Schedules 4 and 5 to the Act (ss 40–61) make provisions for notification requirements and foreign travel restriction orders for persons sentenced or made subject of a hospital order for this offence. See PNLD ref S1136 to check whether these sections are in force, see also p xxvii for a summary of the Act.

PNLD ref number

D8706

4.4.2 **Fund-raising**

Section 15 of the Terrorism Act 2000 provides for the offences of fund-raising.

Offences

(1) A person commits an offence if he—
  (a) invites another to **provide money or other property**, and
  (b) intends that it should be used, or has reasonable cause to suspect that it may be used, for the purposes of **terrorism**.

(2) A person commits an offence if he—
  (a) receives money or other **property**, and
  (b) intends that it should be used, or has reasonable cause to suspect that it may be used, for the purposes of terrorism.

(3) A person commits an offence if he—
  (a) provides money or other property, and
  (b) knows or has reasonable cause to suspect that it will or may be used for the purposes of terrorism.

Terrorism Act 2000, s 15

Points to prove

Section 15(1) and (2)

✓ date and location
✓ invited another to provide/received/provided
✓ money/other property
✓ intending that it should be used *or*
✓ having reasonable cause to suspect that it might be used
✓ for the purposes of terrorism

Section 15(3)

✓ date and location
✓ provided
✓ money/property
✓ knowing/having reasonable cause to suspect
✓ it would/might be used
✓ for the purposes of terrorism

Meanings

Provision of money or other property

Is a reference to its being given, lent or otherwise made available, whether or not for consideration (Terrorism Act 2000, s 15(4)).

Terrorism (see **4.1**).

Property

Includes property wherever situated and whether real or personal, heritable (inheritable) or moveable, and things in action (eg copyright, trademark, rights of repayment of loaned money) and other intangible (eg goodwill of business) or incorporeal property (eg mortgages, leases etc) (Terrorism Act 2000, s 121).

Defences

There are four defences to the offences contained in sections 15–18 of the Terrorism Act 2000 (see **4.4.8**).

Police powers

Power of arrest—section 41 of the Terrorism Act 2000 (see **5.3.1**)

Power to stop and search—section 43 of the Terrorism Act 2000 (see **5.2.1**)

Notes

(a) A forfeiture order may also be made when sentencing for this offence (see **4.4.12**).

(b) When a disclosure is made to a constable under this section then they must inform a member of the Serious Organised Crime Agency as soon as practicable (Terrorism Act 2000, s 21C).

(c) This offence applies to acts done outside the UK by any person (see **5.7.1**).

(d) If it appears that this offence is connected fully or partly to another country outside of the UK, the Attorney General must consent.

(e) *Counter-Terrorism Act 2008*—Sections 22 to 27 of the Act make provision for post-charge questioning of a person if the offence is a terrorism offence or the offence has a terrorist connection. This offence is a terrorism offence for the purposes of the Act. See PNLD ref S1136 to check whether these sections are in force, see also p xxvii for a summary of the Act.

(f) *Counter-Terrorism Act 2008*—Section 28 makes provisions for this offence to be tried in any place in the UK if it was committed in the UK. See PNLD ref S1136 to check whether this section is in force, see also p xxvii for a summary of the Act.

(g) *Counter-Terrorism Act 2008*—Part IV of and Schedules 4 and 5 to the Act (ss 40–61) make provisions for notification requirements and foreign travel restriction orders for persons sentenced or made subject of a hospital order for this offence. See PNLD ref S1136 to check whether these sections are in force, see also p xxvii for a summary of the Act.

PNLD reference numbers

H3558, H3559, H3560, D8707

DPP✓ **DPP/AG consent required:** Terrorism Act 2000 s 117 (see 5.7.4).

🕐 **Time limit for prosecution:** None.

♿ **Summary:** Maximum six months' imprisonment and/or fine not exceeding the statutory maximum.

▥ **Indictment:** Maximum 14 years' imprisonment and/or fine.

4.4.3 Using money and property for terrorism

Section 16 of the Terrorism Act 2000 creates the offence of using or possessing money or property for the purposes of terrorism.

Offences

(1) A person commits an offence if he uses money or other **property** for the purposes of **terrorism**.
(2) A person commits an offence if he—
  (a) possesses money or other property, and
  (b) intends that it should be used, or has reasonable cause to suspect that it may be used, for the purposes of terrorism.

Terrorism Act 2000, s 16

Points to prove

Section 16(1)

✓ date and location
✓ used
✓ money/property
✓ for the purposes of terrorism

Section 16(2)

✓ date and location

✓ possessed
✓ money/property
✓ intending/having reasonable cause to suspect that it might be used
✓ for the purposes of terrorism

Meanings

Property (see **4.4.2**).

Terrorism (see **4.1.2**).

Defences

There are four defences to the offences contained in sections 15–18 of the Terrorism Act 2000 (see **4.4.8**).

Police powers

Power of arrest—section 41 of the Terrorism Act 2000 (see 5.3.1)

Power to stop and search—section 43 of the Terrorism Act 2000 (see 5.2.1)

Notes

(a) This offence applies to acts done outside the UK by any person (see **5.7.1**).

(b) A forfeiture order may also be made when sentencing for this offence (see **4.4.12**).

(c) When a disclosure is made to a constable under this section then they must inform a member of the Serious Organised Crime Agency as soon as practicable (Terrorism Act 2000, s 21C).

(d) If it appears that this offence is connected fully or partly to another country outside of the UK, the Attorney General must consent.

(e) *Counter-Terrorism Act 2008*—Sections 22 to 27 of the Act make provision for post-charge questioning of a person if the offence is a terrorism offence or the offence has a terrorist connection. This offence is a terrorism offence for the purposes of the Act. See PNLD ref S1136 to check whether these sections are in force, see also p xxvii for a summary of the Act.

(f) *Counter-Terrorism Act 2008*—Section 28 makes provisions for this offence to be tried in any place in the UK if it was committed in the UK. See PNLD ref S1136 to check whether this section is in force, see also p xxvii for a summary of the Act.

(g) *Counter-Terrorism Act 2008*—Part IV of and Schedules 4 and 5 to the Act (ss 40–61) make provisions for notification requirements and foreign travel restriction orders for persons sentenced or made subject of a hospital order for this offence. See PNLD ref S1136 to check whether these sections are in force, see also p xxvii for a summary of the Act.

Related cases

R (on the application of O'Driscoll) v Secretary of State for the Home Department [2002] EWHC 2477 In order to prove an offence under section 16 of the Terrorism Act 2000, specific intent or state of mind must be proved. If the organization was properly proscribed under section 3 of the same Act, then section 16 is proportionate and compatible with human rights.

PNLD reference numbers

H3561, H3562, D8708

DPP/AG consent required: Terrorism Act 2000, s 117 (see **5.7.4**).

Time limit for prosecution: None.

Summary: Maximum six months' imprisonment and/or a fine not exceeding the statutory maximum.

Indictment: Maximum 14 years' imprisonment and/or a fine.

4.4.4 Arranging availability of money and property for use in terrorism

Section 17 of the Terrorism Act 2000 details the offence of arranging funds or property for the purposes of terrorism.

> ### Offence
>
> A person commits an offence if—
> (a) he enters into or becomes concerned in an arrangement as a result of which money or other **property** is made available or is to be made available to another, and
> (b) he knows or has reasonable cause to suspect that it will or may be used for the purposes of **terrorism**.
>
> Terrorism Act 2000, s 17(1)

Points to prove

- ✓ date and location
- ✓ entered into/became concerned in arrangement
- ✓ whereby money/property was/was to be made available to
- ✓ another person knowing/having reasonable cause to suspect it would/might be used
- ✓ for the purposes of terrorism

Meanings

Property (see **4.4.2**).

Terrorism (see **4.1.2**).

Defences

There are four defences to the offences contained in sections 15–18 of the Terrorism Act 2000 (see **4.4.8**).

Police powers

Power of arrest—section 41 of the Terrorism Act 2000 (see 5.3.1)

Power to stop and search—section 43 of the Terrorism Act 2000 (see 5.2.1)

Notes

(a) This offence covers those who instigate an arrangement and also those who become involved in an existing arrangement.

(b) When a disclosure is made to a constable under this section then they must inform a member of the Serious Organised Crime Agency as soon as practicable (Terrorism Act 2000, s 21C).

(c) A forfeiture order may also be made when sentencing for this offence (see **4.4.12**).

(d) This offence applies to acts done outside the UK by any person (see **5.7.1**).

(e) If it appears that this offence is connected fully or partly to another country outside of the UK, the Attorney General must consent.

(f) *Counter-Terrorism Act 2008*—Sections 22 to 27 of the Act make provision for post-charge questioning of a person if the offence is a terrorism offence or the offence has a terrorist connection. This offence is a terrorism offence for the purposes of the Act.

See PNLD ref S1136 to check whether these sections are in force, see also p xxvii for a summary of the Act.

(g) *Counter-Terrorism Act 2008*—Section 28 makes provisions for this offence to be tried in any place in the UK if it was committed in the UK. See PNLD ref S1136 to check whether this section is in force, see also p xxvii for a summary of the Act.

(h) *Counter-Terrorism Act 2008*—Part IV of and Schedules 4 and 5 to the Act (ss 40–61) make provisions for notification requirements and foreign travel restriction orders for persons sentenced or made subject of a hospital order for this offence. See PNLD ref S1136 to check whether these sections are in force, see also p xxvii for a summary of the Act.

PNLD reference numbers

H3563, D8709

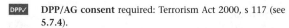 **DPP/AG consent** required: Terrorism Act 2000, s 117 (see 5.7.4).

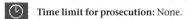 **Time limit for prosecution:** None.

Summary: Maximum six months' imprisonment and/or a fine not exceeding the statutory maximum.

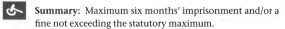 **Indictment:** Maximum 14 years' imprisonment and/or a fine.

4.4.5 Facilitate retention or control of terrorist property/money laundering

Section 18 of the Terrorism Act 2000 creates the offence of laundering terrorist property for the purposes of terrorism.

Offence

A person commits an offence if he enters into or becomes concerned in an arrangement which facilitates the retention or control by or on behalf of another person of **terrorist property**—

(a) by concealment,

(b) by removal from the jurisdiction,

(c) by transfer to nominees, or

(d) in any other way.

Terrorism Act 2000, s 18(1)

Points to prove

✓ date and location
✓ entered into/concerned in an arrangement
✓ for retention/control by/on behalf of another
✓ of terrorist property
✓ by concealment/removal from jurisdiction/transfer to nominee/other means

---

Meanings

Terrorist property (see **4.4.2**).

Defences

It is a defence for a person charged with an offence under subsection (1) to prove that he did not know and had no reasonable cause to suspect that the arrangement related to terrorist property.

Terrorism Act 2000, s 18(2)

The burden of proof is on the defendant to prove that he did not know or had no reasonable cause to suspect that the arrangement related to terrorist property.

There are four other defences to the offences contained in sections 15–18 of the Terrorism Act 2000 (see **4.4.8**).

Police powers

Power of arrest—section 41 of the Terrorism Act 2000 (see **5.3.1**)

Power to stop and search—section 43 of the Terrorism Act 2000 (see **5.2.1**)

Notes

(a) This offence covers funding used directly for terrorism purposes but also covers funding which is not directly linked to terrorism such as payment to relatives of paramilitary/terrorist prisoners.

(b) When a disclosure is made to a constable under this section then they must inform a member of the Serious Organised Crime Agency as soon as practicable (Terrorism Act 2000, s 21C).

(c) This offence applies to acts done outside the UK by any person (see **5.7.1**).

(d) There are orders from the United Nations which create further offences of making funds available and dealing with funds of those who have been designated (suspected to be involved in terrorism).

(e) A forfeiture order may also be made when sentencing for this offence (see **4.4.12**).

(f) If it appears that this offence is connected fully or partly to another country outside of the UK, the Attorney General must consent.

(g) *Counter-Terrorism Act 2008*—Sections 22 to 27 of the Act make provision for post-charge questioning of a person if the offence is a terrorism offence or the offence has a terrorist connection. This offence is a terrorism offence for the purposes of the Act. See PNLD ref S1136 to check whether these sections are in force, see also p xxvii for a summary of the Act.

(h) *Counter-Terrorism Act 2008*—Section 28 makes provisions for this offence to be tried in any place in the UK if it was committed in the UK. See PNLD ref S1136 to check whether this section is in force, see also p xxvii for a summary of the Act.

(i) *Counter-Terrorism Act 2008*—Section 77 of the Act makes a slight amendment to section 19(1)(b) and inserts section 22A into the Terrorism Act 2000 which contains a definition of the term 'employment'. See PNLD reference numbers D8711, D20525, and D22177 for details. see also p xxvii for a summary of the Act.

PNLD reference numbers

H3564, D8710

 **DPP/AG consent** required: Terrorism Act 2000, s 117 (see **5.7.4**).

Time limit for prosecution: None.

Summary: Maximum six months' imprisonment and/or a fine not exceeding the statutory maximum.

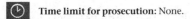 **Indictment:** Maximum 14 years' imprisonment and/or a fine.

4.4.6 **Duty to disclose information relating to terrorism finance offences**

Section 19 of the Terrorism Act 2000 creates a duty to disclose information relating to certain offences under this Act and an offence of failing to do so.

Offences

(1) This section applies where a person—
  (a) believes or suspects that another person has committed an offence under sections 15–18, and
  (b) bases his belief or suspicion on information which comes to his attention in the course of a trade, profession, business or employment.
(2) The person commits an offence if he does not disclose to a **constable** as soon as is reasonably practicable—
  (a) his belief or suspicion, and
  (b) the information on which it is based.

Terrorism Act 2000, s 19(1) and (2)

Points to prove

✓ date and location
✓ failed to disclose to a constable
✓ as soon as reasonably practicable
✓ belief/suspicion and information on which knowledge/suspicion based
✓ that another person had committed an offence under sections 15–18 of the Terrorism Act 2000
✓ that belief/suspicion based on information
✓ which had come to his/her attention in the course of trade/profession/business/employment

Meanings

Constable

Includes a member of the Serious Organised Crime Agency authorized by its Director General for that purpose (Terrorism Act 2000, s 19(7B)).

Defence

(3) It is a defence for a person charged with an offence under subsection (2) to prove that he had a reasonable excuse for not making the disclosure.

(4) Where—

    (a) a person is in employment,

    (b) his employer has established a procedure for the making of disclosures of the matters specified in subsection (2), and

    (c) he is charged with an offence under that subsection, it is a defence for him to prove that he disclosed the matters specified in that subsection in accordance with the procedure.

Terrorism Act 2000, s 19(3) and (4)

With reference to the defence provided by subsection 19(3) above, unlike similar provisions in, for example, drug trafficking legislation, the person handling the terrorist property must demonstrate not only that he genuinely did not believe it necessary to make a disclosure but also that it was reasonable not to do so. In this way an objective standard applies to the likes of bankers and accountants in their recognition of circumstances which should be seen as being linked to terrorism.

Subsection (4) allows for the reporting of such suspicions to others where there is a set procedure for doing so, such as a money laundering reporting officer within the organization.

Police powers

Power of arrest—section 41 of the Terrorism Act 2000 (see 5.3.1)

Power to stop and search—section 43 of the Terrorism Act 2000 (see 5.2.1)

Notes

(a) Subsection 19(1) requires banks and other businesses to report any suspicion they may have that someone is laundering terrorist money or committing any of the other terrorist property offences (sections 15–18, see **4.4.2–4.4.5**).

(b) This is a very extensive duty as the suspicion is based on those raised by an individual during the course of their work and they must have a reasonable excuse not to disclose this information to the police or other intermediary (see defence above).

(c) Section 19 preserves the exemption in respect of a professional legal adviser's privileged material as long as the material came to him in privileged circumstances and the reason is not to further a criminal purpose.

(d) Privileged circumstances in this section mean that the information is obtained from a client or a client's representative, in connection with the provision of legal advice by the adviser to the client, from a person seeking legal advice from the adviser, or from the person's representative, or from any person, for the purpose of actual or contemplated legal proceedings (Terrorism Act 2000, s 19(6)).

(e) This offence has a global element to it, if the person has been in possession of a thing or taken an action and if he had committed that offence had he been in the UK at the time when he did, then he still commits the offence (Terrorism Act 2000, s 19(7)).

(f) Although this duty is confined to business relationships, family members could commit this offence if they fail to disclose their suspicions about relatives if they are involved in a business relationship with those family members.

(g) When a disclosure is made to a constable under this section then he must inform a member of the Serious Organised Crime Agency as soon as practicable (Terrorism Act 2000, s 21C).

PNLD reference numbers

H3778, D8711

DPP/   **DPP/AG consent** required: Terrorism Act 2000, s 117 (see 5.7.4).

Time limit for prosecution: None.

Summary: Maximum six months' imprisonment and/or a fine not exceeding the statutory maximum.

Indictment: Maximum five years' imprisonment and/or a fine.

4.4.7 Permission to disclose information relating to terrorism finance offences

Section 20 of the Terrorism Act 2000 provides permission for disclosures to be made under section 19 of the Act.

(1) A person may disclose to a **constable**—

(a) a suspicion or belief that any money or other **property** is **terrorist property** or is derived from terrorist property;

(b) any matter on which the suspicion or belief is based.

(2) A person may make a disclosure to a constable in the circumstances mentioned in section 19(1) and (2).

(3) Subsections (1) and (2) shall have effect notwithstanding any restriction on the disclosure of information imposed by statute or otherwise.

(4) Where—

(a) a person is in employment, and

(b) his employer has established a procedure for the making of disclosures of the kinds mentioned in subsection (1) and section 19(2), subsections (1) and (2) shall have effect in relation to that person as if any reference to disclosure to a constable included a reference to disclosure in accordance with the procedure.

Terrorism Act 2000, s 20(1)–(4)

Meanings

Constable (see **4.4.6**).

Property (see **4.4.2**).

Terrorist property (see **4.4.2**).

Notes

(a) This section means that businesses, etc can make disclosures without fear of breaching any other legal restrictions, such as the Official Secrets Act 1989, or any potential civil actions.

(b) When a disclosure is made to a constable under this section then he must inform a member of the Serious Organised Crime Agency as soon as practicable (Terrorism Act 2000, s 21C).

(c) See **4.4.10** for a similar provision for those in the regulated sector.

PNLD reference number

D8712

4.4.8 **Exemptions of liability**

Sections 21, 21ZA, 21ZB and 21ZC of the Terrorism Act 2000 provide specific exemptions from criminal liability in relation to acts done and transactions undertaken when dealing with terrorist property. Each defence has a similar premise in that they provide protection for those who make a disclosure, before, during, or after becoming involved in a transaction,

(1) A person does not commit an offence under sections 15–18, if he is acting with the express consent of a **constable**.

(2) Subject to subsections (3) and (4), a person does not commit an offence under sections 15–18 by involvement in **a transaction or arrangement relating to money or other property** if he discloses to a constable—

    (a) his suspicion or belief that the money or other **property** is **terrorist property**, and

    (b) the information on which his suspicion or belief is based.

(3) Subsection (2) applies only where a person makes a disclosure—

    (a) after he becomes concerned in the transaction concerned,

    (b) on his own initiative, and

    (c) as soon as is reasonably practicable.

(4) Subsection (2) does not apply to a person if—

    (a) a constable forbids him to continue his involvement in the transaction or arrangement to which the disclosure relates, and

    (b) he continues his involvement.

Terrorism Act 2000, s 21(1)–(4)

Meanings

Constable (see **4.4.6**).

Property (see **4.4.2**).

Terrorist property (see **4.4.2**).

Transaction or arrangement relating to money or other property
Includes a reference to use or possession (Terrorism Act, s 21(7)).

Defence

(5) It is a defence for a person charged with an offence under sections 15(2) and (3) and 16, 17 or 18, to prove that—

    (a) he intended to make a disclosure of the kind mentioned in subsections (2) and (3), and

> (b) there is reasonable excuse for his failure to do so
> (6) Where—
>   (a) a person is in employment, and
>   (b) his employer has established a procedure for the making of disclo-
>   sures of the same kind as may be made to a constable under sub-
>   section (2), this section shall have effect in relation to that person
>   as if any reference to disclosure to a constable included a reference
>   to disclosure in accordance with the procedure.
>
> *Terrorism Act 2000, s 21(5) and (6)*

Subsection (6) allows for the reporting of such suspicions to others
where there is a set procedure for doing so, such as a money laundering reporting officer within the organization.

Notes

(a) Subsection 21(1) allows for the activities of informants who
may have been involved with terrorist property if they are to
conceal their identity.

(b) Subsections 21(2) to (4) make it possible for someone involved
with such property to avoid prosecution by telling the police as
soon as is reasonably practical and to stop any involvement if
asked to do so by the police.

  (1) A person does not commit an offence under any of sections
    15 to 18 by involvement in a transaction or an arrangement
    relating to money or other property if, before becoming
    involved, the person—
    (a) discloses to an authorised officer the person's suspicion
      or belief that the money or other property is terrorist
      property and the information on which the suspicion or
      belief is based, and
    (b) has the authorised officer's consent to becoming
      involved in the transaction or arrangement.
  (2) A person is treated as having an authorised officer's consent
    if before the end of the notice period the person does not
    receive notice from an authorised officer that consent is
    refused.

Terrorism Act 2000, s 21ZA

(c) This covers the situation where the person has made a disclosure to an authorized officer before the transaction has been
carried out and continues with the transaction with the permission of that officer.

(d) An authorized officer in this section and the others below is an appropriately authorized member of staff from the Serious Organised Crime Agency.

(e) The notice period in this section is seven working days, starting the day after the disclosure is made.

  (1) A person does not commit an offence under any of sections 15 to 18 by involvement in a transaction or an arrangement relating to money or other property if, after becoming involved, the person discloses to an authorised officer—

    (a) the person's suspicion or belief that the money or other property is terrorist property, and

    (b) the information on which the suspicion or belief is based.

  (2) This section applies only where—

    (a) there is a reasonable excuse for the person's failure to make the disclosure before becoming involved in the transaction or arrangement, and

    (b) the disclosure is made on the person's own initiative and as soon as it is reasonably practicable for the person to make it.

  (3) This section does not apply to a person if—

    (a) an authorised officer forbids the person to continue involvement in the transaction or arrangement to which the disclosure relates, and

    (b) the person continues that involvement.

Terrorism Act 2000, s 21ZB

(f) This section covers the situation where a person becomes involved in a transaction and then discloses the fact to an authorized officer as long as the person has a reasonable excuse for failing to make the disclosure before becoming involved.

(g) If the person continues with the transaction after being told not to by an authorized officer then he cannot rely on this defence.

(h) *Counter-Terrorism Act 2008*—Sections 22 to 27 of the Act make provision for post-charge questioning of a person if the offence is a terrorism offence or the offence has a terrorist connection. This offence is a terrorism offence for the purposes of the Act. See PNLD ref S1136 to check whether these sections are in force, see also p xxvii for a summary of the Act.

(i) *Counter-Terrorism Act 2008*—Section 28 makes provisions for this offence to be tried in any place in the UK if it was committed in the UK. See PNLD ref S1136 to check whether this section is in force, see also p xxvii for a summary of the Act.

Defence

It is a defence for a person charged with an offence under any of sections 15 to 18 to prove that—
(a) the person intended to make a disclosure of the kind mentioned in section 21ZA or 21ZB, and
(b) there is a reasonable excuse for the person's failure to do so.

Terrorism Act 2000, s 21ZC

This section covers those who have failed to make a disclosure but have a reasonable excuse for failing to do so.

PNLD reference numbers

D8713, D21661, D21662, D21663.

4.4.9 Disclosures and co-operation in the regulated sector

Section 21A of the Terrorism Act 2000 creates the offence of a person working in the regulated sector (ie banking) failing to disclose information.

Offence

(1) A person commits an offence if each of the following three conditions is satisfied.
(2) The first condition is that he—
    (a) knows or suspects, or
    (b) has reasonable grounds for knowing or suspecting,
    that another person has committed, or attempted to commit, an offence under sections 15–18.
(3) The second condition is that the information or other matter—
    (a) on which his knowledge or suspicion is based, or
    (b) which gives reasonable grounds for such knowledge or suspicion,
    came to him in the course of **a business in the regulated sector.**
(4) The third condition is that he does not disclose the information or other matter to a constable or a **nominated officer** as soon as is practicable after it comes to him.

Terrorism Act 2000, s 21A

Points to prove

- ✓ date and location
- ✓ in the course of a business in the regulated sector
- ✓ knowing or suspecting *or*
- ✓ having reasonable grounds for knowing or suspecting
- ✓ that another person has committed an offence under section 15–18 of the Terrorism Act 2000
- ✓ failed to disclose that information/other matter
- ✓ to a constable/nominated officer
- ✓ as soon as is practicable

Meanings

A business in the regulated sector

Simply put, is a business that carries on financial duties that are regulated by the Financial Services Authority (ie banks, building societies, bureaux de change, accountants, investment establishments). The full complex definition can be found in Schedule 3A to the Terrorism Act 2000 (not reproduced here).

A disclosure to a nominated officer

Is a disclosure which—

(a) is made to a person nominated by the alleged offender's employer to receive disclosures under this section, and

(b) is made in the course of the alleged offender's employment and in accordance with the procedure established by the employer for the purpose.

Defence

(5) But a person does not commit an offence under this section if—

    (a) he has a reasonable excuse for not disclosing the information or other matter;

    (b) he is a professional legal adviser, or relevant professional adviser, and the information or other matter came to him in privileged circumstances; or

    (c) subsection (5A) applies to him.

(5A) This subsection applies to a person if

    (a) the person is employed by, or is in partnership with, a professional legal adviser or relevant professional adviser to provide the adviser with assistance or support,

(b) the information or other matter comes to the person in connection with the provision of such assistance or support, and

(c) the information or other matter came to the adviser in privileged circumstances.

Terrorism Act 2000, s 21A(5) and (5A)

Notes

(a) The requirement to pass on information where there are reasonable grounds to know or suspect that someone has committed an offence lays down an objective test for criminal liability. In recognition of this subsection (6) provides that the court must take any guidance issued by the supervisory authority or any other appropriate authority into account when determining whether an offence has been committed. That guidance has to be approved by the Treasury and is published in a manner approved by the Treasury so as to bring it to the attention of persons likely to be affected by it. There is a long list of supervisory authorities contained in Schedule 3. Examples are, the Commissioners for Her Majesty's Revenue and Customs, the Financial Services Authority, the Gambling Commission, the Office of Fair Trading and the Secretary of State.

(b) An appropriate body is any body which regulates or is representative of any trade, profession, business or employment carried on by the alleged offender (Terrorism Act 2000, s 21A(13)).

(c) Information is obtained in privileged circumstances if it is communicated or given—

- by (or by a representative of) a client of his in connection with the giving by the adviser of legal advice to the client,
- by (or by a representative of) a person seeking legal advice from the adviser, or
- by a person in connection with legal proceedings or contemplated legal proceedings.

But this does not apply to information or other matter which is communicated or given with a view to furthering a criminal purpose (Terrorism Act 2000, s 21A(8) and (9)).

Police powers

Power of arrest—section 41 of the Terrorism Act 2000 (see 5.3.1)

Power to stop and search—section 43 of the Terrorism Act 2000 (see 5.2.1)

Notes

(a) This provision is only directed at persons who are carrying out activities in the regulated sector (see **4.4.9**), it reflects the fact that they should be expected to exercise a higher level of diligence in handling transactions than those engaged in other business. Where a business carries out some activities which are specified in Schedule 3A, Part 1 and some which are not, then it is only to the extent that information is obtained in the course of the specified activities that are covered by these provisions.

(b) This offence has a global element to it, if the person has been in possession of a thing or taken an action and if he had committed that offence had he been in the UK at the time when he did, then he still commits the offence (Terrorism Act 2000, s 21A(11)).

(c) When a disclosure is made to a constable under this section then he must inform a member of the Serious Organised Crime Agency as soon as practicable (Terrorism Act 2000, s 21C).

(d) See **4.4.7** for those not in the regulated sector.

PNLD reference numbers

H3573, D10407, D10409

DPP✓ **DPP/AG consent** required: Terrorism Act 2000, s 117 (see **5.7.4**).

🕐 **Time limit for prosecution:** None.

♿ **Summary:** Maximum six months' imprisonment and/or a fine not exceeding the statutory maximum.

▦ **Indictment:** Maximum five years' imprisonment and/or a fine.

4.4.10 Permission to disclose information relating to terrorism offences in the regulated sector

Section 21B of the Terrorism Act 2000 provides that those in the regulated sector (ie banking, etc) can disclose information where disclosure would normally be restricted.

(1) A disclosure which satisfies the following three conditions is not to be taken to breach any restriction on the disclosure of information (however imposed).

(2) The first condition is that the information or other matter disclosed came to the person making the disclosure (the discloser) in the course of a business in the regulated sector.

(3) The second condition is that the information or other matter—
   (a) causes the discloser to know or suspect, or
   (b) gives him reasonable grounds for knowing or suspect-
       ing, that another person has committed or attempted to
       commit an offence under sections 15–18.
(4) The third condition is that the **disclosure** is made to a con-
    stable or a **nominated officer** as soon as is practicable after the
    information or other matter comes to the discloser.

Terrorism Act 2000, s 21B(1)–(4)

Meanings

A disclosure to a nominated officer

Is a disclosure which is made to a person nominated by the discloser's employer to receive disclosures under this section, and is made
in the course of the discloser's employment and in accordance with
the procedure established by the employer for the purpose (Terrorism Act 2000, s 21(B)(5)).

Constable

The reference to a constable includes a reference to a person authorized for the purposes of this section by the Director General of the
Serious Organised Crime Agency, (Terrorism Act 2000, s 21(B)(7)).

Business in the regulated sector (see 4.4.9).

Note

This section means that banks, building societies, etc can make
disclosures without fear of breaching any other legal restrictions,
such as the Official Secrets Act 1989 or any potential civil actions.
See **4.4.7** for those not in the regulated sector.

PNLD reference number

D10408

4.4.11 **Tipping off**

Section 21D of the Terrorism Act 2000 creates the offence of tipping
off, for example, a member of banking staff telling a customer that
he had been reported for a suspected terrorist finance offence. Sections 21E to 21G provide the exceptions to this offence.

Offences

(1) A person commits an offence if—
   (a) the person discloses any matter within subsection (2);
   (b) the disclosure is likely to prejudice any investigation that might be conducted following the disclosure referred to in that subsection; and
   (c) the information on which the disclosure is based came to the person in the course of a **business in the regulated sector**.

(2) The matters are that the person or another person has made a disclosure under a provision of this part—
   (a) to a constable,
   (b) in accordance with a procedure established by that person's employer for the making of disclosures under that provision,
   (c) to a nominated officer, or
   (d) to a member of staff of the Serious Organised Crime Agency authorised for the purposes of that provision by the Director General of that Agency, of information that came to that person in the course of a business in the regulated sector.

(3) A person commits an offence if—
   (a) the person discloses that an investigation into allegations that an offence under this part has been committed is being contemplated or is being carried out;
   (b) the disclosure is likely to prejudice that investigation; and
   (c) the information on which the disclosure is based came to the person in the course of a business in the regulated sector.

Terrorism Act 2000, s 21D(1)–(3)

Points to prove

- ✓ date and location
- ✓ made a disclosure
- ✓ that an investigation
- ✓ into allegations that an offence under Part III of the Terrorism Act 2000
- ✓ had been committed/was being contemplated/was being carried out
- ✓ knowing/suspecting the disclosure was likely to prejudice that investigation
- ✓ and the information on which the disclosure was based
- ✓ came to you in the course of a business in the regulated sector

Meanings

Business in the regulated sector (see **4.4.9.**).

Defences

Sections 21E–21G of the Terrorism Act 2000 set out the exceptions to the tipping off offence under section 21D.

(1) An employee, officer or partner of an undertaking does not commit an offence under section 21D if the disclosure is to an employee, officer or partner of the same undertaking.

(2) A person does not commit an offence under section 21D in respect of a disclosure by a credit institution or a financial institution if—

    (a) the disclosure is to a credit institution or a financial institution,

    (b) the institution to whom the disclosure is made is situated in an EEA State or in a country or territory imposing equivalent money laundering requirements, and

    (c) both the institution making the disclosure and the institution to whom it is made belong to the same group.

(3) In subsection (2) 'group' has the same meaning as in Directive 2002/87/EC of the European Parliament and of the Council of 16th December 2002 on the supplementary supervision of credit institutions, insurance undertakings and investment firms in a financial conglomerate.

(4) A professional legal adviser or a relevant professional adviser does not commit an offence under section 21D if—

    (a) the disclosure is to a professional legal adviser or a relevant professional adviser,

    (b) both the person making the disclosure and the person to whom it is made carry on business in an EEA state or in a country or territory imposing equivalent money laundering requirements, and

    (c) those persons perform their professional activities within different undertakings that share common ownership, management or control.

Terrorism Act 2000, s 21E

This section covers those who disclose to other employees, partners, another financial institution, or other legal or professional adviser. Simplistically put the disclosure must be to a person/organization who are part of the same overall company and who are in an EEA state or a country which has similar money laundering provisions.

(1) This section applies to a disclosure—

    (a) by a credit institution to another credit institution,

    (b) by a financial institution to another financial institution,

(c) by a professional legal adviser to another professional legal adviser, or

(d) by a relevant professional adviser of a particular kind to another relevant professional adviser of the same kind.

(2) A person does not commit an offence under section 21D in respect of a disclosure to which this section applies if—

(a) the disclosure relates to—

(i) a client or former client of the institution or adviser making the disclosure and the institution or adviser to whom it is made,

(ii) a transaction involving them both, or

(iii) the provision of a service involving them both;

(b) the disclosure is for the purpose only of preventing an offence under this part of this Act;

(c) the institution or adviser to whom the disclosure is made is situated in an EEA State or in a country or territory imposing equivalent money laundering requirements; and

(d) the institution or adviser making the disclosure and the institution or adviser to whom it is made are subject to equivalent duties of professional confidentiality and the protection of personal data (within the meaning of section 1 of the Data Protection Act 1998).

Terrorism Act 2000, s 21F(2)(d)

This covers those mentioned in subsection (1) who make a disclosure to another and that disclosure involves a client or former client of either one of them and the service or transaction concerns them both. The disclosure must also only relate to preventing an offence under this part and they both must be under similar duties of confidentiality and also be in an EEA state or a country with similar money laundering provisions.

In this section, relevant professional adviser means an accountant, auditor or tax adviser who is a member of a professional body which is established for accountants, auditors or tax advisers (as the case may be) and which makes provision for—

(a) testing the competence of those seeking admission to membership of such a body as a condition for such admission; and

(b) imposing and maintaining professional and ethical standards for its members, as well as imposing sanctions for non-compliance with those standards (Terrorism Act 2000, s 21H).

Credit and financial institutions are organizations such as banks and building societies, a full definition can be found in Schedule 3A.

Defences

(1) A person does not commit an offence under section 21D if the disclosure is—
   (a) to the authority that is the supervisory authority for that person by virtue of the Money Laundering Regulations 2007 (S.I. 2007/2157); or
   (b) for the purpose of—
      (i) the detection, investigation or prosecution of a criminal offence (whether in the United Kingdom or elsewhere),
      (ii) an investigation under the Proceeds of Crime Act 2002, or
      (iii) the enforcement of any order of a court under that Act.

(2) A professional legal adviser or a relevant professional adviser does not commit an offence under section 21D if the disclosure—
   (a) is to the adviser's client, and
   (b) is made for the purpose of dissuading the client from engaging in conduct amounting to an offence.

(3) A person does not commit an offence under section 21D(1) if the person does not know or suspect that the disclosure is likely to have the effect mentioned in section 21D(1)(b).

(4) A person does not commit an offence under section 21D(3) if the person does not know or suspect that the disclosure is likely to have the effect mentioned in section 21D(3)(b).

Terrorism Act 2000, s 21G

Police powers

Power of arrest—section 41 of the Terrorism Act 2000 (see 5.3.1)

Power to stop and search—section 43 of the Terrorism Act 2000 (see 5.2.1)

Notes

(a) The section prohibits the persons, in the course of business in the regulated sector (ie banking etc, see **4.4.9**), from disclosing to the customer concerned or to other third persons the fact that information about known or suspected money laundering or terrorist financing has been transmitted and/or that a money laundering or terrorist financing investigation is being, or may be, carried out.

(b) *Counter-Terrorism Act 2008*—Sections 22 to 27 of the Act make provision for post-charge questioning of a person if the offence is a terrorism offence or the offence has a terrorist connection. This offence is a terrorism offence for the purposes of the Act.

See PNLD ref S1136 to check whether these sections are in force, see also p xxvii for a summary of the Act.

(c) *Counter-Terrorism Act 2008*—Section 28 makes provisions for this offence to be tried in any place in the UK if it was committed in the UK. See PNLD ref S1136 to check whether this section is in force, see also p xxvii for a summary of the Act.

(d) *Counter-Terrorism Act 2008*—Sections 34 to 36 of the Act make further provisions with regards to forfeiture. Sections 35 and 36 insert sections 23A and 23B respectively into TACT. Section 37 of the Act amends Schedule 4 to the Terrorism Act 2000 (TACT) to allow victims to be compensated by the courts in certain circumstances. See PNLD ref S399 and D8700 to check whether these sections and amendments are in force, see also p xxvii for a summary of the Act.

PNLD reference numbers

H9233, D21665, D21666, D21667, D21668

 Time limit for prosecution: None.

 Summary: Maximum three months' imprisonment and/or a fine not exceeding the statutory maximum.

 Indictment: Maximum two years' imprisonment and/or a fine.

4.4.12 **Forfeiture of terrorist cash**

Section 23 of the Terrorism Act 2000 gives details of the forfeiture orders available to the courts where a person has been convicted of an offence under sections 15–18 (terrorist property and finance offences) of this Act.

(1) The court by or before which a person is convicted of an offence under any of sections 15–18 may make a forfeiture order in accordance with the provisions of this section.

(2) Where a person is convicted of an offence under section 15(1) or (2) or 16 the court may order the forfeiture of any money or other **property**—

(a) which, at the time of the offence, he had in his possession or under his control, and

(b) which, at that time, he intended should be used, or had reasonable cause to suspect might be used, for the purposes of **terrorism**.

(3) Where a person is convicted of an offence under section 15(3) the court may order the forfeiture of any money or other property—

    (a) which, at the time of the offence, he had in his possession or under his control, and

    (b) which, at that time, he knew or had reasonable cause to suspect would or might be used for the purposes of terrorism.

(4) Where a person is convicted of an offence under section 17 the court may order the forfeiture of the money or other property—

    (a) to which the arrangement in question related, and

    (b) which, at the time of the offence, he knew or had reasonable cause to suspect would or might be used for the purposes of terrorism.

(5) Where a person is convicted of an offence under section 18 the court may order the forfeiture of the money or other property to which the arrangement in question related.

(6) Where a person is convicted of an offence under sections 15–18, the court may order the forfeiture of any money or other property which wholly or partly, and directly or indirectly, is received by any person as a payment or other reward in connection with the commission of the offence.

Terrorism Act 2000, s 23(1)–(6)

Meanings

Property (see **4.4.2**).

Terrorism (see **4.2.1**).

Police powers

Under Schedule 4, paragraph 7(1), a constable may seize any property subject to a restraint order for the purpose of preventing it from being removed from Great Britain (see note (d) below).

Notes

(a) Subsection 23(6) closes a loophole by allowing the forfeiture of the proceeds of a terrorist property offence, for example if an accountant prepared accounts on behalf of a proscribed organization which facilitates the retention or control of the organization's money, the money he is paid for this task can be forfeited under this section. Previously the money could not be forfeited because it was not intended or suspected for use in terrorism nor could it be confiscated under the Criminal Justice Act 1988 because that confiscation regime does not include terrorist property offences.

(b) This is a 'criminal forfeiture' ie forfeiture following conviction of a criminal offence (for civil forfeiture see **4.4.17**).

(c) Where someone other than the convicted person claims to be the owner of or have an interest in anything to be forfeited under this section, they will have an opportunity to be heard by the court (Terrorism Act, s 23(7)).

(d) Schedule 4 to the Terrorism Act 2000 makes some further provisions about forfeiture orders. The court can order property (other than money or land) to be sold, require the forfeited property to be handed over to a proper officer (officer of the court) or a constable, appoint a receiver to deal with the property and order any part of the proceeds to a person with a valid claim under section 23(7).

(e) Schedule 4 also allows for the making of a restraint order by the High Court which prevents a person accused of an offence under sections 14–30 from selling/disposing of their property in order to avoid forfeiture. Applications for restraint orders may be made at an early stage of an investigation, even before proceedings have been formally instituted. Although a restraint order is formally made by the High Court, the prosecution can apply without notice to any other parties (ex parte) to a judge in chambers for the issue of such an order. This is because in some instances it is vital to act as quickly as possible.

PNLD reference numbers

D8714, D8755, D8756, D8757, D8758

4.4.13 **Freezing orders—contents**

Sections 4 to 16 of the Anti-terrorism, Crime and Security Act 2001 contain measures to allow the UK to take action to freeze the assets of overseas persons or governments who are threatening the economic interests of the UK or the life or property of UK residents. These provisions will allow the UK to impose sanctions in cases of urgency, where neither the United Nations nor the European Union has yet agreed a course of action, or in cases where it is appropriate for the UK to impose sanctions independently. Section 5 of and Schedule 3 to the Anti-terrorism, Crime and Security Act 2001 detail the contents of a freezing order.

(1) A freezing order is an order which prohibits persons from **making funds available to or for the benefit of a person** or persons specified in the order.

(2) The order must provide that these are the persons who are prohibited—
   (a) all persons in the United Kingdom, and
   (b) all persons elsewhere who are **nationals of the United Kingdom** or are bodies incorporated under the law of any part of the United Kingdom or are Scottish partnerships.

(3) The order may specify the following (and only the following) as the person or persons to whom or for whose benefit **funds** are not to be made available—
   (a) the person or persons reasonably believed by the Treasury to have taken or to be likely to take the action referred to in section 4;
   (b) any person the Treasury reasonably believes has provided or is likely to provide assistance (directly or indirectly) to that person or any of those persons.

(4) A person may be specified under subsection (3) by—
   (a) being named in the order, or
   (b) falling within a description of persons set out in the order.

(5) The description must be such that a reasonable person would know whether he fell within it.

(6) Funds are financial assets and economic benefits of any kind.

Anti-terrorism, Crime and Security Act 2001, s 5

Meanings

Making funds available to or for the benefit of a person

The freezing order must specify what this means in each case, but it can include—

(a) allowing a person to withdraw from an account;
(b) honouring a cheque payable to a person;
(c) crediting a person's account with interest;
(d) releasing documents of title (such as share certificates) held on a person's behalf;
(e) making available the proceeds of realization of a person's property;
(f) making a payment to or for a person's benefit (for instance, under a contract or as a gift or under any enactment such as the enactments relating to social security);
(g) such other acts as the order may specify (Anti-terrorism, Crime and Security Act 2001, Schedule 3).

A national of the United Kingdom

Is an individual who is a British citizen, a British Overseas Territories citizen, a British National (Overseas) or a British Overseas citizen, a person who under the British Nationality Act 1981 is a British subject, or a British protected person within the meaning of that Act (Anti-terrorism, Crime and Security Act 2001, s 9).

Funds

Include gold, cash, deposits, securities (such as stocks, shares and debentures) and such other matters as the order may specify (Anti-terrorism, Crime and Security Act 2001, Sch 3, para 2).

Notes

(a) Paragraph 4 of Schedule 3 to the Anti-terrorism, Crime and Security Act 2001 provides that a freezing order must include provisions for authorizing funds to be made available (for example for basic living expenses or legal costs) subject to conditions set out by the Treasury. The Treasury may charge fees to cover the administrative costs of granting such a licence.

(b) Paragraph 5 of Schedule 3 specifies that a freezing order may provide that a person must provide information or a document if it is reasonably needed in order to establish whether an offence under the order has been committed. The requirement to provide information or a document may be made by the Treasury or a person authorized by the Treasury. The requirement is to do so, in a certain time period and at a place set out in the order. The order may provide that the requirement to provide information is not to be taken to breach any restriction on the disclosure of information. However, the requirement does not apply to information or documents subject to legal privilege, except to the extent that the information or document is held with the intention of furthering a criminal purpose.

(c) Paragraph 6 of Schedule 3 provides that a freezing order may include a provision requiring a person to disclose information if three conditions apply. First, the person required to disclose must be specified in the order. Secondly, the person must know or suspect, or have grounds to know or suspect, that a person specified in a freezing order is a customer of his or has dealings with him. Thirdly, the information must have come to him in the course of a business in the regulated sector. The freezing order may include provisions: that the requirement to disclose information is not a breach of any restriction on the disclosure of information; on the use to which the information may be put and further disclosures; and that the obligation to disclose does not apply to privileged information except where the information is held with the intention of furthering a criminal purpose.

(d) Paragraph 10 of Schedule 3 provides that compensation may be paid in certain circumstances if the person has suffered loss. The entitlement to compensation may be made subject to a requirement that the claimant has behaved reasonably (for example by mitigating his loss).

(e) The Treasury can make a freezing order if two conditions are satisfied. First, the Treasury must reasonably believe that action threatening the UK's economy (or part of it) or the life or property of UK nationals or residents has taken place or is likely to take place. Secondly, the persons involved in the action must be resident outside the UK or be an overseas government (ie a foreign perpetrator) (Anti-terrorism, Crime and Security Act 2001, s 4).

(f) The Treasury is required to keep under review whether any freezing order should be kept in force or amended and a freezing order lapses after two years starting with the day on which it was made (Anti-terrorism, Crime and Security Act 2001, ss 7 and 8).

(g) Freezing orders are made by the government by statutory instrument. The freezing order must be approved by resolution of both Houses within 28 days of being made otherwise it will cease to have effect (Anti-terrorism, Crime and Security Act 2001, s 10).

PNLD reference numbers

D10304, D10305, D10307, D10384-94

4.4.14 **Freezing orders—offences**

Schedule 3 to the Anti-terrorism, Crime and Security Act 2001 creates the offences relating to freezing orders.

Offences

(1) A **freezing order** may include any of the provisions set out in this paragraph.

(2) A person commits an offence if he fails to comply with a prohibition imposed by the order.

(3) A person commits an offence if he engages in an activity knowing or intending that it will enable or facilitate the commission by another person of an offence under a provision included under sub-paragraph (2).

(4) A person commits an offence if—

    (a) he fails without reasonable excuse to provide information, or to produce a document, in response to a requirement made under the order;

    (b) he provides information, or produces a document, which he knows is false in a material particular in response to such a requirement or with a view to obtaining a licence under the order;

    (c) he recklessly provides information, or produces a document, which is false in a material particular in response to such a requirement or with a view to obtaining a licence under the order;

    (d) he fails without reasonable excuse to disclose information as required by a provision included under paragraph 6.

Anti-terrorism, Crime and Security Act 2001, Sch 3, para 7(1)–(4)

Points to prove

Paragraph 7(2) of Schedule 3

✓ failure
✓ to comply with a prohibition
✓ imposed by a freezing order

Paragraph 7(3) of Schedule 3

✓ engaged in an activity
✓ knowing/intending that it would
✓ enable/facilitate another person
✓ not to comply with a prohibition
✓ imposed by a freezing order

Paragraph 7(4)(a) of Schedule 3

✓ failed without reasonable excuse
✓ to provide information/produce a document
✓ in response to a requirement made
✓ by a freezing order

Paragraph 7(4)(b), (c) of Schedule 3

✓ provided information/produced a document/recklessly provided information/recklessly produced a document
✓ which you knew was false in a material particular
✓ in response to a requirement imposed by or
✓ with a view to obtaining a licence under paragraph 4 of Schedule 3 to the Anti-terrorism, Crime and Security Act 2001
✓ in respect of a freezing order

Paragraph 7(4)(d)
- ✓ failed without reasonable excuse
- ✓ to disclose information
- ✓ as required by a provision included in paragraph 6 of Schedule 3 to the Anti-terrorism, Crime and Security Act 2001

Meanings

Freezing order (see **4.4.13**).

Licence (see **4.4.13 note (a)**).

Defence

A person does not commit an offence under a provision included under subparagraph (2) or (3) if he proves that he did not know and had no reason to suppose that the person to whom or for whose benefit funds were made available, or were to be made available, was the person (or one of the persons) specified in the freezing order as a person to whom or for whose benefit funds are not to be made available.

Anti-terrorism, Crime and Security Act 2001, Sch 3, para 7(5)

Police powers

Power of arrest—section 41 of the Terrorism Act 2000 (see **5.3.1**)

Power to stop and search—section 43 of the Terrorism Act 2000 (see **5.2.1**)

Notes

(a) A freezing order *may* contain a provision that if an offence under this Schedule is committed by a body corporate and it can be proved the offence was committed with the knowledge or assistance of an officer of the company (manager, director, company secretary etc) then they may also commit the offence and be proceeded against (Anti-terrorism, Crime and Security Act 2001, Schedule 3), (see **5.7.2**).

(b) A freezing order *may* contain a provision that the consent of the DPP or the Treasury is required before proceedings can be instituted (Anti-terrorism, Crime and Security Act 2001, Schedule 3, para 8(2)).

PNLD reference numbers

H4773, H4774, H4775, H4776, H4777, H4778, H4779, H4780, H4782
D10390, D10391

Offences in subparas (2) and (3)

🕐 **Time limit for prosecution:** None.

▥ **Indictment:** Maximum two years' imprisonment and/or a fine.

♿ **Summary:** Maximum six months' imprisonment and/or to a fine not exceeding the statutory maximum.

Offence in subpara (4)

🕐 **Time limit for prosecution:** A freezing order *may* contain a provision which states that an information relating to an offence under the order which is triable by a magistrates court in England and Wales may be tried if it is laid at any time in the period of one year starting with the date of the commission of the offence. Otherwise the time limit for prosecution would be six months.

♿ **Summary:** Maximum six months' imprisonment and/or a fine not exceeding level 5 on the standard scale.

4.4.15 **Financial information**

Section 38 of and Schedule 6 to the Terrorism Act 2000 provide a power to investigate terrorist finance. A police officer of at least the rank of Superintendent may apply for a disclosure order that requires a financial institution to provide customer information. The purpose of such an order is to enable a constable to identify accounts in relation to terrorist investigations. It is therefore intended to be used earlier in an investigation than production and explanation orders under Schedule 5 to the Act (see **5.1.4** and **5.1.6**).

Police power

1(1) Where an order has been made under this paragraph in relation to a **terrorist investigation**, a constable named in the order may require a **financial institution** to which the order applies to provide **customer information** for the purposes of the investigation.

(1A) The order may provide that it applies to—
    (a) all financial institutions,
    (b) a particular description, or particular descriptions, of financial institutions, or
    (c) a particular financial institution or particular financial institutions.
 (2) The information shall be provided—
    (a) in such manner and within such time as the constable may specify, and
    (b) notwithstanding any restriction on the disclosure of information imposed by statute or otherwise.

Criteria for making order

5 An order under paragraph 1 may be made only if the person making it is satisfied that-
    (a) the order is sought for the purposes of a terrorist investigation,
    (b) the tracing of **terrorist property** is desirable for the purposes of the investigation, and
    (c) the order will enhance the effectiveness of the investigation.

Terrorism Act 2000, Sch 6, para 1(1)–(2)

Meanings

Terrorist investigation (see **5.1**).

Financial institution

Means

(a) a person who has permission under Part 4 of the Financial Services and Markets Act 2000 to accept deposits,
(b) *repealed*
(c) a credit union (within the meaning of the Credit Unions Act 1979 or the Credit Unions (Northern Ireland) Order 1985),
(d) a person carrying on a **relevant regulated activity**,
(e) the National Savings Bank,
(f) a person who carries out an activity for the purposes of raising money authorized to be raised under the National Loans Act 1968 under the auspices of the Director of National Savings,
(g) a European institution carrying on a home regulated activity (within the meaning of Directive 2006/48/EC of the European Parliament and of the Council of 14 June 2006 relating to the taking up and pursuit of the business of credit institutions),
(h) a person carrying out an activity specified in any of points 1 to 12 and 14 of Annex 1 to that Directive, and

(i) a person who carries on an insurance business in accordance with an authorization pursuant to Article 4 or 51 of Directive 2002/83/EC of the European Parliament and of the Council of 5 November 2002 concerning life assurance (Terrorism Act 2000, Sch 6, para 6(1)).

An institution which ceases to be a financial institution for the purposes of this Schedule (whether by virtue of sub-paragraph (2)(b) or otherwise) shall continue to be treated as a financial institution for the purposes of any requirement under paragraph 1 to provide customer information which relates to a time when the institution was a financial institution (Terrorism Act 2000, Sch 6, para 6(3)).

Relevant regulated activity

Means

(a) dealing in investments as principal or as agent,
(b) arranging deals in investments,
(ba) operating a multilateral trading facility,
(c) managing investments,
(d) safeguarding and administering investments,
(e) sending dematerialised instructions,
(f) establishing etc collective investment schemes,
(g) advising on investments (Terrorism Act 2000, Sch 6, para 6(1A)).

Customer information

Means

(a) information whether a **business relationship** exists or existed between a financial institution and a particular person ('a customer'),
(b) a customer's account number,
(c) a customer's full name,
(d) a customer's date of birth,
(e) a customer's address or former address,
(f) the date on which a business relationship between a financial institution and a customer begins or ends,
(g) any evidence of a customer's identity obtained by a financial institution in pursuance of or for the purposes of any legislation relating to money laundering, and
(h) the identity of a person sharing an account with a customer.

A business relationship exists between a financial institution and a person only if—

(a) there is an arrangement between them designed to facilitate the carrying out of frequent or regular transactions between them, and

(b) the total amount of payments to be made in the course of the arrangement is neither known nor capable of being ascertained when the arrangement is made (Terrorism Act 2000, Sch 6 para 7(1) and (2)).

There is also the possibility for the Secretary of State to make an order to provide for a class of information to be customer information for the purposes of this Schedule, or to cease to be customer information for the purposes of this Schedule (Terrorism Act 2000, Sch 6 para 7(3)). No such order has been made to date.

Terrorist property

Means

(a) money or other property which is likely to be used for the purposes of terrorism (including any resources of a proscribed organization),
(b) proceeds of the commission of acts of terrorism, and
(c) proceeds of acts carried out for the purposes of terrorism

(Terrorism Act 2000, s 14(1), for details see **4.4.1**).

Notes

(a) This method of investigation is sometimes known as a 'general bank circular' investigation. It allows the police to find out whether a financial institution holds accounts in particular names. Where more detailed information is required, a production order under Schedule 5 will be necessary, see **5.1.4**, or an account monitoring order under Schedule 6A, see **4.4.16**.
(b) Only a police officer of at least the rank of Superintendent can apply for an order under this Schedule (Terrorism Act 2000, Sch 6 para 2(a)).
(c) An order under paragraph 1 may be made only by a Circuit Judge or a District Judge (magistrates' courts) (Terrorism Act 2000, Sch 6 para 3(a)).
(d) The investigation may include money or other property intended for use in terrorism as well as any proceeds of terrorist acts.
(e) *Offence—failure to comply* An institution which fails to comply with a requirement under paragraph 1 of Schedule 6 commits an offence. It is a defence to prove that the information required was not in the institution's possession, or that it was not reasonably practicable for the institution to comply with the requirement, for example where the amount of information required would be huge. The penalty on summary conviction is a fine not exceeding level 5 on the standard scale (Terrorism Act 2000, Sch 6, para 1(3)–(5)).

(f) Where the offence is committed by an institution and it is proved that the offence—
  • was committed with the consent or connivance of an officer of the institution, or
  • was attributable to neglect on the part of an officer of the institution, the officer, as well as the institution, shall be guilty of the offence. The penalty for an individual on summary conviction is maximum six months imprisonment and/or a fine not exceeding level 5 on the standard scale.

In the case of an institution which is a body corporate, 'officer' includes—

(a) a director, manager, or secretary,
(b) a person purporting to act as a director, manager, or secretary, and
(c) if the affairs of the body are managed by its members, a member.
  In the case of an institution which is a partnership, 'officer' means a partner.

  In the case of an institution which is an unincorporated association (other than a partnership), 'officer' means a person concerned in the management or control of the association.
  (Terrorism Act 2000, Sch 6, para 8).

(g) *Self-incrimination*—Where a financial institution provides customer information under Schedule 8 this information is not admissible in evidence in criminal proceedings against the institution or any of its officers or employees. It may, however, be used in proceedings for an offence under paragraph 1(3) (including proceedings brought by virtue of paragraph 8, see note (f) above) (Terrorism Act 2000, Sch 6, para 9).

(h) *Counter-Terrorism Act 2008*—Section 28 of the Act makes provision for the offence in paragraph 1 of Schedule 6 to be tried at any place in the UK if it was committed in the UK. See PNLD reference number S1136 to check whether this section is in force.

PNLD reference numbers

D8772, D8773, D8774, D8775

4.4.16 **Account monitoring orders**

Section 38A of and Schedule 6A to the Terrorism Act 2000 provide for account monitoring orders. Such orders can be imposed on financial institutions. The financial institution then has to provide specified information in relation to an account (for example, details of all transactions passing through the account) for a maximum of up to 90 days for the purpose of a terrorist investigation.

Police power

(4) An account monitoring order is an order that the **financial institution** specified in the application for the order must—
  (a) for the period specified in the order,
  (b) in the manner so specified,
  (c) at or by the time or times so specified, and
  (d) at the place or places so specified,
  provide information of the description specified in the application to an appropriate officer.

(1) **A judge** may, on an application made to him by an **appropriate officer**, make an account monitoring order if he is satisfied that—
  (a) the order is sought for the purposes of a **terrorist investigation**,
  (b) the tracing of **terrorist property** is desirable for the purposes of the investigation, and
  (c) the order will enhance the effectiveness of the investigation.

(2) The application for an account monitoring order must state that the order is sought against the financial institution specified in the application in relation to information which—
  (a) relates to an account or accounts held at the institution by the person specified in the application (whether solely or jointly with another), and
  (b) is of the description so specified.

(3) The application for an account monitoring order may specify information relating to—
  (a) all accounts held by the person specified in the application for the order at the financial institution so specified,
  (b) a particular description, or particular descriptions, of accounts so held, or
  (c) a particular account, or particular accounts, so held.

Terrorism Act 2000, Sch 6A, para 2(4), (1)–(3)

Meanings

Financial institution (see **5.1.7**).

A judge

Means a Circuit Judge (Terrorism Act 2000, Sch 6A, para 1(2)(a)).

Appropriate officer

Means a police officer (Terrorism Act 2000, Sch 6A, para 1(4)(a)).

Terrorist investigation (see **5.1**).

Terrorist property (see **4.4.15**).

Notes

(a) The information would normally be provided in the form of a bank statement.

(b) Orders under Schedule 6A to the Terrorism Act 2000 differ from those in Schedule 6. The main differences are that they relate to transactions, not to customer information; and they can allow for real-time disclosure rather than a single response to a request.

(c) *Applications*—An application for an account monitoring order may be made ex parte to a judge in chambers (that means without the financial institution being present). The description of information specified in an application for an account monitoring order may be varied by the person who made the application. This is necessary so that an application does not fail completely where the judge is prepared to make the order in relation to certain of the information specified but not all. This flexibility avoids the need for a further application to be made. If the application was made by a police officer, the description of information specified in it may be varied by a different police officer (Terrorism Act 2000, Sch 6A, para 3).

(d) *Discharge or variation*—The person who applied for the account monitoring order and any person affected by the order may make an application to the Crown Court to discharge or vary the order. If the application was made by a police officer, a different officer may make such an application. The court may then discharge or vary the order (Terrorism Act 2000, Sch 6A, para 4 and para 1(3)(a)).

(e) *Duration*—The period stated in an account monitoring order must not exceed the period of 90 days beginning with the day on which the order is made (Terrorism Act 2000, Sch 6A, para 2(5)).

(f) *Effect*—Paragraph 6(2) provides that the order must be complied with in spite of any restrictions on the disclosure of information (however imposed). This is necessary as the information which is described in the order will be held by the financial institution subject to various restrictions on its disclosure to third parties. This makes it clear that the order has effect, and must be complied with, despite the existence of such restrictions.

(g) *Evidence*—Statements made by financial institutions in response to an account monitoring order may only exceptionally be used in evidence against it in criminal proceedings. The exceptions are proceedings for contempt of court; proceedings under section 23 of the Terrorism Act 2000 where the financial institution has been convicted of an offence under any of sections 15 to 18 (see **4.4.2–4.4.5**); and on a prosecution for an offence where, in giving evidence, the financial institution makes a statement inconsistent with a statement made in response to an account monitoring order (in the latter case the statement may only be used if evidence relating to it is adduced, or a question relating to it is asked, by or on behalf of the financial institution in the proceedings arising out of the prosecution) (Terrorism Act 2000, Sch 6A, para 7).

(h) *Breach of the order*—An account monitoring order is an order of the court (Terrorism Act 2000, Sch 6A, para 6(1)). If a person breaches the order, he commits the offence of contempt of court.

PNLD reference number

D10406

4.4.17 **Forfeiture orders**

Section 1 of and Schedule 1 to the Anti-terrorism, Crime and Security Act 2001 provide for the forfeiture of terrorist cash. Cash which is intended to be used for the purposes of terrorism, consists of the resources of an organization which is a proscribed organization, or is, or represents, property obtained through terrorism, may be forfeited in civil proceedings before a magistrates' court. This is possible even where no criminal proceedings have been brought for an offence in connection with the cash.

Police powers

Seizure of cash

(1) An **authorised officer** may seize any **cash** if he has reasonable grounds for suspecting that it is **terrorist cash**.

(2) An authorised officer may also seize cash part of which he has reasonable grounds for suspecting to be terrorist cash if it is not reasonably practicable to seize only that part.

Anti-terrorism, Crime and Security Act 2001, Sch 1, para 2

Detention of seized cash

(1) While the authorised officer continues to have reasonable grounds for his suspicion, cash seized under this Schedule may be detained initially for a period of 48 hours.

Anti-terrorism, Crime and Security Act 2001, Sch 1, para 3(1)

Meanings

Authorised officer

Means a constable, a customs officer, or an immigration officer (Anti-terrorism, Crime and Security Act 2001, Sch 1, para 19).

Customs officer

Means an officer of Customs and Revenue.

Immigration officer

Means a person appointed as an immigration officer under paragraph 1 of Schedule 2 to the Immigration Act 1971 (Anti-terrorism, Crime and Security Act 2001, Sch 1, para 19).

Note: the powers to seize and detain cash provided in Schedule 1 to the Anti-terrorism, Crime and Security Act 2001 are available to police officers, immigration officers, and customs officers.

However, according to the Code of Practice for authorized officers (see **5.1.7**) immigration and customs officers should only exceptionally exercise these. Where an officer, while exercising powers under other Acts, suspects that cash found is liable to be seized he should alert a police officer as soon as possible to continue the investigation (see **Appendix 4, Code of Practice, para 6**).

Cash

Means

(a) coins and notes in any currency,

(b) postal orders,

(c) cheques of any kind, including travellers' cheques,

(d) bankers drafts,

(e) bearer bonds and bearer shares, found at any place in the UK (Anti-terrorism, Crime and Security Act 2001, Sch 1, para 1(2)).

This does not include counterfeit cash, but see note (f) below.

Terrorist cash

Means cash which—

(a) is intended to be used **for the purposes of terrorism**, or

(b) consists of resources of an organization which is a **proscribed organization**, or

(c) is property **earmarked as terrorist property** (Anti-terrorism, Crime and Security Act 2001, s 1 and Sch 1, para 1(2)).

The definition of cash is intended to cover the most readily realisable monetary instruments used by terrorists.

For the purposes of terrorism

Includes anything done or intended to be done for the benefit of a proscribed organization (Anti-terrorism, Crime and Security Act 2001, Sch 1, para 19(4)).

Proscribed organization (see **4.2.1**).

Property

(1) Property is all property wherever situated and includes—
  (a) money,
  (b) all forms of property, real or personal, heritable or moveable,
  (c) things in action and other intangible or incorporeal property.

(2) Any reference to a person's property (whether expressed as a reference to the property he holds or otherwise) is to be read as follows.

(3) In relation to land, it is a reference to any interest which he holds in the land.

(4) In relation to property other than land, it is a reference—
  (a) to the property (if it belongs to him), or
  (b) to any other interest which he holds in the property (Anti-terrorism, Crime and Security Act 2001, Sch 1, para 17).

Property earmarked as terrorist property

(1) **Property obtained through terrorism** is earmarked as terrorist property.

(2) But if property obtained through terrorism has been disposed of (since it was so obtained), it is earmarked as terrorist property only if it is held by a person into whose hands it may be followed.

(3) Earmarked property obtained through terrorism may be followed into the hands of a person obtaining it on a disposal by—
  (a) the person who obtained the property through terrorism, or
  (b) a person into whose hands it may (by virtue of this sub-paragraph) be followed (Anti-terrorism, Crime and Security Act 2001, Sch 1, para 12).

See note (m) below.

Property obtained through terrorism

(1) A person obtains property through terrorism if he obtains property by or in return for **acts of terrorism**, or acts carried out for the purposes of terrorism.
(2) In deciding whether any property was obtained through terrorism—
  (a) it is immaterial whether or not any money, goods or services were provided in order to put the person in question in a position to carry out the acts,
  (b) it is not necessary to show that the act was of a particular kind if it is shown that the property was obtained through acts of one of a number of kinds, each of which would have been an act of terrorism, or an act carried out for the purposes of terrorism (Anti-terrorism, Crime and Security Act 2001, Sch 1, para 11).

Acts of terrorism (see **4.1**).

Notes

(a) These forfeiture powers may be exercised in relation to any cash whether or not any proceedings have been brought for an offence in connection with the cash (Anti-terrorism, Crime and Security Act 2001, s 1(2)).
(b) An authorized officer may use *reasonable force* when exercising these powers of seizure and detention (Terrorism Act 2000, Sch 14, para 3).
(c) An authorized officer may also *enter a vehicle*, aircraft, hovercraft, train, or vessel for the purpose of seizing and detaining cash (Terrorism Act 2000, Sch 14, para 2).
(d) There is a Code of Practice for authorized officers acting under Schedule 1. This gives more detailed guidance on the exercise of powers under this Schedule. See **4.4.18** and for the full text, see **Appendix 3**.
(e) There are no minimum or maximum limits on the amount of cash that may be seized.

(f) These provisions do not apply to counterfeit cash. Such cash could be seized under section 24 of the Forgery and Counterfeiting Act 1981.

(g) *Extension of detention of seized cash by court order*—Under the Anti-terrorism, Crime and Security Act 2001, Sch 1, para 3(2) a magistrates' court can make an order to extend the period for which cash or any part of it may be detained.

(h) The magistrates' court (or justice of the peace if first order, see note (k) below) may make the order if satisfied, in relation to any cash to be further detained, that one of the following conditions is met.

First condition: reasonable grounds for suspecting that the cash is intended to be used for the purposes of terrorism and that either—

(a) its continued detention is justified while its intended use is further investigated or consideration is given to bringing (in the UK or elsewhere) proceedings against any person for an offence with which the cash is connected, or

(b) proceedings against any person for an offence with which the cash is connected have been started and have not been concluded.

Second condition: reasonable grounds for suspecting that the cash consists of resources of an organization which is a proscribed organization and that either—

(a) its continued detention is justified while investigation is made into whether or not it consists of such resources or consideration is given to bringing (in the UK or elsewhere) proceedings against any person for an offence with which the cash is connected, or

(b) proceedings against any person for an offence with which the cash is connected have been started and have not been concluded.

Third condition: reasonable grounds for suspecting that the cash is property earmarked as terrorist property and that either—

(a) its continued detention is justified while its derivation is further investigated or consideration is given to bringing (in the UK or elsewhere) proceedings against any person for an offence with which the cash is connected, or

(b) proceedings against any person for an offence with which the cash is connected have been started and have not been concluded (Anti-terrorism, Crime and Security Act 2001, Sch 1, para 3(5)–(8)).

(i) *Application*—The application for an order under sub-paragraph (2) may be made by the Commissioners of Customs and Excise or an authorized officer, ie a constable, immigration, or customs officer (Anti-terrorism, Crime and Security Act 2001, Sch 1, para 3(5)).

(j) *Duration*—Detention of cash may be authorized for up to three months from the date of the order, and, in the case of any further orders, up to two years from the date of the first order (Anti-terrorism, Crime and Security Act 2001, Sch 1, para 3(2)).

(k) *First order*—A first order under sub-paragraph (2) to extend the period of detention of seized cash may be made by a justice of the peace. The application to a justice of the peace for such an order may be made and heard without notice of the application or hearing having been given to any of the persons affected by the application or to the legal representative of such a person, and may be heard and determined in private in the absence of persons so affected and of their legal representatives (Anti-terrorism, Crime and Security Act 2001, Sch 1, para 3(3A)). The person affected will have the opportunity to challenge the making of the order at a later date because he will be served with a copy of it (para 3(4)) and can apply for it to be discharged (para 5).

(l) *Notice*—An order under sub-paragraph (2) must provide for notice to be given to persons affected by it (Anti-terrorism, Crime and Security Act 2001, Sch 1, para 3(4)).

(m) *Terrorist property*—Paragraphs 11–16 of Schedule 1 make detailed provisions about property earmarked as terrorist property. For tracing property, mixing property, accruing profits and exceptions refer to Schedule 1 (not reproduced here).

(n) *Handling of detained cash*—Paragraphs 4 and 5 of Schedule 1 make provision for the payment of detained cash into an interest-bearing account and for the release of such cash.

(o) *Forfeiture*—While cash is detained under Schedule 1, an application for its forfeiture may be made. Paragraphs 6 to 8 of Schedule 1 set out the procedure for doing this and how to appeal against the forfeiture. Note that these are civil proceedings and that this is a different procedure from the one provided for in section 23 of and Schedule 4 to the Terrorism Act 2000 which applies where a person had been convicted of a terrorist property or finance offence (see **4.4.12**).

(p) *Victims/compensation*—Paragraphs 9 and 10 of Schedule 1 make provision for persons to apply to the magistrates' court for the release of their cash and for compensation.

(q) *Counter-Terrorism Act 2008*—Section 83 of the Act inserts a new
sub-paragraph 3(1A) into Schedule 1 of the Anti-terrorism,
Crime and Security Act 2001 which clarifies that in determining the period of 48 hours in sub-paragraph 3(1) any Saturday
or Sunday, Christmas Day, Good Friday, and any bank holiday
are to be disregarded. See PNLD reference number D10369 for
details.

4.4.18 Code of practice for authorized officers

The Code of Practice for authorized officers acting under Schedule
1 to the Anti-terrorism, Crime and Security Act 2001 issued under
Schedule 14 to the Terrorism Act 2000 applies to all authorizing
officers, ie constables, immigration officers, and customs officers,
exercising functions under Schedule 1 (see **4.4.17**). It does not apply
in the exercise of other powers of seizure, detention, or forfeiture
under other Acts, for example under the Drug Trafficking Act 1994.

Notes

(a) The Code should be available at all police stations and at police
offices at ports (for ports, see **5.4**) where the powers are, or are
likely to be, used, for consultation by the police and the public.
(b) Failure by an officer to observe a provision of a code does not
of itself make him liable to criminal or civil proceedings (Terrorism Act 2000, Sch 14, para 6(2)).
(c) For the full text of the code, see **Appendix 3**.

Chapter 5

Terrorist Investigations

5.1 Meaning of Terrorist Investigation

Section 32 of the Terrorism Act 2000 defines the term 'terrorist investigation'. This definition applies, for example, to powers to use cordons, to obtain search warrants, production orders and explanation orders; and to make financial information orders. There is also an offence in section 39 of 'tipping off' in relation to a terrorist investigation (see **5.1.8**).

Terrorist investigation means an investigation of—

(a) the commission, preparation, or instigation of **acts of terrorism**,
(b) an act which appears to have been done for the purposes of terrorism,
(c) the resources of a **proscribed organisation**,
(d) the possibility of making an order under section 3(3), or
(e) the commission, preparation, or instigation of an offence under this Act or under Part 1 sections 1–20 of the Terrorism Act 2006 other than an offence under section 1 [*encouragement of terrorism*] or 2 [*dissemination of terrorist publication*] of that Act.

Meanings

Acts of terrorism (see **4.1.2**).

Proscribed organization (see **4.2.1**).

Notes

(a) The terms used in the definition of 'terrorist investigation' will often cover not only investigations into possible criminal offences, but also other forms of preparatory work, such as in relation to proscription or transnational terrorism finances, and protective work.

(b) For details on the offences in sections 1 and 2 of the Terrorism Act 2006 see **4.3.1** and **4.3.2**.

PNLD reference number

D8722

5.1.1 Obtaining of information—powers under Schedule 5

Section 37 of and Schedule 5 to the Terrorism Act 2000 set out the procedure for obtaining information in terrorist investigations, either by warrant or order of the court or by the authority of a police officer. The powers differ from those under the Police and Criminal Evidence Act 1984 (PACE), but there are similarities. Essentially, searches under Schedule 5 require that the search is part of a terrorist investigation (see definition above **5.1**); it does not need to be connected to a specific offence as the PACE powers. The other notable extension of power is that it is possible to obtain excluded material and to conduct an 'area search' of non-residential premises. Schedule 5 also creates a number of offences, where searches are obstructed, false statements made, etc. When undertaking financial investigations the powers provided in Schedule 6 (see **4.4.15**) or account monitoring orders, Schedule 6A (see **4.4.16**), might be more appropriate.

Schedule 5 provides the following powers—

1. Search warrant under paragraph 1 (see **5.1.2**)
   * power to enter and search premises, search persons, seize and retain relevant material
   * constable may apply to justice of the peace
   * specific or all premises warrant, may include residential premises
   * *not* excepted material
   * urgency: written order by Superintendent (see **5.1.2, note (m)**)
2. Search warrant under paragraph 2 (see **5.1.3**)
   * power to enter and search premises, search persons, seize and retain relevant material
   * Superintendent may apply to justice of the peace
   * justice need not be satisfied that warrant likely to be necessary
   * specific premises warrant, *not* residential premises
   * *not* excepted material

3. Authority to search under paragraph 3—cordons (see **5.2.5**)
   - power to enter and search premises, search persons, seize and retain relevant material
   - authority by Superintendent (urgency: constable)
   - in cordoned area
   - *not* excepted material
4. Production order under paragraph 5 (see **5.1.4**)
   - production of and access to excluded and special procedure material
   - constable may apply to Circuit Judge
5. Search warrant under paragraphs 11 and 12—excluded and special procedure material (see **5.1.5**)
   - power to enter and search premises, search persons, seize and retain relevant material, including excluded and special procedure material
   - constable may apply to Circuit Judge
   - specific or all premises warrant, may include residential premises
   - urgency: written order by Superintendent (see **5.1.5**, **note (l)**)
6. Explanation orders under paragraph 13 (see **5.1.6**)
   - order to provide explanation of material seized under paragraph 1 or 11/produced under paragraph 5
   - constable may apply to Circuit Judge
   - different powers are appropriate depending on the different types of material that are the subject of the search, production order etc. Some do not apply to **excepted material**, some allow the search for **excluded material** or **special procedure material**. No power allows the search or seizure of **items subject to legal privilege**.

Meanings

Excepted material is any of the following—

(a) 'excluded material',
(b) 'items subject to legal privilege', and
(c) 'special procedure material'

as defined in sections 11, 10 and 14 of the Police and Criminal Evidence Act 1984 (Terrorism Act 2000, Sch 5, para 4).

Excluded material

Means—

(a) personal records which a person has acquired or created in the course of any trade, business, profession, or other occupation or for the purposes of any paid or unpaid office and which he holds in confidence;

(b) human tissue or tissue fluid which has been taken for the purposes of diagnosis or medical treatment and which a person holds in confidence;

(c) journalistic material which a person holds in confidence and which consists of documents or of other records.

A person holds personal records and human tissue or fluid material in confidence if he holds it subject to an express or implied undertaking to hold it in confidence; or to a restriction on disclosure or an obligation of secrecy contained in any enactment, including an enactment contained in an Act passed after this Act.

A person holds journalistic material in confidence if he holds it subject to such an undertaking, restriction, or obligation; and it has been continuously held (by one or more persons) subject to such an undertaking, restriction, or obligation since it was first acquired or created for the purposes of journalism (Police and Criminal Evidence Act 1984, s 11).

Special procedure material

Means—

- journalistic material, other than excluded material and
- material, other than items subject to legal privilege and excluded material, in the possession of a person who acquired or created it in the course of any trade, business, profession, or other occupation or for the purpose of any paid or unpaid office; and holds it subject—
    (i) to an express or implied undertaking to hold it in confidence; or
    (ii) to a restriction on disclosure or an obligation of secrecy contained in any enactment.

Where material is acquired by an employee from his employer and in the course of his employment, or by a company from an associated company, it is only special procedure material if it was special procedure material immediately before the acquisition.

Where material is created by an employee in the course of his employment, it is only special procedure material if it would have been special procedure material had his employer created it.

Where material is created by a company on behalf of an associated company, it is only special procedure material if it would have been special procedure material had the associated company created it (Police and Criminal Evidence Act 1984, s 14).

Items subject to legal privilege

Means—

(a) communications between a professional legal adviser and his client or any person representing his client made in connection with the giving of legal advice to the client;

(b) communications between a professional legal adviser and his client or any person representing his client or between such an adviser or his client or any such representative and any other person made in connection with or in contemplation of legal proceedings and for the purposes of such proceedings; and

(c) items enclosed with or referred to in such communications and made in connection with the giving of legal advice; or in connection with or in contemplation of legal proceedings and for the purposes of such proceedings, when they are in the possession of a person who is entitled to possession of them.

Items held with the intention of furthering a criminal purpose are not items subject to legal privilege (Police and Criminal Evidence Act 1984, s 10).

Related cases

R v Inner London Crown Court ex p Baines and Baines (a firm) [1988] QB 579; R v Guildhall Magistrates' Court, ex p Primlaks Holdings Co (Panama) Inc [1990] 1 QB 261 'Legal privilege' relates to legal advice in connection with proceedings rather than legal documents in general.

R v R [1994] 1 WLR 758 A blood sample provided by the defendant to his doctor for a DNA test which his solicitors had requested was privileged.

Privilege does not apply to:

R v Leeds Magistrates' Court, ex p Dumbleton [1993] Crim LR 866, DC Forged documents.

R v Manchester Crown Court, ex p Rogers [1999] 1 WLR 832 Records of time spent with a client on attendance notes, time sheets or fee records.

R v Central Criminal Court, ex p Francis and Francis (a firm) [1989] AC 346; R (on the application of Hallinan Blackburn-Gittings & Nott (a firm)) v Middlesex Guildhall Crown Court [2004] EWHC 2726 (Admin) Items held with the intention of either the holder or any other person of furthering a criminal purpose (including the perverting of justice) (Police and Criminal Evidence Act 1984, s 10(2)).

PNLD reference numbers

D8766, C99, C97, C283, C1176

5.1.2 **Search warrants**

Paragraph 1 of Schedule 5 to the Terrorism Act 2000 provides for warrants to enter and search premises, search persons, seize and retain relevant material.

(1) A constable may apply to a justice of the peace for the issue of a warrant under this paragraph for the purposes of a **terrorist investigation**.

(2) A warrant under this paragraph shall authorise any constable—
   (a) to enter **premises mentioned in sub-paragraph (2A)**,
   (b) to search the premises and any person found there, and
   (c) to seize and retain any **relevant material** which is found on a search under paragraph (b).

(5) Subject to paragraph 2, a justice may grant an application under this paragraph if satisfied-
   (a) that the warrant is sought for the purposes of a terrorist investigation,
   (b) that there are reasonable grounds for believing that there is material on premises to which the application relates which is likely to be of substantial value, whether by itself or together with other material, to a terrorist investigation and which does not consist of or include **excepted material** (within the meaning of paragraph 4 below),
   (c) that the issue of a warrant is likely to be necessary in the circumstances of the case, and
   (d) in the case of an application for an all premises warrant, that it is not reasonably practicable to specify in the application all the premises which the person so specified occupies or controls and which might need to be searched.

Terrorism Act 2000, Sch 5, para 1(1), (2) and (5)

Meanings

Terrorist investigation (see **5.1**).

Premises mentioned in sub-paragraph (2A).

These are:

(a) one or more sets of premises specified in the application (in which case the application is for a 'specific premises warrant'); or

(b) any premises occupied or controlled by a person specified in the application, including such sets of premises as are so specified (in which case the application is for an 'all premises warrant') (Terrorism Act 2000, Sch 5, para 1(2A)).

Material is relevant

If the constable has reasonable grounds for believing that—

(a) it is likely to be of substantial value, whether by itself or together with other material, to a terrorist investigation, and
(b) it must be seized in order to prevent it from being concealed, lost, damaged, altered or destroyed (Terrorism Act 2000, Sch 5, para 1(3)).

Excepted material (see **5.1.1**).

Notes

(a) The seizure and retention of *items subject to legal privilege* (see **5.1.1**) cannot be authorized by a warrant under this provision (Terrorism Act 2000, Sch 5, para 1(4)(a)).
(b) For access to excluded and special procedure material see **5.1.4** and **5.1.5**. This may include government material, see **5.1.4**, **note (f)** and paragraph 9 of Schedule 5.
(c) *Removal of clothing* under this provision: a constable may only require a person to remove headgear, footwear, an outer coat, a jacket, or gloves in public (Terrorism Act 2000, Sch 5, para 1(4)(b)).
(d) A constable may if necessary use *reasonable force* for the purpose of exercising a power of entry, search, or seizure (Terrorism Act 2000, s 114(2)).
(e) The power to search premises includes the power to search a container (Terrorism Act 2000, s 116(1)).
(f) If something is found during a search that is not relevant to the specific investigation, but to a different terrorist investigation, the item may be seized and it is not necessary to return to court to get a further warrant; for example, a search is conducted as part of an investigation into the publication of material that is glorifying terrorism; during the search chemicals are found that might be used to build bombs.
(g) The power to seize and retain materials attracts additional powers under the Criminal Justice and Police Act 2001, ss 50, 51 and 55. Section 50 allows the seizure of bulk material in order to sift through it at another place where it is not reasonably practicable to sift through it at the place where it was found. Where only part of an item would be legally seizable, section 50 provides for the removal of the whole item where it is not

reasonably practicable to separate the part that may otherwise lawfully be seized from the rest, for example, where material is on a computer. Section 51 provides similar powers where items are found on a person who is lawfully searched; for example, where a person carries a computer or a bag full of material that needs to be examined. Section 55 provides that any excluded or special procedure material must be returned as soon as practicable, unless it is not reasonably practicable to separate it from other lawfully seized material without prejudicing that material's use.

(h) Section 21 of the Police and Criminal Evidence Act 1984 provides a person, from whom material has been lawfully seized by the police, with certain rights to access to and/or copies of it.

(i) Section 22 of the Police and Criminal Evidence Act 1984 provides directions and powers in relation to items that have been seized by the police.

(j) As in the Police and Criminal Evidence Act 1984, the warrant may be a 'specific premises warrant' or an 'all premises warrant'. For a specific premises warrant one or more sets of premises must be specified in the warrant (and in the application); the all premises warrant applies to any premises occupied or controlled by a person specified in the warrant, including those premises specified in the warrant.

(k) *Duration*—Entry and search under a warrant must be within three months from the date of its issue (Police and Criminal Evidence Act 1984, s 16(3)).

(l) There is also a power to require a person to provide an explanation of the material seized in pursuance of a warrant under paragraph 1, see **5.1.6**.

(m) *Urgent cases*—The same authority that may be given by a search warrant under paragraph 1 may in urgent cases be given to a constable by a police officer of at least the rank of Superintendent by a written order signed by him. Such an order may only be made if the officer has reasonable grounds for believing that the case is one of great emergency, *and* that immediate action is necessary. Where such an order is made particulars of the case must be notified as soon as is reasonably practicable to the Secretary of State. It is an offence to wilfully obstruct a search made under such an order (maximum penalty on summary conviction three months imprisonment and/or a fine not exceeding level 4 on the standard scale) (Terrorism Act 2000, Sch 5, para 15).

(n) If a police officer of at least the rank of Superintendent has reasonable grounds for believing that the case is one of great emergency he may by a written notice signed by him require any person specified in the notice to provide an explanation of any material seized in pursuance of an order under paragraph 15 (Terrorism Act 2000, Sch 5, para 16(1)). Paragraphs 13(2)–(4) and 14 shall apply to a notice under this paragraph as they apply to an order under paragraph 13, see **5.1.6**. It is an offence to fail to comply with a notice under paragraph 16. It is a defence to this offence if the person can show that he had a reasonable excuse for his failure. The maximum penalty on summary conviction is six months imprisonment and/or a fine not exceeding level 5 on the standard scale (Terrorism Act 2000, Sch 5, para 16(3)–(5)).

(o) *Counter-Terrorism Act 2008*—Sections 1 to 9 of the Act provide further powers to remove documents for examination, etc. For a summary of the Act see p xxvii. See PNLD reference number S1136 to check whether these sections are in force.

PNLD reference numbers

D8764, D8771

5.1.3 Search warrants—non-residential premises

Paragraph 2 of Schedule 5 provides for a further power to enter and search premises. It is wider than the one in paragraph 1 (see **5.1.2**): a justice of the peace need not be satisfied that the issue of the warrant is likely to be necessary. Such an application must be made by a Superintendent and covers only non-residential premises.

(1) This paragraph applies where an application for a specific premises warrant is made under paragraph 1 and—
   (a) the application is made by a police officer of at least the rank of superintendent,
   (b) the application does not relate to **residential premises**, and
   (c) the justice to whom the application is made is not satisfied of the matter referred to in paragraph 1(5)(c) [*warrant likely to be necessary*, see **5.1.2**].
(2) The justice may grant the application if satisfied of the matters referred to in paragraph 1(5)(a) and (b) [*terrorist investigation and reasonable grounds to believe material of substantial value is on premises*, see **5.1.2**].

Terrorism Act 2000, Sch 5, para 2

Meanings

Residential premises

Means any premises which the officer making the application has reasonable grounds for believing are used wholly or mainly as a dwelling (Terrorism Act 2000, Sch 5, para 2(4)).

Notes

(a) There is no equivalent power to this in the Police and Criminal Evidence Act 1984.

(b) This power may, for example, be used to search a number of premises in a specific area where it is suspected that terrorists are active, but where the exact location of the premises is not known. The power has been used, for example, to search rows of lock-up garages.

(c) *Duration*—the powers under paragraph 1(2)(a) and (2)(b) (to enter and search the premises and persons found therein) are only exercisable within 24 hours beginning with the time the warrant is issued (Terrorism Act 2000, Sch 5, para 2(3)). The power to seize and retain material found on such a search is exercisable within three months from the date of the issue of the warrant (Police and Criminal Evidence Act 1984, s 16(3)).

(d) Section 21 of the Police and Criminal Evidence Act 1984 provides a person, from whom material has been lawfully seized by the police, with certain rights of access to and/or copies of it.

(e) Section 22 of the Police and Criminal Evidence Act 1984 provides directions and powers in relation to items that have been seized by the police.

PNLD reference number

D8765

5.1.4 Production orders—excluded and special procedure material

Production of and access to excluded and special procedure material is provided for in paragraph 5 of Schedule 5 to the Terrorism Act 2000. There is also an option to search for such material; it applies where an order under paragraph 5 has not been complied with, if it is not practicable to communicate with the person concerned or if immediate access is necessary (see **5.1.5**).

5(1) A constable may apply to a Circuit Judge for an order under this paragraph for the purposes of a **terrorist investigation**.

(2) An application for an order shall relate to particular material, or material of a particular description, which consists of or includes **excluded material** or **special procedure material**.

(3) An order under this paragraph may require a specified person—
   (a) to produce to a constable within a specified period for seizure and retention any material which he has in his possession, custody or power and to which the application relates;
   (b) to give a constable access to any material of the kind mentioned in paragraph (a) within a specified period;
   (c) to state to the best of his knowledge and belief the location of material to which the application relates if it is not in, and it will not come into, his possession, custody or power within the period specified under paragraph (a) or (b).

(4) For the purposes of this paragraph—
   (a) an order may specify a person only if he appears to the Circuit Judge to have in his possession, custody or power any of the material to which the application relates, and
   (b) a period specified in an order shall be the period of seven days beginning with the date of the order unless it appears to the judge that a different period would be appropriate in the particular circumstances of the application.

(5) Where a Circuit Judge makes an order under sub-paragraph (3)(b) in relation to material on any premises, he may, on the application of a constable, order any person who appears to the judge to be entitled to grant entry to the premises to allow any constable to enter the premises to obtain access to the material.

6(1) A Circuit Judge may grant an application under paragraph 5 if satisfied—
   (a) that the material to which the application relates consists of or includes excluded material or special procedure material,
   (b) that it does not include **items subject to legal privilege**, and
   (c) that the conditions in sub-paragraph (2) and (3) are satisfied in respect of that material.

(2) The first condition is that—
   (a) the order is sought for the purpose of a terrorist investigation, and

    (b) there are reasonable grounds for believing that the material is **likely to be of substantial value**, whether by itself or together with other material, to a terrorist investigation.

(3) The second condition is that there are reasonable grounds for believing that it is in the public interest that the material should be produced or that access to it should be given having regard-

    (a) to the benefit likely to accrue to a terrorist investigation if the material is obtained, and

    (b) to the circumstances under which the person concerned has any of the material in his possession, custody or power.

Terrorism Act 2000, Sch 5, paras 5 and 6

Meanings

Terrorist investigation (see **5.1.1**).

Excluded material (see **5.1.1**).

Special procedure material (see **5.1.1**).

Items subject to legal privilege (see **5.1.1**).

Likely to be of substantial value (see related case below).

Notes

(a) Special procedure material may be seized under any of the three powers set out in Schedule 5, paragraphs 1–3 (see **5.1.2**, **5.1.3** and **5.2.4**); however, if it is intentionally sought, the power in paragraph 5 of Schedule 5 should be used.

(b) Paragraph 7 of Schedule 5 provides that an order may also extend to material that comes into existence within 28 days from the day of the date of the order and may be made in relation to a person who the Circuit Judge thinks is likely to have any of the material to which the application relates in his possession, custody or power within that period (Terrorism Act 2000, Sch 5, para 7(1)).

(c) There is no requirement that the notice be given to the possessor of the materials or that the material must be potential 'evidence' for a court case.

(d) *Items subject to legal privilege* are exempt from any orders under Schedule 5, including paragraph 5 (Terrorism Act 2000, Sch 5, para 8(1)(a)).

(e) Paragraph 5 has effect notwithstanding any restrictions on disclosure of information imposed by statute or otherwise (Terrorism Act 2000, Sch 5, para 8(1)(b)).

(f) *Government material*—An order made under paragraph 5 may also cover material in the possession, custody, or power of a government department (for details see paragraph 9 of Schedule 5 which is not reproduced here).

(g) *Material on computer*—Where the application under paragraph 5 relates to information contained in a computer, an order under paragraph 5(3)(a) to produce to a constable for seizure and retention any material has effect as an order to produce the material in a form in which it can be taken away and in which it is visible and legible; and an order under paragraph 5(3)(b) to give a constable access to material has effect as an order to give access to the material in a form in which it is visible and legible (Terrorism Act 2000, Sch 5, para 8(2)).

(h) This power may be used to obtain journalistic material. However, the rights of journalists to protect their sources and the freedom of expression need to be balanced with the needs of the police investigation. See related case below.

(i) Where an order under paragraph 5 has not been complied with the police may apply for a warrant to search for excluded and special procedure material, see **5.1.5**.

(j) There is also a power to require a person to provide an explanation of the material produced or made available to a constable under paragraph 5, see **5.1.6**.

Related case

Malik v Manchester Crown Court [2008] EWHC 1362 Where material that is relevant for a terrorist investigation is in the possession of a journalist, there is a potential conflict between the interests of the state in ensuring that the police are able to conduct terrorist investigations as effectively as possible and the rights of a journalist to protect his confidential sources. These rights of a journalist are important, but are not absolute. It is for the police to satisfy the court that the balance should be struck in favour of making a production order. When exercising discretion the judge has to take into account Article 10 of the European Convention on Human Rights (freedom of expression). A production order cannot be made if and to the extent that it would violate a person's Convention rights.

Paragraph 6(2)(b) should be given its plain and ordinary meaning: 'likely' means 'probable'. A 'substantial value' is a value which is more than minimal: it must be significant. The judge has to be satisfied that there are reasonable grounds for believing that the material is likely to be of substantial value, mere suspicion will not suffice.

5.1.5 Search warrants—excluded and special procedure material

Paragraphs 11 and 12 of Schedule 5 to the Terrorism Act 2000 provide for warrants to enter and search premises, search persons, seize and retain relevant material, including excluded and special procedure material. It applies where an order under paragraph 5 (see **5.1.4**) has not been complied with, if it is not practicable to communicate with the person concerned or if immediate access is necessary.

11(1) A constable may apply to a Circuit Judge for the issue of a warrant under this paragraph for the purposes of a **terrorist investigation**.

  (2) A warrant under this paragraph shall authorise any constable—

   (a) to enter **premises mentioned in sub-paragraph (3A)**,

   (b) to search the premises and any person found there, and

   (c) to seize and retain any **relevant material** which is found on a search under paragraph (b).

12(1) A Circuit Judge may grant an application for a specific premises warrant under paragraph 11 if satisfied that an order made under paragraph 5 in relation to material on the premises specified in the application has not been complied with.

  (2) A Circuit Judge may also grant an application for a specific premises warrant under paragraph 11 if satisfied that there are reasonable grounds for believing that—

   (a) there is material on premises specified in the application which consists of or includes **excluded material** or **special procedure material** but does not include items subject to legal privilege, and

   (b) the conditions in sub-paragraphs (3) and (4) are satisfied.

(2A) A Circuit Judge or a District Judge (magistrates' courts) may grant an application for an all premises warrant under paragraph 11 if satisfied—

   (a) that an order made under paragraph 5 has not been complied with, and

   (b) that the person specified in the application is also specified in the order.

(2B) A Circuit Judge or a District Judge (magistrates' courts) may also grant an application for an all premises warrant under paragraph 11 if satisfied that there are reasonable grounds for believing—

   (a) that there is material on premises to which the application relates which consists of or includes excluded material or special procedure material but does not include items subject to legal privilege, and

    (b) that the conditions in sub-paragraphs (3) and (4) are met.

(3) The first condition is that—

    (a) the warrant is sought for the purposes of a terrorist investigation, and

    (b) the material is likely to be of substantial value, whether by itself or together with other material, to a terrorist investigation.

(4) The second condition is that it is not appropriate to make an order under paragraph 5 in relation to the material because-

    (a) it is not practicable to communicate with any person entitled to produce the material,

    (b) it is not practicable to communicate with any person entitled to grant access to the material or entitled to grant entry to premises to which the application for the warrant relates, or

    (c) a terrorist investigation may be seriously prejudiced unless a constable can secure immediate access to the material.

Terrorism Act 2000, Sch 5, paras 11(1)
and (2) and 12(1)–(4)

Meanings

Terrorist investigation (see **5.1**).

Premises mentioned in sub-paragraph (3A).

These are—

(a) one or more sets of premises specified in the application (in which case the application is for a 'specific premises warrant'); or

(b) any premises occupied or controlled by a person specified in the application, including such sets of premises as are so specified (in which case the application is for an 'all premises warrant') (Terrorism Act 2000, Sch 5, para 11(3A)).

Material is relevant

If the constable has reasonable grounds for believing that it is **likely to be of substantial value**, whether by itself or together with other material, to a terrorist investigation (Terrorism Act 2000, Sch 5, para 11(4)).

Likely to be of substantial value (see related case in **5.1.4**).

Excluded material (see **5.1.1**).

Special procedure material (see **5.1.1**).

Notes

(a) *Items subject to legal privilege*—The seizure and retention of such items (see **5.1.1**) cannot be authorized by a warrant under this provision (see **5.1.1**, Terrorism Act 2000, Sch 5, para 11(3)(a)).

(b) *Removal of clothing*—Under this provision a constable may only require a person to remove headgear, footwear, an outer coat, a jacket, or gloves in public (Terrorism Act 2000, Sch 5, para 11(3)(b)).

(c) The power to search premises includes the power to search a container (Terrorism Act 2000, s 116(1)).

(d) A constable may if necessary use *reasonable force* for the purpose of exercising a power of entry, search, or seizure (Terrorism Act 2000, s 114(2)).

(e) The power to seize and retain material attracts additional powers under the Criminal Justice and Police Act 2001, ss 50 and 51, namely additional powers of seizure from premises and additional powers of seizure from the person. For details see **5.1.2, note (g)**.

(f) Section 21 of the Police and Criminal Evidence Act 1984 provides a person, from whom material has been lawfully seized by the police, with certain rights of access to and/or copies of it.

(g) Section 22 of the Police and Criminal Evidence Act 1984 provides directions and powers in relation to items that have been seized by the police.

(h) The warrant may be a specific premises warrant or an all premises warrant, see **5.1.2, note (j)**.

(i) *Duration*—Entry and search under a warrant must be within three months from the date of its issue (Police and Criminal Evidence Act 1984, s 16(3)).

(j) There is also a power to require a person to provide an explanation of the material seized in pursuance of a warrant under paragraph 11, see **5.1.6**.

(k) *Urgent cases*—The same authority that may be given by a search warrant under paragraph 11 may in urgent cases be given to a constable by a police officer of at least the rank of Superintendent by a written order signed by him. Such an order may only be made if the officer has reasonable grounds for believing that the case is one of great emergency, *and* that immediate action is necessary. Where such an order is made particulars of the case must be notified as soon as is reasonably practicable to the Secretary of State. It is an offence to wilfully obstruct a search made under such an order (maximum penalty on summary conviction three months imprisonment and/or a fine not exceeding level 4 on the standard scale) (Terrorism Act 2000, Sch 5, para 15).

(l) If a police officer of at least the rank of Superintendent has reasonable grounds for believing that the case is one of great emergency he may by a written notice signed by him require any person specified in the notice to provide an explanation of any material seized in pursuance of an order under paragraph 15 (Terrorism Act 2000, Sch 5, para 16(1)), see also **5.1.2, note (n)**.

(m) *Counter-Terrorism Act 2008*—Sections 1 to 9 of the Act provide further powers to remove documents for examination etc. For a summary of the Act see p xxvii. See PNLD reference number S1136 to check whether these sections are in force.

PNLD reference number

D8769

5.1.6 **Explanation orders**

Paragraph 13 of Schedule 5 to the Terrorism Act 2000 provides another investigatory power linked to the search powers in paragraph 1 (search of premises, see **5.1.2**) and paragraph 11 (search for excluded and special procedure material, see **5.1.5**) and the production order under paragraph 5 (excluded and special procedure material, see **5.1.4**). Where material has been seized or given to the police under these provisions a constable may apply for an order requiring a person to provide an explanation of that material.

Police power to require explanation of material

(1) A constable may apply to a Circuit Judge for an order under this paragraph requiring any person specified in the order to provide an explanation of any material—
   (a) seized in pursuance of a warrant under paragraph 1 or 11, or
   (b) produced or made available to a constable under paragraph 5.

Terrorism Act 2000, Sch 5, para 13(1)

Notes

(a) For search powers in paragraph 1 (search of premises) see **5.1.2**, and paragraph 11 (search for excluded and special procedure material) see **5.1.5**.

(b) For production orders under paragraph 5 (excluded and special procedure material) see **5.1.4**.

(c) There is no equivalent power to this in the Police and Criminal Evidence Act 1984.

(d) The order must not include legally privileged material (see **5.1.1**); it must not require a person to disclose information which he would be entitled to refuse to disclose on grounds of legal professional privilege in proceedings in the High Court. However, a lawyer may be required to provide the name and address of his client (Terrorism Act 2000, Sch 5, para 13(2) and (3)).

(e) It is an offence if a person, in purported compliance with an order under paragraph 13, makes a statement which he knows to be false or misleading in a material particular, or recklessly makes a statement which is false or misleading in a material particular. This is an either way offence, the maximum penalty on conviction on indictment is imprisonment up to two years and/or a fine, on summary conviction imprisonment up to six months and/or a fine not exceeding the statutory maximum (Terrorism Act 2000, Sch 5, para 14).

(f) Where an order under paragraph 13 requires a person to explain material, he may make a statement orally or in writing (Terrorism Act 2000, Sch 5, para 13(4)(a)).

(g) Such a statement may only be used as evidence against the person on a prosecution for an offence under paragraph 14 (see **note (e)** above, Terrorism Act 2000, Sch 5, para 13(4)(b)). The statement must not be used as evidence in any other case; this would contravene Article 6 of the European Convention of Human Rights (right against self-incrimination).

PNLD reference number

D8770

5.1.7 **Disclosure of information**

Part 3 (sections 17 to 20) of the Anti-terrorism, Crime and Security Act 2001 deals with the disclosure of information. Section 17 of the Act clarifies and extends a number of information disclosure provisions available to individuals working in public authorities.

(1) This section applies to the provisions listed in Schedule 4, so far as they authorise the disclosure of **information**.

(2) Each of the provisions to which this section applies shall have effect, in relation to the disclosure of information by or on behalf of a **public authority**, as if the purposes for which the disclosure of information is authorised by that provision included each of the following-

    (a) the purposes of any **criminal investigation** whatever which is being or may be carried out, whether in the United Kingdom or elsewhere;

    (b) the purposes of any criminal proceedings whatever which have been or may be initiated, whether in the United Kingdom or elsewhere;

    (c) the purposes of the initiation or bringing to an end of any such investigation or proceedings;

    (d) the purpose of facilitating a determination of whether any such investigation or proceedings should be initiated or brought to an end.

(5) No disclosure of information shall be made by virtue of this section unless the public authority by which the disclosure is made is satisfied that the making of the disclosure is proportionate to what is sought to be achieved by it.

(6) Nothing in this section shall be taken to prejudice any power to disclose information which exists apart from this section.

Anti-terrorism, Crime and Security Act 2001,
s 17(1),(2),(5) and (6)

Meanings

Information

Includes—

(a) documents; and

(b) in relation to a disclosure authorized by a provision to which section 17 applies, anything that falls to be treated as information for the purposes of that provision (Anti-terrorism, Crime and Security Act 2001, s 20(1)).

Public authority

Includes—

(a) a court or tribunal, and

(b) any person certain of whose functions are functions of a public nature,

but does not include either House of Parliament or a person exercising functions in connection with proceedings in

Parliament (Anti-terrorism, Crime and Security Act 2001, s 20(1), Human Rights Act, s 6(3)).

Criminal investigation

Means an investigation of any criminal conduct, including an investigation of alleged or suspected criminal conduct and an investigation of whether criminal conduct has taken place (Anti-terrorism, Crime and Security Act 2001, s 20(1)). Note that these powers are not confined to terrorism investigations.

Conduct

Includes acts, omissions, and statements (Anti-terrorism, Crime and Security Act 2001, s 20(3)).

Criminal conduct

Means any conduct which—

(a) constitutes one or more criminal offences under the law of a part of the UK; or

(b) is, or corresponds to, conduct which, if it all took place in a particular part of the UK, would constitute one or more offences under the law of that part of the UK (Anti-terrorism, Crime and Security Act 2001, s 20(3)).

Proceedings outside the UK shall not be taken to be criminal proceedings unless the conduct with which the defendant in those proceedings is charged is criminal conduct or conduct which, to a substantial extent, consists of criminal conduct (Anti-terrorism, Crime and Security Act 2001, s 20(2)).

Notes

(a) The powers are listed in Schedule 4 and include, for example, section 28(7) of the Health and Safety at Work etc. Act 1974 (restriction on disclosure of information re investigations by Health and Safety Executive/inspectors of enforcing authorities), section 59(1) of the Data Protection Act 1998 (confidentiality of information obtained by Information Commissioner/staff/agent) and section 23(4) of the Civil Aviation Act 1982 (disclosure of information by Civil Aviation Authority).

(b) Section 17 of the Anti-terrorism, Crime and Security Act 2001 permits disclosure to assist any criminal investigation or criminal proceedings being carried out in the UK or abroad or to facilitate whether or not such investigations or proceedings should begin or end. The powers provided in this section do not limit any other powers to disclose that exists apart from this section.

(c) In determining whether they may disclose information, public authorities must ensure that their disclosure is proportionate to that which is intended by disclosing.

(d) *Overseas investigations/proceedings*—Section 18 of the Anti-terrorism, Crime and Security Act 2001 enables the Secretary of State to prohibit the disclosure of information for the purposes of overseas criminal investigations or criminal proceedings that would otherwise be permitted by section 17 or, without section 17, by the provisions modified by that section.

Overseas proceedings are criminal proceedings which are taking place, or will or may take place, in a country or territory outside the UK; and criminal investigations which are, or will or may be, conducted by an authority of any such country or territory.

This power may be exercised where it appears that the overseas investigation or proceedings relates to a matter in respect of which it would be more appropriate for any jurisdiction or investigation to be exercised or carried out by the authorities of the UK or a third country. The implication is that it may not be in the UK's national security interests to entrust information to every foreign power that seeks it, or even to some friendly powers which are treading on the toes of British security operations. Any person who knowingly makes a disclosure prohibited by the Secretary of State pursuant to section 17 commits an offence.

(e) *HM Revenue and Customs*—Section 19 of the Anti-terrorism, Crime and Security Act 2001 applies to information held by HM Commissioners for Revenue and Customs. It provides that no obligation of secrecy, with the exception of the Data Protection Act 1998 requirements, prevents the voluntary disclosure of information on the authority of the relevant Commissioners made for the following purposes: facilitating the carrying out by any of the intelligence services of any of that service's functions; for the purpose of any criminal investigation or criminal proceedings in the UK or abroad or to begin or end such investigation or proceedings or to determine to do so (Anti-terrorism, Crime and Security Act 2001, s 19(2)). Without the provision in section 19 staff of the HM Commissioners for Revenue and Customs would not be authorized to make such a disclosure. For further guidance refer to the 'Anti-terrorism, Crime and Security Act 2001: Code of Practice on the disclosure of information' (<http://www.hmrc.gov.uk/pdfs/cop_at.pdf>).

(f) *Proportionality*—The person who makes the disclosure has to be satisfied that the making of the disclosure is proportionate to what is sought to be achieved by it (Anti-terrorism, Crime and Security Act 2001, s 19(3)).

(g) *Further disclosure*—Disclosed information cannot be further disclosed by the recipient except for the purposes permitted for original disclosures and with the consent of the relevant Commissioners (Anti-terrorism, Crime and Security Act 2001, s 19(5)).

(h) Much of the information falling within section 17 can have little relevance to terrorism —the Schedule 4 list includes, for example, the Merchant Shipping (Liner Conferences) Act 1982 and the Diseases of Fish Act 1983. Furthermore, the powers are not confined to terrorism investigations but relate to crimes in general. The definition of 'criminal investigation' in section 20 means not only an investigation of any criminal conduct, including an investigation of alleged or suspected criminal conduct, but also an investigation of whether criminal conduct has taken place.

(i) *Sharing of information*—There are some other statutory sharing arrangements (affecting the Customs under the Commissioners for Revenue and Customs Act 2005 and the Department of Social Security under the Social Security Administration (Fraud) Act 1997 and the Finance Act 1997), otherwise, one official body has no authority to inform another of merely suspicious activity or simply on request and there may be offences if disclosure is made outside these bounds.

PNLD reference numbers

D10311, D10312, H4751, D10313, D10314

5.1.8 **Disclosure of information—offence**

Section 39 of the Terrorism Act 2000 creates two offences relating to the disclosure of certain material relevant to a terrorist investigation. These offences are sometimes called 'tipping off'.

Offence

(1) Subsection (2) applies where a person knows or has reasonable cause to suspect that a constable is **conducting** or proposes to conduct a **terrorist investigation**.

(2) The person commits an offence if he—

   (a) discloses to another anything which is likely to prejudice the investigation, or

   (b) **interferes with material** which is likely to be relevant to the investigation.

(3) Subsection (4) applies where a person knows or has reasonable cause to suspect that a disclosure has been or will be made under any of sections 19 to 21B or 38B.

(4) The person commits an offence if he—

    (a) discloses to another anything which is likely to prejudice an investigation resulting from the disclosure under that section, or

    (b) interferes with material which is likely to be relevant to an investigation resulting from the disclosure under that section.

Terrorism Act 2000, s 39(1)–(4)

Points to prove

Offence in section 39(2)

- ✓ date and location
- ✓ knew/had reasonable cause to suspect that
- ✓ a constable
- ✓ was conducting/proposing to conduct
- ✓ a terrorist investigation
- ✓ disclosed to another
- ✓ something which was likely to prejudice the investigation

   or

- ✓ interfered with material
- ✓ which was likely to be relevant to the investigation

Points to prove

Offence in section 39(4)

- ✓ date and location
- ✓ knew/had reasonable cause to suspect
- ✓ that a disclosure had been/was to be made
- ✓ under section 19/20/21/21A/21B/38B of the Terrorism Act 2000
- ✓ disclosed information/other matter
- ✓ likely to prejudice investigation conducted following disclosure

   or

- ✓ interfered with material
- ✓ likely to be relevant to an investigation
- ✓ resulting from the disclosure

Meanings

Terrorist investigation (see **5.1**).

Conducting a terrorist investigation

Includes a reference to taking part in the conduct of, or assisting, a terrorist investigation (Terrorism Act 2000, s 39(8)(a)).

A person interferes with material

If he falsifies it, conceals it, destroys it or disposes of it, or if he causes or permits another to do any of those things (Terrorism Act 2000, s 39(8)(b)).

Defence

It is a defence for a person charged with an offence under subsection (2) or (4) to prove—

(a) that he did not know and had no reasonable cause to suspect that the disclosure or interference was likely to affect a terrorist investigation, or

(b) that he had a reasonable excuse for the disclosure or interference.

Terrorism Act 2000, s 39(5)

In relation to the defence in section 39(5)(a), section 118 of the Terrorism Act 2000 shifts the burden of proof to the prosecution where the defendant adduces evidence that is sufficient to raise this defence (for details see **4.3.10**). This does not apply to the defence in section 39(5)(b).

Police powers

If suspected terrorist:

Power of arrest—section 41 of the Terrorism Act 2000 (see **5.3.1**)

Power to stop and search—section 43 of the Terrorism Act 2000 (see **5.2.1**)

If the person is not suspected of being a terrorist consider using PACE powers (such as ss 24, 17, 18, and 32 of PACE) but see **5.3.1** for drawbacks on using PACE powers for potential terrorists.

Notes

(a) No offence is committed where the disclosure is made by a professional legal adviser either to his client or his client's

---

representative when giving legal advice to the client or to another person for the purpose of actual or contemplated proceedings, and without a view to furthering a criminal purpose (Terrorism Act 2000, s 39(6)).

(b) No offence is committed where the disclosure is of a matter within section 21D(2) or (3)(a) (terrorist property: tipping off, see **4.4.11**), and the information on which the disclosure is based came to the person in the course of a business in the regulated sector. For the meaning of 'business in the regulated sector', see **4.4.9**.

(c) See also section 19 of the Terrorism Act 2000 which creates a duty to disclose information relating to certain financial offences under the Act and an offence of failing to do so, see **4.4.6**, as well as further provisions on disclosure in sections 20 to 21B and 38B, see **4.4.7–4.4.10, 5.1.9**.

(d) *Counter-Terrorism Act 2008*—Sections 19 to 21 of the Act make provision on the disclosure of information and the intelligence services (see PNLD reference numbers D23724, D23725 and D23726). Section 28 of the Act makes provision for this offence to be tried at any place in the UK if it was committed in the UK. For a summary of the Act see p xxvii. See PNLD reference number S1136 to check whether this section is in force.

PNLD reference numbers

H3774, H3775, H3776, H3777, D8727

DPP✓	**DPP/AG consent required**: Terrorism Act 2006, s 117 (see **5.7.4**).
🕐	**Time limit for prosecution**: None.
♿	**Summary**: Maximum six months' imprisonment and/or fine not exceeding the statutory maximum.
▦	**Indictment**: Maximum five years' imprisonment and/or fine.

5.1.9 Fail to disclose information about acts of terrorism

Section 38B of the Terrorism Act 2000 provides for the offence of failing to disclose information about acts of terrorism which may be of material assistance.

5 Terrorist Investigations

(1) This section applies where a person has information which he knows or believes might be of material assistance—
    (a) in preventing the commission by another person of an act of **terrorism**, or
    (b) in securing the apprehension, prosecution or conviction of another person, in the United Kingdom, for an offence involving the **commission, preparation or instigation of an act of terrorism.**

(2) The person commits an offence if he does not disclose the information as soon as reasonably practicable in accordance with **subsection (3).**

Terrorism Act 2000, s 38B(1) and (2)

Points to prove

✓ date and location
✓ knowing/believing
✓ that you had information
✓ which might be of material assistance in
✓ preventing the commission by another person of an act of terrorism *or*
  securing the apprehension/prosecution/conviction of another person in the UK
✓ for an offence involving the commission/preparation/instigation of an act of terrorism
✓ failed to disclose that information
✓ as soon as reasonably practicable
✓ to a constable

Meanings

Terrorism (see **4.1.1**).

Commission, preparation or instigation of an act of terrorism (see **4.1.3**).

Subsection (3)

Means disclosure made to a constable.

Police powers

If suspected terrorist:

Power of arrest—section 41 of the Terrorism Act 2000 (see **5.3.1**)

Power to stop and search—section 43 of the Terrorism Act 2000 (see **5.2.1**)

If the person is not suspected of being a terrorist then consider using PACE powers of arrest but see **5.3.1** for drawbacks on using PACE powers for potential terrorists.

Defence

It is a defence for a person charged with an offence under subsection (2) to prove that he had a reasonable excuse for not making the disclosure.

Terrorism Act 2000, s 38B(4)

Notes

(a) For non terrorism-related offences there is no legal duty to report information to the police, only a moral one. This section creates a legal duty to report information to the police. However, the person must *know* or *believe* that the information will be of material assistance so suspicion is not enough to commit the offence.

(b) The information must also relate to the possible prevention of an act of terrorism or to the apprehension, prosecution, or conviction of a person involved in the commission, instigation, or preparation of an act of terrorism. This points to the fact that there must be an act of terrorism that has or is going to occur.

(c) Home Office Circular 7/2002 provides that this duty relates to every person and having a familial and legal relationship with a person does not grant immunity from the obligation to disclose information. This would cover family members who are not involved in terrorism but know or believe that a family member is and even the relationship between a client and a solicitor.

(d) This offence could be committed in a number of ways, by failing to tell the police anything at all, by refusing to answer questions or by relating false information.

(e) *Extraterritorial jurisdiction*—Proceedings for an offence can be taken, and the offence can be regarded as having been committed in any place where the person to be charged is or has been since he first believed or knew about information that might be of assistance in the prevention of terrorism or bringing a terrorist to justice (Terrorism Act 2000, s 38B(6)). This allows a person resident in the UK to be charged with the offence even if he was outside the UK at the time he became aware of the information.

(f) Charges under this offence could be possible in four different scenarios. First, where there is evidence that an accomplice or conspirator is involved in an act of terrorism and the evidence against them is weak, section 38B could be used. Secondly, where the police have discovered an active terrorist organization, section 38B could be used to prosecute those less involved. Thirdly, where evidence in a terrorist plot is not enough to charge the main offenders, section 38B could be used for those less involved. Fourthly, those persons who have been coerced into aiding terrorists, for example by loaning cars, section 38B could be considered (Clive Walker, *Blackstone's Guide to The Anti-Terrorism Legislation*, 2002).

(g) *Counter-Terrorism Act 2008*—Sections 19–21 make provision on the disclosure of information and the intelligence services. See PNLD reference numbers D23724, D23725 and D23726.

(h) *Counter-Terrorism Act 2008*—Sections 22–27 make provision for the post-charge questioning of a person if the offence is a terrorism offence or the offence has a terrorism connection. This offence is a terrorism offence for the purposes of the Act. See PNLD ref S1136 to check whether these sections are in force.

(i) *Counter-Terrorism Act 2008*—Section 28 makes provisions for this offence to be tried in any place in the UK if it is committed in the UK. See PNLD ref S1136 to check whether this section is in force.

(j) *Counter-Terrorism Act 2008*—Part IV and Schedules 4 and 5 (ss 40–61) make provisions for notification requirements and foreign travel restriction orders for persons sentenced or made subject of a hospital order for this offence. For a summary of the Act see p xxvii. See PNLD ref S1136 to check whether these sections are in force.

PNLD reference numbers

H3571, D10405

 Time limit for prosecution: None.

 Summary: Maximum six months' imprisonment and/or a fine not exceeding the statutory maximum.

 Indictment: Maximum five years' imprisonment and/or a fine.

5.2 **Stop and Search and Other Powers**

This part sets out officers' powers in relation to stopping and searching people and vehicles and powers relating to placing cordons and parking restrictions under the Terrorism Act 2000.

5.2.1 **Power to stop and search**

Section 43 of the Terrorism Act 2000 provides a police officer with a power to stop and search anyone whom he reasonably suspects is a terrorist or search anyone who has been arrested under section 41 (see **5.3.1**).

Police powers

(1) A constable may stop and search a person whom he reasonably suspects to be a **terrorist** to discover whether he has in his possession anything which may constitute evidence that he is a terrorist.

(2) A constable may search a person arrested under section 41 to discover whether he has in his possession anything which may constitute evidence that he is a terrorist.

Terrorism Act 2000, s 43

Meanings

Terrorism (see **4.1.3**).

Notes

(a) Section 43(1) is a very wide ranging and controversial power, it is much wider than the powers under section 1 of the Police and Criminal Evidence Act 1984 as no reason is needed other than a reasonable suspicion that the person is a terrorist (as defined by section 40, see **4.1**) which is a very low-level requirement and covers many possibilities. However, it is not as controversial as the stop and search power under section 44 (see **5.2.2**), which does not even require reasonable suspicion to be established against any individual and is invoked much more frequently than section 43(1).

(b) The search must be carried out by a person of the same sex (s 43(3)).

(c) Any material that the constable believes is evidence that the person is a terrorist can be seized and retained (s 43(4)). This material can be taken away and examined elsewhere (Criminal Justice and Police Act 2001, s 51) See **5.2.3** for more details.

(d) This power can be used in any part of the UK (s 43(5)).

(e) This section does not limit where the power can be used but if it is in a private place then the constable would have to have some other lawful reason or consent for being on the premises.

(f) See also **3.4.5**.

(g) *Counter-Terrorism Act 2008*—Sections 1–9 provide further powers o remove documents for examination etc. See PNLD ref S1136 to check whether these sections are in force.

PNLD reference number

D8731

5.2.2 Authorizations to invoke powers to stop and search without reasonable suspicion

Section 44 of the Terrorism Act 2000 describes the procedure whereby a constable is authorized to stop and search persons and vehicles in order to prevent acts of terrorism.

Police powers

(1) An authorisation under this subsection authorises any constable in uniform to stop a vehicle in an area or at a place specified in the authorisation and to search—

(a) the **vehicle**;

(b) the **driver** of the vehicle;

(c) a passenger in the vehicle;

(d) anything in or on the vehicle or carried by the driver or a passenger.

(2) An authorisation under this subsection authorises any constable in uniform to stop a pedestrian in an area or at a place specified in the authorisation and to search—

(a) the pedestrian;

(b) anything carried by him.

Terrorism Act 2000, s 44

Meanings

Vehicle

Includes an aircraft, hovercraft, train or vessel (Terrorism Act 2000, s 121).

Driver

In relation to an aircraft, hovercraft or vessel, means the captain, pilot or other person with control of the aircraft, hovercraft or vessel or any member of its crew and, in relation to a train, includes any member of its crew (s 44(5A)).

Notes

(a) Section 44 has two distinct powers, section 44(1) allows a constable to stop and search a vehicle (and driver and passengers) in a place/area specified in the authorization. Section 44(2) is the same power for pedestrians. The purpose of the search to is discover articles which the constable reasonably suspects are intended to be used in connection with terrorism, see **5.2.3**.

(b) The authorization can only be given if it is considered by the person giving the authorization to be advantageous to preventing acts of terrorism (s 44(3)). This means that in the specified area any person/vehicle can be searched but see related cases below for restrictions.

(c) A constable must be in uniform to exercise the power under this section.

(d) The authorization may be given by a police officer of at least the rank of Assistant Chief Constable or for the Metropolitan and City of London Police, an officer of at least the rank of Commander (s 44(4)). Acting ranks can give an authorization.

(e) In the cases of British Transport Police, Ministry of Defence Police, and Civil Nuclear Constabulary, an authorization may be given by an Assistant Chief Constable, if the area is one where an officer of one of the above forces has power and privileges, but may not be given in any other circumstances (s 44(4A), (4B) and (4C)). Acting ranks can give an authorization.

(f) If an authorization is given orally then it must be confirmed in writing as soon as is practicable (s 44(5)).

(g) An authorization can include internal waters adjacent to the place mentioned in the authorization or part of those internal waters. Internal waters means any waters in the UK that do not form part of any police area.

(h) An authorization can only last for a period of 28 days.

(i) The Secretary of State must be informed within 48 hours that an authorization has been made otherwise it will cease to have effect (s 46(2) and (4)). He can cancel an authorization with effect from a specified time and can substitute an earlier date specified in the authorization (s 46(5) and (6)).

(j) An authorization can be renewed by the person who gave it or by someone who could have given it and each time it is renewed, **notes (h) and (i)** above apply again on each renewal (s 46(7)).

(k) Home Office Circular 27/2008 provides guidance for forces in issuing standard authorizations under section 44 and the National Police Improvement Agency has issued Practice Advice on Stop and Search in relation to the Terrorism Act (2007). These should be considered by anyone planning to make an authorization.

(l) Failure to comply with an authorization/requirement under this section is an offence, see **5.2.4.**

(m) See also Police and Criminal Evidence Act 1984 Code A, paras 2.19–2.26 and 4.4.

Related case

R (on application of Gillan and another) v Metropolitan Police Commissioner [2006] UKHL 12 This case covered several points but the main one was on the use of the word 'expedient' in the legislation. In section 44(3) the word 'expedient' was distinct from the word 'necessary' in its meaning. In the dispensing of the requirement of reasonable suspicion there was a dispensing of the normal requirements of a police officer when exercising his powers of stop and search, however these types of searches are strictly regulated. So the implementing constable is not free to act arbitrarily and must not stop and search people who are obviously not terrorist suspects, and the absence of a requirement of reasonable suspicion is not tantamount to carte blanche. Authorizations should only be given if considered to be 'of significant practical value and utility in seeking to achieve ... the prevention of acts of terrorism'. Furthermore, the power does not permit ethnic profiling: 'the mere fact that the person appears to be of Asian origin is not a legitimate reason for its exercise'. While an appearance which suggests that the person is of Asian origin may attract the constable's initial attention when alerted about 'Jihadist' terrorism, a further factor must be in the mind of the constable who is implementing the power, even if on the spur of the moment and subjectively felt, otherwise the selection may be inherently discriminatory and unlawful. The other main point is that this power does not breach human rights because the length and degree of interference with liberty involved is considered to be too trifling to call it 'detention' under Article 5, and interference for the prevention of terrorism can be justifiable in relation to privacy rights (Article 8) and rights to demonstrate (Articles 10 and 11).

PNLD reference numbers

D8731, D8734, C1037

5.2.3 Exercise of power to stop and search

Section 45 of the Terrorism Act 2000 provides the procedure for exercising the power of stop and search under section 44.

(1) The power conferred by an authorisation under section 44(1) or (2)—

    (a) may be exercised only for the purpose of searching for articles of a kind which could be used in connection with **terrorism**, and

    (b) may be exercised whether or not the constable has grounds for suspecting the presence of articles of that kind.

Terrorism Act 2000, s 45(1)

Meanings

Terrorism (see **4.1**).

Police powers

(2) A constable may seize and retain an article which he discovers in the course of a search by virtue of section 44(1) or (2) and which he reasonably suspects is intended to be used in connection with terrorism.

(3) A constable exercising the power conferred by an authorisation may not require a person to remove any clothing in public except for headgear, footwear, an outer coat, a jacket, or gloves.

(4) Where a constable proposes to search a person or vehicle by virtue of section 44(1) or (2) he may detain the person or

vehicle for such time as is reasonably required to permit the search to be carried out at or near the place where the person or vehicle is stopped.

Terrorism Act 2000, s 45(2), (3), (4)

Notes

(a) This power is much wider-ranging than those under section 1 of the Police and Criminal Evidence Act 1984 in that the officer does not need to have reasonable suspicion in order to stop the person, but see related cases in **5.2.2** for restrictions.

(b) A suitably designated community support officer has the same powers as a constable under this section.

(c) A person stopped under section 44 can apply for a written statement to confirm that he was stopped. The application must be made within 12 months beginning on the date the person or vehicle was stopped (s 45(5) and (6)).

PNLD reference number

D8733

5.2.4 Offences related to stop and search

Section 47 of the Terrorism Act 2000 creates the offences relating to stop and search under section 44.

Offence

A person commits an offence if he—

(a) fails to stop a vehicle when required to do so by a constable in the exercise of the power conferred by an **authorisation under section 44(1)**;

(b) fails to stop when required to do so by a constable in the exercise of the power conferred by an **authorisation under section 44(2)**;

(c) **wilfully obstructs** a constable in the exercise of the power conferred by an authorisation under section 44(1) or (2).

Terrorism Act 2000, s 47(1).

Points to prove

Section 47(1)(a)

✓ date and location
✓ failed to stop vehicle
✓ when required by constable in uniform
✓ exercising stop and search powers under section 44(1)

Section 47(1)(b)

✓ date and location
✓ failed to stop
✓ when required to
✓ by constable in uniform
✓ exercising stop and search powers under section 44(2)
   (person)

Section 47(1)(c)

✓ date and location
✓ wilfully obstructed a constable in uniform
✓ exercising stop and search powers under section 44(1)
   (vehicle) or (2)(person)

Meanings

Authorization under section 44(1) or (2) (see 5.2.3).

Wilfully obstructs

For the act to be 'wilful' in this context it has to be deliberate. The obstruction must usually be some form of positive act which prevents, or makes it more difficult, for the officer to carry out his duty. It need not be the offender's specific purpose to obstruct, provided that he is aware that his intended act will do so. Such obstruction often takes the form of standing in the way (or some other similar action of a physical nature) whilst an officer is trying to make an arrest.

Police powers

If suspected terrorist:

Power of arrest—section 41 of the Terrorism Act 2000 (see 5.3.1)

Power to stop and search—section 43 of the Terrorism Act 2000 (see 5.2.1)

If the person is not suspected to be a terrorist, consider using PACE powers (such as ss 24, 17, 18, and 32 of PACE) but see **5.3.1** for drawbacks on using PACE powers for potential terrorists.

PNLD reference numbers

H3565, H3566, H3567, H3568, D8735

DPP✓ **DPP/AG consent required:** Terrorism Act 2000 s 117 (see 5.7.4).

🕐 **Time limit for prosecution:** Six months.

♿ **Summary:** Maximum six months' imprisonment and/or a fine not exceeding level five on the standard scale.

5.2.5 **Cordons**

Section 34 of the Terrorism Act 2000 provides for the police to place a cordon around an area for the purposes of a terrorist investigation.

Police powers

(1) **Subject to subsections 34(1A)(1B) and (2), a designation under section 33** may only be made where the area is outside Northern Ireland and is wholly or partly within a police area, by an officer for the police area who is of at least the rank of superintendent.

Terrorism Act 2000, s 34(1)

Meanings

Subject to subsections 34(1A)(1B)

Is reference to the fact that the British Transport Police and the Ministry of Defence Police can only authorize cordons in or in the vicinity of premises policed by them. Also, in the case of the Ministry of Defence, they can police any area covered by the Ministry of Defence Police Act 1987. They cannot cordon areas under any other circumstances (s 34(1C)).

Subject to subsections 34(2)

A constable of any rank can place a cordon if he considers it necessary by reason of urgency.

A designation under section 33

Means that an area can be cordoned off for the purposes of a **terrorist investigation** if the person making it considers it expedient to do so.

Terrorist investigation (see **5.1**).

Notes

(a) A cordon gives the police powers to cordon off an area involved in a terrorist incident or one that they believe may be or become involved in one. Whilst it is a wide-ranging power, the benefits of stopping terrorist acts, protecting the public, and preventing the loss or contamination of any potential evidence at the scene must outweigh the inconvenience and draconian measure of the cordon.

(b) If a constable makes a designation under section 34(2) then he must do so in writing and also inform an officer of at least the rank of Superintendent as soon as possible. The officer who is told of the designation can confirm or cancel it. If it is cancelled it must be done in writing, giving the reasons for the cancellation (s 34(3) and (4)).

(c) A designation can be made orally but must be confirmed in writing as soon as practicable (s 33(3)).

(d) Whosoever makes the designation should arrange for the area to be cordoned off with tape marked with police or in any other appropriate way (s 33(4)).

(e) The initial cordon cannot last for a period longer than 14 days. The person who made the designation or another person who is authorized to do so can extend the period of designation in writing but cannot extend for a period longer than 14 days, giving a total period of 28 days (s 35).

(f) See **5.2.7** for offences related to cordons.

(g) There is a power to authorize a search of premises in a cordoned area (see **5.2.6**).

(h) Section 116 of the Terrorism Act 2000 provides an additional offence of failing to stop a vehicle when requested to do so by an officer. Note below also applies to this offence.

(i) *Counter-Terrorism Act 2008*—Section 28 makes provisions for this offence to be tried any place in the UK if it was committed in the UK. For a summary of the Act see p xxvii. See PNLD ref S1136 to check whether this section is in force.

PNLD reference numbers

D8723, D8724

5.2.6 **Police power to search and enter in cordoned area**

Paragraph 3 of Schedule 5 to the Terrorism Act 2000 provides specific powers to enter and search premises, search persons, and seize and retain relevant material which applies to premises in a cordoned area.

(1) Subject to sub-paragraph (2), a police officer of at least the rank of superintendent may by written authority signed by him authorise a search of specified premises which are wholly or partly within a cordoned area.

(3) An authorisation under this paragraph shall authorise any constable—
   (a) to enter the premises specified in the authority,
   (b) to search the premises and any person found there,
   (c) to seize and retain any relevant material (within the meaning of paragraph 1(3) which is found on a search under paragraph (b).

(6) An authorisation under this paragraph shall not be given unless the person giving it has reasonable grounds for believing that there is material to be found on the premises which-
   (a) is likely to be of substantial value, whether by itself or together with other material, to a terrorist investigation, and
   (b) does not consist of or include excepted material.

Terrorism Act 2000, Sch 5, para 3(1), (3) and (6)

Meanings

Cordoned area (see **5.2.5**).

Material is relevant

If the constable has reasonable grounds for believing that—

(a) it is likely to be of substantial value, whether by itself or together with other material, to a terrorist investigation, and
(b) it must be seized in order to prevent it from being concealed, lost, damaged, altered or destroyed (Terrorism Act 2000, Sch 5 para 1(3)).

Excepted material (see **5.1.1**).

Notes

(a) *Urgency*—A constable who is not of at least the rank of Superintendent may give an authorization under paragraph 3 if he considers it necessary by reason of urgency (Terrorism Act 2000, Sch 5, para 3(2)).
(b) *Duration*—The powers to enter and search premises and persons found there may be exercised on one or more occasions

and at any time during the period when the designation of the cordoned area under section 33 of the Terrorism Act 2000 has effect, see **5.2.5** (Terrorism Act 2000, Sch 5, para 3(4)).

(c) *Items subject to legal privilege*—The seizure and retention of such items (see **5.1.1**) cannot be authorized by a warrant under this provision (Terrorism Act 2000, Sch 5, para 3(5)(a)). Where access to excluded or special procedure material is required, see **5.1.4** and **5.1.5**.

(d) *Removal of clothing*—Under this provision a constable may only require a person to remove headgear, footwear, an outer coat, a jacket, or gloves (Terrorism Act 2000, Sch 5, para 3(5)(b)).

(e) *Use of force*—A constable may, if necessary, use reasonable force for the purpose of exercising a power of entry, search or seizure (Terrorism Act 2000, s 114(2)).

(f) *Additional powers*—The power to seize and retain materials attracts additional powers under the Criminal Justice and Police Act 2001, ss 50, 51 and 55, namely additional powers of seizure from premises and additional powers of seizure from the person; there is an obligation to return excluded and special procedure material. For details see **5.1.2**, **note (g)**.

(g) Section 21 of the Police and Criminal Evidence Act 1984 provides a person, from whom material has been lawfully seized by the police, with certain rights to access to and/or copies of it.

(h) Section 22 of the Police and Criminal Evidence Act 1984 provides directions and powers in relation to items that have been seized by the police.

(i) *Offence*—It is an offence to wilfully obstruct a search under paragraph 3 (summary, maximum three months' imprisonment and/or fine not exceeding level 4 on the standard scale) (Terrorism Act 2000, Sch 5, para 3(7) and (8)).

(j) *Counter-Terrorism Act 2008*—Sections 1 to 9 of the Act provide further powers to remove documents for examination, etc. For a summary of the Act see p xxvii. See PNLD reference number S1136 to check whether these sections are in force.

PNLD reference number

D8765

5.2.7 **Offences related to cordons**

Section 36 of the Terrorism Act 2000 provides police powers and offences related to cordons.

Police powers

(1) A constable in uniform may—
  (a) order a person in a cordoned area to leave it immediately;
  (b) order a person immediately to leave premises which are wholly or partly in or adjacent to a cordoned area;
  (c) order the driver or person in charge of a vehicle in a cordoned area to move it from the area immediately;
  (d) arrange for the removal of a vehicle from a cordoned area;
  (e) arrange for the movement of a vehicle within a cordoned area;
  (f) prohibit or restrict access to a cordoned area by pedestrians or vehicles.

Terrorism Act 2000, s 36(1)

Offence

A person commits an offence if he fails to comply with an order, prohibition or restriction imposed by virtue of subsection (1).

Terrorism Act 2000, s 36(2)

Points to prove

Section 36(1)(a)

✓ date and location
✓ failed to comply when ordered by a constable in uniform
✓ to leave
✓ a cordoned area immediately

Section 36(1)(b)

✓ date and location
✓ failed to comply with an order by a constable in uniform
✓ to leave premises
✓ wholly/partly within/adjacent to
✓ a cordoned area

Section 36(1)(c)

✓ date and location
✓ being the driver/person in charge of a vehicle
✓ within a cordoned area
✓ failed to move the vehicle immediately
✓ when ordered to do so by a constable in uniform 36(2)

Section 36(1)(f)

✓ date and location
✓ being a pedestrian/driver of a vehicle
✓ failed to comply with
✓ a prohibition/restriction of access to a cordoned area
✓ imposed by a constable in uniform

Meanings

Order, prohibition or restriction imposed by virtue of subsection (1). See police powers above.

Defences

It is a defence for a person charged with an offence under subsection (2) to prove that he had a reasonable excuse for his failure.

Terrorism Act 2000, s 36(3)

Police powers

If suspected terrorist:

Power of arrest—section 41 of the Terrorism Act 2000 (see **5.3.1**)

Power to stop and search—section 43 of the Terrorism Act 2000 (see **5.2.1**)

If the person is not suspected to be a terrorist, consider using PACE powers (such as ss 24, 17, 18, and 32 of PACE) but see **5.3.1** for drawbacks on using PACE powers for potential terrorists.

Notes

(a) A community support officer has the same powers as a constable under this section.

(b) A cordon gives the police powers to cordon off an area involved in a terrorist incident or one that they believe may be or become involved in one. Whilst it is a wide-ranging power, the benefits of stopping terrorist acts and preventing the loss of any potential scene and evidence must outweigh the inconvenience and draconian measure of the cordon.

PNLD reference numbers

H3782, H3783, H3784, H3794, D8726

 Time limit for prosecution: Six months.

 Summary: Maximum three months' imprisonment and/or a fine not exceeding level four on the standard scale.

5.2.8 Power to restrict parking

Section 48 of the Terrorism Act 2000 provides the police with a power to restrict parking in specified areas.

Police powers

(1) An authorisation under this section authorises any constable in uniform to prohibit or restrict the **parking** of **vehicles** on a **road** specified in the authorisation.

Terrorism Act 2000, s 48(1)

(2) A constable exercising the power conferred by an authorisation under section 48 may suspend a parking place.

Terrorism Act 2000, s49(2)

Meanings

Parking

Means leaving a vehicle or permitting it to remain at rest (s 52).

Vehicle

Means any vehicle, whether or not it is in a fit state for use on roads, and includes any chassis or body, with or without wheels, appearing to have formed part of such a vehicle, and any load carried by, and anything attached to, such a vehicle (Road Traffic Regulation Act 1984, s 99(5)).

Road

Means any highway and any other road to which the public has access, and includes bridges over which a road passes. It always includes obvious public highways, footpaths and bridle ways maintained by government agencies or local authorities (Road Traffic Act 1988, s 192(1)).

Notes

(a) An authorization under this section may only be given if it is considered expedient to prevent acts of terrorism (s 48(2)).

(b) The authorization may be given by an officer of at least the rank of Assistant Chief Constable or a Commander for the Metropolitan and City of London Police (s 48(3)).

(c) An authorization may be given orally but if it is, it should be confirmed in writing as soon as practicable (s 48(4)).

(d) The power under this section shall be exercised by the placing of a traffic sign on the road concerned (s 49(1)). Traffic sign has been given the same meaning as that in the Road Traffic Regulation Act 1984 (s 64) which is any object or device (whether fixed or portable) for conveying to traffic on roads or any specified class of traffic, warnings, information, requirements, restrictions or prohibitions of any description (specified by regulations or authorised by the Secretary of State) and any line or mark on a road for so conveying such warnings, information, requirements, restrictions or prohibitions.

(e) If a constable suspends a parking place under s 49(2) then any vehicle contravening this can be towed away (s 49(3)).

(f) The period specified in this section cannot exceed 28 days but can be renewed in writing by the person who gave the authorization or who is authorized to do so (s 50(2) and (3)).

(g) There are also the powers to divert traffic for the purposes of preventing terrorism under section 22C of the Road Traffic Regulation Act 1984.

PNLD reference numbers

D8736, D8737

5.2.9 **Offences related to parking restrictions**

Section 51 of the Terrorism Act 2000 creates the offences related to parking where parking is prohibited or restricted for the prevention of acts of terrorism.

Offence

(1) A person commits an offence if he parks a **vehicle** in contravention of a prohibition or restriction imposed by virtue of **section 48**.
(2) A person commits an offence if-
  (a) he is the **driver** or other person in charge of a vehicle which has been permitted to remain at rest in contravention of any prohibition or restriction imposed by virtue of section 48, and
  (b) he fails to move the vehicle when ordered to do so by a constable in uniform.

Terrorism Act 2000, s 51(1) and (2)

Points to prove

Section 51(1)

✓ date and location
✓ park vehicle
✓ in contravention of prohibition/restriction under section 48

Section 51(2)

✓ date and location
✓ driver/person in charge of vehicle
✓ permitted to rest on a road
✓ in contravention of prohibition/restriction under section 48
✓ failed to move the vehicle
✓ when ordered by constable in uniform

Meanings

Vehicle (see 5.2.8).

Section 48 (see 5.2.8).

Driver

Means, in relation to a vehicle which has been left on any road, the person who was driving it when it was left there (s 52).

Defence

It is a defence for a person charged with an offence under this section to prove that he had a reasonable excuse for the act or omission in question.

Terrorism Act 2000, s 51(3)

It will be for the court to decide what constitutes a reasonable excuse.

Displaying a disabled badge does not in itself constitute a reasonable excuse (s 51(4)).

Police powers

If suspected terrorist:

Power of arrest—section 41 of the Terrorism Act 2000 (see **5.3.1**)

Power to stop and search—section 43 of the Terrorism Act 2000 (see **5.2.1**)

If the person is not suspected of being a terrorist then consider using PACE powers (such as ss 24, 17, 18, and 32 of PACE) but see **5.3.1** for drawbacks on using PACE powers for potential terrorists.

PNLD reference numbers

H3569, H3570, D8738

 Time limit for prosecution: Six months.

 Summary:

    51(1) A fine not exceeding level four on the standard scale.

    51(2) Maximum three months' imprisonment and/or a fine not exceeding level four on the standard scale.

5.3 **Arrest and Detention**

Section 41 of and Schedule 8 to the Terrorism Act 2000 deal with the arrest and detention of suspected terrorists. Police and Criminal Evidence Act 1984 Code of Practice H deals with the detention, treatment, and questioning by police officers of persons arrested under section 41 of the Terrorism Act 2000 and detained in police custody under section 41 of and Schedule 8 to the Act. Code H can be found in full at **Appendix 1**. Code H is primarily based on Code C, in each of the 'Notes' sections, the relevant differences between Code C and Code H are summarized.

5.3.1 **Power of arrest**

Section 41 of the Terrorism Act 2000 creates a power of arrest for those suspected to be terrorists. There is no need to satisfy the necessity test but an officer must have reasonable suspicion that the person is a terrorist.

Police powers

(1) A constable may arrest without a warrant a person whom he reasonably suspects to be a **terrorist**.

Terrorism Act 2000, s 41(1).

Meanings

Terrorist

Means a person who—

is or has been concerned in the commission, preparation or instigation of acts of terrorism or has committed one of a list of offences (eg weapons training, money laundering, directing a terrorist organization) (see **4.1**).

Notes

(a) This is a very broad power of arrest and there is no need for the necessity test to be fulfilled as with those arrested under the Police and Criminal Evidence Act 1984 (PACE): the only requirement is to reasonably suspect that the person is a terrorist. This means that an arrest can be made at a time when the police believe it should be made even though under PACE provisions there may not be enough evidence to arrest a person in connection with a specific offence.

(b) A person can be detained on the authority of the police under this section for 48 hours from the time of arrest (s 41(3))—if no extensions are sought under Schedule 8 (see **5.3.11**) then the person must be released. For those detained initially under Schedule 7 and subsequently arrested under section 41 the time begins when the examination under that Schedule began (see **5.4.1**).

(c) If a person suspected of being a terrorist is arrested using PACE provisions, the provisions under the Terrorism Act (TACT) will not be available unless further offences are disclosed. If there is any reasonable suspicion that the person is involved in terrorism, it is advisable to use the power of arrest under section 41 and not section 24 of PACE, for two reasons. First, once arrested, due to the very sensitive nature of this type of investigation, there is no requirement that the suspect be given detailed information of the reasons for the arrest; both the suspect and any representatives need only be informed of legal grounds and basic factual details (eg you are suspected of being a terrorist and have been arrested and detained under section 41 of the Terrorism Act 2000, (see **note (f)** below). Not having to give full details allows greater flexibility in the investigation and the tactics of interrogation. Secondly, suspects arrested under TACT are subject to extra powers of detention after arrest—up to 28 days rather than 96 hours (see **5.3.5**, **5.3.10** and **5.3.11**).

(d) This power of arrest is not to be used indiscriminately; there must be real and reasonable suspicion (see related cases) and it is normally exercised only against terrorism related to Irish or international causes.

(e) When arresting anyone under this section, it is advisable, for safety reasons, to give the terrorist suspect another identification number other than a collar number, such as the number on the back of the warrant card, from which it is much more difficult to identify a person (check force policy for local procedures). Also when talking to colleagues in the company of a terrorist suspect, do not use any personal details such as nicknames or first names which could possibly lead to indentification, instead it might be advisable to address colleagues by rank (check force policy for local procedures).

(f) *Code H*—Code H states that the custody record shall record and the detained person shall be informed, that the person was arrested under section 41 and the grounds for the arrest. However, where the grounds of arrest are reasons of a sensitive nature, the grounds can initially be recorded that the person is a terrorist in line with section 40(1)(a) or (b), (see **4.1**). However, Article 5.2 of the European Convention allows only a few hours' delay in giving some indication as to the nature of the offences and charges, but those details may be deduced from a later interrogation (For code H in full see Appendix 1).

(g) This power of arrest can be used across the UK (s 41(9)).

(h) The rest of section 41 deals with the detention of a suspect which is covered in **5.3.8**, **5.3.9** and **5.3.11**.

(i) See **5.4** for those detained at ports who could be later arrested under section 41.

(j) See also **3.4.3**.

Related cases

O'Hara v Chief Constable of the Royal Ulster Constabulary [1997] AC 286 The test for whether a police officer had reasonable suspicion for arrest (under previous terrorism legislation) was a simple one—what was in the mind of the officer when the arrest was made. The components involve both a genuine and subjective suspicion in the mind of the arresting officer that the arrestee has been concerned in acts of terrorism and also objectively reasonable grounds for forming such a suspicion. Thus there is an objective element to the test in that the grounds must be reasonable. Reasonable suspicion can be formed by the officer based on information he has been told either by a superior officer or an informant, there is no need to prove that the information was true. Reasonable grounds for suspicion must be taken in light of the whole situation which includes the information and the context in which it was received.

Raissi v Metropolitan Police Commissioner [2007] EWHC 2842 (QB), [2007] All ER (D) 494 (Nov) QBD A was arrested as a suspected terrorist. She was the wife of a prime suspect thought to be involved in the bombings on 11 September 2001, and she had been with him in a foreign country when it was believed that he may have undergone terrorist training (at the same time and location of one of the perpetrators of the bombings). It was reasonable for the officer to suspect that she may be a terrorist. B was also arrested as a suspected terrorist, he was the brother of the prime suspect, thought by the officer to be a close brother who lived nearby. The officer had also been influenced by the fact that he had been informed that family links played a part in terrorist activity. This did not pass the threshold of reasonable suspicion and the arrest of the brother was unlawful.

PNLD reference numbers

D8729, C1529

5.3.2 **Warrants—enter and search of premises for purposes of arrest**

Section 42 of the Terrorism Act 2000 sets out the procedure to follow when making an application to a justice of the peace for the issue of a warrant to search premises in order to make an arrest under section 41 of the Act (see **5.3.1**).

42(1) A justice of the peace may on the application of a constable issue a warrant in relation to specified premises if he is satisfied that there are reasonable grounds for suspecting that a person whom the constable reasonably suspects to be a **person falling within section 40(1)(b)** is to be found there.

42(2) A warrant under this section shall authorise any constable to enter and search the specified premises for the purpose of arresting the person referred to in subsection (1) under section 41 (arrest without warrant).

Terrorism Act 2000, s 42

Meanings

Person falling within section 40(1)(b)

Is a person who is or has been concerned in the commission, preparation, or instigation of acts of terrorism.

Acts of terrorism (see **4.1**).

Note

For arrests without warrant under section 41, see **5.3.1**.

PNLD reference number

D8730

5.3.3 **Places of detention and methods of identification**

Paragraphs 1 and 2 of Schedule 8 to the Terrorism Act 2000 provide for places of detention for those arrested under section 41 and the means to identify them.

1(1) The Secretary of State shall **designate places** at which persons may be detained under **Schedule 7** or section 41.

2(1) An **authorised person** may take any steps which are reasonably necessary for—
  (a) photographing the detained person,
  (b) measuring him, or
  (c) identifying him.

Terrorism Act 2000, Sch 8, paras 1 and 2

Meanings

Designated places

In England and Wales, there has been the designation of any police
station or prison or (additionally for persons under 18) any Young
Offender Institution, Secure Training Centre or other place of
safety. In practice, a number of police stations in Britain have been
equipped to hold terrorist suspects in conditions of sufficient security—most notably at Paddington Green Police Station in London.

Schedule 7

Refers to those detained at ports (see **5.4.1**).

Authorised person

Means a constable, a prison officer, a person authorized by the Secretary of State, and in the case of a person detained under Schedule
7, an examining officer (a constable, an immigration officer, and a
customs officer (see **5.4.1**).

Notes

(a) A constable must take a person arrested under section 41 as
   soon as is reasonably practicable to the police station he considers most appropriate (para 1(4)). Most forces will have police
   stations designated for terrorist suspects and those should be
   used. Where it is considered appropriate, in the best interests of
   all concerned and after risk assessments have been carried out,
   a terrorist suspect could be taken to cells in another force if the
   arresting force does not have the correct facilities.
(b) *Custody area*—The custody area should be completely sterile
   and contain no files, newspapers, radios, or televisions. The
   terrorist suspect should be placed in a forensically-sealed cell
   where they will undergo a thorough forensic examination. The
   custody record should be all on paper and not on the normal
   computer system used for PACE prisoners (unless force policy
   dictates otherwise). Normally, there should not be any computer terminals in the cell area, this is because the information
   contained therein is very sensitive.

(c) *Review*—A review (under Sch 8, para.21) of the detention must be done **first** before anything else, detention must be authorized in person by the review officer (see **5.3.8**) present at the police station before any other steps are taken. If appropriate it could be done from outside the cell. Failure to authorize detention could lead to valuable evidence being found inadmissible. If a review is not done first there must be a justifiable reason.

(d) *Welfare*—The welfare of the detained person is paramount and is an area that will be open to legal challenges. The detained person by the very nature of their arrest and detention is a vulnerable person and consideration should be given to constant supervision (CCTV) to ensure their welfare.

(e) *Code H key points*—There is **no** provision for bail before charge for anyone detained under section 41 (paragraph 1.6). If a detainee is taken to hospital to receive medical treatment, unlike under PACE, the clock **does not** stop (Note 1L). The review officer (at this point an Inspector not involved in the investigation, (see **5.3.10**), not the custody officer is responsible for authorizing detention (Note 3H)). Where practicable, provisions should be made to allow a detained person to practice their religion (separate prayer room, appropriate food and clothing, and religious books) (paragraph 8.8 and Note 8D). This is an important part of a detained person's welfare, forces should ensure that religious observances are followed, such as uncontaminated religious books, allowing the person to pray at the appropriate times and even waking them up during the rest period if they so request.

(f) *Code H continued*—The record of arrest need not show a specific offence, only that the person has been arrested under section 41 (paragraph 3.4 and Note 3G). Risk assessments do not form part of the custody record and should not be shown to the detained person or their legal representative (paragraph 3.8). It is advisable to keep these in a completely separate location and not as part of the custody package. Reading material (including main religious texts) should be made available to the detained person where praticable unless it interferes with the investigation or prevents or hinders statutory duties or those under this Code (paragraph 8.10). If practicable brief outdoor exercise should be offered, where this is not possible and where facilities exist, indoor exercise should be offered instead (paragraph 8.7). Exercise should be offered on each occasion even if it has been refused previously and the custody record updated. Detained persons must be visited every hour by custody staff. At least once every 24 hours, the detained person who is held for more than 96 hours should be visited by a healthcare professional (paragraph 9.1). Some forces use designated doctors to carry out these visits, check force policy. There is no requirement for the identity of officers or police staff to be disclosed in terrorism cases (paragraph 2.8), see also **note (i)** below.

(g) Reasonable force may be used where appropriate in order to photograph, identify, or measure the detained person (Terrorism Act 2000, s 114).

(h) If a person is arrested in one part of the UK but all or part of his detention takes place in another then he shall be detained in accordance with the parts of Schedule 8 applicable to the part of the country in which he is in detention (para 1(6)). There are slight differences in the law for Scotland and Northern Ireland, so if in the unusual circumstances, a person is arrested in Scotland but detained in England, the law relating to England should be adhered to.

(i) When arresting anyone under this section, it is advisable, for safety reasons, to give the terrorist suspect another identification number other than a collar number, such as the number on the back of the warrant card, from which it is much more difficult to identify a person (check force policy for local procedures). Also when talking to colleagues in the company of a terrorist suspect, do not use any personal details such as nicknames or first names which could possibly lead to identification, instead it might be advisable to address colleagues by rank (check force policy for local procedures).

(j) Under paragraph 2 of Schedule 8 there is no power to fingerprint or take samples only to measure, identify, and photograph (see also Code H 3.12–3.13.). The power to take samples is under paragraphs 10 and 12 of Schedule 8 (see **5.3.6**).

(k) There is nothing in Schedule 8 to prevent a detained person being taken elsewhere to be measured, identified, and photographed.

(l) If a person is detained under Schedule 7 (those detained at ports, see **5.4.1**) he may be transported to other places in order to examine him, establish his nationality or citizenship or make arrangements for him to be sent to another country or territory outside the UK (para 1(3)).

(m) *Counter-Terrorism Act 2008*—Sections 22–27 make provision for post-charge questioning of a person if the offence is a terrorism offence or the offence has a terrorist connection. For a summary of the Act see p xxvii. See PNLD ref S1136 to check whether these sections are in force.

PNLD reference numbers

D8786

5.3.4 **Recording of interviews and Codes of Practice**

Paragraphs 3 and 4 of Schedule 8 to the Terrorism Act 2000 details how interviews shall be recorded. These paragraphs states that there shall be a code of practice (see Terrorism Act 2000 (Code of Practice on Audio Recording of Interviews) (No 2) Order 2001 (SI 2001/189) see **Appendix 2** for the full code of practice) for the audio recording of interviews with terrorist suspects and any interviews conducted must abide by that code. It also states that there may be a code of practice for the video recording of interviews, this is not yet compulsory in Britain (but is in Northern Ireland).

Notes

(a) A breach of the code of practice by a constable is not an offence in itself, nor will it leave him open to civil proceedings (para 4(6)).

(b) The codes of practice are, however, admissible in any criminal and civil proceedings and can be taken into account where considered to be appropriate (para 4(7)).

(c) *Code H*—An appropriate adult could be required to leave the interview if the interviewing officer considers that their behaviour is hindering the interview. A Superintendent, or if one is not readily available an Inspector should be consulted (paragraph 11.10). Officers should consider the effect of prolonged detention on any information provided by the detained person, particularly if it has not been mentioned previously when asked (Note 11D). Detained persons and their legal representatives should, where practicable, be made aware of the general reasons why there are extended periods (over 24 hours) between interviews (paragraph 12.9 and Note 12C).

PNLD reference number

D8787

5.3.5 **Detained person—status and rights**

Paragraphs 5–9 of Schedule 8 to the Terrorism Act 2000 sets out a detained persons status and his rights.

5   A detained person shall be deemed to be in **legal custody** throughout the period of his detention.

6(1)   Subject to paragraph 8, **a person detained under Schedule 7** or **section 41** at a police station in England or Wales shall be entitled, if he so requests, to have one named person informed as soon as is reasonably practicable that he is being detained there.

7(1)   Subject to paragraphs 8 and 9, a person detained under Schedule 7 or section 41 at a police station in England or Wales shall be entitled, if he so requests, to consult a solicitor as soon as is reasonably practicable, privately and at any time.

Terrorism Act 2000, Sch 8, paras 5, 6(1) and 7(1)

Meanings

Legal custody

Means from arrival at the police station.

A person detained under Schedule 7

Means a person detained at a port (see **5.4**).

A person detained under section 41

Means a person arrested as a suspected terrorist (see **5.3.1**).

Police powers

8(1)   Subject to sub-paragraph (2), an officer of at least the rank of superintendent may authorise a delay—
    (a)   in informing the person named by a detained person under paragraph 6;
    (b)   in permitting a detained person to consult a solicitor under paragraph 7.

9(1)   A direction under this paragraph may provide that a detained person who wishes to exercise the right under paragraph 7 may consult a solicitor only in the sight and hearing of a qualified officer [*see* **note 1** *for meaning of qualified officer*]

9(2)   A direction under this paragraph may be given where the person is detained at a police station in England or Wales, by an officer of at least the rank of Commander or Assistant Chief Constable.

Terrorism Act 2000, Sch 8, paras 8(1) and 9(1) and (2)

Notes

(a) A person who can be informed under paragraph 6 must be a friend, relative or someone who would have an interest in the welfare of the detained person (para 6(2)). If the person is transferred to another police station he has the right to have a person informed of the transfer (para 6(3)).

(b) A detained person also has the right, subject to certain conditions (see **5.3.5**) to be able to consult a solicitor privately and at any time (para 7(1)). Such a request and the time it was made must be recorded (para 7(2)).

(c) A Superintendent can delay the right to have someone informed or the right to consult a solicitor (para 8(1)). Where a person is detained under section 41 he must be allowed to exercise his right to inform a person of his whereabouts and to consult a solicitor within 48 hours (para 8(2)). The right to consult with a lawyer is viewed by the courts as very important in any consideration of whether the person has been treated fairly. The police should also consider whether the reasons for refusal in relation to one lawyer might apply to another lawyer.

(d) A Superintendent can only give an authorization to delay these rights if he has reasonable grounds for *believing* that to allow the suspect to exercise these rights will have any of the following consequences (para 8(5)):

- interference with or harm to evidence of a serious offence (indictable offence or an offence, or conspiracy or attempt to commit an offence under section 40(1)(a) (see **4.1**))
- interference with or physical injury to any person
- alerting of persons suspected of, but not yet arrested for, a serious offence
- the hindering of recovering property obtained as a result of a serious offence or in respect of which a forfeiture order could be made under section 23 of the Terrorism Act 2000 (see **4.4.12**)
- interference with the gathering of information about the commission, instigation, or preparation of acts of terrorism
- alerting of a person making it more difficult to prevent an act of terrorism (see **4.1**) and
- alerting of a person making it more difficult to secure a(ny) person's apprehension, prosecution, or conviction in connection with the commission, instigation, or preparation an act of terrorism (para 8(4)).

(e) A Superintendent can also delay these rights if he has reasonable grounds for believing that the detained person has benefited from his criminal conduct (obtained property or pecuniary advantage) or that the recovery of property constituting the benefit will be hindered by informing a named person or allowing the person to seek advice from a solicitor.

(f) Where an authorization is given orally, it must be confirmed in writing as soon as reasonably practicable and the detained person should also be informed as soon as reasonably practicable (para 8(6) and (7)).

(g) If the reason for the delay ceases to exist then there must be no further delay in allowing the detained person their rights (para 8(8)).

(h) *Code H* (see **Appendix 1** for full Code)—Where appropriate, the detained person should be allowed to receive visitors, friends, family, or others likely to be concerned with their welfare. Risk assessments and close liaison with the investigating team should always be carried out prior to this occurring (paragraph 5.4 and Note 5B). Official visitors should also be permitted, as long as the detained person consents and after consultation with the officer with overall responsibility for the investigation. An official visitor must not compromise safety or security or unduly delay the investigation (Note 5C includes examples of official visitors). Officers must consider the risk of the detained person passing on information to associates if they are permitted to have writing materials or be allowed to communicate via telephone (paragraph 5.6 and Note 5G).

(i) Paragraph 9(1) of Schedule 8, which allows for a consultation to occur between legal representative and his client in the hearing of a police officer, is a controversial one and could undermine one of the most important rights a detained person has—the right to seek independent legal advice. Home Office Circular 42/2003, which was produced after the case of **Brennan** (see related cases below) states that this power should only be used exceptionally after a careful assessment encompassing applicability and proportionality (see also Code H, paragraph 6.5).

(j) The Home Office Circular also states that even if the police believe that such consequences will occur the restriction should only be imposed if it is proportionate to do so in the light of all the circumstances of the case. Factors that should be taken into account in reaching this evaluation are:

- whether the suspect has been initially co-operative and has been answering questions: if the suspect has been co-operating and making admissions that could prejudice his defence, it may indicate that the suspect is in need of legal advice and as such requires uninhibited access to his solicitor;

- whether the suspect could be considered vulnerable: a court could rule that a vulnerable suspect has more need of solicitor access. A suspect may have an obvious vulnerability such as a physical or sensory disability. Equally, they may be made vulnerable through restricted language ability and cultural differences. However, there will equally be cases when the vulnerability of the suspect is not immediately obvious but could be deduced from behavioural and response patterns. Such vulnerabilities would need careful assessment and might include some form of mental impairment, drug dependency or a condition that is controlled by medication. Further, overwhelming or prolonged emotional distress might be interpreted as vulnerability (para 15 of HOC 42/2003).

(k) If the police choose to exercise this power (to have a police officer within hearing of legal consultation) it is essential that they can show that one of the consequences in para 8(4) (see **note (d)** above) would occur if there was not a police officer present during the detained person's consultation with his solicitor (para 14 of HOC 42/2003).

(l) A qualified officer for the purposes of paragraph 9 is a uniformed Inspector of the force concerned, with no connection to the detained person's case (Sch 8, para 9(4)).

(m) Once the reason for the direction under paragraph 9 ceases to exist then the detained person can consult with his solicitor in private (para 9(5)).

(n) *Counter-Terrorism Act 2008*—Section 82 makes a minor amendment to para 9(3) of Schedule 8 to the Terrorism Act 2000. For a summary of the Act see p xxvii. See PNLD ref D8700 for details.

Related cases

Brennan v UK (2002) 34 EHRR 18 This is a Northern Ireland case and the power exercised was under section 45 of the Northern Ireland (Emergency Provisions) Act 1991 which is a similar provision to paragraph 9 of Schedule 8 to the Terrorism Act 2000. The European Court of Human Rights held that there had been a breach of Article 6(3)(c) (right to legal assistance) because the defendant's first consultation with his solicitor was in hearing of a police officer and would have prevented him from speaking freely. However, it was held that access to a solicitor may be restricted subject to the police showing good reason, see **notes (i) and (j)** above.

PNLD reference numbers

D8788, D8789, D19341

5.3.6 **Taking of fingerprints and samples**

Paragraphs 10–13 of Schedule 8 to the Terrorism Act 2000 provide for the taking of samples from terrorist suspects and what may be done with them when they have been taken.

Police powers

10(2) **Fingerprints** may be taken from the detained person only if they are taken by a constable—
    (a) with the **appropriate consent** given in writing, or
    (b) without that consent under sub-paragraph (4).

10(3) A **non-intimate sample** may be taken from the detained person only if it is taken by a constable—
    (a) with the appropriate consent given in writing, or
    (b) without that consent under sub-paragraph (4).

10(4) Fingerprints or a non-intimate sample may be taken from the detained person without the appropriate consent only if—
    (a) he is detained at a police station and a police officer of at least the rank of superintendent authorises the fingerprints or sample to be taken, or
    (b) he has been convicted of a **recordable offence** and, where a non-intimate sample is to be taken, he was convicted of the offence on or after 10th April 1995.

10(5) An **intimate sample** may be taken from the detained person only if—
    (a) he is detained at a police station,
    (b) the appropriate consent is given in writing,
    (c) a police officer of at least the rank of superintendent authorises the sample to be taken, and
    (d) subject to paragraph 13(2) and (3), the sample is taken by a constable.

Terrorism Act 2000, Sch 8, para 10(2)–(5)

Meanings

Fingerprints

In relation to any person, means a record (in any form and produced by any method) of the skin pattern and other physical characteristics or features of any of that person's fingers or either of his palms (Police and Criminal Evidence Act 1984 (PACE), s 65).

Appropriate consent

Means—

(a) in relation to a person who has attained the age of 17 years, the consent of that person;

(b) in relation to a person who has not attained that age but has attained the age of 14 years, the consent of that person and his parent or guardian; and

(c) in relation to a person who has not attained the age of 14 years, the consent of his parent or guardian (PACE, s 65).

Non-intimate sample

Means—

(a) a sample of hair other than pubic hair;

(b) a sample taken from a nail or from under a nail;

(c) a swab taken from any part of a person's body other than a part from which a swab taken would be an intimate sample;

(d) saliva;

(e) a skin impression—which in relation to any person, means any record (other than a fingerprint) which is a record (in any form and produced by any method) of the skin pattern and other physical characteristics or features of the whole or any part of his foot or of any other part of his body (PACE, s 65).

Recordable offence

Means any offence punishable with a term of imprisonment and some other non-imprisonable offences specified by the Secretary of State, for example, firearms, begging, public order, and fail to provide a specimen of breath (PACE, s 118).

Intimate sample

Means—

(a) a sample of blood, semen or any other tissue, fluid, urine or pubic hair;

(b) a dental impression;

(c) a swab taken from any part of a person's genitals (including pubic hair) or from a person's body orifice other than the mouth (PACE, s 65).

Notes

(a) An intimate sample may only be taken with consent (in writing) and the authorization of an officer of at least the rank of Superintendent. This is mainly because intimate samples (except for a urine sample) require a third party professional to take it and their ethical codes will not permit them to take a sample by force. If an intimate sample is refused without good cause, adverse inferences can be drawn by the courts (para 13(1)). Intimate samples, other than urine, must be taken by a registered medical practitioner or dentist on the authority of a constable (para 13(2) and (3)).

(b) For an authorization to be given for the taking of fingerprints and non-intimate samples without consent an officer must be satisfied that the fingerprints of the detained person will facilitate the ascertainment of that person's identity; and that person has refused to identify himself or the officer has reasonable grounds for suspecting that that person is not who he claims to be (para 10(6A)). Further, an officer may also only give such an authorization if—

   (i) in the case of a person detained under section 41, the officer reasonably suspects that the person has been involved in an offence under any of the provisions mentioned in section 40(1)(a) (see **4.1**), and the officer reasonably believes that the fingerprints or sample will tend to confirm or disprove his involvement, or

   (ii) in any case, the officer is satisfied that the taking of the fingerprints or sample from the person is necessary in order to assist in determining whether he falls within section 40(1)(b) (commission, preparation, or instigation of acts of terrorism) (para 10(6)).

(c) If an authorization is given orally, it should be confirmed in writing as soon as reasonably practicable (para 10(7)).

(d) Before fingerprints are taken under this paragraph the detained person shall be informed that they may be used for the purposes of a speculative search under section 63(A) of PACE and also paragraph 14(4) of Schedule 8 (see **5.3.7**) and if they were taken with consent or under section 10(4)(b) (convicted of a recordable offence) the reason that they were taken (para 11(1)).

(e) If the samples (non-intimate and fingerprints) are to be taken without consent the detained person shall be told that authorization has been given, why it has been given and where relevant the nature of the offence he is suspected of being involved in (para 11(2)).

(f) After the samples have been taken, it shall be recorded (as soon as reasonably practicable) that the person has been told what will happen to the samples and where authorization was given, the fact it was given and the reasons why and that appropriate consent was given (para 11(3)).

(g) Where a sample of hair (other than pubic) is to be taken, they can be taken by either cutting or plucking hair from roots so

long as no more are taken than is necessary for a sufficient
sample (para 13(4)).

(h) Reasonable force may be used where appropriate in order to
take samples (other than intimate) under this paragraph
(Terrorism Act 2000, s 114).

(i) If two or more non-intimate samples have been taken under
paragraph 10 and they have proved to be insufficient and the
person has been released from custody, an intimate sample
may be taken (with consent in writing and authorization from
a Superintendent) by a constable or medical practitioner or
dentist (para 12(2)). Notes **(c)**, **(d)** and **(e)** above apply to any
sample taken under paragraph 12(2).

PNLD reference numbers

D8790, D8791

5.3.7 **Checking of fingerprints and samples**

Paragraph 14 of Schedule 8 to the Terrorism Act 2000 states what
can be done with fingerprints taken under paragraphs 10 and 12.

14(1) This paragraph applies to—
(a) **fingerprints** or **samples** taken under **paragraph 10** or
12, and
(b) information derived from those samples.

14(2) The fingerprints and samples may be retained but shall not
be used by any person except for the purposes of a terrorist
investigation or for purposes related to the prevention or
detection of **crime**, the investigation of an offence or the
conduct of a prosecution.

Terrorism Act 2000, Sch 8, para 14(1) and (2)

Meanings

Fingerprints (see 5.3.6).

Samples (see 5.3.6).

Paragraph 10 or 12 (see 5.3.6).

Crime
Means—

(a) a reference to crime includes a reference to any conduct
which—

(i) constitutes one or more criminal offences (whether under the law of a part of the UK or of a country or territory outside the UK); or

(ii) is, or corresponds to, any conduct which, if it all took place in any one part of the UK, would constitute one or more criminal offences; and

(b) the references to an investigation and to a prosecution include references, respectively, to any investigation outside the United Kingdom of any crime or suspected crime and to a prosecution brought in respect of any crime in a country or territory outside the UK (para 14(4A)).

Notes

(a) Paragraph 14(2)–(3) provides that samples taken under paragraphs 10 and 12 can be checked against those taken under section 63A(1) of the Police and Criminal Evidence Act 1984 and those taken under previous terrorism provisions (section 15(9) of, or paragraph 7(5) of Schedule 5 to, the Prevention of Terrorism (Temporary Provisions) Act 1989) as long as they are for the purposes of a terrorist investigation or for the purposes related to the prevention or detection of crime, the investigation of an offence, or the conduct of a prosecution. Intelligence checks could be carried out as this would be covered by the prevention and detection of crime but those to identify a person cannot be made under this paragraph and must be made under paragraph 10, (see **5.3.6, note (b)**).

(b) There is no provision for the destruction of fingerprints and samples taken under this provision but the Data Protection Act 1988 and Article 8 of the ECHR (right to private life) require that retention be kept under review.

(c) This paragraph (other than sub-paragraph (4)) applies to fingerprints or samples (including information derived from those samples) taken under section 15(9) of, or paragraph 7(5) of Schedule 5 to, the Prevention of Terrorism (Temporary Provisions) Act 1989 (no longer in force) as it applies to fingerprints or samples (including information derived from those samples) taken under paragraph 10 or 12 (para 14(5)).

(d) *Counter-Terrorism Act 2008*—Section 14 amends the Police and Criminal Evidence Act 1984 (ss 63A and 64) to allow checks to be made, by those with access, to fingerprints and samples held by the Security Service and the Secret Intelligence Service. For a summary of the Act see p xxvii. See PNLD ref S2 to check whether these amendments are in force.

PNLD reference numbers

D8792

5.3.8 **Reviews of detention**

Paragraphs 21 and 22 of Schedule 8 to the Terrorism Act 2000 provide details of when reviews should be carried out and when they can be postponed.

21(1) A person's detention shall be periodically reviewed by a **review officer**.

21(2) The first review shall be carried out as soon as is reasonably practicable after the time of the person's arrest.

21(3) Subsequent reviews shall, subject to **paragraph 22**, be carried out at intervals of not more than 12 hours.

21(4) No review of a person's detention shall be carried out after **a warrant extending his detention has been issued under Part III**.

Terrorism Act 2000, Sch 8, para 21(1)–(4)

Meanings

Review officer (see **5.3.10**).

Paragraph 22 (see notes (d), (e), and (f) below).

A warrant extending detention under Part III (see **5.3.11**).

Notes

(a) Paragraph 21(4) is an important paragraph in that it provides that after 48 hours (the initial detention period) strictly speaking no reviews need be carried out. However, to ensure the welfare of the detained person is maintained it would be advisable to ensure the reviews continue. These reviews are not statutory reviews as these have now been passed onto a higher authority (the courts) but become reviews of the detained person's welfare and would be more than likely to be done by the custody officer.

(b) The review must be done **first** before anything else. Detention must be authorized before any other steps are taken. If appropriate it could be done from outside the cell. Failure to authorize detention could lead to valuable evidence being found inadmissible. If a review is not done first there must be a justifiable reason.

(c) Reviews of those detained for terrorism offences must be done in person and cannot be carried out by telephone.

(d) Reviews can be postponed if at the time the review is supposed to go ahead, the detained person is being interviewed by police officers and the review officer feels that the investigation may be prejudiced if the review was carried out, or if there is no review officer available, or if it is not practicable for any other reason to carry out the review (para 22(1)).

(e) Where a review has been postponed it shall be carried out as soon as reasonably practicable (para 22(2)).

(f) In order to calculate when the next review should take place, a postponed review will be deemed to have taken place at the latest time in accordance with paragraph 21 (para 22(3)).

(g) *Code H*—When reviewing a detained person's detention, no officer should question the detained person about his involvement in any offence or with regards to any comments he may make with regards to his continued detention (para 14.2).

PNLD reference numbers

D8793

5.3.9 **Grounds for continued detention**

Paragraph 23 of Schedule 8 to the Terrorism Act 2000 sets out when detention can be continued for those held under section 41.

Police powers

(1) A **review officer** may authorise a person's continued detention only if satisfied that it is necessary—

(a) to obtain **relevant evidence** whether by questioning him or otherwise,

(b) to preserve relevant evidence,

(ba) pending the result of an examination or analysis of any relevant evidence or, of anything the examination or analysis of which is to be or is being carried out with a view to obtaining relevant evidence,

(c) pending a decision whether to apply to the Secretary of State for a **deportation notice** to be served on the detained person,

(d) pending the making of an application to the Secretary of State for a deportation notice to be served on the detained person,

(e) pending consideration by the Secretary of State whether to serve a deportation notice on the detained person, or

(f) pending a decision whether the detained person should be charged with an offence.

Terrorism Act 2000, Sch 8, para 23(1)

Meanings

Review officer (see **5.3.10**).

Relevant evidence

Means evidence which—

(a) relates to the commission by the detained person of an offence under any of the provisions mentioned in section 40(1)(a) (see **4.1**) or

(b) indicates that the detained person falls within section 40(1)(b) (para 23(4)).

Deportation notice

Means notice of a decision to make a deportation order under the Immigration Act 1971 (para 23(5)).

Notes

(a) The review officer must ensure that before he authorizes continued detention under this paragraph, (all subsections except (ba)) that the procedure/investigation is being carried out diligently and expeditiously (para 23(2)).

(b) Reviews of those detained for terrorism offences must be done in person and cannot be carried out by telephone.

PNLD reference number

D8794

5.3.10 Detention—review officer, representations and record of review

Paragraphs 24–28 of Schedule 8 to the Terrorism Act 2000 deal with the review officer and the procedures he must carry out when reviewing detention.

24(1) The review officer shall be an officer who has not been directly involved in the investigation in connection with which the person is detained.

24(2) In the case of a review carried out within the period of 24 hours beginning with the time of arrest, the review officer shall be an officer of at least the rank of inspector.

24(3) In the case of any other review, the review officer shall be an officer of at least the rank of superintendent.

26(1) Before determining whether to authorise a person's continued detention, a review officer shall give either of the following persons an opportunity to make representations about the detention—
   (a) the detained person, or
   (b) a solicitor representing him who is available at the time of the review.

27(1) Where a review officer authorises continued detention he shall inform the detained person—
   (a) of any of his rights under **paragraphs 6 and 7** which he has not yet exercised, and
   (b) if the exercise of any of his rights under either of those paragraphs is being delayed in accordance with the provisions of paragraph 8, of the fact that it is being so delayed.

28(1) A review officer carrying out a review shall make a written record of the outcome of the review and of any of the following which apply—
   (a) the grounds upon which continued detention is authorised,
   (b) the reason for postponement of the review
   (c) the fact that the detained person has been informed as required under paragraph 27(1),
   (d) the officer's conclusion on the matter considered under paragraph 27(2)(a),
   (e) the fact that he has taken action under paragraph 27(2)(b), and
   (f) the fact that the detained person is being detained by virtue of section 41(5) or (6).

Terrorism Act 2000, Sch 8, paras 24(1), (2), (3), 26(1), 27(1) and 28(1)

Meanings

Paragraph 6 and 7

Means the right to have someone informed and the right to legal advice (see **5.3.5**).

Notes

(a) *Review officer*—Where the review officer is an officer below the rank of Superintendent, and a higher ranking officer gives him directions relating to the detained person which contradict his duties under Schedule 8, the review officer must refer the matter to an officer of at least the rank of Superintendent without delay (para 25(1) and (2)).

(b) *Representations*—These may be made orally or in writing (para 26(2)) and the review officer can refuse to hear oral representations from the detained person if he considers that he is unfit because of his condition or behaviour (para 26(3)).

(c) *Rights*—Where a review officer authorizes continued detention and the detained person has had his rights under paragraphs 6 and 7 delayed (right to have someone informed and right to legal advice) he shall consider whether the reasons for the delay continue and if he believes they no longer exist he shall inform the officer who authorized the delay of his opinion (unless it was he who made the decision) (para 27(2)).

(d) *Written record*—A written record of the outcome must be made in the presence of the detained person and he must be informed whether the review officer is authorizing detention and if so, on what grounds. If the detained person is incapable of understanding what is being said to him, violent or likely to become so or in need of medical attention then the above does not apply (para 28(2), (3)).

(e) Reviews of those detained for terrorism offences must be done in person and cannot be carried out by telephone.

PNLD reference numbers

D8795, D8796, D8797

5.3.11 **Warrant of further detention**

Paragraphs 29–37 of Schedule 8 to the Terrorism Act 2000 set out the procedure for extending detention under section 41.

29(2) A warrant of further detention—
    (a) shall authorise the further detention under **section 41** of a specified person for a specified period, and
    (b) shall state the time at which it is issued.

30(1) An **application for a warrant shall be made**—
    (a) during the **period mentioned in section 41(3)**, or
    (b) within six hours of the end of that period.

31 An application for a warrant may not be heard unless the person to whom it relates has been given a notice stating—
    (a) that the application has been made,
    (b) the time at which the application was made,
    (c) the time at which it is to be heard, and
    (d) the grounds upon which further detention is sought.

32(1) A **judicial authority** may issue a warrant of further detention only if satisfied that—
    (a) there are reasonable grounds for believing that the further detention of the person to whom the application relates is necessary as mentioned in **subparagraph (1A)**, and
    (b) the investigation in connection with which the person is detained is being conducted diligently and expeditiously.

33(1) The person to whom an application relates shall—
    (a) be given an opportunity to make oral or written representations to the judicial authority about the application, and
    (b) subject to **sub-paragraph (3)**, be entitled to be legally represented at the hearing.

34(1) The person who has made an application for a warrant may apply to the judicial authority for an order that specified information upon which he intends to rely be withheld from—
    (a) the person to whom the application relates, and
    (b) anyone representing him.

Terrorism Act, Sch 8, paras 29(2), 30(1),
31, 32(1), 33(1), 34(1)

Meanings

Section 41 (see **5.3.1**).

Application for a warrant shall be made

An application for a warrant is made when written or oral notice of an intention to make the application is given to a judicial authority (para 30(3)).

Period mentioned in section 41(3)

This is 48 hours.

Judicial authority

Means in England and Wales, a District Judge (magistrates' courts) who is designated for the purpose of this Part by the Secretary of State (para 29(4)).

Subparagraph (1A)

See **note (d)** below.

Subparagraph (3)

See **note (e)** below and related cases for more information.

Notes

(a) *Warrant of further detention*—A Crown Prosecutor or a police officer of at least the rank of Superintendent may apply for a warrant of further detention (para 29(1)). A warrant of further detention shall be issued for a period of **seven days** (see below). The seven days shall start at the time the person was arrested under section 41 or if he was detained under Schedule 7 (see **5.4.1**) the time when his examination under that Schedule began (para 29(3)). A warrant of further detention may be for a shorter period of time, if the application so requests or if the judicial authority is satisfied that it would be inappropriate for it to be for a period of seven days (para 29(3A)). For further extensions see **note (i)** below.

(b) *Time limits*—An application must be made within 54 hours (48 hours plus six hours) para 30(1) (the extra six hours given for the practicalities of getting a high-security detainee to court) and a judicial authority hearing an application after 48 hours shall dismiss it if he considers that it would have been reasonably practicable to make it within 48 hours (para 30(1), (2)).

(c) *Notice*—Notice must be given to the detained person and the application shall not be heard unless this has been done (para 31).

(d) *Grounds for extension*—The further detention of a person is necessary as mentioned in this sub-paragraph if it is necessary—
   (i) to obtain relevant evidence whether by questioning him or otherwise;
   (ii) to preserve relevant evidence; or
   (iii) pending the result of an examination or analysis of any relevant evidence or of anything the examination or analysis of which is to be or is being carried out with a view to obtaining relevant evidence (para 32(1A)). Relevant evidence means evidence which relates to any of the offences mentioned in s40(1)(a) (see **4.1**) or which indicates that he is or has been involved in the commission, preparation, or instigation of acts of terrorism (see **4.1**) (para 32(2)).

(e) *Representation*—a judicial authority shall adjourn the hearing of an application, if the person is not legally represented, is entitled to be and wishes to be (para 33(2)). A judicial authority may exclude from any part of the hearing, the person to whom the application relates or anyone representing him (para 33(3)), see related cases.

(f) *Hearing*—A judicial authority may, after giving the opportunity for representations to be made by the applicant (police or CPS) and/or by or on behalf of the detained person, direct that the hearing shall go ahead not in the presence of the detained person or his representative but by some other means so that they can see and be seen by the judicial authority (for example by live television link) (para 33(4) and (5)). If the detained person wishes to make representations about such a direction then he must do so using the means specified in the direction (live link etc) (para 33(6)). A judicial authority shall adjourn the hearing of a direction under this sub paragraph, if the person is not legally represented, is entitled to be and wishes to be (para 33(7)). A judicial authority is only able to make such a direction if he has been notified (and it has not been withdrawn) by the Secretary of State that there are the facilities available at the place where the person is detained (para 33(8)). If the judicial authority is able to make such a direction but chooses not to do so, it shall state the reasons why (para 33(9)).

(g) *Information*—The police or CPS can apply for an order to withhold certain information from the detained person and his legal representative. The judicial authority will grant the order only if he is satisfied that one of the following will occur if the information was disclosed—

  (i) evidence of an offence under any of the provisions mentioned in section 40(1)(a) (see **4.1**) would be interfered with or harmed,

  (ii) the recovery of property obtained as a result of an offence under any of those provisions would be hindered,

  (iii) the recovery of property in respect of which a forfeiture order could be made under section 23 (of the Terrorism Act 2000, see **4.4.12**) would be hindered,

  (iv) the apprehension, prosecution, or conviction of a person who is suspected of falling within section 40(1)(a) or (b) would be made more difficult as a result of his being alerted,

  (v) the prevention of an act of terrorism (see **4.1**) would be made more difficult as a result of a person being alerted,

  (vi) the gathering of information about the commission, preparation or instigation of an act of terrorism would be interfered with, or

(vii) a person would be interfered with or physically injured (para 34(2)).

A judicial authority may also make such an order if he is satisfied that the person has benefited from his criminal conduct and if that information was disclosed, recovery of the benefit would be hindered (para 34(3)). The judicial authority shall direct that the detained person and his legal representative be excluded from the hearing of the application under this paragraph (para 34(4)) See related cases also.

(h) *Adjournment*—An adjournment for the application of a warrant of further detention can only be given if the hearing is adjourned to a date before the end of the 48-hour period from when the person was arrested but this does not apply to an adjournment under para 33(2) (an adjournment for the detained person to obtain legal representation if he is so wishes) (para 35).

(i) *Extensions of warrants*—A Superintendent or above or a Crown Prosecutor may apply for an extension of a warrant of further detention (para 36(1)). If it is the first application of this kind and would extend the period of detention to no more than 14 days from the time of the arrest or the time when the examination began under Schedule 7 (see **5.4.1**), a judicial authority (District Judge, magistrates' court) will hear the application. In any other case it must be a senior judge (High Court or High Court of Justiciary in Scotland) (para 36(1A) and (1B)). Warrants of detention can be extended for a maximum period of seven days at any one time and for a total period of 28 days (para 36(3)). The judicial authority or senior judge can make the warrant for a shorter period of time than seven days, if the applicant requests it or if they feel it would be inappropriate to extend it for the length of time requested (para 36(3AA)). **Notes (c) and (d)** above apply to extensions to warrants of further detention as they do to warrants of further detention and where it says judicial authority, where appropriate it should read senior judge (para 36(4)). The warrant should be endorsed with the new specified period of time of detention (para 36(2). A hearing for an application to extend detention may only be adjourned if it is to a date before the expiration of the specified time in the warrant, this does not apply to an adjournment under para 33(2) (an adjournment for the detained person to obtain legal representation if he is so wishes) (para 36(5) and (6))).

(j) *Code H* (full Code H can be found at **Appendix 1**)—Where a detained person has been detained for more than 14 days, he should be transferred to a designated prison as soon as practicable since prisons are considered to have better facilities for detainees than police stations. The transfer might not be made if the detained person requests to stay at the police station (and that request can be accommodated) or there are reasonable grounds to believe that transferring the person to a prison would significantly hinder a terrorist investigation (see **5.1**) or prevent it from being carried out diligently and expeditiously or it would delay the charge or release of the person (para 14.5). Once the detained person has been transferred to prison, Code H will cease to apply (and Prison Rules will apply) but will re-apply at any time the person is transferred back to police detention (para 14.8). The legal representative, family and friends should be informed of the transfer of the detained person (para 14.10).

(k) If it appears to the police officer in charge of the detained person's detention that any of the matters (obtain evidence by questioning or preserve evidence) on which the last detention was based, has changed then he must release the person from custody immediately or tell the person who does have custody of the detained person and they in turn must release them immediately (para 37).

Related cases

Ward v Police Service of Northern Ireland [2007] UKHL 50 A detained person and his solicitor were excluded from part of a hearing for a warrant of further detention so that the judge could question the police with regards to the remaining topics they wished to interview the detained person about. The detained person and his legal representative were not informed of the information that had been discussed. This was permitted within the parameters of paragraph 33 and was also of benefit to the detained person so that the judge could satisfy himself that the police did have grounds to detain him further. Even so, the House of Lords warned that judges who exclude take upon themselves an enhanced duty to check the reasons for extended detention.

PNLD reference numbers

D8786–D8799, D8951, D8952, C1558

5.4 **Ports Control**

Section 53 of and Schedule 7 to the Terrorism Act 2000 provide powers for the control of ports, ie airports and seaports. The port controls are in addition to any powers under the Immigration Act 1971 which regulates entry into and stay in the UK generally (not included in this book). Unlike the immigration control, the security controls at ports do not give examining officers power on their own authority to refuse entry and place no requirements on travellers to obtain leave to enter the country. Another difference from the immigration powers is that these measures can apply to travel within the UK (see **5.4.1, note (e)**).

Further police powers are set out in the Aviation Security Act 1982 and the Immigration, Asylum and Nationality Act 2006. Offences relating to the security of airports and aircraft can be found in the Aviation Security Act 1982 and the Air Navigation Order 2005 which also provide police powers. The Aviation and Maritime Security Act 1990 is concerned with the security of ships and harbours. And the offence of trespass on an aerodrome is set out in the Civil Aviation Act 1982. For measures aimed at enhancing the security of ships and ports see the Ship and Port Facility (Security) Regulations 2004 (as amended) (not included in this book).

See **2.6.3** on the UK Border Agency and **3.4.9** on ports and border policing, as well as **3.4.10** on practical aspects of Schedule 7 to the Terrorism Act 2000. Also refer to the case studies 'Glasgow Airport, 30 June 2007' (**2.7**) and 'Trans-Atlantic airline plot, 10 August 2006' (**2.8.1**).

5.4.1 **Power to stop, question, and detain**

Schedule 7 to the Terrorism Act 2000 allows examining officers (constables, immigration and customs officers) to stop, question, and detain persons at ports for up to nine hours to determine whether the person is or has been concerned in the commission, preparation, or instigation of acts of terrorism.

Police powers

2(1) An **examining officer** may question a person to whom this paragraph applies for the purpose of determining whether he appears to be a **person falling within section 40(1)(b)**.

2(2) This paragraph applies to a person if—
- (a) he is at a **port** or in **the border area**, and
- (b) the examining officer **believes** that the person's presence at the port or in the area is connected with his entering or leaving Great Britain or Northern Ireland or his travelling by air within Great Britain or within Northern Ireland.

2(3) This paragraph also applies to a person on a **ship** or aircraft which has arrived at any place in Great Britain or Northern Ireland (whether from within or outside Great Britain or Northern Ireland).

2(4) An examining officer may exercise his powers under this paragraph whether or not he has grounds for suspecting that a person falls within section 40(1)(b).

5 A person who is questioned under paragraph 2 or 3 must—
- (a) give the examining officer any information in his possession which the officer requests;
- (b) give the examining officer on request either a valid passport which includes a photograph or another document which establishes his identity;
- (c) declare whether he has with him documents of a kind specified by the examining officer;
- (d) give the examining officer on request any document which he has with him and which is of a kind specified by the officer.

Terrorism Act 2000, Sch 7, paras 2 and 5

Meanings

Examining officer

Means any of the following—

(a) a constable,

(b) an **immigration officer**, and

(c) a **customs officer** who is designated for the purpose of this Schedule by the Secretary of State and the Commissioners of Customs and Excise (Terrorism Act 2000, Sch 7, para 1(1)).

Immigration officer

Means a person appointed as an immigration officer under paragraph 1 of Schedule 2 to the Immigration Act 1971 (Terrorism Act 2000, s 121).

Customs officer

Means an officer of Revenue and Customs (Terrorism Act 2000, s 121).

Note: Most port control powers provided in Schedule 7 to the Terrorism Act 2000 are available to police officers, immigration officers, and customs officers.

However, according to the Code of Practice for Examining Officers (see **5.4.9**) immigration and customs officer should only exceptionally exercise their functions and only when a police officer is not readily available or on specific request by a police officer (rank of sergeant or above); such action should be authorized by an officer of a certain rank (for details see Code of Practice, para 6, see **Appendix 4**).

A person falls within section 40(1)(b)

If he is or has been concerned in the commission, preparation, or instigation of acts of terrorism (see **4.1.3**).

Acts of terrorism (see **4.1.2**).

Port

Includes an airport and a hoverport (Terrorism Act 2000, Sch 7, para 1(2)).

And a place shall be treated as a port in relation to a person if an examining officer believes that the person—

(a) has gone there for the purpose of embarking on a ship or aircraft, or
(b) has arrived there on disembarking from a ship or aircraft (Terrorism Act 2000, Sch 7, para 1(3)).

It also includes a railway station or other places where—

(a) persons embark or disembark or
(b) goods are loaded or unloaded,

on or from a through train (international services) or shuttle train (trains carrying road traffic between England and France), as the case may be (Channel Tunnel (International Arrangements) Order 1993 (SI 1993/1813)), see **note (w)** below.

The border area

Refers to the area no more than one mile from the border between Northern Ireland and the Republic of Ireland (Terrorism Act 2000, Sch 7, para 4).

Belief

Should be justifiable and will depend on the individual circumstances (see **note (e)** below).

Ship

Includes a hovercraft (Terrorism Act 2000, Sch 7, para 1(2)).

5 Terrorist Investigations

Notes

(a) The purpose of questioning and associated powers is to determine whether a person appears to be someone who is or has been concerned in the commission, preparation, or instigation of acts of terrorism. The powers must not be used for any other purpose. They are in addition to the power of arrest under section 41 of the Terrorism Act 2000 (see **5.3.1**).

(b) There is no need for reasonable suspicion that the person is concerned in the commission, preparation, or instigation of acts of terrorism (Sch 7, para 2(4) and s 40(1)(b)) (for the definition of terrorism and s 40(1)(b), see **4.1**). This means that the power is wider than normal powers available to police, immigration, or customs officers. Thus, the powers can be exercised routinely as well as allowing more specific operations.

(c) Unless a person is arrested he does not have to be cautioned.

(d) Examination is a form of checking travellers distinct from detention and arrest. Examination and examination whilst under detention are two separate procedures. Examination may or may not involve formal detention or arrest; in most cases examination will not require detention. Detention might be necessary where the person does not co-operate or insists on leaving. If there is reasonable suspicion of the person being a terrorist and a period of detention for questioning and carrying out checks on identity and forensic tests may be required, then the power of arrest under section 41 (see **5.3.1**) is likely to be more appropriate.

(e) The examining officer must believe that a person's presence at the port is connected with his entering or leaving Great Britain or his travelling by air within Great Britain. For examples see paragraph 7 of the Code of Practice for Examining Officers (see **Appendix 4**—note that the Code did not yet include the amendment of paragraph 2 of Schedule 7 to extend to persons travelling by air within Great Britain). The powers also apply to a person on a ship or an aircraft which has arrived at any place in Great Britain. Note that the powers in Schedule 7 cannot be used if someone is travelling within Great Britain unless the person is travelling by air. Note also that people travelling within the Common Travel Area (UK, Republic of Ireland, Channel Islands and the Isle of Man) may not routinely carry passports as a primary means of identification.

(f) The power to stop, question, and detain must be exercised in a way that causes as little embarrassment or offence as possible to a person who has no terrorist connections. Bear in mind that there is no need for reasonable suspicion for a person's involvement in terrorism. Also avoid discriminating against persons on the grounds of race, colour, religion, creed, gender, or sexual orientation (see also Code of Practice for Examining Officers, para 10 and notes for guidance, **Appendix 4**).

(g) The length of examination should be kept to a minimum. Once an examination lasts for one hour, an explanatory notice of examination should be served by the examining officer on the person as set out in the Annex to the Code of Practice (see **Appendix 4**) and explained to him or her. Examinations must not exceed nine hours, see **note (s)** below.

(h) Depending on the length of the examination ensure that refreshments are available at regular intervals.

(i) Where questioning is done by an immigration or customs officer and it appears necessary to continue the examination, the person should be referred to a police officer. For details see paragraph 12 of the Code of Practice for Examining Officers (see **Appendix 4**).

(j) *Certain information* should be given to a detained person:
   • that he is not under arrest or caution, but detained under the provisions of Schedule 7 of the Terrorism Act 2000
   • that this does not mean he is suspected of being involved in terrorism, but that the purpose of the questioning is to establish whether he appears to be such a person
   • that he is under a duty to give all information in his possession which is requested by the officer
   • that failure to comply is an offence (see **5.4.8**).

   See also paragraph 35 of the Code of Practice for Examining Officers and Annex A (Form of notice of duties and rights) (see **Appendix 4**).

(k) *Juveniles and other vulnerable people* should only be questioned after special consideration. They should be questioned in the presence of a parent, guardian or responsible person, and if travelling on their own, of a social worker or other person not connected to the police. Bear in mind that children, especially if on their own, may be easily intimidated; on the other hand they may be vulnerable to exploitation by adults using them for terrorist aims. For further details refer to paragraphs 15–18 of the Code of Practice for Examining Officers (see **Appendix 4**).

(l) Interviews with a person detained under Schedule 7 do not have to be audio recorded, unless they take place at a police station. The Code of Practice on Audio Recording of Interviews applies to interviews under Schedule 7 (see **5.3.4**). Code of Practice E does not apply to such interviews.

(m) 'Information' requested by an examining officer includes electronic devices and data and passwords to access that data. Where the information is located elsewhere, for example on another server, and is accessed via a mobile phone or internet connection, further authority, such as a warrant, would be required (see **Appendix 4**).

(n) Where an examining officer exercises the power to question under paragraph 2 he may stop a person or vehicle, and detain a person. For the purpose of detaining a person an examining officer may authorize the person's removal from a ship, aircraft, or vehicle (this includes a train, Sch 7, para 1(2)), Schedule 7, paragraph 6. There is also a power of search, see **5.4.2** below.

(o) An examining officer may also *enter a vehicle*, aircraft, hovercraft, train, or vessel for the purpose of stopping, questioning, or detaining a person (Terrorism Act 2000, Sch 14, para 2).

(p) An examining officer may *not use reasonable force* for the purpose of exercising a power under paragraph 2, ie questioning a person. The use of force is expressly excluded in section 114 which allows the use of reasonable force in the exercise of other powers under the Act. However, if a person fails to co-operate when stopped and questioned this might lead to sufficient suspicion for an arrest under section 41 of the Terrorism Act 2000 (see **5.3.1**).

(q) Where a person is detained under this power he has to be treated in the same way as a person arrested and detained under section 41 of the Terrorism Act 2000, the provisions of Part 1 of Schedule 8 to the Terrorism Act 2000 apply (Sch 7, para 6(3)). This means that the powers provided in Schedule 8 also apply, so that, for example, a person who is being examined whilst in detention may be photographed, measured and identified (Sch 8, para 2). For details, rights of the detained person and police powers see **5.3.5**.

(r) With the consent of the individual, fingerprints may be taken at the port of entry. However, where consent has been refused the person should be taken to a police station because of the greater security offered.

(s) A person may be detained and/or examined under this power for up to nine hours. The relevant time begins when his examination begins (Sch 7, para 6(4)). An examination begins as soon as a person or vehicle has been stopped and screening questions (used to identify the individual and his travel patterns) have been asked. A longer detention is only possible if the person is arrested (see also related case below). Note that if a person is later arrested under section 41 of the Terrorism Act 2000 or under section 24 of the Police and Criminal Evidence

Act 1984 the relevant time is still counted from the time when his examination under Schedule 7 has begun (see also **5.3.1** and **Appendix 4**).

(t) Any document that has been given to the examining officer in accordance with paragraph 5(d) may be detained, see **5.4.3**.

(u) Records should be made of all examinations. For details see paragraphs 13–14 of the Code of Practice for Examining Officers (see **Appendix 4**).

(v) Where an examining officer acquires information in the exercise of the power to question a person, this information may be supplied to the Secretary of State for use in relation to immigration, to the Commissioners for Customs and Excise or a customs officer, to a constable, to the Director of the Serious Organised Crime Agency, and to a person specified by order of the Secretary of State for use of a kind specified in the order. A customs or immigration officer may supply such information to an examining officer (Terrorism Act 2000, Sch 14, para 4).

(w) The powers also apply to persons embarking on or disembarking from trains that have arrived in Great Britain through the Channel Tunnel System, international trains (through trains; for example from Brussels to London) as well as so-called shuttle trains which carry road traffic between England and France.

Related case

Breen v Chief Constable of Dumfries and Galloway [1997] SLT 826 The time limit for detention must not be exceeded for the purpose of considering the case.

PNLD reference numbers

D8776, D8777

5.4.2 **Searches**

In order to check whether there are persons that an examining officer (constable, immigration and customs officer) might want to question under paragraph 2 of Schedule 7 to the Terrorism Act 2000 (see **5.4.1**) an examining officer or an authorized person (see **note (i)**) may search ships or aircraft. If a person is questioned under this Schedule there is a power to search the person, his belongings, the ship or aircraft, or vehicles. There is also a power to examine unaccompanied baggage or goods to determine whether they have been used in the commission, preparation, or instigation of acts of terrorism.

Police powers

7   For the purpose of satisfying himself whether there are any persons whom he may wish to question under paragraph 2 an examining **officer** may—

(a) search a **ship** or aircraft;

(b) search anything on a ship or aircraft;

(c) search anything which he reasonably believes has been, or is about to be, on a ship or aircraft.

8(1) An examining officer who questions a person under paragraph 2 may, for the purpose of determining whether he falls within section 40(1)(b)—

(a) search the person;

(b) search anything which he has with him, or which belongs to him, and which is on a ship or aircraft;

(c) search anything which he has with him, or which belongs to him, and which the examining officer reasonably believes has been, or is about to be, on a ship or aircraft;

(d) search a ship or aircraft for anything falling within paragraph (b);

(e) search a **vehicle** which is on a ship or aircraft;

(f) search a vehicle which the examining officer reasonably believes has been, or is about to be, on a ship or aircraft.

9(1) An examining officer may examine goods to which this paragraph applies for the purpose of determining whether they have been used in the commission, preparation or instigation of acts of terrorism.

9(2) This paragraph applies to—

(a) **goods** which have arrived in or are about to leave Great Britain or Northern Ireland on a ship or vehicle, and

(b) goods which have arrived at or are about to leave any place in Great Britain or Northern Ireland on an aircraft (whether the place they have come from or are going to is within or outside Great Britain or Northern Ireland).

9(4) An examining officer may board a ship or aircraft or enter a vehicle for the purpose of determining whether to exercise his power under this paragraph.

Terrorism Act 2000, Sch 7, paras 7, 8(1) and 9

Meanings

Examining officer

Means constable, immigration officer and customs officer (see **5.4.1**).

Ship

Includes a hovercraft (Terrorism Act 2000, Sch 7, para 1(2)).

Vehicle

Includes a train (Terrorism Act 2000, Sch 7, para 1(2)).

Goods

Includes property of any description, and containers (Terrorism Act 2000, Sch 7, para 9(3)).

Notes

(a) These powers of search must not be used for any other purpose than to determine whether the person appears to be someone who is, or has been, involved in the commission, preparation, or instigation of terrorism. However, searches may be carried out for other purposes under other powers, for example under section 43 of the Terrorism Act 2000 (see **5.2.1**) or under the Police and Criminal Evidence Act 1984.

(b) An examining officer may *use reasonable force* for the purpose of a search if necessary (Terrorism Act 2000, Sch 14, para 3).

(c) The Code of Practice for Examining Officers applies to searches under Schedule 7 (see **Appendix 4**).
Note that PACE Code A does not apply to such searches.

(d) The search of the person must be carried out by someone of the same sex (Terrorism Act 2000, Sch 7, para 8(3)).

(e) Searches of baggage do not have to be carried out by a person of the same sex, but should be if the person objects; see further paragraph 23 of the Code of Practice for Examining Officers (see **Appendix 4**).

(f) As when questioning a person, every effort should be made to avoid potential embarrassment, see **5.4.1** and paragraphs 23–24 of the Code of Practice (see **Appendix 4**).

(g) Where an officer searches a person and is not in uniform he should show evidence of his authority, such as a warrant card. If requested, sufficient information to identify the officer in case of a query or complaint should be given, such as collar number and location. It is not necessary to give a name; and in certain circumstances it might be appropriate not to do so. See further paragraphs 26–27 of the Code of Practice (see **Appendix 4**).

(h) *Strip searches* (searches involving the removal of more than outer clothing) should not be undertaken routinely and should only be considered necessary where the person is in police custody as result of detention under Schedule 7. However, if the examining officer has reasonable grounds to suspect that a person has concealed something which may be evidence that the person is involved in terrorism or which might have been used for such a purpose a strip search may take place at a port. For details on how to conduct a strip search refer to paragraphs 30–32 of the Code of Practice for Examining Officers (see also **Appendix 4**).

(i) An examining officer may authorize a person to carry out on his behalf a search or examination under any of paragraphs 7 to 9. The authorized person may also board a ship or an aircraft in accordance with paragraph 9(4) (Terrorism Act 2000, Sch 7, para 10).

(j) An examining officer may enter a vehicle, aircraft, hovercraft, train or vessel for the purpose of a search (Terrorism Act 2000, Sch 14, para 2).

(k) Anything searched or found during a search or examined may be detained, see **5.4.3**.

(l) As a result of a search, offences other than terrorism offences may be discovered, for example in relation to drugs. These can be dealt with using general police powers.

(m) Where an examining officer acquires information in the exercise of the power to search this information may be supplied to others, for details see **5.4.1, note (v)**.

(n) The powers also apply to trains that have arrived in Great Britain through the Channel Tunnel System, international trains (through trains; for example from Brussels to London) as well as so called shuttle trains which carry road traffic between England and France (Channel Tunnel (International Arrangements) Order 1993 (SI 1993/1813)).

PNLD reference number

D8778

5.4.3 **Detention of property**

During controls at ports certain property may be detained by an examining officer (constable, immigration and customs officer) for future examination, as evidence or in connection with deportation orders. This power covers any property which has been searched or found during a search under paragraph 8 or examined under paragraph 9 (see **5.4.2**). It also applies to documents which have been given to the examining officer under Schedule 7, paragraph 5(d) to the Terrorism Act 2000 (see **5.4.1**).

Police powers

(1) This paragraph applies to anything which—
- (a) is given to an **examining officer** in accordance with paragraph 5(d) *(i. e. documents requested by the officer when questioning under paragraph 2)*,
- (b) is searched or found on a search under paragraph 8, or
- (c) is examined under paragraph 9.

(2) An examining officer may detain the thing—
- (a) for the purpose of examination, for a period not exceeding seven days beginning with the day on which the detention commences,
- (b) while he believes that it may be needed for use as evidence in criminal proceedings, *or*
- (c) while he believes that it may be needed in connection with a decision by the Secretary of State whether to make a deportation order under the Immigration Act 1971.

Terrorism Act 2000, Sch 7, para 11

Meanings

Examining officer

Means constable, immigration officer and customs officer (see 5.4.1).

Notes

- (a) This power may be exercised by an examining officer or by a person authorized by an examining officer to carry out a search or examination on his behalf under paragraphs 7 to 9 (Terrorism Act 2000, Sch 7, para 10).
- (b) An examining officer may enter a *vehicle* for the purpose of exercising this power (Terrorism Act 2000, Sch 14, para 2).
- (c) An examining officer may if necessary use *reasonable force* for the purpose of exercising this power (Terrorism Act 2000, Sch 14, para 3).
- (d) The powers also apply to trains that have arrived in Great Britain through the Channel Tunnel System, international trains (through trains, for example from Brussels to London) as well as so called shuttle trains which carry road traffic between England and France (Channel Tunnel (International Arrangements) Order 1993 (SI 1993/1813)).

PNLD reference number

D8779

5.4.4 **Designated ports**

Paragraph 12 of Schedule 7 to the Terrorism Act 2000 provides that ships and aircraft on journeys between Great Britain, Northern Ireland, the Isle of Man, and the Channel Islands may only use designated ports for the embarking or disembarking of passengers unless a different arrangement is approved by an examining officer. Captains of aircraft carrying passengers other than for reward may allow their passengers to embark from, or disembark at, non-designated airports provided they give 12 hours' notice to a constable in the relevant area.

(1) This paragraph applies to a journey—
   (a) to Great Britain from the Republic of Ireland, Northern Ireland or any of the Islands,
   (b) from Great Britain to any of those places,
   (c) to Northern Ireland from Great Britain, the Republic of Ireland or any of the Islands, or
   (d) from Northern Ireland to any of those places.

(2) Where a **ship** or aircraft is employed to carry passengers for reward on a journey to which this paragraph applies the owners or agents of the ship or aircraft shall not arrange for it to call at a port in Great Britain or Northern Ireland for the purpose of disembarking or embarking passengers unless—
   (a) the port is a **designated port**, or
   (b) an **examining officer** approves the arrangement.

(3) Where an aircraft is employed on a journey to which this paragraph applies otherwise than to carry passengers for reward, the **captain** of the aircraft shall not permit it to call at or leave a port in Great Britain or Northern Ireland unless—
   (a) the port is a designated port, or
   (b) he gives at least 12 hours' notice in writing to a constable for the police area in which the port is situated (or, where the port is in Northern Ireland, to a member of the Police Service of Northern Ireland).

Terrorism Act 2000, Sch 7, para 12

Meanings

Ship

Includes a hovercraft (Terrorism Act 2000, Sch 7, para 1(2)).

Port

Includes an airport and a hoverport (Terrorism Act 2000, Sch 7, para 1(2)).

Designated port

Is a port which appears in the table in Schedule 7 (see below).

Examining officer

Means constable, immigration officer, and customs officer (see **5.4.1**).

Captain

Means master of a ship or commander of an aircraft (Terrorism Act 2000, Sch 7, para 1(2)).

Notes

(a) A designated port is a port which appears in the table included in Schedule 7 (see below). This table includes many air and sea ports used for commercial passenger and freight traffic. These are mainly ports with Irish connection. Some ports are not listed, such as Dover. In such ports normal border controls apply. However, much of the provision of Schedule 7 to the Terrorism Act 2000 still applies whether the port is designated or not.

(b) The following are designated seaports and airports in England and Wales:

Seaports

Fishguard

Fleetwood

Heysham

Holyhead

Pembroke Dock

Plymouth

Poole Harbour

Port of Liverpool

Portsmouth Continental Ferry Port

Southampton

Swansea

Torquay

Weymouth

Airports

Biggin Hill

Birmingham

Blackpool

Bournemouth (Hurn)

Bristol

Cambridge

Cardiff

Carlisle

Coventry

East Midlands

Exeter

Gloucester/Cheltenham (Staverton)

Humberside

Leeds/Bradford

Liverpool

London-City

London-Gatwick

London-Heathrow

Luton

Lydd

Manchester

Manston

Newcastle

Norwich

Plymouth

Sheffield City

Southampton

Southend

Stansted

Teesside

(c) Contravention of the prohibitions in paragraphs 12(2) and 12(3) is an offence, see **5.4.8**.

PNLD reference numbers

D8780, D8785

5.4.5 **Embarkation and disembarkation**

Paragraphs 13 to 15 of Schedule 7 to the Terrorism Act 2000 provide controls for the embarkation and disembarkation of passengers at ports, including airports and hoverports.

Notes

(a) The Secretary of State may give a written notice to the owners or agents of ships and aircraft in order to designate control areas in any port in the UK and specify conditions on and restrictions for the embarkation or disembarkation of passengers in a control area. The receiver of such a notice has to take all reasonable steps to ensure that passengers do not (dis)embark at the port outside that control area and that all conditions and restrictions specified in the notice are complied with (Terrorism Act 2000, Sch 7, para 13). Failure to comply is an offence, see **5.4.8**.

(b) A control area in a port is designated by the Secretary of State by giving a written notice to the ports managers (ie the persons concerned with the management of a port). The notice may require that the port manager provides specified facilities in the control area for the (dis)embarkation and examination of passengers under Schedule 7. The notice can also contain conditions and restrictions relating to the (dis)embarkation of passengers in a control area and require that notices with specified information about the ports and border controls under the Terrorism Act 2000 are displayed in specified locations in a certain form.

(c) Port managers have to take all reasonable steps to comply with requirements set out in such a notice; failure to comply is an offence, (Terrorism Act 2000, Sch 7, para 14) see **5.4.8**.

(d) It was hoped that the Home Secretary would not have to give formal notice designating control areas and that it would prove possible to agree appropriate arrangements at a local level without having to invoke the power. Currently, no control areas have been designated.

(e) Paragraph 15 of Schedule 7 to the Terrorism Act 2000 provides that where a ship which is employed to carry passengers for reward, or an aircraft arrives in or leaves Great Britain from or for the Republic of Ireland, Northern Ireland or any of the Islands (the so-called Common Travel Area or CTA), the captain shall ensure—

(i) that passengers and members of the crew do not disembark at a port unless either they have been examined by an examining officer or they disembark in accordance with arrangements approved by an examining officer;

(ii) that passengers and members of the crew do not embark at a port except in accordance with arrangements approved by an examining officer;

(iii) where a person is to be examined under this Schedule on board the ship or aircraft, that he is presented for examination in an orderly manner (Paragraph 15(2) of Schedule 7 to the Terrorism Act 2000).

Failure to comply is an offence, see **5.4.8**.

(f) Where the disembarkation requirements on arrival in the UK under paragraph 27 of Schedule 2 to the Immigration Act 1971 apply (ie the 'normal' immigration requirements re examination of passengers by immigration officers), the requirements of paragraph (2)(a) above are in addition to the requirements of paragraph 27 of that Schedule.

(g) The controls on embarkation and disembarkation also apply to trains that have arrived in Great Britain through the Channel Tunnel System, international trains (through trains, eg from Brussels to London) as well as so-called shuttle trains which carry road traffic between England and France (Channel Tunnel (International Arrangements) Order 1993 (SI 1993/1813)).

PNLD reference number

D8781

5.4.6 **Carding**

Paragraph 16 of Schedule 7 to the Terrorism Act 2000 provides for a landing and embarkation card scheme for passengers. This process is known as 'carding' and allows for basic information to be collected directly from passengers, aside from the information provided by the carrier (see **5.4.7**).

This scheme applies to persons who (dis)embark in Great Britain from ships, including hovercraft, and aircraft which have come from or are going to the Republic of Ireland, Northern Ireland, the Channel Islands, or the Isle of Man—and equally in Northern Ireland for ships and aircraft coming from or going to Great Britain, the Republic of Ireland or any of the Islands (the Common Travel Area (CTA)).

For other journeys the normal border controls apply such as under section 32 of the Immigration, Asylum and Nationality Act 2006, see **5.4.11**, and under paragraph 17 of Schedule 7 to the Terrorism Act 2000, see **5.4.7**.

Notes

(a) If required by an examining officer (constable, immigration officer, and customs officer, see **5.4.1**) persons have to complete a card and produce it to the officer. The form of the card and the required information is set out in Parts 1 (Landing Card) and 2 (Embarkation Card) of the Schedule to the Terrorism Act 2000 (Carding) Order 2001 (SI 2001/426)). An example of a landing/embarkation card can be found in Annex C of the Home Office Circular 3/2001. Cards have to be supplied by the police.

(b) A landing/embarkation card may be required whether or not the examining officer suspects the person is involved in terrorism. Bear in mind that, as with questioning (see **5.4.1, note (f)**), it might be embarrassing or cause offence to a person who has no terrorist connections and who might feel victimized.

(c) Passengers not travelling within the CTA should not be asked to complete cards. However, they might be asked to provide information by other means if they are subject to an examination under paragraph 2 of Schedule 7 (see **5.4.1**).

(d) Under paragraph 18 of Schedule 7 to the Terrorism Act 2000 it is an offence wilfully to fail to comply with this requirement, see **5.4.8**.

(e) Where an examining officer acquires information under the carding provisions this may be supplied to others, for details see **5.4.1, note (v)**.

(f) Carding does not apply to the Channel Tunnel.

PNLD reference numbers

D8782, D10141, D3152

5.4.7 **Provision of passenger information**

Paragraph 17 of Schedule 7 to the Terrorism Act 2000 allows examining officers (constables, immigration and customs officers) to require owners and agents of ships and aircraft to provide certain passenger information. Passengers and members of the crew have to provide information as required to the agent or owner.

(1) This paragraph applies to a **ship** or aircraft which—

   (a) arrives or is expected to arrive in any place in the United Kingdom (whether from another place in the United Kingdom or from outside the United Kingdom), or
   (b) leaves or is expected to leave the United Kingdom.

(2) If an **examining officer** gives the owners or agents of a ship or aircraft to which this paragraph applies a written request to provide **specified information**, the owners or agents shall comply with the request as soon as is reasonably practicable.

(3) A request to an owner or agent may relate—
   (a) to a particular ship or aircraft,
   (b) to all ships or aircraft of the owner or agent to which this paragraph applies, or
   (c) to specified ships or aircraft.

(4) Information may be specified in a request only if it is of a kind which is prescribed by order of the Secretary of State and which relates—
   (a) to passengers,
   (b) to crew,
   (c) to vehicles belonging to passengers or crew, or
   (d) to goods.

(5) A passenger or member of the crew on a ship or aircraft shall give the **captain** any information required for the purpose of enabling the owners or agents to comply with a request under this paragraph.

Terrorism Act 2000, Sch 7, para 17(1)–(5)

Meanings

Ship

Includes a hovercraft (Terrorism Act 2000, Sch 7, para 1(2)).

Examining officer

Means constable, immigration officer, and customs officer (see **5.4.1**).

Specified information

1. The following information about passengers or crew, namely—
    (a) the person's—
       (i)   full name,
       (ii) gender,
       (iii) date and place of birth,
       (iv) home address, and
       (v)   nationality; and

(b) where the person has a travel document—
    (i) the type of document,
    (ii) its number,
    (iii) its country of issue, and
    (iv) its expiry date.

2 The number of items that a passenger has placed in the hold of an aircraft.

3 The following information about any vehicle belonging to passengers or crew, namely, its registration number.

4 The following information about goods carried on a vehicle, namely—
    (a) a brief description of them,
    (b) the address from which the goods were collected,
    (c) the address to which the goods are to be delivered, and
    (d) the registration number of that vehicle.

5 The following information about goods which are not carried on a vehicle, namely-
    (a) a brief description of them,
    (b) the method of payment for the carriage of the goods, and
    (c) the name or number of any container in which the goods are placed.

Schedule 7 to the Terrorism Act 2000
(Information) Order 2002, Sch

Captain

Means master of a ship or commander of an aircraft (Terrorism Act 2000, Sch 7, para 1(2)).

Notes

(a) Information provided by shippers and carriers is of great value to port officers. Knowing who is or what is carried on aircraft or ships may enable the police to make further important enquiries. It is therefore essential that the information provided is accurate, adequate and given high level of importance by transport operators.

(b) Failure of the owner, agent, of passengers or members of the crew to comply with a request for information is an offence, see **5.4.8**.

(c) Where an examining officer acquires information in the exercise of the power to search this information may be supplied to others, for details see **5.4.1, note (v)**.

(d) The requirements for the provision of passenger information under paragraph 17 of Schedule 7 to the Terrorism Act 2000 do not apply to the Channel Tunnel.

PNLD reference numbers

D8783, D10142

5.4.8 Offences in relation to ports controls

Paragraph 18 of Schedule 7 to the Terrorism Act 2000 creates a range of offences in relation to ports controls under that Schedule. There are three different offences: failure to comply with a duty; contravention of a prohibition; and obstruction of a search or examination.

Offences

A person commits an offence if he—
(a) wilfully fails to comply with a duty imposed under or by virtue of this Schedule,
(b) wilfully contravenes a prohibition imposed under or by virtue of this Schedule, or
(c) wilfully obstructs, or seeks to frustrate, a search or examination under or by virtue of this Schedule.

Terrorism Act 2000, Sch 7, para 18(1)

Points to prove

Offence in para 18(1)(a) of Sch 7

✓ date and location
✓ wilfully
✓ failed to comply with a duty imposed by Schedule 7 to the Terrorism Act 2000

Offence in para 18(1)(b) of Sch 7

✓ date and location
✓ wilfully
✓ contravened
✓ a prohibition imposed under/by virtue of Schedule 7 to the Terrorism Act 2000

Offence in para 18(1)(c) of Sch 7

✓ date and location
✓ wilfully
✓ obstructed/sought to frustrate
✓ a search/examination under/by virtue of Schedule 7 to the Terrorism Act 2000

Police powers

If suspected terrorist:

Power of arrest—section 41 of the Terrorism Act 2000 (see **5.3.1**)

Power to stop and search—section 43 of the Terrorism Act 2000 (see **5.2.1**)

If the person is not suspected to be a terrorist, consider using PACE powers (such as ss 24, 17, 18, and 32 of PACE) but see **5.3.1** for drawbacks on using PACE powers for potential terrorists.

Notes

(a) The following duties are set out in Schedule 7 of the Terrorism Act 2000:
  - give information/passport/document to examining officer on request, paragraph 5 (see **5.4.1**)
  - owner/agent of ship/aircraft ensure that passengers do not (dis)embark outside control area/that specified conditions/ restrictions are met/complied with, paragraph 13(2) (see **5.4.5**)
  - ports manager comply with notice, paragraph 14(2) (see **5.4.5**)
  - captain to ensure that passengers/crew do not (dis)embark other than arranged with examining officer/that person who is examined is presented in orderly manner, paragraph 15(2) (see **5.4.5**)
  - owner/agent of ship/aircraft to supply passengers with cards as specified, paragraph 16(2) (see **5.4.6**)
  - owner/agent of ship/aircraft to comply with request, paragraph 17(2) (see **5.4.7**)
  - passenger/member of crew give captain information as required, paragraph 17(5) (see **5.4.7**)

(b) The following prohibitions are set out in Schedule 7 of the Terrorism Act 2000:
  - owner/agent of ship/aircraft must not arrange for ship/aircraft to call at port unless designated port/arrangement with examining officer, paragraph 12(2) (see **5.4.4**).
  - captain of aircraft must not permit aircraft to call at/leave a port unless designated port/giving 12 hours' notice, paragraph 12(3) (see **5.4.4**).

(c) For searches and examinations under Schedule 7 see **5.4.1** and **5.4.2** above.

(d) The offence requires that the person acted 'wilfully' not just 'knowingly'. That means that the offence might not be committed if, for example, a carrier makes every effort to collect the requested information but it is simply not possible for some reason, even within a reasonable timescale.

(e) *Counter-Terrorism Act 2008*—Section 28 of the Act makes provision for this offence to be tried at any place in the UK if it was committed in the UK. See PNLD reference number S1136 to check whether this section is in force.

PNLD reference numbers

H3797, H3798, H3799, D8784

 Time limit for prosecution: Six months.

 Summary: Maximum three months' imprisonment and/or fine not exceeding level four on the standard scale.

5.4.9 Code of Practice for Examining Officers

The Code of Practice for Examining Officers issued under Schedule 14 to the Terrorism Act 2000 applies to all examining officers, ie constables, immigration officers and customs officers (see **5.4.1**) exercising functions under the Terrorism Act 2000 (see **5.4.1–5.4.7**). It does not apply in the exercise of powers under other Acts, for example under the Immigration Act 1971, the Customs and Excise Management Act 1979 or the Immigration, Asylum and Nationality Act 2006.

Notes

(a) The code should be available at all police stations and at police offices at ports where the powers are, or are likely to be, used, for consultation by the police and the public.

(b) Failure by an officer to observe a provision of a code does not of itself make him liable to criminal or civil proceedings (Terrorism Act 2000, Sch 14, para 6(2)).

For the full text of the Code see **Appendix 4**.

PNLD reference number

D1623

5.4.10 **Police powers in airports**

The policing of airports is provided for in part III (sections 24B–31) of the Aviation Security Act 1982. It gives police officers powers to stop and search persons, vehicles and aircraft for stolen or prohibited articles in any airport. It also deals with the policing of designated airports.

Power to stop and search at aerodromes

(1) Subject to subsection (2) below, a constable may search—
    (a) any person, vehicle or aircraft in an **aerodrome**, or
    (b) anything which is in or on such a vehicle or aircraft, for stolen or **prohibited articles**.
(2) This section does not give a constable power to search a person, vehicle or aircraft, or anything in or on a vehicle or aircraft, unless he has reasonable grounds for suspecting that he will find stolen or prohibited articles.
(3) For the purposes of exercising the power conferred by subsection (1) above, a constable may—
    (a) enter any part of an aerodrome;
    (b) detain a person, vehicle or aircraft;
    (c) board an aircraft.

Aviation Security Act 1982, s 24B(1)–(3)

Meanings

Aerodrome

Means the aggregate of the land, buildings, and works comprised in an aerodrome within the meaning of the Civil Aviation Act 1982 and (if and so far as not comprised in an aerodrome as defined in that Act) any land, building, or works situated within the boundaries of an area designated, by an order made by the Secretary of State which is for the time being in force, as constituting the area of an aerodrome for the purposes of this Act (Aviation Security Act 1982, s 38(1)).

Aerodrome within the meaning of the Civil Aviation Act 1982

Means any area of land or water designed, equipped, set apart or commonly used for affording facilities for the landing and departure of aircraft and includes any area or space, whether on the ground, on the roof of a building or elsewhere, which is designed, equipped or set apart for affording facilities for the landing and departure of aircraft capable of descending or climbing vertically (Civil Aviation Act 1982, s 105).

The term aerodrome is used rather than airport, as it has wider meaning and covers major airports as well as airfields used only by private flying clubs.

Prohibited article

An article is prohibited if it is an article—

(a) made or adapted for use in the course of or in connection with **criminal conduct**, or
(b) intended by the person having it with him for such use by him or by some other person (Aviation Security Act 1982, s 24B(5)).

Criminal conduct

Means conduct which—

(a) constitutes an offence in the part of the UK in which the aerodrome is situated, or
(b) would constitute an offence in that part of the UK if it occurred there (Aviation Security Act 1982, s 24B(6)).

Notes

(a) *Power to seize articles*—If a constable discovers an article which he has reasonable grounds for suspecting to be a stolen or prohibited article, he may seize it (Aviation Security Act 1982, s 24B(4)).
(b) A warrant is not necessary to exercise the powers under this section (Aviation Security Act 1982, s 24B(8)).
(c) This section does not authorize a constable to enter a dwelling (Aviation Security Act 1982, s 24B(9)).
(d) Further police powers are available at designated airports under sections 25 to 29 of the Aviation Security Act 1982. They apply only to designated airports. These are Heathrow, Stansted, Gatwick, Birmingham, and Manchester. Constables may enter any part of such an airport, section 26, and have powers to stop and search to prevent theft, section 27.

PNLD reference number

D20441

5.4.11 Passenger and crew information: police powers

Section 32 of the Immigration, Asylum and Nationality Act 2006 provides police powers to gather information in respect of ships and aircraft arriving (or expected to arrive) or leaving (or expected to leave) the United Kingdom. A police officer of at least the rank of superintendent may request passenger or crew information or information about the flight from the owner or agent of a ship or aircraft.

(1) This section applies to ships and aircraft which are—
    (a) arriving, or expected to arrive, in the United Kingdom, or
    (b) leaving, or expected to leave, the UK.

(2) The owner or agent of a ship or aircraft shall comply with any requirement imposed by a constable of the rank of superintendent or above to provide **passenger or service information**.

(3) A passenger or member of crew shall provide to the owner or agent of a ship or aircraft any information that he requires for the purpose of complying with a requirement imposed by virtue of subsection (2).

    Immigration, Asylum and Nationality Act 2006, s 32(1)–(3)

Meanings

Passenger or service information

Relates to—

(a) passengers,
(b) members of crew, or
(c) a voyage or flight

and is specified in Schedules 3 and 4 to the Immigration and Police (Passenger, Crew and Service Information) Order 2008 (SI 2008/5). Examples of what is listed in the Schedule include: information as provided on the passenger's or member of crew's travel document (full name, gender, date of birth, nationality, etc), the vehicle registration number of any vehicle in which the passenger is travelling, flight numbers, ship name, name of carrier, scheduled departure and arrival times.

Notes

(a) A requirement to provide information under section 32(2) may only be imposed by a police officer if he thinks it necessary for police purposes (Immigration, Asylum and Nationality Act 2006, s 32(4)). Police purposes means any of the following—
    (i) the prevention, detection, investigation, or prosecution of criminal offences;
    (ii) safeguarding national security;
    (iii) such other purposes as may be specified (Immigration and Asylum Act 1999, s 21(3)).

(b) A requirement to provide information under section 32(2)—
  (i) must be in writing,
  (ii) may apply generally or only to one or more specified ships or aircraft,
  (iii) must specify a period, not exceeding six months and beginning with the date on which it is imposed, during which it has effect,
  (iv) must state—
    • the information required, and
    • the date or time by which it is to be provided.
(c) These powers also apply to trains that have arrived in Great Britain through the Channel Tunnel System, international trains (through trains; for example from Brussels to London) as well as so called shuttle trains which carry road traffic between England and France (Channel Tunnel (International Arrangements) Order 1993 SI 1993/1813).
(d) Failure to comply with a requirement imposed under section 32(2) or (3) is an offence (summary, penalty maximum three months' imprisonment and/or fine not exceeding level 4 on the standard scale).

PNLD reference numbers

H9304, H9303, D21703, D21705

5.4.12 **Hijacking aircraft**

Section 1 of the Aviation Security Act 1982 creates the offence of hijacking an aircraft in flight.

Offence

A person on board an aircraft **in flight** who unlawfully, by the use of force or by threats of any kind, seizes the aircraft or exercises control of it commits the offence of hijacking, whatever his nationality, whatever the State in which the aircraft is registered and whether the aircraft is in the United Kingdom or elsewhere, but subject to subsection (2) below.

Aviation Security Act 1982, s 1(1)

> ### Points to prove
> ✓ date and location
> ✓ being on board an aircraft in flight
> ✓ unlawfully
> ✓ by use of force/threats
> ✓ seized/exercised control of aircraft

Meanings

In flight

The period during which an aircraft is in flight shall be deemed to include any period from the moment when all its external doors are closed following embarkation until the moment when any such door is opened for disembarkation, and, in the case of a forced landing, any period until the competent authorities take over responsibility for the aircraft and for persons and property on board, and anything done on board an aircraft while in flight over any part of the UK shall be treated as done in that part of the UK(Aviation Security Act 1982, s 38(3)).

Defence

See related case below.

Police powers

If suspected terrorist:

Power of arrest—section 41 of the Terrorism Act 2000 (see 5.3.1)

Power to stop and search—section 43 of the Terrorism Act 2000 (see 5.2.1)

If the person is not suspected of being a terrorist consider using PACE powers (such as ss 24, 17, 18, and 32 of PACE) but see 5.3.1 for drawbacks on using PACE powers for potential terrorists.

Power of arrest—section 7(1) of the Aviation Security Act 1982:

(1) Where a constable has reasonable cause to suspect that a person about to embark on an aircraft in the UK, or a person on board such an aircraft, intends to commit, in relation to the aircraft, an offence under any of the preceding provisions of this Part of

this Act (other than section 4), the constable may prohibit him from travelling on board the aircraft, and for the purpose of enforcing that prohibition the constable—

(a) may prevent him from embarking on the aircraft or, as the case may be, may remove him from the aircraft; and

(b) may arrest him without warrant and detain him for so long as may be necessary for that purpose.

Aviation Security Act 1982, s 7(1)

It is an offence to intentionally obstruct a person acting in the exercise of this power (Aviation Security Act 1982, s 7(2), either way, summary: maximum fine not exceeding the statutory maximum, on indictment: maximum two years' imprisonment and/or fine).

Powers of commander of the aircraft—section 94 of the Civil Aviation Act 1982:

The commander of an aircraft in flight (that means from the time the external doors are closed following embarkation until doors are opened for disembarkation) has certain powers, for example to restrain persons on board whose actions jeopardize the safety of the aircraft or persons on board. Police officers may use these powers at the request or with the authority of the commander of the aircraft. For details see section 94 of the Civil Aviation Act 1982 (not reproduced here).

Notes

(a) This offence applies to acts done outside the UK regardless of the nationality of the offender or the place of registration of the aircraft with two exceptions: the offence does not apply if the aircraft is used in **military**, customs, or police service, or both the place of take-off and the place of landing are in the **territory** of the State in which the aircraft is registered, unless—

(i) the person seizing or exercising control of the aircraft is a **UK national**; or

(ii) his act is committed in the UK; or

(iii) the aircraft is registered in the UK or is used in the military or customs service of the UK or in the service of any police force in the UK (Aviation Security Act 1982, s 1(2)).

(b) Certain acts committed in connection with the offence of hijacking are also offences under UK law independent of the nationality of the offender or the place where they are committed.

Meanings

Military service

Includes naval and air force service (Aviation Security Act 1982, s 38(1)). And the territorial waters of any State shall be treated as part of its *territory* (Aviation Security Act 1982, s 1(5)).

UK national

Means an individual who is—

(a) a British citizen, a British overseas territories citizen, a British National (Overseas) or a British Overseas citizen;

(b) a person who under the British Nationality Act 1981 is a British subject; or

(c) a British protected person (within the meaning of that Act) (Aviation Security Act 1982, s 38(1)).

> Without prejudice to section 92 of the Civil Aviation Act 1982 (application of criminal law to aircraft) or to section 2(1)(b) of this Act, where a person (of whatever nationality) does on board any aircraft (wherever registered) and while outside the UK any act which, if done in the UK would constitute the offence of murder, attempted murder, manslaughter, culpable homicide or assault or an offence under section 18 *(wounding with intent)*, 20 *(wounding)*, 21 *(attempting to choke)*, 22 *(using chloroform)*, 23 *(maliciously administer poison)*, 28 *(causing grievous bodily harm by gunpowder)* or 29 *(corrosive substances)* of the Offences Against the Person Act 1861 or section 2 of the Explosive Substances Act 1883 *(cause explosion likely to endanger life or property*, see **5.8.1**), his act shall constitute that offence if it is done in connection with the offence of hijacking committed or attempted by him on board that aircraft.
>
> *Aviation Security Act 1982, s 6(1)*

That means that apart from the offence of hijacking, the offender may have committed any of the offences mentioned in section 6(1) even if the act did not take place in the UK. In addition to this, the offender might have committed further offences under UK law if the aircraft was travelling to the UK, Civil Aviation Act 1982, s 92, or the offence of endangering the safety of aircraft, section 2(1)(b) (see **5.4.13**).

(d) It is also an offence to induce someone to commit this offence outside the UK despite the exception in section 1(2), Aviation Security Act 1982, s 6 (see **5.4.15**).

(e) For the liability of company directors etc. see section 37 of the Aviation Security Act 1982 (see **5.7.2**).

Related case

R v Abdul-Hussain (Mustafa Shakir) [1998] EWCA Crim 3528 Shi'ite Muslims had hijacked a plane and claimed to have done so in order to escape death at hands of Iraqi authorities. The court stated that the defence of duress is available in relation to this offence and the defendants were acquitted on appeal and granted asylum. However, the terror induced in innocent passengers will generally raise issues of proportionality; imminent peril of death or serious injury to the defendant or his dependants has to operate on the mind of the defendant at the time he commits the act so as to overbear his will, but the execution of the threat need not be immediately in prospect. The period of time between the beginning of the peril and the defendant's act is a relevant but not determinative factor; all circumstances of the peril, including the number, identity and status of those creating it, and the opportunities (if any) to avoid it are relevant, initially for the judge and, in appropriate cases, for the jury, when assessing whether the defendant's mind is affected so as to overbear his will.

PNLD reference numbers

H8550, D4310

 AG consent required: Aviation Security Act 1982, s 8(1).

 Time limit for prosecution: None.

Indictment: Maximum life imprisonment.

5.4.13 Destroy, damage, endanger safety of aircraft

Section 2 of the Aviation Security Act 1982 creates the offences of unlawfully destroying or damaging aircraft in flight or in service and unlawfully and intentionally placing or causing to be placed on an aircraft in service or in flight any device or substance likely to destroy the aircraft or endanger its safety.

Offences

(1) It shall, subject to subsection (4) below, be an offence for any person **unlawfully** and intentionally—

    (a) to destroy an **aircraft in service** or so to damage such an aircraft as to render it incapable of flight or as to be likely to endanger its safety **in flight**; or

    (b) to commit on board an aircraft in flight any **act of violence** which is likely to endanger the safety of the aircraft.

(2) It shall also, subject to subsection (4) below, be an offence for any person unlawfully and intentionally to place, or cause to be placed, on an aircraft in service any device or substance which is likely to destroy the aircraft, or is likely so to damage it as to render it incapable of flight or as to be likely to endanger its safety in flight; but nothing in this subsection shall be construed as limiting the circumstances in which the commission of any act—

    (a) may constitute an offence under subsection (1) above, or

    (b) may constitute attempting or conspiring to commit, or aiding, abetting, counselling or procuring, or being art and part in, the commission of such an offence.

Aviation Security Act 1982, s 2(1) and (2)

Points to prove
Destroy aircraft
✓ date and location
✓ unlawfully and intentionally
✓ destroyed an aircraft in service

Damage aircraft
✓ date and location
✓ unlawfully and intentionally
✓ damaged an aircraft in service
✓ as to render it incapable of flight/be likely to endanger its safety in flight

Endangering aircraft
✓ date and location on board an aircraft in flight
✓ unlawfully and intentionally
✓ committed an act of violence likely to endanger the safety of the aircraft

Placing device on aircraft
✓ date and location
✓ unlawfully and intentionally
✓ placed/caused to be placed on an aircraft
✓ a device/substance which was likely to destroy the aircraft/so to damage it as to render it incapable of flight/as to be likely to endanger its safety in flight

Meanings

Unlawfully

(a) in relation to the commission of an act in the UK, means so as (apart from this Act) to constitute an offence under the law of the part of the UK in which the act is committed, and

(b) in relation to the commission of an act outside the UK, means so that the commission of the act would (apart from this Act) have been an offence under the law of England and Wales if it had been committed in England and Wales or of Scotland if it had been committed in Scotland (Aviation Security Act 1982, s 2(6)).

Aircraft in service/in flight

(a) The period during which an aircraft is in flight shall be deemed to include any period from the moment when all its external doors are closed following embarkation until the moment when any such door is opened for disembarkation, and, in the case of a forced landing, any period until the competent authorities take over responsibility for the aircraft and for persons and property on board; and

(b) an aircraft shall be taken to be in service during the whole of the period which begins with the pre-flight preparation of the aircraft for a flight and ends 24 hours after the aircraft lands having completed that flight, and also at any time (not falling within that period) while, in accordance with the preceding paragraph, the aircraft is in flight,

and anything done on board an aircraft while in flight over any part of the UK shall be treated as done in that part of the UK (Aviation Security Act 1982, s 38(3)).

Act of violence

Means—

(a) any act done in the UK which constitutes the offence of murder, attempted murder, manslaughter, culpable homicide or assault or an offence under section 18, 20, 21, 22, 23, 24, 28 or 29 of the Offences Against the Person Act 1861 or under section 2 of the Explosive Substances Act 1883 (see **5.8.1**), and

(b) any act done outside the UK, which, if done in the UK, would constitute such an offence as is mentioned in paragraph (a) above (Aviation Security Act 1982, s 2(7)).

Police powers

If suspected terrorist:

Power of arrest—section 41 of the Terrorism Act 2000 (see 5.3.1)

Power to stop and search—section 43 of the Terrorism Act 2000 (see 5.2.1)

If the person is not suspected to be a terrorist consider using PACE powers (such as ss 24, 17, 18, and 32 of PACE) but see **5.3.1** for drawbacks on using PACE powers for potential terrorists.

Power of arrest—section 7(1) of the Aviation Security Act 1982 (see 5.4.12), includes power to prohibit from travelling on board the aircraft, to prevent from embarking on or remove from aircraft, arrest and detain.

Powers of commander of the aircraft—section 94 of the Civil Aviation Act 1982 (see **5.4.12**)

Notes

(a) This offence applies to acts done outside the UK regardless of the nationality of the offender and the State in which the aircraft is registered (Aviation Security Act 1982, s 2(3)) with the following exceptions. The offences do not apply to any act committed in relation to an aircraft used in **military**, customs or police service unless the act is committed in the UK, or where the act is committed outside the UK, the person committing it is a UK national (Aviation Security Act 1982, s 2(3) and (4)).

Meanings

Military service

Includes naval and air force service (Aviation Security Act 1982, s 39(1)).

UK national (see **5.4.12**)

(b) It is also an offence to induce someone to commit this offence outside the UK despite the exception in section 2(4), Aviation Security Act 1982, s 6 (see **5.4.15**).

(c) For the liability of company directors, etc see section 37 of the Aviation Security Act 1982 (see **5.7.2**).

(d) It is also an offence to destroy or damage property associated with air navigation facilities where the destruction or damage is likely to endanger the safety of aircraft in flight; and also to communicate false information where that information endangers the safety of aircraft in flight (Aviation Security Act 1982, s 3).

(e) See also Flight training (see **2.3.1** and **4.3.7**).

PNLD reference numbers

H8551, H8552, H8553, H8554, D4311

 AG consent required: Aviation Security Act 1982, s 8(1).

 Time limit for prosecution: None.

Indictment: Maximum life imprisonment.

5.4.14 Possession of dangerous articles on aircraft or in aerodrome

Section 4 of the Aviation Security Act 1982 makes it an offence for a person to have with him or in his baggage dangerous articles, such as firearms, imitation firearms, and explosives, in an aircraft, aerodrome or air navigation installation.

Offence

(1) It shall be an offence for any person without lawful authority or reasonable excuse (the proof of which shall lie on him) **to have with him—**
   (a) in any **aircraft registered in the United Kingdom**, whether at a time when the aircraft is in the United Kingdom or not, or
   (b) in any other aircraft at a time when it is in, or in flight over, the United Kingdom, or
   (c) in any part of an **aerodrome** in the United Kingdom, or
   (d) in any **air navigation installation** in the United Kingdom which does not form part of an aerodrome,
   any article to which this section applies.

(2) This section applies to the following articles, that is to say—
   (a) any **firearm,** or any article having the appearance of being a firearm, whether capable of being discharged or not;
   (b) any **explosive,** any article manufactured or adapted (whether in the form of a bomb, grenade or otherwise) so as to have the appearance of being an explosive, whether it is capable of producing a practical effect by explosion or not, or any article marked or labelled so as to indicate that it is or contains an explosive; and
   (c) any **article** (not falling within either of the preceding paragraphs) made or adapted for use for causing injury to or incapacitating a person or for destroying or damaging **property**, or intended by the person having it with him for such use, whether by him or by any other person.

Aviation Security Act 1982, s 4(1) and (2)

Points to prove

✓ date and location
✓ without lawful authority/reasonable excuse had with you
✓ in an aircraft registered in the UK *or*

in any aircraft at a time when it is in, or in flight over, the UK *or*

in any part of an aerodrome *or*

in any air navigation installation - a firearm *or*

an article having the appearance of being a firearm *or*

an explosive *or*

an article manufactured/adapted so as to have the appearance of being an explosive whether capable of producing a practical effect by explosion or not *or*

an article marked/labelled so as to indicate that it is/contains an explosive *or*

an article made/adapted for use for causing injury to/incapacitating any person *or*

an article made/adapted for use for destroying/damaging property *or*

an article intended for use by you/any other person/for causing injury to/incapacitating a person *or*

an article intended for use by you/any other person for destroying/damaging property

Meanings

To have with him

Is explained in section 4(3) and (5) (see **note (a)** below).

Aircraft registered or operating in the UK

Means any aircraft which is either—

(a) an aircraft registered in the UK, or
(b) an aircraft not so registered which is for the time being allocated for use on flights which (otherwise than in exceptional circumstances) include landing at or taking off from one or more aerodromes in the UK (Aviation Security Act 1982, s 38(1)).

Aerodrome (see 5.4.10)

Air navigation installation

Means any building, works, apparatus or equipment used wholly or mainly for the purpose of assisting air traffic control or as an aid to air navigation, together with any land contiguous or adjacent to any such building, works, apparatus or equipment and used wholly or mainly for purposes connected therewith (Aviation Security Act 1982, s 38(1)).

Firearm

Includes an airgun or air pistol (Aviation Security Act 1982, s 38(1)).

Explosive

Means any article manufactured for the purpose of producing a practical effect by explosion, or intended for that purpose by a person having the article with him (Aviation Security Act 1982, s 38(1)).

Article

Includes any substance, whether in solid or liquid form or in the form of a gas or vapour (Aviation Security Act 1982, s 38(1)).

Property

Includes any land, buildings or works, any aircraft or vehicle and any baggage, cargo or other article of any description (Aviation Security Act 1982, s 38(1)).

Police powers

If suspected terrorist:

Power of arrest—section 41 of the Terrorism Act 2000 (see 5.3.1)

Power to stop and search—section 43 of the Terrorism Act 2000 (see 5.2.1)

If the person is not suspected to be a terrorist consider using PACE powers (such as ss 24, 17, 18, and 32 of PACE) but see **5.3.1** for drawbacks on using PACE powers for potential terrorists.

Power of arrest—section 7(1) of the Aviation Security Act 1982 (see **5.4.12**), includes power to prohibit from travelling on board the aircraft, to prevent from embarking or remove from aircraft, arrest and detain.

Powers of commander of the aircraft—section 94 of the Civil Aviation Act 1982 (see 5.4.12)

Notes

(a) A person is regarded as 'having baggage with him' even if he is not actually carrying an item himself, but the baggage is, for example, already checked in. Section 4(3) explains this, but does not limit it to these circumstances (s 4(5)):

(3) For the purposes of this section a person who is for the time being in an aircraft, or in part of an aerodrome, shall be treated as having with him in the aircraft, or in that part of the aerodrome, as the case may be, an article to which this section applies if—

 (a) where he is in an aircraft, the article, or an article in which it is contained, is in the aircraft and has been caused (whether by him or by any other person) to be brought there as being, or as forming part of, his baggage on a flight in the aircraft or has been caused by him to be brought there as being, or as forming part of, any other property to be carried on such a flight, or

 (b) where he is in part of an aerodrome (otherwise than in an aircraft), the article, or an article in which it is contained, is in that or any other part of the aerodrome and has been caused (whether by him or by any other person) to be brought into the aerodrome as being, or as forming part of, his baggage on a flight from that aerodrome or has been caused by him to be brought there as being, or as forming part of, any other property to be carried on such a flight on which he is also to be carried, notwithstanding that the circumstances may be such that (apart from this subsection) he would not be regarded as having the article with him in the aircraft or in a part of the aerodrome, as the case may be.

(5) Nothing in subsection (3) above shall be construed as limiting the circumstances in which a person would, apart from that subsection, be regarded as having an article with him as mentioned in subsection (1) above.

Aviation Security Act 1982, s 4(3) and (5)

 (b) The burden of proof that the defendant had lawful authority or reasonable excuse for having an article with him lies on the defendant.

 (c) For the liability of company directors, etc see section 37 of the Aviation Security Act 1982 (see **5.7.2**).

Related case

DPP v Hynde [1998] 1 All ER 649 A butterfly knife by its very design is necessarily made for the purpose of injury to the person.

PNLD reference numbers

H8142, H8143, H8144, D4313, D4314

Time limit for prosecution: None.

 Summary: Maximum three months' imprisonment and/or fine not exceeding the statutory maximum.

 Indictment: Maximum five years' imprisonment and/or fine.

5.4.15 Induce or assist commission of offence re aircraft

Section 6(2) of the Aviation Security Act 1982 makes it an offence to induce or assist the commission of other offences under this Act where this would otherwise not be an offence under UK.

Offence

It shall be an offence for any person in the United Kingdom to induce or assist the commission outside the United Kingdom of any act which—

(a) would, but for subsection (2) of section 1 *[hijacking]* of this Act, be an offence under that section; or

(b) would, but for subsection (4) of section 2 *[destroy/damage/endanger safety of aircraft]* of this Act, be an offence under that section; or

(c) would, but for subsection (5) or (6) of section 3 *[destroy or damage property likely to endanger aircraft]* of this Act, be an offence under that section.

Aviation Security Act 1982, s 6(2)

Points to prove

✓ date and location
✓ induced the commission outside the UK of an act of
✓ hijacking under s 1(1) of the Aviation Security Act 1982 *or*
destroying/damaging/endangering the safety of an aircraft under s 2(1) of the Act *or*
destroying/damaging/interfering with the operation of property used for the provision of air navigation facilities under s 3(1) of the Act

---

Police powers

If suspected terrorist:

Power of arrest—section 41 of the Terrorism Act 2000 (see **5.3.1**)

Power to stop and search—section 43 of the Terrorism Act 2000 (see **5.2.1**)

If the person is not suspected of being a terrorist consider using PACE powers (such as ss 24, 17, 18, and 32 of PACE) but see **5.3.1** for drawbacks on using PACE powers for potential terrorists.

Power of arrest—section 7(1) of the Aviation Security Act 1982 (see **5.4.12**), includes power to prohibit from travelling on board the aircraft, to prevent from embarking on or remove from aircraft, arrest and detain.

Powers of commander of the aircraft—section 94 of the Civil Aviation Act 1982 (see **5.4.12**)

Notes

(a) The offences of hijacking, section 1 (see **5.4.12**), destroying, damaging or endangering the safety of aircraft, section 2 (**5.4.13**), and destroying or damaging property used for the provision of air navigation facilities likely to endanger aircraft, section 3, are all subject to some exceptions, for example, if committed outside the UK by a non UK national. The purpose of section 6(2) is to ensure that a person can be prosecuted if he, while in the UK, induces or assists another person outside the UK who is not a UK national and who therefore does not commit an offence under UK law himself.

(b) Section 8 of the Accessories and Abettors Act 1861 does apply to the offences under sections 1, 2 and 3; the normal rules on aiding and abetting therefore apply to these offences in addition to section 6 (see **5.8.6**).

(c) For the liability of company directors, etc see section 37 of the Aviation Security Act 1982 (see **5.7.2**).

PNLD reference numbers

H8561, D4318

AG✓   **AG consent required:** Aviation Security Act 1982, s 8(1).

🕐   **Time limit for prosecution:** None.

▥   **Indictment:** Maximum life imprisonment.

5.4.16 **Unauthorized presence in restricted zone of an airport**

Section 21C of the Aviation Security Act 1982 creates the offence of unauthorized presence on board an aircraft.

Offence

A person shall not—

(a) go, with or without a vehicle, onto any part of a **restricted zone** of—
  (i) an **aerodrome**, or
  (ii) an **air navigation installation** which does not form part of an aerodrome, except with the permission of the **manager** of the aerodrome, the authority responsible for the air navigation installation or a person acting on behalf of that manager or authority, and in accordance with any conditions subject to which that permission is for the time being granted, or

(b) remain on any part of such a restricted zone after being requested to leave by the manager of the aerodrome, the authority responsible for the air navigation installation or a person acting on behalf of that manager or authority.

Aviation Security Act 1982, s 21C(1)

Points to prove

Enter restricted zone without permission

✓ date and location
✓ without lawful authority/reasonable excuse
✓ went on to part of the restricted zone of an aerodrome/of an air navigation installation not forming part of an aerodrome
✓ without the permission
✓ of the manager/person acting on behalf of manager

Breach entry of restricted zone

- ✓ date and location
- ✓ without lawful authority/reasonable excuse
- ✓ went onto part of a restricted zone of an aerodrome/of an air navigation installation not forming part of an aerodrome
- ✓ in breach of condition subject to which you had been granted permission to enter the restricted zone
- ✓ by the manager of the aerodrome/person acting on behalf of manager

Fail to leave restricted zone on request

- ✓ date and location
- ✓ without lawful authority/reasonable excuse
- ✓ remained on part of a restricted zone of an aerodrome/of an air navigation installation not forming part of an aerodrome
- ✓ when requested to leave
- ✓ by the manager/person acting on behalf of manager

Meanings

Restricted zone

In relation to an aerodrome or air navigation installation, means any part of the aerodrome or installation designated under section 11A of this Act or, where the whole of the aerodrome or installation is so designated, that aerodrome or installation, Aviation Security Act 1982, s 24A.

Aerodrome (see 5.4.10)

Air navigation installation

Means any building, works, apparatus or equipment used wholly or mainly for the purpose of assisting air traffic control or as an aid to air navigation, together with any land contiguous or adjacent to any such building, works, apparatus or equipment and used wholly or mainly for purposes connected therewith (Aviation Security Act 1982, s 38(1)).

Manager

In relation to an aerodrome, means the person (whether the Civil Aviation Authority, a local authority or any other person) by whom the aerodrome is managed (Aviation Security Act 1982, s 38).

Police powers

Power of arrest—section 41 of the Terrorism Act 2000 (see **5.3.1**)

Power to stop and search—section 43 of the Terrorism Act 2000 (see **5.2.1**)

A constable, the manager of an aerodrome or a person acting on his behalf may use reasonable force to remove a person who fails to comply with a request under section 21C(1)(b) (Aviation Security Act 1982, s 21C(4)).

If the person is not suspected to be a terrorist, consider using PACE powers (such as ss 24, 17, 18, and 32 of PACE) but see **5.3.1** for drawbacks on using PACE powers for potential terrorists.

Notes

(a) The offences in section 21C(1)(a) do not apply unless it is proved that, at the material time, notices stating that the area concerned was a restricted zone were posted so as to be readily seen and read by persons entering the restricted zone (Aviation Security Act 1982, s 21C(2)).

(b) A person is permitted to have access to a restricted zone of an aerodrome or air navigation installation if he is permitted to enter that zone or if arrangements exist for permitting any of his employees or agents to enter that zone (Aviation Security Act 1982, s 24A(2)).

(c) For the liability of company directors, etc see section 37 of the Aviation Security Act 1982 (see **5.7.2**).

(d) See also the offences of unauthorized presence on board an aircraft (**5.4.17**).

PNLD reference numbers

H4228, H4229, H4230, H2730, H2732, H2734, D4330

 Time limit for prosecution: Six months.

 Summary: Fine not exceeding level five on the standard scale.

5.4.17 Unauthorized presence on board an aircraft

Section 21D of the Aviation Security Act 1982 creates the offence of unauthorized presence on board an aircraft.

Offence

(1) A person shall not—
   (a) get into or onto an aircraft at an **aerodrome** in the United King-
       dom except with the permission of the **operator** of the aircraft or
       a person acting on his behalf, or
   (b) remain on an aircraft at such an aerodrome after being requested
       to leave by the operator of the aircraft or a person acting on his
       behalf.
(2) A person who contravenes subsection (1) above without lawful
   authority or reasonable excuse shall be guilty of an offence (...).

Aviation Security Act 1982, s 21D(1) and (2)

Points to prove

Board aircraft without permission

- ✓ date and location
- ✓ without lawful authority/reasonable excuse
- ✓ at an aerodrome
- ✓ got into/onto an aircraft
- ✓ without the permission
- ✓ of the operator of the aircraft/person acting on operator's
  behalf

Fail/refuse to leave aircraft on request

- ✓ date and location
- ✓ without lawful authority/reasonable excuse
- ✓ at an aerodrome
- ✓ remained on an aircraft
- ✓ after being requested to leave by
- ✓ operator of aircraft/person acting on operator's behalf

Meanings

Aerodrome (see **5.4.13**).

Operator

In relation to an aircraft, means the person having the management
of the aircraft for the time being or, in relation to a time, at that time
(Civil Aviation Act 1982, s 105).

Police powers

If suspected terrorist:

Power of arrest—section 41 of the Terrorism Act 2000 (see **5.3.1**)

Power to stop and search—section 43 of the Terrorism Act 2000 (see **5.2.1**)

A constable, the operator of an aircraft or a person acting on his behalf may use reasonable force to remove a person who fails to comply with a request under section 21D(1)(b) (Aviation Security Act 1982, s 21D(3)).

If the person is not suspected to be a terrorist, consider using PACE powers (such as ss 24, 17, 18, and 32 of PACE) but see **5.3.1** for drawbacks on using PACE powers for potential terrorists.

Notes

(a) For the liability of company directors, etc see section 37 of the Aviation Security Act 1982 (see **5.7.2**).
(b) See also the offences of unauthorized presence in a restricted zone of an aerodrome (**5.4.16**).

PNLD reference numbers

H4231, H4232, D4331

 Time limit for prosecution: Six months.

 Summary: Fine not exceeding level five on the standard scale.

5.4.18 Obstruction or impersonation of authorized person

Section 21E of the Aviation Security Act 1982 provides the offences of intentionally obstructing an authorized person in the execution of his duties and of falsely pretending to be an authorized person.

> ### Offence
>
> A person who—
> (a) intentionally obstructs an **authorised person** acting in the exercise of a power conferred on him by or under this Part of this Act, or
> (b) falsely pretends to be an authorised person, commits an offence.
>
> Aviation Security Act 1982, s 21E(1)

Points to prove

✓ date and location

✓ intentionally obstructed/falsely pretended to be

✓ an authorized person acting in exercise of power under Aviation Security Act 1982

Meanings

Authorized person

Means a person authorized in writing by the Secretary of State for the purposes of part II of the Aviation Security Act 1982 (Protection of Aircraft, Aerodromes and Air Navigation Installations Against Acts of Violence, sections 10–24A) (Aviation Security Act 1982, s 24A).

Police powers

If suspected terrorist:

Power of arrest—section 41 of the Terrorism Act 2000 (see **5.3.1**)

Power to stop and search—section 43 of the Terrorism Act 2000 (see **5.2.1**)

If the person is not suspected to be a terrorist, consider using PACE powers (such as ss 24, 17, 18, and 32 of PACE) but see **5.3.1** for drawbacks on using PACE powers for potential terrorists.

PNLD reference numbers

H4233, H4234, D4332

Obstruct authorized person

🕐 **Time limit for prosecution:** None.

♿ **Summary:** Fine not exceeding statutory maximum.

▦ **Indictment:** Maximum two years' imprisonment and/or fine.

Pretend to be authorized person

🕐 **Time limit for prosecution:** Six months.

♿ **Summary:** Fine not exceeding level five on the standard scale.

5.4.19 Endangering safety of an aircraft, a person, or property

Article 73 of the Air Navigation Order 2005 (SI 2005/1970) creates the offence of endangering the safety of an aircraft.

Offence

A person shall not recklessly or negligently act in a manner likely to endanger an aircraft, or any person therein.

Air Navigation Order 2005, art 73

Points to prove

✓ date and location
✓ recklessly act in a manner
✓ likely to endanger aircraft/person therein

Police powers

If suspected terrorist:

Power of arrest—section 41 of the Terrorism Act 2000 (see 5.3.1)

Power to stop and search—section 43 of the Terrorism Act 2000 (see 5.2.1)

If the person is not suspected to be a terrorist, consider using PACE powers (such as ss 24, 17, 18, and 32 of PACE) but see **5.3.1** for drawbacks on using PACE powers for potential terrorists.

Powers of commander of the aircraft—section 94 of the Civil Aviation Act 1982 (see 5.4.12)

Note

The offence applies to offences committed in the UK, and to acts committed on aircraft which are UK registered or which are foreign registered but within the UK or over UK territorial waters, regardless of the nationality of the offender, for details see articles 149 and 150 of the Air Navigation Order 2005.

PNLD reference numbers

H8120, D17026

 Time limit for prosecution: None.

 Summary: Fine not exceeding the statutory maximum.

 Indictment: Maximum five years imprisonment and/or fine.

5.4.20 Cause or permit aircraft to endanger person or property

Article 74 of the Air Navigation Order 2005 (SI 2005/1970) creates the offence of causing or permitting an aircraft to endanger the safety of any person or property.

Offence

A person shall not recklessly or negligently act in a manner likely to endanger an aircraft, or any person therein.

Air Navigation Order 2005, art 74

Points to prove

✓ date and location
✓ recklessly/negligently
✓ caused/permitted an aircraft
✓ to endanger persons/property

Police powers

If suspected terrorist:

Power of arrest—section 41 of the Terrorism Act 2000 (see 5.3.1)

Power to stop and search—section 43 of the Terrorism Act 2000 (see 5.2.1)

If the person is not suspected to be a terrorist, consider using PACE powers (such as ss 24, 17, 18, and 32 of PACE) but see **5.3.1** for drawbacks on using PACE powers for potential terrorists.

Powers of commander of the aircraft—section 94 of the Civil Aviation Act 1982 (see 5.4.12)

Note

The offence applies to offences committed in the UK, and to acts committed on aircraft which are UK registered or which are foreign registered but within the UK or over UK territorial waters, regardless of the nationality of the offender, see articles 149 and 150 of the Air Navigation Order 2005.

PNLD reference numbers

H8122, D17027

 Time limit for prosecution: None.

 Summary: Fine not exceeding the statutory maximum.

 Indictment: Maximum two years' imprisonment and/or fine.

5.4.21 **Endangering safety at aerodromes**

Section 1 of the Aviation and Maritime Security Act 1990 creates offences of endangering safety at aerodromes.

Offence

(1) It is an offence for any person by means of any device, substance or weapon intentionally to commit at an **aerodrome** serving international civil aviation any **act of violence** which—
   (a) causes or is likely to cause death or serious personal injury, and
   (b) endangers or is likely to endanger the safe operation of the aerodrome or the safety of persons at the aerodrome.
(2) It is also, subject to subsection (4) below, an offence for any person by means of any device, substance or weapon **unlawfully** and intentionally—
   (a) to destroy or seriously to damage-
      (i) property used for the provision of any facilities at an aerodrome serving international civil aviation (including any apparatus or equipment so used), or

---

(ii)   any aircraft which is at such an aerodrome but is not in service, or

(b) to disrupt the services of such an aerodrome, in such a way as to endanger or be likely to endanger the safe operation of the aerodrome or the safety of persons at the aerodrome.

Aviation and Maritime Security Act 1990, s 1(1) and (2)

Points to prove

Offence under section 1(1)

- ✓ date and location
- ✓ by means of device(s)/substance(s)/weapon(s)
- ✓ at an aerodrome serving international civil aviation
- ✓ intentionally
- ✓ committed an act of violence
- ✓ which caused serious personal injury/death/which was likely to cause death/serious personal injury
- ✓ and endangered/was likely to endanger
- ✓ the safe operation of/safety of persons at aerodrome

Offence under section 1(2)

- ✓ date and location
- ✓ by means of device(s)/substance(s)/weapon(s)
- ✓ at an aerodrome serving international civil aviation
- ✓ unlawfully and intentionally
- ✓ disrupted the services of the aerodrome in such way as to
  or
- ✓ destroyed/seriously damaged property used for provision of facilities/aircraft not in service at that aerodrome in such way as to
- ✓ endanger/be likely to endanger safe operation of aerodrome/safety of persons at aerodrome

Meanings

Aerodrome

Has the same meaning as in the Civil Aviation Act 1982 (see **5.4.10**).

Act of violence

Means—

(a) any act done in the UK which constitutes the offence of mur-
    der, attempted murder, manslaughter, culpable homicide, or
    assault or an offence under section 18, 20, 21, 22, 23, 24, 28,
    or 29 of the Offences Against the Person Act 1861 (see **5.8.3**)
    or under section 2 of the Explosive Substances Act 1883 (see
    5.8.1.1), and

(b) any act done outside the UK which, if done in the UK,
    would constitute such an offence as is mentioned in para-
    graph (a) above (Aviation and Maritime Security Act 1990,
    s 1(9)).

Unlawfully

Means—

(a) in relation to the commission of an act in the UK, means so
    as (apart from this section) to constitute an offence under
    the law of the part of the UK in which the act is committed,
    and

(b) in relation to the commission of an act outside the UK, means
    so that the commission of the act would (apart from this
    section) have been an offence under the law of England and
    Wales if it had been committed in England and Wales or of
    Scotland if it had been committed in Scotland (Aviation and
    Maritime Security Act 1990, s 1(9)).

Police powers

If suspected terrorist:

Power of arrest—section 41 of the Terrorism Act 2000 (see 5.3.1)

Power to stop and search—section 43 of the Terrorism Act 2000
    (see **5.2.1**)

If the person is not suspected to be a terrorist, consider using PACE
powers (such as ss 24, 17, 18, and 32 of PACE) but see **5.3.1** for drawbacks on using PACE powers for potential terrorists.

Note

This offence applies to acts done outside the UK regardless of the
nationality of the offender with one exception: subsection (2)(a)(ii)
above does not apply to any act committed in relation to an aircraft
used in **military**, customs, or police **service** unless—

(i) the act is committed in the UK, or

(ii) where the act is committed outside the UK, the person committing it is a UK national (Aviation and Maritime Security Act 1990, s 1(3) and (4)).

Meanings

Military service

Includes naval and air force service (Aviation Security Act 1982, s 38(1)).

UK national

Means an individual who is—

(a) a British citizen, a British overseas territories citizen, a British National (Overseas) or a British Overseas citizen;

(b) a person who under the British Nationality Act 1981 is a British subject; or

(c) a British protected person (within the meaning of that Act) (Aviation Security Act 1982, s 38(1)).

Notes

(a) Section 50 of the Aviation and Maritime Security Act 1990 provides for offences committed by a body corporate (see **5.7.2**).

(b) The Aviation and Maritime Security Act 1990 contains further offences regarding the safety of ships and fixed platforms, such as hijacking of ships (section 9), seizing or exercising control of fixed platforms (section 10) and endangering safe navigation (section 12). In addition to this, the Act provides powers for the protection of ships and harbour areas against acts of violence; the Secretary of State may, for example, impose restrictions on ships (section 21) or require other persons to carry out searches in harbour areas (sections 22 and 23).

PNLD reference numbers

D4315, H4211, H4212, H4454, H4455, H4456

AG consent required: Aviation and Maritime Security Act 1990, s 1(7).

Time limit for prosecution: None.

Indictment: Maximum life imprisonment.

5.4.22 **Trespass on licensed aerodromes**

Section 39 of the Civil Aviation Act 1982 creates the offence of trespassing on licensed aerodromes.

Offence

Subject to subsection (2) below, if any person trespasses on any land forming part of an **aerodrome licensed** in pursuance of an **Air Navigation Order**, he shall be liable on summary conviction to a fine not exceeding level 3 on the standard scale.

Civil Aviation Act 1982, s 39(1)

Points to prove

✓ date and location
✓ trespassed
✓ on land forming part of a licensed aerodrome

Meanings

Subject to subsection (2) below (see defence).

Aerodrome

Means any area of land or water designed, equipped, set apart or commonly used for affording facilities for the landing and departure of aircraft and includes any area or space, whether on the ground, on the roof of a building or elsewhere, which is designed, equipped or set apart for affording facilities for the landing and departure of aircraft capable of descending or climbing vertically (Civil Aviation Act 1982, s 105(1)).

Licensed aerodromes

Means licensed under Art 128 of the Air Navigation Order 2005 (SI 2005/1970).

Air Navigation Order

Means an Order in Council under section 60 of the Civil Aviation Act 1982, the most relevant being the Air Navigation Order 2005 (Civil Aviation Act 1982, s 105(1)).

Defence

No person shall be liable under this section unless it is proved that, at the material time, notices warning trespassers of their liability under this section were posted so as to be readily seen and read by members of the public, in such positions on or near the boundary of the aerodrome as appear to the court to be proper.

Civil Aviation Act 1982, s 39(2)

Police powers

Power of arrest—section 41 of the Terrorism Act 2000 (see **5.3.1**)

Power to stop and search—section 43 of the Terrorism Act 2000 (see **5.2.1**)

If the person is not suspected of being a terrorist consider using PACE powers (such as ss 24, 17, 18, and 32 of PACE) but see **5.3.1** for drawbacks on using PACE powers for potential terrorists.

Note

See also the offence of unauthorized presence in restricted zone of an airport (see **5.4.16**).

PNLD reference number

D4347

 Time limit for prosecution: Six months.

 Summary: Fine not exceeding level three on the standard scale.

5.5 **Chemical, Biological, Radiological, and Nuclear**

Various Acts contain provisions dealing with chemical, biological, radioactive, and nuclear weapons and/or material. The Terrorism Act 2006 creates offences relating to radioactive devices and materials and nuclear facilities. The Anti-terrorism, Crime and Security Act 2001 creates offences relating to the use of nuclear weapons and pathogens and toxins. Further provisions deal with the security of the nuclear industry, trespassing on nuclear sites, the use of noxious substances, and biological and chemical weapons.

See also **1.6.7** and the case study 'CBRN Resilience Programme' (in **2.4.4**) as well as Protecting National Security (**2.7**).

5.5.1 **Making and possession of radioactive devices or materials**

Section 9 of the Terrorism Act 2006 creates the offence of making or possessing radioactive devices or materials. This offence is specifically terrorism-related and adds to other offences relating to nuclear weapons and other nuclear material which are not terrorism-related.

Offence

A person commits an offence if—

(a) he makes or has in his possession a **radioactive device**, or

(b) he has in his possession **radioactive material**,

with the intention of using the device or material in the course of or in connection with the commission or preparation of an **act of terrorism** or for the purposes of terrorism, or of making it available to be so used.

Terrorism Act 2006, s 9(1)

> **Points to prove**
> ✓ date and location
> ✓ made/possessed radioactive device/material
> ✓ intending to use it in the course of/in connection with the commission/preparation of an act of terrorism **or** for the purposes of terrorism **or** to make it available to be so used

Meanings

Radioactive device

Means—

(a) a nuclear weapon or other nuclear explosive device;
(b) a radioactive material dispersal device;
(c) a radiation-emitting device.

Radioactive material

Means nuclear material or any other radioactive substance which—

(a) contains nuclides that undergo spontaneous disintegration in a process accompanied by the emission of one or more types of ionising radiation, such as alpha radiation, beta radiation, neutron particles or gamma rays; and

(b) is capable, owing to its radiological or fissile properties, of—
  (i) causing serious bodily injury to a person;
  (ii) causing serious damage to property;
  (iii) endangering a person's life; or
  (iv) creating a serious risk to the health or safety of **the public**.

Terrorism Act 2006, s 9(4)

This definition can include (under 'radioactive material dispersal device') a 'dirty bomb' in which an explosive causes radioactive material to disperse, with the effect that the radiation causes danger.

The public

Means the public of any part of the UK or of a country or territory outside the UK, or any section of the public (Terrorism Act 2006, s 20(3)).

Device

Includes any of the following, whether or not fixed to land, namely, machinery, equipment, appliances, tanks, containers, pipes and conduits.

Nuclear material

Has the same meaning as in the Nuclear Material (Offences) Act 1983 (Terrorism Act 2006, 9(5)). Section 6 of the Nuclear Material (Offences) Act 1983 defines 'nuclear material' as material which, within the meaning of the Convention on the Physical Protection of Nuclear Material, is nuclear material used for peaceful purposes. It covers particular types of plutonium and uranium, such as uranium-233 and any material containing such uranium or plutonium.

Terrorism/act of terrorism (see 4.1).

Police powers

Power of arrest—section 41 of the Terrorism Act 2000 (see 5.3.1)

Power to stop and search—section 43 of the Terrorism Act 2000 (see 5.2.1)

Notes

(a) It is irrelevant whether the act of terrorism to which an intention relates is a particular act of terrorism, an act of terrorism of a particular description, or an act of terrorism generally (Terrorism Act 2006, s 9(2)).

(b) *Extra territorial jurisdiction*—This offence applies to acts done outside the UK regardless of the nationality of the offender (Terrorism Act 2006, s 17, see **5.7.1.1**).

(c) *Corporate liability*—For the liability of company directors, etc see section 18 of the Terrorism Act 2006 (see **5.7.2.1**).

(d) Also consider the offences of 'misuse of radioactive devices or material and misuse and damage of facilities' (see **5.5.2**) and 'terrorist threats relating to radioactive devices, material or facilities' (see **5.5.3**) and the offences concerning nuclear weapons, section 47 of the Anti-terrorism, Crime and Security Act 2001 (see **5.5.4**).

(e) *Counter-Terrorism Act 2008*—Section 28 of the Act makes provision for this offence to be tried at any place in the UK if it was committed in the UK. See PNLD reference number S1136 to check whether this section is in force.

(f) *Counter-Terrorism Act 2008—forfeiture orders*—Section 38 of the Act inserts a new section 11A into the Terrorism Act 2000 which provides that the court on conviction of this offence may order the forfeiture of any radioactive device or radioactive material, or any nuclear facility, made or used in committing this offence. For a summary of the Act see p xxvii. Check PNLD reference number S399 to see whether section 11A is in force.

(g) *Counter-Terrorism Act 2008—notification requirements*—Sections 40 to 61 of the Act make provision for notification requirements for persons sentenced, or made subject to a hospital order. For a summary of the Act see p xxvii. See PNLD reference number S1136 to check whether these sections are in force.

PNLD reference numbers

H8460, H8465, D18580

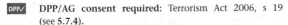 **DPP/AG consent required:** Terrorism Act 2006, s 19 (see **5.7.4**).

Time limit for prosecution: None.

Indictment: Maximum life imprisonment.

5.5.2 **Misuse of radioactive devices and materials and misuse or damage of facilities**

Section 10 of the Terrorism Act 2006 makes it an offence to misuse radioactive devices or material and to misuse or damage nuclear facilities in connection with terrorism. It adds to other offences in relation to nuclear weapons (see **5.5.4**).

Offences

(1) A person commits an offence if he uses—
   (a) a **radioactive device**, or
   (b) **radioactive material**, in the course of or in connection with the commission of an **act of terrorism** or for the purposes of **terrorism**.

(2) A person commits an offence if, in the course of or in connection with the commission of an act of terrorism or for the purposes of terrorism, he uses or damages a **nuclear facility** in a manner which—
   (a) causes a release of radioactive material; or
   (b) creates or increases a risk that such material will be released.

Terrorism Act 2006, s 10(1) and (2)

Points to prove

Offence in s 10(1)

✓ date and location
✓ used a radioactive device/radioactive material
✓ in the course of/in connection with the commission of an act of terrorism/for the purposes of terrorism

Offence in s 10(2)

✓ date and location
✓ used/damaged a nuclear facility
✓ in a manner which caused a release of radioactive material
  or
  created/increased a risk that radioactive material would be released
✓ in the course of/in connection with the commission of an act of terrorism/for the purposes of terrorism

---

Meanings

Radioactive device and radioactive material (see 5.5.1).

Terrorism/act of terrorism (see 4.1).

Nuclear facility

Means—

(a) a **nuclear reactor**, including a reactor installed in or on any **transportation device** for use as an energy source in order to propel it or for any other purpose; or
(b) a plant or conveyance being used for the production, storage, processing or transport of radioactive material (Terrorism Act 2006, s 10(4)).

Nuclear reactor

Means any plant (including any machinery, equipment or appliance, whether affixed to land or not) designed or adapted for the production of atomic energy by a fission process in which a controlled chain reaction can be maintained without an additional source of neutrons (Terrorism Act 2006, s 10(5), and Nuclear Installations Act 1965, s 26).

Transportation device

Means any vehicle or any space object (that includes the component parts of a space object, its launch vehicle and the component parts of that) (Terrorism Act 2006, s 10(5), and Outer Space Act 1986, s 13(1)).

Police powers

Power of arrest—section 41 of the Terrorism Act 2000 (see **5.3.1**)

Power to stop and search—section 43 of the Terrorism Act 2000 (see **5.2.1**)

Notes

(a) *Extraterritorial jurisdiction*—This offence applies to acts done outside the UK regardless of the nationality of the offender (Terrorism Act 2006, s 17, see **5.7.1.1**).

(b) Also see the offences of 'making and possession of radioactive devices or material' (see **5.5.1**) and 'terrorist threats relating to radioactive devices, material or facilities' (see **5.5.3**) and the offences concerning nuclear weapons under section 47 of the Anti-terrorism, Crime and Security Act 2001 (see **5.5.4**).

(c) *Corporate liability*—For the liability of company directors, etc see section 18 of the Terrorism Act 2006 (see **5.7.2.1**).

(d) *Counter-Terrorism Act 2008*—Section 28 of the Act makes provision for this offence to be tried at any place in the UK if it was committed in the UK. See PNLD reference number S1136 to check whether this section is in force.

(e) *Counter-Terrorism Act 2008—forfeiture orders*—Section 38 of the Act inserts a new section 11A into the Terrorism Act 2000 which provides that the court on conviction of this offence may order the forfeiture of any radioactive device or radioactive material, or any nuclear facility, made or used in committing this offence. Check PNLD reference number S399 to see whether section 11A is in force.

(f) *Counter-Terrorism Act 2008—notification requirements*—Sections 40 to 61 of the Act make provision for notification requirements for persons sentenced, or made subject to a hospital order. For a summary of the Act see p xxvii. See PNLD reference number S1136 to check whether these sections are in force.

PNLD reference numbers

H8461, H8463, D18581

DPP✓ **DPP/AG consent required:** Terrorism Act 2006, s 19 (see **5.7.4**).

🕐 **Time limit for prosecution:** None.

▥ **Indictment:** Maximum life imprisonment.

5.5.3 **Terrorist threats relating to radioactive devices and materials or facilities**

Section 11 of the Terrorism Act 2006 creates offences concerning the making of threats relating to radioactive devices, radioactive material or nuclear facilities in connection with terrorism. It adds to the offences under section 113 of the Anti-terrorism, Crime and Security Act 2001 in relation to noxious substances or things (see **5.5.15**).

Offences

(1) A person commits an offence if, in the course of or in connection with the commission of an **act of terrorism** or for the purposes of terrorism—

   (a) he makes a demand—

      (i) for the supply to himself or to another of a **radioactive device** or of **radioactive material**;

      (ii) for a **nuclear facility** to be made available to himself or to another; or

      (iii) for access to such a facility to be given to himself or to another;

   (b) he supports the demand with a threat that he or another will take action if the demand is not met; and

   (c) the circumstances and manner of the threat are such that it is reasonable for the person to whom it is made to assume that there is real risk that the threat will be carried out if the demand is not met.

(2) A person commits an offence if—

   (a) he makes a threat falling within subsection (3) in the course of or in connection with the commission of an act of terrorism or for the purposes of terrorism; and

   (b) the circumstances and manner of the threat are such that it is reasonable for the person to whom it is made to assume that there is real risk that the threat will be carried out, or would be carried out if demands made in association with the threat are not met.

(3) A threat falls within this subsection if it is—

   (a) a threat to use radioactive material;

   (b) a threat to use a radioactive device; or

   (c) a threat to use or damage a nuclear facility in a manner that releases radioactive material or creates or increases a risk that such material will be released.

Terrorism Act 2006, s 11(1)–(3)

Points to prove

Offence in s 11(1)

✓ date and location
✓ in the course of/in connection with the commission of an act of terrorism/for the purposes of terrorism
✓ made a demand
✓ for the supply to yourself/another of a radioactive device/material **or**
for a nuclear facility to be made available to yourself/another **or**
for access to a nuclear facility to be given to yourself/another **and**
✓ supported the demand with a threat
✓ that you/another would take action if the demand was not met **and**
✓ the circumstances and manner of the threat were such
✓ that it was reasonable for the person to whom it was made
✓ to assume that there was a real risk
✓ that the threat would be carried out if the demand was not met

Offence in s 11(2)

✓ date and location
✓ made a threat
✓ to use radioactive material/radioactive device **or**
✓ to use/damage a nuclear facility in a manner that releases radioactive material/creates/increases a risk that such material would be released
✓ in the course of/in connection with the commission of an act of terrorism/for the purposes of terrorism
✓ the circumstances and manner of the threat were such
✓ that it was reasonable for the person to whom it was made
✓ to assume that there was a real risk
✓ that the threat would be carried out if the demand was not met

Meanings

Terrorism/act of terrorism (see **4.1**).

Radioactive device and radioactive material (see **5.5.1**).

Nuclear facility (see 5.5.2).

Police powers

Power of arrest—section 41 of the Terrorism Act 2000 (see 5.3.1)

Power to stop and search—section 43 of the Terrorism Act 2000 (see 5.2.1)

Notes

(a) The offences are similar to blackmail. Both offences are completed by making the threat alone. No radioactive device or material actually needs to exist.

(b) The offences can only be committed in relation to terrorism, not Convention offences (see 5.7.3). Also, they can be committed 'in the course of or in connection with' acts of terrorism, but not in preparation for acts of terrorism.

(c) The offence only takes place if the threat is credible looking at the circumstances and manner in which it was made.

(d) *Extraterritorial jurisdiction*—The offences apply to acts done outside the UK regardless of the nationality of the offender (Terrorism Act 2006, s 17, see 5.7.1.1).

(e) Also see the offences of 'making and possession of radioactive devices or material' (see 5.5.1) and 'misuse of radioactive devices or material and misuse and damage of facilities' (see 5.5.2), the offences concerning nuclear weapons under section 47 of the Anti-terrorism, Crime and Security Act 2001 (see 5.5.4) and the offences under section 113 of the Anti-terrorism, Crime and Security Act 2001 in relation to noxious substances or things (see 5.5.7).

(f) *Corporate liability*—For the liability of company directors etc. see section 18 of the Terrorism Act 2006 (see 5.7.2.1).

(g) *Counter-Terrorism Act 2008*—Section 28 of the Act makes provision for this offence to be tried at any place in the UK if it was committed in the UK. See PNLD reference number S1136 to check whether this section is in force.

(h) *Counter-Terrorism Act 2008—forfeiture orders*—Section 38 of the Act inserts a new section 11A into the Terrorism Act 2000 which provides that the court on conviction of this offence may order the forfeiture of any radioactive device or radioactive material, or any nuclear facility, which is the subject of a demand under section 11(1) or a threat falling within section 11(3). Check PNLD reference number S399 to see whether section 11A is in force.

(i) *Counter-Terrorism Act 2008—notification requirements*—Sections 40 to 61 of the Act make provision for notification requirements for persons sentenced, or made subject to a hospital order. For a summary of the Act see p xxvii. See PNLD reference number S1136 to check whether these sections are in force.

PNLD reference numbers

H8462, H8464, D18582

 DPP/AG consent required: Terrorism Act 2006, s 19 (see **5.7.4**).

 Time limit for prosecution: None.

 Indictment: Maximum life imprisonment.

5.5.4 Use etc of nuclear weapons

Section 47 of the Anti-terrorism, Crime and Security Act 2001 creates offences regarding the use of nuclear weapons.

Offence

A person who—

(a) knowingly causes a **nuclear weapon** explosion;
(b) develops or produces, or **participates in the development or production of, a nuclear** weapon
(c) has a nuclear weapon in his possession;
(d) participates in the transfer of a nuclear weapon; or
(e) engages in military preparations, or in preparations of a military nature, intending to use, or threaten to use, a nuclear weapon,

is guilty of an offence.

Anti-terrorism, Crime and Security Act 2001, s 47(1)

Points to prove

Offence in section 47(1)(a)

✓ date and location
✓ knowingly
✓ caused
✓ a nuclear weapon explosion

Offence in section 47(1)(b)

✓ date and location
✓ developed/produced *or*
✓ participated in the development/production of
✓ a nuclear weapon

Offence in section 47(1)(c)

✓ date and location
✓ possessed
✓ a nuclear weapon

Offence in section 47(1)(d)

✓ date and location
✓ participated in the transfer of
✓ a nuclear weapon

Offence in section 47(1)(e)

✓ date and location
✓ engaged in military preparations/in preparations of a military nature
✓ intending to use/threatening to use
✓ a nuclear weapon

Meanings

Nuclear weapon

Includes a nuclear explosive device that is not intended for use as a weapon (Anti-terrorism, Crime and Security Act 2001, s 47(6)). In this way, a 'dirty bomb' is covered.

A person participates in the development or production of a nuclear weapon

If he does any act which—

    (a) facilitates the development by another of the capability to produce or use a nuclear weapon,

or

    (b) facilitates the making by another of a nuclear weapon, knowing or having reason to believe that his act has (or will have) that effect (Anti-terrorism, Crime and Security Act 2001, s 47(3)).

A person participates in the transfer of a nuclear weapon

If—

    (a) he buys or otherwise acquires it or agrees with another to do so;

(b) he sells or otherwise disposes of it or agrees with another to do so; or

(c) he makes arrangements under which another person either acquires or disposes of it or agrees with a third person to do so (Anti-terrorism, Crime and Security Act 2001, s 47(4)).

Defence

(1) In proceedings for an offence under section 47(1)(c) or (d) relating to an object it is a defence for the accused to show that he did not know and had no reason to believe that the object was a nuclear weapon.

(2) But he shall be taken to have shown that fact if—
   (a) sufficient evidence is adduced to raise an issue with respect to it; and
   (b) the contrary is not proved by the prosecution beyond reasonable doubt.

(3) In proceedings for such an offence it is also a defence for the accused to show that he knew or believed that the object was a nuclear weapon but, as soon as reasonably practicable after he first knew or believed that fact, he took all reasonable steps to inform the Secretary of State or a constable of his knowledge or belief.

Anti-terrorism, Crime and Security Act 2001, s 48 (1)–(3)

Police powers

Power of entry to search for evidence relating to nuclear weapons, etc—section 52 of the Anti-terrorism, Crime and Security Act 2001 (see 5.5.6)

If suspected terrorist:

Power of arrest—section 41 of the Terrorism Act 2000 (see 5.3.1)

Power to stop and search—section 43 of the Terrorism Act 2000 (see 5.2.1)

If the person is not suspected to be a terrorist, consider using PACE powers (such as ss 24, 17, 18, and 32 of PACE) but see 5.3.1 for drawbacks on using PACE powers for potential terrorists.

Notes

(a) Section 48 of the Anti-terrorism, Crime and Security Act 2001 makes exceptions for actions carried out in the course of an armed conflict or for actions authorized by the Secretary of State.

(b) *Extraterritorial jurisdiction*—The offence applies to acts done outside the UK, but only if they are done by a UK person (Anti-terrorism, Crime and Security Act 2001, s 47(7)).

UK person

Means a UK national, a Scottish partnership or a body incorporated under the law of a part of the UK.

UK national

Is an individual who is—

(a) a British citizen, a British overseas territories citizen, a British National (Overseas) or a British Overseas citizen;

(b) a person who under the British Nationality Act 1981 is a British subject; or

(c) a British protected person within the meaning of that Act. (Anti-terrorism, Crime and Security Act 2001, s 56).

Where the offence is committed outside the UK proceedings may be taken, and the offence may for incidental purposes be treated as having been committed, in any part of the UK (Anti-terrorism, Crime and Security Act 2001, s 51(1)).

Where a person aids, abets, counsels or procures, or incites, a person who is not a UK person to commit this offence outside the UK, see **5.5.5**.

(c) *Revenue and Customs prosecutions*—Proceedings for this offence (including an offence of aiding, abetting, counselling or procuring the commission of, or attempting or conspiring to commit, this offence, or an offence of encouraging or assisting crime under the Serious Crime Act 2007) may be instituted by the Director of Revenue and Customs Prosecutions or by order of the Commissioners for Her Majesty's Revenue and Customs if it appears to the Director or to the Commissioners that the offence has involved—

(i) the development or production outside the UK of a nuclear weapon;

(ii) the movement of a nuclear weapon into or out of any country or territory;

(iii) any proposal or attempt to do anything falling within paragraph (a) or (b).
(Anti-terrorism, Crime and Security Act 2001, s 53).

(d) *Corporate liability*—See section 54(3) of the Anti-terrorism, Crime and Security Act 2001 (see **5.7.2.2**).

PNLD reference numbers

H4752, H4753, H4754, H4755, H4756, D10327

 AG consent required: Anti-terrorism, Crime and Security Act 2001, s 55.

 Time limit for prosecution: None.

Indictment: Maximum life imprisonment.

5.5.5 Assisting or inducing certain weapons-related acts overseas

Section 50 of the Anti-terrorism, Crime and Security Act 2001 makes it an offence to aid, abet, counsel or procure, or encourages or assists offences relating to nuclear weapons, chemical weapons or biological agents and toxins outside the UK.

Offence

A person who aids, abets, counsels or procures, or **incites**, a person who is not a **United Kingdom person** to do **a relevant act** outside the United Kingdom is guilty of an offence.

Anti-terrorism, Crime and Security Act 2001, s 50(1)

Points to prove

✓ date and location
✓ aided, abetted, counselled or procured
✓ person who is not a UK person
✓ to do an act
✓ outside the UK
✓ which, if committed by a UK person, would constitute a contravention of
✓ section 1 of the Biological Weapons Act 1974 *or*
 section 2 of the Chemical Weapons Act 1996 *or*
 section 47 of the Anti-terrorism, Crime and Security Act 2001

Meanings

A relevant act

Is an act that, if done by a UK person, would contravene any of the following provisions—

- (a) section 1 of the Biological Weapons Act 1974 (offences relating to biological agents and toxins, see **5.5.17**);
- (b) section 2 of the Chemical Weapons Act 1996 (offences relating to chemical weapons, see **5.5.18**); or
- (c) section 47 above (offences relating to nuclear weapons, see **5.5.4**).

Incites

Refers to the offences of encouraging or assisting crime under the Serious Crime Act 2007.

UK person (see **5.5.4**).

Defence

A person accused of an offence under this section in relation to a relevant act which would contravene a provision mentioned in subsection (2) may raise any defence which would be open to a person accused of the corresponding offence ancillary to an offence under that provision.

Anti-terrorism, Crime and Security Act 2001, s 50(4))

Police powers

Power of entry to search for evidence relating to nuclear weapons, etc—section 52 of the Anti-terrorism, Crime and Security Act 2001 (see **5.5.6**)

If suspected terrorist:

Power of arrest—section 41 of the Terrorism Act 2000 (see **5.3.1**)

Power to stop and search—section 43 of the Terrorism Act 2000 (see **5.2.1**)

If the person is not suspected to be a terrorist, consider using PACE powers (such as ss 24, 17, 18, and 32 of PACE) but see **5.3.1** for drawbacks on using PACE powers for potential terrorists.

Notes

- (a) *Extra-territorial jurisdiction*—This offence applies to acts done outside the UK, but only if they are done by a UK person (Anti-terrorism, Crime and Security Act 2001, s 50(6)). Where the offence is committed outside the UK proceedings may be taken, and the offence may for incidental purposes be treated as having been committed, in any part of the UK (Anti-terrorism, Crime and Security Act 2001, s 51(1)).

(b) *Revenue and Customs prosecutions*—Proceedings for this offence may be instituted by the Director of Revenue and Customs Prosecutions or by order of the Commissioners for Her Majesty's Revenue and Customs, for details see **5.5.4** (Anti-terrorism, Crime and Security Act 2001, s 53).

(c) *Corporate liability*—See section 54(3) of the Anti-terrorism, Crime and Security Act 2001 (**5.7.2.2**).

PNLD reference numbers

H4757, H4758, D10330

 AG consent required: Anti-terrorism, Crime and Security Act 2001, s 55.

 Time limit for prosecution: None.

 Indictment: Maximum life imprisonment.

5.5.6 Power of entry to search for evidence relating to nuclear weapons, etc

Section 52 of the Anti-terrorism, Crime and Security Act 2001 provides powers of entry under warrant to authorized officers of the Secretary of State and accompanying police officers to search for evidence for the commission of an offence under sections 47 and 50 (see **5.5.4** and **5.5.5**).

Powers

(1) If—

a justice of the peace is satisfied on information on oath that there are reasonable grounds for suspecting that evidence of the commission of an offence under section 47 *[use etc. of nuclear weapons, see 5.5.4]* or 50 *[assisting or inducing certain weapons-related acts overseas, see 5.5.5]* is to be found on any premises;

he may issue a warrant authorising an **authorised officer** to enter the premises, if necessary by force, at any time within one month from the time of the issue of the warrant and to search them.

(2) The powers of a person who enters the premises under the authority of the warrant include power—

(a) to take with him such other persons and such equipment as appear to him to be necessary;

(b) to inspect, seize and retain any substance, equipment or document found on the premises;

(c) to require any document or other information which is held in electronic form and is accessible from the premises to be produced in a form—

(i) in which he can read and copy it; or

(ii) from which it can readily be produced in a form in which he can read and copy it;

(d) to copy any document which he has reasonable cause to believe may be required as evidence for the purposes of proceedings in respect of an offence under section 47 or 50.

(3) A constable who enters premises under the authority of a warrant or by virtue of subsection (2)(a) may—

(a) give such assistance as an authorised officer may request for the purpose of facilitating the exercise of any power under this section; and

(b) search or cause to be searched any person on the premises who the constable has reasonable cause to believe may have in his possession any document or other thing which may be required as evidence for the purposes of proceedings in respect of an offence under section 47 or 50.

Anti-terrorism, Crime and Security Act 2001, s 52(1)–(3)

Meanings

Authorised officer

Means an authorized officer of the Secretary of State (Anti-terrorism, Crime and Security Act 2001, s 52(8)).

Notes

(a) There is no provision for the police to obtain a warrant directly, but they may be permitted to accompany authorized officers.

(b) The powers conferred by a warrant under this section shall only be exercisable, if the warrant so provides, in the presence of a constable (Anti-terrorism, Crime and Security Act 2001, s 52(5)).

(c) No constable shall search a person of the opposite sex (Anti-terrorism, Crime and Security Act 2001, s 52(4)).

(d) It is an offence to wilfully obstruct an authorized officer in the exercise of a power conferred by a warrant under section 52, or to fail without reasonable excuse to comply with a reasonable request made by an authorized officer or a constable for the purpose of facilitating the exercise of such a power (either way, summary: fine not exceeding the statutory maximum, on indictment: maximum two years' imprisonment and/or fine, Anti-terrorism, Crime and Security Act 2001, s 52(6) and (7)).

(e) *Counter-Terrorism Act 2008*—Sections 1 to 9 of the Act provide further powers to remove documents for examination etc for searches under section 52(1) or (3)(b). For a summary of the Act see p xxvii. See PNLD reference number S1136 to check whether these sections are in force.

PNLD reference numbers

H4759, H4760, D10332

5.5.7 **Security of nuclear industry**

Section 79 of the Anti-terrorism, Crime and Security Act 2001 makes it an offence to disclose information which might prejudice the security of a nuclear site or nuclear material.

Offence

A person is guilty of an offence if he **discloses** any information or thing the **disclosure** of which might prejudice the security of any **nuclear site** or of any **nuclear material**—

(a) with the intention of prejudicing that security; or

(b) being reckless as to whether the disclosure might prejudice that security.

Anti-terrorism, Crime and Security Act 2001, s 79(1)

Points to prove

✓ disclosed
✓ information/thing
✓ the disclosure of which might prejudice
✓ the security of any nuclear site/material
✓ with the intention of prejudicing that security *or* being reckless as to whether the disclosure might prejudice that security

Meanings

Disclose and disclosure

In relation to a thing, include parting with possession of it (Anti-terrorism, Crime and Security Act 2001, s 79(4)).

Nuclear site

Means a site in the UK (including a site occupied by or on behalf of the Crown) which is (or is expected to be) used for any purpose mentioned in section 1(1) of the Nuclear Installations Act 1965 (such as the installation or operating of a nuclear reactor or other installation designed or adapted for the production or use of atomic energy storage or the processing or disposal of nuclear fuel).

Nuclear material

Means—

- (a) any fissile material in the form of-
  - (i) uranium metal, alloy or chemical compound; or
  - (ii) plutonium metal, alloy or chemical compound;
- (b) any other fissile material prescribed by regulations made by the Secretary of State (Energy Act 2004, s 71(1)).

A reference to nuclear material

Is a reference to—

- (a) nuclear material which is being held on any nuclear site, or
- (b) nuclear material anywhere in the world which is being transported to or from a nuclear site or carried on board a **British ship**, (including nuclear material which is expected to be so held, transported or carried) (Anti-terrorism, Crime and Security Act 2001, s 79(2)).

British ship

Means a ship (including a ship belonging to Her Majesty) which is registered in the UK (Anti-terrorism, Crime and Security Act 2001, s 79(4)).

Police powers

If suspected terrorist:

Power of arrest—section 41 of the Terrorism Act 2000 (see 5.3.1)

Power to stop and search—section 43 of the Terrorism Act 2000 (see 5.2.1)

If the person is not suspected to be a terrorist, consider using PACE powers (such as ss 24, 17, 18, and 32 of PACE) but see **5.3.1** for drawbacks on using PACE powers for potential terrorists.

Notes

(a) Unlike under most sections of the Official Secrets Act 1989, section 79 makes no reference to whether the information is already in the public domain or whether it might be in the wider public interest to disclose it.

(b) *Extraterritorial jurisdiction*—The offence applies to acts done outside the UK, but only if they are done by a UK person. And proceedings for an offence committed outside the UK may be taken, and the offence may for incidental purposes be treated as having been committed, in any place in the UK. (Anti-terrorism, Crime and Security Act 2001, s 79(5) and (6)). 'UK person' means a UK national, a Scottish partnership or a body incorporated under the law of any part of the UK. For this purpose a UK national is an individual who is—

 (i) a British citizen, a British overseas territories citizen, a British National (Overseas) or a British Overseas citizen;

 (ii) a person who under the British Nationality Act 1981 is a British subject; or

 (iii) a British protected person within the meaning of that Act (Anti-terrorism, Crime and Security Act 2001, s 81(2) and (3)).

(c) Section 80 of the Anti-terrorism, Crime and Security Act 2001 creates a similar offence in relation to disclosures of uranium enrichment technology (either way offence, maximum penalty on summary conviction imprisonment of six months and/or fine not exceeding the statutory maximum, on indictment seven years imprisonment and/or fine). See also the Uranium Enrichment Technology (Prohibition on Disclosure) Regulations 2004 (SI 2004/1818) which make it an offence to make disclosures of uranium enrichment technology unless such disclosures are exempt.

(d) Further provisions dealing with the security of nuclear premises and of transport of nuclear material and the security of sensitive nuclear information can be found in the Nuclear Industries Security Regulations 2003 (SI 2003/403, as amended by SI 2006/2815). `

PNLD reference numbers

H4764, D10355, H4765, D10356

AG✓ **AG consent required:** Anti-terrorism, Crime and Security Act 2001, s 81(1).

🕐 **Time limit for prosecution:** None.

Summary: Maximum six months' imprisonment and/or fine not exceeding the statutory maximum.

 Indictment: Maximum seven years' imprisonment and/or fine.

5.5.8 **Trespassing on a nuclear/designated site**

Section 128 of the Serious Organised Crime and Police Act 2005 creates the offence of trespassing on a nuclear or designated site.

Offence

A person commits an offence if he enters, or is on, any **protected site** in England and Wales or Northern Ireland as a **trespasser.**

Serious Organised and Police Act 2005, s 128(1)

Points to prove

✓ date and location
✓ as a trespasser
✓ entered/were on
✓ a protected site *or*
  a designated site designated by the Secretary of State

Meanings

Protected site

Means a nuclear site or a designated site (Serious Organised Crime and Police Act 2005, s 128(1A)).

Nuclear site

Means (all licensed nuclear sites)—

  (a) so much of any premises in respect of which a nuclear site licence (within the meaning of the Nuclear Installations Act 1965) is for the time being in force as lies within the outer perimeter of the protection provided for those premises; and

---

(b) so much of any other premises of which premises falling within paragraph (a) form a part as lies within that outer perimeter (Serious Organised Crime and Police Act 2005, s 128(1B).

Designated site

Means a site designated by the Secretary of State (Serious Organised Crime and Police Act 2005, section 128(2)). Examples of current designated sites are RAF bases, Buckingham Palace, Thames House, St James's Palace, 10 Downing Street, and Palace of Westminster. A full list can be found in the Serious Organised Crime and Police Act 2005 (Designated Sites under Section 128) Order 2007 (SI 2007/930)).

Trespasser

Means a person who is on any premises without the owner or occupier's consent or without lawful excuse.

Police powers

If suspected terrorist:

Power of arrest—section 41 of the Terrorism Act 2000 (see 5.3.1)

Power to stop and search—section 43 of the Terrorism Act 2000 (see 5.2.1)

If the person is not suspected to be a terrorist, consider using PACE powers (such as ss 24, 17, 18, and 32 of PACE) but see **5.3.1** for drawbacks on using PACE powers for potential terrorists.

Defence

It is a defence for a person charged with an offence under this section to prove that he did not know, and had no reasonable cause to suspect, that the site in relation to which the offence is alleged to have been committed was a protected site.

Serious Organised and Police Act 2005, s 128(4)

It is for the defendant to prove this defence. This is viewed as appropriate because in such a case the facts to be proved would be within the defendant's own knowledge (Home Office Circular 18/2007).

Notes

(a) A person who is on any protected site as a trespasser does not cease to be a trespasser by virtue of being allowed time to leave the site (Serious Organised Crime and Police Act 2005, s 128(7)).

(b) Home Office Circular 18/2007 provides some additional guidance. The background to this offence being created is the high profile security breaches at Buckingham Palace and Windsor Castle and it was felt that a specific offence in cases such as these was needed to give officers a power of arrest where no other offences had been committed. It also provides that good practice when encountering a trespasser at such sites would be to warn the individual verbally that the site is a protected site under section 128 of the Serious Organised Crime and Police Act 2005 and that trespass on the site is a criminal offence. This would ensure that even if the individual could prove he met the defence in respect of original entry to the site, he could still be proceeded against if he did not subsequently leave the site following the warning.

(c) Section 131(1) of the Serious Organised Crime and Police Act 2005 provides that the rights with regards to freedom to roam do not apply to protected sites.

(d) The Secretary of State (with the consent of the landowner) may display any signs he considers appropriate to inform the public with regards to the designated site (Serious Organised Crime and Police Act 2005, s 131).

PNLD reference numbers

H6614, D16684, D20007

 AG consent required: Serious Organised Crime and Police Act 2005, s 128(6).

 Time limit for prosecution: Six months.

 Summary: Maximum six months and/or fine not exceeding level five on standard scale.

5.5.9 Pathogens and toxins

Part 7 (sections 58–75) of the Anti-terrorism, Crime and Security Act 2001 deals with the control of pathogens and toxins. Section 58 and Schedule 5 set out to which pathogens and toxins the requirements under Part 7 apply.

The list in Schedule 5 (not reproduced here, but see also amendments to the list in the Schedule 5 to the Anti-terrorism, Crime and Security Act 2001 (Modification) Order 2007 (SI 2007/929)) comprises the pathogens and toxins that potentially pose the greatest risk to human life if misused by terrorists. The list includes viruses (organisms that can only reproduce within the cells of other organisms, such as the Ebola virus, pandemic strains of influenza viruses, the Polio virus, the rabies virus), rickettsiae (bacteria which cannot survive outside the cells of animals), bacteria (single-celled organisms that multiply by cell division an do not possess a nucleus, such as anthrax), fungi and toxins (poisonous agents especially a poisonous substance produced by a living organism including a genetically modified organism, such as ricin).

The provisions in Part 7 use the term 'dangerous substance'.

Meaning

Dangerous substance

Means—

(a) anything which consists of or includes a substance for the time being mentioned in Schedule 5; or

(b) anything which is infected with or otherwise carries any such substance.

Anti-terrorism, Crime and Security Act 2001, s 58(4)

PNLD reference numbers

D10337, D10396

5.5.10 **Duty to notify Secretary of State**

Section 59 of the Anti-terrorism, Crime and Security Act 2001 places a duty on the occupiers of premises to notify the Secretary of State before keeping or using any dangerous substance there. Occupiers of premises holding these substances must notify the Secretary of State within one month.

(1) The **occupier** of any premises must give a notice to the Secretary of State before any **dangerous substance** is kept or used there.

(4) A notice under this section must—

    (a) identify the premises in which the substance is kept or used;

    (b) identify any building or site of which the premises form part; and

    (c) contain such other particulars (if any) as may be prescribed.

Anti-terrorism, Crime and Security Act 2001, s 59(1) and (4)

Meanings

Occupier

Includes a partnership or unincorporated association and, in relation to premises that are unoccupied, means any person entitled to occupy the premises (Anti-terrorism, Crime and Security Act 2001, s 74(1)).

Dangerous substance (see **5.5.9**).

Notes

(a) The occupier of any premises in respect of which a notice has been given may withdraw the notice if no dangerous substance is kept or used there (Anti-terrorism, Crime and Security Act 2001, s 59(3)).

(b) The list of substances in Schedule 5 may be amended by the Secretary of State. And where a substance which is kept or used in any premises becomes a dangerous substance by virtue of a modification of Schedule 5, but no other dangerous substance is kept or used there, the occupier of the premises must give a notice under section 59 within one month beginning with the day on which that modification comes into force (Anti-terrorism, Crime and Security Act 2001, s 59(6)).

(c) The police may require information about the security of dangerous substances and about persons with access to such substances from the owner of premises in respect of which a notice under section 59 is in force (see **5.5.11**).

(d) Failure to comply with this duty is an offence (see **5.5.14**).

PNLD reference number

D10338

5.5.11 Information about security of dangerous substances and about persons with access to such substances

Sections 60 and 61 of the Anti-terrorism, Crime and Security Act 2001 give the police the power to require information about the security of dangerous substances and about persons with access to such substances.

Police power

Information about security of dangerous substances

(1) A constable may give to the **occupier** of any **relevant premises** a notice requiring him to give the **chief officer of police** such information as is specified or described in the notice by a time so specified and in a form and manner so specified.

(2) The required information must relate to—

    (a) any **dangerous substance** kept or used in the premises; or

    (b) the **measures taken** (whether by the occupier or any other person) **to ensure the security of any such substance**.

Anti-terrorism, Crime and Security Act 2001, s 60(1) and (2)

Police power

Information about persons with access to dangerous substances

(1) A police officer of at least the rank of inspector may give to the occupier of any relevant premises a notice requiring him to give the chief officer of police a list of—

    (a) each person who has access to any dangerous substance kept or used there;

    (b) each person who, in such circumstances as are specified or described in the notice, has access to such part of the premises as is so specified or described;

    (c) each person who, in such circumstances as are specified or described in the notice, has access to the premises; or

    (d) each person who, in such circumstances as are specified or described in the notice, has access to any building or site of which the premises form part.

(7) Any list under this section must—

    (a) identify the access which the person has, or is proposed to have;

    (b) state the full name of that person, his date of birth, his address and his nationality; and

    (c) contain such other matters (if any) as may be prescribed.

Anti-terrorism, Crime and Security Act 2001, s 61(1) and (7)

Meanings

Occupier (see 5.5.10).

Relevant premises

Means any premises—

    (a) in which any dangerous substance is kept or used, or

(b) in respect of which a notice under section 59 (see **5.5.10**) is in force (Anti-terrorism, Crime and Security Act 2001, s 60(4)).

Chief officer of police

Means the chief officer of police for the area in which the premises are situated (Anti-terrorism, Crime and Security Act 2001, s 74(1)).

Dangerous substance (see 5.5.9).

Measures taken to ensure the security of any dangerous substance kept or used in any relevant premises

Include—

(a) measures taken to ensure the security of any building or site of which the premises form part; and
(b) measures taken for the purpose of ensuring access to the substance is given only to those whose activities require access and only in circumstances that ensure the security of the substance (Anti-terrorism, Crime and Security Act 2001, s 60(3)).

Notes

(a) A list under section 61(1) must be given before the end of the period of one month beginning with the day on which the notice is given (Anti-terrorism, Crime and Security Act 2001, s 61(2)).
(b) Where a list under section 61(1) is given, the occupier of the premises must secure that only persons mentioned in the list are given the access identified in the list relating to them. A supplementary list may be given of other persons to whom it is proposed to give access. Where a supplementary list is given, the occupier of the premises must secure that persons mentioned in that list do not have the proposed access relating to them until the end of the period of 30 days beginning with the day on which that list is given. But the chief officer of police may direct that a person may have such access before the end of that period. (Anti-terrorism, Crime and Security Act 2001, s 61(3), (4) and (5)).
(c) A person who is required to do an act in response to a notice under section 60 may appeal to the magistrates' court, on the grounds that it is unreasonable to do the act (Anti-terrorism, Crime and Security Act 2001, s 71).
(d) Failure of the occupier of the premises to comply with a request by the police is an offence (see **5.5.14**).

PNLD reference numbers

D10339, D10340

5.5.12 Directions requiring security measures, disposal of dangerous substances and denial of access

Sections 62 to 64 of the Anti-terrorism, Crime and Security Act 2001 enable the police to require the occupier of premises holding dangerous substances to make improvements to the security arrangements operating there. Further, they give the Secretary of State the power to require the disposal of dangerous substances and denial of access to such premises.

Police power

(1) A constable may give directions to the **occupier** of any **relevant premises** requiring him to take such **measures** to ensure the security of any **dangerous substance** kept or used there as are specified or described in the directions by a time so specified.

(2) The directions may—
   (a) specify or describe the substances in relation to the security of which the measures relate; and
   (b) require the occupier to give a notice to the **chief officer of police** before any other dangerous substance specified or described in the directions is kept or used in the premises.

Anti-terrorism, Crime and Security Act 2001, s 62

Meanings

Occupier (see **5.5.10**).

Relevant premises (see **5.5.11**).

Measures taken to ensure the security of any dangerous substance

These are to be construed in accordance with section 60 (see **5.5.11**).
Anti-terrorism, Crime and Security Act 2001, s 74(2)

Dangerous substance (see **5.5.9**).

Chief officer of police (see **5.5.11**).

Notes

(a) Where the Secretary of State has reasonable grounds for believing that adequate measures to secure the security of any dangerous substance kept or used in any relevant premises are not being taken and are unlikely to be taken, he may give a direction to the occupier requiring the disposal of the substance (Anti-terrorism, Crime and Security Act 2001, s 63).

(b) The Secretary of State may also give directions to the occupier of relevant premises requiring that certain persons must not have access to dangerous substances, to (certain parts of) the premises or buildings or sites which form part of the premises if he believes that the direction is necessary in the interest of national security (Anti-terrorism, Crime and Security Act 2001, s 64).

(c) Where a direction is given under section 64 denying access an appeal may be made to the Pathogens Access Appeal Commission (Anti-terrorism, Crime and Security Act 2001, s 70 and Sch 6).

(d) A person who is required to do an act in response to directions under section 62 or 63 may appeal to the magistrates' court, on the grounds that it is unreasonable to do the act (Anti-terrorism, Crime and Security Act 2001, s 71).

(e) Failure to comply with a direction under this section is an offence, see **5.5.14**.

PNLD reference numbers

D10341, D10342, D10343

5.5.13 **Powers of entry to assess security measures and search warrants**

Sections 65 and 66 of the Anti-terrorism, Crime and Security Act 2001 provide for powers of entry to premises on which dangerous substances are kept.

Police power

(1) A constable may, on giving notice under this section, enter any **relevant premises**, or any building or site of which the premises form part, at a reasonable time for the purpose of assessing

the **measures** taken to ensure the security of any **dangerous substance** kept or used in the premises.

(4) A constable who has entered any premises, building or site by virtue of subsection (1) may for the purpose mentioned in that subsection—
   (a) search the premises, building or site;
   (b) require any person who appears to the constable to be in charge of the premises, building or site to facilitate any such inspection; and
   (c) require any such person to answer any question.
      Anti-terrorism, Crime and Security Act 2001, s 65(1) and (4)

Search warrant

(1) If, in England and Wales or Northern Ireland, on an application made by a constable a justice of the peace is satisfied that there are reasonable grounds for believing—
   (a) that a dangerous substance is kept or used in any premises but that no notice under section 59 (see *5.5.10*) is in force in respect of the premises, or
   (b) that the occupier of any relevant premises is failing to comply with any direction given to him under section 62 or 63 (see *5.5.12*),

   and that any of the conditions mentioned in subsection (4) apply, he may issue a warrant authorising a constable to enter the premises, if necessary by force, and to search them.

(3) A constable may seize and retain anything which he believes is or contains a dangerous substance.

(4) The conditions mentioned in subsection (1) are—
   (a) that it is not practicable to communicate with any person entitled to grant entry to the premises;
   (b) that it is practicable to communicate with a person entitled to grant entry to the premises but it is not practicable to communicate with any person entitled to grant access to any substance which may be a dangerous substance;
   (c) that entry to the premises will not be granted unless a warrant is produced;
   (d) that the purpose of a search may be frustrated or seriously prejudiced unless a constable arriving at the premises can secure immediate entry to them.
      Anti-terrorism, Crime and Security Act 2001, s 66

Meanings

Relevant premises (see 5.5.11).

Measures taken to ensure the security of any dangerous substance (see 5.5.11).

Dangerous substance (see 5.5.9).

Notes

(a) The notice must be given to the occupier of the premises, or (as the case may be) the occupier of the building or site of which the premises form part, at least 2 working days before the proposed entry (Anti-terrorism, Crime and Security Act 2001, s 65(2)). For the meaning of 'occupier' see **5.5.10**.

(b) The notice must set out the purpose mentioned in subsection (1) (Anti-terrorism, Crime and Security Act 2001, s 65(3)).

(c) Under this section a constable may take with him such other persons as appear to him to be necessary (Anti-terrorism, Crime and Security Act 2001, s 65(5)).

PNLD reference numbers

D10344, D10345

5.5.14 Offences relating to pathogens and toxins

Section 67 of the Anti-terrorism, Crime and Security Act 2001 makes it an offence for occupiers of premises to fail, without reasonable excuse, to comply with any duty or directions imposed by this part 7 (sections 58–75) of the Act in relation to the security of pathogens and toxins.

Offences

(1) An occupier who fails without reasonable excuse to comply with any duty or direction imposed on him by or under this Part is guilty of an offence.

(2) A person who, in giving any information to a person exercising functions under this Part, knowingly or recklessly makes a statement which is false or misleading in a material particular is guilty of an offence.

Anti-terrorism, Crime and Security Act 2001, s 67(1) and (2)

Points to prove

Offence in section 67(1)

- ✓ date and location
- ✓ being the occupier of premises
- ✓ failed without reasonable excuse
- ✓ to comply with a duty/direction imposed by or under Part 7 of the Anti-terrorism, Crime and Security Act 2001

Offence in section 67(2)

- ✓ date and location
- ✓ made a statement
- ✓ which was false/misleading in a material particular
- ✓ when providing information
- ✓ to a person exercising functions under Part 7 of the Anti-terrorism, Crime and Security Act 2001

Meanings.

Occupier (see 5.5.10)

Duty or direction imposed on him by or under this Part (Part 7, sections 58–75).

Duty to notify the Secretary of State before keeping or using any dangerous substance (see **5.5.10**); duty to give information about security of dangerous substances (see **5.5.10**); duty to give information about persons with access to dangerous substances (see **5.5.11**); duty to take security measures re/to dispose of dangerous substances/to deny access (see **5.5.12**).

Police powers

If suspected terrorist:

Power of arrest—section 41 of the Terrorism Act 2000 (see 5.3.1)

Power to stop and search—section 43 of the Terrorism Act 2000 (see 5.2.1)

If the person is not suspected to be a terrorist, consider using PACE powers (such as ss 24, 17, 18, and 32 of PACE) but see **5.3.1** for drawbacks on using PACE powers for potential terrorists.

Notes

(a) The offence in section 67(2) may be relevant where a person gives information under section 59 (duty to notify Secretary of State about dangerous substances, see **5.5.8**) or under sections 60 and 61 (information about security of dangerous substances and persons with access to such substances, see **5.5.9**).

(b) *Corporate liability*—For the liability of company directors, etc see section 68 of the Anti-terrorism, Crime and Security Act 2001 (see **5.7.2.3**).

(c) Proceedings for an offence alleged to have been committed by a partnership or an unincorporated association must be brought in the name of the partnership or association; for details see section 69 of the Anti-terrorism, Crime and Security Act 2001 (not reproduced here).

PNLD reference numbers

H4762, H4763, D10346

 Time limit for prosecution: None.

 Summary: Maximum six months' imprisonment and/or fine not exceeding the statutory maximum.

 Indictment: Maximum five years' imprisonment and/or fine.

5.5.15 Use of noxious substances or things to cause harm and intimidate

Sections 113, 113A and 113B of the Anti-terrorism, Crime and Security Act 2001 deal with the offence of using noxious substances or things to cause harm and intimidate.

Offence

(1) A person who takes any **action** which—

    (a) involves the use of a noxious **substance** or other noxious thing;

    (b) has an effect falling within subsection (2); and

    (c) is designed to influence the **government** or international governmental organisation or to intimidate the **public** or a section of the public,

is guilty of an offence.

---

(3) A person who—
  (a) makes a threat that he or another will take any action falling within subsection (1); and
  (b) intends thereby to induce in a person anywhere in the world the fear that the threat is likely to be carried out,
  is guilty of an offence.

Anti-terrorism, Crime and Security Act 2001, s 113(1) and (3)

Points to prove

Use noxious substance/thing to cause violence/damage (s 113(1))

- ✓ date and location
- ✓ committed an act
- ✓ anywhere in the world
- ✓ designed to influence the government/intimidate the public/a section of the public
- ✓ which caused/was likely to cause
- ✓ serious violence against a person/serious damage to real/personal property
- ✓ which involved the use of a noxious substance/thing

Commit act to induce fear/endanger life or health (s 113(1))

- ✓ date and location
- ✓ committed an act
- ✓ anywhere in the world
- ✓ designed to influence the government/to intimidate the public/a section of the public
- ✓ had/was likely to have the effect of
- ✓ endangering human life/creating a serious risk to the health/safety
- ✓ of the public/a section of the public
- ✓ which involved the use of a noxious substance/thing

Threaten use of noxious substance (s 113(3))

- ✓ date and location
- ✓ made a threat that you/another
- ✓ designed to influence the government/intimidate the public/section of the public
- ✓ that you/another would take action
- ✓ involving the use of a noxious substance/thing
- ✓ to cause serious violence against a person anywhere in the world or

> to cause serious damage to real or personal property any-
> where in the world *or*
> have the effect of endangering human life *or*
> creating a serious risk to the health/safety of the public/sec-
> tion of the public *or*
> have the effect of inducing in members of the public
> ✓ the fear that the action was likely to endanger their lives or
> ✓ create a serious risk to their health or safety and
> ✓ intending thereby to induce in a person
> ✓ anywhere in the world
> ✓ the fear that the threat was likely to be carried out

Meanings

Action

Has an effect falling within this subsection if it—

(a) causes serious violence against a person anywhere in the world;
(b) causes serious damage to real or personal property anywhere in
    the world;
(c) endangers human life or creates a serious risk to the health or
    safety of the public or a section of the public; or
(d) induces in members of the public the fear that the action is
    likely to endanger their lives or create a serious risk to their
    health or safety;

but any effect on the person taking the action is to be disregarded
(Anti-terrorism, Crime and Security Act 2001, s 113(2)).

Substance

Includes any biological agent and any other natural or artificial substance (whatever its form, origin, or method of production) (Anti-
terrorism, Crime and Security Act 2001, s 115).

The government

Means the government of the UK, a part of the UK or of a country
other than the UK (Anti-terrorism, Crime and Security Act 2001,
s 113(5)).

The public

Includes the public of a country other than the UK (Anti-terrorism,
Crime and Security Act 2001, s 113(5)).

Police powers

If suspected terrorist:

Power of arrest—section 41 of the Terrorism Act 2000 (see 5.3.1)

Power to stop and search—section 43 of the Terrorism Act 2000 (see 5.2.1)

If the person is not suspected to be a terrorist, consider using PACE powers of arrest but see **5.3.1** for drawbacks on using PACE powers for potential terrorists.

Power to stop and search—section 43 of the Terrorism Act 2000 (see 5.2.1)

Notes

(a) The offence—the action or threat—must originate in the UK even if its effect is felt outside the UK.

(b) This section is designed to cover those individuals who seek to cause havoc by, for example sending anthrax through the post, or damaging fields or polluting water supplies. The scope of the offences includes someone acting or threatening to act in the UK at the time. For example, sending a parcel containing anthrax from the UK to someone in France with the intention of causing harm there.

(c) For a person to be guilty of an offence under section 113(3) it is not necessary for him to have any particular person in mind.

(d) *Extraterritorial jurisdiction*—This offence applies to conduct done within the UK and also to conduct done outside of the UK providing two conditions are satisfied. The first condition is that the conduct is done for the purpose of advancing a political, religious or ideological cause (see **note (g)** below). The second condition is that the conduct is by a UK national or a UK resident; or by any person done to, or in relation to, a UK national, a UK resident or a protected person; or by any person done in circumstances which fall within section 63D(1)(b) and (c) or (3)(b) and (c) of the Terrorism Act 2000 (commission of offences abroad see **5.7.1**). For the purposes of this section it is immaterial whether a person knows that another is a UK national, a UK resident or a protected person (Anti-terrorism, Crime and Security Act 2001, s 113A(1)–(3) and (5)).

(e) Proceedings for an offence committed under section 113 outside the UK may be taken, and the offence may for incidental purposes be treated as having been committed, in any part of the UK (Anti-terrorism, Crime and Security Act 2001, s 113B(1) and (2)).

(f) *Counter-Terrorism Act 2008*—Section 28 of the Act makes provision for this offence to be tried at any place in the UK if it was

committed in the UK. For a summary of the Act see p xxvii.
See PNLD reference number S1136 to check whether this
section is in force.

(g) *Counter-Terrorism Act 2008*—Section 75 of the Act amends the
definition of terrorism to include conduct done for the purpose
of advancing a **racial** cause. For a summary of the Act see p
xxvii. See PNLD reference number D12307 to check whether
this amendment to section 113A is in force.

PNLD reference numbers

H4766-4769, H4781, D10365, D12307, D12308

AG✓ **AG consent required:** Anti-terrorism, Crime and Security
Act 2001, s 113B (where offence committed outside UK).

🕐 **Time limit for prosecution:** None.

♿ **Summary:** Maximum six months' imprisonment and/or
fine not exceeding the statutory maximum.

▦ **Indictment:** Maximum 14 years' imprisonment and/or
fine.

5.5.16 Hoaxes involving noxious substances or things

Section 114 of the Anti-terrorism, Crime and Security Act 2001
creates similar offences for biological, chemical, and nuclear
hoaxes.

Offences

(1) A person is guilty of an offence if he—
(a) places any **substance** or other thing in any place whatever; or
(b) sends any substance or other thing from one place to another (by
post, rail or any other means whatever);
with the **intention** of inducing in a **person** anywhere in the world a
belief that it is likely to be (or contain) a noxious substance or other
noxious thing and thereby endanger human life or create a serious risk
to human health.

(2) A person is guilty of an offence if he communicates any information which he knows or believes to be false with the intention of inducing in a person anywhere in the world a belief that a noxious substance or other noxious thing is likely to be present (whether at the time the information is communicated or later) in any place and thereby endanger human life or create a serious risk to human health.

Anti-terrorism, Crime and Security Act 2001, s 114(1) and (2)

Points to prove

Section 114(1) offence

- ✓ date and location
- ✓ placed/sent
- ✓ a substance/thing
- ✓ intending
- ✓ to induce in a person
- ✓ a belief that it is likely to be/contain a noxious substance/thing
- ✓ thereby endanger human life/create a serious risk to human health

Section 114(2) offence

- ✓ date and location
- ✓ communicated information
- ✓ which you knew/believed to be false
- ✓ intending
- ✓ to induce in a person
- ✓ anywhere in the world
- ✓ a belief that a noxious substance/thing
- ✓ was likely to be present in any place
- ✓ thereby endanger human life/create a serious risk to human health

---

Meanings

Substance

Includes any biological agent and any other natural or artificial substance (whatever its form, origin, or method of production) (Anti-terrorism, Crime and Security Act 2001, s 115).

Intention

Is not defined but has to be proved. It can be proved by drawing on two sources of information or by a combination of both.

1. By admissions made by the defendant in interview with reference to his state of mind at the time of commission of the offence and his answers to questions with regard to his actions and intentions at the time of the offence.
2. By inference from the circumstances the offence, any evidence from witnesses, the defendant's actions and property found on him or in his control, such as a motor vehicle for transporting property. To prove intent, an officer needs to take all this into account, the important thing is that he has to prove the defendant's state of mind at the time.

Person

It is not necessary to have any particular person in mind.

Police powers

If suspected terrorist:

Power of arrest— section 41 of the Terrorism Act 2000 (see 5.3.1)

Power to stop and search—section 43 of the Terrorism Act 2000 (see 5.2.1)

If the person is not suspected to be a terrorist, consider using PACE powers of arrest but see **5.3.1** for drawbacks on using PACE powers for potential terrorists.

Note

A related offence is food contamination contrary to section 38 of the Public Order Act 1986. It is an offence under section 38(1) to intend to cause alarm, injury, or loss by contamination or interference with goods or by making it appear that goods have been contaminated or interfered with in a place where goods of that description are consumed, used, sold, or otherwise supplied. It is also an offence under section 38(2) to make threats or claims relating to along these lines (s 38(2)) or to possess materials under section 38(3) with a view to the committing of a section 38(1) offence (s 38(3)). Section 38 responded to a small number of well-publicized incidents of 'consumer terrorism', a minority of which could involve animal rights activists or an individual trying to blackmail a manufacturer or supermarket chain. Goods includes substances whether natural or manufactured and whether or not incorporated in or mixed with other goods. The court should be made aware of the disruptions and anxiety that was caused by the hoax, for example, how much time and expense was wasted by the hoax.

PNLD reference numbers

H4771, H4772, D10366

 Time limit for prosecution: None.

 Summary: Maximum six months' imprisonment and/or a fine not exceeding the statutory maximum.

 Indictment: Maximum seven years' imprisonment.

5.5.17 **Biological Weapons**

Section 1 of the Biological Weapons Act 1974 makes it an offence to develop, produce, stockpile, acquire, retain, or transfer biological agents, toxins and weapons.

Offences

(1) No person shall develop, produce, stockpile, acquire or retain—
   (a) any **biological agent** or **toxin** of a type and in a quantity that has no justification for **prophylactic**, protective or other peaceful purposes; or
   (b) any weapon, equipment or means of delivery designed to use biological agents or toxins for hostile purposes or in armed conflict.

(1A) A person shall not—
   (a) transfer any biological agent or toxin to another person or enter into an agreement to do so, or
   (b) make arrangements under which another person transfers any biological agent or toxin or enters into an agreement with a third person to do so,

if the biological agent or toxin is likely to be kept or used (whether by the transferee or any other person) otherwise than for prophylactic, protective or other peaceful purposes and he knows or has reason to believe that that is the case.

Biological Weapons Act 1974, s 1(1)–(1A)

Points to prove

Section 1(1)

✓ date and location
✓ developed/produced/stockpiled/acquired/retained
✓ a biological agent/toxin of a type and in a quantity that has no justification for prophylactic/protective/other peaceful purpose *or*

  a weapon/equipment/means of delivery designed to use biological agents/toxins for hostile purposes/in armed conflict

Section 1(1A)(a)

✓ date and location
✓ transferred/entered into an agreement to transfer
✓ a biological agent/toxin
✓ to another person
✓ when the biological agent/toxin was likely to be kept or used (whether by the transferee or any other person) otherwise than for prophylactic/protective/other peaceful purposes
✓ knowing/having reason to believe that that was the case

Section 1(1A)(b)

✓ date and location
✓ made arrangements under which another person transferred a biological agent/toxin

  or

  entered into an agreement with a third person to transfer a biological agent/toxin

✓ when the biological agent/toxin was likely to be kept or used (whether by the transferee or any other person) otherwise than for prophylactic/protective/other peaceful purposes
✓ knowing/having reason to believe that that was the case

Meanings

Biological agent

Means any microbial or other biological agent.

Toxin

Means any toxin, whatever its origin or method of production.

Prophylactic

Intended to prevent disease.

Police powers

If suspected terrorist:

Power of arrest—section 41 of the Terrorism Act 2000 (see **5.3.1**)

Power to stop and search—section 43 of the Terrorism Act 2000 (see **5.2.1**)

If the person is not suspected to be a terrorist, consider using PACE powers of arrest but see **5.3.1** for drawbacks on using PACE powers for potential terrorists.

Power of entry and search under section 4 of Biological Weapons Act 1974:

4(1) If a justice of the peace is satisfied by information on oath, or in Scotland the sheriff or a magistrate or justice of the peace is satisfied by evidence on oath, that there is reasonable ground for suspecting that an offence under section 1 of this Act has been, or is about to be, committed, he may grant a search warrant authorising a constable—

    (a) to enter, at any time within three months from the date of the warrant, any premises or place named therein, if necessary by force, and to search the premises or place and every person found therein;

    (b) to inspect any document found in the premises or place or in the possession of any person found therein, and to take copies of, or seize or detain any such document;

    (c) to inspect, seize and detain any equipment so found; and

    (d) to inspect, sample, seize and detain any substance so found.

4(2) A warrant issued under subsection (1) above, authorising a constable to take the steps mentioned in that subsection, may also authorise any person named in the warrant to accompany the constable and assist him in taking any of those steps.

Biological Weapons Act 1974, s 4

Notes

(a) *Extraterritorial jurisdiction*—Section 1A of the Biological Weapons Act 1974 extends the application of section 1 to acts done outside the UK by UK persons.

(b) *Revenue and Customs prosecutions*—Commissioners for Her Majesty's Revenue and Customs can prosecute offences under this section (Biological Weapons Act 1974, s 1B).

(c) *Corporate liability*—Where an offence under this section has been committed by a body corporate, with the knowledge or negligence of any director, manager, secretary, etc then both shall be guilty and liable to prosecution (Biological Weapons Act 1974, s 3).

PNLD reference numbers

D15596–98, D15600, D15601

 AG consent required: Biological Weapons Act 1974, s 2.

 Time limit for prosecution: None.

Indictment: Life imprisonment.

5.5.18 **Chemical Weapons**

Section 2 of the Chemical Weapons Act 1996 sets out offences related to chemical weapons.

Offence

No person shall—
(a) use a **chemical weapon**;
(b) develop or produce a chemical weapon;
(c) have a chemical weapon in his possession;
(d) participate in the **transfer** of a chemical weapon;
(e) engage in military preparations, or in preparations of a military nature, intending to use a chemical weapon.

Chemical Weapons Act 1996, s 2(1)

Points to prove

Section 2(1)(a)–(d)

✓ date and location
✓ use/develop/produce/possess/participate in transfer of
✓ a chemical weapon

> **Section 2(1)(e)**
> ✓ date and location
> ✓ engaged in military preparations/preparations of a military
>   nature
> ✓ with the intention
> ✓ to use
> ✓ a chemical weapon

Meanings

Chemical weapon

Means—

(a) toxic chemicals and their precursors;
(b) munitions and other devices designed to cause death or harm
    through the toxic properties of toxic chemicals released by
    them;
(c) equipment designed for use in connection with munitions and
    devices falling within paragraph (b) (Chemical Weapons Act
    1996, s 1(1)).

A precursor is a chemical reactant which takes part at any stage in
the production (by whatever method) of a toxic chemical (Chemical
Weapons Act 1996, s 1(6)).

Transfer

A person participates in the transfer of an object if—

he acquires or disposes of the object or enters into a contract to
acquire or dispose of it, or he makes arrangements under which
another person acquires or disposes of the object or another person
enters into a contract to acquire or dispose of it. To acquire an object
is to buy it, hire it, borrow it or accept it as a gift; to dispose of an
object is to sell it, let it on hire, lend it or give it (Chemical Weapons
Act 1996 s 2(4) and (5)).

Police powers

If suspected terrorist:

Power of arrest—section 41 of the Terrorism Act 2000 (see 5.3.1)

Power to stop and search—section 43 of the Terrorism Act 2000
  (see **5.2.1**)

If the person is not suspected to be a terrorist, consider using PACE
powers (such as ss 24, 17, 18, and 32 of PACE) but see **5.3.1** for drawbacks on using PACE powers for potential terrorists.

Defence

(6) In proceedings for an offence under subsection (1)(a), (c) or (d) relating to an object it is a defence for the accused to prove—

   (a) that he neither knew nor suspected nor had reason to suspect that the object was a chemical weapon, or

   (b) that he knew or suspected it to be a chemical weapon and as soon as reasonably practicable after he first so knew or suspected he took all reasonable steps to inform the Secretary of State or a constable of his knowledge or suspicion.

(7) Nothing in subsection (6) prejudices any defence which it is open to a person charged with an offence under this section to raise apart from that subsection.

Chemical Weapons Act 1996, s 2(6) and (7)

Notes

(a) For the purposes of section 2(1) an object will not be a chemical weapon if it is used or a person does an act with the intention that the object will be used only for permitted purposes. Permitted purposes are—peaceful purposes; purposes related to protection against toxic chemicals; legitimate military purposes; purposes of enforcing the law. Legitimate military purposes are all military purposes except those which depend on the use of the toxic properties of chemicals as a method of warfare in circumstances where the main object is to cause death, permanent harm or temporary incapacity to humans or animals. A toxic chemical is a chemical which through its chemical action on life processes can cause death, permanent harm or temporary incapacity to humans or animals; and the origin, method of production and place of production are immaterial. As to whether or not something falls within permitted purpose the types and quantities of objects will be taken into account (Chemical Weapons Act 1996, ss 1(3)–(5) and 2(2) and (3)).

(b) *Extraterritorial jurisdiction*—This offence applies to acts done within and outside of the UK (Chemical Weapons Act 1996, s 3).

(c) There are other offences in the Act that have not been reproduced here. The most serious offences of use of chemical weapons, and creating chemical weapons production facilities under sections 2 (see above) and 11, which are punishable by life imprisonment. The middle range offences of providing false or misleading information under sections 9, 17, 20, 21, 22 and

23, disclosure of confidential information under section 32, and use of Schedule 1 chemicals under section 19 are each punishable by a fine, imprisonment, or both. The lesser offences of failure to provide information under section 9, failure to comply with a notice under section 22, failure to comply with a regulation under section 23, offences connected with inspections under section 26, and destruction of objects, etc, under section 17 attract a fine alone.

PNLD reference numbers

H5251–55, D11802

 AG consent required: Chemical Weapons Act 1996, s 31(1).

 Time limit for prosecution: None.

 Indictment: Life imprisonment.

5.6 **Control Orders**

A control order is an order that imposes certain obligations on an individual which is intended to prevent him from involvement in terrorism thus protecting the public from further terrorist acts. There are two different types of control orders, non-derogating (see **5.6.2**) and derogating (see **5.6.3**). A non-derogating control order is an order that is compatible with Article 5 of the European Convention on Human Rights and a derogating control order is one that is not compatible with Article 5 and can only be made on the condition of issuing a valid notice under Article 15. A control order is made where there is not enough evidence of a terrorism-related offence to put the individual before the courts but the authorities suspect that the individual is involved in terrorism and that the public need protecting from this potential threat, see also **3.4.6**.

5.6.1 **Power to make control orders**

Section 1 of the Prevention of Terrorism Act 2005 sets out who has the power to make control orders and examples of what obligations may be imposed.

(2) The power to make a **control order** against an individual shall be exercisable—
  (a) except in the case of an order imposing obligations that are incompatible with the individual's right to liberty under **Article 5 of the Human Rights Convention**, by the Secretary of State; and
  (b) in the case of an order imposing obligations that are or include **derogating** obligations, by the court on an application by the Secretary of State.

Prevention of Terrorism Act 2005, s 1(2)

Meanings

Control order

Means an order against an individual that imposes obligations on him for purposes connected with protecting members of the public from a risk of terrorism (Prevention of Terrorism Act 2005, s 1(1)).

Article 5 of the Human Rights Convention

Means the right to liberty and security of person (see also related cases below).

Derogating obligation

Means an obligation on an individual which is incompatible with his right to liberty under Article 5 of the Human Rights Convention; but is of a description of obligations which, for the purposes of the designation of a designated derogation, is set out in the designation order (Prevention of Terrorism Act 2005, s 1(10)). Derogation means that the order would be a breach/violation of Article 5 and that the UK can suspend the application of that Article in this circumstance by reference to Article 15 which applies when there is an emergency threatening the life of the nation. An example of this would be to place a person on a curfew at home for 24 hours a day, seven days a week.

Derogate

To suspend.

Notes

(a) The Secretary of State may impose any obligations that he considers necessary to prevent/restrict an individual's involvement in terrorism-related activity (see note (b) below). These may include the following—

(i) a prohibition or restriction on his possession or use of specified articles or substances;

(ii) a prohibition or restriction on his use of specified services or specified facilities, or on his carrying on specified activities;

(iii) a restriction in respect of his work or other occupation, or in respect of his business;

(iv) a restriction on his association or communications with specified persons or with other persons generally;

(v) a restriction in respect of his place of residence or on the persons to whom he gives access to his place of residence;

(vi) a prohibition on his being at specified places or within a specified area at specified times or on specified days;

(vii) a prohibition or restriction on his movements to, from or within the UK, a specified part of the UK or a specified place or area within the UK (this includes a requirement for him to remain at a particular place or area, whether generally or between certain times—house arrest);

(viii)   a requirement on him to comply with such other prohibitions or restrictions on his movements as may be imposed, for a period not exceeding 24 hours, by directions given to him in the specified manner, by a specified person and for the purpose of securing compliance with other obligations imposed by or under the order;

(ix)   a requirement on him to surrender his passport, or anything in his possession to which a prohibition or restriction imposed by the order relates, to a specified person for a period not exceeding the period for which the order remains in force;

(x)   a requirement on him to give access to specified persons to his place of residence or to other premises to which he has power to grant access;

(xi)   a requirement on him to allow specified persons to search that place or any such premises for the purpose of ascertaining whether obligations imposed by or under the order have been, are being or are about to be contravened;

(xii)   a requirement on him to allow specified persons, either for that purpose or for the purpose of securing that the order is complied with, to remove anything found in that place or on any such premises and to subject it to tests or to retain it for a period not exceeding the period for which the order remains in force;

(xiii)   a requirement on him to allow himself to be photographed;

(xiv)   a requirement on him to co-operate with specified arrangements for enabling his movements, communications or other activities to be monitored by electronic or other means (includes, submitting to procedures required by the arrangements; wearing or otherwise using apparatus approved by or in accordance with the arrangements; maintaining such apparatus in the specified manner; complying with directions given by persons carrying out functions for the purposes of those arrangements);

(xv)   a requirement on him to comply with a demand made in the specified manner to provide information to a specified person in accordance with the demand (includes, in particular, advance information about his proposed movements or other activities);

(xvi)   a requirement on him to report to a specified person at specified times and places (Prevention of Terrorism Act 2005, s 1(4)).

(b) Terrorism-related activity is any one or more of the following—

(i) the commission, preparation, or instigation of acts of terrorism (see **4.1**);

(ii) conduct which facilitates the commission, preparation, or instigation of such acts, or which is intended to do so;

(iii) conduct which gives encouragement to the commission, preparation, or instigation of such acts, or which is intended to do so;

(iv) conduct which gives support or assistance to individuals who are known or believed to be involved in terrorism-related activity; and for the purposes of this subsection it is immaterial whether the acts of terrorism in question are specific acts of terrorism or acts of terrorism generally (Prevention of Terrorism Act 2005, s 1(9)).

(c) A particular obligation on the control order may be waived, either on one or more occasions if the person subject to the control order gets prior permission from a specified person (Secretary of State)(Prevention of Terrorism Act 2005, s 1(8)).

Related cases

Guzzardi v Italy (1980) 3 EHRR 333 'In order to determine whether someone has been "deprived of his liberty" within the meaning of Article 5, the starting point must be his concrete situation and account must be taken of a whole range of criteria such as the type, duration, effects and manner of implementation of the measure in question . . .' (para 92).

PNLD reference numbers

D15490, D15491

5.6.2 **Non-derogating control orders**

Section 2 of the Prevention of Terrorism Act 2005 specifies the grounds when a non-derogating control order can be made. Section 3 sets out the courts' responsibilities towards non-derogating control orders, see **note (f)**. Section 7 outlines the procedure for changing any of the obligations contained in a non-derogating control order.

2(1) The Secretary of State may make a **control order** against an individual if he—

(a) has reasonable grounds for suspecting that the individual is or has been involved in **terrorism-related activity**; and

(b) considers that it is necessary, for purposes connected with protecting members of the public from a risk of **terrorism**, to make a control order imposing obligations on that individual.

Prevention of Terrorism Act 2005, s 2(1)

Meanings

Control order (see **5.6.1**).

Terrorism-related activity

Is any one or more of the following—

(a) the commission, preparation, or instigation of acts of terrorism;
(b) conduct which facilitates the commission, preparation, or instigation of such acts, or which is intended to do so;
(c) conduct which gives encouragement to the commission, preparation, or instigation of such acts, or which is intended to do so;
(d) conduct which gives support or assistance to individuals who are known or believed to be involved in terrorism-related activity;

and for the purposes of this subsection it is immaterial whether the acts of terrorism in question are specific acts of terrorism or acts of terrorism generally (Prevention of Terrorism Act 2005, s 1(9)).

Terrorism (see **4.1.1**).

Police powers

(9) For the purpose of delivering a notice under subsection (8) [*notice of change to/renewal of order*] to the controlled person a constable or a person authorised for the purpose by the Secretary of State may [*if necessary by force*]—
    (a) enter any premises where he has reasonable grounds for believing that person to be; and
    (b) search those premises for him.

Prevention of Terrorism Act 2005, s 7(9)

See **note (g)** below for more detail.

Notes

(a) A non-derogating control order is a control order which imposes obligations on an individual that do not interfere with his right to liberty and security. Each control order is tailored to the individual and the particular risk they pose. An example of an obligation that would be non-derogating is that a person would be subject to a curfew of up to 16 hours a day whereas if it were derogating, the curfew would be 24 hours a day. Since the introduction of this legislation there have been 31 people subject to control orders, all of them non-derogating. The latest figures (from February 2008) state that there are currently five such orders in force. An order may be issued against British citizens or against foreigners.

(b) The obligations imposed do not only have to deal with the activities that gave rise for the control order in the first place but can cover prevention of any terrorism-related activity (Prevention of Terrorism Act 2005, s 2(9)).

(c) A non-derogating control order will last for 12 months, but may be renewed. It must state the date when it ceases to have effect (Prevention of Terrorism Act 2005, s 2(4) and (5)).

(d) The Secretary of State can renew the control order, with or without modifications if he considers that it is necessary, for protecting members of the public from a risk of terrorism, for an order imposing obligations on the controlled person to continue in force; and if he considers that the obligations to be imposed by the renewed order are necessary for preventing or restricting involvement by that person in terrorism-related activity (Prevention of Terrorism Act 2005, s 2(6)).

(e) The renewal of a control order will begin from when the order would have ceased to have effect or at the start of the seventh day after the renewal, whichever is the earliest (Prevention of Terrorism Act 2005, s 2(7)).

(f) Section 3 of the Prevention of Terrorism Act 2005 outlines the supervisory duties and responsibilities of the court in relation to the non-derogating orders. The court must oversee the applications from the Home Secretary and give permission for the application to go ahead. It also looks at those orders made by the Home Secretary in emergencies where permission has not or could not be sought before the order was made. Albeit the 'permission' can be given without the individual's knowledge or presence the court must give them the opportunity to make representations in certain circumstances within seven days of the court giving 'permission' about the directions given. The court has the power to quash the order completely, quash one or more obligations within the order and return the order to the Home Secretary for modifications.

(g) Non-derogating control orders can be also changed and modified by the person subject to the order (on application) or the Secretary of State. The person subject to the order can apply to the Secretary of State for a change or revocation of the order if there a has been a change in circumstances which affects the control order. The Secretary of State can also at any time revoke the order, relax or remove an obligation within the order or modify any of the obligations in the order which he considers necessary for purposes connected with preventing or restricting involvement by the controlled person in terrorism-related activity. These changes can also be made with the mutual consent of both parties. However, the Secretary of State may not make any changes to the obligations which would turn it into a derogating control order. If a change is made then the person subject to the control order must be given notice of the change, see police powers above. (Prevention of Terrorism Act 2005, s 7(1)–(3) and (8) and (10)).

(h) *Counter-Terrorism Act 2008*—Sections 78–81 make amendments to provisions relating to control orders. Section 78 inserts ss 7A–7C into the Prevention of Terrorism Act 2005. These are powers of entry and search for police officers for those subject to control orders. Sections 79–81 of the Act make other amendments relating to control orders. See PNLD reference numbers D23916–18 for details.

(i) *Counter-Terrorism Act 2008*—Sections 1–9 provide further powers tot remove documents for examination for offences in ss 7A–7C of the Prevention of Terrorism Act 2005. See PNLD reference numbers S1136 and S823 to check whether these sections are in force.

(j) *Counter-Terrorism Act 2008*—Section 10 amends the Police and Criminal Evidence Act 1984 (PACE) (ss 61, 63 63A, 64, and 65) to allow police to take without consent fingerprints and samples of those persons subject to a control order. The fingerprints and samples can also be retained and checked against other fingerprints and samples as per other PACE samples. For a summary of the Act see p xxvii. See PNLD reference number S2 to check whether these amendments are in force.

Related cases

Secretary of State for the Home Department v E [2007] UKHL 47 A curfew of 12 hours was acceptable and did not breach Article 5. E was confined to his own home and had his family around him. The range of his curfew restricted his movement but did not deprive him of his liberty.

JJ v Secretary of State for the Home Department [2007] UKHL 45 An 18-hour curfew was viewed as illegal. Lord Brown stated in this case that up to 16 hours' curfew would be acceptable to him before there could be any challenges over breaches of Article 5. As a result of his guidance, the Home Office has revised orders above 16 hours and has adopted 16 hours as the outer limit.

PNLD reference numbers

D15492, D15493, D15494, D15500, C1519

5.6.3 **Derogating control orders**

Section 4 of the Prevention of Terrorism Act 2005 sets out the court's responsibilities for making derogating control orders. These are control orders that are not compatible with Article 5 of the Human Rights Convention.

(3) At the preliminary hearing, the court may make a control order against the individual in question if it appears to the court—

  (a) that there is material which (if not disproved) is capable of being relied on by the court as establishing that the individual is or has been involved in terrorism-related activity;

  (b) that there are reasonable grounds for believing that the imposition of obligations on that individual is necessary for purposes connected with protecting members of the public from a risk of terrorism;

  (c) that the risk arises out of, or is associated with, a public emergency in respect of which there is a designated derogation from the whole or a part of Article 5 of the Human Rights Convention; and

  (d) that the obligations that there are reasonable grounds for believing should be imposed on the individual are or include derogating obligations of a description set out for the purposes of the designated derogation in the designation order.

Prevention of Terrorism Act 2005, s 4(3)

Meanings

Control order (see **5.6.1**).

Terrorism-related activity (see **5.6.2**).

Designated derogation

Any derogation (detraction) by the UK from an Article of the Convention, or of any protocol to the Convention which is designated for the purposes of this Act in an order made by the Secretary of State (Human Rights Act 1998, s 14(1)). Derogation means that the order would be a breach/violation of Article 5 and that the UK can suspend the application of that Article in this circumstance.

Article 5 of the Human Rights Convention

Means the right to liberty and security of person.

Derogating obligation

Means an obligation on an individual which—

(a) is incompatible with his right to liberty under Article 5 of the Human Rights Convention; but
(b) is of a description of obligations which, for the purposes of the designation of a designated derogation, is set out in the designation order (Prevention of Terrorism Act 2005, s 1(10)).

Derogation means that the order would be a breach/violation of Article 5 and that the UK can suspend the application of that Article in this circumstance.

Designation order

In relation to a designated derogation, means the order under section 14(1) of the Human Rights Act 1998 by which the derogation is designated (Prevention of Terrorism Act 2005, s 1(10)). This is the administrative procedure of suspending the application of Article 5 in these circumstances.

Police powers

7(9) For the purpose of delivering a notice under subsection (8) (notice of change to/renewal of order) to the controlled person a constable or a person authorised for the purpose by the Secretary of State may (if necessary by force)—
   (a) enter any premises where he has reasonable grounds for believing that person to be; and
   (b) search those premises for him.

Prevention of Terrorism Act 2005, s 7(9)

See **note (i)** below for more details.

Notes

(a) A derogating control order is one which is incompatible with Article 5 of the Human Rights Convention and would be so extensive that it would deprive a person of his liberty, not merely restrict his movements as with non-derogating control orders. It is for this reason that the court (Queens Bench Division) determines whether to make these types of control orders. An example of an obligation that would be derogating is a person on a 24-hour curfew. At the time of writing there are no derogating control orders in force in the UK.

(b) The obligations imposed do not only have to deal with the activities that gave rise for the control order in the first place but can cover prevention of any terrorism-related activity (Prevention of Terrorism Act 2005, s 4(13)).

(c) The Secretary of State makes an application to the court who must immediately hold a preliminary hearing to determine whether to make a derogating control order against an individual. The hearing can be held without the presence of the individual and without his having been given notice or the chance to make representations about the order. If the court does decide to make such an order then it must give a direction to hold a full hearing to decide whether to confirm the order (with or without modifications). The reasons that the court must consider are listed above at section 4(3) (Prevention of Terrorism Act 2005, s 4(1), (2), and (3)).

(d) At a full hearing the court may confirm (with or without modifications) or revoke the order. The court may only confirm the order if—

   (i) it is satisfied, on the balance of probabilities, that the controlled person is an individual who is or has been involved in terrorism-related activity;

   (ii) it considers that the imposition of obligations on the controlled person is necessary for purposes connected with protecting members of the public from a risk of terrorism;

   (iii) it appears to the court that the risk is one arising out of, or is associated with, a public emergency in respect of which there is a designated derogation from the whole or a part of Article 5 of the Human Rights Convention; and

   (iv) the obligations to be imposed by the order or (as the case may be) by the order as modified are or include derogating obligations of a description set out for the purposes of the designated derogation in the designation order.

(e) A derogating control order is valid for six months (starting with the day it is made) unless it is revoked, renewed or ceases to have effect under section 6 (ie there has been no order within the relevant time to confirm that the Secretary of State has the power to impose derogating obligations) (Prevention of Terrorism Act 2005, s 4(8)).

(f) A control order can be renewed for a period of six months, by the court, on application by the Secretary of State only if—

   (i) the court considers that it is necessary, for purposes connected with protecting members of the public from a risk of terrorism, for a derogating control order to continue in force against the controlled person;

   (ii) it appears to the court that the risk is one arising out of, or is associated with, a public emergency in respect of which there is a designated derogation from the whole or a part of Article 5 of the Human Rights Convention;

  (iii) the derogating obligations that the court considers should continue in force are of a description that continues to be set out for the purposes of the designated derogation in the designation order; and

  (iv) the court considers that the obligations to be imposed by the renewed order are necessary for purposes connected with preventing or restricting involvement by that person in terrorism-related activity.

(g) This renewal can be exercised on as many occasions as the court sees fit but only if the above conditions are satisfied on each occasion (Prevention of Terrorism Act 2005, s 4(9) and (10)).

(h) The renewal of a control order will begin from when the order would have ceased to have effect or at the start of the seventh day after the renewal, whichever is the earliest (Prevention of Terrorism Act 2005, s 4(9)).

(i) A derogating control order will only have effect if the relevant derogation (suspension) is still in force and it is not more than 12 months since the derogation was made. Alternatively after the Secretary of State has made an order stating that it remains necessary for him to have the power to impose derogating obligations (Prevention of Terrorism Act, s 6).

(j) The person subject to the derogating control order or the Secretary of State can both apply to the court to make changes to or revoke the order. The court can modify the control order, if it is to relax or remove an obligation, if both parties agree (Secretary of State and person subject to the control order) or if the court considers it necessary for purposes connected with preventing or restricting the controlled person's involvement in terrorism-related activity. The court cannot impose further derogating obligations as part of the modification unless it considers it necessary for purposes connected with protecting members of the public from a risk of terrorism, and it appears to the court that the risk arises out of, or is associated with, the public emergency in respect of which there is a designated derogation. If a change is made then the person subject to the control order must be given notice of the change, see police powers above. If the court considers that derogating obligations need no longer apply to a derogating control order then it must revoke the whole of the order. (Prevention of Terrorism Act 2005, s 7(4)–(8) and (10)).

(k) *Counter-Terrorism Act 2008*—Sections 78–81 make amendments to provisions relating to control orders. Section 78 inserts ss 7A–7C into the Prevention of Terrorism Act 2005. These are powers of entry and search for police officers for those subject to control orders. Sections 79–81 of the Act make other amendments relating to control orders. See PNLD re S823 to see whether these provisions are in force.

(l) *Counter-Terrorism Act 2008*—Sections 1–9 provide further powers tot remove documents for examination for offences in ss 7A–7C of the Prevention of Terrorism Act 2005. See PNLD refs S1136 and S823 to check whether these sections are in force.

(m) *Counter-Terrorism Act 2008*—Section 10 amends the Police and Criminal Evidence Act 1984 (PACE) (ss 61, 63, 63A, 64, and 65) to allow police to take without consent fingerprints and samples of those persons subject to a control order. The fingerprints and samples can also be retained and checked against other fingerprints and samples as per other PACE samples. For a summary of the Act see p xxvii. See PNLD ref S2 to check whether these amendments are in force.

PNLD reference numbers

D15495, D15496

5.6.4 **Arrest and detention pending control order**

Section 5 of the Prevention of Terrorism Act 2005 sets out that an individual can be arrested pending a derogating control order being made, for how long and where that person can be detained.

Police powers

(1) A constable may arrest and detain an individual if—
   (a) the Secretary of State has made an application to the court for a **derogating control order** to be made against that individual; and
   (b) the constable considers that the individual's arrest and detention is necessary to ensure that he is available to be given notice of the order if it is made.

Prevention of Terrorism Act 2005, s 5(1)

Meanings

A derogating control order (see **5.6.3**).

Notes

(a) This power does not apply to non-derogating control orders.

(b) The constable must take the arrested individual to a designated place (see **5.3.3**) as soon as practicable after the arrest. A designated place is a police station that has the appropriate cells to detain possible terrorist suspects (Prevention of Terrorism Act 2005, s 5(2)).

(c) A person can be detained for 48 hours under this section. This can be extended for a further period of 48 hours by the court if it considers it necessary so that the individual can be given notice of any derogating control order (Prevention of Terrorism Act 2005, s 5(3) and (4)).

(d) Once the person becomes subject to a derogating control order or the control order is not made, he must be released (Prevention of Terrorism Act 2005, s 5(5)).

(e) Code of Practice H (see **Appendix 1**) does not apply to those detained under this section and there is no other equivalent Code of Practice.

(f) A constable can exercise this power in the whole of the UK (Prevention of Terrorism Act 2005, s 5(6)).

(g) A person detained under this section is deemed to be in police detention for the purpose of the Police and Criminal Evidence Act 1984 and is also subject to certain provisions of Schedule 8 to the Terrorism Act 2000, subject to some amendments.

Para 1(6)—if a person is arrested in one part of the UK and detained in another, the relevant parts of Schedule 8 shall apply to where he is detained (see **5.3.3**)

Para 2—take relevant steps to identify the person (amended so that only a constable can take the steps) (see **5.3.3**)

Para 6—right to have someone informed (see **5.3.5**)

Para 7—right to legal advice (see **5.3.5**)

Para 8—Superintendents' authority to delay rights (amended so as not to include right to exercise these rights within 48 hours and right to delay with regard to benefiting from criminal conduct) (see **5.3.5**)

Para 9—the authorization for police officer to be present during legal consultation (see **5.3.5**) (Prevention of Terrorism Act 2005, s 5(8)).

(h) Section 5(9) states that the detention may be incompatible with the right to liberty under Article 5 provided there is a designated derogation in connection with the 2005 Act powers which arises from the same public emergency as the derogation in connection with derogating control orders. This simply ensures that an Article 15 derogation notice is a condition to the issuance of a derogating control order.

PNLD reference number

D15497

5.6.5 **Criminal investigations during control orders**

Section 8 of the Prevention of Terrorism Act 2005 provides duties for the Secretary of State to consult with the police prior to making a control order where he thinks there maybe enough evidence to prosecute for a terrorism-related offence.

This section applies where it appears to the Secretary of State—
    (a) that the involvement in terrorism-related activity of which an individual is suspected may have involved the commission of an offence relating to terrorism; and
    (b) that the commission of that offence is being or would fall to be investigated by a police force.

Prevention of Terrorism Act 2005, s 8(1)

Meanings

Terrorism-related activity (see **5.6.2**).

Terrorism (see **4.1.1**).

Notes

(a) This section provides that if the Secretary of State thinks that there is enough evidence to suggest that the person subject to an application for a control order may have committed an offence relating to terrorism then he must check with the chief officer of police, before making the control order, to see if it is being investigated or should be investigated by the police (Prevention of Terrorism Act 2005, s 8(1)).

(b) Before applying for, or making a control order, the Secretary of State must check with the chief officer of police as to whether there is enough evidence for a realistic chance of prosecution (Prevention of Terrorism Act 2005, s 8(2)).

(c) The Secretary of State must inform the chief officer of police when a control order has been made and it will then be the duty of the chief officer of police to ensure that the investigation into the individual's conduct is kept under review with a view to prosecution throughout the duration of the control order (Prevention of Terrorism Act 2005, s 8(3) and (4)).

(d) If he considers it appropriate, once the control order has been made, the chief officer of police must consult with the Director of Public Prosecutions with regards to his investigation into the conduct of the individual (Prevention of Terrorism Act 2005, s 8(5)).

(e) *Counter-Terrorism Act 2008*—Sections 78–81 make amendments to provisions relating to control orders. Section 78 inserts ss 7A–7C into the Prevention of Terrorism Act 2005. These are powers of entry and search for police officers for those subject to control orders. Sections 79–81 of the Act make other amendments relating to control orders. See PNLD ref S823 to see whether these provisions are in force.

(f) *Counter-Terrorism Act 2008*—Sections 1–9 provide further powers to remove documents for examination for offences in ss 7A–7C of the Prevention of Terrorism Act 2005. See PNLD refs S1136 and S823 to check whether these sections are in force.

(g) *Counter-Terrorism Act 2008*—Section 10 amends the Police and Criminal Evidence Act 1984 (PACE) (ss 61, 63, 63A, 64, and 65) to allow police to take without consent fingerprints and samples of those persons subject to a control order. The fingerprints and samples can also be retained and checked against other fingerprints and samples as per other PACE samples. For a summary of the Act see p xxvii. See PNLD ref S2 to check whether these amendments are in force.

Related cases

Secretary of State for the Home Department v E [2007] UKHL 47 Proof of a lack of evidence to secure a prosecution for a terrorism-related offence is not a pre-requisite for making a non-derogating control order and a duty to prosecute wherever possible under section 8(2) was not a qualifying condition in this respect and a failure to observe it does not make the control order invalid. The Secretary of State has a duty to consult the police but not to make a clear decision about a possible prosecution as this would weaken what should be an expeditious and effective procedure. The Secretary of State must also provide the police with information in his possession that may assist a possible prosecution. The police must keep the situation under review and the Secretary of State must ensure that the review is significant. A control order would only be found to be invalid if the duties under section 8(2) and (4) were not carried out and if they had been carried out the individual could and should have faced prosecution with a reasonable chance of success.

PNLD reference numbers

D15501, C1519

5.6.6 **Offences related to control orders**

Section 9 of the Prevention of Terrorism Act 2005 provides the offences related to control orders.

Offences

(1) A person who, without reasonable excuse, contravenes an obligation imposed on him by a **control order** is guilty of an offence.

(2) A person is guilty of an offence if—

(a) a control order by which he is bound at a time when he leaves the United Kingdom requires him, whenever he enters the United Kingdom, to report to a specified person that he is or has been the subject of such an order;

(b) he re-enters the United Kingdom after the order has ceased to have effect;

(c) the occasion on which he re-enters the United Kingdom is the first occasion on which he does so after leaving while the order was in force; and

(d) on that occasion he fails, without reasonable excuse, to report to the specified person in the manner that was required by the order.

(3) A person is guilty of an offence if he intentionally obstructs the exercise by any person of **a power conferred by section 7(9)**.

Prevention of Terrorism Act 2005, s 9(1)–(3)

Points to prove

Section 9(1)

✓ date and location
✓ subject of derogating/non-derogating control order
✓ made by court/Secretary of State on (date)
✓ contravened an obligation
✓ without reasonable excuse

Section 9(2)

✓ date and location
✓ having left the UK on a date
✓ when a derogating/non-derogating control order was in existence
✓ which required to report to a specified person on return to the UK
✓ failed to report to that person in the manner that was required by that order

Section 9(3)

✓ date and location
✓ intentionally obstructed a PC/an authorized person
✓ whilst delivering a notice under section 7(8) of the Prevention of Terrorism Act 2005
✓ relating to a control order/the renewal or modification of a control order

Meanings

Control order (see 5.6.1).

A power conferred by section 7(9)

Means the power to enter and search premises for the purpose of delivering a notice under sub-section (8) to the controlled person a constable or a person authorised for the purpose by the Secretary of State may (if necessary by force)—

(a) enter any premises where he has reasonable grounds for believing that person to be; and
(b) search those premises for him.

Police powers

Power of arrest—section 41 of the Terrorism Act 2000 (see 5.3.1)

Power to stop and search—section 43 of the Terrorism Act 2000 (see 5.2.1)

Note

The courts cannot give a conditional discharge to a person convicted under section 9(1) or (2).

 Time limit for prosecution: None.

Section 9(1) and (2)

 Summary: Maximum six months' imprisonment and/or a fine not exceeding the statutory maximum.

 Indictment: Maximum five years' imprisonment and/or a fine.

Section 9(3)

 Summary: Maximum six months' imprisonment and/or fine not exceeding level five on the standard scale.

PNLD reference numbers

H8034, H8035, H8036, D15502

5.6.7 Appeals and court powers

Section 10 of the Prevention of Terrorism Act 2005 sets out when a person subject to a control order can appeal against a control order and the powers of the court in dealing with such appeals.

(1) Where—
  (a) a **non-derogating control order** has been renewed, or
  (b) an obligation imposed by such an order has been modified without the consent of the controlled person,
  the controlled person may appeal to the court against the renewal or modification.

Prevention of Terrorism Act 2005, s 10(1)

Meanings

Non-derogating control order (see 5.6.2).

Notes

(a) Where a renewal includes modifications to the control order, the person can appeal against any or all of the obligations not just those recently made on the renewal (Prevention of Terrorism Act 2005, s 10(2)).

(b) The person subject to the control order can apply to the Secretary of State for the revocation or modification of the control order. He can then appeal to the court on any of the decisions made by the Secretary of State on the application (Prevention of Terrorism Act 2005, s 10(3)).

(c) The task of the court when hearing an appeal, is to determine whether or not a decision of the Secretary of State was flawed. These decisions are—that it is necessary, for protecting members of the public from a risk of terrorism, for a control order to continue in force; and/or that the obligations to be imposed by the renewed order, or the obligations to which the application for revocation relates, are necessary for preventing or restricting involvement by that person in terrorism-related activity (Prevention of Terrorism Act 2005, s 10(4)).

(d) When the court hears an appeal against a modification or non-modification of a control order, it must determine whether or not a decision made by the Secretary of State is flawed. The decision is, in the case of an appeal against a modification, his decision that the modification is necessary for purposes connected with preventing or restricting involvement by the controlled person in terrorism-related activity. In the case of an appeal against a decision on an application for the modification of an obligation, his decision that the obligation continues to be necessary for that purpose (Prevention of Terrorism Act 2005, s 10(5)).

(e) If the court finds that the decision of the Secretary of State is flawed then the court must either quash the renewal of the order; quash one or more obligations imposed by the order; or give directions to the Secretary of State for the revocation of the order or for the modification of the obligations it imposes. In every other case the court must dismiss the appeal (Prevention of Terrorism Act 2005, s 10(7) and (8)).

PNLD reference number

D15503

5.7 **Other Issues**

5.7.1 **Commission of offence abroad**

Generally, a person can only be prosecuted in the UK for acts done on UK territory. However, there are some exceptions to this rule. Certain offences or Acts include provisions that extend offences to acts done by UK citizens abroad. Others even extend the offence to acts done by anybody in any place; see for example the offence of hijacking aircraft (see **5.4.12**). Most of the time, the extent of each offence is provided for in the section or Act creating the offence. If a particular offence can be committed abroad, this is set out in the notes to each offence in this handbook.

There are some provisions that extend UK jurisdiction to acts done abroad for a number of offences. These are explained in this chapter, namely section 17 of the Terrorism Act 2006 and sections 62–63E of the Terrorism Act 2000.

Note

Counter-Terrorism Act 2008—notification requirements—Sections 40 to 61 of the Act make provision for notification requirements for persons sentenced, or made subject to a hospital order. This applies to offences in respect of which there is jurisdiction by virtue of any of sections 62 to 63D of the Terrorism Act 2000 and section 17 of the Terrorism Act 2006. For a summary of the Act see p xxvii. See PNLD reference number S1136 to check whether these sections are in force.

5.7.1.1 Section 17 of the Terrorism Act 2006

Section 17 of the Terrorism Act 2006 provides extra-territorial jurisdiction in relation to a number of offences relating to terrorism regardless of the nationality of the offender.

(1) If—
    (a) a person does anything outside the United Kingdom, and
    (b) his action, if done in a part of the United Kingdom, would
        constitute an **offence falling within subsection (2)**,
    he shall be guilty in that part of the United Kingdom of the
    offence.

(3) Subsection (1) applies irrespective of whether the person is a British citizen or, in the case of a company, a company incorporated in a part of the United Kingdom.

Terrorism Act 2006, s 17(1) and (3)

Meanings

Offences falling within subsection (2)

(under the Terrorism Act 2006)

encouragement of terrorism, s 1 (see **4.3.1**).

training for terrorist acts, s 6 (see **4.3.7**).

attendance at a place used for terrorist training, s 8 (see **4.3.8**).

making and possession of radioactive devices and material, s 9 (see **5.5.1**).

misuse of radioactive devices and materials and misuse or damage of facilities, s 10 (see **5.5.2**).

terrorist threats relating to radioactive devices and materials or facilities (s 11, see **5.5.3**).

(under the Terrorism Act 2000)

membership of proscribed organizations, s 11(1) (see **4.2.2**).

weapons training, s 54 (see **4.3.9**).

conspiracy to commit an offence falling within this subsection (see **5.8.6**).

encouraging/assisting an offender (see **5.8.6**).

attempting to commit such an offence (see **5.8.6**).

aiding, abetting, counselling or procuring the commission of such an offence (see **5.8.6**).

Notes

(a) Extra-territorial jurisdiction applies irrespective of whether or not the person is a British citizen or, in the case of a company, a company incorporated in a part of the UK (Terrorism Act 2006, s 17(3)).

(b) If one of the offences listed above is committed wholly or partly outside the UK, proceedings for the offence may be taken at any place in the UK; and the offence may for all incidental purposes be treated as having been committed at any such place (Terrorism Act 2006, s 17(4)).

(c) The extra-territorial jurisdiction set out in this section is required to give effect to a number of international treaties which require the UK and other states who are party to the treaty to take jurisdiction in respect of offences committed anywhere by nationals of any state and of anyone present on UK territory if the UK does not extradite that person to the state where the offence was committed. The main purpose of this is to avoid the situation where a criminal can hide in another country, for example the UK, if the country where he committed the offence does not, for whatever reason, conduct a prosecution and/or request his extradition.

(d) At the moment, even though there is an International Criminal Court, its jurisdiction does not explicitly refer to terrorism, so terrorism-related offences would still be prosecuted by national authorities. Theoretically, anybody suspected of having committed any of the offences listed in section 17(2) anywhere in the world could be prosecuted in the UK. In the view of Lord Carlile, the independent reviewer of the Terrorism Act 2000 and other anti-terrorist legislation, it could hardly be considered wrong to arrest and prosecute a major international terrorist if he happened to transit through the UK and be apprehended here; or a UK national involved in terrorism offences in other parts of the world. In this way, terrorism offences are made into international crimes, though that position has not been adopted by international law or most other national jurisdictions except for some international offences, such as the hijacking of aircraft (see Aviation Security Act 1982), hostage-taking (see Taking of Hostages Act 1982), or attacks on diplomats (see Internationally Protected Persons Act 1978). The discretion whether or not to prosecute is important and sensitive in this context since some might view armed resistance to oppressive regimes as being justified. See also 'Consents to prosecution', 5.7.4.

5.7.1.2 Section 62 of the Terrorism Act 2000

Section 62 of the Terrorism Act 2000 provides extra-territorial jurisdiction in relation to a number of terrorism-related bombing offences.

(1) If—

    (a) a person does anything outside the United Kingdom as an act of terrorism or for the purposes of terrorism, and

(b) his action would have constituted the commission of one
of the offences listed in subsection (2) if it had been done in
the United Kingdom,

he shall be guilty of the offence.

Terrorism Act 2000, s 62(1)

Meanings

Offences listed in subsection (1)(b)

(under the Explosive Substances Act 1883)

cause explosion endangering life or property, s 2 (see **5.8.1**).

do act/conspire/possess to cause explosion endangering life or property, s 3 (see **5.8.1**).

punishment of accessories, s 5 (see **5.8.1**).

(under the Biological Weapons Act 1974)

develop/produce, etc biological weapons, s 1 (see **5.5.17**).

(under the Chemical Weapons Act 1996)

use of chemical weapons, s 2 (see **5.5.18**).

Terrorism Act 2000, s 62(2).

Notes

(a) This applies irrespective of whether the person is a British
citizen or not or, in the case of a company, a company incorporated in a part of the UK.

(b) The extra-territorial jurisdiction set out in this section was
required to enable the UK to ratify the United Nations Convention for the Suppression of Terrorist Bombings 1997. It enables
the UK to meet its obligations under the Convention to either
extradite the suspect or prosecute him. Where, for example,
a foreign national cannot be extradited to another country
(granted asylum in the UK, threat of torture abroad) he may be
prosecuted in the UK under this provision.

5.7.1.3 Section 63 of the Terrorism Act 2000

Section 63 of the Terrorism Act 2000 provides for extra-territorial
jurisdiction for certain terrorist finance offences (see **4.4.2–4.4.5**).

(1) If—

(a) a person does anything outside the United Kingdom, and

    (b) his action would have constituted the commission of an offence under any of sections 15 to 18 if it had been done in the United Kingdom,

he shall be guilty of the offence.

Terrorism Act 2000, s 63(1)

Meanings

Offences under any of sections 15 to 18

These are fund raising (s 15, see **4.4.2**), use and possession of money or property (s 16, see **4.4.3**), arranging funds or property (s 17, see **4.4.4**) and money laundering (s 18, see **4.4.5**).

Notes

(a) Extra-territorial jurisdiction applies irrespective of whether the person is a British citizen or, in the case of a company, a company incorporated in a part of the UK.

(b) This provision is based on the United Nations Convention for the Suppression of the Financing of Terrorism 1999. It allows the UK to either extradite a suspect or prosecute in the UK where extradition might not be possible or desired.

5.7.1.4 Section 63A of the Terrorism Act 2000

Section 63A of the Terrorism Act 2000 provides for extra-territorial jurisdiction for the terrorism-related offences in sections 56–61 of the Terrorism Act 2000 where these are committed by UK residents or UK nationals.

If—

    (a) a **United Kingdom national** or a **United Kingdom resident** does anything outside the United Kingdom, and

    (b) his action, if done in any part of the United Kingdom, would have constituted an **offence under any of sections 56 to 61**,

he shall be guilty in that part of the United Kingdom of the offence.

Terrorism Act 2000, s 63A(1)

Meanings

UK national

Means an individual who is—

   (a) a British citizen, a British overseas territories citizen, a
       British National (Overseas) or a British Overseas citizen,
   (b) a person who under the British Nationality Act 1981 is a
       British subject, or
   (c) a British protected person within the meaning of that Act
       (Terrorism Act 2000, s 63A(2)).

UK resident

Means an individual who is resident in the UK (Terrorism Act 2000,
s 63A(3)).

Offences under any of sections 56 to 61

These are directing a terrorist organization (s 56, see **4.2.5**), possession of articles for terrorist purpose (s 57, see **4.3.10**), collection of
information (s 58, see **4.3.11**), inciting terrorism overseas (s 59 for
England and Wales, see **4.3.5**, ss 60 and 61 for Northern Ireland and
Scotland).

Notes

(a) The effect of this section is that acts committed outside the UK
    by UK nationals or residents can be prosecuted in the UK. (This
    section and sections 63B–63E implement the European Union
    Framework Decision of 13 June 2002 on combating terrorism).
(b) Where such an extra-territorial offence is created, extra-
    territorial jurisdiction is automatically taken over secondary
    and inchoate offences, such as aiding, abetting, attempting,
    inciting, conspiring, counselling, or procuring. That means
    that not only could the principal offender be prosecuted, but
    also someone who aided and abetted, etc.

5.7.1.5 Section 63B of the Terrorism Act 2000

Section 63B of the Terrorism Act 2000 provides for extra-territorial
jurisdiction where terrorist attacks are committed abroad by UK
nationals or residents.

(1) If—
   (a) a **United Kingdom national** or a **United Kingdom resi-
       dent** does anything outside the United Kingdom as an **act
       of terrorism or** for the purposes of terrorism, and
   (b) his action, if done in any part of the United Kingdom,
       would have constituted an offence listed in subsection (2),
   he shall be guilty in that part of the United Kingdom of the
   offence.

Terrorism Act 2000, s 63B(1)

Meanings

UK national (see **5.7.1.4**).

UK resident (see **5.7.1.4**).

Act of terrorism (see **4.1.2**).

Offence listed in subsection (2)

(a) murder (see **5.8.4**), manslaughter(see **5.8.4**), culpable homicide, rape, assault causing injury, assault to injury, kidnapping (see **5.8.3.5**), abduction or false imprisonment,

(b) an offence under section 4, 16 (see **5.8.3.4**), 18 (see **5.8.3.3**), 20 (see **5.8.3.2**), 21, 22, 23, 24, 28, 29, 30 or 64 of the Offences Against the Person Act 1861 (see **5.8.3**),

(c) an offence under any of sections 1 to 5 of the Forgery and Counterfeiting Act 1981,

(d) the uttering of a forged document or an offence under section 46A of the Criminal Law (Consolidation) (Scotland) Act 1995,

(e) an offence under section 1 or 2 of the Criminal Damage Act 1971 (see **5.8.5**),

(f) an offence under Article 3 or 4 of the Criminal Damage (Northern Ireland) Order 1977,

(g) malicious mischief,

(h) wilful fire-raising. (Terrorism Act 2000, s 63B(2)).

Note

These offences could normally not be prosecuted in the UK, even though committed by UK nationals or residents; the effect of this section is that a prosecution for such offences in the UK is possible where they are related to a terrorist attack.

> AG✓ **AG consent required:** Proceedings may only be started by or with the consent of the Attorney General (Terrorism Act 2000, s 63E(1)).

5.7.1.6 Sections 63C and 63D of the Terrorism Act 2000

Sections 63C and 63D of the Terrorism Act 2000 make further provision for extra-territorial jurisdiction for a number of terrorism-related offences. Section 63C concerns offences committed against UK nationals or residents and 'protected persons' outside the UK as an act of terrorism or for the purposes of terrorism. The nationality or residence of the offender is irrelevant. 'Protected persons' include all diplomatic and consular staff, whether UK nationals or not; they are defined in section 63C(3). The offences are listed in section 63C(2) and include murder (see **5.8.4**), manslaughter, kidnapping and a number of offences under the Offences Against the Person Act 1861 (see **5.8.3**) and under the Forgery and Counterfeiting Act 1981. Section 63D gives UK jurisdiction over the offence of criminal damage or threat of criminal damage (Criminal Damage Act 1971, ss 1 and 2) where it is committed as a terrorist attack or threatened attack against the residential or working premises or vehicles of protected persons when a protected person is in, or likely to be, on the premises or in the vehicle. For the purposes of sections 63C and 63D it is immaterial whether a person knows that another person is a UK national or resident or a protected person (Terrorism Act 2000, s 63E(3)). Proceedings may only be started by or with the consent of the Attorney General, unless the offence is under one of the following Acts: the Internationally Protected Persons Act 1978, the Suppression of Terrorism Act 1978, the Nuclear Material (Offences) Act 1983, the United Nations Personnel Act 1997 (Terrorism Act 2000, s 63E(1) and (2)).

PNLD reference numbers

D18583, D8746, D8747, D12302, D12303, D12304, D12305, D12306

5.7.2 **Company Directors' Liability**

Certain offences may not only be committed by individuals, but by companies. The provisions below set out the liability of company directors, managers, secretaries, and other similar officers of a body corporate for certain terrorism-related offences.

5.7.2.1 Section 18 of the Terrorism Act 2006

Where an **offence under this Part** [*Part 1, sections 1-20*] is committed by a **body corporate** and is proved to have been committed with the consent or connivance of—
(a) a **director,** manager, secretary or other similar officer of the body corporate, or
(b) a person who was purporting to act in any such capacity, he (as well as the body corporate) is guilty of that offence and shall be liable to be proceeded against and punished accordingly.

Terrorism Act 2006, s 18(1)

Meanings

Offences under Part 1 of the Terrorism Act 2006

- encouragement of terrorism, section 1 (see **4.3.1**)
- dissemination of terrorist publications, section 2 (see **4.3.2**)
- preparation of terrorist acts, section 5 (see **4.3.6**)
- training for terrorist acts, section 6 (see **4.3.7**)
- attendance at a place used for terrorist training, section 8 (see **4.3.8**)
- making and possession of radioactive devices and material, section 9 (see **5.5.1**)
- misuse of radioactive devices and materials and misuse or damage of facilities, section 10 (see **5.5.2**)
- terrorist threats relating to radioactive devices and materials or facilities (section 11, see **5.5.3**)

Body corporate

Is the legal term for a corporation. It is distinct from a natural person, although it has many of the same legal rights.

Director

In relation to a body corporate whose affairs are managed by its members, means a member of the body corporate (Terrorism Act 2000, s 18(3)).

Note

Of the offences in sections 1–20 of the Terrorism Act 2006 a corporate body is most likely to be prosecuted for an offence under section 2 for disseminating terrorist publications. Both, the senior officer (or officers, if consent, connivance, or neglect can be proved against each) and the body corporate will be liable for the offence.

5.7.2.2 Section 54 of the Anti-terrorism, Crime and Security Act 2001 (weapons of mass destruction)

Section 54 lays out individual liability of the relevant senior office holder in a body corporate, in addition to corporate responsibility, in relation to certain offences concerning weapons of mass destruction.

> Where an **offence under section 47, 50 or subsection (1)** above committed by a body corporate is proved to have been committed with the consent or connivance of, or to be attributable to any neglect on the part of—

(a) a **director**, manager, secretary or other similar officer of the body corporate; or

(b) any person who was purporting to act in any such capacity, he as well as the body corporate shall be guilty of that offence and shall be liable to be proceeded against and punished accordingly.

Anti-terrorism, Crime and Security Act 2001, s 54(3)

Meanings

Offence under section 47, 50 or subsection (1) above

- use, etc of nuclear weapon, section 47 (see **5.5.4**)
- assisting or inducing certain weapons-related acts overseas, section 50 (see **5.5.5**)
- make false/misleading statement re section 47/50 statement, section 54(1)

Director

In relation to a body corporate whose affairs are managed by its members, means a member of the body corporate (Anti-terrorism, Crime and Security Act 2001, s 54(4).

5.7.2.3 Section 68 of the Anti-terrorism, Crime and Security Act 2001 (security of pathogens and toxins)

Section 68 of the Anti-terrorism, Crime and Security Act 2001 concerns offences committed by a body corporate, as the occupier of premises under Part 7 which deals with the security of pathogens and toxins. It enables the prosecution of certain officers or employees, in addition to the body corporate.

If an offence under this Part (Part 7, sections 58–75) committed by a body corporate is shown to have been committed with the consent or connivance of, or to be attributable to any neglect on the part of—

(a) any officer, or

(b) any other employee of the body corporate who is in charge of any relevant premises or the access to any dangerous substance kept or used there,

he, as well as the body corporate, is guilty of the offence and liable to be proceeded against and punished accordingly.

Anti-terrorism, Crime and Security Act 2001, 68(1)

Meanings

Offences under Part 7 of the Anti-terrorism, Crime and Security Act 2001

Failure of occupier of premises to comply with duty/direction or making false/misleading statement when giving information, section 67 (see **5.5.14**).

Officer

In relation to a body corporate, means—

(a) any director, manager, secretary, or other similar officer of the body corporate; or

(b) any person purporting to act in any such capacity (Anti-terrorism, Crime and Security Act 2001, s 68(2)).

Notes

(a) Where the affairs of a body corporate are managed by its members, this section applies in relation to the acts and defaults of a member in connection with his functions of management as if he were a director of the body corporate (Anti-terrorism, Crime and Security Act 2001, s 68(3)).

(b) Section 69 clarifies how the provisions relating to offences apply to an unincorporated association or partnership where it is the occupier of the premises.

5.7.2.4 Further provisions

Section 37 of the Aviation Security Act 1982 makes provisions for the commission of offences under that Act by bodies corporate; so does section 50 of the Aviation and Maritime Security Act 1990 for offences committed under that Act. Paragraph 8 of Schedule 6 to the Terrorism Act 2000 deals with offences committed by a financial institution under paragraph 1(3) (failure to comply with requirement re financial information, see **4.4.15**).

A further provision dealing with the commission of offences by a body corporate is included in Schedule 3 to the Anti-terrorism, Crime and Security Act 2001 (para 9, re freezing orders); paragraph 9 states that a freezing order may provide that where an offence has been committed by a body corporate with the consent, connivance or by neglect of a director, manager, secretary or other similar officer, then he is also liable for the offence.

PNLD reference numbers

D18584, D10334, D10347, D4338, D12876

5.7.3 **Convention offences**

The term 'Convention offences' is used in a number of offences created by the Terrorism Act 2006. They are intended to cover the terrorist offences in the Council of Europe Convention for the Prevention of Terrorism 2005. The offences in the Terrorism Act 2006 cover actions that relate to acts of terrorism **and** Convention offences.

Meanings

Convention offence

Means an offence listed in Schedule 1 of the Terrorism Act 2006 or an equivalent offence under the law of a country or territory outside the UK (Terrorism Act 2006, s 20).

Schedule 1 to the Terrorism Act 2006 contains a list of Convention offences:

- Explosives offences under the Offences Against the Person Act 1861
  - causing injury by explosion, section 28
  - causing explosions, section 29
  - handling or placing explosives, section 30.
- Explosives offences under the Explosive Substances Act 1883
  - causing an explosion likely to endanger life, section 2 (see **5.8.1.1**)
  - preparation of explosives, section 3 (see **5.8.1.2**)
  - ancillary offences, section 5.
- Biological weapons offences under the Biological Weapons Act 1974
  - development, etc of biological weapons, section 1 (see **5.5.17**).
- Offences against internationally protected persons under the Internationally Protected Persons Act 1978
  - attacks against protected persons committed outside the UK (s 1(1)(a)), if the offence is committed (whether in the UK or elsewhere) in relation to a protected person,
  - attacks on relevant premises, etc (s 1(1)(b)), if the offence is committed (whether in the UK or elsewhere) in connection with an attack on relevant premises or on a vehicle ordinarily

used by a protected person, and at a time when a protected person is in or on the premises or vehicle
  • threats, etc in relation to protected persons, section 1(3).
• Hostage-taking under the Taking of Hostages Act 1982
  • hostage-taking, section 1.
• Hijacking and other offences against aircraft under the Aviation Security Act 1982
  • hijacking, section 1 (see **5.4.12**)
  • destroying, damaging or endangering safety of aircraft, section 2 (see **5.4.13**)
  • other acts endangering or likely to endanger safety of aircraft, section 3
  • ancillary offences, section 6(2) (see **5.4.15**).
• Offences involving nuclear material under the Nuclear Material (Offences) Act 1983
  • offences in relation to nuclear material committed outside the UK, section 1, if the offence is committed (whether in the UK or elsewhere) in relation to or by means of nuclear material
  • offence involving preparatory acts and threats in relation to nuclear material, section 2.
• Offences under the Aviation and Maritime Security Act 1990
  • endangering safety at aerodromes, section 1 (see **5.4.21**)
  • hijacking of ships, section 9
  • seizing or exercising control of fixed platforms, section 10
  • destroying ships or fixed platforms or endangering their safety, section 11
  • other acts endangering or likely to endanger safe navigation, section 12
  • offences involving threats relating to ships or fixed platforms, section 13
  • ancillary offences, section 14.
• Offences involving chemical weapons under the Chemical Weapons Act 1996
  • use, development etc. of chemical weapons, section 2 (see **5.5.18**).
• Offences relating to terrorist funds under the Terrorism Act 2000
  • terrorist fund-raising, section 15 (see **4.4.2**)
  • use or possession of terrorist funds, section 16 (see **4.4.3**)
  • funding arrangements for terrorism, section 17 (see **4.4.4**)
  • money laundering of terrorist funds, section 18 (see **4.4.5**).

- Offences relating to directing terrorist organizations under the Terrorism Act 2000
  - directing a terrorist organization, section 56 (see **4.2.5**).
- Offences involving nuclear weapons under the Anti-terrorism, Crime and Security Act 2001
  - use, development etc of nuclear weapons, section 47 (see **5.5.4**).
- Conspiracy, etc
  - conspiracy to commit a Convention offence
  - inciting the commission of a Convention offence
  - attempting to commit a Convention offence
  - aiding, abetting, counselling, or procuring the commission of a Convention offence (see **5.8.6**).

PNLD reference number

D18590

5.7.4 **Consents to prosecution**

The prosecution of a number of terrorism-related offences requires the consent of either the Director of Public Prosecutions (DPP) or the Attorney General (AG).

The main provisions setting out consent to prosecution are section 117 of the Terrorism Act 2000 and section 19 of the Terrorism Act 2006. They provide that for certain offences proceedings for the offence shall not be instituted in England and Wales without the consent of the DPP; but if it appears to the DPP that such an offence has been committed [outside the UK or—*see note below*] for a purpose wholly or partly connected with the affairs of a country other than the UK, his consent for the purposes of this section may be given only with the permission of the AG.

A number of other Acts make similar provision, for example, section 8(1) of the Aviation Security Act 1982 provides that for most of the offences under that Act the consent of the AG is required.

Where consent is required for the prosecution of a particular offence this is stated in this handbook for each offence with an icon at the end of the chapter.

Note

Counter-Terrorism Act 2008—Section 29 of the Act inserted 'outside the United Kingdom' into these sections. This means that the Attorney General's consent is now required where it appears that the offence has been committed outside the United Kingdom.

PNLD reference numbers

D8751, D18585

5.8 **Alternative Offences**

The following section deals with alternative criminal offences to those terrorism-related offences. This section contains only the information that is relevant to a terrorist investigation.

5.8.1 **Explosives offences**

The Explosive Substances Act 1883 creates offences relating to causing explosions.

5.8.1.1 **Cause explosion likely to endanger life or property**

Section 2 of the Explosive Substances Act 1883 creates the offence of causing an explosion likely to endanger life or property.

Offence

A person who in the United Kingdom or (being a citizen of the United Kingdom and Colonies) or in the Republic of Ireland **unlawfully** and **maliciously** causes by any **explosive substance** an explosion of a nature likely to endanger life or to cause serious injury to property shall, whether any injury to person or property has been actually caused or not, be guilty of an offence.

Explosive Substances Act 1883, s 2

Points to prove
- ✓ date and location
- ✓ unlawfully and maliciously
- ✓ cause by an explosive substance
- ✓ an explosion
- ✓ of a nature likely to
- ✓ endanger life/cause serious injury to property

Meanings

Unlawfully

Means without excuse or justification at law.

Maliciously

Means malice (ill-will or an evil motive) must be present. 'Maliciously requires either an actual intention to do the particular kind of harm that was done or recklessness whether any such harm should occur or not; it is neither limited to, nor does it require, any ill-will towards the person injured' (**R v Cunningham [1957] 2 All ER 412, CA**).

Explosive substance

Shall be deemed to include any materials for making any explosive substance; also any apparatus, machine, implement, or materials used, or intended to be used, or adapted for causing, or aiding in causing, any explosion in or with any explosive substance; also any part of any such apparatus, machine, or implement (Explosive Substances Act 1883, s 9).

In **R v Wheatley [1979] 1 All ER 954** it was also held that the above definition should also incorporate that found in section 3 of the Explosives Act 1875.

Explosive

(1) Means gunpowder, nitro-glycerine, dynamite, gun-cotton, blasting powders, fulminate of mercury or of other metals, coloured fires, and every other substance, whether similar to those above mentioned or not, used or manufactured with a view to produce a practical effect by explosion or a pyrotechnic effect; and
(2) Includes fog-signals, fireworks, fuses, rockets, percussion caps, detonators, cartridges, ammunition of all descriptions, and every adaptation or preparation of an explosive as above defined.

Police powers

Power of arrest—section 24 of the Police and Criminal Evidence Act 1984

Powers of entry and search—sections 17, 18 and 32 of the Police and Criminal Evidence Act 1984

Section 73 of the Explosives Act 1875 provides a constable with a power of entry, search and seizure where he believes an offence under the Explosives Act 1875 or the Explosive Substances Act 1883 has been or is being committed.

> Where any of the following officers,—namely, any ... constable, if such constable or officer is specially authorised either
> (a) by warrant of a justice (which warrant such justice may grant upon reasonable ground being assigned on oath), or
> (b) (where it appears to a superintendent or other officer of police of equal or superior rank, or to a Government inspector, that the case is one of emergency and that the delay in obtaining a warrant would be likely to endanger life), by a written order from such superintendent, officer or inspector—
> has reasonable cause to believe that any offence has been or is being committed with respect to an explosive in any place (whether a building or not, or a carriage, boat or ship), or that any explosive is in any such place in contravention of this Act, or that the provisions of this Act are not duly observed in any such place, such officer may, on producing, if demanded, ..., in the case of any other officer his authority, enter at any time, and if needs be by force, and as well on Sunday as on other days, the said place, and every part thereof, and examine the same, and search for explosives therein, and take samples of any explosive and ingredient of an explosive therein, and any substance reasonably supposed to be an explosive, or such ingredient which may be found therein.

Explosives Act 1875, s 73

Notes

(a) Forensic evidence is very important in these cases and should be gathered with great care so as to avoid arguments about origin or contamination.

(b) For this offence to be committed there is no requirement that actual injury be caused, just that the explosion was of a nature that could have caused serious injury to people or property.

(c) If a person does anything outside the UK as an act of terrorism or for the purposes of terrorism and his action would have constituted the commission of an offence under this section or section 3 (see below) or section 5 (see below), he is guilty of an offence (Terrorism Act 2000, s 62, see **5.7.1**).

(d) Any person (who is a British citizen) who assists in the commission of an offence in this Act in any way shall be treated as a principal (main offender) (Explosive Substances Act 1883, s 5).

(e) Any person who obstructs a constable or refuses him admission to the place he wishes to enter and search using his powers under section 73 of the Explosives Act 1875 commits an offence. It is an either way offence, the penalty is a fine and the defendant shall also forfeit all explosives and ingredients that were in his possession or under his control at the time.

(f) If the constable enters under section 73 using a written order from a Superintendent, the Superintendent must send a report to the Secretary of State detailing everything the constable did under the order.

PNLD reference numbers

H4477, D3740

 AG consent required: Explosive Substances Act 1883, s 7.

 Time limit for prosecution: None.

Indictment: Life imprisonment.

5.8.1.2 Preparation of explosives

Section 3 of the Explosive Substances Act 1883 sets out four other offences in relation to explosive substances.

Offences

A person who in the United Kingdom or a **dependency** or (being a citizen of the United Kingdom and Colonies) elsewhere **unlawfully** and **maliciously**—

(a) does any act with **intent** to cause, or conspires to cause, by an **explosive substance** an explosion of a nature likely to endanger life, or cause serious injury to property, whether in the United Kingdom or elsewhere, or

(b) makes or has in his possession or under his control an explosive substance with intent by means thereof to endanger life, or cause serious injury to property, whether in the United Kingdom or elsewhere, or to enable any other person so to do,

shall, whether any explosion does or does not take place, and whether any injury to person or property is actually caused or not, be guilty of an offence, and the explosive substance shall be forfeited.

Explosive Substances Act 1883, s 3(1).

Points to prove

Section 3(1)(a)

- ✓ date and location
- ✓ unlawfully and maliciously
- ✓ did an act
- ✓ with intent
- ✓ to cause an explosion likely to
- ✓ endanger life/cause serious injury to property

Section 3(1)(a)

- ✓ date and location
- ✓ unlawfully and maliciously
- ✓ conspired
- ✓ to cause an explosion likely to
- ✓ endanger life/cause serious injury to property

Section 3(1)(b)

- ✓ date and location
- ✓ unlawfully and maliciously
- ✓ made
- ✓ an explosive substance
- ✓ with intent
- ✓ to endanger life/cause serious injury to property or
- ✓ enable another so to do

Section 3(1)(b)

- ✓ date and location
- ✓ unlawfully and maliciously
- ✓ had in your possession or
  under your control
- ✓ an explosive substance
- ✓ with intent
- ✓ to endanger life or
  cause serious injury to property or
  enable another so to do

Meanings

Dependency

Means the Channel Islands, the Isle of Man and any colony, other than a colony for whose external relations a country other than the UK is responsible.

Unlawfully (see **5.8.1.1**).

Maliciously (see **5.8.1.1**).

Intent

Intention is not defined but has to be proved. It can be proved by drawing on two sources of information or by a combination of both.

1. By admissions made by the defendant in interview with reference to his state of mind at the time of commission of the offence and his answers to questions with regard to his actions and intentions at the time of the offence.
2. By inference from the circumstances the offence, any evidence from witnesses, the defendant's actions and property found on him or in his control, such as a motor vehicle for transporting property. To prove intent, an officer needs to take all this into account, the important thing is that he has to prove the defendant's state of mind at the time.

Explosive substance (see above).

Police powers

Power of arrest—section 24 of the Police and Criminal Evidence Act 1984

Powers of entry and search—sections 17, 18 and 32 of the Police and Criminal Evidence Act 1984

Notes

(a) For this offence to be committed there is no requirement that actual injury be caused, just that the explosion was of a nature that could have caused serious injury to people or property.
(b) Forensic evidence is very important in these cases and should be gathered with great care so as to avoid arguments about origin or contamination.
(c) If a person does anything outside the UK as an act of terrorism or for the purposes of terrorism and his action would have constituted the commission of an offence under this section or section 3 (see below) or section 5 (see note (d) below), he is guilty of an offence (Terrorism Act 2000, s 62, see **5.7.1**).
(d) Any person (who is a British citizen) who assists in the commission of an offence in this Act in any way shall be treated as a principal (main offender) (Explosive Substances Act 1883, s 5).

PNLD reference numbers

H4468, H4469, H4478, H4479, D3741

| AG✓ | **AG consent required:** Explosive Substances Act 1883, s 7. |

| 🕐 | **Time limit for prosecution:** None. |

| ▥ | **Indictment:** Life imprisonment. |

5.8.1.3 Making or possessing an explosive substance in suspicious circumstances

Section 4 of the Explosive Substances Act 1883 sets out the offence of making or possessing explosive substances in suspicious circumstances.

Offence

Any person who makes or knowingly has in his possession or under his control any **explosive substance**, under such circumstances as to give rise to a reasonable suspicion that he is not making it or does not have it in his possession or under his control for a **lawful object**, shall, unless he can show that he made it or had it in his possession or under his control for a lawful object, be guilty of **felony**, and, on conviction, shall be liable to **penal servitude** for a term not exceeding fourteen years, or to imprisonment for a term not exceeding two years with or without **hard labour**, and the explosive substance shall be forfeited.

Explosive Substances Act 1883, s 4(1).

Points to prove

Made explosive substance

- ✓ date and location
- ✓ made explosive substance
- ✓ under circumstances giving reasonable suspicion
- ✓ not making it for a lawful object

Possessed or had explosive substance under his control

- ✓ date and location
- ✓ knowingly
- ✓ possessed/had under his/her control explosive substance
- ✓ under circumstances giving reasonable suspicion
- ✓ not for lawful object

Meanings

Explosive substance (see **5.8.1.1**).

Lawful object
Means lawful purpose.

Felony, penal servitude and hard labour
These are historical terms that are no longer current. The penalty is imprisonment only, there is no hard labour. See below for maximum sentence.

Police powers

Power of arrest—section 24 of the Police and Criminal Evidence Act 1984

Powers of entry and search—sections 17, 18 and 32 of the Police and Criminal Evidence Act 1984

Note

Any person (who is a British citizen) who assists in the commission of an offence in this Act in any way shall be treated as a principal (main offender) (Explosive Substances Act 1883, s 5).

Related cases

R v Berry [1994] 2 All ER 913 It is the responsibility of the prosecution to prove that the accused 'knowingly' was in possession of a substance and knew it was an explosive substance as defined and that he possessed it under such circumstances as to give rise to reasonable suspicion that he did not have it for a lawful object. The accused then has to show that he possessed it for a lawful object.

A-G's Reference (No 2 of 1983) [1984] 1 All ER 988 The term 'lawful object' could include, in limited circumstances, possession of explosive substances for the purpose of self defence.

PNLD reference numbers

H1722, H2166, D3742, C691

 AG consent required: Explosive Substances Act 1883, s 7.

 Time limit for prosecution: None.

 Indictment: Maximum 14 years' imprisonment.

5.8.2 **Bomb hoaxes**

Section 51 of the Criminal Law Act 1977 provides the offences related to bomb hoaxes.

Offences

(1) A person who—
   (a) places any **article** in any place whatever; or
   (b) dispatches any article by post, rail or any other means whatever of sending things from one place to another,
   with the **intention** (in either case) of inducing in some other **person** a belief that it is likely to explode or ignite and thereby cause personal injury or damage to property is guilty of an offence.
(2) A person who communicates any information which he knows or believes to be false to another person with the intention of inducing in him or any other person a false belief that a bomb or other thing liable to explode or ignite is present in any place or location whatever is guilty of an offence.

Criminal Law Act 1977, s 51(1)–(2)

Points to prove

Section 51(1) offence

✓ date and location
✓ placed in any place or dispatched by post/rail/other means of sending things
✓ an article
✓ with intent
✓ to induce in another the belief
✓ that the article
✓ was likely to explode/ignite
✓ and cause personal injury/damage to property

Section 51(2) offence

✓ date and location
✓ communicated
✓ information
✓ you knew/believed to be false
✓ to another person
✓ with intent
✓ of inducing a false belief in that person/any other person
✓ that bomb/thing was in place or location and
✓ was liable to explode/ignite at that place/location was present

Meanings

Article

This includes substances.

Intention

Intention is not defined but has to be proved. It can be proved by drawing on two sources of information or by a combination of both.

1. By admissions made by the defendant in interview with reference to his state of mind at the time of commission of the offence and his answers to questions with regard to his actions and intentions at the time of the offence.
2. By inference from the circumstances of the offence, any evidence from witnesses, the defendant's actions and property found on him or in his control, such as a motor vehicle for transporting property. To prove intent, an officer needs to take all this into account, the important thing is that he has to prove the defendant's state of mind at the time.

Person

It is not necessary to have any particular person in mind.

Police powers

Power of arrest—section 24 of the Police and Criminal Evidence Act 1984

Powers of entry and search—sections 17, 18 and 32 of the Police and Criminal Evidence Act 1984

Notes

(a) Section 51(1) concerns the placing or dispatching of articles with the intention that people believe that the articles are bombs or explosive devices, whereas section 51(2) concerns people who communicate false information intending others to believe there is a bomb or explosive device likely to explode.
(b) This section does not require a specific place or location to be given.

Related cases

R v Webb [1995] 27 LS Gaz R 31, CA The hoax message does not have to give a specific place or location.

PNLD reference numbers

H2056, H2057, H2102, D1420, C376

 Time limit for prosecution: None.

 Summary: Maximum six months' imprisonment and/or a fine not exceeding the statutory maximum.

 Indictment: Maximum seven years' imprisonment.

5.8.3 Offences against the person

The explanations about the following offences have been modified to include only the information considered relevant for a terrorist investigation.

5.8.3.1 Assault occasioning actual bodily harm (AOABH)

Section 47 of the Offences Against the Person Act creates the offence of assault occasioning actual bodily harm.

Offence

Whosoever shall be convicted upon an indictment of any assault occasioning **actual bodily harm** shall be guilty of an offence.

Offences Against the Person Act 1861, s 47

Points to prove

- ✓ date and location
- ✓ unlawfully
- ✓ assaulted
- ✓ another person
- ✓ occasioning him/her
- ✓ actual bodily harm

Meanings

Actual bodily harm

Has been defined as 'any hurt which interferes with health or comfort but not to a considerable degree'.

Police powers

Power of arrest—section 24 of the Police and Criminal Evidence Act 1984

Powers of entry and search—sections 17, 18 and 32 of the Police and Criminal Evidence Act 1984

Notes

(a) CPS guidance states that this offence is committed when a person assaults another, thereby causing actual bodily harm to that other person.

(b) Bodily harm has its ordinary meaning and is that which is calculated to interfere with the health or comfort of the victim, but must be more than transient or trifling.

(c) CPS charging standards and guidance give examples of injuries which could amount to 'actual bodily harm'—loss or breaking of a tooth or teeth; temporary loss of sensory functions (includes loss of consciousness); extensive or multiple bruising; displaced broken nose; minor fractures; minor cuts (not superficial), may require stitches (medical treatment); psychiatric injury (proved by appropriate expert evidence) which is more than fear, distress, or panic.

(d) A conviction can be obtained if actual bodily harm is caused to the victim by some action which is the natural and reasonably foreseeable result of what the defendant said or did.

(e) Consider section 20 or 18 of the Offences Against the Person Act 1861 for more serious injuries, (see **5.8.3.2** and **5.8.3.3**) for more details.

(f) If racially or religiously aggravated, the more serious racially/religiously aggravated offence should be considered.

(g) Ensure that visible injuries are photographed.

(h) Include in CJA witness statement details of the injuries, circumstances of the incident, include any evidence as to intent or recklessness.

(i) Obtain medical evidence (hospital or doctor).

Defences

Accident (as long as malice is not present)

Self-defence

In cases of self-defence—'A jury must decide whether a defendant honestly believed that the circumstances were such as required him to use force to defend himself from an attack or threatened attack; the jury has then to decide whether the force used was reasonable in the circumstances' (R v Owino [1996] 2 Cr App R 128, CA and DPP v Armstrong-Braun [1999] Crim LR 417.

Related cases

H v DPP [2007] EWHC 960, QBD It is not necessary to identify which particular injury had been caused by which defendant provided that some injury resulting in actual bodily harm had been caused by the defendant.

R v Savage; R v Parmenter [1992] 1 AC 699 HL No intent to cause injury is needed for assault occasioning actual bodily harm.

PNLD reference numbers

H4722, H4723, H479, D374, D377, C202, C1475

 Time limit for prosecution: None.

 Summary: Maximum six months' imprisonment and/or a fine not exceeding the statutory maximum.

 Indictment: Maximum five years' imprisonment.

5.8.3.2 Wounding or inflicting grievous bodily harm

Section 20 of the Offences Against the Person Act 1861 provides the offence of 'wounding or inflicting grievous bodily harm'.

Offence

Whosoever shall **unlawfully** and **maliciously wound** or **inflict** any **grievous bodily harm** upon any other person, either with or without any weapon or instrument shall be guilty of an offence.

Offences Against the Person Act 1861, s 20

Points to prove

✓ date and location
✓ unlawfully
✓ maliciously
✓ wounded/inflicted grievous bodily harm
✓ upon another person

Meanings

Unlawfully

Means without excuse or justification at law.

Maliciously

Means malice (ill-will or an evil motive) must be present. 'Maliciously requires either an actual intention to do the particular kind of harm that was done or recklessness whether any such harm should occur or not; it is neither limited to, nor does it require, any ill-will towards the person injured' (**R v Cunningham [1957] 2 All ER 412, CA**).

Recklessness

Is one element of the term 'maliciously'. In **R v Cunningham [1957] 2 All ER 412, CA** it was held that the prosecution have to prove that the defendant was aware of the existence of the risk but nonetheless had gone on and taken it.

Wound

Means any break in the continuity of the whole skin.

Inflict

Does not have as wide a meaning as 'cause'—grievous bodily harm can be inflicted without there being an assault.

Grievous bodily harm

Means 'serious or really serious harm' (**R v Saunders [1985] Crim LR 230, CA**). Bodily harm can include inflicting/causing a psychiatric harm/illness (silent/heavy breathing/menacing telephone calls—**R v Ireland [1998] AC 147, HL**). It could include psychiatric injury, in serious cases, as well as physical injury (stalking victim— **R v Burstow [1997] 4 All ER 225, HL**).

Police powers

Power of arrest—section 24 of the Police and Criminal Evidence Act 1984

Powers of entry and search—sections 17, 18 and 32 of the Police and Criminal Evidence Act 1984

Notes

(a) If it appears possible that the target of the attack was not the actual victim, then the 'doctrine of transferred malice' provides that if a person mistakenly causes injury to a person other than the person who he intended to attack, he will commit the same offence as if he had injured the intended victim. The doctrine only applies if the crime remains the same and the harm done must be of the same kind as the harm intended (**R v Latimer (1886) 17 QBD 359, QBD**).

(b) As wounding and grievous bodily harm are both different, the distinction as to which offence is appropriate should be made.

(c) A section 47 assault (AOABH, see **5.8.3.1**) can be an alternative verdict if it includes implications of assault occasioning actual bodily harm.

(d) Where appropriate, consider the more serious racially/religiously aggravated offence.

(e) The distinction between 'wound' and 'GBH' must be identified and considered, as they do not have the same meaning. Where both a wound and grievous bodily harm have been inflicted, choose which part of s 20 reflects the true nature of the offence (**R v McCready [1978] 1 WLR 1376, CA**).

(f) The prosecution must prove under section 20 that either the defendant intended, or actually foresaw, that the act would cause harm and that the defendant was aware of the existence of the risk but nonetheless went on to take it. It is not necessary to prove these elements in relation to the extent of the specific injuries received.

(g) The section 18 offence (see **5.8.3.3**) requires intent while section 20 is 'unlawfully and maliciously'.

(h) A section 47 assault (see **5.8.3.1**) can be an alternative verdict to section 20 if it includes implications of assault occasioning actual bodily harm.

(i) Consideration must be given to CPS advice and the specific guidance for unlawful wounding/inflicting GBH which is as follows—the distinction between charges under section 18 and section 20 is one of intent. The gravity of the injury resulting is not the determining factor, although it may provide some evidence of intent.

(j) Wounding means the breaking of the continuity of the whole of the outer skin, or the inner skin within the cheek or lip. It does not include the rupturing of internal blood vessels. Wounds within this definition are sometimes minor, such as a small cut or laceration. Such minor injuries should more appropriately be charged under section 47. Section 20 should be reserved for those wounds considered to be serious (thus equating the offences with the infliction of grievous, or serious, bodily harm under the other part of the section).

(k) Grievous bodily harm means serious bodily harm. Examples of this are—injury resulting in permanent disability or permanent loss of sensory function; injury which results in more than minor permanent, visible disfigurement; broken or displaced limbs or bones, including fractured skull, compound fractures, broken cheekbone, jaw, ribs, etc; injuries which cause substantial loss of blood, usually necessitating a transfusion; injuries resulting in lengthy treatment or incapacity; psychiatric injury. As with assault occasioning actual bodily harm expert evidence is essential to prove the injury.

(l) Obtain medical evidence to prove extent of injury.

(m) Obtain photographs of victim's injuries.

(n) 'Cunningham malice' will suffice. It is enough that the defendant should have foreseen that some physical harm might result—of whatever character.

Defences

A general defence may be available to a section 20 offence (see **5.8.3.1**).

Related cases

R v Wilson & Jenkins [1983] 3 All ER 448, HL Frightened by the defendant the victim jumps through a window and breaks a leg. Grievous bodily harm has been 'inflicted' by the offender by inducing substantial fear, even though there is no direct application of force.

R v Martin [1881–85] All ER 699, CA The defendant came out of a theatre, extinguished the lights, and placed a bar across the doorway. Panic was intended to be the natural consequences of his actions but, if in the ensuing panic, people suffered serious injuries the defendant will have 'inflicted GBH' on those people.

Attorney-General's Reference (No 3 of 1994) [1996] 2 All ER 10 The doctrine of transferred malice was accepted where the defendant stabbed his girlfriend knowing she was pregnant and the knife penetrated the foetus.

R v Cunningham [1957] 2 All ER 412, CA Meaning of 'maliciously' and recklessness test (above).

R v Savage [1992] 1 AC 699, HL and **DPP v Parmenter [1991] 3 WLR 914, HL** See above.

R v Wilson and Jenkins [1983] 3 All ER 448, HL 'Grievous bodily harm may be inflicted either by: directly and violently assaulting the victim; or something intentionally done which although in itself is not a direct application of force to the body of the victim, does directly result in force being applied to the body of the victim so that he suffers grievous bodily harm'.

PNLD reference numbers

H4720, H4721, H478, D373, D41, C44, C202, C45

 Time limit for prosecution: None.

 Summary: Maximum six months' imprisonment and/or a fine not exceeding the statutory maximum.

 Indictment: Maximum five years' imprisonment.

5.8.3.3 Wounding or grievous bodily harm—with intent

Section 18 of the Offences Against the Person Act 1861, creates the offences of 'wounding or causing grievous bodily harm with intent'.

> **Offence**
>
> Whosoever shall **unlawfully** and **maliciously** by **any means whatsoever wound** or cause any **grievous bodily harm** to any person **with intent** to do some grievous bodily harm to any person, or with intent to resist or prevent the lawful apprehension or detainer of any person, shall be guilty of an offence.
>
> Offences Against the Person Act 1861, s 18

Points to prove
- ✓ date and location
- ✓ unlawfully and maliciously
- ✓ cause grievous bodily harm or wounded a person
- ✓ with intent to
- ✓ do grievous bodily harm or resist/prevent lawful apprehension/detention of self/another

Meanings

The meanings given here have invariably been derived from case law.

Unlawfully (see **5.8.3.2**).

Maliciously (see **5.8.3.2**).

Any means whatsoever

This is given its literal meaning. The only thing that must be proved is a connection between the means used and the harm caused.

Wound (see 5.8.3.2).

Cause

This has been defined as 'anything that produces a result or effect'.

Grievous bodily harm (see 5.8.2).

Intent (see 5.8.2).

Resist

The Oxford Dictionary defines resist as 'to strive against; to oppose; try to impede or refuse to comply with'.

Prevent

The Oxford Dictionary defines prevent as 'to stop from happening or doing something; hinder; make impossible'.

Police powers

Power of arrest—section 24 of the Police and Criminal Evidence Act 1984

Powers of entry and search—sections 17, 18 and 32 of the Police and Criminal Evidence Act 1984

Notes

(a) Cause has a wider meaning than 'inflict'. All that needs to be proved is some connection between the action (the means used) and the injury (sometimes called the chain of causation). There does not need to be a direct application of force. The issue of causation is separate from the test for intent. An example would be where the defendant intends to assault a person and kicks down a door, making the victim jump out of the window to escape thereby suffering harm/injuries. There is clearly a causal link between the actions of the defendant and the victim's injuries and the chain of causation is unbroken.

(b) Intent must be proved either from verbal admissions on interview and/or other and incriminating evidence (eg subsequent actions).

(c) In relation to the offence of wounding or causing GBH with intent to resist or prevent the lawful arrest/detention of any person the following points must be proved—the arrest/

detention must be lawful and the person concerned must know that an arrest is being made on him or another person.

(d) Section 18 does not come under racially or religiously aggravated assaults. However, the courts must consider such matters when determining sentence.

(e) The essential ingredient here is intent: either a specific intent to cause grievous bodily harm or intent to resist arrest. Proof is required that the defendant specifically intended to cause grievous bodily harm. Knowledge that grievous bodily harm was a virtually certain consequence of his action will not amount to an intention, but it will be good evidence from which a court can infer such an intention. Other factors which may indicate the specific intent include—

- a repeated or planned attack;
- deliberate selection of a weapon or adaptation of an article to cause injury, such as breaking a glass before an attack;
- making prior threats;
- using an offensive weapon against, or kicking, the victim's head.

(f) Proof is required that the wound/GBH was inflicted maliciously. This means that the defendant must have foreseen some harm—although not necessarily the specific type or gravity of injury suffered or inflicted.

(g) Generally an assault under this section may take one of four different forms—

- wounding with intent to do grievous bodily harm;
- causing grievous bodily harm, with intent to do grievous bodily harm;
- wounding with intent to resist or prevent the lawful arrest/ detention of self/any person;
- maliciously causing grievous bodily harm with intent to resist or prevent the lawful arrest of self/any person.

(h) Where evidence of intent is absent, but a wound or grievous bodily harm is still caused, then both section 18 and section 20 should be included on the indictment.

(i) Consideration must be given to CPS advice and the specific guidance for wounding/causing GBH with intent—the distinction between charges under section 18 and section 20 is one of intent. The gravity of the injury resulting is not the determining factor, although it may provide some evidence of intent. In cases involving grievous bodily harm, remember that section 20 requires the infliction of harm, whereas section 18 requires the causing of harm, although this distinction has been greatly reduced by the decisions in **R v Ireland [1998] AC 147, HL** and **R v Burstow [1997] 4 All ER 225, HL** (see 2.3.1).

(j) A section 18 offence includes wounding or causing grievous bodily harm with intent to resist or prevent the lawful detention of any person. This part of section 18 is of assistance in more serious assaults upon police officers, where the evidence of an intention to prevent arrest is clear, but the evidence of intent to cause grievous bodily harm is in doubt.

(k) Section 6(3) of the Criminal Law Act 1967 permits a conviction of section 20: inflicting grievous bodily harm in respect of a count for section 18 causing grievous bodily harm with intent as 'cause' includes 'inflict' (**R v Wilson and Jenkins [1983] 3 All ER 448, HL**).

(l) Obtain medical evidence to prove extent of injury.

(m) Obtain photographs of victim's injuries.

Defences (see **5.8.3.1**).

Related cases

R v Belfon [1976] 3 All ER 46, CA For the offence of wounding with intent the prosecution must prove that the defendant wounded the victim; the wounding was deliberate and unjustified; with intent to cause really serious bodily harm; and the test of intent is subjective.

R v Roberts (1972) 56 Cr App R 95, CA A victim of an ongoing sexual assault jumped out of a car to escape and was seriously injured in doing so. The court considered the actions of a victim which could affect the 'chain of causation' and applied a 'causation test' to determine whether the harm/injury was the natural result of what the assailant had said or done—

- if the victim's actions are reasonable ones which could be foreseen and were acceptable under the circumstances, then the defendant will be liable for injuries resulting from them.
- if the harm/injury to the victim is really brought by a voluntary act on the part of the victim which could not reasonably be foreseen, then the chain of causation between the defendant's actions and the harm/injury received will be broken and the defendant will not be liable for them.

PNLD reference numbers

H2282, H2294, H476, H477, H5105, H5106, D366 - D371, D41, C115

 Time limit for prosecution: None.

 Indictment: Life imprisonment.

5.8.3.4 Threats to kill

Section 16 of the Offences Against the Person Act 1861 provides the offence of threats to kill. The offence of 'threats to kill' is a serious offence, particularly in its effect on the victim. Generally speaking, the threats are often made during a heated argument or a moment of aggression and it is not unusual for the case to fail to reach the courts owing to lack of proof of the required intent.

Offence

A person who, without lawful excuse makes to another a threat **intending** that the other would fear it would be carried out, to kill that other or a third person shall be guilty of an offence.

Offences Against the Person Act 1861, s 16

Points to prove

✓ date and location
✓ without lawful excuse
✓ made threat to kill
✓ intending to cause fear threat would be carried out

Meanings

Intending (see 'intent' at 5.8.2).

Police powers

Power of arrest—section 24 of the Police and Criminal Evidence Act 1984

Powers of entry and search—sections 17, 18 and 32 of the Police and Criminal Evidence Act 1984

Notes

(a) There is no need to show that the defendant intended to kill anyone. The relevant intent has to be that the person receiving the threat would fear the threat (to kill them or a third person) would be carried out.

(b) The onus is on the prosecution to prove that there was no lawful excuse for making a threat. The jury should be directed to any facts that could give rise to a defence of lawful excuse which was reasonable. It is for the jury to decide what is reasonable and what amounts to a threat.

(c) Consider hearsay and bad character admissibility under the Criminal Justice Act 2003.

(d) Proof of the mens rea ('guilty mind'), is required, that means the intention that the other person would fear the threat would be carried out to kill that person or a third person.

(e) Evidence of previous history between the parties is admissible as tending to prove that the defendant intended his words to be taken seriously.

(f) Detail in file and CJA witness statements the following points:

- nature of the threats made—exact words used and in what context, include any previous threats made;

- the fact that the threat was understood by the person to whom it was made and that the person feared the threat would be carried out;

- describe the full circumstances of the incident, antecedent history details of the relationship between the defendant and complainant.

(g) Does the defendant have a lawful excuse (defence) for making the threat?

(h) Consider whether or not there are any 'aggravating' circumstances such as racial or religious motivation or terrorism.

(i) See case study at **3.1.8**.

Defences

The specific statutory defence to this offence is having a lawful excuse. Such excuse could arise from a number of sources, including the prevention of crime or self-defence.

The defence will only apply if it was reasonable in all the circumstances to make the threat.

Related cases

R v Rizwan Mawji [2003] EWCA Crim 3067, CA Where a threat to kill was made to a victim by e-mail and s/he printed that e-mail, it could be adduced in evidence after s/he had given oral evidence without offending the rules of hearsay.

R v Williams (Clarence Ivor) (1987) 84 Cr App R 299, CA On a charge of threats to kill, evidence of a previous assault is admissible by the judge as it went to the seriousness of the threat and tended to prove that the accused intended his victim to take the threat seriously.

R v Cousins [1982] 2 All ER 115, CA A lawful excuse can exist if a threat to kill is made for the prevention of crime or for self-defence, provided that it is reasonable in the circumstances to make such a threat.

PNLD reference numbers

H2144, D6785

 Time limit for prosecution: None.

 Summary: Maximum six months' imprisonment and/or a fine not exceeding the statutory maximum.

 Indictment: Maximum ten years' imprisonment.

5.8.3.5 Kidnap

Kidnapping is an offence at common law.

Offence

The taking or carrying away of one person by another, by force or **fraud**, without the consent of the person so taken or carried away, and without lawful excuse.

Points to prove

✓ date and location
✓ without lawful excuse
✓ by force/fraud
✓ took/carried away
✓ another person
✓ without his consent

Meanings

Fraud

Means deceit/guile/trick. It should not be confused with the narrower meaning given to it for the purposes of consent in sexual offences.

Notes

(a) The important points to prove are the deprivation of liberty and carrying away even where a short distance is involved— and the absence of consent.

(b) In the case of a child it is the child's consent that should be considered (rather than the parent/guardian) and in the case of a very young child, absence of consent may be inferred.

Defences

Consent or lawful excuse.

Related cases

R v Hendy-Freegard [2007] EWCA Crim 1236, CA The victim must have been deprived of their liberty by the kidnapper for the offence to be made out. Inducing a person by deception to move from one place to another unaccompanied by the 'kidnapper' could not constitute a taking and carrying away or deprivation of liberty.

R v Wellard [1978] 3 All ER 161, CA The defendant purported to be a police officer and escorted/placed a female victim into his car a short distance away. It was held that the ingredients of the offence of kidnapping are: that the victim was deprived of their liberty; and carried away from the place where they wanted to be without lawful excuse.

R v Cort [2003] 3 WLR 1300, CA The defendant went to bus stops telling lone women that the bus they were waiting for had broken down and offering/providing lifts in his vehicle. The fact that the defendant had lied about the absence of the buses meant that, although they had gotten into the car voluntarily, the women had not given true consent to the journey and the offences of kidnap (and attempts) were complete.

PNLD reference numbers

H2156, H5104, D489, C1520, C135

 Time limit for prosecution: None.

 Indictment: Life imprisonment and/or unlimited fine.

5.8.4 **Murder and manslaughter**

The offence of murder comes under the common law and is defined as:

> ### Offence (at common law)
>
> Where a person of **sound mind and discretion unlawfully kills** any reasonable creature in being and **under the Queen's peace**, with intent to kill or cause grievous bodily harm.

Points to prove
- ✓ date and location
- ✓ unlawfully
- ✓ killed
- ✓ a human being
- ✓ with intent to kill or cause grievous bodily harm

Meanings

Sound mind and discretion

Every person of the age of discretion is presumed to be sane and accountable for his actions, unless the contrary is proved. This means anyone who is not insane or is under ten years old.

Unlawfully

Means without lawful authority, legal justification, or excuse.

Kills

This is 'the act' ('actus reus') which is the substantial cause of death (stabbed, shot, strangled, suffocated, poisoned, etc).

Reasonable creature in being

Any human being, including a baby born alive having an independent existence from its mother.

Under the Queen's peace

This is meant to exclude killing in the course of war. A British subject takes the Queen's peace with them everywhere in the world.

Intent

Intention is not defined but has to be proved. It can be proved by drawing on two sources of information or by a combination of both.

1. By admissions made by the defendant in interview with reference to his state of mind at the time of commission of the offence and his answers to questions with regard to his actions and intentions at the time of the offence.
2. By inference from the circumstances of the offence, any evidence from witnesses, the defendant's actions and property found on him or in his control, such as a motor vehicle for transporting property. To prove intent, an officer needs to take all this into account, the important thing is that he has to prove the defendant's state of mind at the time.

Cause/causation

If there is an 'intervening factor' between the defendant's actions and the death of the victim, the jury will consider whether the defendant's act contributed significantly to the death.

Grievous bodily harm

Means 'serious or really serious harm' **(R v Saunders [1985] Crim LR 230, CA)**. Bodily harm can include inflicting/causing a psychiatric harm/illness (silent/heavy breathing/menacing telephone calls—R v Ireland [1998] AC 147, HL). It could include psychiatric injury, in serious cases, as well as physical injury (stalking victim—R v Burstow [1997] 4 All ER 225, HL).

Police powers

Power of arrest—section 24 of the Police and Criminal Evidence Act 1984

Powers of entry and search—sections 17, 18 and 32 of the Police and Criminal Evidence Act 1984

Notes

(a) If a defendant wishes to plead insanity, they will be judged on McNaughten's Rules from **McNaughten's Case (1843) 10 Cl & F 200**. This examines the extent to which, at the time of the commission of the offence, the person was 'labouring under such defect of reason from disease of the mind that either: (a) the defendant did not know what he was doing, or (b) he did know what he was doing but did not know it was wrong.'

(b) The onus is on the prosecution to prove that the killing was unlawful.

(c) If a person intentionally causes grievous bodily harm and the victim subsequently dies as a result, he is guilty of murder.

(d) Traditionally it required 'malice aforethought', but practically it is the relevant intent that will determine whether an unlawful killing is murder or manslaughter.

(e) The jury will consider whether the defendant's act contributed significantly to the death by applying the 'substantial test' as set out in **R v Smith [1959] 2 All ER 193, Court Martial CA**.

(f) Whether the defendant intended or foresaw the results of his actions will be determined by a number of factors.

(g) The defendant's act must be the substantial cause of death.

(h) The killing must be causally related to the acts of the defendant and not through an intervening factor which breaks the chain of causation. If there is doubt whether death was caused by some supervening event (such as medical negligence when treated), the prosecution do not have to prove that the supervening event was not a significant cause of death.

(i) Intention has to be proved (see above).

(j) The date of the offence is the actual date of death.

(k) Consent of the Attorney-General is required where the injury was sustained more than three years before death; or the accused has been previously convicted of the offence alleged to be connected with the death.

(l) If a person is suffering from a terminal disease and receives a wound that hastens their death, this killing would (with the required intent) be murder or manslaughter.

(m) A murder or manslaughter committed by a British citizen outside the UK may be tried in this country as if it had been committed here (Offences Against the Person Act 1861, s 9, and the British Nationality Act 1948, s 3).

(n) Motivation will form a key part of any prosecution and will also be relevant in considering the availability of special or general defences. Motivation, such as revenge, would mean that a person has had time to think/reflect so negating the defence of provocation (no sudden and temporary loss of self-control) and increasing the likelihood that the defendant foresaw the consequences of his actions and therefore that he intended them to happen.

(o) The only mens rea that will suffice for attempted murder is an intent to kill and the defence of diminished responsibility cannot be used in answer to such a charge.

(p) Section 2(1) of the Suicide Act 1961 creates the offence of aiding and abetting a suicide: 'A person who aids, abets, counsels or procures the suicide of another, or an attempt by another, shall be liable on conviction on indictment to imprisonment for a term not exceeding 14 years.'

Defences to murder

Insanity

See the meaning of 'sound mind and discretion' and explanatory notes as to 'insanity'.

Lawful killing

Means with lawful authority; legal justification or excuse

Self-defence

At war

This is self explanatory, not being under the 'Queen's peace' (see meaning above).

Specific defences

Provocation

Where on a charge of murder there is evidence on which the jury can find that the person charged was provoked (whether by things done or by things said or by both together) to lose his self-control, the question whether the provocation was enough to make a reasonable man do as he did shall be left to be determined by the jury; and in determining that question the jury shall take into account everything both done and said according to the effect which, in their opinion, it would have on a reasonable man (Homicide Act 1957, s 3).

Diminished responsibility

Where a person kills or is party to the killing of another, he shall not be convicted of murder if he was suffering from such abnormality of mind (whether arising from a condition of arrested or retarded development of mind or any inherent causes or induced by disease or injury) as substantially impaired his mental responsibility for his acts and omissions in doing or being party to the killing (Homicide Act 1957, s 2(1)).

Suicide pact

Means a common agreement between two or more persons having for its object the death of all of them, whether or not each is to take his own life, but nothing done by a person who enters into a suicide pact shall be treated as done by him in pursuance of the pact unless it is done while he has the settled intention of dying in pursuance of the pact (Homicide Act 1957, s 4(3)).

Related cases

R v Byrne [1960] 3 All ER 1, CA An abnormality of mind (diminished responsibility defence) is a 'state of mind so different from that of ordinary, reasonable human beings that they would call it abnormal'.

R v Smith [1959] 2 All ER 193, Court Martial CA Only if the second cause is so overwhelming as to make the original wound merely part of the history can it be said that the death does not flow from the wound.

R v Malcherek; R v Steel [1981] 2 All ER 422 A defendant (who causes injury) necessitating medical treatment could not argue that the sole cause of death was the doctor's action in switching the life support system off.

R v Moloney [1985] 1 All ER 1025, HL The jury has to decide whether the defendant intended to kill or cause grievous bodily harm.

R v Smith [2001] 1 AC 146, HL Provocation requires some act by the victim, which causes the defendant a sudden temporary loss of self-control. The considerations for the jury in such cases are technically complex and require a consideration of both subjective and objective elements.

PNLD reference numbers

H2172, H2173, D6753–D6763, C342

 Time limit for prosecution: None.

 Indictment: Life imprisonment.

5.8.4.1 Soliciting to commit murder

Section 4 of the Offences Against the Person Act 1861 sets out the offence of soliciting to commit murder.

> **Offence**
>
> Whosoever shall **solicit**, encourage, persuade or **endeavour** to persuade, or shall propose to any person, to **murder** any other person, whether he be a **subject of her Majesty** or not, and whether he be within the **Queen's dominions** or not, shall be guilty of an offence.
>
> Offences Against the Person Act 1861, s 4

Points to prove
- ✓ date and location
- ✓ solicited/encouraged/persuaded/endeavour to persuade/ proposed to murder another person

---

Meanings

Solicit

The Oxford Dictionary defines it as 'ask for or try to obtain (something) from someone, ask for something from'.

Endeavour

The Oxford Dictionary defines it as 'try hard to do or achieve something'.

Murder (see 5.8.4).

Subject of her Majesty

Means a British subject.

Queen's dominions

Means within independent countries under Sovereign authority (eg Australia).

Police powers

Power of arrest—section 24 of the Police and Criminal Evidence Act 1984

Powers of entry and search—sections 17, 18 and 32 of the Police and Criminal Evidence Act 1984

Notes

(a) To constitute soliciting there must be some communication between the accused and the person solicited, however it is not necessary to prove that the mind of the person solicited was affected by the soliciting. In the absence of actual communication, there may be a conviction of attempted solicitation. In the case of **R v Banks (1873) 12 Cox 393** the solicitation was by letter with no evidence of it having been received by the person solicited.

(b) The publication and circulation of an article in a newspaper may be an encouragement, or endeavour to persuade to murder, even though not addressed to any person in particular.

(c) The intended victim need not be identified; need not be a British subject or even be in the country. Solicitation against a particular class is sufficient, for example a particular race or religion.

Related cases

R v Winter [2007] EWCA Crim 3493 Section 4 of the Offences Against the Person Act 1861 was sufficiently wide enough to include soliciting a person to act as a secondary party to murder. Such an offence can be committed by numerous persons playing their part, it matters not whether they played no part in the actual killing. There is a difference between soliciting and assisting murder and for solicitation the jury must be satisfied that someone had formed a plan in advance of encouraging others to join in.

R v Abu Hamza [2006] EWCA Crim 2918 The common law principle is that an inchoate offence could not be committed unless the conduct planned or incited would, if enacted, be an indictable offence in England, but section 4 of the Offences Against the Person Act 1861 was an exception to the rule. The loophole that Parliament sought to close when enacting this section was to deal with the conduct of visitors in England in relation to murders or attempted murders outside the jurisdiction. In light of this it would not be sensible to restrict the offence to murderers who were British citizens. Section 4 does not imply that conspirators or those incited should be British citizens either. Murder is such a grave crime that it would be absurd to distinguish between inciting a British citizen within the English jurisdiction to commit it and inciting a foreigner to do so.

PNLD reference numbers

H9210, H9211, D6784, C1547, C1490

 Time limit for prosecution: None.

 Indictment: Life imprisonment, although case law shows that seven years' imprisonment has been the common maximum penalty.

5.8.4.2 Manslaughter

Manslaughter is an offence at common law and is defined as:

Offence

Manslaughter is the unlawful killing of another human being which can either be a voluntary or involuntary manslaughter offence.

Points to prove

✓ date and location
✓ unlawful act or gross negligence
✓ killed
✓ a human being

Meanings

Unlawful killing (see 'murder' at **5.8.4**).

Voluntary manslaughter

This occurs when a murder charge is reduced to voluntary manslaughter by reason of one of the specific defences to murder (see above).

Involuntary manslaughter

Is an unlawful killing without an intention to kill or cause grievous bodily harm. Apart from the required intent, the elements of the offence are the same as for murder (see above). Manslaughter can be caused by:

- unlawful act (not omission): The unlawful act must be unlawful in itself (eg another criminal offence such as an assault or a threat to kill) and must involve a risk that someone would be harmed by it;
- gross negligence (involving breach of duty): gross negligence manslaughter requires a breach of a duty of care owed by the defendant to the victim under circumstances where the defendant's conduct was serious enough to amount to a crime.

Police powers

Power of arrest—section 24 of the Police and Criminal Evidence Act 1984

Powers of entry and search—sections 17, 18 and 32 of the Police and Criminal Evidence Act 1984

Notes

(a) The previous convictions or past behaviour of the defendant in homicide cases may well be relevant, both to the issue of mens rea/intent and also to sentence.

(b) The burden of proof in relation to claiming diminished responsibility or acting in pursuance of a suicide pact lies with the defendant.

(c) Acts having fatal consequences for another person can arise in a number of forms—from workplace accidents to calculated acts of violence.

(d) Motivation will form a key part of any prosecution and will also be relevant in considering the availability of special or general defences. Motivation such as revenge would mean that a person has had time to think/reflect so negating the defence of provocation (no sudden and temporary loss of self-control) and increasing the likelihood that the defendant foresaw the consequences of their actions and therefore that they intended them to happen.

(e) The only mens rea that will suffice for attempted murder is an intention to kill and the defence of diminished responsibility cannot be used in answer to such a charge.

(f) Section 2(1) of the Suicide Act 1961 creates the offence of aiding and abetting a suicide (see note (p) at **5.8.4**).

Related cases

R v Roberts, Day I and Day M [2001] EWCA Crim 1594, An intent to cause GBH is murder but an intention only to do some lesser harm is manslaughter.

R v Prentice, and Hollaway Adomako Sulman [1993] 4 All ER 935, HL Manslaughter by gross negligence requires—

• that the defendant owed a duty of care to the victim;
• a breach of that duty;
• which caused the victim's death; and
• in circumstances where the defendant's conduct was so bad as to amount to a criminal act.

PNLD reference numbers

H2169, H2097, D6780, D6781, D6782, C236, C673

 Time limit for prosecution: None.

 Indictment: Life imprisonment.

5.8.5 **Criminal damage**

Section 1 of the Criminal Damage Act 1971 creates the offence of simple 'criminal damage'. The offence of criminal damage is designed to protect people's property from the unlawful actions of others.

Offences

A person who without lawful excuse **destroys** or **damages** any **property** belonging to another **intending** to destroy or damage any such property or being **reckless** as to whether any such property would be destroyed or damaged shall be guilty of an offence.

Criminal Damage Act 1971, s 1(1)

Points to prove

✓ date and location
✓ without lawful excuse
✓ destroyed/damaged
✓ property to value of
✓ intending to
✓ destroy/damage such property or
✓ being reckless whether it was destroyed/damaged.

Meanings

Destroys

Means property becomes incapable of being repaired and can only be replaced.

Damaged

Means the property has suffered some physical harm, impairment, or deterioration.

Property

Means property of a tangible nature, whether real or personal, including money and—

(a) including wild creatures which have been tamed or are ordinarily kept in captivity, and any other wild creatures or their carcasses if, but only if, they have been reduced into possession which has not been lost or abandoned or are in the course of being reduced into possession; but

---

(b) not including mushrooms growing wild on any land or flowers, fruit or foliage of a plant growing wild on any land (s10(1)).

Belonging to another

This is property that belongs to another person who has custody or control of it, or who has a right or an interest in it, or has a charge over it.

Intending

Intention is not defined but has to be proved. It can be proved by drawing on two sources of information or by a combination of both.

1. By admissions made by the defendant in interview with reference to his state of mind at the time of commission of the offence and his answers to questions with regard to his actions and intentions at the time of the offence.
2. By inference from the circumstances of the offence, any evidence from witnesses, the defendant's actions and property found on him or in his control, such as a motor vehicle for transporting property. To prove intent, an officer needs to take all this into account, the important thing is that he has to prove the defendant's state of mind at the time.

Reckless

The test set out in **R v G and R [2003] UKHL 50** applies, which states that a person acts 'recklessly' for the purposes of section 1 with respect to—

- circumstances where that person is aware of a risk that exists or will exist;
- a result when s/he is aware of a risk that it will occur;

  and it is, in the circumstances known to him, unreasonable to take the risk.

The first part provides for those existing or future circumstances known to the defendant which, in the circumstances as known to him, made it unreasonable to take the risk he took. An example would be a tramp taking shelter in a barn full of dry hay. Aware of the risk, he lights a fire to boil water for a cup of tea, and sets the barn alight.

The second part of the test applies if the person is aware that the result of his actions are a risk and, in the circumstances as known to him, it would be unreasonable to take that risk. An example would be an adult who lets off a large rocket and ignores instructions which state that the firework should be launched from a tube embedded in the ground and instead launches it from a bottle standing upright on the pavement. As a result the rocket goes through the window of a house opposite and causes a fire.

The case of **G and R** involved two children aged 11 and 12 who set fire to a shop when lighting newspapers in a yard at the back. It was argued in their defence that, although the act might have been an obvious risk to the average person, it might not be obvious to such young children. The House of Lords agreed and overturned the previous 'objective' test in the case of **R v Caldwell [1981] 1 All ER 961**.

Police powers

Power of arrest—section 24 of the Police and Criminal Evidence Act 1984

Powers of entry and search—sections 17, 18 and 32 of the Police and Criminal Evidence Act 1984

Section 6 of the Criminal Damage Act 1971 provides for a warrant to search for and seize anything in the custody or control of a suspect on his premises having reasonable cause to believe, has been used or is intended for use without lawful excuse to either destroy or damage property belonging to another or in a way likely to endanger the life of another.

Notes

(a) The important thing to prove or disprove (in addition to the damage itself) is the state of mind (intent) or that the defendant was reckless in his actions, in destroying/damaging the property.

(b) If property has been destroyed, the value specified in the charge should reflect the full replacement cost.

(c) Charging that property was both 'destroyed' and 'damaged' is an unnecessary duplication, so wherever possible a choice should be made.

(d) If the destruction or damage has been caused by fire, an offence of arson under section 1(3) should be charged.

(e) Consider the more serious offence of racially or religiously aggravated criminal damage where appropriate.

(f) Where the value of the damage is below £5,000, the offence would normally be tried at a magistrates' court.

(g) If the full offence is not committed consider attempted criminal damage.

(h) The same incident may involve separate activities, some causing ordinary damage and some damage by fire (for example, protestors break into a laboratory building, smash laboratory equipment and set fire to some files). In such circumstances they are separate offences and best charged as such.

Defence

Lawful excuse

(1) This section applies to any offence under section 1(1) and any offence under section 2 or 3 other than one involving a threat by the person charged to destroy or damage property in a way which he knows is likely to endanger the life of another or involving an intent by the person charged to use or cause or permit the use of something in his custody or under his control so to destroy or damage property.

(2) A person charged with an offence to which this section applies shall, whether or not he would be treated for the purposes of this Act as having a lawful excuse apart from this subsection, be treated for those purposes as having a lawful excuse—

   (a) if at the time of the act or acts alleged to constitute the offence he believed that the person or persons whom he believed to be entitled to consent to the destruction of or damage to the property in question had so consented, or would have so consented to it if he or they had known of the destruction or damage and its circumstances; or

   (b) if he destroyed or damaged or threatened to destroy or damage the property in question or, in the case of a charge of an offence under section 3, intended to use or cause or permit the use of something to destroy or damage it, in order to protect property belonging to himself or another or a right or interest in property which was or which he believed to be vested in himself or another, and at the time of the act or acts alleged to constitute the offence he believed—

      (i) that the property, right or interest was in immediate need of protection; and

      (ii) that the means of protection adopted or proposed to be adopted were or would be reasonable having regard to all the circumstances.

(3) For the purposes of this section it is immaterial whether a belief is justified or not if it is honestly held.

Protect life or property

(4) For the purposes of sub-section (2) above a right or interest in property includes any right or privilege in or over land, whether created by grant, licence or otherwise.

(5) This section shall not be construed as casting doubt on any defence recognized by law as a defence to criminal charges.

Criminal Damage Act 1971, s 5(1)–(5)

The courts have accepted that damage caused to protect life, prevent injury, or stop unlawful imprisonment of a person is also a valid defence (**R v Baker, The Times, 26 November 1996**).

Related cases

R v Jones and others; Ayliffe and others v DPP, Swain v DPP [2006] UKHL 16, HL The defendants took part in protests at military bases against the war in Iraq and damaged the perimeter fence and vehicles. They claimed that this damage was done to prevent the international crime of aggression and so they had a 'lawful excuse' under section 5. It was held that the right of citizens to use force or cause damage on their own initiative is limited when not defending their own person or property and furthermore does not cover customary international law.

Johnson v DPP [1994] Crim LR 673, QBD When lawful excuse is the defence, two questions need to be asked. The first is an objective question (eg whether the act of damage was done in order to protect property); and the second, a subjective question (whether the defendant believed that the property was in immediate need of protection and the means of protection used were reasonable).

Chamberlain v Lindon, The Times, 6 April 1998 The requirement of immediacy (under section 5(2)(b)(i) above) will still be satisfied if the threat to property (or rights in property) is already taking place. Here, the defendant was charged with criminal damage after destroying a wall erected by his neighbour which obstructed a right of access to his property. The court held that the defendant had a lawful excuse for his action because the obstruction to his rights had already happened and he believed that his rights would be further prejudiced if the wall remained in place.

Drake v DPP [1994] Crim LR 855, QBD Damage must affect the integrity of the object damaged.

PNLD reference numbers

H2081, H2082, H2090, D127, D128, D140, D37

 Time limit for prosecution: None.

 Summary: Value below £5,000: Maximum three months imprisonment and/or a fine not exceeding level four on the standard scale. Value of or exceeding £5,000: Maximum six months' imprisonment and/or a fine not exceeding the statutory maximum.

 Indictment: Maximum ten years' imprisonment.

5.8.5.1 Damage with intent to endanger life and arson

The offence of damage with intent to endanger life is also known as aggravated damage. This and arson are serious offences because of their potential to have disastrous effects on other people's lives and the wider community.

This section is presented in two parts: damage with intent to endanger life and then arson.

5.8.5.2 Damage with intent to endanger life

Section 1(2) of the Criminal Damage Act 1971 creates the serious offence of destroying or damaging property intending that, or being reckless as to whether life would be endangered.

Offence

A person who without lawful excuse, destroys or damages any property, whether belonging to himself or another—
(a) intending to destroy or damage any property or being reckless as to whether any property would be destroyed or damaged; and
(b) intending by the destruction or damage to endanger the life of another or being reckless as to whether the life of another would be thereby endangered;
shall be guilty of an offence.

Criminal Damage Act 1971, s 1(2)

Points to prove

✓ date and location
✓ without lawful excuse
✓ destroy/damage
✓ property
✓ whether belonging to self or another
✓ with intent to destroy/damage or reckless destroy/damage *and*
✓ intending by destruction/damage to endanger life of another *or*
✓ being reckless as to whether such life would thereby be endangered.

Meanings

Lawful excuse (see Defence at **5.8.5**).

Intent (see **5.8.5**).

Destroy (see **5.8.5**).

Damage (see **5.8.5**).

Property (see **5.8.5**).

Belonging to another (see **5.8.5**).

Endanger life

This does not require an attempt to kill nor for any actual injury to occur. It is sufficient that life was endangered.

Reckless (see above).

Police powers

Power of arrest—section 24 of the Police and Criminal Evidence Act 1984

Powers of entry and search—sections 17, 18 and 32 of the Police and Criminal Evidence Act 1984

Notes

(a) Consider attempted murder or manslaughter where appropriate (see **5.8.4**).

(b) No actual injury need occur; all that is required is evidence that life was endangered. For example, if a jealous person cuts the brake pipe of his rival's car, no harm may actually come to the intended victim, but the potential for harm exists. Either intention to endanger the life of another or recklessness in that regard must be proved and the potential for harm to someone other than the defendant must be proved.

(c) The actual damage caused must also be the cause of the danger. For example, shooting at a person in a room (through a window) both endangers life and damages the window, but it is not the damage that endangers the life.

(d) The same incident may involve separate activities, some causing ordinary damage and some damage by fire (for example, protestors break into a laboratory building, smash laboratory equipment, and set fire to some files). In such circumstances they are separate offences and best charged as such.

(e) Damage by fire is arson (see **5.8.5.3**).

Defence

See **5.8.5**.

Related cases

R v Webster & others [1995] 2 All ER 168, CA Intent to damage causing injury/endangerment to life. Two similar cases related to the offence of 'damage with intent to endanger life'. In the first case, the defendants pushed a coping stone from a bridge onto a moving railway carriage. No one was injured. The court decided that the principal intention of the defendants was not for the stone to directly injure the passengers, therefore the offence of 'damage intending to endanger life' had not been committed. However, the court substituted a conviction for the offence of 'recklessness causing damage which could endanger life' (eg the debris that flew around the carriage following the incident). In the second case, the defendants threw bricks at a police car from a stolen car, aiming for its windscreen. The windscreen broke and injured one of the officers. In that case, the victim's resultant loss of vision would be sufficient for a conviction for the offence of causing damage with intent to endanger life. Establishing intention is important, so therefore ask in interview what the offender's intentions were or what he perceived the outcome of his actions would be.

R v Hardie [1984] 3 All ER 848, CA Recklessness after defendant has taken drugs is insufficient as defendant could not form the necessary mens rea.

R v Steer [1988] AC 111 The actual damage caused must give rise to the danger to life, not just the act of causing the damage.

PNLD reference numbers

H4369, H4372, H469, D130, D132

 Time limit for prosecution: None.

 Indictment: Life imprisonment.

5.8.5.3 Arson

Section 1(3) of the Criminal Damage Act 1971 creates the offence of 'arson'.

> #### Offence
>
> An offence committed under this section by **destroying** or **damaging property** by fire shall be charged as arson.
>
> Criminal Damage Act 1971, s 1(3)

Points to prove

Arson

- ✓ date and location
- ✓ without lawful excuse
- ✓ destroyed/damaged
- ✓ by fire
- ✓ property with intent to destroy/damage it
- ✓ or being reckless as to whether such property was destroyed/damaged

Arson—endanger life

- ✓ all points to prove for arson (above) and
- ✓ intending by that destruction/damage to endanger life of another or
- ✓ being reckless as to whether life of another would thereby be endangered

Meanings

Destroy (see 5.8.5).

Damage (see 5.8.5).

Property (see 5.8.5).

Police powers

Power of arrest—section 24 of the Police and Criminal Evidence Act 1984

Powers of entry and search—sections 17, 18 and 32 of the Police and Criminal Evidence Act 1984

Notes

(a) For the offence to be complete, some of the damage must be by fire; this does not include smoke damage. It is enough, however, that wood is charred (**R v Parker (1839) 9 C & P 45**).

(b) Intention or recklessness must be proved. A burglar who accidentally dropped a lighted match used for illumination could be reckless.

(c) The same incident may involve separate activities, some causing ordinary damage and some damage by fire. These are separate offences and should be so charged.

(d) Most arsons involve the use of 'accelerants' such as petrol or lighter fuel to start the fire. If it is suspected that accelerants might have been used, special procedures need to be implemented in order to obtain forensic samples. An accelerant is used to increase the speed of a chemical reaction. For police purposes, this usually means something to speed up the spread of a fire during an arson attack. Accelerants (such as petrol) are volatile and will evaporate if left in the open air. Do not confuse accelerants with oils and greases, which demand different treatment.

(e) Procedures for the careful preservation and packaging which must be carried out to enable the detection of accelerants can be divided into three basic areas - clothing, at the scene, fragile items.

(f) Submit the control sample of the suspected accelerant in a clean metal container with a well-fitting cap, sealed inside a nylon bag. If no metal can is available, use a clean glass container but protect any rubber insert in the cap with a nylon film. For this purpose cut up part of one of the nylon bags, and use the rest as a control—see below. Isolate from all other samples.

(g) Control sample of nylon bag used to seal any sample: in a case where a nylon bag has been employed to seal a sample, a control nylon bag from the same batch as the one used to contain the samples should be submitted. This should be sealed but should only contain air.

(h) Important—never dry out items suspected of containing fire accelerants before packaging. Never store or transport items for examination for the presence of fire accelerant materials, in close proximity to a control sample of fire accelerant or anything taken from the defendant. Even a suspicion of contamination will destroy the evidential value of the samples.

Related cases

R v Drayton [2005] EWCA Crim 2013, CA A charge of causing criminal damage by fire under s 1(3) still constitutes a charge of arson even if 'arson' is not specifically stated in the charge.

PNLD reference numbers

H4372, H470, H471, H5101, H5102, D133, D655–D658, C1140

 Summary: Maximum six months' imprisonment and/or a fine not exceeding level five on the standard scale.

 Indictment: Life imprisonment.

5.8.5.4 Threats to destroy or damage property

Section 2 of the Criminal Damage Act 1971 creates specific offences relating to threats to destroy or damage property.

Offence

A person who without lawful excuse makes to another a threat, intending that the other would fear it would be carried out—
(a) to destroy or damage any property belonging to that other or a third person; or
(b) to destroy or damage his own property in way which he knows is likely to endanger the life of that other or a third person

shall be guilty of an offence.

Criminal Damage Act 1971, s 2

Points to prove

✓ date and location
✓ without lawful excuse
✓ threatened to destroy/damage property of a person
✓ intending
✓ a person would fear that the threat would be carried out

Threaten damage own property to endanger life

✓ date and location
✓ without lawful excuse
✓ threatened to destroy/damage
✓ your own property
✓ in a way you knew
✓ was likely to endanger life of another
✓ intending a person would fear threat would be carried out.

Meanings

Lawful excuse (see 5.8.5).

Intending (see 5.8.5).

Destroy (see 5.8.5).

Damage (see 5.8.5).

Property (see 5.8.5).

Endanger life (5.8.5.2).

Police powers

Power of arrest—section 24 of the Police and Criminal Evidence Act 1984

Powers of entry and search—sections 17, 18 and 32 of the Police and Criminal Evidence Act 1984

Notes

(a) It is not necessary to show the other person is actually in fear that the threat will be carried out; what has to be proved is that the defendant intended the other to fear it will be carried out.

(b) It does not matter that the defendant may not actually intend to carry out the threats and/or the victim may not even believe them. The offender's intention to create such a fear is sufficient—and necessary—to complete the offence.

(c) The test for whether the action amounts to a threat is objective, ie 'would the reasonable person conclude that a threat had been made?' (**R v Cakmak and others [2002] EWCA Crim 500**). Only intention will do; unlike section 1 there is no mention of recklessness in this section.

(d) The threat must be to another person, and can relate to a third party such as 'I will smash up your son's car if you don't do what I say'. The threat is to one person about his or a third person's property.

(e) In section 2(b) above, the offender can threaten to damage his own property in a way that is likely to endanger the life of another, such as a landlord threatening to burn down a house he owns if a tenant will not leave.

(f) In relation to the meaning of 'threats in criminal damage', two points must be considered—the type of conduct threatened; and the threat itself. There is no specific requirement for the threatened act to be immediate and a threat to do damage to a property at some time in the future may well suffice; each case will depend on the circumstances surrounding it.

Defence
Lawful excuse will be a defence under section 5 (see **5.8.5**).

PNLD reference numbers

H2278, H2280, D134

 Time limit for prosecution: None.

Summary: Maximum six months' imprisonment and/or a fine not exceeding the statutory maximum.

Indictment: Maximum ten years' imprisonment.

5.8.6 Encouraging or assisting an offence, conspiracy, aid and abet and attempt

5.8.6.1 Encouraging or assisting an offence

Sections 44 to 46 of the Serious Crime Act 2007 provide for the offences of encouraging or assisting an offence, these offences replace the common law offence of incitement.

Offences

44 (1) A person commits an offence if—
    (a) he does an act capable of encouraging or assisting the commission of an offence; and
    (b) he intends to encourage or assist its commission.

45   A person commits an offence if—
    (a) he does an act capable of encouraging or assisting the commission of an offence; and
    (b) he believes—
      (i) that the offence will be committed; and
      (ii) that his act will encourage or assist its commission.

46 (1) A person commits an offence if—
    (a) he does an act capable of encouraging or assisting the commission of one or more of a number of offences; and
    (b) he believes—
      (i) that one or more of those offences will be committed (but has no belief as to which); and
      (ii) that his act will encourage or assist the commission of one or more of them.

Serious Crime Act 2007, ss 44, 45, and 46

Meanings

An act capable of encouraging or assisting the commission of an offence

A person doing an act that is capable of encouraging the commission of an offence includes a reference to his doing so by threatening another person or otherwise putting pressure on another person to commit the offence.

A person doing an act that is capable of encouraging or assisting the commission of an offence includes a reference to his doing so by—

(a) taking steps to reduce the possibility of criminal proceedings being brought in respect of that offence;
(b) failing to take reasonable steps to discharge a duty.

But a person is not to be regarded as doing an act that is capable of encouraging or assisting the commission of an offence merely because he fails to respond to a constable's request for assistance in preventing a breach of the peace (Serious Crime Act 2007, s 65).

Police powers

Power of arrest—section 24 of the Police and Criminal Evidence Act 1984

Powers of entry and search—sections 17, 18 and 32 of the Police and Criminal Evidence Act 1984

If suspected terrorist then:

Power of arrest—section 41 of the Terrorism Act 2000, see **5.3.1**

Powers to stop and search—section 43 of the Terrorism Act 2000, see **5.2.1**

Defences

(1) A person is not guilty of an offence under this part *[part 2 (sections 44–67)]* if he proves—
   a) that he knew certain circumstances existed; and
   b) that it was reasonable for him to act as he did in those circumstances.
(2) A person is not guilty of an offence under this part if he proves—
   (a) that he believed certain circumstances to exist;
   (b) that his belief was reasonable; and
   (c) that it was reasonable for him to act as he did in the circumstances as he believed them to be.

Serious Crime Act 2007, s 50(1) and (2)

Factors that are to be taken into account when assessing reasonableness are—the seriousness of the anticipated offence (or, in the case of an offence under section 46, the offences specified in the indictment); any purpose for which he claims to have been acting; any authority by which he claims to have been acting (Serious Crime Act 2007 s 50(3)).

Note

There are details for the requirement of proof and other provisions for these offences contained in sections 47–49 of the Serious Crime Act 2007 (not reproduced here).

PNLD reference numbers

D21841–47

Penalty—as per the anticipated or reference offence.

5.8.6.2 Conspiracy

Section 1 of the Criminal Law Act 1977 sets out the offence of conspiracy.

Offence

If a person agrees with any other person or persons that a **course of conduct** shall be pursued which, if the agreement is carried out in accordance with their intentions either—

(a) will necessarily amount to or involve the commission of any offence or offences by one or more of the parties to the agreement; or

(b) would do so but for the existence of facts which render the commission of the offence or any of the offences impossible,

he is guilty of **conspiracy** to commit the offence or offences in question.

Criminal Law Act 1977, s 1(1)

Points to prove

✓ date and location
✓ conspired
✓ with
✓ person(s)
✓ to commit an offence

Meanings

Course of conduct

It is the course of conduct agreed upon that is critical. If that course involves an act to be carried out by an innocent party, the fact that he does not carry it out and thereby prevents the commission of the substantive offence, does not absolve the other parties to the agreement from liability (**R v Bolton (1992) 94 Cr App R 74**).

A course of conduct may be actual physical acts which the parties propose shall be done or it might include the consequences which they intend to follow from their conduct and the relevant circumstances which they know or believe or intend to exist. If it goes outside their intentions, there is no conspiracy. But there will still be primary liability for the consequences, eg A and B agree to cause GBH to X. X dies as a result. They are guilty of conspiracy to commit GBH. They are not guilty of conspiracy to murder. But they are guilty of murder.

Conspiracy

Means to agree together to plot, to scheme together, to devise together.

Police powers

Power of arrest—section 24 of the Police and Criminal Evidence Act 1984

Powers of entry and search—sections 17, 18 and 32 of the Police and Criminal Evidence Act 1984

Notes

(a) The offence of conspiracy lies between incitement and attempt and to some extent is a form of preventive measure to enable a legal intervention in a series of conduct to be carried out at an early stage to prevent a crime being committed.

(b) Conspiracy is a preliminary phase to the commission of many crimes but it is also a crime in its own right. The essence of the offence of conspiracy is an agreement. To constitute the offence, what occurs must go beyond the negotiation stage or intention and become a matter of agreement. This agreement could be indicated by letter, telephone, hand shake, nod, or bodily movement. Negotiations prior to a conspiracy could involve incitements by the parties to the negotiation. Therefore if a person pulls out at the planning stage before an agreement, there is no conspiracy. For example, a man is approached by a gang and asked if he knows anyone who is interested in taking part in a payroll robbery. He introduces a man to the gang who initially says he is interested but after discussion he refuses to take part and pulls out. This is only negotiation. An agreement had not been reached—**R v Walker [1962] Crim LR 458**.

(c) Nothing needs be done in pursuit of an agreement. The offence is complete with the agreement.

(d) Repentance, lack of opportunity or failure are all immaterial. The fact that a person withdraws from the agreement can only be used as mitigation.

(e) Section 1(1)(b) is very similar to the 'impossibility rule' in criminal attempts.

(f) Section 4 of the Criminal Law Act 1977 sets out the restriction on institution of proceedings where the defendants conspired to commit a summary only offence (the consent of the Director of Public Prosecution is required), and where the offence is subject to time limits re the institution of proceedings.

(g) Where the substantive offence includes an element of intent, it is advisable to specify this in the charge even though it may appear superfluous eg Conspired together with [specify person] to wound [specify person] with intent to do him grievous bodily harm.

(h) *Practical examples*—in relation to subsection 1(1)(a)—

    (i)   Two men agree to go out and break into a jeweller's to steal. Will their conduct necessarily amount to the commission of an offence by at least one of them? Yes, burglary; therefore once the agreement is reached a conspiracy exists.

    (ii)   Two men agree to embark on a simple burglary, unknown to his accomplice one of the men has with him a firearm. Is there a conspiracy? Yes, but only to burglary not aggravated burglary. The course of conduct agreed upon did not include the taking of a firearm.

Practical examples—in relation to subsection 1(1)(b)—

    (i)   Two men agree to rape a woman. They go to her home but find she is no longer there. Conspiracy.

    (ii)   Two men agree to go on a safe blowing expedition, but when they arrive they find their explosives are not capable of blowing the safe. Conspiracy.

    (iii)   Two men agree to extract cocaine from a substance they have acquired from C. Though the substance contains no cocaine, they are guilty of conspiracy to produce controlled drugs (since they are guilty in the light of the facts they believed them to be)—**DPP v Nock [1978] AC 979**.

Consider the situation where two men agree to a burglary at a house but on arrival discover the police and fire brigade are present as a result of a fire next door.

Do these circumstances fit part (b) the 'impossible'? No, the offence still could be committed and would come under part (a).

(i) Where liability for any offence may be incurred without knowledge on the part of the person committing it of any particular fact or circumstances necessary for the commission of the offence, a person shall nevertheless not be guilty of conspiracy to commit that offence by virtue of sub-section (1) above unless he and at least one other party to the agreement intend or know that that fact or circumstance shall or will exist at the time when the conduct constituting the offence is to take place.

For example, A and B agree to have intercourse with X unsure as to whether she consents or not. X does not consent. A and B are guilty of rape since recklessness as to consent is sufficient mens rea. But they are not guilty of conspiracy since they do not have knowledge or belief as to lack of consent.

It may not be necessary to show that the persons accused of conspiracy were in direct communication with each other. Provided they have a common design then it may be proper that they be indicted even if they have not been in touch with each other until they stand in the dock (**R v Meyrick and Rubiffi (1929) 21 Cr App R 94**).

It is quite possible for a number of conspirators to deal only with one person at the hub and for them all to be members of the same conspiracy. The issue in such a situation is whether they were aware that the scheme to which they attached themselves went beyond their agreement with the person at the hub. Equally, it is possible for there to be but one conspiracy where A agrees with B, B agrees with C and so on. These are referred to as 'wheel' and 'chain' conspiracies respectively.

For example, A (the brains) knows B (a good villain) who knows C (a driver) who knows D (the heavy) who knows E (a gun dealer) who knows F (a farmer whose premises they can use after the job), etc. Only one knows one and does not meet the others (chain conspiracy). Each of the conspirators by entering into a common agreement makes the others his agents. The agreement must be a shared 'common' one and not two or more distinct conspiracies in relation to different persons or property as was arguably the case in **Meyrick**.

5.8.6.3 Conspiracy to commit offences abroad

Section 1A of the Criminal Law Act 1977 provides the offence of conspiring to commit offences abroad. In order for this offence to be committed, four conditions must be satisfied.

1. That the pursuit of the agreed course of conduct would at some stage involve an act by one or more of the parties or the

happening of some other event intended to take place outside the UK;

2. That the act or event is an offence in that place;
3. That the agreement would satisfy section 1(1) of the Criminal Law Act 1977 but for the fact that the offence would be an offence triable in England Wales if carried out as intended;
4. That—

   (i) a party to the agreement (or an agent) did anything in relation to the agreement in England and Wales before its formation; or

   (ii) a party to the agreement became a party in England and Wales (by joining in person or through an agent); or

   (iii) a party to the agreement, (or a party's agent), did or omitted anything in England and Wales in pursuance of the agreement.

1A(6) In the application of this Part of this Act to an agreement in the case of which each of the above conditions is satisfied, a reference to an offence is to be read as a reference to what would be the offence in question but for the fact that it is not an offence triable in England and Wales.

Criminal Law Act 1977, s 1A

The Attorney General's consent is required.

Related cases

R v Kenning and others [2008] EWCA Crim 1534 Agreement to aid and abet is not capable of being a criminal conspiracy in law. It was, however possible for persons to agree to aid and abet an offence that they intended or expected would be committed by someone who was not a party to the agreement but it was difficult to regard such an agreement constituting a criminal conspiracy for the purpose of section 1(1) of the Criminal Law Act 1977.

PNLD reference numbers

D5906, D5907, D5912, C1924

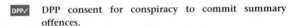 **DPP consent for conspiracy to commit summary offences.**

 **Time limit for prosecution:** As per substantive offence.

Summary and indictment: As per substantive offence.

5.8.6.4 Aid and abet

Section 8 of the Accessories and Abettors Act 1861 creates the offence of aiding and abetting for indictable offences and section 44 of the Magistrates' Courts Act 1980 creates the offence for summary and either way offences.

Offences

Whosoever shall **aid**, **abet**, **counsel** or **procure** the commission of any indictable offence whether the same be an offence at common law or by virtue of any Act passed or to be passed, shall be liable to be tried, indicted and punished as a **principal offender**.

Accessories and Abettors Act 1861, s 8

44(1) A person who aids, abets, counsels or procures the commission by another person of a summary offence shall be guilty of the like offence and may be tried (whether or not he is charged as a principal) either by a court having jurisdiction to try that other person or by a court having by virtue of his own offence jurisdiction to try him.

44(2) Any offence consisting in aiding, abetting, counselling or procuring the commission of an offence triable either way (other than an **offence listed in Schedule 1** to this Act) shall by virtue of this subsection be triable either way.

Magistrates' Courts Act 1980, s 44

Meanings

Aid

Means to provide help or assistance to a principal offender, whether before or at the time of commission of the offence.

Abet

Is difficult to describe, but such an activity could include where an individual incites, instigates, or encourages the principal to commit the offence.

Counsel

Means to advise or solicit the commission of an offence.

Procure

Means 'obtaining by care and effort'. A course of action is procured by setting out to see that it happens and taking the appropriate steps to produce that happening. A causal link must be established between what the procurer did and what the principal did.

Principal offender

Means the party whose act is the most immediate cause of the guilty deed.

Offence listed in Schedule 1

A full list can be found on PNLD at D9821, examples are, section 20 of the Offences Against the Person Act 1861, common law offences of public nuisance and outraging public decency and section 1 of the Perjury Act 1911.

Police powers

Power of arrest—section 24 of the Police and Criminal Evidence Act 1984

Powers of entry and search—sections 17, 18 and 32 of the Police and Criminal Evidence Act 1984

Note

To be convicted as an 'aider or abettor' a person must have knowledge of all the circumstances which constitute the offence. Whether the 'aider' realizes that the particular circumstances constitute an offence is immaterial.

Related cases

R v Kenning and others [2008] EWCA Crim 1534 Agreement to aid and abet is not capable of being a criminal conspiracy in law. There could be no conviction for aiding, abetting, counselling, or procuring an offence unless the actus reus (criminal conduct) of the substantive offence actually occurred and under section 1(4)(b) of the Criminal Attempts Act 1981 there was no offence of attempting to aid, abet, counsel, or procure the commission of an offence. It was, however possible for persons to agree to aid and abet an offence that they intended or expected would be committed by someone who was not a party to the agreement but it was difficult to regard such an agreement constituting a criminal conspiracy for the purpose of section 1(1) of the 1977 Act.

R v Loukes [1996] Crim LR 341 Offence must have occurred for it to be aided and abetted.

PNLD reference numbers

D920, D923, D9256, C1924, C425

 Time limit for prosecution: As per principal offence.

 Summary: As per principal offence.

 Indictment: As per principal offence.

5.8.6.5 Attempts

Section 1 of the Criminal Attempts Act 1981 provides the offence of attempting to commit a criminal offence.

Offence

If, with **intent** to commit **an offence to which this section applies**, a person does an act which is **more than merely preparatory** to the commission of the offence, he is guilty of attempting to commit the offence.

Criminal Attempts Act 1981, s 1(1)

Meanings

Intent

Intention is not defined but has to be proved. It can be proved by drawing on two sources of information or by a combination of both.

1. By admissions made by the defendant in interview with reference to his state of mind at the time of commission of the offence and his answers to questions with regard to his actions and intentions at the time of the offence.
2. By inference from the circumstances the offence, any evidence from witnesses, the defendant's actions and property found on him or in his control, such as a motor vehicle for transporting property. To prove intent, an officer needs to take all this into account, the important thing is that he has to prove the defendant's state of mind at the time.

An offence to which this section applies

All indictable offences, except for conspiracy, aiding and abetting and assisting offender offences (Criminal Attempts Act 1981, s 1(4)).

More than merely preparatory

The offence of attempt is complete if he does an act which is a step towards the commission of the specific crime, which is immediately and not remotely connected with the commission of it, and the doing of which cannot reasonably be regarded as having any other purpose than the commission of the specific crime. The main point to remember is that an attempt is not the same as the intent to commit an offence. If an act is merely preparatory (eg obtaining an insurance claim form to make a false claim), then it is not an attempt. There would have to be some other act such as actually filling the form out and posting it. Mere intent is not enough. See related cases below for more.

Police powers

Power of arrest—section 24 of the Police and Criminal Evidence Act 1984

Powers of entry and search—sections 17, 18 and 32 of the Police and Criminal Evidence Act 1984

Note

Criminal attempt offences are only possible where the principal offence is either an indictable offence or one that is triable either way. Attempts to commit summary offences are not recognized in law. However, an anomaly exists in that criminal damage is an 'either way' offence which, if the amount damaged totals under £5,000, can be treated by magistrates as a summary offence. Such an attempt is still an 'either way' offence (which can be tried summarily), it is not a purely summary offence in the normal sense (**R v Bristol Justices ex parte Edgar (1998)**). A suspect can be charged with attempting to damage property under £5,000.

Related cases

Davey v Lee [1967] 2 All ER 423 An attempt to commit a crime is an act done with intent to commit that crime, and forming part of a series of acts which would constitute the actual commission if it were not interrupted. The Lord Chief Justice also stated that the test that should be applied was the one set out in Archbold which is 'the actus reus necessary to constitute an attempt is complete if the prisoner does an act which is a step towards the commission of the specific crime, which is immediately and not merely remotely connected with the commission of it, and the doing of which cannot reasonably be regarded as having any other purpose than the commission of the specific crime'.

R v Tosti and White [1997] Crim LR 746 Examining a padlock to break in could be an attempt.

R v Geddes [1996] Crim LR 894 G was seen by a teacher in the boys' lavatory block at a school. A cider can with G's fingerprints was in one of the cubicles. His rucksack, containing a large kitchen knife, some rope and a roll of masking tape, was found in some nearby bushes. He was charged and convicted of attempted child abduction, the prosecution putting forward the argument that G had been hiding in the lavatories to abduct a child. G appealed on the grounds that he had not attempted to commit the offence. The appeal was upheld and G's conviction quashed. The difference between a 'preparatory act' and an 'attempt' is not always easy to define. In this case, G's intentions were not really in doubt, he had made preparations, equipped himself and put himself in a position where he could carry out the attack. However, the statutory test for an attempt requires an answer to the question:

Has the defendant actually tried to commit the offence in question? G had never had any communication with, nor had he confronted any schoolboy. In view of this the court had to conclude that he had not got to the stage where he could have been said to attempt an abduction.

PNLD reference numbers

D20, D162, D161, C491, C443, C172

Police and Criminal Evidence Act 1984, Code of Practice H

Code of Practice in Connection with the Detention, Treatment and Questioning by Police Officers of Persons under Section 41 of, and Schedule 8 to, the Terrorism Act 2000

1 General

1.1 This Code of Practice applies to, and only to, persons arrested under section 41 of the Terrorism Act 2000 (TACT) and detained in police custody under those provisions and Schedule 8 of the Act. References to detention under this provision that were previously included in PACE Code C—Code for the Detention, Treatment, and Questioning of Persons by Police Officers, no longer apply.

1.2 The Code ceases to apply at any point that a detainee is:
(a) Charged with an offence
(b) Released without charge, or
(c) Transferred to a prison, see section 14.5.

1.3 References to an offence in this Code include being concerned in the commission, preparation or instigation of acts of terrorism.

1.4 This Code's provisions do not apply to detention of individuals under any other terrorism legislation. This Code does not apply to people:

(i) Detained under section 5(1) of the Prevention of Terrorism Act 2005.

(ii) Detained for examination under TACT Schedule 7 and to whom the Code of Practice issued under that Act, Schedule 14, paragraph 6 applies;

(iii) Detained for searches under stop and search powers.

The provisions for the detention, treatment and questioning by police officers of persons other than those in police detention following arrest under section 41 of TACT, are set out in Code C issued under section 66(1) of the Police & Criminal Evidence Act (PACE)1984 (PACE Code C).

1.5 All persons in custody must be dealt with expeditiously, and released as soon as the need for detention no longer applies.

1.6 There is no provision for bail under TACT prior to charge.

1.7 An officer must perform the assigned duties in this Code as soon as practicable. An officer will not be in breach of this Code if delay is justifiable and reasonable steps are taken to prevent unnecessary delay. The custody record shall show when a delay has occurred and the reason. See *Note 1H*.

1.8 This Code of Practice must be readily available at all police stations for consultation by:
• police officers
• police staff
• detained persons
• members of the public.

1.9 The provisions of this Code:
• include the *Annexes*
• do not include the *Notes for Guidance*.

1.10 If an officer has any suspicion, or is told in good faith, that a person of any age may be mentally disordered or otherwise mentally vulnerable, in the absence of clear evidence to dispel that suspicion, the person shall be treated as such for the purposes of this Code. See *Note 1G*.

1.11 For the purposes of this Code, a juvenile is any person under the age of 17. If anyone appears to be under 17, and there is no clear evidence that they are 17 or over, they shall be treated as a juvenile for the purposes of this Code.

1.12 If a person appears to be blind, seriously visually impaired, deaf, unable to read or speak or has difficulty orally because of a speech impediment, they shall be treated as such for the purposes of this Code in the absence of clear evidence to the contrary.

1.13 'The appropriate adult' means, in the case of a:
(a) juvenile:
   (i) the parent, guardian or, if the juvenile is in local authority or voluntary organisation care, or is otherwise being looked after under the Children Act 1989, a person representing that authority or organisation;
   (ii) a social worker of a local authority social services department;
   (iii) failing these, some other responsible adult aged 18 or over who is not a police officer or employed by the police.
(b) person who is mentally disordered or mentally vulnerable: See *Note 1D*.
   (i) a relative, guardian or other person responsible for their care or custody;
   (ii) someone experienced in dealing with mentally disordered or mentally vulnerable people but who is not a police officer or employed by the police;
   (iii) failing these, some other responsible adult aged 18 or over who is not a police officer or employed by the police.

1.14 If this Code requires a person be given certain information, they do not have to be given it if at the time they are incapable of understanding what is said, are violent or may become violent or in urgent need of medical attention, but they must be given it as soon as practicable.

1.15 References to a custody officer include any:-
• police officer; or
• designated staff custody officer acting in the exercise or performance of the powers and duties conferred or imposed on them by their designation, performing the functions of a custody officer. See *Note 1J*.

1.16 When this Code requires the prior authority or agreement of an officer of at least inspector or superintendent rank, that authority may be given by a sergeant or chief inspector authorised by section 107 of PACE to perform the functions of the higher rank under TACT.

1.17 In this Code:

(a) 'designated person' means a person other than a police officer, designated under the Police Reform Act 2002, Part 4 who has specified powers and duties of police officers conferred or imposed on them;

(b) reference to a police officer includes a designated person acting in the exercise or performance of the powers and duties conferred or imposed on them by their designation.

1.18 Designated persons are entitled to use reasonable force as follows:-

(a) when exercising a power conferred on them which allows a police officer exercising that power to use reasonable force, a designated person has the same entitlement to use force; and

(b) at other times when carrying out duties conferred or imposed on them that also entitle them to use reasonable force, for example:
   - when at a police station carrying out the duty to keep detainees for whom they are responsible under control and to assist any other police officer or designated person to keep any detainee under control and to prevent their escape.
   - when securing, or assisting any other police officer or designated person in securing, the detention of a person at a police station.
   - when escorting, or assisting any other police officer or designated person in escorting, a detainee within a police station.
   - for the purpose of saving life or limb; or
   - preventing serious damage to property.

1.19 Nothing in this Code prevents the custody officer, or other officer given custody of the detainee, from allowing police staff who are not designated persons to carry out individual procedures or tasks at the police station if the law allows. However, the officer remains responsible for making sure the procedures and tasks are carried out correctly in accordance with the Codes of Practice. Any such person must be:

(a) a person employed by a police authority maintaining a police force and under the control and direction of the Chief Officer of that force;

(b) employed by a person with whom a police authority has a contract for the provision of services relating to persons arrested or otherwise in custody.

1.20 Designated persons and other police staff must have regard to any relevant provisions of this Code.

1.21 References to pocket books include any official report book issued to police officers or other police staff.

Notes for guidance

1A Although certain sections of this Code apply specifically to people in custody at police stations, those there voluntarily to assist with an investigation should be treated with no less consideration, e.g. offered refreshments at appropriate times, and enjoy an absolute right to obtain legal advice or communicate with anyone outside the police station.

1B A person, including a parent or guardian, should not be an appropriate adult if they:
- *are*
  - *suspected of involvement in the offence or involvement in the commission, preparation or instigation of acts of terrorism*
  - *the victim*
  - *a witness*
  - *involved in the investigation*
- *received admissions prior to attending to act as the appropriate adult.*
Note: If a juvenile's parent is estranged from the juvenile, they should not be asked to act as the appropriate adult if the juvenile expressly and specifically objects to their presence.

1C If a juvenile admits an offence to, or in the presence of, a social worker or member of a youth offending team other than during the time that person is acting as the juvenile's appropriate adult, another appropriate adult should be appointed in the interest of fairness.

1D In the case of people who are mentally disordered or otherwise mentally vulnerable, it may be more satisfactory if the appropriate adult is someone experienced or trained in their care rather than a relative lacking such qualifications. But if the detainee prefers a relative to a better qualified stranger or objects to a particular person their wishes should, if practicable, be respected.

1E *A detainee should always be given an opportunity, when an appropriate adult is called to the police station, to consult privately with a solicitor in the appropriate adult's absence if they want. An appropriate adult is not subject to legal privilege.*

1F *A solicitor or independent custody visitor (formerly a lay visitor) present at the police station in that capacity may not be the appropriate adult.*

1G *'Mentally vulnerable' applies to any detainee who, because of their mental state or capacity, may not understand the significance of what is said, of questions or of their replies. 'Mental disorder' is defined in the Mental Health Act 1983, section 1(2) as 'mental illness, arrested or incomplete development of mind, psychopathic disorder and any other disorder or disability of mind'. When the custody officer has any doubt about the mental state or capacity of a detainee, that detainee should be treated as mentally vulnerable and an appropriate adult called.*

1H *Paragraph 1.7 is intended to cover delays which may occur in processing detainees e.g. if:*
* *a large number of suspects are brought into the station simultaneously to be placed in custody;*
* *interview rooms are all being used;*
* *there are difficulties contacting an appropriate adult, solicitor or interpreter.*

1I *The custody officer must remind the appropriate adult and detainee about the right to legal advice and record any reasons for waiving it in accordance with section 6.*

1J *The designation of police staff custody officers applies only in police areas where an order commencing the provisions of the Police Reform Act 2002, section 38 and Schedule 4A, for designating police staff custody officers is in effect.*

1K *This Code does not affect the principle that all citizens have a duty to help police officers to prevent crime and discover offenders. This is a civic rather than a legal duty; but when a police officer is trying to discover whether, or by whom, an offence has been committed he is entitled to question any person from whom he thinks useful information can be obtained, subject to the restrictions imposed by this Code. A person's declaration that he is unwilling to reply does not alter this entitlement.*

1L If a person is moved from a police station to receive medical treatment, or for any other reason, the period of detention is still calculated from the time of arrest under section 41 of TACT (or, if a person was being detained under TACT Schedule 7 when arrested, from the time at which the examination under Schedule 7 began).

1M Under Paragraph 1 of Schedule 8 to TACT, all police stations are designated for detention of persons arrested under section 41 of TACT. Paragraph 4 of Schedule 8 requires that the constable who arrests a person under section 41 takes him as soon as practicable to the police station which he considers is 'most appropriate'.

2 Custody records

2.1 When a person is brought to a police station:
• under TACT section 41 arrest,
• or is arrested under TACT section 41 at the police station having attended there voluntarily,
   they should be brought before the custody officer as soon as practicable after their arrival at the station or, if appropriate, following arrest after attending the police station voluntarily. See *Note 3H*. A person is deemed to be 'at a police station' for these purposes if they are within the boundary of any building or enclosed yard which forms part of that police station.

2.2 A separate custody record must be opened as soon as practicable for each person brought to a police station under arrest or arrested at the station having gone there voluntarily. All information recorded under this Code must be recorded as soon as practicable in the custody record unless otherwise specified. Any audio or video recording made in the custody area is not part of the custody record.

2.3 If any action requires the authority of an officer of a specified rank, this must be noted in the custody record, subject to paragraph 2.8.

2.4 The custody officer is responsible for the custody record's accuracy and completeness and for making sure the record or copy of the record accompanies a detainee if they are transferred to another police station. The record shall show the:
• time and reason for transfer;
• time a person is released from detention.

2.5 A solicitor or appropriate adult must be permitted to consult a detainee's custody record as soon as practicable after their arrival at the station and at any other time whilst the person is detained.

Arrangements for this access must be agreed with the custody officer and may not unreasonably interfere with the custody officer's duties or the justifiable needs of the investigation.

2.6 When a detainee leaves police detention or is taken before a court they, their legal representative or appropriate adult shall be given, on request, a copy of the custody record as soon as practicable. This entitlement lasts for 12 months after release.

2.7 The detainee, appropriate adult or legal representative shall be permitted to inspect the original custody record once the detained person is no longer held under the provisions of TACT section 41 and Schedule 8, provided they give reasonable notice of their request. Any such inspection shall be noted in the custody record.

2.8 All entries in custody records must be timed and identified by the maker. Nothing in this Code requires the identity of officers or other police staff to be recorded or disclosed in the case of enquiries linked to the investigation of terrorism. In these cases, they shall use their warrant or other identification numbers and the name of their police station. See *Note 2A*. If records are entered on computer these shall also be timed and contain the operator's identification.

2.9 The fact and time of any detainee's refusal to sign a custody record, when asked in accordance with this Code, must be recorded.

Note for guidance

2A The purpose of paragraph 2.8 is to protect those involved in terrorist investigations or arrests of terrorist suspects from the possibility that those arrested, their associates or other individuals or groups may threaten or cause harm to those involved.

3 Initial action

(a) Detained persons—normal procedure

3.1 When a person is brought to a police station under arrest or arrested at the station having gone there voluntarily, the custody officer must make sure the person is told clearly about the following continuing rights which may be exercised at any stage during the period in custody:

(i)   the right to have someone informed of their arrest as in *section 5;*

(ii) the right to consult privately with a solicitor and that free inde-
      pendent legal advice is available;
(iii) the right to consult this Code of Practice. See *Note 3D*.

3.2 The detainee must also be given:
- a written notice setting out:
  – the above three rights;
  – the arrangements for obtaining legal advice;
  – the right to a copy of the custody record as in paragraph 2.6;
  – the caution in the terms prescribed in section 10.
- an additional written notice briefly setting out their entitlements
  while in custody. See *Notes 3A and 3B*.

Note: The detainee shall be asked to sign the custody record to
acknowledge receipt of these notices. Any refusal must be recorded
on the custody record.

3.3 A citizen of an independent Commonwealth country or a
national of a foreign country, including the Republic of Ireland,
must be informed as soon as practicable about their rights of communication with their High Commission, Embassy or Consulate.
See *section 7*.

3.4 The custody officer shall:
- record that the person was arrested under section 41 of TACT and
  the reason(s) for the arrest on the custody record. See *paragraph
  10.2 and Note for Guidance 3G;*
- note on the custody record any comment the detainee makes
  in relation to the arresting officer's account but shall not invite
  comment. If the arresting officer is not physically present when
  the detainee is brought to a police station, the arresting officer's
  account must be made available to the custody officer remotely or
  by a third party on the arresting officer's behalf;
- note any comment the detainee makes in respect of the decision
  to detain them but shall not invite comment;
- not put specific questions to the detainee regarding their involvement in any offence, nor in respect of any comments they may
  make in response to the arresting officer's account or the decision
  to place them in detention. See *paragraphs 14.1 and 14.2 and Notes
  for Guidance 3H, 14A and 14B.* Such an exchange is likely to constitute an interview as in paragraph 11.1 and require the associated
  safe guards in section 11.

See *paragraph 5.9 of the Code of Practice issued under TACT Schedule 8
Paragraph 3* in respect of unsolicited comments. If the first review of

detention is carried out at this time, see paragraphs 14.1 and 14.2, and Part II of Schedule 8 to the Terrorism Act 2000 in respect of action by the review officer.

3.5 The custody officer shall:

(a) ask the detainee, whether at this time, they:
  (i) would like legal advice, see section 6;
  (ii) want someone informed of their detention, see section 5;

(b) ask the detainee to sign the custody record to confirm their decisions in respect of (a);

(c) determine whether the detainee:
  (i) is, or might be, in need of medical treatment or attention, see section 9;
  (ii) requires:
    • an appropriate adult;
    • help to check documentation;
    • an interpreter;

(d) record the decision in respect of (c).

3.6 When determining these needs the custody officer is responsible for initiating an assessment to consider whether the detainee is likely to present specific risks to custody staff, any individual who may have contact with detainee (e.g. legal advisers, medical staff), or themselves. Such assessments should always include a check on the Police National Computer, to be carried out as soon as practicable, to identify any risks highlighted in relation to the detainee. Although such assessments are primarily the custody officer's responsibility, it will be necessary to obtain information from other sources, especially the investigation team. See *Note 3E*, the arresting officer or an appropriate health care professional, see *paragraph 9.15*. Reasons for delaying the initiation or completion of the assessment must be recorded.

3.7 Chief Officers should ensure that arrangements for proper and effective risk assessments required by *paragraph 3.6* are implemented in respect of all detainees at police stations in their area.

3.8 Risk assessments must follow a structured process which clearly defines the categories of risk to be considered and the results must be incorporated in the detainee's custody record. The custody officer is responsible for making sure those responsible for the detainee's custody are appropriately briefed about the risks. The content of any risk assessment and any analysis of the level of risk relating to the person's detention is not required to be shown or provided to the detainee or any person acting on behalf of the detainee. If no specific risks are identified by the assessment, that should be noted in the custody record. See *Note 3F and paragraph 9.15*.

3.9 Custody officers are responsible for implementing the response to any specific risk assessment, which should include for example:
• reducing opportunities for self harm;
• calling a health care professional;
• increasing levels of monitoring or observation;
• reducing the risk to those who come into contact with the detainee.
See *Note for Guidance 3F*.

3.10 Risk assessment is an ongoing process and assessments must always be subject to review if circumstances change.

3.11 If video cameras are installed in the custody area, notices shall be prominently displayed showing cameras are in use. Any request to have video cameras switched off shall be refused.

3.12 A constable, prison officer or other person authorised by the Secretary of State may take any steps which are reasonably necessary for
(a) photographing the detained person
(b) measuring him, or
(c) identifying him.

3.13 Paragraph 3.12 concerns the power in TACT Schedule 8 Paragraph 2. The power in TACT Schedule 8 Paragraph 2 does not cover the taking of fingerprints, intimate samples or non-intimate samples, which is covered in TACT Schedule 8 paragraphs 10–15.

(b) Detained persons—special groups

3.14 If the detainee appears deaf or there is doubt about their hearing or speaking ability or ability to understand English, and the custody officer cannot establish effective communication, the custody officer must, as soon as practicable, call an interpreter for assistance in the action under *paragraphs 3.1–3.5*. See *section 13*.

3.15 If the detainee is a juvenile, the custody officer must, if it is practicable, ascertain the identity of a person responsible for their welfare. That person:
• may be:
  – the parent or guardian;

– if the juvenile is in local authority or voluntary organisation care, or is otherwise being looked after under the Children Act 1989, a person appointed by that authority or organisation to have responsibility for the juvenile's welfare;

– any other person who has, for the time being, assumed responsibility for the juvenile's welfare.

- must be informed as soon as practicable that the juvenile has been arrested, why they have been arrested and where they are detained. This right is in addition to the juvenile's right in section 5 not to be held incommunicado. See *Note 3C.*

3.16 If a juvenile is known to be subject to a court order under which a person or organisation is given any degree of statutory responsibility to supervise or otherwise monitor them, reasonable steps must also be taken to notify that person or organisation (the 'responsible officer'). The responsible officer will normally be a member of a Youth Offending Team, except for a curfew order which involves electronic monitoring when the contractor providing the monitoring will normally be the responsible officer.

3.17 If the detainee is a juvenile, mentally disordered or otherwise mentally vulnerable, the custody officer must, as soon as practicable:

- inform the appropriate adult, who in the case of a juvenile may or may not be a person responsible for their welfare, as in *paragraph 3.15,* of:
  – the grounds for their detention;
  – their whereabouts.
- ask the adult to come to the police station to see the detainee.

3.18 If the appropriate adult is:

- already at the police station, the provisions of *paragraphs 3.1 to 3.5* must be complied with in the appropriate adult's presence;
- not at the station when these provisions are complied with, they must be complied with again in the presence of the appropriate adult when they arrive.

3.19 The detainee shall be advised that:

- the duties of the appropriate adult include giving advice and assistance;
- they can consult privately with the appropriate adult at any time.

3.20 If the detainee, or appropriate adult on the detainee's behalf, asks for a solicitor to be called to give legal advice, the provisions of *section 6* apply.

3.21 If the detainee is blind, seriously visually impaired or unable to read, the custody officer shall make sure their solicitor, relative, appropriate adult or some other person likely to take an interest in them and not involved in the investigation is available to help check any documentation. When this Code requires written consent or signing the person assisting may be asked to sign instead, if the detainee prefers. This paragraph does not require an appropriate adult to be called solely to assist in checking and signing documentation for a person who is not a juvenile, or mentally disordered or otherwise mentally vulnerable (see *paragraph 3.17*).

(c) Documentation

3.22 The grounds for a person's detention shall be recorded, in the person's presence if practicable.

3.23 Action taken under *paragraphs 3.14 to 3.22* shall be recorded.

Notes for guidance

3A The notice of entitlements should:
* *list the entitlements in this Code, including:*
  - *visits and contact with outside parties where practicable, including specialc provisions for Commonwealth citizens and foreign nationals;*
  - *reasonable standards of physical comfort;*
  - *adequate food and drink;*
  - *access to toilets and washing facilities, clothing, medical attention, and exercise when practicable.*
* *mention the:*
  - *provisions relating to the conduct of interviews;*
  - *circumstances in which an appropriate adult should be available to assist the detainee and their statutory rights to make representation whenever the period of their detention is reviewed.*

3B In addition to notices in English, translations should be available in Welsh, the main minority ethnic languages and the principal European languages whenever they are likely to be helpful. Audio versions of the notice should also be made available.

3C If the juvenile is in local authority or voluntary organisation care but living with their parents or other adults responsible for their welfare, although there is no legal obligation to inform them, they should normally be contacted, as well as the authority or organisation unless suspected of involvement in the offence concerned. Even if the juvenile is not living with their parents, consideration should be given to informing them.

3D *The right to consult this or other relevant Codes of Practice does not entitle the person concerned to delay unreasonably any necessary investigative or administrative action whilst they do so. Examples of action which need not be delayed unreasonably include:*
- *searching detainees at the police station;*
- *taking fingerprints or non-intimate samples without consent for evidential purposes.*

3E *The investigation team will include any officer involved in questioning a suspect, gathering or analysing evidence in relation to the offences of which the detainee is suspected of having committed. Should a custody officer require information from the investigation team, the first point of contact should be the officer in charge of the investigation.*

3F *Home Office Circular 32/2000 provides more detailed guidance on risk assessments and identifies key risk areas which should always be considered. This should be read with the Guidance on Safer Detention & Handling of Persons in Police Custody issued by the National Centre for Policing Excellence in conjunction with the Home Office and Association of Chief Police Officers.*

3G *Arrests under TACT section 41 can only be made where an officer has reasonable grounds to suspect that the individual concerned is a "terrorist". This differs from the PACE power of arrest in that it need not be linked to a specific offence. There may also be circumstances where an arrest under TACT is made on the grounds of sensitive information which can not be disclosed. In such circumstances, the grounds for arrest may be given in terms of the interpretation of a "terrorist" set out in TACT sections 40(1)(a) or 40(1)(b).*

3H *For the purpose of arrests under TACT section 41, the review officer is responsible for authorising detention (see Paragraphs 14.1 and 14.2, and Notes for Guidance 14A and 14B). The review officer's role is explained in TACT Schedule 8 Part II. A person may be detained after arrest pending the first review, which must take place as soon as practicable after the person's arrest.*

4 Detainee's property

(a) Action

4.1 The custody officer is responsible for:

(a) ascertaining what property a detainee:

    (i) has with them when they come to the police station, either on first arrival at the police station or any subsequent arrivals at a police station in connection with that detention.

    (ii) might have acquired for an unlawful or harmful purpose while in custody;

(b) the safekeeping of any property taken from a detainee which remains at the police station. The custody officer may search the detainee or authorise their being searched to the extent they consider necessary, provided a search of intimate parts of the body or involving the removal of more than outer clothing is only made as in *Annex A*. A search may only be carried out by an officer of the same sex as the detainee. See *Note 4A*.

4.2 Detainees may retain clothing and personal effects at their own risk unless the custody officer considers they may use them to cause harm to themselves or others, interfere with evidence, damage property, effect an escape or they are needed as evidence. In this event the custody officer may withhold such articles as they consider necessary and must tell the detainee why.

4.3 Personal effects are those items a detainee may lawfully need, use or refer to while in detention but do not include cash and other items of value.

(b) Documentation

4.4 It is a matter for the custody officer to determine whether a record should be made of the property a detained person has with him or had taken from him on arrest (see *Note for Guidance 4D*). Any record made is not required to be kept as part of the custody record but the custody record should be noted as to where such a record exists. Whenever a record is made the detainee shall be allowed to check and sign the record of property as correct. Any refusal to sign shall be recorded.

4.5 If a detainee is not allowed to keep any article of clothing or personal effects, the reason must be recorded.

Notes for guidance

4A PACE, Section 54(1) and paragraph 4.1 require a detainee to be searched when it is clear the custody officer will have continuing duties in relation to that detainee or when that detainee's behaviour or offence makes an inventory appropriate. They do not require every detainee to be searched, e.g. if it is clear a person will only be detained for a short period and is not to be placed in a cell, the custody officer may decide not to search them. In such a case the custody record will be endorsed 'not searched', paragraph 4.4 will not apply, and the detainee will be invited to sign the entry. If the detainee refuses, the custody officer will be obliged to ascertain what property they have in accordance with paragraph 4.1.

4B Paragraph 4.4 does not require the custody officer to record on the custody record property in the detainee's possession on arrest if, by virtue of its nature, quantity or size, it is not practicable to remove it to the police station.

4C Paragraph 4.4 does not require items of clothing worn by the person be recorded unless withheld by the custody officer as in paragraph 4.2.

4D Section 43(2) of TACT allows a constable to search a person who has been arrested under section 41 to discover whether he has anything in his possession that may constitute evidence that he is a terrorist.

5 Right not to be held incommunicado

(a) Action

5.1 Any person arrested and held in custody at a police station or other premises may, on request, have one named person who is a friend, relative or a person known to them who is likely to take an interest in their welfare informed at public expense of their where-abouts as soon as practicable. If the person cannot be contacted the detainee may choose up to two alternatives. If they cannot be contacted, the person in charge of detention or the investigation has discretion to allow further attempts until the information has been conveyed. See *Notes 5D and 5E*.

5.2 The exercise of the above right in respect of each person nominated may be delayed only in accordance with *Annex B*.

5.3 The above right may be exercised each time a detainee is taken to another police station or returned to a police station having been previously transferred to prison. This Code does not afford such a right to a person on transfer to a prison, where a detainee's rights will be governed by Prison Rules, see *paragraph 14.8*.

5.4 If the detainee agrees, they may receive visits from friends, family or others likely to take an interest in their welfare, at the custody officer's discretion. Custody Officers should liaise closely with the investigation team (see *Note 3E*) to allow risk assessments to be made where particular visitors have been requested by the detainee or identified themselves to police. In circumstances where the nature of the investigation means that such requests can not be met, consideration should be given, in conjunction with a representative of the relevant scheme, to increasing the frequency of visits from independent visitor schemes. See *Notes 5B and 5C*.

5.5 If a friend, relative or person with an interest in the detainee's welfare enquires about their whereabouts, this information shall be given if the suspect agrees and *Annex B* does not apply. See *Note 5E*.

5.6 The detainee shall be given writing materials, on request, and allowed to telephone one person for a reasonable time. See Notes 5A and 5F. Either or both these privileges may be denied or delayed if an officer of inspector rank or above considers sending a letter or making a telephone call may result in any of the consequences in *Annex B paragraphs 1 and 2,* particularly in relation to the making of a telephone call in a language which an officer listening to the call (see *paragraph 5.7*) does not understand. See *note 5G*. Nothing in this paragraph permits the restriction or denial of the rights in *paragraphs 5.1 and 6.1*.

5.7 Before any letter or message is sent, or telephone call made, the detainee shall be informed that what they say in any letter, call or message (other than in a communication to a solicitor) may be read or listened to and may be given in evidence. A telephone call may be terminated if it is being abused. See *Note 5G*. The costs can be at public expense at the custody officer's discretion.

5.8 Any delay or denial of the rights in this section should be proportionate and should last no longer than necessary.

(b) Documentation

5.9 A record must be kept of any:

(a) request made under this section and the action taken;

(b) letters, messages or telephone calls made or received or visit received;

(c) refusal by the detainee to have information about them given to an outside enquirer, or any refusal to see a visitor. The detainee must be asked to countersign the record accordingly and any refusal recorded.

Notes for guidance

5A A person may request an interpreter to interpret a telephone call or translate a letter.

5B At the custody officer's discretion (and subject to the detainee's consent), visits from friends, family or others likely to take an interest in the detainee's welfare, should be allowed when possible, subject to sufficient personnel being available to supervise a visit and any possible hindrance to the investigation. Custody Officers should bear in mind the exceptional nature of prolonged TACT detention and consider the potential benefits that visits may bring to the health and welfare of detainees who are held for extended periods.

5C Official visitors should be given access following consultation with the officer who has overall responsibility for the investigation provided the detainee consents, and they do not compromise safety or security or unduly delay or interfere with the progress of an investigation. Official visitors should still be required to provide appropriate dentification and subject to any screening process in place at the place of detention. Official visitors may include:

- *An accredited faith representative*
- *Members of either House of Parliament*
- *Public officials needing to interview the prisoner in the course of their duties*
- *Other persons visiting with the approval of the officer who has overall responsibility for the investigation*
- *Consular officials visiting a detainee who is a national of the country they represent subject to Annex F.*

Visits from appropriate members of the Independent Custody Visitors Scheme should be dealt with in accordance with the separate Code of Practice on Independent Custody Visiting.

5D If the detainee does not know anyone to contact for advice or support or cannot contact a friend or relative, the custody officer should bear in mind any local voluntary bodies or other organisations that might be able to help. Paragraph 6.1 applies if legal advice is required.

5E In some circumstances it may not be appropriate to use the telephone to disclose information under paragraphs 5.1 and 5.5.

5F The telephone call at paragraph 5.6 is in addition to any communication under paragraphs 5.1 and 6.1. Further calls may be made at the custody officer's discretion.

5G The nature of terrorism investigations means that officers should have particular regard to the possibility of suspects attempting to pass information which may be detrimental to public safety, or to an investigation.

6 Right to legal advice

(a) Action

6.1 Unless *Annex B* applies, all detainees must be informed that they may at any time consult and communicate privately with a solicitor, whether in person, in writing or by telephone, and that free independent legal advice is available from the duty solicitor. Where an appropriate adult is in attendance, they must also be informed of this right. See *paragraph 3.1, Note 1I, Note 6B and Note 6I.*

6.2 A poster advertising the right to legal advice must be prominently displayed in the charging area of every police station. See *Note 6G.*

6.3 No police officer should, at any time, do or say anything with the intention of dissuading a detainee from obtaining legal advice.

6.4 The exercise of the right of access to legal advice may be delayed exceptionally only as in *Annex B*. Whenever legal advice is requested, and unless *Annex B* applies, the custody officer must act without delay to secure the provision of such advice. If, on being informed or reminded of this right, the detainee declines to speak to a solicitor in person, the officer should point out that the right includes the right to speak with a solicitor on the telephone (see *paragraph 5.6*). If the detainee continues to waive this right the officer should ask them why and any reasons should be recorded on the custody record or the interview record as appropriate. Reminders of the right to legal advice must be given as in *paragraphs 3.5, 11.3,* and the PACE Code D on the Identification of Persons by Police Officers (PACE Code D), *paragraphs 3.19(ii) and 6.2*. Once it is clear a detainee does not want to speak to a solicitor in person or by telephone they should cease to be asked their reasons. See *Note 6J*.

6.5 An officer of the rank of Commander or Assistant Chief Constable may give a direction under TACT Schedule 8 paragraph 9 that a detainee may only consult a solicitor within the sight and hearing of a qualified officer. Such a direction may only be given if the officer has reasonable grounds to believe that if it were not, it may result in one of the consequences set out in TACT Schedule 8 paragraphs 8(4) or 8(5)(c). See *Annex B paragraph 3 and Note 6I*. A 'qualified officer' means a police officer who:

(a) is at least the rank of inspector;

(b) is of the uniformed branch of the force of which the officer giving the direction is a member, and

(c) in the opinion of the officer giving the direction, has no connection with the detained person's case. Officers considering the use of this power should first refer to Home Office Circular 40/2003.

6.6 In the case of a juvenile, an appropriate adult should consider whether legal advice from a solicitor is required. If the juvenile indicates that they do not want legal advice, the appropriate adult has the right to ask for a solicitor to attend if this would be in the best interests of the person. However, the detained person cannot be forced to see the solicitor if he is adamant that he does not wish to do so.

6.7 A detainee who wants legal advice may not be interviewed or continue to be interviewed until they have received such advice unless:

(a) *Annex B* applies, when the restriction on drawing adverse inferences from silence in *Annex C* will apply because the detainee is not allowed an opportunity to consult a solicitor; or

(b) an officer of superintendent rank or above has reasonable grounds for believing that:

  (i) the consequent delay might:

  - lead to interference with, or harm to, evidence connected with an offence;
  - lead to interference with, or physical harm to, other people;
  - lead to serious loss of, or damage to, property;

- lead to alerting other people suspected of having committed an offence but not yet arrested for it;
- hinder the recovery of property obtained in consequence of the commission of an offence.

(ii) when a solicitor, including a duty solicitor, has been contacted and has agreed to attend, awaiting their arrival would cause unreasonable delay to the process of investigation.

Note: In these cases the restriction on drawing adverse inferences from silence in *Annex C* will apply because the detainee is not allowed an opportunity to consult a solicitor.

(c) the solicitor the detainee has nominated or selected from a list:
   (i) cannot be contacted;
   (ii) has previously indicated they do not wish to be contacted; or
   (iii) having been contacted, has declined to attend; and the detainee has been advised of the Duty Solicitor Scheme but has declined to ask for the duty solicitor.

In these circumstances the interview may be started or continued without further delay provided an officer of inspector rank or above has agreed to the interview proceeding.

Note: The restriction on drawing adverse inferences from silence in *Annex C* will not apply because the detainee is allowed an opportunity to consult the duty solicitor.

(d) the detainee changes their mind, about wanting legal advice. In these circumstances the interview may be started or continued without delay provided that:
   (i) the detainee agrees to do so , in writing or on the interview record made in accordance with the Code of Practice issued under TACT Schedule 8 Paragraph 3; and
   (ii) an officer of inspector rank or above has inquired about the detainee's reasons for their change of mind and gives authority for the interview to proceed.

Confirmation of the detainee's agreement, their change of mind, the reasons for it if given and, subject to *paragraph 2.8*, the name of the authorising officer shall be recorded in the written interview record or the interview record made in accordance with the Code of Practice issued under Paragraph 3 of Schedule 8 to the Terrorism Act. See *Note 6H*.

Note: In these circumstances the restriction on drawing adverse inferences from silence in *Annex C* will not apply because the detainee is allowed an opportunity to consult a solicitor if they wish.

6.8 If *paragraph 6.7(a)* applies, where the reason for authorising the delay ceases to apply, there may be no further delay in permitting the exercise of the right in the absence of a further authorisation unless *paragraph 6.7 (b), (c) or (d)* applies.

6.9 A detainee who has been permitted to consult a solicitor shall be entitled on request to have the solicitor present when they are interviewed unless one of the exceptions in *paragraph 6.7* applies.

6.10 The solicitor may only be required to leave the interview if their conduct is such that the interviewer is unable properly to put questions to the suspect. See *Notes 6C and 6D*.

6.11 If the interviewer considers a solicitor is acting in such a way, they will stop the interview and consult an officer not below superintendent rank, if one is readily available, and otherwise an officer not below inspector rank not connected with the investigation. After speaking to the solicitor, the officer consulted will decide if the interview should continue in the presence of that solicitor. If they decide it should not, the suspect will be given the opportunity to consult another solicitor before the interview continues and that solicitor given an opportunity to be present at the interview. See *Note 6D*.

6.12 The removal of a solicitor from an interview is a serious step and, if it occurs, the officer of superintendent rank or above who took the decision will consider if the incident should be reported to the Law Society. If the decision to remove the solicitor has been taken by an officer below superintendent rank, the facts must be reported to an officer of superintendent rank or above who will similarly consider whether a report to the Law Society would be appropriate. When the solicitor concerned is a duty solicitor, the report should be both to the Law Society and to the Legal Services Commission.

6.13 'Solicitor' in this Code means:
- a solicitor who holds a current practising certificate.
- an accredited or probationary representative included on the register of representatives maintained by the Legal Services Commission.

6.14 An accredited or probationary representative sent to provide advice by, and on behalf of, a solicitor shall be admitted to the police station for this purpose unless an officer of inspector rank or above considers such a visit will hinder the investigation and directs otherwise. Hindering the investigation does not include giving proper legal advice to a detainee as in Note 6C. Once admitted to the police station, *paragraphs 6.7 to 6.11* apply.

6.15 In exercising their discretion under *paragraph 6.14,* the officer should take into account in particular:
• whether:
  – the identity and status of an accredited or probationary representative have been satisfactorily established;
  – they are of suitable character to provide legal advice,
  – any other matters in any written letter of authorisation provided by the solicitor on whose behalf the person is attending the police station. See *Note 6E.*

6.16 If the inspector refuses access to an accredited or probationary representative or a decision is taken that such a person should not be permitted to remain at an interview, the inspector must notify the solicitor on whose behalf the representative was acting and give them an opportunity to make alternative arrangements. The detainee must be informed and the custody record noted.

6.17 If a solicitor arrives at the station to see a particular person, that person must, unless *Annex B* applies, be so informed whether or not they are being interviewed and asked if they would like to see the solicitor. This applies even if the detainee has declined legal advice or, having requested it, subsequently agreed to be interviewed without receiving advice. The solicitor's attendance and the detainee's decision must be noted in the custody record.

(b) Documentation

6.18 Any request for legal advice and the action taken shall be recorded.

6.19 A record shall be made in the interview record if a detainee asks for legal advice and an interview is begun either in the absence of a solicitor or their representative, or they have been required to leave an interview.

Notes for Guidance

6A If paragraph 6.7(b) applies, the officer should, if practicable, ask the solicitor for an estimate of how long it will take to come to the station and relate this to the time detention is permitted, the time of day (i.e. whether the rest period under paragraph 12.2 is imminent) and the requirements of other investigations. If the solicitor is on their way or is to set off immediately, it will not normally be appropriate to begin an interview before they arrive. If it appears necessary to begin an interview before the solicitor's arrival, they should be given an indication of how long the police would be able to wait so there is an opportunity to make arrangements for someone else to provide legal advice. Nothing within this section is intended to prevent police from ascertaining immediately after the arrest of an individual whether a threat to public safety exists (see paragraph 11.2).

6B A detainee who asks for legal advice should be given an opportunity to consult a specific solicitor or another solicitor from that solicitor's firm or the duty solicitor. If advice is not available by these means, or they do not want to consult the duty solicitor, the detainee should be given an opportunity to choose a solicitor from a list of those willing to provide legal advice. If this solicitor is unavailable, they may choose up to two alternatives. If these attempts are unsuccessful, the custody officer has discretion to allow further attempts until a solicitor has been contacted and agrees to provide legal advice. Apart from carrying out these duties, an officer must not advise the suspect about any particular firm of solicitors.

6C A detainee has a right to free legal advice and to be represented by a solicitor. The solicitor's only role in the police station is to protect and advance the legal rights of their client. On occasions this may require the solicitor to give advice which has the effect of the client avoiding giving evidence which strengthens a prosecution case. The solicitor may intervene in order to seek clarification, challenge an improper question to their client or the manner in which it is put, advise their client not to reply to particular questions, or if they wish to give their client further legal advice. Paragraph 6.9 only applies if the solicitor's approach or conduct prevents or unreasonably obstructs proper questions being put to the suspect or the suspect's response being recorded. Examples of unacceptable conduct include answering questions on a suspect's behalf or providing written replies for the suspect to quote.

6D An officer who takes the decision to exclude a solicitor must be in a position to satisfy the court the decision was properly made. In order to do this they may need to witness what is happening.

6E If an officer of at least inspector rank considers a particular solicitor or firm of solicitors is persistently sending probationary representatives who are unsuited to provide legal advice, they should inform an officer of at least superintendent rank, who may wish to take the matter up with the Law Society.

6F Subject to the constraints of Annex B, a solicitor may advise more than one client in an investigation if they wish. Any question of a conflict of interest is for the solicitor under their professional code of conduct. If, however, waiting for a solicitor to give advice to one client may lead to unreasonable delay to the interview with another, the provisions of paragraph 6.7(b) may apply.

6G In addition to a poster in English, a poster or posters containing translations into Welsh, the main minority ethnic languages and the principal European languages should be displayed wherever they are likely to be helpful and it is practicable to do so.

6H Paragraph 6.7(d) requires the authorisation of an officer of inspector rank or above to the continuation of an interview when a detainee who wanted legal advice changes their mind. It is permissible for such authorisation to be given over the telephone, if the authorising officer is able to satisfy themselves about the reason for the detainee's change of mind and is satisfied it is proper to continue the interview in those circumstances.

6I Whenever a detainee exercises their right to legal advice by consulting or communicating with a solicitor, they must be allowed to do so in private. This right to consult or communicate in private is fundamental. Except as allowed by the Terrorism Act 2000, Schedule 8, paragraph 9, if the requirement for privacy is compromised because what is said or written by the detainee or solicitor for the purpose of giving and receiving legal advice is overheard, listened to, or read by others without the informed consent of the detainee, the right will effectively have been denied. When a detainee chooses to speak to a solicitor on the telephone, they should be allowed to do so in private unless a direction under Schedule 8, paragraph 9 of the Terrorism Act 2000 has been given.

7 Citizens of independent Commonwealth countries or foreign nationals

(a) Action

7.1 Any citizen of an independent Commonwealth country or a national of a foreign country, including the Republic of Ireland, may communicate at any time with the appropriate High Commission, Embassy or Consulate. The detainee must be informed as soon as practicable of:

- this right;
- their right, upon request, to have their High Commission, Embassy or Consulate told of their whereabouts and the grounds for their detention. Such a request should be acted upon as soon as practicable.

7.2 If a detainee is a citizen of a country with which a bilateral consular convention or agreement is in force requiring notification of arrest, the appropriate High Commission, Embassy or Consulate shall be informed as soon as practicable, subject to *paragraph 7.4*. The countries to which this applies as at 1 April 2003 are listed in *Annex F*.

7.3 Consular officers may visit one of their nationals in police detention to talk to them and, if required, to arrange for legal advice. Such visits shall take place out of the hearing of a police officer.

7.4 Notwithstanding the provisions of consular conventions, if the detainee is a political refugee whether for reasons of race, nationality, political opinion or religion, or is seeking political asylum, consular officers shall not be informed of the arrest of one of their nationals or given access or information about them except at the detainee's express request.

(b) Documentation

7.5 A record shall be made when a detainee is informed of their rights under this section and of any communications with a High Commission, Embassy or Consulate.

Note for guidance

7A The exercise of the rights in this section may not be interfered with even though Annex B applies.

8 Conditions of detention

(a) Action

8.1 So far as it is practicable, not more than one detainee should be detained in each cell.

8.2 Cells in use must be adequately heated, cleaned and ventilated. They must be adequately lit, subject to such dimming as is compatible with safety and security to allow people detained overnight to sleep. No additional restraints shall be used within a locked cell unless absolutely necessary and then only restraint equipment, approved for use in that force by the Chief Officer, which is reasonable and necessary in the circumstances having regard to the detainee's demeanour and with a view to ensuring their safety and the safety of others. If a detainee is deaf, mentally disordered or otherwise mentally vulnerable, particular care must be taken when deciding whether to use any form of approved restraints.

8.3 Blankets, mattresses, pillows and other bedding supplied shall be of a reasonable standard and in a clean and sanitary condition.

8.4 Access to toilet and washing facilities must be provided.

8.5 If it is necessary to remove a detainee's clothes for the purposes of investigation, for hygiene, health reasons or cleaning, replacement clothing of a reasonable standard of comfort and cleanliness shall be provided. A detainee may not be interviewed unless adequate clothing has been offered.

8.6 At least two light meals and one main meal should be offered in any 24 hour period. See *Note 8B*. Drinks should be provided at meal times and upon reasonable request between meals. Whenever necessary, advice shall be sought from the appropriate health care professional, see *Note 9A*, on medical and dietary matters. As far as practicable, meals provided shall offer a varied diet and meet any specific dietary needs or religious beliefs the detainee may have. Detainees should also be made aware that the meals offered meet such needs. The detainee may, at the custody officer's discretion, have meals supplied by their family or friends at their expense. See *Note 8A*.

8.7 Brief outdoor exercise shall be offered daily if practicable. Where facilities exist, indoor exercise shall be offered as an alternative if outside conditions are such that a detainee can not be reasonably expected to take outdoor exercise (e.g., in cold or wet weather) or if requested by the detainee or for reasons of security. See *Note 8C*.

8.8 Where practicable, provision should be made for detainees to practice religious observance. Consideration should be given to providing a separate room which can be used as a prayer room. The supply of appropriate food and clothing, and suitable provision for prayer facilities, such as uncontaminated copies of religious books, should also be considered. See *Note 8D*.

8.9 A juvenile shall not be placed in a cell unless no other secure accommodation is available and the custody officer considers it is not practicable to supervise them if they are not placed in a cell or that cell provides more comfortable accommodation than other secure accommodation in the station. A juvenile may not be placed in a cell with a detained adult.

8.10 Police stations should keep a reasonable supply of reading material available for detainees, including but not limited to, the main religious texts. See *Note 8D*. Detainees should be made aware that such material is available and reasonable requests for such material should be met as soon as practicable unless to do so would:

(i) interfere with the investigation; or
(ii) prevent or delay an officer from discharging his statutory duties, or those in this Code.

If such a request is refused on the grounds of (i) or (ii) above, this should be noted in the custody record and met as soon as possible after those grounds cease to apply.

(b) Documentation

8.11 A record must be kept of replacement clothing and meals offered.

8.12 The use of any restraints on a detainee whilst in a cell, the reasons for it and, if appropriate, the arrangements for enhanced supervision of the detainee whilst so restrained, shall be recorded. See *paragraph 3.9*.

Notes for guidance

8A In deciding whether to allow meals to be supplied by family or friends, the custody officer is entitled to take account of the risk of items being concealed in any food or package and the officer's duties and responsibilities under food handling legislation. If an officer needs to examine food or other items supplied by family and friends before deciding whether they can be given to the detainee, he should inform the person who has brought the item to the police station of this and the reasons for doing so.

8B Meals should, so far as practicable, be offered at recognised meal times, or at other times that take account of when the detainee last had a meal.

8C In light of the potential for detaining individuals for extended periods of time, the overriding principle should be to accommodate a period of exercise, except where to do so would hinder the investigation, delay the detainee's release or charge, or it is declined by the detainee.

8D Police forces should consult with representatives of the main religious communities to ensure the provision for religious observance is adequate, and to seek advice on the appropriate storage and handling of religious texts or other religious items.

9 Care and treatment of detained persons

(a) General

9.1 Notwithstanding other requirements for medical attention as set out in this section, detainees who are held for more than 96 hours must be visited by a health care professional at least once every 24 hours.

9.2 Nothing in this section prevents the police from calling the police surgeon or, if appropriate, some other health care professional, to examine a detainee for the purposes of obtaining evidence relating to any offence in which the detainee is suspected of being involved. See *Note 9A.*

9.3 If a complaint is made by, or on behalf of, a detainee about their treatment since their arrest, or it comes to notice that a detainee may have been treated improperly, a report must be made as soon as practicable to an officer of inspector rank or above not connected with the investigation. If the matter concerns a possible assault or the possibility of the unnecessary or unreasonable use of force, an appropriate health care professional must also be called as soon as practicable.

9.4 Detainees should be visited at least every hour. If no reasonably foreseeable risk was identified in a risk assessment, see *paragraphs 3.6–3.10,* there is no need to wake a sleeping detainee. Those suspected of being intoxicated through drink or drugs or having swallowed drugs, see *Note 9C,* or whose level of consciousness causes concern must, subject to any clinical directions given by the appropriate health care professional, see *paragraph 9.15:*
• be visited and roused at least every half hour
• have their condition assessed as in *Annex H*
• and clinical treatment arranged if appropriate

See *Notes 9B, 9C and 9G.*

9.5 When arrangements are made to secure clinical attention for a detainee, the custody officer must make sure all relevant information which might assist in the treatment of the detainee's condition is made available to the responsible health care professional. This applies whether or not the health care professional asks for such information. Any officer or police staff with relevant information must inform the custody officer as soon as practicable.

(b) Clinical treatment and attention

9.6 The custody officer must make sure a detainee receives appropriate clinical attention as soon as reasonably practicable if the person:

(a) appears to be suffering from physical illness; or
(b) is injured; or
(c) appears to be suffering from a mental disorder; or
(d) appears to need clinical attention.

9.7 This applies even if the detainee makes no request for clinical attention and whether or not they have already received clinical attention elsewhere. If the need for attention appears urgent, e.g. when indicated as in *Annex H,* the nearest available health care professional or an ambulance must be called immediately.

9.8 The custody officer must also consider the need for clinical attention as set out in *Note 9C* in relation to those suffering the effects of alcohol or drugs.

9.9 If it appears to the custody officer, or they are told, that a person brought to a station under arrest may be suffering from an infectious disease or condition, the custody officer must take reasonable steps to safeguard the health of the detainee and others at the station. In deciding what action to take, advice must be sought from an appropriate health care professional. See *Note 9D.* The custody officer has discretion to isolate the person and their property until clinical directions have been obtained.

9.10 If a detainee requests a clinical examination, an appropriate health care professional must be called as soon as practicable to assess the detainee's clinical needs. If a safe and appropriate care plan cannot be provided, the police surgeon's advice must be sought. The detainee may also be examined by a medical practitioner of their choice at their expense.

9.11 If a detainee is required to take or apply any medication in compliance with clinical directions prescribed before their detention, the custody officer must consult the appropriate health care professional before the use of the medication. Subject to the restrictions in *paragraph 9.12*, the custody officer is responsible for the safe-keeping of any medication and for making sure the detainee is given the opportunity to take or apply prescribed or approved medication. Any such consultation and its outcome shall be noted in the custody record.

9.12 No police officer may administer or supervise the self-administration of medically prescribed controlled drugs of the types and forms listed in the Misuse of Drugs Regulations 2001, Schedule 2 or 3. A detainee may only self-administer such drugs under the personal supervision of the registered medical practitioner authorising their use. Drugs listed in Schedule 4 or 5 may be distributed by the custody officer for self administration if they have consulted the registered medical practitioner authorising their use, this may be done by telephone, and both parties are satisfied self-administration will not expose the detainee, police officers or anyone else to the risk of harm or injury.

9.13 When appropriate health care professionals administer drugs or other medications, or supervise their self-administration, it must be within current medicines legislation and the scope of practice as determined by their relevant professional body.

9.14 If a detainee has in their possession, or claims to need, medication relating to a heart condition, diabetes, epilepsy or a condition of comparable potential seriousness then, even though paragraph 9.6 may not apply, the advice of the appropriate health care professional must be obtained.

9.15 Whenever the appropriate health care professional is called in accordance with this section to examine or treat a detainee, the custody officer shall ask for their opinion about:
- any risks or problems which police need to take into account when making decisions about the detainee's continued detention;
- when to carry out an interview if applicable; and
- the need for safeguards.

9.16 When clinical directions are given by the appropriate health care professional, whether orally or in writing, and the custody officer has any doubts or is in any way uncertain about any aspect of the directions, the custody officer shall ask for clarification. It is particularly important that directions concerning the frequency of visits are clear, precise and capable of being implemented. See Note 9E.

(c) Documentation

9.17 A record must be made in the custody record of:

(a) the arrangements made for an examination by an appropriate health care professional under *paragraph 9.3* and of any complaint reported under that paragraph together with any relevant remarks by the custody officer;

(b) any arrangements made in accordance with *paragraph 9.6;*

(c) any request for a clinical examination under *paragraph 9.10* and any arrangements made in response;

(d) the injury, ailment, condition or other reason which made it necessary to make the arrangements in (a) to (c). See *Note 9F;*

(e) any clinical directions and advice, including any further clarifications, given to police by a health care professional concerning the care and treatment of the detainee in connection with any of the arrangements made in (a) to (c). See *Note 9E;*

(f) if applicable, the responses received when attempting to rouse a person using the procedure in *Annex H*. See *Note 9G.*

9.18 If a health care professional does not record their clinical findings in the custody record, the record must show where they are recorded. See *Note 9F*. However, information which is necessary to custody staff to ensure the effective ongoing care and well being of the detainee must be recorded openly in the custody record, see *paragraph 3.8 and Annex G, paragraph 7.*

9.19 Subject to the requirements of *Section 4,* the custody record shall include:

• a record of all medication a detainee has in their possession on arrival at the police station;

• a note of any such medication they claim to need but do not have with them.

Notes for guidance

9A A 'health care professional' means a clinically qualified person working within the scope of practice as determined by their relevant professional body. Whether a health care professional is 'appropriate' depends on the circumstances of the duties they carry out at the time.

9B Whenever possible juveniles and mentally vulnerable detainees should be visited more frequently.

9C A detainee who appears drunk or behaves abnormally may be suffering from illness, the effects of drugs or may have sustained injury, particularly a head injury which is not apparent. A detainee needing or dependent on certain drugs, including alcohol, may experience harmful effects within a short time of being deprived of their supply. In these circumstances, when there is any doubt, police should always act urgently to call an appropriate health care professional or an ambulance. Paragraph 9.6 does not apply to minor ailments or injuries which do not need attention. However, all such ailments or injuries must be recorded in the custody record and any doubt must be resolved in favour of calling the appropriate health care professional.

9D It is important to respect a person's right to privacy and information about their health must be kept confidential and only disclosed with their consent or in accordance with clinical advice when it is necessary to protect the detainee's health or that of others who come into contact with them.

9E The custody officer should always seek to clarify directions that the detainee requires constant observation or supervision and should ask the appropriate health care professional to explain precisely what action needs to be taken to implement such directions.

9F Paragraphs 9.17 and 9.18 do not require any information about the cause of any injury, ailment or condition to be recorded on the custody record if it appears capable of providing evidence of an offence.

9G The purpose of recording a person's responses when attempting to rouse them using the procedure in Annex H is to enable any change in the individual's consciousness level to be noted and clinical treatment arranged if appropriate.

10 Cautions

(a) When a caution must be given

10.1 A person whom there are grounds to suspect of an offence, see *Note 10A*, must be cautioned before any questions about an offence, or further questions if the answers provide the grounds for suspicion, are put to them if either the suspect's answers or silence, (i.e. failure or refusal to answer or answer satisfactorily) may be given in evidence to a court in a prosecution.

10.2 A person who is arrested, or further arrested, must be informed at the time, or as soon as practicable thereafter, that they are under arrest and the grounds for their arrest, see *paragraph 3.4, Note 3G and Note 10B.*

10.3 As per section 3 of PACE Code G, a person who is arrested, or further arrested, must also be cautioned unless:
(a) it is impracticable to do so by reason of their condition or behaviour at the time;
(b) they have already been cautioned immediately prior to arrest as in *paragraph 10.1.*

(b) Terms of the cautions

10.4 The caution which must be given on:
(a) arrest;
(b) all other occasions before a person is charged or informed they may be prosecuted, see PACE Code C, section 16. Should, unless the restriction on drawing adverse inferences from silence applies, see *Annex C,* be in the following terms: 'You do not have to say anything. But it may harm your defence if you do not mention when questioned something which you later rely on in Court. Anything you do say may be given in evidence.' See *Note 10F.*

10.5 *Annex C, paragraph 2* sets out the alternative terms of the caution to be used when the restriction on drawing adverse inferences from silence applies.

10.6 Minor deviations from the words of any caution given in accordance with this Code do not constitute a breach of this Code, provided the sense of the relevant caution is preserved. See *Note 10C.*

10.7 After any break in questioning under caution, the person being questioned must be made aware they remain under caution. If there is any doubt the relevant caution should be given again in full when the interview resumes. See *Note 10D.*

10.8 When, despite being cautioned, a person fails to co-operate or to answer particular questions which may affect their immediate

treatment, the person should be informed of any relevant consequences and that those consequences are not affected by the caution. Examples are when a person's refusal to provide:

- their name and address when charged may make them liable to
  detention;
- particulars and information in accordance with a statutory
  requirement.

(c) Special warnings under the Criminal Justice and Public Order Act 1994, sections 36 and 37

10.9 When a suspect interviewed at a police station or authorised
place of detention after arrest fails or refuses to answer certain questions, or to answer satisfactorily, after due warning, see *Note 10E*,
a court or jury may draw such inferences as appear proper under
the Criminal Justice and Public Order Act 1994, sections 36 and 37.
Such inferences may only be drawn when:

(a) the restriction on drawing adverse inferences from silence, see
Annex C, does not apply; and

(b) the suspect is arrested by a constable and fails or refuses to
account for any objects, marks or substances, or marks on such
objects found:
- on their person;
- in or on their clothing or footwear;
- otherwise in their possession; or
- in the place they were arrested;

(c) the arrested suspect was found by a constable at a place at or
about the time the offence for which that officer has arrested
them is alleged to have been committed, and the suspect fails or
refuses to account for their presence there.

When the restriction on drawing adverse inferences from silence
applies, the suspect may still be asked to account for any of the
matters in (b) or (c) but the special warning described in *paragraph
10.10* will not apply and must not be given.

10.10 For an inference to be drawn when a suspect fails or refuses to
answer a question about one of these matters or to answer it satisfactorily, the suspect must first be told in ordinary language:

(a) what offence is being investigated;

(b) what fact they are being asked to account for;

(c) this fact may be due to them taking part in the commission of
the offence;

(d) a court may draw a proper inference if they fail or refuse to
account for this fact;

(e) a record is being made of the interview and it may be given in evidence if they are brought to trial.

(d) Juveniles and persons who are mentally disordered or otherwise mentally vulnerable

10.11 If a juvenile or a person who is mentally disordered or otherwise mentally vulnerable is cautioned in the absence of the appropriate adult, the caution must be repeated in the adult's presence.

(e) Documentation

10.12 A record shall be made when a caution is given under this section, either in the interviewer's pocket book or in the interview record.

Notes for guidance

10A There must be some reasonable, objective grounds for the suspicion, based on known facts or information which are relevant to the likelihood the offence has been committed and the person to be questioned committed it.

10B An arrested person must be given sufficient information to enable them to understand that they have been deprived of their liberty and the reason they have been arrested, e.g. when a person is arrested on suspicion of committing an offence they must be informed of the suspected offence's nature, when and where it was committed. See Note 3G. The suspect must also be informed of the reason or reasons why the arrest is considered necessary. Vague or technical language should be avoided.

10C If it appears a person does not understand the caution, the person giving it should explain it in their own words.

10D It may be necessary to show to the court that nothing occurred during an interview break or between interviews which influenced the suspect's recorded evidence. After a break in an interview or at the beginning of a subsequent interview, the interviewing officer should summarise the reason for the break and confirm this with the suspect.

10E The Criminal Justice and Public Order Act 1994, sections 36 and 37 apply only to suspects who have been arrested by a constable or Customs and Excise officer and are given the relevant warning by the police or customs officer who made the arrest or who is investigating the offence.

They do not apply to any interviews with suspects who have not been arrested.

10F Nothing in this Code requires a caution to be given or repeated when informing a person not under arrest they may be prosecuted for an offence. However, a court will not be able to draw any inferences under the Criminal Justice and Public Order Act 1994, section 34, if the person was not cautioned.

11 Interviews—general

(a) Action

11.1 An interview in this Code is the questioning of a person arrested on suspicion of being a terrorist which, under *paragraph 10.1*, must be carried out under caution. Whenever a person is interviewed they must be informed of the grounds for arrest. See *Note 3G*.

11.2 Following a decision to arrest a suspect, they must not be interviewed about the relevant offence except at a place designated for detention under Schedule 8 paragraph 1 of the Terrorism Act 2000, unless the consequent delay would be likely to:

(a) lead to:
- interference with, or harm to, evidence connected with an offence;
- interference with, or physical harm to, other people; or
- serious loss of, or damage to, property;

(b) lead to alerting other people suspected of committing an offence but not yet arrested for it; or

(c) hinder the recovery of property obtained in consequence of the commission of an offence.

Interviewing in any of these circumstances shall cease once the relevant risk has been averted or the necessary questions have been put in order to attempt to avert that risk.

11.3 Immediately prior to the commencement or re-commencement of any interview at a designated place of detention, the interviewer should remind the suspect of their entitlement to free legal advice and that the interview can be delayed for legal advice to be obtained, unless one of the exceptions in *paragraph 6.7* applies. It is the interviewer's responsibility to make sure all reminders are recorded in the interview record.

11.4 At the beginning of an interview the interviewer, after cautioning the suspect, see *section 10*, shall put to them any significant statement or silence which occurred in the presence and hearing of a police officer or other police staff before the start of the interview and which have not been put to the suspect in the course of a previous interview. See *Note 11A.* The interviewer shall ask the suspect whether they confirm or deny that earlier statement or silence and if they want to add anything.

11.5 A significant statement is one which appears capable of being used in evidence against the suspect, in particular a direct admission of guilt. A significant silence is a failure or refusal to answer a question or answer satisfactorily when under caution, which might, allowing for the restriction on drawing adverse inferences from silence, see *Annex C,* give rise to an inference under the Criminal Justice and Public Order Act 1994, Part III.

11.6 No interviewer may try to obtain answers or elicit a statement by the use of oppression. Except as in *paragraph 10.8,* no interviewer shall indicate, except to answer a direct question, what action will be taken by the police if the person being questioned answers questions, makes a statement or refuses to do either. If the person asks directly what action will be taken if they answer questions, make a statement or refuse to do either, the interviewer may inform them what action the police propose to take provided that action is itself proper and warranted.

11.7 The interview or further interview of a person about an offence with which that person has not been charged or for which they have not been informed they may be prosecuted, must cease when:
(a) the officer in charge of the investigation is satisfied all the questions they consider relevant to obtaining accurate and reliable information about the offence have been put to the suspect, this includes allowing the suspect an opportunity to give an innocent explanation and asking questions to test if the explanation is accurate and reliable, e.g. to clear up ambiguities or clarify what the suspect said;
(b) the officer in charge of the investigation has taken account of any other available evidence; and
(c) the officer in charge of the investigation, or in the case of a detained suspect, the custody officer, see PACE Code C paragraph 16.1, reasonably believes there is sufficient evidence to provide a realistic prospect of conviction for that offence. See *Note 11B.*

(b) Interview records

11.8 Interview records should be made in accordance with the Code of Practice issued under Schedule 8 Paragraph 3 to the Terrorism Act where the interview takes place at a designated place of detention.

(c) Juveniles and mentally disordered or otherwise mentally vulnerable people

11.9 A juvenile or person who is mentally disordered or otherwise mentally vulnerable must not be interviewed regarding their involvement or suspected involvement in a criminal offence or offences, or asked to provide or sign a written statement under caution or record of interview, in the absence of the appropriate adult unless *paragraphs 11.2, 11.11 to 11.13* apply. See *Note 11C.*

11.10 If an appropriate adult is present at an interview, they shall be informed:
- they are not expected to act simply as an observer; and
- the purpose of their presence is to:
  – advise the person being interviewed;
  – observe whether the interview is being conducted properly and fairly;
  – facilitate communication with the person being interviewed.

The appropriate adult may be required to leave the interview if their conduct is such that the interviewer is unable properly to put questions to the suspect. This will include situations where the appropriate adult's approach or conduct prevents or unreasonably obstructs proper questions being put to the suspect or the suspect's responses being recorded. If the interviewer considers an appropriate adult is acting in such a way, they will stop the interview and consult an officer not below superintendent rank, if one is readily available, and otherwise an officer not below inspector rank not connected with the investigation. After speaking to the appropriate adult, the officer consulted will decide if the interview should continue without the attendance of that appropriate adult. If they decide it should not, another appropriate adult should be obtained before the interview continues, unless the provisions of *paragraph 11.11* below apply.

(d) Vulnerable suspects—urgent interviews at police stations

11.11 The following persons may not be interviewed unless an officer of superintendent rank or above considers delay will lead to the consequences in *paragraph 11.2(a) to (c)*, and is satisfied the interview would not significantly harm the person's physical or mental state (see *Annex G*):

(a) a juvenile or person who is mentally disordered or otherwise mentally vulnerable if at the time of the interview the appropriate adult is not present;

(b) anyone other than in (a) who at the time of the interview appears unable to:
   • appreciate the significance of questions and their answers; or
   • understand what is happening because of the effects of drink, drugs or any illness, ailment or condition;

(c) a person who has difficulty understanding English or has a hearing disability, if at the time of the interview an interpreter is not present.

11.12 These interviews may not continue once sufficient information has been obtained to avert the consequences in *paragraph 11.2(a) to (c)*.

11.13 A record shall be made of the grounds for any decision to interview a person under *paragraph 11.11*.

Notes for guidance

11A *Paragraph 11.4 does not prevent the interviewer from putting significant statements and silences to a suspect again at a later stage or a further interview.*

11B *The Criminal Procedure and Investigations Act 1996 Code of Practice, paragraph 3.4 states 'In conducting an investigation, the investigator should pursue all reasonable lines of enquiry, whether these point towards or away from the suspect. What is reasonable will depend on the particular circumstances.' Interviewers should keep this in mind when deciding what questions to ask in an interview.*

11C *Although juveniles or people who are mentally disordered or otherwise mentally vulnerable are often capable of providing reliable evidence, they may, without knowing or wishing to do so, be particularly prone in certain circumstances to provide information that may be unreliable, misleading or self-incriminating. Special care should always be taken when questioning such a person, and the appropriate adult should be involved if* *there is any doubt about a person's age, mental state or capacity. Because of the risk of unreliable evidence it is also important to obtain corroboration of any facts admitted whenever possible.*

11D *Consideration should be given to the effect of extended detention on a detainee and any subsequent information they provide, especially if it relates to information on matters that they have failed to provide previously in response to similar questioning. See Annex G.*

11E *Significant statements described in paragraph 11.4 will always be relevant to the offence and must be recorded. When a suspect agrees to read records of interviews and other comments and sign them as correct, they should be asked to endorse the record with, e.g. 'I agree that this is a correct record of what was said' and add their signature. If the suspect does not agree with the record, the interviewer should record the details of any disagreement and ask the suspect to read these details and sign them to the effect that they accurately reflect their disagreement. Any refusal to sign should be recorded.*

12 Interviews in police stations

(a) Action

12.1 If a police officer wants to interview or conduct enquiries which require the presence of a detainee, the custody officer is responsible for deciding whether to deliver the detainee into the officer's custody.

12.2 Except as below, in any period of 24 hours a detainee must be allowed a continuous period of at least 8 hours for rest, free from questioning, travel or any interruption in connection with the investigation concerned. This period should normally be at night or other appropriate time which takes account of when the detainee last slept or rested. If a detainee is arrested at a police station after going there voluntarily, the period of 24 hours runs from the time of their arrest (or, if a person was being detained under TACT Schedule 7 when arrested, from the time at which the examination under Schedule 7 began) and not the time of arrival at the police station. The period may not be interrupted or delayed, except:

(a) when there are reasonable grounds for believing not delaying or interrupting the period would:

    (i)   involve a risk of harm to people or serious loss of, or damage to, property;

    (ii)   delay unnecessarily the person's release from custody;

    (iii) otherwise prejudice the outcome of the investigation;

(b) at the request of the detainee, their appropriate adult or legal representative;

(c) when a delay or interruption is necessary in order to:

    (i)   comply with the legal obligations and duties arising under *section 14;*

    (ii) to take action required under *section 9* or in accordance with medical advice.

If the period is interrupted in accordance with (a), a fresh period must be allowed. Interruptions under (b) and (c), do not require a fresh period to be allowed.

12.3 Before a detainee is interviewed the custody officer, in consultation with the officer in charge of the investigation and appropriate health care professionals as necessary, shall assess whether the detainee is fit enough to be interviewed. This means determining and considering the risks to the detainee's physical and mental state if the interview took place and determining what safeguards are needed to allow the interview to take place. The custody officer shall not allow a detainee to be interviewed if the custody officer considers it would cause significant harm to the detainee's physical or mental state. Vulnerable suspects listed at *paragraph 11.11* shall be treated as always being at some risk during an interview and these persons may not be interviewed except in accordance with *paragraphs 11.11 to 11.13.*

12.4 As far as practicable interviews shall take place in interview rooms which are adequately heated, lit and ventilated.

12.5 A suspect whose detention without charge has been authorised under TACT Schedule 8, because the detention is necessary for an interview to obtain evidence of the offence for which they have been arrested, may choose not to answer questions but police do not require the suspect's consent or agreement to interview them for this purpose. If a suspect takes steps to prevent themselves being questioned or further questioned, e.g. by refusing to leave their cell to go to a suitable interview room or by trying to leave the interview room, they shall be advised their consent or agreement to interview is not required. The suspect shall be cautioned as in section 10, and informed if they fail or refuse to co-operate, the interview may take place in the cell and that their failure or refusal to co-operate may be given in evidence. The suspect shall then be invited to co-operate and go into the interview room.

12.6 People being questioned or making statements shall not be required to stand.

12.7 Before the interview commences each interviewer shall, subject to the qualification at *paragraph 2.8,* identify themselves and any other persons present to the interviewee.

12.8 Breaks from interviewing should be made at recognised meal times or at other times that take account of when an interviewee last had a meal. Short refreshment breaks shall be provided at approximately two hour intervals, subject to the interviewer's discretion to delay a break if there are reasonable grounds for believing it would:
(i)   involve a:
    • risk of harm to people;
    • serious loss of, or damage to, property;
(ii) unnecessarily delay the detainee's release;
(iii) otherwise prejudice the outcome of the investigation. See *Note 12B.*

12.9 During extended periods where no interviews take place, because of the need to gather further evidence or analyse existing evidence, detainees and their legal representative shall be informed that the investigation into the relevant offence remains ongoing. If practicable, the detainee and legal representative should also be made aware in general terms of any reasons for long gaps between interviews. Consideration should be given to allowing visits, more frequent exercise, or for reading or writing materials to be offered, see *paragraph 5.4, section 8 and Note 12C.*

12.10 If during the interview a complaint is made by or on behalf of the interviewee concerning the provisions of this Code, the interviewer should:
(a) record it in the interview record;
(b) inform the custody officer, who is then responsible for dealing with it as in *section 9.*

(b) Documentation

12.11 A record must be made of the:
• time a detainee is not in the custody of the custody officer, and why; or
• reason for any refusal to deliver the detainee out of that custody

12.12 A record shall be made of:
(a) the reasons it was not practicable to use an interview room; and
(b) any action taken as in *paragraph 12.5.*

The record shall be made on the custody record or in the interview record for action taken whilst an interview record is being kept, with a brief reference to this effect in the custody record.

12.13 Any decision to delay a break in an interview must be recorded, with reasons, in the interview record.

12.14 All written statements made at police stations under caution shall be written on forms provided for the purpose.

12.15 All written statements made under caution shall be taken in accordance with *Annex D*. Before a person makes a written statement under caution at a police station they shall be reminded about the right to legal advice. See *Note 12A*.

Notes for guidance

12A It is not normally necessary to ask for a written statement if the interview was recorded in writing and the record signed in accordance with the Code of Practice issued under TACT Schedule 8 Paragraph 3. Statements under caution should normally be taken in these circumstances only at the person's express wish. A person may however be asked if they want to make such a statement.

12B Meal breaks should normally last at least 45 minutes and shorter breaks after two hours should last at least 15 minutes. If the interviewer delays a break in accordance with paragraph 12.8 and prolongs the interview, a longer break should be provided. If there is a short interview, and another short interview is contemplated, the length of the break may be reduced if there are reasonable grounds to believe this is necessary to avoid any of the consequences in paragraph 12.8(i) to (iii).

12C Consideration should be given to the matters referred to in paragraph 12.9 after a period of over 24 hours without questioning. This is to ensure that extended periods of detention without an indication that the investigation remains ongoing do not contribute to a deterioration of the detainee's well-being.

13 Interpreters

(a) General

13.1 Chief officers are responsible for making sure appropriate arrangements are in place for provision of suitably qualified interpreters for people who:

- are deaf;
- do not understand English.

Whenever possible, interpreters should be drawn from the National Register of Public Service Interpreters (NRPSI) or the Council for the Advancement of Communication with Deaf People (CACDP) Directory of British Sign Language/English Interpreters.

(b) Foreign languages

13.2 Unless *paragraphs 11.2, 11.11 to 11.13* apply, a person must not be interviewed in the absence of a person capable of interpreting if:

(a) they have difficulty understanding English;

(b) the interviewer cannot speak the person's own language;

(c) the person wants an interpreter present.

13.3 The interviewer shall make sure the interpreter makes a note of the interview at the time in the person's language for use in the event of the interpreter being called to give evidence, and certifies its accuracy. The interviewer should allow sufficient time for the interpreter to note each question and answer after each is put, given and interpreted. The person should be allowed to read the record or have it read to them and sign it as correct or indicate the respects in which they consider it inaccurate. If the interview is audibly recorded or visually recorded with sound, the Code of Practice issued under paragraph 3 of Schedule 8 to the Terrorism Act 2000 will apply.

13.4 In the case of a person making a statement to a police officer or other police staff other than in English:

(a) the interpreter shall record the statement in the language it is made;

(b) the person shall be invited to sign it;

(c) an official English translation shall be made in due course.

(c) Deaf people and people with speech difficulties

13.5 If a person appears to be deaf or there is doubt about their hearing or speaking ability, they must not be interviewed in the absence of an interpreter unless they agree in writing to being interviewed without one or *paragraphs 11.2, 11.11 to 11.13* apply.

13.6 An interpreter should also be called if a juvenile is interviewed and the parent or guardian present as the appropriate adult appears to be deaf or there is doubt about their hearing or speaking ability, unless they agree in writing to the interview proceeding without one or *paragraphs 11.2, 11.11 to 11.13* apply.

13.7 The interviewer shall make sure the interpreter is allowed to read the interview record and certify its accuracy in the event of the interpreter being called to give evidence. If the interview is audibly recorded or visually recorded, the Code of Practice issued under TACT Schedule 8 Paragraph 3 will apply.

(d) Additional rules for detained persons

13.8 All reasonable attempts should be made to make the detainee understand that interpreters will be provided at public expense.

13.9 If *paragraph 6.1* applies and the detainee cannot communicate with the solicitor because of language, hearing or speech difficulties, an interpreter must be called. The interpreter may not be a police officer or any other police staff when interpretation is needed for the purposes of obtaining legal advice. In all other cases a police officer or other police staff may only interpret if the detainee and the appropriate adult, if applicable, give their agreement in writing or if the interview is audibly recorded or visually recorded as in the Code of Practice issued under TACT Schedule 8 Paragraph 3.

13.10 When the custody officer cannot establish effective communication with a person charged with an offence who appears deaf or there is doubt about their ability to hear, speak or to understand English, arrangements must be made as soon as practicable for an interpreter to explain the offence and any other information given by the custody officer.

(e) Documentation

13.11 Action taken to call an interpreter under this section and any agreement to be interviewed in the absence of an interpreter must be recorded.

14 Reviews and Extensions of Detention

(a) Reviews and Extensions of Detention

14.1 The powers and duties of the review officer are in the Terrorism Act 2000, Schedule 8, Part II. See *Notes 14A and 14B*. A review officer should carry out his duties at the police station where the detainee is held, and be allowed such access to the detainee as is necessary for him to exercise those duties.

14.2 For the purposes of reviewing a person's detention, no officer shall put specific questions to the detainee:
- regarding their involvement in any offence; or
- in respect of any comments they may make:
  – when given the opportunity to make representations; or
  – in response to a decision to keep them in detention or extend the maximum period of detention.

Such an exchange could constitute an interview as in *paragraph 11.1* and would be subject to the associated safeguards in *section 11* and, in respect of a person who has been charged see PACE Code C Section 16.8.

14.3 If detention is necessary for longer than 48 hours, a police officer of at least superintendent rank, or a Crown Prosecutor may apply for warrants of further detention under the Terrorism Act 2000, Schedule 8, Part III.

14.4 When an application for a warrant of further or extended detention is sought under Paragraph 29 or 36 of Schedule 8, the detained person and their representative must be informed of their rights in respect of the application. These include:
a) the right to a written or oral notice of the warrant. See *Note 14G*.
b) the right to make oral or written representations to the judicial authority about the application.
c) the right to be present and legally represented at the hearing of the application, unless specifically excluded by the judicial authority.
d) their right to free legal advice (see *section 6* of this Code).

(b) Transfer of detained persons to Prison

14.5 Where a warrant is issued which authorises detention beyond a period of 14 days from the time of arrest (or if a person was being detained under TACT Schedule 7, from the time at which the examination under Schedule 7 began), the detainee must be transferred from detention in a police station to detention in a designated prison as soon as is practicable, unless:
a) the detainee specifically requests to remain in detention at a police station and that request can be accommodated, or
b) there are reasonable grounds to believe that transferring a person to a prison would:
   i)   significantly hinder a terrorism investigation;
   ii) delay charging of the detainee or his release from custody, or

    iii)   otherwise prevent the investigation from being conducted diligently and expeditiously.

If any of the grounds in (b)(i) to (iii) above are relied upon, these must be presented to the judicial authority as part of the application for the warrant that would extend detention beyond a period of 14 days from the time of arrest (or if a person was being detained under TACT Schedule 7, from the time at which the examination under Schedule 7 began) See *Note 14J*.

14.6 If a person remains in detention at a police station under a warrant of further detention as described at *section 14.5*, they must be transferred to a prison as soon as practicable after the grounds at (b)(i) to (iii) of that section cease to apply.

14.7 Police should maintain an agreement with the National Offender Management Service (NOMS) that stipulates named prisons to which individuals may be transferred under this section. This should be made with regard to ensuring detainees are moved to the most suitable prison for the purposes of the investigation and their welfare, and should include provision for the transfer of male, female and juvenile detainees. Police should ensure that the Governor of a prison to which they intend to transfer a detainee is given reasonable notice of this. Where practicable, this should be no later than the point at which a warrant is applied for that would take the period of detention beyond 14 days.

14.8 Following a detained person's transfer to a designated prison, their detention will be governed by the terms of Schedule 8 and Prison Rules, and this Code of Practice will not apply during any period that the person remains in prison detention. The Code will once more apply if a detained person is transferred back from prison detention to police detention. In order to enable the Governor to arrange for the production of the detainee back into police custody, police should give notice to the Governor of the relevant prison as soon as possible of any decision to transfer a detainee from prison back to a police station. Any transfer between a prison and a police station should be conducted by police, and this Code will be applicable during the period of transit. See Note 14K. A detainee should only remain in police custody having been transferred back from a prison, for as long as is necessary for the purpose of the investigation.

14.9 The investigating team and custody officer should provide as much information as necessary to enable the relevant prison authorities to provide appropriate facilities to detain an individual. This should include, but not be limited to:

(i)   medical assessments

(ii)   security and risk assessments

(iii) details of the detained person's legal representatives

(iv)   details of any individuals from whom the detained person has requested visits, or who have requested to visit the detained person.

14.10 Where a detainee is to be transferred to prison, the custody officer should inform the detainee's legal adviser beforehand that the transfer is to take place (including the name of the prison). The custody officer should also make all reasonable attempts to inform:

- family or friends who have been informed previously of the detainee's detention; and
- the person who was initially informed of the detainee's detention as at *paragraph 5.1*.

(c) Documentation

14.11 It is the responsibility of the officer who gives any reminders as at *paragraph 14.4*, to ensure that these are noted in the custody record, as well any comments made by the detained person upon being told of those rights.

14.12 The grounds for, and extent of, any delay in conducting a review shall be recorded.

14.13 Any written representations shall be retained.

14.14 A record shall be made as soon as practicable about the outcome of each review or determination whether to extend the maximum detention period without charge or an application for a warrant of further detention or its extension.

14.15 Any decision not to transfer a detained person to a designated prison under paragraph 14.5, must be recorded, along with the reasons for this decision. If a request under *paragraph 14.5(a)* is not accommodated, the reasons for this should also be recorded.

Notes for guidance

14A   TACT Schedule 8 Part II sets out the procedures for review of detention up to 48 hours from the time of arrest under TACT section 41 (or if a person was being detained under TACT Schedule 7, from the time at which the examination under Schedule 7 began). These include provisions for the requirement to review detention, postponing a review, grounds for continued detention, designating a review officer, representations, rights of the detained person and keeping a record. The review officer's role ends after a warrant has been issued for extension of detention under Part III of Schedule 8.

14B *Section 24(1) of the Terrorism Act 2006, amended the grounds contained within the 2000 Act on which a review officer may authorise continued detention. Continued detention may be authorised if it is necessary—*

a) *to obtain relevant evidence whether by questioning him or otherwise*

b) *to preserve relevant evidence*

c) *while awaiting the result of an examination or analysis of relevant evidence*

d) *for the examination or analysis of anything with a view to obtaining relevant evidence*

e) *pending a decision to apply to the Secretary of State for a deportation notice to be served on the detainee, the making of any such application, or the consideration of any such application by the Secretary of State*

f) *pending a decision to charge the detainee with an offence.*

14C *Applications for warrants to extend detention beyond 48 hours, may be made for periods of days at a time (initially under TACT Schedule 8 paragraph 29, and extensions thereafter under TACT Schedule 8, Paragraph 36), up to a maximum period of 28 days from the time of arrest (or if a person was being detained under TACT Schedule 7, from the time at which the examination under Schedule 7 began). Applications may be made for shorter periods than 7 days, which must be specified. The judicial authority may also substitute a shorter period if he feels a period of 7 days is inappropriate.*

14D *Unless Note 14F applies, applications for warrants that would take the total period of detention up to 14 days or less should be made to a judicial authority, meaning a District Judge (magistrates' court) designated by the Lord Chancellor to hear such applications.*

14E *Any application for a warrant which would take the period of detention beyond 14 days from the time of arrest (or if a person was being detained under TACT Schedule 7, from the time at which the examination under Schedule 7 began), must be made to a High Court Judge.*

14F If an application has been made to a High Court Judge for a warrant which would take detention beyond 14 days, and the High Court Judge instead issues a warrant for a period of time which would not take detention beyond 14 days, further applications for extension of detention must also be made to a High Court Judge, regardless of the period of time to which they refer.

14G TACT Schedule 8 Paragraph 31 requires a notice to be given to the detained person if a warrant is sought for further detention. This must be provided before the judicial hearing of the application for that warrant and must include:

a) notification that the application for a warrant has been made
b) the time at which the application was made
c) the time at which the application is to be heard
d) the grounds on which further detention is sought.

A notice must also be provided each time an application is made to extend an existing warrant.

14H An officer applying for an order under TACT Schedule 8 Paragraph 34 to withhold specified information on which he intends to rely when applying for a warrant of further detention, may make the application for the order orally or in writing. The most appropriate method of application will depend on the circumstances of the case and the need to ensure fairness to the detainee.

14I Where facilities exist, hearings relating to extension of detention under Part III of Schedule 8 may take place using video conferencing facilities provided that the requirements set out in Schedule 8 are still met. However, if the judicial authority requires the detained person to be physically present at any hearing, this should be complied with as soon as practicable. Paragraphs 33(4) to 33(9) of TACT Schedule 8 govern the relevant conduct of hearings.

14J Transfer to prison is intended to ensure that individuals who are detained for extended periods of time are held in a place designed for longer periods of detention than police stations. Prison will provide detainees with a greater range of facilities more appropriate to longer detention periods.

14K The Code will only apply as is appropriate to the conditions of detention during the period of transit. There is obviously no requirement to provide such things as bed linen or reading materials for the journey between prison and police station.

15 Charging

15.1 Charging of detained persons is covered by PACE and guidance issued under PACE by the Director of Public Prosecutions. General guidance on charging can be found in section 16 of PACE Code C.

16 Testing persons for the presence of specified Class A drugs

16.1 The provisions for drug testing under section 63B of PACE (as amended by section 5 of the Criminal Justice Act 2003 and section 7 of the Drugs Act 2005), do not apply to detention under TACT section 41 and Schedule 8. Guidance on these provisions can be found in section 17 of PACE Code C.

Annex A—Intimate and Strip Searches

A Intimate search

1. An intimate search consists of the physical examination of a person's body orifices other than the mouth. The intrusive nature of such searches means the actual and potential risks associated with intimate searches must never be underestimated.

(a) Action

2. Body orifices other than the mouth may be searched only if authorised by an officer of inspector rank or above who has reasonable grounds for believing that the person may have concealed on themselves anything which they could and might use to cause physical injury to themselves or others at the station and the officer has reasonable grounds for believing that an intimate search is the only means of removing those items.

3. Before the search begins, a police officer, designated detention officer or staff custody officer, must tell the detainee:-
(a) that the authority to carry out the search has been given;
(b) the grounds for giving the authorisation and for believing that the article cannot be removed without an intimate search.

4. An intimate search may only be carried out by a registered medical practitioner or registered nurse, unless an officer of at least inspector rank considers this is not practicable, in which case a police officer may carry out the search. See *Notes A1 to A5*.

5. Any proposal for a search under *paragraph 2* to be carried out by someone other than a registered medical practitioner or registered nurse must only be considered as a last resort and when the authorising officer is satisfied the risks associated with allowing the item to remain with the detainee outweigh the risks associated with removing it. See *Notes A1 to A5*.

6. An intimate search at a police station of a juvenile or mentally disordered or otherwise mentally vulnerable person may take place only in the presence of an appropriate adult of the same sex, unless the detainee specifically requests a particular adult of the opposite sex who is readily available. In the case of a juvenile the search may take place in the absence of the appropriate adult only if the juvenile signifies in the presence of the appropriate adult they do not want the adult present during the search and the adult agrees. A record shall be made of the juvenile's decision and signed by the appropriate adult.

7. When an intimate search under *paragraph 2* is carried out by a police officer, the officer must be of the same sex as the detainee. A minimum of two people, other than the detainee, must be present during the search. Subject to *paragraph 6,* no person of the opposite sex who is not a medical practitioner or nurse shall be present, nor shall anyone whose presence is unnecessary. The search shall be conducted with proper regard to the sensitivity and vulnerability of the detainee.

(b) Documentation

8. In the case of an intimate search under *paragraph 2,* the following shall be recorded as soon as practicable, in the detainee's custody record:

- the authorisation to carry out the search;
- the grounds for giving the authorisation;
- the grounds for believing the article could not be removed without an intimate search;
- which parts of the detainee's body were searched;
- who carried out the search;
- who was present;
- the result.

9. If an intimate search is carried out by a police officer, the reason why it was impracticable for a registered medical practitioner or registered nurse to conduct it must be recorded.

B Strip search

10. A strip search is a search involving the removal of more than outer clothing. In this Code, outer clothing includes shoes and socks.

(a) Action

11. A strip search may take place only if it is considered necessary to remove an article which a detainee would not be allowed to keep, and the officer reasonably considers the detainee might have concealed such an article. Strip searches shall not be routinely carried out if there is no reason to consider that articles are concealed. The conduct of strip searches.

12. When strip searches are conducted:

(a) a police officer carrying out a strip search must be the same sex as the detainee;

(b) the search shall take place in an area where the detainee cannot be seen by anyone who does not need to be present, nor by a member of the opposite sex except an appropriate adult who has been specifically requested by the detainee;

(c) except in cases of urgency, where there is risk of serious harm to the detainee or to others, whenever a strip search involves exposure of intimate body parts, there must be at least two people present other than the detainee, and if the search is of a juvenile or mentally disordered or otherwise mentally vulnerable person, one of the people must be the appropriate adult. Except in urgent cases as above, a search of a juvenile may take place in the absence of the appropriate adult only if the juvenile signifies in the presence of the appropriate adult that they do not want the adult to be present during the search and the adult agrees. A record shall be made of the juvenile's decision and signed by the appropriate adult. The presence of more than two people, other than an appropriate adult, shall be permitted only in the most exceptional circumstances;

(d) the search shall be conducted with proper regard to the sensitivity and vulnerability of the detainee in these circumstances and every reasonable effort shall be made to secure the detainee's co-operation and minimise embarrassment. Detainees who are searched shall not normally be required to remove all their clothes at the same time, e.g. a person should be allowed to remove clothing above the waist and redress before removing further clothing;

(e) if necessary to assist the search, the detainee may be required to hold their arms in the air or to stand with their legs apart and bend forward so a visual examination may be made of the genital and anal areas provided no physical contact is made with any body orifice;

(f) if articles are found, the detainee shall be asked to hand them over. If articles are found within any body orifice other than the mouth, and the detainee refuses to hand them over, their removal would constitute an intimate search, which must be carried out as in *Part A*;

(g) a strip search shall be conducted as quickly as possible, and the detainee allowed to dress as soon as the procedure is complete.

(b) Documentation

13. A record shall be made on the custody record of a strip search including the reason it was considered necessary, those present and any result.

Notes for guidance

A1 Before authorising any intimate search, the authorising officer must make every reasonable effort to persuade the detainee to hand the article over without a search. If the detainee agrees, a registered medical practitioner or registered nurse should whenever possible be asked to assess the risks involved and, if necessary, attend to assist the detainee.

A2 If the detainee does not agree to hand the article over without a search, the authorising officer must carefully review all the relevant factors before authorising an intimate search. In particular, the officer must consider whether the grounds for believing an article may be concealed are reasonable.

A3 If authority is given for a search under paragraph 2, a registered medical practitioner or registered nurse shall be consulted whenever possible. The presumption should be that the search will be conducted by the registered medical practitioner or registered nurse and the authorising officer must make every reasonable effort to persuade the detainee to allow the medical practitioner or nurse to conduct the search.

A4 A constable should only be authorised to carry out a search as a last resort and when all other approaches have failed. In these circumstances, the authorising officer must be satisfied the detainee might use the article for one or more of the purposes in paragraph 2 and the physical injury likely to be caused is sufficiently severe to justify authorising a constable to carry out the search.

A5 If an officer has any doubts whether to authorise an intimate search by a constable, the officer should seek advice from an officer of superintendent rank or above.

Annex B—Delay in Notifying Arrest or Allowing Acces to Legal Advice for Persons Detained Under the Terrorism Act 2000.

A Delays under TACT Schedule 8

1. The rights as in *sections 5 or 6*, may be delayed if the person is detained under the Terrorism Act 2000, section 41, has not yet been charged with an offence and an officer of superintendent rank or above has reasonable grounds for believing the exercise of either right will have one of the following consequences:

(a) interference with or harm to evidence of a serious offence,

(b) interference with or physical injury to any person,

(c) the alerting of persons who are suspected of having committed a serious offence but who have not been arrested for it,

(d) the hindering of the recovery of property obtained as a result of a serious offence or in respect of which a forfeiture order could be made under section 23,

(e) interference with the gathering of information about the commission, preparation or instigation of acts of terrorism,

(f) the alerting of a person and thereby making it more difficult to prevent an act of terrorism, or

(g) the alerting of a person and thereby making it more difficult to secure a person's apprehension, prosecution or conviction in connection with the commission, preparation or instigation of an act of terrorism.

2. These rights may also be delayed if the officer has reasonable grounds for believing that:

(a) the detained person has benefited from his criminal conduct (to be decided in accordance with Part 2 of the Proceeds of Crime Act 2002), and

(b) the recovery of the value of the property constituting the benefit will be hindered by—

    (i) informing the named person of the detained person's detention (in the case of an authorisation under Paragraph 8(1)(a) of Schedule 8 to TACT,

       or

    (ii) the exercise of the right under paragraph 7 (in the case of an authorisation under Paragraph 8(1)(b) of Schedule 8 to TACT.

3. Authority to delay a detainee's right to consult privately with a solicitor may be given only if the authorising officer has reasonable grounds to believe the solicitor the detainee wants to consult will, inadvertently or otherwise, pass on a message from the detainee or act in some other way which will have any of the consequences specified under paragraph 8 of Schedule 8 to the Terrorism Act 2000. In these circumstances the detainee must be allowed to choose another solicitor. See *Note B3*.

4. If the detainee wishes to see a solicitor, access to that solicitor may not be delayed on the grounds they might advise the detainee not to answer questions or the solicitor was initially asked to attend the police station by someone else. In the latter case the detainee must be told the solicitor has come to the police station at another person's request, and must be asked to sign the custody record to signify whether they want to see the solicitor.

5. The fact the grounds for delaying notification of arrest may be satisfied does not automatically mean the grounds for delaying access to legal advice will also be satisfied.

6. These rights may be delayed only for as long as is necessary but not beyond 48 hours from the time of arrest (or if a person was being detained under TACT Schedule 7, from the time at which the examination under Schedule 7 began). If the above grounds cease to apply within this time the detainee must as soon as practicable be asked if they wish to exercise either right, the custody record noted accordingly, and action taken in accordance with the relevant section of this Code.

7. A person must be allowed to consult a solicitor for a reasonable time before any court hearing.

B Documentation

8. The grounds for action under this Annex shall be recorded and the detainee informed of them as soon as practicable.

9. Any reply given by a detainee under paragraph 6 must be recorded and the detainee asked to endorse the record in relation to whether they want to receive legal advice at this point.

C Cautions and special warnings

10. When a suspect detained at a police station is interviewed during any period for which access to legal advice has been delayed under this Annex, the court or jury may not draw adverse inferences from their silence.

Notes for guidance

B1 *Even if Annex B applies in the case of a juvenile, or a person who is mentally disordered or otherwise mentally vulnerable, action to inform the appropriate adult and the person responsible for a juvenile's welfare if that is a different person, must nevertheless be taken as in paragraph 3.15 and 3.17.*

B2 *In the case of Commonwealth citizens and foreign nationals, see Note 7A.*

B3 *A decision to delay access to a specific solicitor is likely to be a rare occurrence and only when it can be shown the suspect is capable of mis-leading that particular solicitor and there is more than a substantial risk that the suspect will succeed in causing information to be conveyed which will lead to one or more of the specified consequences.*

Annex C—Restriction on Drawing Adverse Inferences from Silence and Terms of the Caution when the Restriction Applies

(a) The restriction on drawing adverse inferences from silence

1. The Criminal Justice and Public Order Act 1994, sections 34, 36 and 37 as amended by the Youth Justice and Criminal Evidence Act 1999, section 58 describe the conditions under which adverse infer-ences may be drawn from a person's failure or refusal to say any-thing about their involvement in the offence when interviewed, after being charged or informed they may be prosecuted. These provisions are subject to an overriding restriction on the ability of a court or jury to draw adverse inferences from a person's silence. This restriction applies:

(a) to any detainee at a police station who, before being inter-viewed, see *section 11*, or being charged or informed they may be prosecuted, see *section 15*, has:

    (i) asked for legal advice, see *section 6, paragraph 6.1*;

    (ii) not been allowed an opportunity to consult a solicitor, including the duty solicitor, as in this Code; and

(iii) not changed their mind about wanting legal advice, see *section 6, paragraph 6.7(c).* Note the condition in (ii) will:
- apply when a detainee who has asked for legal advice is interviewed before speaking to a solicitor as in *section 6, paragraph 6.6(a) or (b).*
- not apply if the detained person declines to ask for the duty solicitor, see *section 6, paragraphs 6.7(b) and (c);*

(b) to any person charged with, or informed they may be prosecuted for, an offence who:

(i) has had brought to their notice a written statement made by another person or the content of an interview with another person which relates to that offence, see PACE Code C *section 16, paragraph 16.6;*

(ii) is interviewed about that offence, see PACE Code C *section 16, paragraph 16.8;* or

(iii) makes a written statement about that offence, see *Annex D paragraphs 4 and 9*

(b) Terms of the caution when the restriction applies

2. When a requirement to caution arises at a time when the restriction on drawing adverse inferences from silence applies, the caution shall be: 'You do not have to say anything, but anything you do say may be given in evidence.'

3. Whenever the restriction either begins to apply or ceases to apply after a caution has already been given, the person shall be re-cautioned in the appropriate terms. The changed position on drawing inferences and that the previous caution no longer applies shall also be explained to the detainee in ordinary language. See *Note C1.*

Notes for guidance

C1 The following is suggested as a framework to help explain changes in the position on drawing adverse inferences if the restriction on drawing adverse inferences from silence:

(a) begins to apply:

'*The caution you were previously given no longer applies. This is because after that caution:*

(i) you asked to speak to a solicitor but have not yet been allowed an opportunity to speak to a solicitor. See paragraph 1(a); or

(ii) you have been charged with/informed you may be prosecuted. See paragraph 1(b).

'This means that from now on, adverse inferences cannot be drawn at court and your defence will not be harmed just because you choose to say nothing. Please listen carefully to the caution I am about to give you because it will apply from now on. You will see that it does not say any-thing about your defence being harmed.'

(b) ceases to apply before or at the time the person is charged or informed they may be prosecuted, see paragraph 1(a);

'The caution you were previously given no longer applies. This is because after that caution you have been allowed an opportunity to speak to a solicitor. Please listen carefully to the caution I am about to give you because it will apply from now on. It explains how your defence at court may be affected if you choose to say nothing.'

Annex D—Written Statements Under Caution

(a) Written by a person under caution

1. A person shall always be invited to write down what they want to say.

2. A person who has not been charged with, or informed they may be prosecuted for, any offence to which the statement they want to write relates, shall:

(a) unless the statement is made at a time when the restriction on drawing adverse inferences from silence applies, see *Annex C*, be asked to write out and sign the following before writing what they want to say: 'I make this statement of my own free will. I understand that I do not have to say anything but that it may harm my defence if I do not mention when questioned some-thing which I later rely on in court. This statement may be given in evidence.';

(b) if the statement is made at a time when the restriction on draw-ing adverse inferences from silence applies, be asked to write out and sign the following before writing what they want to say; 'I make this statement of my own free will. I understand that I do not have to say anything. This statement may be given in evidence.'

3. When a person, on the occasion of being charged with or informed they may be prosecuted for any offence, asks to make a statement which relates to any such offence and wants to write it they shall:

(a) unless the restriction on drawing adverse inferences from silence, see *Annex C*, applied when they were so charged or informed they may be prosecuted, be asked to write out and sign the following before writing what they want to say:

'I make this statement of my own free will. I understand that I do not have to say anything but that it may harm my defence if I do not mention when questioned something which I later rely on in court. This statement may be given in evidence.';

(b) if the restriction on drawing adverse inferences from silence applied when they were so charged or informed they may be prosecuted, be asked to write out and sign the following before writing what they want to say:

'I make this statement of my own free will. I understand that I do not have to say anything. This statement may be given in evidence.'

4. When a person, who has already been charged with or informed they may be prosecuted for any offence, asks to make a statement which relates to any such offence and wants to write it they shall be asked to write out and sign the following before writing what they want to say:

'I make this statement of my own free will. I understand that I do not have to say anything. This statement may be given in evidence.';

5. Any person writing their own statement shall be allowed to do so without any prompting except a police officer or other police staff may indicate to them which matters are material or question any ambiguity in the statement.

(b) Written by a police officer or other police staff

6. If a person says they would like someone to write the statement for them, a police officer, or other police staff shall write the statement.

7. If the person has not been charged with, or informed they may be prosecuted for, any offence to which the statement they want to make relates they shall, before starting, be asked to sign, or make their mark, to the following:

(a) unless the statement is made at a time when the restriction on drawing adverse inferences from silence applies, see *Annex C:*

'I, ..., wish to make a statement. I want someone to write down what I say. I understand that I do not have to say anything but that it may harm my defence if I do not mention when questioned something which I later rely on in court. This statement may be given in evidence.';

(b) if the statement is made at a time when the restriction on drawing adverse inferences from silence applies:

'I, ..., wish to make a statement. I want someone to write down what I say. I understand that I do not have to say anything. This statement may be given in evidence.'

8. If, on the occasion of being charged with or informed they may be prosecuted for any offence, the person asks to make a statement which relates to any such offence they shall before starting be asked to sign, or make their mark to, the following:

(a) unless the restriction on drawing adverse inferences from silence applied, see *Annex C*, when they were so charged or informed they may be prosecuted:

'I, ..., wish to make a statement. I want someone to write down what I say. I understand that I do not have to say anything but that it may harm my defence if I do not mention when questioned something which I later rely on in court. This statement may be given in evidence.';

(b) if the restriction on drawing adverse inferences from silence applied when they were so charged or informed they may be prosecuted:

'I, ..., wish to make a statement. I want someone to write down what I say. I understand that I do not have to say anything. This statement may be given in evidence.'

9. If, having already been charged with or informed they may be prosecuted for any offence, a person asks to make a statement which relates to any such offence they shall before starting, be asked to sign, or make their mark to:

'I, ..., wish to make a statement. I want someone to write down what I say. I understand that I do not have to say anything. This statement may be given in evidence.'

10. The person writing the statement must take down the exact words spoken by the person making it and must not edit or paraphrase it. Any questions that are necessary, e.g. to make it more intelligible, and the answers given must be recorded at the same time on the statement form.

11. When the writing of a statement is finished the person making it shall be asked to read it and to make any corrections, alterations or additions they want. When they have finished reading they shall be asked to write and sign or make their mark on the following certificate at the end of the statement:

'I have read the above statement, and I have been able to correct, alter or add anything I wish. This statement is true. I have made it of my own free will.'

12. If the person making the statement cannot read, or refuses to read it, or to write the above mentioned certificate at the end of it or to sign it, the person taking the statement shall read it to them and ask them if they would like to correct, alter or add anything and to put their signature or make their mark at the end. The person taking the statement shall certify on the statement itself what has occurred.

Annex E—Summary of Provisions Relating to Mentally Disordered and Otherwise Mentally Vulnerable People

1. If an officer has any suspicion, or is told in good faith, that a person of any age may be mentally disordered or otherwise mentally vulnerable, or mentally incapable of understanding the significance of questions or their replies that person shall be treated as mentally disordered or otherwise mentally vulnerable for the purposes of this Code. See *paragraph 1.10*.

2. In the case of a person who is mentally disordered or otherwise mentally vulnerable, 'the appropriate adult' means:

(a) a relative, guardian or other person responsible for their care or custody;

(b) someone experienced in dealing with mentally disordered or mentally vulnerable people but who is not a police officer or employed by the police;

(c) failing these, some other responsible adult aged 18 or over who is not a police officer or employed by the police. See *paragraph 1.13(b) and Note 1D*.

3. If the detention of a person who is mentally vulnerable or appears to be suffering from a mental disorder is authorised by the review officer (see *paragraphs 14.1 and 14.2 and Notes for Guidance 14A and 14B*), the custody officer must as soon as practicable inform the appropriate adult of the grounds for detention and the person's whereabouts, and ask the adult to come to the police station to see them. If the appropriate adult: is already at the station when information is given as in *paragraphs 3.1 to 3.5* the information must be given in their presence is not at the station when the provisions of *paragraph 3.1 to 3.5* are complied with these provisions must be complied with again in their presence once they arrive. See *paragraphs 3.15 to 3.16 4*. If the appropriate adult, having been informed of the right to legal advice, considers legal advice should be taken, the provisions of *section 6* apply as if the mentally disordered or otherwise mentally vulnerable person had requested access to legal advice. See *paragraph 3.20 and Note E1*.

5. The custody officer must make sure a person receives appropriate clinical attention as soon as reasonably practicable if the person appears to be suffering from a mental disorder or in urgent cases immediately call the nearest health care professional or an ambulance. It is not intended these provisions delay the transfer of a detainee to a place of safety under the Mental Health Act 1983, section 136 if that is applicable. If an assessment under that Act is to take place at a police station, the custody officer must consider whether an appropriate health care professional should be called to conduct an initial clinical check on the detainee. See *paragraph 9.6 and 9.8*.

6. If a mentally disordered or otherwise mentally vulnerable person is cautioned in the absence of the appropriate adult, the caution must be repeated in the appropriate adult's presence. See *paragraph 10.11*.

7. A mentally disordered or otherwise mentally vulnerable person must not be interviewed or asked to provide or sign a written statement in the absence of the appropriate adult unless the provisions of *paragraphs 11.2 or 11.11 to 11.13* apply. Questioning in these circumstances may not continue in the absence of the appropriate adult once sufficient information to avert the risk has been obtained. A record shall be made of the grounds for any decision to begin an interview in these circumstances. See *paragraphs 11.2, 11.9 and 11.11 to 11.13*.

8. If the appropriate adult is present at an interview, they shall be informed they are not expected to act simply as an observer and the purposes of their presence are to:
• advise the interviewee
• observe whether or not the interview is being conducted properly and fairly facilitate communication with the interviewee. See *paragraph 11.10*.

9. If the custody officer charges a mentally disordered or otherwise mentally vulnerable person with an offence or takes such other action as is appropriate when there is sufficient evidence for a prosecution this must be done in the presence of the appropriate adult. The written notice embodying any charge must be given to the appropriate adult. See *paragraphs PACE Code C Section 16*.

10. An intimate or strip search of a mentally disordered or otherwise mentally vulnerable person may take place only in the presence of the appropriate adult of the same sex, unless the detainee specifically requests the presence of a particular adult of the opposite sex. A strip search may take place in the absence of an appropriate adult only in cases of urgency when there is a risk of serious harm to the detainee or others. See *Annex A, paragraphs 6 and 12(c)*.

11. Particular care must be taken when deciding whether to use any form of approved restraints on a mentally disordered or otherwise mentally vulnerable person in a locked cell. See *paragraph 8.2*.

Notes for guidance

E1 The purpose of the provision at paragraph 3.20 is to protect the rights of a mentally disordered or otherwise mentally vulnerable detained person who does not understand the significance of what is said to them. If the detained person wants to exercise the right to legal advice, the appropriate action should be taken and not delayed until the appropriate adult arrives. A mentally disordered or otherwise mentally vulnerable detained person should always be given an opportunity, when an appropriate adult is called to the police station, to consult privately with a solicitor in the absence of the appropriate adult if they want.

E2 Although people who are mentally disordered or otherwise mentally vulnerable are often capable of providing reliable evidence, they may, without knowing or wanting to do so, be particularly prone in certain circumstances to provide information that may be unreliable, misleading or self-incriminating. Special care should always be taken when questioning such a person, and the appropriate adult should be involved if there is any doubt about a person's mental state or capacity. Because of the risk of unreliable evidence, it is important to obtain corroboration of any facts admitted whenever possible.

E3 Because of the risks referred to in Note E2, which the presence of the appropriate adult is intended to minimise, officers of superintendent rank or above should exercise their discretion to authorise the commencement of an interview in the appropriate adult's absence only in exceptional cases, if it is necessary to avert an immediate risk of serious harm. See paragraphs 11.2, 11.11 to 11.13.

Annex F—Countries with which Bilateral Consular Conventions or Agreements Requiring Notification of the Arrest and Detention of their Nationals are in Force.

Armenia	Kazakhstan
Austria	Macedonia
Azerbaijan	Mexico
Belarus	Moldova
Belgium	Mongolia
Bosnia-Herzegovina	Norway
Bulgaria	Poland
China*	Romania
Croatia	Russia
Cuba	Slovak Republic
Czech Republic	Slovenia
Denmark	Spain
Egypt	Sweden
France	Tajikistan
Georgia	Turkmenistan
German Federal Republic	Ukraine
Greece	USA
Hungary	Uzbekistan
Italy	Yugoslavia
Japan	

* Police are required to inform Chinese officials of arrest/detention in the Manchester consular district only. This comprises Derbyshire, Durham, Greater Manchester, Lancashire, Merseyside, North, South and West Yorkshire, and Tyne and Wear.

Annex G—Fitness to be Interviewed

1. This Annex contains general guidance to help police officers and health care professionals assess whether a detainee might be at risk in an interview.

2. A detainee may be at risk in a interview if it is considered that:
(a) conducting the interview could significantly harm the detainee's physical or mental state;
(b) anything the detainee says in the interview about their involvement or suspected involvement in the offence about which they are being interviewed might be considered unreliable in subsequent court proceedings because of their physical or mental state.

3. In assessing whether the detainee should be interviewed, the following must be considered:

(a) how the detainee's physical or mental state might affect their ability to understand the nature and purpose of the interview, to comprehend what is being asked and to appreciate the significance of any answers given and make rational decisions about whether they want to say anything;

(b) the extent to which the detainee's replies may be affected by their physical or mental condition rather than representing a rational and accurate explanation of their involvement in the offence;

(c) how the nature of the interview, which could include particularly probing questions, might affect the detainee.

4. It is essential health care professionals who are consulted consider the functional ability of the detainee rather than simply relying on a medical diagnosis, e.g. it is possible for a person with severe mental illness to be fit for interview.

5. Health care professionals should advise on the need for an appropriate adult to be present, whether reassessment of the person's fitness for interview may be necessary if the interview lasts beyond a specified time, and whether a further specialist opinion may be required.

6. When health care professionals identify risks they should be asked to quantify the risks. They should inform the custody officer:
• whether the person's condition:
  – is likely to improve
  – will require or be amenable to treatment; and
• indicate how long it may take for such improvement to take effect.

7. The role of the health care professional is to consider the risks and advise the custody officer of the outcome of that consideration. The health care professional's determination and any advice or recommendations should be made in writing and form part of the custody record.

8. Once the health care professional has provided that information, it is a matter for the custody officer to decide whether or not to allow the interview to go ahead and if the interview is to proceed, to determine what safeguards are needed. Nothing prevents safeguards being provided in addition to those required under the Code. An example might be to have an appropriate health care professional present during the interview, in addition to an appropriate adult, in order constantly to monitor the person's condition and how it is being affected by the interview.

Annex H—Detained Person: Observation List

1. If any detainee fails to meet any of the following criteria, an appropriate health care professional or an ambulance must be called.

2. When assessing the level of rousability, consider:

Rousability—can they be woken?
- go into the cell
- call their name
- shake gently

Response to questions—can they give appropriate answers to questions such as:
- What's your name?
- Where do you live?
- Where do you think you are?

Response to commands—can they respond appropriately to commands such as:
- Open your eyes!
- Lift one arm, now the other arm!

3. Remember to take into account the possibility or presence of other illnesses, injury, or mental condition, a person who is drowsy and smells of alcohol may also have the following:
- Diabetes
- Epilepsy
- Head injury
- Drug intoxication or overdose
- Stroke

Appendix 2

The Terrorism Act 2000—Code of Practice for Audio Recording of Interviews

Section 1 General

1.1 This Code of Practice applies to the audio taping of interviews with persons arrested under section 41 or detained by a police officer at a police station under Schedule 7 of the Terrorism Act 2000 ('the Act').

1.2 This Code of Practice must be readily available at all police stations for consultation by police officers, arrested or detained persons, members of the public, appropriate adults and solicitors.

1.3 In this code reference to a 'POLICE STATION' includes any place which is designated by the Secretary of State under paragraph 1(1) of Schedule 8 to the Act as a place at which persons may be detained under section 41.

1.4 The notes for guidance included are not provisions of this code. They form guidance to police officers and others about its application and interpretation.

1.5 Nothing in this code shall be taken as detracting in any way from the legal responsibilities of interviewing officers in conducting an interview with a detained person.

1.6 In this code 'APPROPRIATE ADULT' means:
(i) in the case of a juvenile or, in Scotland, a child:
    (a) his parent or guardian (where they are not involved in the case); or, if he is in care, the care authority or voluntary organisation. The term 'IN CARE' is used in this code to cover all cases in which a juvenile is 'LOOKED AFTER' by a local authority under the terms of the Children Act 1989, the Children (Northern Ireland) Order 1995 or the Children (Scotland) Act 1995;
    (b) a social worker; or

(c) failing either of the above, another responsible adult aged 18 or over who is not a police officer or employed by the police.

(ii) in the case of a person who is mentally disordered or mentally handicapped:

(a) a relative, guardian or other person responsible for his care or custody;

(b) someone who has experience of dealing with mentally disordered or mentally handicapped people but who is not a police officer or employed by the police; or

(c) failing either of the above, some other responsible adult aged 18 or over who is not a police officer or employed by the police.

'MENTAL DISORDER' is a generic term which has the meaning given to it in section 1(2) of the Mental Health Act 1983, that is, 'mental illness, arrested or incomplete development of mind, psychopathic disorder and any other disorder or disability of mind' and which includes reference to 'mental handicap' as defined in Article 3(1) of the Mental Health (Northern Ireland) Order 1986 as 'a state of arrested or incomplete development of mind which includes significant impairment of intelligence and social functioning'.

1.7 In this code 'SOLICITOR' means:

In Northern Ireland a solicitor qualified to practice in accordance with the Solicitors (Northern Ireland) Order 1976 or the Solicitors Act 1974.

In England and Wales a solicitor who holds a current practising certificate, a trainee solicitor, a duty solicitor representative or an accredited representative included on the register of representatives maintained by the Legal Aid Board.

In Scotland a solicitor who is entitled to practise in terms of the Solicitor (Scotland) Act 1980.

1.8 In this code the term 'RELEVANT PROSECUTING AUTHORITY' includes the Director of Public Prosecutions in England & Wales, the Director of Public Prosecutions for Northern Ireland and the Procurator Fiscal & Lord Advocate in Scotland and any other body or person, other than the police, with a statutory responsibility for prosecution and to whom the police report the investigation of any criminal offence.

1.9 If anyone appears to be under the age of 17 then he shall be treated as a juvenile for the purposes of this code. In Scotland, a child is anyone under the age of 16 except where that person is between 16 and 18 and is the subject of a supervision requirement of a Children's Hearing.

1.10 Only officers who have been trained for the purpose can carry out tape-recorded interviews under this code.

Notes for guidance

1A In the case of people who are mentally disordered or mentally handicapped, it may in certain circumstances be more satisfactory for all concerned if the appropriate adult is one who has experience or training in their care rather than a relative lacking such qualifications. But if the person himself prefers a relative to a better qualified stranger or objects to a particular person as the appropriate adult, his wishes should if practicable be respected.

1B It is important to bear in mind that, although juveniles or people who are mentally disordered or mentally handicapped are often capable of providing reliable evidence, they may, without knowing or wishing to do so, be particularly prone in certain circumstances to provide information which is unreliable, misleading or self-incriminating. Special care should therefore always be exercised in questioning such a person, and the appropriate adult should always be involved, if there is any doubt about a person's age, mental state or capacity. Because of the risk of unreliable evidence it is also important to obtain corroboration of any facts admitted whenever possible.

1C Reasonable effort should be made to allow access to a solicitor from an outside jurisdiction provided the solicitor is entitled to practice.

Section 2 Recording and Sealing of Master Tapes

2.1 The audio recording of interviews shall be carried out openly so as to instill confidence in the integrity of the tape as an impartial and accurate record of the interview. (See Note 2A)

2.2 One tape, referred to in this Code as the master tape, will be sealed before it leaves the presence of the detained person. A second tape will be used as a working copy. The master tape is either one of the tapes used in the twin or triple deck tape-recorder or the only tape used in single deck machines. The working copy is either the second tape used in a twin or triple deck machine or a copy of the master tape made by a single deck machine.

Appendix 2: Code of Practice for Audio Recording Interviews

Notes for Guidance

2A. Interviewing officers will wish to arrange that, as far as possible, audio recording arrangements are unobtrusive. It must be clear to the detained person, however, that there is no opportunity to interfere with the recording equipment or the tapes.

2B. The purpose of sealing the master tape before it leaves the presence of the detained person is to establish his confidence that the integrity of the tape is preserved. Where a single deck machine is used the working copy of the master tape must be made in the presence of the suspect without the master tape having left his sight. The working copy shall be used for making further copies where the need arises. The recorder will be capable of recording voices and will have a time coding or other security device.

Section 3 Interviews to be audio recorded

When audio recording is required

3.1 Subject to paragraph 3.5 below, audio recording shall be used for any interview with a person detained under section 41 of the Act or detained at a police station under Schedule 7 to that Act.

3.2 Audio recording shall also be used in an interview with a person suspected on reasonable grounds of an offence under section 1 of the Official Secrets Act 1911 (offences prejudicial to the safety or interests of the State).

3.3 The whole of each interview shall be audio recorded, including the taking and reading back of any statement.

When audio recording is NOT required

3.4 Audio recording is not required for people being examined under Schedule 7 to the Act unless they are detained at a police station.

Note

An 'examination' can only take place at a port or airport and must end after 9 hours (Schedule 7 of the Terrorism Act 2000).

3.5 A uniformed officer not below the rank of inspector who is not involved with the investigation (the authorising officer) may authorise the interviewing officer not to audio record the interview where it is not reasonably practicable to do so because of failure of the equipment or the non-availability of a suitable interview room or recorder, and the authorising officer considers on reasonable grounds that the interview should not be delayed until the failure has been rectified or a suitable room or recorder becomes available. In all cases the authorising officer shall make a note in specific terms of the reasons for not audio recording.

Notes for Guidance

3A No person who is unfit through drink or drugs to the extent that they are unable to appreciate the significance of questions put to them or their answers may be questioned in that condition. A medical officer or medical practitioner can give advice about whether or not a person is fit to be interviewed.

3B A decision not to audio record an interview for any reason may be the subject of comment if a case comes to court. The authorising officer should therefore be prepared to justify his decision in each case.

Section 4 The Interview

(a) Commencement of interview

4.1 When the detained person is brought into the interview room the interviewing officer (the police officer conducting the interview or any of such officers, if there are more than one) shall, without delay, but in the sight of the detained person, load the recorder with previously unused tapes and set it to record. The tapes must be unwrapped or otherwise opened in the presence of the detained person. (See Note 4A)

Notes for Guidance

4A The interviewing officer should attempt to estimate the likely length of the interview and ensure the appropriate number of unused tapes, and labels with which to seal the master tapes are available in the interview room.

4.2 (i) The interviewing officer shall then tell the detained person formally about the audio recording.

He shall state:-

(a) that the interview is being audio recorded;
(b) the date, time of commencement and place of the interview;
(c) his name (or his warrant or other identification numbers) and rank and the name (or warrant or other identification numbers) and rank of any other police officer present;
(d) the name of the detained person and any other person present (eg solicitor); and

(e) that the detained person will be given a notice about what will happen to the tapes.

(ii) When the interviewing officer identifies himself and his rank in accordance with sub-paragraph 4.2(i)(c) above, any other police officer present shall then also state his name (or warrant or other identification number) and rank.

(iii) When the interviewing officer states the name of the detained person and any other person present, in accordance with sub-paragraph 4.2 (i)(d) above, he shall invite each such person to identify himself for the purpose of the tape. (See Note 4B)

Notes for Guidance

4B It is necessary, for the purpose of voice identification in the recording, for the interviewing officer to ask the detained person and any other persons present to identify themselves.

(iv) Any person entering the interview room after the interview has commenced shall be invited by the interviewing officer to identify himself for the purpose of the tape and state the reason for which he has entered the interview room.

(b) Interviews under section 41

4.3 Unless in accordance with paragraphs 8 and 16 of Schedule 8 of the Act access to independent legal advice has been delayed (the reasons for which should be communicated to the detained person and recorded as soon as is reasonably practicable), the interviewing officer shall remind the detained person of his right to free and independent legal advice and that he can speak to a solicitor privately. Immediately prior to the commencement or re-commencement of any interview at a police station, the interviewing officer should remind the detained person of his entitlement to legal advice and that the interview can be delayed for this purpose.

4.4 The interviewing officer shall then advise the detained person in the following terms:

In England and Wales

'you do not have to say anything. But it may harm your defence if you do not mention when questioned something which you later rely on in court. Anything you do say may be given in evidence.'

In Northern Ireland

'you do not have to say anything, but I must caution you that if you do not mention when questioned something which you later rely on in court, it may harm your defence. If you do say anything it may be given in evidence.'

In Scotland

'you are not bound to answer, but if you do your answers will be tape-recorded and may be noted and may be used in evidence. Do you understand.'

Further cautions may be appropriate during the course of the interview where, for example, fresh evidence suggests further offences may have been committed.

4.5 Minor deviations from the form of words set out in the above paragraphs do not constitute a breach of this Code provided the sense is preserved.

(c) Special warnings under Sections 36 and 37 of the Criminal Justice and Public Order Act 1994 (England and Wales) and Articles 5 and 6 of the Criminal Evidence (Northern Ireland) Order 1988

4.6 When a suspect who is interviewed after arrest fails or refuses to answer certain questions, or to answer them satisfactorily, after due warning, a court or jury may draw a proper inference from this silence under section 36 and section 37 of the Criminal Justice and Public Order Act 1994 or Articles 5 and 6 of the Criminal Evidence (Northern Ireland) Order 1988. This applies when:

(a) a suspect is arrested by a constable and there is found on his person, or in or on his clothing or footwear, or otherwise in his possession, or in the place where he was arrested, any objects, marks or substances, or marks on such objects, and the person fails or refuses to account for the objects, marks or substances found; or

(b) an arrested person was found by a constable at a place or at about the time the offence for which he was arrested is alleged to have been committed, and the person fails or refuses to account for his presence at that place.

4.7 For an inference to be drawn from a suspect's failure or refusal to answer a question about one of these matters or to answer it satisfactorily, the interviewing officer must first tell him in ordinary language:

(a) what offence he is investigating;

(b) what fact he is asking the suspect to account for;

(c) that he believes this fact may be due to the suspect's taking part in the commission of the offence in question;

(d) that a court may draw a proper inference from his silence if he fails or refuses to account for the fact about which he is being questioned;

(e) that a record is being made of the interview and may be given in evidence if he is brought to trial.

(d) Interviews of those detained at a police station under Schedule 7 to the Act

Note

i.e someome originally detained at a port or airport who is being 'examined' within 9 hours of the detention.

4.8 The interviewing officer shall inform the detained person that he is not under arrest or caution but that he is being detained under the provisions of Schedule 7 of the Act. He will explain that this in itself does not mean that the interviewer suspects that the detained person is or has been concerned in the commission preparation or instigation of acts of terrorism and that the purpose of the questioning is to enable the interviewer to determine whether the detained person appears to be such a person.

4.9 The interviewer shall advise the detained person that, in accordance with paragraph 5 of Schedule 7 to the Act, he has a duty to give the interviewer all the information in his possession which the interviewer requests in connection with his determining whether the person is or has been concerned in the commission, preparation or instigation of acts of terrorism.

4.10 He shall also advise the detained person that if he deliberately fails to comply with the interviewer's request he may be guilty of an offence under paragraph 18(1) of Schedule 7 to the Act.

4.11 The interviewer shall inform the detained person that he may, if he wishes, at public expense, inform a relative or someone close to him, or known to him, or someone who is likely to take an interest in his welfare that he is being questioned and where he is. The interviewers shall also advise the detained person that he can, if he wishes, also consult a solicitor, either in person, in writing or by telephone and that the interview can be delayed for this purpose.

(e) Interviews with the deaf or with those who do not understand English

4.12 If a person appears to be deaf or there is doubt about his hearing or speaking ability, he must not be interviewed in the absence of an interpreter unless he agrees in writing to be interviewed without one or unless an officer of the rank of superintendent or above considers that delaying the interview would be likely:

(a) to lead to interference with or harm to evidence connected with an offence or interference with or physical harm to other people;

(b) to lead to the alerting of other people suspected of having committed an offence but not yet arrested for it; or

(c) to hinder the recovery of property obtained in consequence of the commission of an offence.

Questioning in these circumstances may not continue once sufficient information to avert the immediate risk has been obtained. A record shall be made of the grounds for any decision to interview a person under this paragraph.

4.13 If the detained person is deaf, or there is doubt about his hearing ability, the interviewing officer shall take a verbatim contemporaneous note of the interview, in addition to audio recording it in accordance with the provisions of this code. (See Note 4C)

Notes for Guidance

4C Paragraph 4.13 is intended to give the deaf equivalent rights of first hand access to the full interview record.

4.14 Except where an officer of the rank of superintendent or above believes that (a), (b) or (c) in paragraph 4.12 above applies, a person must not be interviewed in the absence of a person capable of acting as interpreter if:

(a) he has difficulty in understanding English;

(b) the interviewing officer cannot understand the person's own language; and

(c) the person wishes an interpreter to be present.

4.15 Where paragraph 4.3 applies and the person concerned cannot communicate with the solicitor, whether because of language, hearing or speech difficulties, the interpreter must be called. The interpreter may be a police officer except where interpretation is needed for the purposes of obtaining legal advice.

(f) Objections and complaints by the detained person

4.16 If the detained person raises objections to the interview being audio recorded either at the outset or during the interview or during a break in the interview, the interviewing officer shall remind him (see sub-paragraph 4.2 (i)(a)) that the interview is being audio recorded and that his objections are being recorded on tape. When any objections have been recorded or the detained person has refused to have his objections recorded, the interviewing officer shall, before turning off the recorder, give his reasons for doing so and then turn it off. He shall then make a verbatim written record of the interview. If the interviewing officer reasonably considers that he should proceed to put questions to the detained person with the recorder still on, he may do so. The detained person's attention shall be drawn to the fact that the recorder is still operating. (See Note 4D)

Notes for Guidance

4D The interviewing officer should bear in mind that his decision to continue recording against the wishes of the detained person may be the subject of comment if the case comes to court. He may wish to consider, however, reminding the interviewee that audio-recording is an added safeguard in the interview process and, where appropriate, seek a view from the interviewee's legal representative before switching off the tape recorder.

4.17 If in the course of an interview a complaint is made by the person being questioned, or on his behalf, about his detention, treatment and questioning or if the complaint is that the provisions of this Code have not been observed, then the interviewing officer shall record it in the interview record and inform the custody officer (in Scotland, the duty officer), or those carrying out the functions of a custody officer, who is then responsible for dealing with the complaint in accordance with recognised procedures. In Northern Ireland, any complaint should be communicated to the Office of the Police Ombudsman as soon as possible. (See Note 4E)

Notes for Guidance

4E Where the custody officer is called immediately to deal with the complaint, wherever possible the tape recorder should be left to run until the custody officer has entered the interview room and spoken to the person being interviewed. Continuation or termination of the interview should be at the discretion of the interviewing officer pending the instigation of recognised complaints procedures in England and Wales, Scotland and Northern Ireland. Where the complaint concerns a matter not connected with this code or with the detained person's detention, treatment or questioning, the decision to continue with the interview is at the discretion of the interviewing officer. Where the interviewing officer decides to continue with the interview the person being interviewed shall be told that the complaint will be brought to the attention of the custody officer or duty officer (in Northern Ireland the Office of the Police Ombudsman) at the conclusion of the interview. When the interview is concluded the interviewing officer must, as soon as practicable, inform the custody officer of the existence and nature of the complaint made.

4.18 If the detained person indicates that he wishes to tell a police officer about matters not directly connected with the matter about which he is being interviewed and that he is unwilling for these matters to be audio recorded, he shall be given the opportunity to tell a police officer about these matters after the conclusion of the interview. Consideration should be given as to whether a separate caution is appropriate in those circumstances.

(g) Changing tapes

4.19 When the recorder indicates that the tapes have only a short time left to run, the interviewing officer shall tell the detained person that the tapes are coming to an end and round off that part of the interview. If the officer wishes to continue the interview but does not already have a second set of tapes, he shall obtain a set. The detained person shall not be left unattended in the interview room. The interviewing officer shall remove the tapes from the recorder and insert the new tapes which shall be unwrapped or otherwise opened in the detained person's presence. The recorder shall then be set to record on the new tapes. When more than one set of tapes has been used, care must be taken to ensure there is no confusion between the sets of tapes. This must be done by marking each set of tapes with the same identification number immediately it is removed from the recorder.

(h) Taking a break during interview

4.20 When a break is to be taken during the course of an interview and the interview room is to be vacated by the detained person, the fact that a break is to be taken, the reason for it and the time shall be audio recorded. The tapes shall then be removed from the recorder and the procedures for the conclusion of an interview set out below shall be followed.

4.21 When a break is to be a short one and both the detained person and the interviewing officer are to remain in the interview room the fact that a break is to be taken, the reason for it and the time shall be audio recorded. The recorder may be turned off: there is, however, no need to remove the tape and when the interview is recommenced the recording shall be continued on the same tape. The time at which the interview recommences shall be audio recorded.

4.22 When there is a break in questioning under caution the interviewing officer must ensure that the person being questioned is reminded of their right to legal advice and also that he is aware that he remains under caution. If there is any doubt the caution must be given again in full when the interview resumes. (See Notes 4F and 4G)

Notes for Guidance

4F In considering whether to caution again after a break in an interview, the interviewing officer should bear in mind that he may have to satisfy a court that the detained person understood he was still under caution when the interview resumed (or during the course of the interview itself).

4G The officer should bear in mind that it may be necessary to show to the court that nothing occurred during a break in an interview or between interviews which influenced the detained person's recorded evidence. The officer should consider, therefore, after a break in an interview or at the beginning of a subsequent interview summarising on tape the reason for the break and confirming this with the detained person.

(i) Failure of recording equipment

4.23 If there is a failure of equipment which can be rectified quickly, for example by inserting new tapes, the procedures set out in paragraph 4.19 shall be followed, and when the recording is resumed the interviewing officer shall explain what has happened and audio record the time the interview recommences. If, however, it is not possible to continue recording on that particular recorder and no replacement recorder or other suitably equipped interview room is readily available, the interview may continue without being audio recorded. In such circumstances the authorisation procedures in paragraph 3.5 above shall be followed. (See Note 4H)

Notes for Guidance

4H If one of the tapes breaks during the interview it should be sealed as a master tape in the presence of the detained person and the interview resumed where it left off. The unbroken tape should be copied and the original sealed as a master tape in the detained person's presence, if necessary after the interview. If equipment for copying the unbroken tape is not readily available, both tapes should be sealed in the presence of the detained person and the interview begun again.

(j) Removing tapes from the recorder

4.24 Where tapes are removed from the recorder in the course of an interview, they shall be retained and the procedures set out in paragraph 4.26 followed.

(k) Conclusion of interview

4.25 At the conclusion of the interview, the detained person shall be offered the opportunity to clarify anything he has said and to add anything he may wish.

4.26 At the conclusion of the interview, including the taking and reading back of any written statement, the time shall be recorded and the recorder switched off. The master tape, as selected by the detained person, shall be sealed with a master tape label and treated as an exhibit (in Scotland, a production). The interviewing officer shall sign the label (a warrant or other identification number may be used) and ask the detained person and any other third party present to sign it also. If the detained person or third party refuses to sign the label, an officer not below the rank of inspector, who is not involved with the investigation, or if one is not available, the custody officer shall be called into the interview room and asked to sign it. (See Note 4I)

Notes for Guidance

4I Where the detained person refuses to sign the label, they should be given an opportunity to place their reasons for so doing on record.

4.27 The detained person or an appropriate adult or an interpreter shall be handed a notice at the end of the first interview which explains: the use which will be made of the tape-recording; the arrangements for access to the tape; that a copy of the tape shall be supplied upon request as soon as practicable if the detained person is charged or informed that he will be prosecuted; the period of retention of the tape; the arrangements for the destruction of the tape. (See Note 4J and the Annex)

Notes for Guidance

4J Only one notice is required to be served on the detained person, or an appropriate adult or an interpreter, and this should be carried out at the end of the first interview.

Section 5 Interview Records of Interviews under Sections 3.5, 4.13 and 4.16 above

5.1 An accurate record must be made of each interview with a detained person, carried out at a police station under paragraph 3.5, paragraph 4.13 or 4.16.

5.2 The record must state the place of the interview, the time it begins and ends, the time the record is made (if different), any breaks in the interview and the names (or warrant or other identification number) and duty station of such officers and all those present; and must be made on the forms provided for this purpose or in the officer's pocket book.

5.3 The record must be made during the course of the interview, unless in the investigating officer's view this would not be practicable or would interfere with the conduct of the interview, and must constitute either a verbatim record of what was said or, failing this, an account of the interview which adequately and accurately summarises it.

5.4 If an interview record is not made during the course of the interview it must be made as soon as practicable after its completion.

5.5 Written interview records must be timed and signed by the maker.

5.6 If an interview record is not completed in the course of the interview the reason must be recorded in the officer's pocket book.

5.7 Unless it is impracticable the person interviewed must be given the opportunity under tape recorded conditions to read the interview record and to sign it as correct or to indicate the respects in which he considers it inaccurate. If the person concerned cannot read or refuses to read the record or to sign it, the senior officer present shall read it to him and ask him whether he would like to sign it as correct (or make his mark) or to indicate the respects in which he considers it inaccurate. The police officer shall then certify on the interview record itself what has occurred. (See Note 5A)

5.8 If an appropriate adult or person's solicitor is present during the interview, he shall also be given the opportunity to read and sign the interview record (or any written statement taken down by a police officer).

5.9 A written record shall also be made of any comments made by a suspected person, including unsolicited comments which are outside the context of an interview but which might be relevant to the offence. Any such record must be timed and signed by the maker. Where practicable the person should be given the opportunity to read and sign it as correct or to indicate the respects in which he considers it inaccurate. (See Note 5B)

5.10 Where an interview has been conducted under paragraph 3.5 or paragraph 4.16 and the detained person is someone to which paragraph 4.14 of the code refers, the interviewing officer shall ensure that the interpreter makes a note of the interview at the time in the language of the person being interviewed for use in the event of his being called to give evidence, and certifies its accuracy. He shall allow sufficient time for the interpreter to make a note of each question and answer after each has been put or given and interpreted. The person shall be given an opportunity to read it or have it read to him and sign it as correct or to indicate the respects in which he considers it inaccurate.

5.11 In the case of a person making a statement in a language other than English:

(a) the interpreter shall take down the statement in the language in which it is made;

(b) the person making the statement shall be invited to sign it; and

(c) an official English translation shall be made in due course.

Notes for Guidance

5A Where a suspect agrees to read the records of interviews and other comments and to sign them as correct, he should be asked to endorse the records with words such as 'I agree that this is a correct record of what was said' and add his signature. Where the suspect does not agree with the record, the officer should record details of any disagreements and then ask the suspect to read these details and then sign them to the effect that they accurately reflect his disagreement. Any refusal to sign when asked to do so shall be recorded.

5B Interviewing officers will wish to consider whether unsolicited relevant comments made during the course of interview should be brought into the interview to assist in establishing them as evidence

Section 6 After the Interview under Section 4

6.1 The interviewing officer shall make a written record of the fact that the interview has taken place, that it has been recorded on audio tape, its time, duration and date. The times during which the recorder has been operating and the identification number of the master tape will be included in the written record.

6.2 Where no further action, including arrest and / or criminal proceedings follow in respect of the person whose interview has been recorded the tapes must nevertheless be kept securely in accordance with section 7.

6.3 Subject as mentioned at paragraph 6.6, where criminal proceedings do follow or are under consideration, the interviewing officer shall prepare, or have prepared on his behalf, a full transcript of the interview or a summary of the interview, which shall be signed by the interviewing officer (see Notes 6A, 6B and 6C). In Scotland the Procurator Fiscal takes full responsibility for the full transcript of the interview tapes.

6.4 Any written statement of evidence prepared by the interviewing officer in relation to what took place at the interview shall refer to the fact that the interview was audio recorded and refer to the master tape as an exhibit (in Scotland, a production) to the statement.

6.5 Subject to paragraph 6.6, the full transcript of the interview or a summary of the interview shall be exhibited to any such written statement of evidence prepared by the interviewing officer under paragraph 6.4. If a full transcript or a summary of the interview, as the case may be, is prepared by a person other than the interviewing officer, the interviewing officer must check that the full transcript or summary of the interview is correct before he signs it, and his written statement must contain a reference to the fact that he has been shown the full transcript or summary of interview, checked it, found it to be correct and signed it.

6.6 The Chief Officer of the Police Force concerned or, where applicable, the relevant prosecuting authority may direct that, in circumstances which he shall specify, neither a full transcript of the interview or a summary of the interview will be required to be included in files submitted for the decision of the relevant Chief Officer or, where applicable, the relevant prosecuting authority. Accordingly, where the specified circumstances arise, paragraphs 6.3 and 6.5 shall not apply unless the Chief Officer or, where applicable, the relevant prosecuting authority after receipt of the file directs that a full transcript of the interview be prepared or a summary of it be prepared in that individual case. (See Note 6D)

6.7 The court shall be made aware of any transcript of the audio-recorded interview which has been made.

Notes for Guidance

6A Prior to preparing the summary of the interview or to checking a summary of interview which has been prepared on his behalf by another person, the interviewing officer may refresh his memory by listening to the working copy of the tape.

6B A person preparing a summary of interview on behalf of the interviewing officer should be a police officer, or other person who has received appropriate training in the preparation of summaries of interview. He should prepare the summary after listening to the tape and if necessary after consultation with the interviewing officer. In Scotland the interviewing officers and their supervisors are responsible for the accuracy of transcripts.

6C The summary of interview should be prepared on the basis that it will be exhibited to the interviewing officer's statement of evidence and that it will be used for the following purposes: to enable the Chief Officer or the relevant prosecuting authority to make informed decisions about the case on the basis of what was said at the interview; for use pursuant to any rule of law permitting the admission of written statements as evidence in court; where applicable, for use as a basis for the conduct of the case by the prosecution, the defence and the court without the necessity for the master tape to be played in court. The summary should, therefore, comprise a balanced account of the interview, including points in mitigation and / or defence made by the detained person. Where an admission is made the question as well as the answer containing the admission should be recorded verbatim in the summary. Care should be taken to bring to the attention of the Chief Officer and / or relevant prosecuting authority, by means of a covering report, any material on the tape which might be regarded by a court as prejudicial or inadmissible. In Scotland a transcript of the salient points will be sent to the Procurator Fiscal and a full transcript is generally prepared by the Procurator Fiscal's office prior to a criminal trial.

6D Where, in the interviewing officer's view, a significant interview occurs, for example, an admission is made, an explanation is provided, inferences may be drawn from a failure to answer questions or there are ambiguous answers, a full transcript will normally be provided. In cases of doubt early consultation with the relevant prosecuting authority is desirable.

Section 7 Tape security

7.1 The officer in charge of each police station at which interviews with detained persons are recorded shall make arrangements for all master tapes to be kept securely and their movements accounted for on the same basis as any material which may be used for evidential purposes, in accordance with Force Standing Orders. (See Note 7A)

7.2 A police officer has no authority to break the seal on a master tape which is required for criminal proceedings. If it is necessary to gain access to the master tape the police shall request the relevant prosecuting authority to seek the authority of the appropriate court for the seal to be broken, the tape copied, and resealed in the presence of an official appointee of the court. In Scotland the relevant authority of the Procurator Fiscal must be obtained. Where no court proceedings have been commenced, but are contemplated or are under consideration, the seal shall be broken, and the tape copied and resealed, in the presence of a legally qualified representative of the relevant prosecuting authority. In either case the detained person or his solicitor shall be informed and given a reasonable opportunity to be present. If the detained person or his solicitor is present he shall be invited to reseal and sign the master tape. If this offer is refused, or neither the detained person nor his solicitor is present, this shall be done by the official appointee of the court or representative of the relevant prosecuting authority, as applicable. (See Note 7B)

7.3 Where no further action including criminal proceedings results, or is under consideration, or where criminal proceedings have been concluded, it is the responsibility of the Chief Officer to establish arrangements for the breaking of the seal on the master tape, where this becomes necessary.

Notes for Guidance

7A This section is concerned with the security of the master tape which will have been sealed at the conclusion of the interview. Care should, however, be taken of working copies of tapes since their loss or destruction may lead unnecessarily to the need to have access to master tapes.

7B 'Legally qualified representative of a relevant prosecuting authority' shall be taken to mean a barrister or solicitor employed by the relevant prosecuting authority or instructed by him to represent him in regard to any matter referred to in paragraph 7.2 above. In Scotland, it may be taken to mean an advocate.

Section 8 Tape Destruction

8.1 At the conclusion of criminal proceedings, or in the event of a direction not to prosecute, the contents of a working copy of the tape shall be completely erased. Such tapes shall not be reissued for the purpose of recording interviews.

8.2 Unless the provisions of the Criminal Procedure and Investigations Act 1996, Code of Practice, apply, or unless civil proceedings have been instigated or it is clear that none will be, master tapes will be destroyed six years after the date of the interview.

Annex

[NAME OF POLICE FORCE]

Audio Recording of Interview

Notice to persons arrested under section 41 OR detained under Schedule 7 of the Terrorism Act 2000 whose interview has been audio recorded. These notices explain how the audio recording will be used and how you or your solicitor can, if you wish, arrange to listen to it if you are prosecuted.

The Use Which will be Made of the Audio Recording

The interview has been audio recorded using a single, twin or triple deck tape recorder. One of the tapes has been sealed in your presence and will be kept securely in case it is needed in court (this tape is known as the "master tape"). The other tape will be a working copy to which the police and you or your solicitor may listen if you wish. Both tapes are protected against tampering.

Arrangements to Access the Tape

If you wish, you or your solicitor may listen to the audio recording by applying to the police officer in charge of the area or Police Commander for the area where this interview took place (in Northern Ireland, the District Commander).

When a Copy of the Tape will be Supplied

If you are charged, or informed that you will be prosecuted, a copy of the tape shall be supplied upon request to you or your solicitor as soon as practicable. Your solicitor can obtain a copy of the tape by applying to the police officer in charge of the area or Police Commander for the area where this interview took place (in Northern Ireland, the District Commander; in Scotland, the Procurator Fiscal).

Retention of Audio Tapes

The master tape has been sealed and will be retained at least until you are acquitted or convicted, or the prosecutor decides not to proceed with the case. You should note that if no further action is taken against you including if criminal proceedings are not instigated against you, and if by the end of six years from the date of your interview a complaint has not been received, or civil proceedings have not been instigated and it is clear that none will be, the master tape of your interview will be destroyed. In all cases, the retention periods as set out in the Criminal Procedure and Investigations Act 1996, Code of Practice, paragraph 5(b), will be followed.

Destruction of Audio Tapes

You or your solicitor may be present to witness the destruction of the master tape. You will be notified of the date and time that the destruction of the master tape will take place.

Important Note

You are entitled to make a complaint about your treatment in police custody at any time.

Code of Practice for Authorised Officers Acting under Schedule 1 of the Anti-terrorism, Crime and Security Act 2001

1. General

1. This code of practice applies to the exercise by an authorised officer of functions of Schedule 1 to the Anti-terrorism, Crime and Security Act 2001 (the Act). The code is issued under paragraph 6(1) of Schedule 14 to the Terrorism Act 2000 (and amended by the Anti-terrorism, Crime and Security Act 2001 (Commencement) Order 2001).

2. 'Authorised officer' for the purpose of this code has the same meaning as in paragraph 19(1) of Schedule 1 to the Act. It therefore applies to an immigration officer and a customs officer when exercising functions under Schedule 1 to the Act as well as to a constable exercising these functions. The code does not apply in other circumstances in which seizure, detention or forfeiture powers are exercised. Nor does the code apply where a customs officer or constable exercises powers of seizure and detention of cash under Part 2 of the Drug Trafficking Act 1994 (DTA).

3. 'Cash' has the same meaning as in paragraph 1 of Schedule 1 to the Act. Reference to an officer's rank includes an officer acting temporarily in that rank.

4. The code should be available at all police stations for consultation by the police and members of the public. It should also be available at police offices at ports (within the meaning of Schedule 7 to the Terrorism Act 2000) where the powers are, or are likely to be used. The code should also form part of the published instructions or guidance for immigration officers and customs officers.

Authority to seize cash

5. Any decision to seize cash under the Act must be authorised:
- where seizure is undertaken by a police constable, by a police officer of the rank of Inspector or above;

- where seizure is undertaken by an immigration officer, by a Chief Immigration Officer;
- where seizure is undertaken by a customs officer, by a Customs Officer Pay Band 7 or above.

Authorisation to seize cash should be obtained prior to actual seizure of the cash itself. Verbal authorisation should be supported by written authorisation as soon as is reasonably practicable.

Use of the powers by immigration and customs officers

6. The powers to seize and detain cash under the Act should only be exercised by an immigration officer or customs officer exceptionally. If such an officer develops a suspicion in the course of exercising his/her powers under the Immigration Act 1971, the Customs and Excise Management Act 1979 or the Police and Criminal Evidence Act 1984 that cash found is liable to be seized under the Act he/she should alert a police officer at the earliest opportunity in order to continue any investigation. The person or persons carrying the cash should be informed of the suspicion and of the action taken (or proposed) to inform the police.

Scope

7. There is no minimum or maximum limit on the amount of cash which may be seized.

8. Under Schedule 1 to the Act an authorised officer may seize and detain cash (for up to 48 hours) where he/she has reasonable grounds for suspecting that the cash:-

(a)
- is intended to be used for the purposes of terrorism;
- consists of resources of a proscribed organisation; or
- is or represents property obtained by or in return for acts of terrorism or acts carried out for the purposes of terrorism (although this is subject to the exceptions set out at paragraph 16 of Schedule 1 to the Act);

   and

(b) is found at any place in the United Kingdom.

Seizure of cash

9. 'Reasonable grounds for suspecting' are likely to depend upon particular circumstances and the authorised officer should take into account such factors as how the cash was discovered, the amount involved, its origins, intended movement, destination, reasons given for a cash as opposed to normal banking transaction, whether the courier(s) and/or the owners of the cash (if different) have any links with terrorists, terrorist groups or sympathisers, whether here or overseas. Where the authorised officer has suspicions about the cash he/she should give the person who has possession of it a reasonable opportunity to provide an explanation on the details of its ownership, origins, purpose, destination and reasons for moving the amount in this way and to provide the authorised officer with supporting documentation. The authorised officer should make clear to the person that anything said will be noted and used in the event that the cash is seized and an application made to the court for its detention or forfeiture.

10. If the authorised officer believes the person has committed an offence and/or is to be arrested he or she should be cautioned and questioned in the normal way. A customs or immigration officer acting in the capacity of an authorised officer may wish or need to refer the matter to a police officer in such instances.

11. The cash should be counted in the presence of the person and another officer. Cash should not be taken out of sight of the person carrying it unless and until it is seized.

12. Where cash is seized, the authorised officer should inform the person carrying it that he suspects that it is cash within one or more of the provision(s) of paragraph 1(1) of Schedule 1 to the Act and the reasons for suspecting this.

13. The authorised officer should physically seize the cash and give a written notification (see Annex) to the person from whom the cash is seized. (This includes the sender and intended recipient of unattended parcels and other containers). This notification explains that an application may be made for detention of the cash within 48 hours of seizure and provides details of the court to which the application will be made. It also advises the person that he or she is entitled to appear at the court hearing either in person or represented by a solicitor. It advises finally that cash will be released no later than the end of the period of 48 hours from the time of seizure unless an order for its further detention is granted.

14. Where the cash is not in sterling, the figure should be entered in the relevant currency. The examining officers should not attempt to convert the currency into sterling. Similarly, where the cash is in different forms (for example, postal orders, ordinary cheques, travellers' cheques, bankers' drafts, bearer bonds or bearer shares) a description and their value should be recorded on the written notification and receipt.

15. The authorised officer should explain the contents of the notification to the person from whom the cash has been taken and what he or she has to do in order to try to get it back. The authorised officer should make every reasonable effort to ensure that the person concerned understands. The person should be asked to sign the statement in the written notification that the content of the notice has been read and understood and the authorised officer should give a copy of the notification to him. If the person refuses to sign the authorised officer should endorse the form "refused to sign" and initial the endorsement.

16. If the person does not appear to understand what is being said or the authorised officer has doubts as to the person's ability to speak English the officer should make every reasonable effort to communicate so as to be satisfied that the person understands what is required of him or her, where necessary, using someone who can act as an interpreter.

Detention of cash seized

17. The authorised officer should record in the written notification the time and date when the cash is first seized. He must release the cash and return it to the person unless a court order is obtained no later than 48 hours after the cash has been first seized.

18. The authorised officer or the Commissioners for Customs and Excise should apply in writing without delay to the relevant court for an order to detain the cash. In Scotland, the authorised officer should report the matter without delay to the procurator fiscal who is responsible for making the application to the sheriff. A copy of the written application should be given to the person from whom the cash has been seized, wherever practicable at the time of the seizure in order to give him/her the maximum time in which to make an application to the court to contest seizure and secure the release of the cash. An application for the detention of cash should be authorised by a police officer of the rank of Inspector or above.

19. Where cash is deposited in an interest bearing account in accordance with paragraph 4 of Schedule 1 to the Act, the authorised officer should ensure a central record is kept of the details of the account and when the cash was deposited. To ensure interest

accrued is accurately accounted, separate records for each cash seizure deposit should be kept.

20. When an order to detain cash has been granted the authorised
officer should keep under review whether continued detention of
the cash is justified. But this does not apply where an application for
forfeiture has been made and not concluded, where an application
has been made under paragraph 9 of Schedule 1 to the Act by a person who claims to be a victim and not concluded or where criminal
proceedings have been commenced in connection with the cash
and not concluded, whether in the United Kingdom or elsewhere.
If for any reason the authorised officer considers he is no longer
justified in detaining the cash he/she should release it and return
it to the person from whom it was seized Where detained cash is to
be released, the authorised officer should inform the court without
delay (in Scotland, the procurator fiscal is responsible for notify-
ing the sheriff that detained cash is to be released). A decision to
release the cash should be authorised by a police officer of the rank
of Inspector or above.

21. An application to renew an order to detain cash beyond 6
months and up to the maximum limit of 2 years (beginning with
the date when the first order was made), should be authorised by a
police officer of the rank of superintendent or above. In Scotland,
the procurator fiscal is responsible for making further applications.

Forfeiture

22. Any application under paragraph 6 of Schedule 1 to the Act
by or on behalf of the authorised officer for the forfeiture of cash
must be authorised by a police officer of the rank of superintendent
or above who, prior to any application being made, should review
the facts in order to be satisfied on the balance of probabilities that
the cash is cash to which Schedule 1 to the Act applies. In Scotland,
applications for the forfeiture of detained cash are made to the sheriff by the Scottish Ministers.

Security of cash seized

23. Any cash seized or received by a constable under the Act should
be handled in accordance with any standing instructions or orders
in force. Without prejudice to any such instructions or orders the
authorised officer who seizes cash should ensure that it is held
in a safe, secure place until either released or lodged in an interest accruing account under paragraph 4 of Schedule 1 to the Act

following a detention order under paragraph 3(2) of Schedule 1 to the Act.

24. Cash seized by an immigration officer or a customs officer must be handed at the earliest opportunity to the police officer with responsibility for investigating whether an application for its continued detention is to be made. The amount delivered to the police officer should be agreed and a receipt given for it by the police officer receiving it.

Annex

NOTIFICATION OF CASH SEIZURE UNDER PARAGRAPH 2 OF SCHEDULE 1 TO THE ANTI-TERRORISM, CRIME AND SECURITY ACT 2001

Under paragraph 2 of Schedule 1 to the Anti-terrorism, Crime and Security Act 2001, cash to the value of .... in.......... (currency) */postal orders */ cheques*/ travellers' cheques*/ bankers' drafts*/ bearer bonds*/ bearer shares* was seized on.......... (date) at.......... (place).

Any application for continued detention of the cash under paragraph 3 of Schedule 1 to the Anti-terrorism, Crime and Security Act 2001 must be made not later than the period of 48 hours from the period beginning with the time when it was seized.

An application will be made by a constable*/ customs officer*/ immigration officer*/ the Commissioners for Customs and Excise* to the magistrates' court at ..../*by the procurator fiscal to the sheriff's court at..........

You will receive a copy of the written application to the court with notification of the hearing. You are entitled to appear in court at the hearing, either in person or represented by a solicitor.

If no application for continued detention of the cash is made within the period of 48 hours mentioned above, the cash seized must be released.

Signed..

Time..

Date..

I .... acknowledge that cash to the value of .... in (currency)*/postal orders*/cheques*/travellers' cheques*/bankers' drafts*/bearer bonds*/bearer shares* has been seized from me and that I have read and understood this notification.

Signed..

Time..

Date..

*Delete as necessary.

Code of Practice for Examining Officers under the Terrorism Act 2000

1. General

1. This code of practice applies to the exercise by examining officers of their functions under the Terrorism Act 2000 ('the Act').

2. The notes for guidance are not provisions of the code but are guidance to examining officers on its application and interpretation.

3. 'Examining Officer' for the purpose of this code has the same meaning as in paragraph 1(1) of Schedule 7 to the Act ('the Schedule'), i.e. a constable, immigration officer or customs officer designated for the purpose of the Schedule by the Secretary of State and the Commissioners of Customs and Excise. The code only applies to immigration or designated customs officers when they are exercising their functions as examining officers under the Act and not in any other circumstances, for example where someone is examined under the Immigration Act 1971 or the Customs and Excise Management Act 1979. The code also applies to members of HM forces in Northern Ireland when exercising such functions as examining officers as the Secretary of State has, by order under Section 97 of the Act, provided for them to perform.

4. For the purposes of this code:
- 'port' and 'border area' have the same meaning as in the Schedule. A place in Northern Ireland is within the border area if it is no more than one mile from the border between Northern Ireland and the Republic of Ireland;
- Common Travel Area ('CTA') has the same meaning as in section 1(3) of the Immigration Act 1971;
- A 'juvenile' (in Scotland, a 'child') means anyone who appears to be under the age of 17 in the absence of clear evidence that he/she is older. In Scotland, a 'child' means anyone under the age 16 except where that person is between 16 and 18 and is the subject of a supervision requirement of a Children's Hearing.

5. The code should be available at all police stations for consultation by the police and members of the public. It should also be available at police offices at ports or in the border area where the powers are, or are likely to be, used. The code should also form part of the published departmental instructions/guidance for immigration officers and customs officers.

Immigration and Customs officers

6. Only exceptionally should an immigration officer or customs officer exercise functions under the Act and only
- when a police officer is not readily available; or
- if specifically requested to do so by a police officer of the rank of sergeant or above.

In all cases, where reasonably practicable, the authority of a Chief Immigration Officer in the case of an immigration officer, or in the case of a customs Officer, a Customs Officer Pay band 7, should be obtained for any action taken under the Act. Where it has not been practicable to achieve prior authorisation, the Chief Immigration Officer or the Customs Officer Pay Band 7 should be notified of the action taken as soon as possible after the exercise of functions has begun.

Scope of the Examination

7. The power to examine someone under the Schedule applies to a person on a ship or aircraft which has arrived in Great Britain or Northern Ireland (see paragraph 2(3) of the Schedule). The power to examine someone under the Schedule also applies where the examining officer *believes* that a person's presence at the port or in the border area (in Northern Ireland) is connected with his entering or leaving Great Britain or Northern Ireland (see paragraph 2(2) of the schedule). 'Belief' should be justifiable and much will depend on the individual circumstances. For example:
- the presence of a member of the public in a controlled, international or Common Travel Area arrivals or departure area or common departure lounge at a port: or
- where someone is waiting to be, is being, or has been checked in for a flight/ferry/train to or from Great Britain or Northern Ireland:
- Where someone is inside, or attending to, a vehicle which is in the process of disembarking or awaiting embarkation at a port from or to Great Britain or Northern Ireland, as the case may be, may be indicators that a person can be examined under the Schedule.

Appendix 4: Code of Practice for Examining Officers

8. These are examples for general guidance only. They are not intended as an exhaustive list. On the other hand it might well not be sufficient that someone is present in a public area at a train station, seaport or airport in the absence of other indications that they are or have been travelling. (See note)

Note for guidance on paragraph 8

Examining officers should be alert to the possibility that someone encountered at, say, an airport in a common departure area might be travelling within Great Britain or Northern Ireland. The examining officer may therefore need to obtain travel details from the person and if it is established that the person is not entering or leaving Great Britain or Northern Ireland the powers contained in the schedule cannot be utilised.

Examination powers

9. The purpose of questioning and associated powers is to determine whether a person appears to be someone who is or has been concerned in the commission, preparation or instigation of acts of terrorism. The powers, which are additional to the powers of arrest under the Act, should not be used for any other purpose. Unless, therefore, the examining officer is arresting the person, he/she need not be cautioned.

10. An examining officer may question a person whether or not he suspects that the person is or has been concerned in the commission, preparation or instigation of an act of terrorism and may stop that person for the purposes of doing so. Examining officers should therefore make every reasonable effort to exercise the power in such a way as to minimise causing embarrassment or offence to a person who has no terrorist connections. The powers to stop and question a person should not be exercised in a way which unfairly discriminates against a person on the grounds of race, colour, religion, creed, gender or sexual orientation. When deciding whether to question a person the examining officer should bear in mind that the primary reason for doing so is to maximise disruption of terrorist movements into and out of the United Kingdom.

Note for guidance on paragraph 10

The selection of people stopped and examined under the port and border area powers should, as far as is practicable given the circumstances at the port or in the area, reflect an objective assessment of the threat posed by various terrorist groups active in and outside the United kingdom. Examining officers should take particular care not to discriminate unfairly against minority ethnic groups in the exercise of these powers. When exercising the powers examining officers should consider such factors as

- known and suspected sources of terrorism
- any information on the origins and/or possible location of terrorist groups
- the possible nature of any current or future terrorist activity
- the means of travel (and documentation) which a group of individuals could use
- local circumstances, such as movements, trends at individual ports or parts of the border area.

11. The examining officer should keep the length of examination to the minimum that is practicable. Once an examination lasts for one hour, an explanatory notice of examination should be served by the examining officer on the person as set out in the Annex to this code. The contents of this notice should be explained to the person by the examining officer. Where a person's examination is protracted or where it is thought likely to be protracted, the examining officer should make arrangements to ensure that the person has the opportunity to have refreshments at regular intervals.

12. Where a person is being questioned by an examining officer who is not a police officer and it appears necessary to continue the examination, the examining officer should refer him/her to a police officer at the port or, in the border area, a police station at the earliest opportunity. The examining officer should agree the time and date of the referral with the police officer receiving the person and both should keep a record of that time and date.

Records of Examinations

13. The examining officer should record in a centrally held record at the port or at a specified police station all examinations which last for more than an hour. The record should include the name of the person examined; the total duration of the examination from the start until completion; whether the person was detained and if so when detention began. The examining officer should also keep a record at the port or, in the border area, at a police station, of all examinations under an hour. (See note)

Note for guidance on paragraph 13
Records of examination that last over an hour should be kept centrally for statistical purposes. Records of examination that last under an hour, however, should also be kept at a port or at a police station in the border area for reference purposes in the event of a complaint or query.

14. The examining officer should keep a record of any examination of someone believed to be an unaccompanied juvenile (or in Scotland, a child). The record should include the name and age (if known) of the juvenile/child. If any of these records are kept by an examining officer who is not also a police officer, the details should be passed to a police officer who has been, is or is to be involved in the examination of the person, as soon as practicable.

Juveniles (children) and other vulnerable people

15. Special care should be taken when considering whether to question someone, where it is evident that the person is a juvenile/child. A juvenile/child travelling with a parent or guardian or responsible person over 18 (for example a teacher, social worker, or group leader where the juvenile is part of an organised party) should be examined in their presence.

16. A juvenile/child aged under 16 travelling alone should not normally be examined in detail unless an adult is present. Where such a juvenile/child is travelling with a friend or relative who is 18 or over, the examining officer should consider allowing that person to be present during any routine examinations unless that person is thought to be exerting influences or pressure which could be detrimental to the juvenile/child's interest. If a more detailed examination is considered necessary it should only take place in the presence of a parent, a guardian, or (if the juvenile/child is in care) a representative of the care authority or voluntary organisation, a social worker, or an adult who is not a police officer or employed by the police and who has been appointed to represent the juvenile/child's interests. The term 'in care' is used in this code to cover all cases in which a juvenile/child is 'looked after' by a local authority under the terms of the Children Act 1989, the Children (Northern Ireland) Order 1995 or is subject to a supervision order under the Children (Scotland) Act 1995.

17. Examining officers should bear in mind that young children can be easily intimidated when examined especially if they are travelling alone but, equally, that they can be vulnerable to exploitation by adults wishing to further terrorist aims. Examining officers are not therefore precluded from examining young children but should do so sparingly, for example where it is believed that the child may be caught up in some way, wittingly or otherwise, in the commission, preparation or instigation of an act of terrorism and the examining officer believes it is necessary in the child's best interests to speak to him/her.

18. These principles apply to other vulnerable people such as those who are mentally disordered or mentally handicapped. 'Mental disorder' is a generic term which has the meaning given to it in Section 1(2) of the Mental Health Act 1983, that is, mental illness, arrested or incomplete development of mind, psychopathic disorder and any other disorder or disability of mind' and which includes reference to 'mental handicap' as defined in Article 3(1) of the Mental Health (NI) Order 1986 as 'a state of arrested or incomplete development of mind which includes significant impairment and social functioning'.

Detention

19. An examining officer may detain a person in order to examine him/her for the purpose set out in paragraph 9 above up to the *maximum time permitted under paragraph 6(4) of the Schedule of 9 hours from the time the person's examination begins.* The examining officer should exercise the power to detain a person and arrange for that person to be taken to a police station for further examination as soon as is practicable if:

Examination cannot, for any reason, proceed or continue at the port or, in the case of the border area, that location, or because it is considered necessary to take the person's fingerprints or other action to identify him/her. (See note)

Where a person is detained under the Schedule at a place other than a police station, the examining officer should inform the detained person that he/she is not under arrest or caution but that he/she is being detained under the provisions of Schedule 7 to the Act. He should explain that this in itself does not necessarily mean that the examining officer suspects the detained person to be concerned in the commission, preparation or instigation of acts of terrorism, and that the purpose of the questioning is to enable the examining officer to determine whether the detained person appears to be such a person. The examining officer should advise the detained person that, under paragraph 5 of Schedule 7 to the Act he/she has a duty to give the officer all the information in his/her possession which the officer requests in connection with his determining whether the person appears to be, or have been, concerned in the commission preparation or instigation of acts of terrorism. The detained person should be reminded also of the duty to comply, under paragraph 18(1) of Schedule 7 to the Act.

Note for guidance on paragraph 19

Examination under the Schedule and detention are not synonymous. A person being examined is not necessarily detained and it is envisaged that most examinations will be conducted without the need to detain the person. Conversely, there may also be occasions when it becomes necessary to detain someone, usually because he/she refuses to co-operate and insists on leaving. In such circumstances, it may not always be necessary to take the person to a police station: detention may be short lived, for example to complete an examination.

Production of information

20. The examining officer should specify, in accordance with paragraph 5 of the Schedule, the kind of information which he expects the person concerned to produce for examination/inspection.

21. The examining officer should give the person concerned a reasonable opportunity to produce information, documents or evidence of identity before conducting a search (see paras 23 to 32 below); and should bear in mind that people travelling to and from Northern Ireland and within the Common Travel Area may not be carrying a passport. An examining officer may nonetheless inspect a passport if one is carried by the person concerned.

22. If the person concerned does not appear to understand what is being said, or if the examining officer doubts the person's ability to understand English, every reasonable effort should be made to communicate with him/her so as to ensure that the person comprehends what is required of him/her, where practicable using someone who can act as an interpreter.

Searches

23. An examining officer may search a person who is being questioned for the purpose set out in paragraph 9 above, and their belongings, including baggage. As under paragraph 10 above every reasonable effort should be made to reduce to a minimum the potential embarrassment or offence that may be caused to a person being searched. A baggage search does not have to be carried out by someone of the same sex, but should be if there is an objection. If it is not practicable to do so, the examining officer should note the objection in the officer's official notebook but may proceed with the search. (See note)

Note for guidance on paragraph 23

Section 114(2) of the Act confers on a "constable" the specific power to use reasonable force, if necessary, for the purpose of exercising a power under the Act (apart from the power to question someone under paragraphs 2 and 3 of the Schedule). Section 114(2) does not, however, confer on an immigration officer or customs officer the power to use reasonable force.

24. A personal search should only be carried out by someone of the same sex. This is a requirement under paragraph 8(3) of the Schedule.

25. The examining officer should bear in mind that the power must not be used for any other purpose than to determine whether the person appears to be someone who is, or has been, concerned in the commission, preparation or instigation of acts of terrorism. This does not, however, necessarily preclude a search being carried out under other powers (for example where the examining officer is a constable and has other powers by virtue of common law or another statute).

26. When a search of a person is carried out the examining officer should, if not uniformed, show a warrant card or similar evidence of his/her authority but need not give his/her name.

27. If requested, the examining officer should nonetheless provide sufficient information to the person (or his/her representative), such as an identification number and location which would enable the officer to be identified in the event of any query or complaint.

Strip Search

28. A strip search is a search involving the removal of more than outer clothing. A strip search should usually only be considered necessary where the individual is in police custody as a result of detention under the Schedule.

29. A strip search at a port may, however, take place where an examining officer has reasonable grounds to suspect that a person has concealed something which may be evidence that he is a person who appears to be, or to have been, concerned in the commission, preparation or instigation of acts of terrorism, or where it is suspected the article itself may have been used for such purposes. Strip searches should not be undertaken routinely.

30. The following procedures should be observed when strip searches are conducted:

(a) an officer carrying out a strip search must be of the same sex as the person searched;

(b) the search should take place in an area where the person being searched cannot be seen by anyone who does not need to be present, nor by a member of the opposite sex (except an appropriate adult whose presence has been specifically requested by the person being searched);

(c) except in cases of urgency, where there is a risk of serious harm to the person being searched or to others, whenever a strip search involves exposure of intimate parts of the body, there should be at least two people present other than the person being searched, and if the search is of a juvenile or a mentally disordered or mentally handicapped person, one of the people should be an appropriate adult. Except in urgent cases as above, a search of a juvenile may take place in the absence of the appropriate adult only if the juvenile signifies, in the presence of the appropriate adult, that he/she prefers the search to be done in the appropriate adult's absence and the appropriate adult agrees. A record should be made of the juvenile's decision and signed by the appropriate adult. The presence of more than two people, other than an appropriate adult, should be permitted only in the most exceptional circumstances;

(d) The search should be conducted with the proper regard to the sensitivity and vulnerability of the person concerned in these circumstances and, every reasonable effort should be made to secure the person's co-operation and minimise embarrassment. Persons who are searched should not normally be required to have all their clothes removed at the same time, for example, a man should be allowed to put on his shirt before removing his trousers and a woman should be allowed to put on her blouse and upper garments before further clothing is removed;

(e) Where necessary to assist the search, the person may be required to hold his/her arms in the air or to stand with his/her legs apart and to bend forward so that a visual examination may be made of the genital and anal areas, provided that no physical contact is made with any body orifice;

(f) If, during the search, articles are found, the person should be asked to hand them over;

(g) A strip search should be conducted as quickly as possible and the person allowed to dress as soon as the procedure is complete.

31. A record should be made of a strip search, including the reason why it was considered necessary to undertake it, those present and the outcome of the search.

32. The above provisions also apply to any person authorised under paragraph 10(1) of the Schedule by an examining officer to carry out a search on the officer's behalf.

Landing/Embarkation Cards

33. Paragraph 34 applies only if an order under paragraph 16 of the Schedule is in force requiring a person (on request by an examining officer) to complete or hand to the officer a landing or embarkation card.

34. The examining officer may require a person to complete a landing/embarkation card whether or not the officer suspects the person is or has been concerned in the commission, preparation or instigation of acts of terrorism. The examining officer should bear in mind that, as with questioning, embarrassment or offence can easily be caused to people who have no terrorist connections and who may feel victimised. The principles referred to in paragraph 10 above therefore also apply when an examining officer requires the completion and handing over of a card.

Notice of Duties and Rights

35. The duties and rights of a person subject to examination as set out in the Annex should be displayed prominently in a place where the person will be able to read them. If the examining officer doubts the person's ability to understand English, every reasonable effort shall be made to communicate the relevant information, where practicable using someone who can act as an interpreter.

Annex A (TACT 1)

The Terrorism Act 2000

General

This notice is to inform you that you are being questioned under the provisions of Schedule 7 to the Terrorism Act 2000 as someone [whose presence at the port of [. . . . . .] is believed to be connected with entering or leaving Great Britain or Northern Ireland] [whose presence within the border area between Northern Ireland and the Republic of Ireland is connected with entering or leaving Northern Ireland]. This in itself does not necessarily mean that the examining officer who is questioning you suspects that you are a person who is, or has been, concerned in the commission, preparation or instigation of acts of terrorism. The purpose of the questioning is to enable him to determine whether you appear to be such a person.

Appendix 4: Code of Practice for Examining Officers

Your duties

You have a duty to be truthful and to give an examining officer all the information in your possession which the officer requests. You must also give to him, if he so requests, a valid passport, or other document which establishes your identity. You must also declare whether you have with you any documents of a kind specified by the officer and, if he so requests, give them to him. The examining officer may also search your luggage.

The examining officer may, for the purpose of examination, detain any document which you have given to him, or anything found during a search of your luggage, for a period not exceeding 7 days (beginning with the day on which the detention commenced).

You may also be asked, or have been asked, to complete and hand to the officer an arrival or embarkation card. If so, you have a duty to comply with that request.

If you deliberately fail to comply with any of these duties, you could be prosecuted under paragraph 18(1) of Schedule 7 to the Terrorism Act 2000.

Your rights

You may, if you so request, have someone close to you, or known to you or likely to take an interest in your welfare, informed that you are being questioned and where you are. You can do this at public expense. You may also consult a solicitor, either in person, in writing or by telephone.

If you wish to have someone informed that you are being questioned, or to consult a solicitor, you should tell the examining officer who will make the necessary arrangements.

If you do not wish to make a request now you can still do so later at any time.

Detention

The examining officer also has the authority to detain you, if necessary, for up to 9 hours from the time your examination began.

Officers' Powers and Duties

Inspectors' powers and duties

5.3.4 Recording of interviews and Codes of Practice (power to require appropriate adult to leave interview in absence of superintendent under Code H para 11.10)

5.3.5 Detained person status and rights (qualified officer under para 9(1) of Sch 8 to the Terrorism Act 2000)

5.3.10 Detention—review officer, representations and record of review (review of detention under para 24 – 28 of Sch 8 to the Terrorism Act 2000)

5.5.11 Information about security of dangerous substances and about persons with access to such substances (power to give notice to occupier re dangerous substances under section 61(1) and (7) of the Anti-terrorism Crime and Security Act 2001)

Superintendents' powers

4.3.3 Use of internet for encouragement of terrorism (power to serve notice under section 3 of the Terrorism Act 2006)

4.4.15 Financial information (power to investigate terrorist finance/to apply for disclosure order that requires financial institution to provide customer information)

5.1.1 Obtaining information (overview of powers under Schedule 5)

5.1.2 Search warrants (urgent cases, see notes (m) and (n))

5.1.3 Application for search warrants—non-residential premises

5.1.5 Search warrants—excluded and special procedure material (urgent cases, see notes (k) and (l))

5.2.5 Designation of cordons

5.2.6 Police power to enter and search premises, search persons, seize and retain relevant material in cordoned area (note (f))

5.3.4 Recording of interviews (Superintendent to be consulted where appropriate adult required to leave interview (see note (c)))

5.3.5 Detained person—status and rights (delay right to have someone informed/right to legal advice)

5.3.6 Taking of fingerprints and samples (without consent and intimate samples)

5.3.10 Detention—review officer, representations and record of review

5.3.11 Warrant of further detention (application for such warrant and extension)

5.4.11 Passenger and crew information: police powers (request such information)

5.6.4 Arrest and detention pending control order (delay right to have someone informed/right to legal advice)

5.8.1.1 Cause explosion likely to endanger life or property (authorise entry/search/seizure in urgent cases)

Assistant Chief Constables'/Commanders' powers

5.2.2 Authorisations to invoke powers to stop and search without reasonable suspicion (power under section 44 of the Terrorism Act 2000)

5.2.8 Power to restrict parking (power under section 48 of the Terrorism Act 2000)

5.3.5 Detained person status and rights (power to give direction that detained person can consult solicitor within hearing of qualified officer under para 9(2) of Sch 8 to the Terrorism Act 2000)

Bibliography and References

Books and Reports

ACPO *Interim Practice Advice on Stop and Search in Relation to the Terrorism Act 2000* (ACPO and NCPE, 2005).

—— *Neighbourhood Policing Performance Guide* (ACPO, 2007).

—— and National Counter-Terrorism Security Office *Counter-Terrorism Protective Security Advice for Cinemas and Theatres* (ACPO, 2008).

—— *National Counter-Terrorism Policing Structure—Building Capacity* (ACPO, 2008).

Baylis, J and Smith, S *The Globalization of World Politics: An Introduction to International Relations* 2nd edn, (Oxford: Oxford University Press, 2007).

Beuter, LE, Bongor, B, Brown, LM, Breckenridge, JN, and Zimbardo, PG *Psychology of Terrorism* (Oxford: Oxford University Press, 2007).

Bowers, R, Jones, A, and Lodge, HD *Blackstone's Guide to the Terrorism Act 2006* (Oxford: Oxford University Press, 2006).

Brown, D *Combating International Crime: The Longer Arm of the Law* (Oxon: Routledge-Cavendish, 2008).

Bruce, S *The Red Hand: Protestant Paramilitaries in Northern Ireland* (Oxford: Oxford University Press, 1992).

Chandler, M and Gunaratna, R *Countering Terrorism: Can We Meet The Threat of Global Violence?* (London: Reakton Books Ltd., 2007).

Combs, CC *Terrorism in the 21st Century* 3rd edn, (New Jersey: Prentice Hall, 2003).

Coogan, P *The IRA* (London: Harper Collins, 1995).

Davies, B *Terrorism: Inside A World Phenomenon* (London: Virgin Books Ltd., 2003).

Flanagan, Sir R *The Review of Policing—Final Report* (2008).

Harfield, C and Harfield, K *Covert Investigation* (Oxford: Oxford University Press, 2005).

HM Government *Countering International Terrorism; The United Kingdom's Strategy* (2006a).

—— *Report into the London Terrorist Attacks on 7 July 2005* (2006b).

Bibliography and References

HM Government *Threat Levels—The System to Assess the Threat from International Terrorism* (2006c).

—— *The Definition of Terrorism—A Report by Lord Carlile of Berriew Q.C. Independent Reviewer of Terrorism Legislation* (2007).

—— *Preventing Violent Extremism—A Strategy for Delivery* (2008a).

—— *Report on the Operation in 2007 of the Terrorism Act 2000 and of the Terrorism Act 2006* (2008b).

—— *The National Security Strategy of the United Kingdom—Security in an Interdependent World* (2008c)

——*The Prevent Strategy—A Guide for Local Partners in England and Wales* (2008d).

HM Revenue & Customs *Protecting Society against Crime and Terrorism* (2006).

Home Office *Extremism: Protecting People and Property* (2001).

—— *Borders, Immigration and Identity Action Plan: Using the National Identity Scheme to strengthen our borders and enforce compliance within the UK* (2006).

—— *Our Shared Values—A Shared Responsibility*: First International Conference on Radicalisation and Political Violence (2007).

——*From The Neighbourhood To The National: Policing Our Communities Together*: Green Paper (2008a).

—— *Working Together To Protect The Public: The Home Office Strategy 2008–11* (2008b).

—— and UK Border Agency *A Strong New Force at the Border* (2008c).

—— and UK Border Agency *Enforcing the Deal—Our Plans for Enforcing the Immigration Laws in the United Kingdom's Communities* (2008d).

Houck, M *Forensic Science: Modern Methods of Solving Crime* (London: Preager, 2007).

Kilcommins, S and Vaughan, B *Terrorism, Rights and the Rule of Law: Negotiating Justice in Ireland* (Devon: Willan Publishing, 2008).

Moloney, E *A Secret History of the IRA* 2nd edn, (London: Pearson Penguin Books, 2007).

Niksch, L *Abu Sayyaf: Target of Philippine—US Anti-Terrorism Co-operation* (Washington: The Library of Congress, 2002).

Patterson, H *Ireland Since 1939: The Persistence of Conflict* (London: Pearson Penguin Books, 2007).

Rapoport, DC *Inside Terrorist Organisations* 2nd edn, (London: Frank Cass, 2001).

Ratcliffe, J *Intelligence-Led Policing* (Devon: Willan Publishing, 2008).

Silke, A *Terrorists, Victims and Society: Psychological Perspectives on Terrorism and its Consequences* (Chichester: Wiley, 2003).

Sinclair, A *An Anatomy of Terror: A History of Terrorism* (London: Macmillan, 2003).

Sterba, JP *Terrorism and International Justice* (Oxford: Oxford University Press, 2003).

Sutherland, Lord *Opinion of the High Court of Justiciary at Camp Zeist, Netherlands* (1998).

Walker, C *Blackstone's Guide to Anti-Terrorism Legislation* (Oxford: Oxford University Press, 2002).

Whittaker, DJ *The Terrorism Reader* (London: Routledge, 2001).

——*Terrorism: Understanding the Global Threat* (London: Longman, 2002).

Online articles

BBC (1983), 'On This Day—Christmas Shoppers Remember Harrods Bomb' <http://news.bbc.co.uk/onthisday/hi/witness/december/17/newsid3327000/3327609.stm> accessed November 2008.

BBC (1988a), 'On This Day—Debris of Disaster' <http://news.bbc.co.uk/onthisday/hi/witness/december/21/newsid3332000/3332069.stm> accessed November 2008.

BBC (1988b), 'On This Day—Harrods Bomb Blast Kills Six' <http://news.bbc.co.uk/onthisday/hi/dates/stories/december/17/newsid2538000/25381.stm> accessed November 2008.

BBC (1997), 'IRA Prisoners Taste Freedom' <http://news.bbc.co.uk/1/hi/uk/40874.stm> accessed November 2008.

BBC (2001a), 'Republican Fugitives Freed on Licence' <http://news.bbc.co.uk/1/hi/northern_ireland/1244975.stm> accessed November 2008.

BBC (2001b), 'Y2K Bomb Plot Man Convicted' <http://news.bbc.co.uk/1/hi/world/americas/1265159.stm> accessed September 2008.

Bibliography and References

BBC (2003a), 'Golden Temple Attack' <http://news.bbc.co.uk/
  go/pr/fr/-/1/hi/world/south_asia/3774035.stm> accessed
  September 2008.

BBC (2003b), 'Profile: Gulbuddin Hekmatyar' <http://news.
  bbc.co.uk/1/hi/world/middle_east/2701547.stm> accessed
  October 2008.

BBC (2005a), 'Call for Police to Solve Sikh Murder' <http://news.
  bbc.co.uk/1/hi/uk/4354435.stm> accessed September 2008.

BBC (2005b), 'Millennium Bomber Gets 22 Years' <http://news.
  bbc.co.uk/go/pr/fr/-/1/hi/world/americas/4722409.stm>
  accessed September 2008.

BBC (2006a), 'Groups Banned by New Terror Law' <http://news.
  bbc.co.uk/1/hi/uk_politics/5188136.stm> accessed October 2008.

BBC (2006b), 'Militants jailed for Bali attacks' <http://news.bbc.
  co.uk/1/hi/world/asia-pacific/5322498.stm> accessed October
  2008.

BBC (2006c), 'Video of 7 July Bomber Released' <http://news.
  bbc.co.uk/2/hi/uk_news/5154714.stm> accessed November
  2008.

BBC (2007a), 'Glasgow Airport attack man dies' <http://
  news.bbc.co.uk/2/hi/uk_news/scotland/glasgow_and_
  west/6928854.stm> accessed October 2008.

BBC (2007b), 'Police Avert car bomb carnage' <http://news.bbc.
  co.uk/2/hi/uk_news/6252276.stm> accessed October 2008.

BBC (2008), 'Profile: Ayman al-Zawahiri' <http://news.bbc.
  co.uk/1/hi/world/middle-east/7216127.stm> accessed June
  2008.

Burgess, M (2002), 'In The Spotlight—Islamic Movement of
  Uzbekistan (IMU)' <http://www.cdi.org/terrorism/imu.cfm>
  accessed October 2008.

CBC News (2005), 'Air India: Key Characters' <http://www.cbc.
  ca/news/background/airindia/key_characters.html> accessed
  September 2008.

Centre for the Protection of National Infrastructure (2008), 'Top
  Ten Security Guidelines' <http://www.cpni.gov.uk> accessed
  October 2008.

Clark, M (2004), 'In The Spotlight—The Islamic Army
  of Aden (IAA)' <http://cdi.org/program/document.
  cfm?DocumentID2679> accessed October 2008

Hensher, P and Margoyles, M (2006), 'The fight against terror: Surveillance UK' The Independent <http://www.independent. co.uk/news/uk/crime/the-fight-against-terror-surveiallnce- uk> accessed October 2008.

G8 Gleneagles (2004), 'Welcome from the Prime Minister Tony Blair' <http://www.g8.gov.uk> accessed October 2008.

History Commons, (2008a) 'Jaish-e-Mohammed (JeM)' <http://www.historycommons.org/entity.jsp?entity=jaish-e- mohammed> accessed September 2008.

History Commons (2008b) 'Profile: Al-Gama'a al-Islamiyya' <http://www.historycommons.org/entity.jsp?entity=al_gama_ a_al-islamiyya1> accessed October 2008.

India Defence (2006), 'Balochistan Liberation Army Targets Quetta' <http://www.india-defence.com/reports-1546> accessed October 2008.

Jenkins, R and McGory, D (2007), 'How Al-Qaeda tried to bring Baghdad to Birmingham' <http://www.timesonline.co.uk/tol/ news/uk/crime/article1308572.ece> accessed October 2008.

Keating, B (2004), 'In the Spotlight—Moroccan Combatant (GICM)' <http://www.cdi.org/program/documentID2227> accessed October 2008.

Keats, A (2002a) 'In the Spotlight—Al-Jihad (Egyptian Islamic Jihad)' <http://www.cdi.org/terrorism/aljihad-pr.cfm> accessed June 2006.

Keats, A (2002b) 'In the Spotlight—Asbat al-Ansar' <http://www. cdi.org/terrorism/asbat-pr.cfm> accessed October 2008.

National Commission on the Terrorist Attacks upon the United States (2002), '9/11 Commission Report' <http://www. gpoaccess.gov/911> accessed September 2008.

National Counter-Terrorism Security Office (2008) 'Who we are, what we do and how we do it' <http://www.nactso.gov.uk> accessed October 2008.

Nine Eleven Finding Answers Foundation (2008), 'Terror Watch—Interview with the Mujahid Abdul Gaffar al-Alamni' <http://www.nefafoundation.org/IslamicJihadUnion> accessed October 2008.

Pike, J and Aftergood, S (2003) 'Moroccan Islamic Combatant Group (GICM)' <http://www.fas.org/irp/world/para/gicm. htm> accessed October 2008.

Protherto, M, (2008) 'Hizbollah builds up covert army for a new assault against Israel' *The Guardian*, <http://www.guardian.co.uk/world/2008/apr/27/israelandthepalestinians.lebanon> accessed April 2008.

Rubin, M (2004), 'Ansar al-Sunna: Iraq's New Terrorist Threat' <http://www.meib.org/articles/0405_iraq1.htm> accessed October 2008.

Sahni, S (1999), 'Who are the Harkat-ul-Ansar?' <http://www.rediff.com.news/1999/dec/31harkat.htm.> accessed October 2008.

Swami, P (2006), 'A Bloody Trail' <http://www.hindunnet.com/thehindu/thscrip/print.pl?file=20060324005102200.htm> accessed September 2008,

Upadhyay, R (2007), 'Harkat-ul-Jihad-al-Islami Bangladesh—A Cocktail of ISI, Al-Qaeda and Taliban' <http://intellibriefs.blogspot.com/2007/08/harkat-ul-jihad-al-islami-bangladesh.html> accessed October 2008.

Zaidi, M, and Watson P (2004), 'Militant Flourishes in Plain Sight' <http://articles.latimes.com/2004/jan/25/world/fg-jihadis25> accessed September 2008.

Newspaper and Journal articles

Beech, G 'Anti-Terrorism Training—9/11 Report: Flight Training' *Jane's Police Review*, 2008.

—— 'Anti-Terrorism Training—Ports/Border' *Jane's Police Review*, 18 July 2008.

—— 'Anti-Terrorism Training—Schedule 7' *Jane's Police Review*, 25 July 2008.

—— 'Anti-Terrorism Training—Stop & Search Section 43' *Jane's Police Review*, 3 October 2008

—— 'Anti-Terrorism Training—Stop & Search Section 44' *Jane's Police Review*, 10 October 2008.

Clarke, P 'Learning from Experience—Counter-Terrorism in the UK since 9/11' The Inaugural Colin Cramphorn Memorial Lecture, Policy Exchange (London, 2007).

Gardham, D and Rayner, G 'British suicide bombers planned to blow airliners out of the sky' *Daily Telegraph*, 4 April 2008.

Fresco, A, McGory, D and Norfolk, A 'Video of Suicide Bomber Released' *The Times*, 6 July 2006.

Manningham-Buller, Dame E 'Partnership and Continuous Improvement in Countering Twenty-First Century Terrorism' *Policing: A Journal of Policy and Practice*, Vol. I, No. 1 (Oxford: Oxford University Press, 2007).

Spencer, P 'Anti-Terrorism Training—Control Orders' *Jane's Police Review*, 20 June 2008.

—— 'Anti-Terrorism Training—Camp Culture' *Jane's Police Review*, 15 August 2008.

Staniforth, A 'Tackling Terrorism—Know Your Enemy' *Jane's Police Review*, 22 February 2008.

—— 'Tackling Terrorism—Action Plan' *Jane's Police Review*, 29 February 2008.

—— 'Tackling Terrorism—Team Effort' *Jane's Police Review*, 7 March 2008.

—— 'Tackling Terrorism—Changing Tactics' *Jane's Police Review*, 14 March 2008.

—— 'Tackling Terrorism—Mind Games' *Jane's Police Review*, 21 March 2008.

—— 'Tackling Terrorism—Chain of Command' *Jane's Police Review*, 28 March 2008.

—— 'Tackling Terrorism—Methods of Mayhem' *Jane's Police Review*, 4 April 2008.

—— 'Tackling Terrorism—Right Balance' *Jane's Police Review*, 11 April 2008.

—— 'Tackling Terrorism—Legal Challenge' *Jane's Police Review*, 18 April 2008.

—— 'Tackling Terrorism—First Line Response' *Jane's Police Review*, 25 April 2008.

—— 'Anti-Terrorism Training—Security' *Jane's Police Review*, 2nd May 2008.

—— 'Anti-Terrorism Training—Terrorism Bill 2008' *Jane's Police Review*, 9 May 2008.

—— 'Anti-Terrorism Training—Terrorism & the Media' *Jane's Police Review*, 16 May 2008.

—— 'Anti-Terrorism Training—Membership' *Jane's Police Review*, 30 May 2008.

—— 'Anti-Terrorism Training—Forensic Awareness' *Jane's Police Review*, 6 June 2008.

—— 'Anti-Terrorism Training—Prevent' *Jane's Police Review*, 13 June 2008.

Bibliography and References

Staniforth, A 'Anti-Terrorism Training—Pursue' *Jane's Police Review*, 27 June 2008.

—— 'Anti-Terrorism Training—Protect' *Jane's Police Review*, 11 July 2008.

—— 'Anti-Terrorism Training—Al-Qaeda' *Jane's Police Review*, 1 August 2008.

—— 'Terrorism and the Olympics—Hitler's Hijack' *Jane's Police Review*, 8 August 2008.

—— 'Terrorism and the Olympics—Munich Massacre' *Jane's Police Review*, 15 August 2008.

——'Anti-terrorism Training—Nationalism' *Jane's Police Review*, 22 August 2008.

—— 'Terrorism and the Olympics—The Olympic Bomber' *Jane's Police Review*, 22 August 2008.

—— 'Anti-Terrorism Training—Suicide Attack' *Jane's Police Review*, 29 August 2008.

—— 'Terrorism and the Olympics—Olympic Spirit' *Jane's Police Review*, 29 August 2008.

—— 'Anti-Terrorism Training—9/11 Report' *Jane's Police Review*, 5 September 2008.

—— 'Anti-Terrorism Training—9/11 Report: Impact' *Jane's Police Review*, 26 September 2008.

—— 'Anti-Terrorism Training—Police Reform' *Jane's Police Review*, 17 October 2008.

—— 'Anti-Terrorism Training—UK Security' *Jane's Police Review*, 24 October 2008.

—— 'Anti-Terrorism Training—42 Days' *Jane's Police Review*, 31 October 2008.

—— 'Anti-Terrorism Training—Hotline' *Jane's Police Review*, 14 November 2008.

—— 'Anti-Terrorism Training—Defining Terrorism' *Jane's Police Review*, 21 November 2008.

Szabo, R 'Anti-Terrorism Training—Hostile Reconnaissance' *Jane's Police Review*, 4 July 2008.

—— 'Anti-Terrorism Training—Inciting' *Jane's Police Review*, 15 August 2008.

Index

Index

Index

Index

Index

Index